SOUTHWEST FRANCE

Delia Gray-Durant

Somerset Books • London
WW Norton • New York

Blue Guide Southwest France
Second edition by this author (Third edition in the USA)

Published by Blue Guides Limited, a Somerset Books Company
49–51 Causton St, London SW1P 4AT
www.blueguides.com
'Blue Guide' is a registered trademark

ISBN 1–905131–13–5

A CIP catalogue record of this book is available from the British Library.

Published in the United States of America by
WW Norton and Company, Inc.
500 Fifth Avenue, New York, NY 10110
USA ISBN 0-393-32893-7

Cover photographs: Top: View of Auch (CRT Midi-Pyrénées, photo: D. Viet).
Bottom: *Le Patio* by Henry Zo (Musée des Beaux-Arts de Pau).
Spine: Detail from the portrait of La Baronne de Crussol by E. Vigée-Lebrun
(Musée des Augustins, Toulouse, photo: Daniel Martin).
Title page: *Le Signe du Lion et le Signe du Bélier*
(Musée des Augustins, Toulouse, photo: Daniel Martin).

All other acknowledgements, photo credits and copyright information are given
on p. 648, which forms part of this copyright page.

About the author
Delia Gray-Durant's association with France began more than 30 years ago when she went to
live and work in Paris. Subsequently she read French and History of Art at University and had
a home in the Midi-Pyrénées. Now she writes books, leads art history tours and spends a large
part of the year in France. She has been writing for *Blue Guides* since 1993 and is also the author
of *Blue Guide Paris and Versailles*.

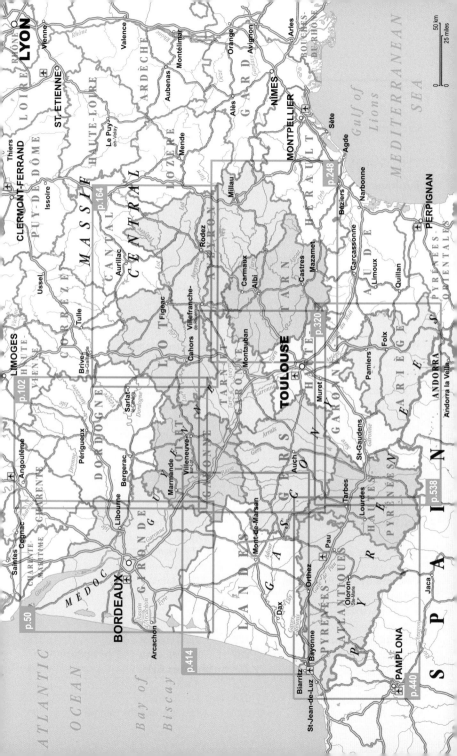

CONTENTS

MAPS & PLANS

PRACTICAL INFORMATION

INTRODUCTION

The routes that for centuries crossed France, leading the devout to the shrine of St James at Compostela in Spain, are busy again with modern-day pilgrims on foot or bicycle. These roads and tracks, with their associated churches, abbeys, bridges and hospices, stretch across the southwest from the church of Notre-Dame-de-la-Fin-des-Terres in Soulac at the tip of the Médoc to the Porte St-Jacques in St-Jean-Pied-de-Port on the threshold of Spain, and have been classified UNESCO World Heritage sites.

Other World Heritage sites in southwest France serve to illustrate the broad sweep of cultural heritage in Aquitaine and Midi-Pyrénées: the Vézère Valley, sometimes described as the Valley of Man, where the unique concentration of prehistoric sites bears witness to the development and creativity of humans some 20,000 years ago; the Juridiction de St-Emilion, the eight parishes which now fall under the authority of the *jurade* whose limits were defined in 1199 by Richard the Lionheart, and which correspond to the vineyards within the St-Emilion *appellation*; and the spectacular amphitheatre formed by the Pyrenees, the Cirque de Gavarnie, an example of the great natural phenomena to be seen in Midi-Pyrénées.

In the past the southwest has suffered its fair share of political upheaval and religious turmoil, but the present remains largely unhurried except at the two poles, Bordeaux in the north and Toulouse in the south. The 6th and 4th largest cities in France respectively, linked by the Garonne, they work like magnets on the region as a whole. Dynamic and prosperous but different in character, they provide a large proportion of the employment and wealth of the two administrative regions, Aquitaine and Midi-Pyrénées. Bordeaux, moulded by the success of its wine trade and of shipping on the Garonne, and via the Gironde estuary to the Atlantic, exudes an aura of calm elegance resulting from the period of urban regeneration that shaped the layout and architecture of the city during the Age of Enlightenment. Toulouse, originally an inland river port, is very much a city of the Midi, a link between the Mediterranean and the Atlantic. Its warm brick façades, Renaissance mansions and pavement life have absorbed the influences of the South of France and of Spain and reinterpreted them in a very individual manner. Each city takes advantage of its riverscapes. The massive scheme in Bordeaux to make full use of the banks of the Garonne, which were formerly made over to commercial shipping, is now coming to its finale and the result is superb.

Between the two urban poles unroll the bucolic landscapes of this largely agricultural region watered by the Dordogne, the Lot and the Tarn. The unhurried present may account for the longevity of the inhabitants in the Gers, although they would probably ascribe it to plenty of unsaturated goose fat and good red wine. And why not? By the time you have got up on a summer's morning and have bought the croissants, everything closes and it is almost time for a siesta.

HISTORICAL SKETCH

Prehistory and early history

The oldest European skeleton, c. 450,000 years old, was discovered in 1971 near Tautavel in the eastern Pyrenees. Man's presence and evolution during the earliest periods is identified by the lithic industry, the production of stone (and bone) tools used by the early hunter-gatherers, and is described as the Palaeolithic or Old Stone Age. The Palaeolithic era is divided into three periods, Lower, Middle and Upper. The bifacial hand axe as well as evidence of controlled fire dates from the Lower Palaeolithic era. During the Middle Palaeolithic, a new technique of stone cutting developed, described as Mousterian (from Le Moustier, Dordogne; *see p. 139*), coinciding with the emergence of *Homo neandertalensis*, the first people known to bury their dead. The Neanderthals were gradually replaced from around 34,000 years ago by Cro-Magnon or modern man (*Homo sapiens sapiens*), first identified at the eponymous rock-shelter between Les Eyzies and Tayac (*see p. 129*). This marks the beginning of the Upper Palaeolithic period which, during the end of the Ice Age in Europe, is divided into five main cultures in southwest France, each spanning five or ten thousand years: Aurignacian, Gravettian (or Perigordian), Solutrean, Magdalenian and Azilian (c. 8,000 years ago). The Aurignacians were the first to produce significant examples of sculpture and engraving, and as time went on early man perfected his tools and enjoyed a relatively comfortable existence. Over 25,000 years, man's creativity developed, reaching a peak with the Magdelenians who were responsible for the sophisticated paintings found at Lascaux and other major sites in the southwest. Organised study of prehistory began piecemeal in the southwest early in the 19th century. Two of the outstanding pioneers of prehistory in the southwest were Abbé Henri Breuil (1877-1962) and Denis Peyrony (1869-1954), as well as E. Riviere, E. Cartailhac, and L. Capitan.

Unique to the southwest of France is the huge wealth of prehistoric painting and sculpture on the walls of caves or rock shelters. Of the 173 decorated sites found in France, some 100 are in Aquitaine, 23 are in the Quercy and 27 in the Pyrenees. The paintings, frequently of animals, must have been of great symbolic importance, given the difficulties associated with creating them. Pebbles, bones and horn were also engraved or carved, the oldest dating from c. 30,000 BP, and the earliest of the relief representations of females, described as Venuses, dates back some 20,000 years.

Mesolithic and Neolithic cultures, corresponding to changes in climate and fauna, mark the evolution from simple to more sophisticated tools, agriculture, pottery, the primitive use of a bow and arrow, communal burials in caves, and megaliths. Towards the beginning of the third millennium BC, metallurgy was introduced into central and southwestern France. The Iron Age was characterised not only by iron tools and weapons, but also by the establishment of hill settlements and often the practice of cremation, when the ashes placed in vessels were buried under barrows or earth mounds, a tradition which seems to have originated in the late Bronze Age. La Tène Celts, who descended from Northern France and beyond some time after the beginning of the 3rd century BC, subjugated or merged with the existing Hallstattians or Aquitains.

The Romans and Franks

When the Romans arrived in the southwest of what they called Gaul in the 2nd century BC, the local Celts had already established commercial links with Roman Narbonne, founded 118 BC. By the second half of the 2nd century BC *Tolosa* (Toulouse), capital of the Celtic tribe, the Volcae Tectosages, accepted an alliance with the Romans and a garrison was established there. The foundation of *Lugdunum Convenarum* (St-Bertrand-de-Comminges) in 72 BC is attributed to Pompey. Two campaigns by Julius Caesar's lieutenant, Crassus, in 56 BC resulted in the submission of the Bituriges-Vivisci (Bordeaux). The Gaulish wars (59–51 BC) against the Romans were led by Vercingetorix (72–46 BC), although the site of his last stand, *Uxellodunum*, the *oppidum* of the Cadurci tribe which fell to Caesar in 51 BC, is still disputed (*see p. 167*). Following the Celtic collapse, *Pax Romana* lasted until the 3rd century AD and urban centres developed such as *Burdigala* (Bordeaux), which became capital of *Aquitania*, *Vesunna* (Périgueux), *Aginum* (Agen) and *Aquae Tarbellicae* (Dax). By the 1st century AD wine imports were replaced by the cultivation of vines in the region and subsequently by the export of wine to the Mediterranean, along with pottery produced in Graufesenque and Montans. Christianity spread through the region during the 3rd century, countered by persecution at the time of the Emperor Diocletian (r. 284–305), producing semi-legendary martyrs such as Saint Sernin (Saturninus) in Toulouse, Sainte Foy (Faith) in Agen, and Saint Front in Périgord.

The most notable new museum in Aquitaine, dedicated entirely to the Gallo-Roman period, is the Musée Gallo-Romain: Vesunna, in Périgueux. A very fine series of antique portrait busts was discovered at Villa Chiragan (Musée St-Raymond), and a magnificent bronze Hercules was found in Bordeaux. There are the remains of several small Gallo-Roman villas with mosaics and painted fragments at Montmaurin (Haute-Garonne), Séviac (Gers), Plassac (Gironde) and Montcaret (Dordogne). The Tour Vésone in Périgueux is the best example of a centrally planned temple existing in France, and here as well as at Bordeaux, Toulouse, Dax (Landes), Bayonne (Pyrénées-Atlantiques), St-Bertrand-de-Comminges and Cahors (Lot) are fragments of Roman civic constructions such as *thermae* or bath complexes, fortifications, and amphitheatres.

The end of Roman domination was precipitated in the 3rd–5th centuries by waves of Germanic tribes such as the Alemani who swept down from the north, followed by the Vandals and Visigoths. They in turn were forced out in 507 by Clovis (r. 481–511), leader of the Franks who left an enduring souvenir in the present name of the former country of the Gauls, and who converted to Christianity c. 500. In the 6th century, Aquitaine was divided by factions of Clovis's dynasty, the Merovingians, and c. 580 the Vascons or Gascons appeared from the southwest. Incursions by Arabs (also called Moors or Saracens) from Iberia northwards through the region were stemmed by Charles Martel (r. 715–41) at Poitiers in 732, although random attacks continued to the mid-8th century.

Charlemagne (742–814), grandson of Charles Martel and son of the first of the Carolingians Pépin the Short, became King of the Franks in 768. From 771, after the death of his brother, he reigned over a vast Christian empire covering much of Europe. Nevertheless, control of the Iberian Peninsula evaded him and the rearguard of his retreating army suffered ignominiously when ambushed at Roncesvalles

PILGRIMAGE

From the 10th century, throughout the Middle Ages and until the Reformation, thousands of pilgrims from all corners of Christendom flocked to Santiago de Compostela on the north-western coast of the Spanish peninsula, intent on the veneration of the relics of St James the Greater. The call to this unlikely place at 'the end of the earth' was based on the association of St James (Sant Iago in Spanish and St Jacques in French), martyred in Jerusalem in AD 44, with *finis terrae*. The momentous discovery of James's tomb and the remains of his companions was attributed to a hermit-shepherd called Pelagius or Pelayo in c. 814, who was led to the sacred remains by a shower of stars. The site took the name *campus stellae*, later Compostela, and a chapel was soon built there. The discovery was reinforced by the miraculous appearance of the saint in the heavens, mounted on a white horse, to assist Ramiro I of Asturias in the Christian reconquest of Spain at the probably mythical battle of Clavijo in 844. St James subsequently became the patron saint of Christian Spain and symbolised the Christian reconquest over the Moors. Promoted by the Church, the reputation of Santiago gained momentum. The first pilgrimage from France was famously made in 950 by Godscalc, Bishop of Le Puy, with 200 companions. Such was the reputation of Santiago that it was declared a Holy City by Pope Alexander II in 1189, on a par with Jerusalem and Rome. From the 12th–14th centuries, pilgrimage to Santiago reached its peak with around 500,000 pilgrims crossing Southwest France. In France pilgrims were referred to as *Roumi* (those who came from Rome), or *Jacquet*, and can be compared to modern tourists in that they acquired souvenirs, recorded their travels, demanded entertainment, and were vulnerable to crime and unscrupulous innkeepers. Aymery Picaud, a priest from the Poitiers region, wrote a guide book for pilgrims, the *Codex Calixtinus*, c. 1120/30. Lodgings sprang up along the way including hospices linked to great abbeys such as Cluny in Burgundy, organised by the Hospitallers of St John, or run by independent groups like the Domerie. Christian hospices offered help to the sick and needy but pilgrims also brought wealth which enabled the building of grander churches. Relics acquired by abbeys and priories along the way were displayed in gorgeous reliquaries such as those that survive at Conques. The typical Romanesque church (12th century) was adapted to meet the needs of clergy and pilgrims, a development epitomised by St-Sernin in Toulouse. A multitude of routes, from Northern Europe, Italy, and Eastern Europe converged on the four major roads which cross Southwest France, including the *Via Podiensis* from Puy-en-Velay and the *Via Turonensis* bringing pilgrims from Northern Europe and Great Britain via Tours. Germans and Eastern Europeans joined the *Via Lemovicensis* at Vezelay in Burgundy; and from the Mediterranean the *Via Tolosana* passed by Arles. These roads came together at St-Palais or Ostabat close to St-Jean-Pied-de-Port before crossing the Pyrenees into Spain over the Col de Somport.

(Roncevaux) in Navarre in 778 (*see p. 476*). Charlemagne was crowned Emperor on Christmas Day 800 and passed on the Kingdom of Aquitaine to his son, Louis the Pious (r. 814–40 with interruptions), but the Carolingian Empire broke down into principalities governed by ennobled vassals. William of Orange (c. 750–812), Count of Toulouse, cousin of Charlemagne, who took control of Languedoc by 793, established one of the most powerful dynasties. They were fiercely challenged by the rival Poitevin dynasty: in the mid-10th century, Ebalus, Count of Poitou and distantly related to William, became the first Duke of Aquitaine (r. 927–34).

The Early Middle Ages

By the late 11th century, crusades against the Turkish 'infidels' who occupied the Holy City of Jerusalem were preached by Pope Urban II throughout France and in 1096 Raymond IV, Count of Toulouse left on the First Crusade to the Holy Land at the head of 100,000 men. The Second Crusade (1147–48) was led by Louis VII of France accompanied by his queen, Eleanor, and in 1190 Richard I of England and Philippe-Auguste of France set out on the Third Crusade. Eleanor of Aquitaine (1122–1204) was to play a role of paramount importance in the history of France, Aquitaine and England resonating over several centuries. The ancient laws of Aquitaine, inherited from the Roman period, allowed women to inherit property and Eleanor, an unusually well-educated young woman, became Duchess of Aquitaine and Countess of Poitou at the death of her father, William X, in 1137. He had made her ward of his overlord, King Louis VI (r. 1108–1137), who married her at the age of 15 to the Dauphin, the future Louis VII (r. 1137–1180). The couple had only daughters. The holy and ascetic Louis was no match for Eleanor, and she did not complain when the king contrived to bring about the dissolution of their marriage on grounds of consanguinity in 1152.

Henry Plantagenet first met Eleanor in Paris in 1151, when he was 18 and she was 29. Eleanor soon married Henry at Poitiers, bringing the Plantagenets the very rich dowry of the Duchy of Aquitaine, encompassing territories from the Loire Valley to the Pyrenees and from the River Rhône to the Atlantic. Henry acceded to the throne of England as Henry II (r. 1154–89), and by 1160 the Plantagenet empire stretched from the border of Scotland to the frontier with Spain including Anjou, Maine, Lorraine and Normandy (inherited from his parents) as well as Aquitaine (Guyenne and Gascony).

Eleanor also laid claim to the Toulousain through her grandmother, Philippa of Toulouse, but never managed to control this valuable link between Aquitaine and the Mediterranean, which also evaded the French for several centuries. In 1169 Eleanor handed over the control of most of Aquitaine to her favourite son, Richard Lion Heart, who acceded to the English throne as Richard I (r. 1189–99). Richard was a political and military rival to Philippe-Auguste of France (r. 1180–1223) who confiscated the territories in Aquitaine from Richard's brother and successor, King John (r. 1199–1216).

Many outstanding examples of architecture and sculpture of the period have survived. The finest examples of the 12th-century pilgrimage church in the Benedictine tradition, laid out in the shape of a Latin cross with transepts, aisles, ambulatory and galleries, are St-Sernin in Toulouse and Ste-Foy in Conques (Aveyron). Specific to the southwest are the domed churches, of which more than 60 once existed, many now altered or rebuilt. Périgueux has two examples. Others include those at Souillac (Lot), Moirax (Lot-et-Garonne) and Cahors, which has the largest dome in diameter. Hispano-Arabic influences, which spread across the Pyrenees to southwest France, are found in the Moorish-style cupolas on intersecting arches at St-Croix in Oloron Ste-Marie and the church of the Hôpital St-Blaise (both in Pyrénées Atlantiques). The most curious church of the period must be the monolithic church carved out of the solid rock below St-Emilion. A remarkable and rare 12th-century belfry stands in Brantôme (Dordogne). Romanesque sculpture picked up influences travelling in both directions along the pilgrimage routes. The most magnificent examples in France of cloister capitals *in situ* are at Moissac (Tarn-et-Garonne). St-Sever (Landes) felt the direct influence of Cluny, but although there are some similarities in the motifs of the capitals with Conques, this last remained independent from Cluny and produced a tympanum in a style akin to churches in the Massif Central. Other good examples of Romanesque carving are at Ste-Quitterie in Aire-sur-l'Adour, Hagetmau and Sorde l'Abbaye (all in the Landes), Cahors, Carennac (Lot), and the more rustic St-Lizier (Ariège). Gathered together in the Musée des Augustins in Toulouse is the largest collection anywhere of 12th-century sculpted capitals, saved from three cloisters demolished in the 19th century. Fortified churches of the 12th–14th centuries are frequent in areas which were contested, especially Aquitaine during English occupation. The belfry—being the tallest building in a village or town without fortifications or a castle—served as the watchtower. At St-Amand-de-Coly is a magnificent *tour-donjon* while St-Avit-Sénieur and Beaumont-en-Périgord have tall towers and other defensive elements (all in the Dordogne).

The Cathars

While lack of discipline in the orthodox Church gave rise to the Gregorian reforms in the 11th century and pilgrimage was on the increase, the Languedoc, under the control of the Counts of Toulouse, presented a degree of religious tolerance, intellectual sophistication, and administrative confusion engendered by internecine rivalry. It became the refuge of the Cathars (from catharsis, meaning purification), also referred to as Albigensians. A fundamentalist Christian sect, entirely pacifist, the Cathars followed a dualist doctrine based on the opposition of Good and Evil, but believed that the true God created only the invisible, spiritual kingdom, which was permanent, whereas all worldly matter was evil emanating from another Principle, the reverse of God, making man in his own likeness. The logical conclusion was that the humanity of Christ was an illusion. The community was divided between the majority or ordinary faithful, and ascetics or preachers known as Perfect or Goodmen, who led an exemplary life of abstinence and charity. Women had equal status. The only Cathar sacrament was the *consolamentum*, which served both in the ordination of priests and as the last rites for ordinary followers.

Although never in the majority, the Cathars through their doctrine, preaching in the vernacular, and failure to exact tithes or taxes, threatened to undermine the authority, wealth and power of the orthodox church. Many attempts were made to bring the

Cathars back to the orthodoxy through debate and disputation, but to no avail. Bernard of Clairvaux (1090–1153), a man of intense religious conviction, had founded the ultra ascetic Cistercian Order at the Abbey of Cîteaux, Burgundy in 1115. Beautifully proportioned Cistercian abbey churches, although not unadulterated, can be found at Beaulieu-en-Rouergue, Loc Dieu and Sylvanès (all in the Aveyron), Cadouin (Dordogne) and Flaran (Gers). Bernard was sent by Pope Innocent III to preach against the Cathar heretics in Toulouse and Albi in 1145, with little effect.

Dominic de Guzman (St Dominic; *see p. 593*), a Spanish cleric, settled in the Languedoc in 1206, and the order of itinerant preachers he gathered around him to counteract the heresy developed into the Dominican order. The heresy also provided an excuse to gain the submission of the powerful Counts of Toulouse. The French king, Philippe II-Auguste (r. 1180-1223), with the support of the pope and the Cistercians, justified an attack on his own people as a religious crusade and gathered an army under the symbol of the Cross which mustered in Lyons in 1209, commanded by the papal legate, Arnaud Amaury. Thus began the Albigensian Crusade (1209–25; *see p. 251*).

The Hundred Years War

The main event leading up to the Hundred Years War was the claim by Edward III of England (r. 1327–77) to the vacant French throne by right of his mother, Isabelle, daughter of Philippe IV. Tensions between the English king's representatives and local administration in Gascony reached a new crisis when Philippe VI (r. 1328–50) declared the Duchy confiscate, escalating the quarrel from one between vassal and overlord to a power struggle between two royal dynasties. War became an almost constant feature from 1337 to 1453, in an endless cycle of siege, battle and intrigue, although few battles were fought between 1348 and 1350 when the population was severely depleted by the Black Death.

By their victory at Poitiers in 1356 Edward and his son, the Black Prince, obtained the Treaty of Brétigny of 1360, whereby much of southwest France reverted to the English king in return for his renunciation of the throne of France. War began again in the southwest, led by Bernard du Guesclin (c. 1320–80), hero of the French cause. Following the English victory at Agincourt in 1415 and the Treaty of Troyes of 1420, the inheritance of the French king Charles VI (r. 1380–1422) was made over to Henry V. The Dauphin and the Armagnacs in Gascony were opposed to this and the war entered a new phase: Joan of Arc (1412–31) made her appearance in 1429, bringing support to the Dauphin who finally defeated the English in Normandy in 1450. Charles VII (r. 1422–61) took the spoils at the Battle of Castillon, near St-Emilion, on 17th July 1453, and the Duchy of Aquitaine was reincorporated into the domain of Royal France.

The castles of the period grew piecemeal and some of the most romantic, ruined or intact, are in the Dordogne, including Beynac, Biron, Castelnau, and Bonaguil which was the last of its kind. The variety and evolution of great castles with towering keeps in the south of the region such as Pau, Foix and Morlanne—in which Gaston Fébus, Count of Foix in the 14th century, had a hand— contrast with the small but perfect Château du Bosquet in remote Aveyron. The most complete medieval fortified bridge, with three towers, is the Pont Valentré which elegantly spans the Lot at Cahors and was built for defence during the Hundred Years War; similar but incomplete is the bridge at Orthez (Pyrénées-Atlantiques). The small fortified hilltop town of Domme (Dordogne) has a magnificent gateway built in 13th-century bossed masonry and Cordes-sur-Ciel (Tarn) still has four early 13th-century gateways and part of its fortifications. Both these are *bastides* (*see p. 358*), of which there are some 300 in the southwest. High-quality medieval domestic architecture is abundant in Figeac (Lot) and also in St-Antonin-Noble-Val and most exceptional are the Gothic houses in Cordes.

The cloister at Cadouin is a fine example of the late Gothic period in the 15th century, built after the destruction wrought by the Hundred Years War. A precious survival from this period is the delicately carved limestone choir enclosure in Albi cathedral. The choir and the uniquely wonderful sculptural group of the *Entombment* at Monestiés (Tarn) were both sponsored by Bishop Louis I d'Amboise in the late 15th century.

During the early 16th century, the late Gothic style of France and Renaissance influences direct from Italy or from the Loire merged to create the pretty early Renaissance or First French Renaissance style. The first decorative imports were the painted vaults of Albi cathedral, and the gable on the west end of the cathedral of Rodez. There are numerous examples of domestic architecture in the style—typified by four-square windows, columns and pilasters and decorated with busts and *rinceaux*. Many châteaux were transformed from forts to homes during the period up to the Wars of Religion, such as the Château de Pau (Pyrénées-Atlantiques), and others were built as a display of their patrons' knowledge of contemporary fashion, such as Puyguilhem, Monbazillac (both in the Dordogne), Assier, Montal (both in the Lot) and Bournazel (Aveyron).

The Wars of Religion

By the mid-16th century the tenets of humanism and the Reformation were infiltrating the region. Protestants (known also as Calvinists or Huguenots) became powerful and widespread in the south of France, where they enjoyed periods of relative tolerance contrasting with moments of violent oppression. Jeanne d'Albret (1528–72), daughter of Henri of Navarre and Marguerite d'Angoulême, the sister of François I, imposed her Protestant faith on much of the Agenais and the Béarn, and passed it on to her son, Henri III of Navarre (*see p. 485*). During the reign of François I (1515–47), anti-Protestant feelings had already developed and they intensified during the reign of Henri II (1547–59). Opposition developed between powerful Catholic families, such the Guise clan and Anne de Montmorency, and the Protestant Bourbons, represented by the Prince de Condé (1522–88), brother of Jeanne d'Albret's husband Antoine de Bourbon, and Admiral Coligny (1519–72). Anti-Protestant opinion escalated into violence. The union between the Protestant Henri III of Navarre and the Catholic Marguerite de Valois (*see p. 92*) did not bring an immediate solution to the religious problems. Henri of Navarre, who had a legitimate claim through his father, acceded to the throne of France in 1589 as Henri IV (1589–1610), the first of the Bourbon line. With the Edict of Nantes (1598), which regulated the legal rights of the Reformed Church in France, he brought about religious harmony and granted both freedom of worship and certain political and military rights to the Protestants.

The Counter-Reformation

Louis XIII (r. 1610–43), however, reunited France under the Catholic banner and exacted severe punishment on Protestant strongholds in the southwest, starting with the dismantling of fortifications at Montauban in 1621. The period 1621–24, first under Constable Luynes (1578–1621) and then with the support of Cardinal Richelieu (1585–1642), was particularly harsh and Protestants were deprived of certain privileges by the Treaty of Alès (1629). Louis established centralised royal authority by creating a body of *Intendants*, but upset the national budget by entering the Thirty Years War. Increasingly heavy taxes imposed on peasants in the Périgord and the Rouergue resulted in insurrections during the 16th and 17th centuries, known as the revolts of the Croquants. As a result of the loss of autonomy in the southwest there was another uprising in 1629. The Governor of Languedoc, the Duc de Montmorency, who had participated in the movement in 1632, was executed in the courtyard of the Capitole in Toulouse in the presence of Louis XIII and Richelieu. This example ensured that during the series of uprisings known as Le Fronde (1649–53), directed against the unpopular Cardinal Mazarin and his financial demands during the minority of Louis XIV, the Midi remained faithful to Mazarin.

With great pomp and ceremony, Louis XIV (r. 1643–1715) married the Infanta Marie-Thérèse of Spain in St-Jean-de-Luz in 1660. He instigated major administrative and financial reforms and continued the Counter-Reformation tendencies of his father with the Revocation of the Edict of Nantes (1685), which resulted in a huge exodus of Protestants from France. The driving force behind the Counter-Reformation was the Council of Trent, a succession of ecumenical councils held between 1545 and 1653 through which the Roman Catholic Church set about a complete revision of its discipline and a reaffirmation of essential dogmas. The physical result of this was the introduction of the Classical and Baroque altarpieces found in every church in France, especially in country regions such as the Pyrenees. The best 17th-century example on any scale is Notre-Dame in Bordeaux. Due to the founding of secular orders (such as the Pénitents blue, white and black), small Baroque chapels appeared, such as the chapels of the Pénitents Noirs in Villefranche-de-Rouergue and in St-Geniez-d'Olt (Aveyron).

Developing trade, the Revolution and Napoleon

One of the greatest engineering projects of the mid-17th century was Pierre-Paul Riquet's Canal Royal du Languedoc, now called the Canal du Midi (1666–81; *see p. 555*). The port of Bordeaux also became the most important in the land during the 18th century, due not only to wine but also to the profitable trade with the colonies in luxury goods, including sugar cane, and the authorisation for trade in slaves. Major works of urban regeneration were undertaken by architects such as the Gabriels and Victor Louis, who between them designed the elegant Place de la Bourse (1733–55), originally Place Royale, dedicated to Louis XV and embellished with Ionic columns; and the austere Grande Théâtre de l'Opéra (1773–80) in the style of the reign of Louis XVI.

The effect of the French Revolution of 1789 was less powerful and less violent in the southwest than in Paris. In Bordeaux, a moderate group of intellectuals, the

Girondins, attempted to control the more violent aspects of the Convention (the Revolutionary Assembly of 1792 to 1795) but were expelled in 1793 and executed. Toulouse remained more supportive of the Convention. In 1790 most of the modern *départements* were formed, maintaining to some extent the boundaries of the old provinces they replaced. The Concordat of July 1801, drawn up by Napoleon and Pope Pius VII, which recognised the alienation of church lands as permanent and the payment of clerical staff by the state, heralded a government-controlled religion during the First Empire. The Napoleonic Wars had a disastrous effect on Bordeaux, which suffered losses during the maritime wars and the embargo that prevented any British imports, or ships that had traded with Britain, coming into French-controlled ports.

Due to the lack of coal—limited to small open-cast mines at Carmaux and Decazeville—the southwest was slow to participate in the industrial revolution. The rail link with Paris was established with Bordeaux in 1852. One of the major regeneration projects of the mid-19th century was the creation of the Landes forest by the drainage and plantation of pines over some million hectares. Conversely, the phylloxera epidemic of the 1870s wiped out entire vineyards in many other parts of the region. Tourism was sparked by the fashion for sea-bathing during the mid-19th century and the patronage of Empress Eugénie and the court of Napoleon III (r. 1852–70), which drew visitors to the Basque coast and was accelerated by the arrival of the railway. While buildings were still being destroyed and demolished there was a parallel impulse to save and restore, reflected in the creation of the Monuments Historiques, an agency for the protection of ancient monuments, under Prosper Mérimée and Eugene Viollet-le-Duc (*see p. 95*).

The twentieth century

Bordeaux, which prides itself on the integration of good modern buildings with old, in 1926 commissioned Le Corbusier for the revolutionary Cité Frugès (Pessac) and he also designed a *château d'eau* (water tower) at Podensac as well as projects at Lège-Cap-Ferret (Gironde). The Villa Natacha at Biarritz has an Art Nouveau interior décor, rare on the Basque coast. In contrast, the Base Sous-Marine (submarine base) was built in Bordeaux during the Second World War. On 11th November 1942, what had been the Free Southern Zone, including Périgueux and Toulouse, was occupied by German forces. Bordeaux was already in the Occupied Zone. The Resistance or *Maquis* was active in certain parts of the southwest, including the Pyrenees (the route to Spain), the Lot and the woodlands of the Périgord. The major positive result of wartime was the development of aviation and the aeronautical industry in Toulouse. The development in the Meriadeck area in Bordeaux in the 1970s introduced avant-garde structures such as the Caisse d'Epargne (1974–80), while nearby are the Ecole Nationale de la Magistrature (1969–73) and the Tribunal de Grande Instance (1994–98) by the Richard Rogers Partnership. Bordeaux has more recently undertaken a vast project to enhance the banks of the Garonne and many other parts of the city with great success. Perhaps it is appropriate to the history of the region that in the 21st century the most celebrated architectural achievement in southwest France is a road: the superb metal and concrete viaduct over the Tarn valley at Millau.

BORDEAUX

Bordeaux is a stately city, prosperous and urbane, as befits the head and heart of the greatest wine-producing area in the world. It developed on the left bank of a great crescent-shaped meander in the Garonne and the combination of water and wine has been the city's raison d'être for many centuries. Its most outstanding feature is the juxtaposition of the river with magnificent 18th- and 19th-century elevations. The full potential of the riverside and other parts of the city is being realised with a huge project of urban regeneration, including the introduction of trams and the pedestrianisation of several streets and squares. In the bid to beautify Bordeaux no detail has been overlooked, including Elizabeth de Portzamparc's designs for street furniture.

It is a visitor-friendly city, not so large as to be intimidating but sizeable enough to offer a variety of artistic, gastronomic and sporting activities. Among many excellent museums are the Musée de l'Aquitaine and the Musée des Beaux Arts; the Cathedral and the Pey-Berland tower are gradually being cleaned and restored; it has a magnificent opera house; and an important wine festival, La Fête le Vin, is held in July. In addition, the improvements are giving Bordeaux a new and vigorous image, of city life overflowing onto the streets and into the pavement cafes.

With around 220,000 inhabitants, plus some 50,000 students, Bordeaux is the ninth city in France and administrative capital of the Region of Aquitaine. It is also the *préfecture* of the Gironde, the largest *département* in France, a vaguely diamond-shaped chunk of land covering 10,000 sq km, which is cleft by the Garonne which, as it flows northwards towards the Atlantic, is swelled by the Dordogne to become the Gironde Estuary.

HISTORY OF BORDEAUX

The merits of Bordeaux's river site were first recognised by a Gallic tribe, the Bituriges-Vivisci, in the 3rd century BC and an important port developed, trading in Cornish tin. In 56 BC there was little resistance to the invading Roman armies of Crassus. During the subsequent Pax Romana, *Burdigala* developed as the administrative capital of *Aquitania* and vines began to be cultivated locally. By the 1st century AD the town had a population of around 20,000 covering some 120ha laid out in a grid pattern but, undefended, it was attacked by Germanic tribes in AD 276; the defenders tore down the public monuments to build walls and *Burdigala* was reduced to some 32ha. The arrival of the Visigoths in AD 409 precipitated the end of the Roman Empire but they in turn were replaced by Clovis, King of the Franks, and Bordeaux was re-established under Frankish rule. By 778 the Carolingian Kingdom of Aquitaine was established, although raids by Saracens and Vikings continued in the 9th and 10th centuries.

Christianity was introduced to Bordeaux towards the end of the 3rd century, and by the 7th century churches and monasteries were established inside and outside the walls.

With the 10th century Aquitaine re-emerged as a duchy and Bordeaux became one of the principal residences of the Dukes. William IX welcomed Pope Urban II in 1096 during the latter's journey to rally support for the first crusade. When William X died on pilgrimage to Compostela in Spain his vast inheritance passed to his daughter, Eleanor, who married the Dauphin of France, the future King Louis VII, in the Cathedral of St-André in 1137. After the dissolution of that marriage in 1152 Eleanor kept her inheritance and promptly married Henry Plantagenet, the future Henry II of England, passing her lands on to him. The people of Bordeaux prospered under English domination, benefiting from the trade, especially in wine, between the two territories belonging to the English Crown. The King-Dukes set up an efficient administrative system and installed their representatives in Bordeaux. The English connection lasted for some 300 years, during which the English developed their appreciation of light red claret wine, and Bordeaux grew in population and wealth. In 1206 Henry III recognised the Jurade (a town council consisting of aldermen and a mayor) which enjoyed a remarkable degree of freedom. By 1220 the town, with about 30,000 inhabitants, had long outgrown the Roman walls. Consequently a new enclosure was constructed to the south and even this had to be further extended between 1302 and 1327.

The Hundred Years War began in 1337, with the first serious attacks on the Guyenne by the French. The Bordelais remained loyal to the English throughout the war despite economic destabilisation compounded by famine and plague. English Bordeaux surrendered on 12th June 1451 and, after the French victory at Castillon in 1453, the whole region returned to France. The French monarch, Charles VII, came down hard on the city, depriving it of many privileges and prohibiting trade with England. He erected defences to control rebellious Bordelais and the local economy was ruined. Under Louis XI (1461–83) there was a change for the better, commerce was reinstated with the English, and a *parlement* (law courts) was established in Bordeaux.

The Renaissance and the age of Humanism brought in its wake serious religious upheaval. Bordeaux, which remained staunchly Catholic, was damaged by Protestant revolts during the Wars of Religion (1568–89). From 1581 Michel de Montaigne, one of the greatest thinkers and writers of the age, as mayor of Bordeaux, reinstated certain privileges. The 17th century was marked by the Counter-Reformation and dominated by Archbishop Cardinal François de Sourdis (*p. 430*), who started the trend for the redevelopment of parts of Bordeaux. After the religious wars ended the city had to face the problems of the Fronde (*see p. 16*), which had repercussions on the wine trade. Conversely there was increasing trade with America and the French West Indies, with the importation of luxury goods including sugar cane.

The Age of Enlightenment has left its mark on Bordeaux's physical aspect. This was the city's golden era. It became the most important port in the kingdom and economic expansion knew no bounds. Trade with the Americas and the Caribbean increased, and from 1716 a royal decree authorising trade in slaves contributed to its wealth. This success is expressed in the grand boulevards and unified architecture introduced by the Intendants (representatives of the king). The Marquis de Tourny (Intendant 1743–57), changed the face of Bordeaux in the 18th century with his pioneering efforts towards healthier urban living, and his work was continued by successive Intendants, Claude Boucher and Dupré de St-Maur. Lawyers and merchants built grand private residences and great patrons funded public buildings. By the time of the Revolution trade was directed primarily towards the French island territories of Martinique, Saint-Dominic and Guadeloupe. One of the major post-Revolution projects on former church land was the Place des Grands-Hommes (c. 1792–97).

At the start of the 19th century the continental blockade on the port imposed by Napoleon put a temporary brake on maritime trade, but once it was lifted confident urban projects were initiated. The first bridge across the Garonne, the Pont de Pierre (1822), was constructed as well as new roads and public monuments, such as that commemorating the Girondins (*see box on p. 25*). The population grew to around 194,000 but a major setback was the series of devastating diseases which virtually wiped out the vineyards. Steam power took over from sail, the docks continued to thrive, and the railway came to Bordeaux in 1852.

The vineyards recovered by the 20th century, but the two world wars, when the French government sought temporary refuge in Bordeaux, took their toll on the city despite there being no serious damage. In the postwar years, the town recovered and continued to expand under two powerful mayors. In 1973 the French mint was transferred from Paris to Pessac on the southwestern periphery of Bordeaux. Bordeaux also has an important share in the aeronautical and space technology, electronics and pharmaceutical industries. The far-reaching urban development projects to enhance the city centre began in 2000 with the first trams up and running in 2003, and should be completed by 2007.

QUARTIER DES GRANDS HOMMES (LE TRIANGLE)

The heart of the city of Bordeaux is Le Triangle, which is created by the three main thoroughfares, Allées de Tourny, Cours de l'Intendance and Cours Georges-Clemenceau. It is the main commercial area, with designer shops, restaurants and cafés. In this area is the Tourist Office on Cours du 30 Juillet, east of Allées de Tourny, the site of the former Café Montesquieu once frequented by Stendhal. Across from it, in the wedge-shaped 18th-century Hôtel Gobineau built by Victor Louis (*see p. 27*), is the Maison du Vin de Bordeaux, decorated inside with two stained-glass windows designed by R. Buthaud. The Allées de Tourny lead south towards Place de la Comédie, the Gallo-Roman site of the ancient forum where a temple dedicated to the goddess Tutellus was demolished in 1675 (fragments known as the Piliers Tutelles are in the Musée d'Aquitaine; *see p. 31*).

The Grand Théâtre and Cours de l'Intendance

The colonnaded façade of the Grand Théâtre (officially the Théâtre de l'Opéra), begun in 1773 and inaugurated in 1780, dominates Place de la Comédie (*guided visits Mon at 11; contact the Tourist Office, T: 05 56 00 66 00*). The unpopular Governor of

Guyenne, Maréchal de Richelieu, commissioned the Parisian architect Victor Louis (1731–1800) to design the theatre, diverting funds earmarked for other public buildings. It became a ballroom in the 19th century, the seat of the National Assembly in 1871, and was used by the French government during both world wars. The imposing Corinthian dodecastyle portico on Place de la Comédie is decorated with twelve female figures representing muses and goddesses. The steps were added in 1846 to raise the entrance above street level. Inside is a Doric vestibule of grandiose proportions with an innovative and monumental stairwell (20m high) decorated with niches and late 19th-century sculptures by Alphonse Dumilâtre, ascending to a loggia covered by a cupola, with Ionic columns. This tour de force was Jean-Louis Garnier's model for the foyer at the Paris Opéra. The charming and elaborate Italian-style auditorium, which has over 1,100 seats, was restored to its original colour scheme of blue, white and gold in 1991. The ceiling was repainted in 1917 by Maurice Roganeau. The new super-deluxe Grand Hôtel de Bordeaux (*see p. 46*), opposite the Grand Théâtre, is due to re-open at time of writing after a complete makeover under the supervision of architect Michel Pétuaud-Létang and interior designer Jacques Garcia.

The Cours de l'Intendance, recently pedestrianised, runs south of Place de la Comédie parallel with the ancient *decumanus*, Rue de la Porte Dijeaux, and roughly on the line of the Roman fortifications. As the town grew its focus shifted and Cours de l'Intendance approximately indicates the division between the medieval town and later developments. A grand and homogenous combination of 17th-, 18th- and 19th-century buildings line Cours de l'Intendance. No. 4, Hôtel du Président de Pichon, dates from 1610–14, and no. 6 has an interior courtyard. On the opposite side, no. 5, with a balcony in wrought iron supported by atlantes with fishy tails, dates from 1785 whereas no. 13 and the arcade, Passage Sarget (with recently opened *salon de thé*) at no. 19, are 19th-century

Rue Martignac and Passage Sarget both lead to Place du Chapelet and the theatrical Baroque **Eglise Notre-Dame** (1684–1707). The work of Pierre-Michel Duplessy in the style of the Counter-Reformation introduced by Vignola's Il Gesù in Rome, this was the church of the Dominican convent. On the façade is a sculpted representation of the Virgin presenting the chapelet (rosary) to St Dominic. The interior is showily elegant with magnificent gilded wrought ironwork, especially around the choir, by Jean Moreau (1781), a splendid original altar and altarpiece in marble with two large supple angels, and a pulpit in carved wood with marble. The nave chapels create narrow sides aisles, and have notable restored *trompe-l'oeil* décor and several early paintings by Frère André (1662–1735). The glass is by Villiets & Hurtrel (19th century) and there is a magnificent organ set off by a wonderful baroque play of curves and counter-curves.

Behind the church, via a narrow passageway on the south side, is Cour Mably, the former Dominican cloisters and chapter house, used for exhibitions and concerts. The exit on the opposite side leads into the circular Place des Grands-Hommes, a hommage to Jean-Jacques Rousseau, Montesquieu and Voltaire, 18th-century philosophers who inspired the Revolution. In the centre is La Grande Ronde, a modern shopping precinct built in 1992 on the site of an old market, with the market now below ground.

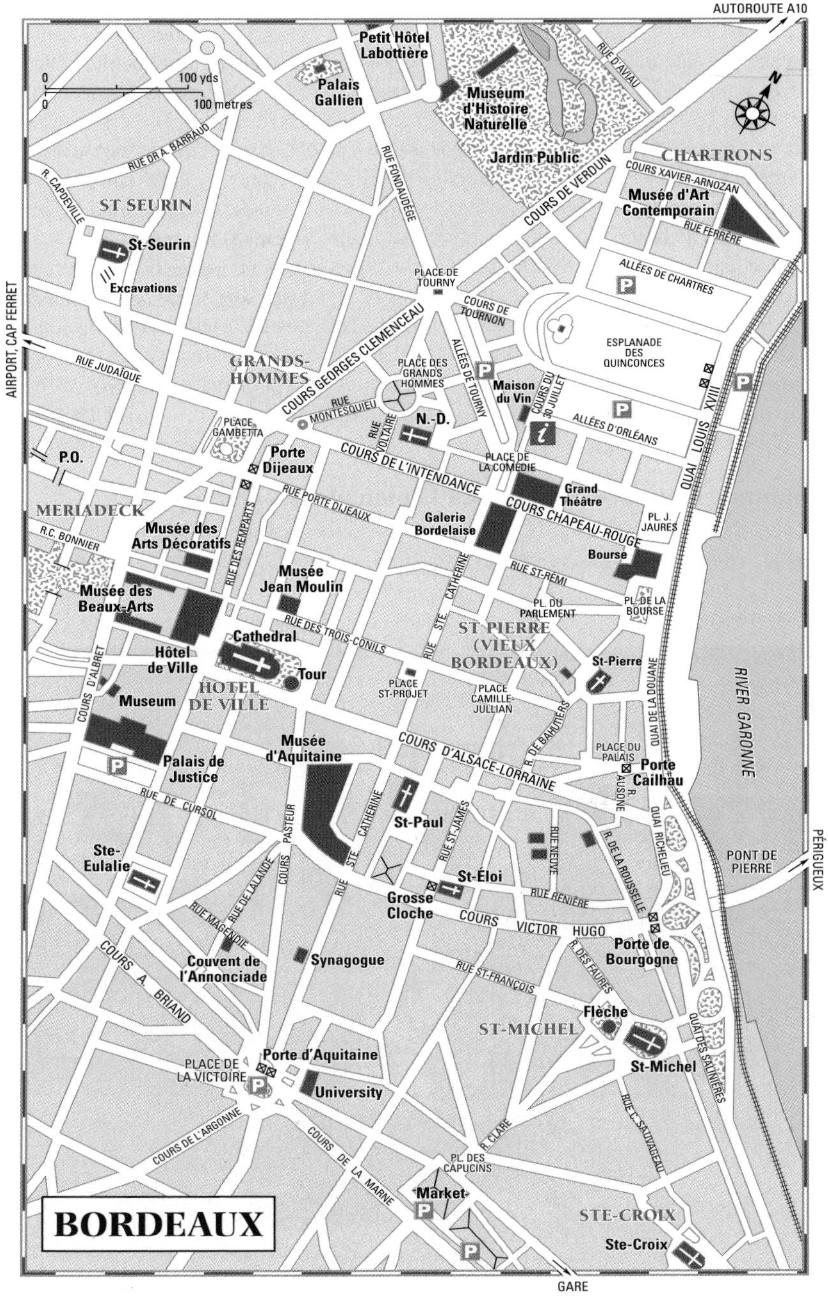
BORDEAUX
AUTOROUTE A10
AIRPORT, CAP FERRET
PÉRIGUEUX
GARE
N
0 100 yds
0 100 metres
Petit Hôtel Labottière
Palais Gallien
Museum d'Histoire Naturelle
Jardin Public
RUE D'AVIAU
CHARTRONS
COURS XAVIER-ARNOZAN
Musée d'Art Contemporain
RUE FERRÈRE
ALLÉES DE CHARTRES
COURS DE VERDUN
RUE FONDAUDÈGE
RUE DR A. BARRAUD
R. CAPDEVILLE
ST SEURIN
St-Seurin
Excavations
PLACE DE TOURNY
COURS DE TOURNON
COURS GEORGES CLEMENCEAU
ALLÉES DE TOURNY
ESPLANADE DES QUINCONCES
RUE JUDAÏQUE
GRANDS-HOMMES
PLACE DES GRANDS HOMMES
Maison du Vin
COURS DU 30 JUILLET
ALLÉES D'ORLÉANS
QUAI LOUIS XVIII
RUE MONTESQUIEU
RUE VOLTAIRE
N.-D.
PLACE GAMBETTA
P.O.
Porte Dijeaux
COURS DE L'INTENDANCE
PLACE DE LA COMÉDIE
Grand Théâtre
MERIADECK
RUE PORTE DIJEAUX
COURS CHAPEAU-ROUGE
PL. J. JAURES
R.C. BONNIER
Musée des Arts Décoratifs
RUE DES REMPARTS
Galerie Bordelaise
Bourse
RUE ST-RÉMI
Musée Jean Moulin
RUE STE CATHERINE
Musée des Beaux-Arts
PL. DU PARLEMENT
PL. DE LA BOURSE
RUE DES TROIS-CONILS
Cathedral
ST PIERRE (VIEUX BORDEAUX)
St-Pierre
Hôtel de Ville
Tour
HOTEL DE VILLE
PLACE ST-PROJET
PLACE CAMILLE-JULLIAN
QUAI DE LA DOUANE
RIVER GARONNE
COURS D'ALBRET
Museum
R. DE BAHUTIERS
Musée d'Aquitaine
COURS D'ALSACE-LORRAINE
PLACE DU PALAIS
Palais de Justice
Porte Cailhau
R. AUSONE
RUE DE CURSOL
COURS PASTEUR
St-Paul
RUE ST-JAMES
RUE NEUVE
R. DE LA ROUSSELLE
QUAI RICHELIEU
PONT DE PIERRE
Ste-Eulalie
RUE DE LALANDE
St-Éloi
Grosse Cloche
RUE RENIÈRE
COURS VICTOR HUGO
RUE MAGENDIE
R. DES FAURES
Porte de Bourgogne
COURS A. BRIAND
Couvent de l'Annonciade
Synagogue
RUE ST-FRANÇOIS
Fleche
ST-MICHEL
St-Michel
QUAI DES SALINIÈRES
PLACE DE LA VICTOIRE
Porte d'Aquitaine
University
RUE C. SAUVAGEAU
COURS DE L'ARGONNE
COURS DE LA MARNE
R. CLARE
PL. DES CAPUCINS
Market
STE-CROIX
Ste-Croix
P

At no. 57 Cours de l'Intendance is the Instituto Cervantes, the Spanish Cultural Centre (*no admission*), where the Spanish painter Francisco Goya lived in exile from 1824 until his death in 1828. Goya was buried in Bordeaux but his body was repatriated in 1889 (*see p. 44*). Set back from the main street is the former Théâtre Français (now a cinema), with a rounded peristyle. At the end of Cours de l'Intendance is Place Gambetta, begun 1743–70 and completed in the 19th century, a lively place where students congregate in the cafes spilling out onto the pavements. To the south is Port Dijeaux, an archway erected at around the same time as the square, marking the start of Rue des Remparts. In this area some of the oldest *mascarons* (*see p. 29*) animate the façades. To the northwest is the old quartier of St-Seurin, which developed outside the walls (*see p. 42*), and southwest is the modern quarter, Mériadeck (*see p. 44*). Cours Georges-Clemenceau links Place Gambetta to Place de Tourny, and on the third side of the Triangle is Allées de Tourny, a wide tree-lined promenade built in 1757 on the site of the first Dominican convent (1227) which is brightened up in winter with a Christmas market.

Monument aux Girondins and Esplanade des Quinconces

Cours de Tournon leads to the Monument aux Girondins (undergoing restoration) a major emblem of Bordeaux on the semicircle created by the Allée de Los Angeles.

Monument aux Girondins (1924).

Dedicated to the Girondins of the Revolution (*see box below*) and to the Republic, the monument combines fountains and a 60m column topped off by an exuberant Liberty 'breaking the chains'. Conceived by Victor Rich and Jean Dumilâtre, the ensemble was first erected 100 years after the Revolution, between 1894 and 1902, but completed only in 1924. It was removed to be melted down in 1943 but discovered still intact in 1945 and re-erected in 1983. The tour de force is the four rearing and plunging aquatic horses with webbed hooves, by Gustave Debrie. Allegorical figures represent the Triumph of the Republic (north) and the Triumph of Concord (south). The French cockerel, as well as Eloquence and History (facing the river), are the only references to the Girondins, whose absence is symbolised by empty pedestals. Beyond the monument is the vast Esplanade des Quinconces (c. 12ha), leading to the Garonne, begun in 1827 on the site of the 15th century Château Trompette.

THE GIRONDINS

This group of revolutionary moderates, who gathered in 1791 under the leadership of Jacques-Pierre Brissot (1754–93), defended liberal ideals. From the educated, professional and merchant classes of Bordeaux, they created a brilliant faction that included lawyers and orators such as Pierre Vergniaud (1753–93) and Armand Gensonné (1758–93). They rebelled against the Jacobin centralism of Paris and set themselves up in direct opposition to the more ruthless Montagnards. The Girondins were finally expelled from the Convention (Revolutionary government) in 1793 and eliminated. One of their heroes, Elie Guadet (1758–94; *see p. 72*), from St-Emilion, was guillotined on Place Gambetta.

The château was built at the end of the Hundred Years War when Aquitaine reverted to the French. Charles VII was resented by the Bordelais who remained loyal to the English, and faced with deprived and rebellious citizens he built the fort to symbolise French power and as protection from possible further English attack. The castle was considerably enlarged at the orders of Louis XIV in 1680 following the problems of the Fronde and a revolt against the Governor of Guyenne, and was demolished in 1816. The name has nothing to do with trumpets, but comes from *tropeyte*, a cordon thrown across the Garonne at various times from the Middle Ages until the 18th century.

The Esplanade is a huge empty area decorated near the river by two rostral columns (1829) glorifying the maritime history of the city and huge statues of Montaigne and Montesquieu erected in 1858. The space is animated every Thursday by the *marché bio* (organic food market) near the columns; and there is an antiques fair which is held here each year for two weeks in November and three weeks in April.

Musée d'Art Contemporain

Open Tues–Sun 11–6; Wed 11–8; closed Mon and holidays; T: 05 56 00 81 50, www.mairie-bordeaux.fr/musees/capc. It has a bookshop and library; terrace restaurant and sushi bar, Le Café du Musée. The exhibition and architecture centre, Arc en Rève (T: 05 56 52 78 36), is in the same building, with bookshop and library.

Known locally as the Entrepôt or CAPC (Centre d'Art Plastique Contemporain), the museum is housed in a converted 19th-century warehouse, L'Entrepôt Lainé, on the corner of Rue Ferrère and Rue Vauban, north of the Esplanade des Quinconces. Typical of port architecture, the warehouse was designed to store 20,000 tons of merchandise from the colonies such as coffee, cocoa, vanilla, spices and timber. The engineer/architect was Claude Deschamps, who also designed the Pont de Pierre (*see p. 31*). The building narrowly avoided demolition in the 1970s and its restoration was entrusted to Jean Pistre and Denis Vallode in 1979. It reopened in its new role in 1984. From the exterior L' Entrepôt is an austere building with a hint of medieval Italy, whereas inside the superimposed arcades and naves create a dimly lit and awesome, church-like space. The building materials—local blond stone, light brick and reddish-brown Oregon pine—are all visible, as are some old graffiti on the walls, and good use is made of the roof-terrace.

The collection

The permanent collection starts with the 1960s. Various trends or movements in contemporary art are covered: Minimalism, American Conceptualism (which emerged as a trend in the 1960s and 1970s, originating with Marcel Duchamp); Italian Arte Povera (a term which the Italian critic Germano Celant used to described poor or impoverished art); English Land Art of the 1970s, represented by Richard Long; and predominantly French and Italian movements of the 1980s such as Figuration Libre and Transavantgarde. The work of present generations is also represented in all forms, figurative or abstract, installation or video. The majority of works are French, although Britain, Italy, Spain and the United States are well represented. Among the many artists shown are Sol LeWitt, Simon Hantai, Jean-Pierre Raynaud, Claude Viallat, Christian Boltanski, Miquel Barcelo, Jose-Maria Sicilia and Susana Solano. There are a few fixed works on the terrace and in the café by Richard Long, Max Neuhaus and Niele Toroni. The collections are regularly rotated to include new acquisitions or trends.

The Jardin Public and the northwest

The Jardin Public, between the Chartrons and St-Seurin districts, was set out by Intendant Tourny in 1746 but spoiled at the Revolution. In 1856 the *jardins à la française* were enlarged and replaced by less formal English-style gardens with ponds, bridges and greenhouses. On the south side is a low colonnaded building with a statue of the Bordelaise painter, Rosa Bonheur. There is also a sculpture of François Mauriac by Zadkine (*see p. 87*), dated 1943. The Botanical Gardens were laid out as part of the Jardin Public and contain a collection of over 3,000 species of living plants.

On the southwest periphery is the wonderfully old-fashioned Musée d'Histoire Naturelle (*open Mon–Fri 11–6; Sat–Sun 2–6; closed Tues and holidays; T: 05 56 48 26 37*), in a house built by R.F. Bonfin at 5 Place Bardineau. Considerable space is given to regional fauna and palaeontology, but there are also specimens from the wider animal world, as well as minerals and fossils. The museum is due for a face-lift but the battalions of birds and animals in their 19th-century vitrines will stay put.

Among the elegant houses in this neighbourhood, notable is the **Petit Hôtel Labottière** at 14 Rue Francis-Martin, a model 18th-century *hôtel particulier* by Etienne Laclotte, which has been carefully restored and furnished by its owners and has two luxury guest apartments (*see p. 47*). Just south, surrounded by smallish houses in Rue Dr Albert-Barraud, is the **Palais Gallien** (*open daily in summer 2–7; in winter confirm with Tourist Office*). This is no palace but the remains of the Roman amphitheatre of *Burdigala*, the oldest monument in Bordeaux. Destroyed by the Barbarians in AD 276, a chunk of it was removed in the 19th century and only an evocative fragment of the great structure, which held 15,000 spectators, is left standing. The monumental gate and a section of the walls and arcades show the characteristic small stonework and brick coursing of Roman construction in Gaul. There is a model of the amphitheatre in the Musée d'Aquitaine (*see p. 31*).

THE QUARTIER ST-PIERRE (VIEUX BORDEAUX)

The melée of the older streets of Bordeaux creates an area of great character. Cours du Chapeau Rouge, perpendicular to the Garonne, was built on the site of the old city ditch outside the Gallo-Roman ramparts and an area of marshland where houses originally had to be built on stilts. All this changed in the 16th century when it became the route for royal processions. The handsome buildings lining it now are mainly 18th-century, although no. 40 (now a branch of the Banque Nationale de Paris), is a 17th-century *hôtel particulier* and no. 18 dates from the end of the 16th century. The land behind the Grand Théâtre is known as îlot Louis, after the architect Victor Louis, who set out to develop the whole area. No. 21, the Hôtel de Saige, is typical of Louis' project. Cours du Chapeau Rouge ends at Place Jean-Jaurès and the Quai de la Douane, one of a succession of quays (*see box below, p. 28*) along the Port de la Lune (Moon Harbour), the old port of Bordeaux on the long curve in the river which is symbolised by a crescent in the city coat of arms.

The magnificent ensemble, **Place de la Bourse** (1733–55), was the first and most enduringly successful 18th-century project in Bordeaux. On the left is the former Hôtel des Fermes du Roy (customs clearance house) and its opposite number the old Palais de la Bourse (Chamber of Commerce), while the central pavilion contains the reinstated American consulate. Intendant Boucher was the instigator but Jacques Gabriel and his son, Jacques-Ange, provided the architectural genius. Jacques, premier architect to Louis XV was bowled over by the potential of the site and set about demolishing a section of the old town and medieval city walls. Giant Ionic columns span the two upper storeys of the pedimented angle pavilions and the central free-standing pavilion, whereas the remaining façades have giant pilasters. The attic storey and high roofs bring a French touch to Italian Baroque, *mascarons* (*see box opposite*) animate the arcaded ground floor and vases balance on the high balustrades.

THE QUAYS OF BORDEAUX

Despite the importance of the river, the city turned its back to it until the end of the 17th century, and only shops or wooden huts stood outside the city walls. Gradually, imposing mansions were built lining the river to impress visitors arriving by ship. The development was in the hands of a few wealthy local families and the principal architects were Bonfin, Chevay, Moulinié, Richefort and Alary. Alterations in the 19th century did not totally destroy the overall effect but in the mid-20th century the port shifted to the right bank, leaving in its wake abandoned dockyard properties and a wide, fast-track highway. The massive project to revitalise and reanimate 4km of the waterfront between the Pont de Pierre and the Cours de la Martinique in the Chartrons district, began in 1999. A wide pedestrian promenade follows the riverbank, with open spaces, trees, grass, and a cycle track. Many of the warehouses have been demolished to open up river vistas and show off the beautiful old properties facing the Gironde, which have been restored to their former glory. Hangar 14 now houses an exhibition space, and other warehouses (15–19) have been converted by architect Claude Marty, and behind the colourful facades are shops and restaurants which overflow onto the terraces completely transforming the Chartrons district (*see p. 44*). Further south, in the St-Michel district, a garden is planned to enhance the Quai Ste-Croix. Trams now (or soon will) serve the most of the city's left bank quays. The right bank is also changing and improving, and affords superb views of the city.

The small section of Bordeaux on the right bank, opposite Place de la Bourse, called La Bastide (formerly the site of a fort or bastion) is also enjoying a 21st-century rejuvenation. It can be identified by the elongated, domed bell-tower of Ste-Marie de la Bastide, built by Paul Abadie in 1865. A cinema, restaurant and brasserie and the Gare d'Orléans (19th century) have been revamped. In its infancy is the Jardin Botanique (*open summer 8–8, winter 8–6; T: 05 56 52 18 77*), the first of its kind in 25 years. It is an open rectangular space, 800m by 70m, opposite Place des Quinconces. It was designed by Catherine Mosbach, and its objective is the study and protection of plant species from different parts of the world. There is a large area given over to pools and aquatic plants, and another representing 11 landscapes of Aquitaine. One of the best night views of the illuminated Place de la Bourse is from the restaurant L'Estaquade (*see p. 48*) in La Bastide.

Place de la Bourse, which set the pattern for other elevations along the quayside, was once graced with the bronze statue of Louis XV. However, this was melted down at the Revolution and only the base has survived in the Musée d'Aquitaine (*see p. 31*). It was replaced in 1864 by the *Three Graces*, and tradition has it that these three beauties represent Queen Victoria, Empress Eugenie and Isabel II, Queen of Spain. So special is Place de la Bourse that it was the first monument in the city to be illuminated at night. The **Musée National des Douanes** (*open Tues–Sun 10–6; closed Mon; T: 05 56 48 82 82*), which retraces the history of the French Customs with the aid of documents, uniforms, weapons, models and tools of the trade, is installed in the former Hôtel des Fermes du Roy.

MASCARONS

The *mascarons* that adorn the façades of Bordeaux were first used in Place de la Bourse and became so popular in 18th-century Bordeaux that some 3,000 have been identified. Usually they are placed above the windows of the first floor, *l'étage noble*, although in Place de la Bourse they are above the ground-floor arcades. There is great variety within the masks, with heads ranging from beautiful to grotesque, from Christian to pagan, and from young to old. Some are original (18th–19th centuries), others are modern remakes. The *mascherone* motif itself was imported from Renaissance Italy.

Around St-Pierre

West of Place de la Bourse are Rue St-Rémi, the continuation of the old Roman road, and Rue Fernand-Philippart, formerly Rue Royale. This is lined with a series of handsome Louis XV-style houses, notably No. 16, with an angle balcony supported by a squinch, typical of the mid-18th century. At the end is the former Place du Marché Royal, now called Place du Parlement, although the *parlement* was never on this site. A charming square (c. 1750), it has a number of original Rococo façades still intact, a few reconstructions to maintain the overall effect, and a 19th-century fountain. Around the square are several eating places with terraces.

The streets beyond follow the medieval layout but the buildings are mainly 17th- and 18th-century. The Quartier St-Pierre, renovated under the Loi Malraux (1970–75), is a living neighbourhood with a mixture of housing, local shops and restaurants. Rue du Parlement St-Pierre leads to the **church of St-Pierre**. The west front (rebuilt 14th–15th centuries) still carries a few original Flamboyant carvings although it was heavily restored in the 19th century when the belfry was added. High aisles light the nave in the style of a hall church, and the chancel has been renovated. Behind the altar is a 17th-century *Pietà*. The church's dedication to the patron of fishermen recalls that Place St-Pierre was built over the site of the ancient Gallo-Roman port at the mouth of the Devèze River which began to silt up in the 6th century. The port was filled in completely during the 12th century and reconstructed further south and the first church was erected. The town walls were extended in the 14th century to contain the urban spread but the remains were demolished in the 18th century. The magnificent Gallo-Roman 2nd/3rd-century bronze *Hercules*, now in the Musée d'Aquitaine (*see p. 31*), was discovered here in the 19th century during excavations.

Square Vinet is a product of the 1970s–80s in an area which has few open spaces, and it has recently been enhanced with *murs-vegetals*, vertical flowerbeds. In Place Camille-Jullian is a monument created from fragments of antique masonry in memory of the archaeologist Jullian and on the angle of Rue Bahutiers and Rue Courcelles are two rare end-15th–16th century buildings, the oldest in Bordeaux. Place du Palais is an 18th-century square named after the 11th-century Château de l'Ombrière (from *ombre*, the shade afforded by the trees which once surrounded it), a fortress-palace built against the ramparts with a tall keep, courtyards, fountains and gardens, which was demolished in 1800. The property of the Dukes of Aquitaine, it was occupied by the English seneschal in the 12th century and was favoured by Eleanor and Henry Plantagenet (*see p. 12*) during their visits to Bordeaux. After the Hundred Years War, the *parlement* used the palace for their assizes. Close by in Rue des Argentiers (silversmith's street) is **Bordeaux Monumental** (*open May–Oct, Mon–Sat 9.30–1 & 2–7, Sun and holidays; 10–1 & 2–6; Nov–April, Mon–Sat 10–1 & 2–6; Sun and holidays 2–6; T: 05 56 48 04 24*). This new exhibition sets out with photographs and text the history of the buildings of Bordeaux and gives an excellent background to a visit to the city.

Between Place du Palais and the river stands **Porte Cailhau** or Porte du Palais (*open daily in summer 2–7; in winter confirm with Tourist Office*), which was built into the old ramparts in 1493–96 and dedicated to Charles VIII. Fortified, with high slate-clad roofs, lantern, dormer windows and Flamboyant decoration, it was both defensive gateway and triumphal arch. Bearing the King's arms on the town side, it commemorates the French conquest of Naples at Fornovo in 1495. On the river side are re-carved images of Charles VIII, Cardinal d'Epinay (Bishop of Bordeaux) and St John the Baptist, patron of the Jurade. It was renovated in the 19th century.

Cours Alsace-Lorraine was built in the 19th century on the site of the south section of the Roman wall to link the Garonne and Place de la Cathédrale. Rue Ausone, on the south side, was named after the Gallo-Roman poet Ausonius, who taught at the university of Burdigala and was proconsul of the Gauls. In Rue de la Rousselle at nos 23–25, is the birthplace of Michel de Montaigne (*see p. 125*), where he was married in 1565 and lived until 1570. Jeanne de Lartigue, wife of Montesquieu, lived in Impasse de la Rue Neuve.

Rue St-James runs into Cours Victor-Hugo under the recently restored **Grosse Cloche** or Porte St-Eloi, a flagship monument and symbol of Bordeaux. The gate in the ancient walls has a 13th century base, was remade in the 15th-18th century, and renovated in the 19th century. It spanned the pilgrim route to Santiago de Compostela (*see p. 11*) in Spain. The adjacent Hôtel de Ville burned down in 1735, but the city coat of arms representing it on the balustrade features the Grosse Cloche, a crescent and waves evoking the Garonne, the leopard of Guyenne, and a crown. The bell, which is suspended from an arch between two sturdy round towers, dates from 1775, and the present clock from 1759. Beside the gate is former church of St-Eloi (11th century) with a pretty 15th-century façade, all heavily restored, where the new magistrates of the Jurade gathered annually to be sworn in, and in this area Montaigne's Essays were printed. Around the Rue du Mirail, the space between the 13th- and 14th-century *enceintes* was occupied by the Jesuits in the 16th century, and has some fine *hôtels particuliers*.

A few fragments of the city walls are still visible at nos 51–53 Cours Victor-Hugo, which is a busy, cosmopolitan street ending at Porte de Bourgogne, a triumphal arch built in 1755 on the quay. Beyond is Place de Bir Hakeim and the Quai des Salinières, the dock for salt used in curing fish and meat in Rue de la Rousselle. The Pont de Pierre (1822) was designed by Claude Deschamps, who resolved for the first time the technical difficulties of throwing a bridge across the Garonne. In the opposite direction, Rue Ste-Catherine links this quartier to the Grands Hommes, which acquired its present rectilinear layout in the 18th century, although it probably follows the ancient cardo running north–south. The name refers to the Santa-Caterina chapel in a church which no longer exists, and the north end of the street was marked until the 18th century by the 12th-century Porta-Médoca (Médoc Gate). The equivalent of Toulouse's Rue St-Rome (*see p. 599*), it has always been a very popular commercial area where almost anything can be purchased and is at its best during the daytime. No. 36 Rue des Ayres is a good example of 17th-century domestic architecture. The former Jesuit church of St-Paul (1663–76) contains, above the main altar, a magnificent marble sculpture by Guillaume Coustou, the *Exaltation of St Francis Xavier*, installed in 1748. Alongside the church at no. 20 is the former mayoral residence with a medieval tower, where Montaigne lived when in office. Further north, at the intersection with Rue des Trois Conils, is the sad little Place St-Projet, where the gibbet once stood, replaced now by the tower of the church, a 15th-century graveyard cross and a fountain of 1738.

QUARTIER DE L'HÔTEL DE VILLE

Musée d'Aquitaine

Open Tues–Sun 11–6, closed Mon and holidays; T: 05 56 01 51 00.

The Musée d'Aquitaine at 20 Cours Pasteur displays the history and archaeology of the modern region of Aquitaine (excluding the Basque region which has its own museum; *see p. 449*). Along with the city rejuvenation project, the museum has been refurbished. Its ambitious temporal span is from the Lower Paleolithic (c. 700,000 years ago) to the 20th century, encompassing regional ethnography, rural and maritime activities, the wine industry, commercial life and the influence of overseas trade. The 19th-century building is the former Faculty of Arts and Sciences, by P.-C. Durand, built on the site of the Couvent des Feuillants. The museum, transferred here in 1985, occupies two floors. The Goupil Museum, in the same building, holds a large collection of prints and photographs 1827–1920 published by Maison Goupil et Cie in Paris.

The exhibits

The Museum begins at the beginning, with prehistory, condensing hundreds of thousands of years of the development of Man according to the rich finds in the southwest of France, into a few rooms.

The exhibits range from primitive stone tools to the reconstruction of a rock shelter of the Middle Palaeolithic period (c. 100,000–35,000 BC), examples of Upper Perigordian flints and the development of tools including the first needles. The progression of cave art is studied through carvings, such as the stone relief of a female figure known as the *Venus of Laussel* (25,000 years old) and small intricate carvings on bone, and the increasing sophistication of rock paintings in the Magdalenian period including a reproduction of the painting of running deer from Lascaux. Neolithic and Bronze Age objects demonstrate the progression from stone to metal, with objects used for funerary rites, in domestic life and for adornment.

Archaeological finds from the Gallo-Roman city of *Burdigala*, from 56 BC onwards, include pieces of monumental architecture and smaller objects relating to economic and social issues. Religious cults and funerary practices are represented by a number of burial urns, altars and stelae, notably that of the child Laetus (late 1st–early 2nd century). Also displayed are the magnificent bronze *Hercules* (2nd century AD; *see p. 30*), mosaics, construction materials, pottery, and treasures lifted from the Garonne riverbed. There is a modern maquette of the Roman theatre, Palais Gallien (*see p. 27*). The evolution from Roman to early Christian Aquitaine introduces sarcophagi, crosses and chrisms, jewellery, capitals and mosaics. Medieval expansion of the Church is addressed by displays on the pilgrimage and religious communities such as La Sauve Majeure. There is a section dedicated to the period when Anglo-Gascon Guyenne was under the control of the English King-Dukes (1154–1453), with objects from daily and religious life, and from England.

The exhibits relating to Bordeaux during the modern period begins after 1453, with the return of Guyenne to France and the establishment of a *parlement* and stock exchange. The Renaissance period is represented by the cenotaph of the writer Michel de Montaigne (*see p. 125*) and twisted columns from the chapel of the Monastery of St-Antoine-des-Feuillants (the site of this museum), where Montaigne was buried in 1592.

The prosperity of the 18th century is evoked by models of merchant ships and fragments of architecture such as the pedestal of the statue of Louis XV from Place de la Bourse (*see p. 27*). The contemporary period has recently been enlarged with a new room devoted to the 20th century.

There is an important ethnological section illustrating the links between rural traditions throughout modern Aquitaine as well as activities specific to certain areas, such as oyster-farming in the Arcachon Basin, the production of cheese from ewes' milk in the Béarn, and wine production in the Bordeaux region. With the development of the port of Bordeaux, the city became the gateway to other continents, and a sample of the various ethnological curiosities and collections that found their way to Bordeaux is displayed in 'Cultures of the World'.

Cathedral of St-André

Until the 18th century the cathedral, on Place Pey-Berland, had a very different aspect from today. Built on marshy land, against the Roman wall to the west, the archbishops' palace was huddled up to the northwest flank. This majestic Gothic edifice, begun in the 13th century, was added to and altered over three centuries. Only when the mania for demolishing and rebuilding took hold in the 18th century was the old archbishops' residence replaced by a new one further north and the obsolete ramparts and cloister finally disappeared. In the early 21st century the Cathedral and Tour Pey-Berland are clean and golden again, freed from years of grime, using a revolutionary laser technique, and further enhanced with the remodelling of Place Pey-Berland which is now a large pedestrian precinct with pavement cafés, while trams glide silently by.

The present cathedral superseded two earlier churches. The first was consecrated in 1096 by Urban II. Here, on 25th July 1137, Eleanor of Aquitaine married the Dauphin of France, the future Louis VII. Of that church only a fragment of the west wall, built in rubble, still stands. It was replaced by a great Romanesque cathedral, possibly domed, which can only be guessed at from the partly 12th-century walls of the nave. That structure was, in its turn, subsumed in the next series of works which began in the 13th century and led to what we now see. In c. 1280 the construction of a new choir and transepts was undertaken in the Gothic or French style, inspired by northern cathedrals such as Amiens. By the mid-14th century there were only two entrances, north and south, when work was speeded up thanks to donations from Bertrand de Got (*see p. 92*), the future Pope Clement V. The wedding of Anne of Austria and Louis XIII took place here in 1616.

The exterior

The north door (c. 1330), always the principal entrance, has been heavily reworked, but the carvings show the Ascension and Last Supper with 10 angels, 12 Apostles and 14 Patriarchs in the intrados. The Porte Royale (1250), east of the north transept, was the private entrance from the medieval archbishops' residence in the northwest angle of the church. Now the door is walled up but it was used in the past by visiting royalty. The sculptures around this portal—*Last Judgement*, Christ and angels, Apostles, bishops and martyrs—owe a debt to Reims. In the 19th century Eugene Viollet-le-Duc (*see p. 95*) took inspiration from the sculptures, which remain untouched, for his restorations to Notre-Dame de Paris. The south façade with a rose window is c. 1400, although the upper part of the north façade was not finished until the 16th century. Extra buttresses, mainly to the south and southwest, were added to support the vaults in the late 15th and early 16th centuries, and the Renaissance 'Gramont' buttress, dominating Porte Royale, is c. 1530. The west front is devoid of ornament because it originally abutted the ramparts and only in 1808 (the old Roman wall having been demolished in the 18th century) was the west door opened, although Paul Abadie's project for the west façade was not carried out. The south door was damaged at the Revolution when it was enlarged to allow a cart to pass through. Spires were not added to the two south towers because of the boggy terrain, and for the same reason the belfry is free-standing.

The interior

From inside the west door is a sweeping view of the vast, aisleless nave, determined by the earlier cathedral, and the Gothic crossing and chancel. When the decision was made to rebuild the cathedral c. 1280, work started in the east end with the five radial chapels. The choir elevation was built 1310–30, and the transepts were completed in large part by c. 1360. There are two elegant rose windows in the transepts with 14th-century tracery in the south and 16th century in the north. The choir has typically tall pointed arcades, small blind triforium and high clerestory windows and is surrounded by a double aisle, the outer one enclosed by wrought-iron grills to create chapels. A plan to rebuild the nave was abandoned and the existing Romanesque building was amended by heightening the walls. Nevertheless, it is still slightly lower than the chancel although the large windows allow more direct light. A fragment of the Romanesque foundations is visible at the base of the north wall. Work continued on the cathedral until the 16th century, including the west vaults of the nave, evident from the jump from clustered piers to a single shaft supporting the roof. The organ loft is built from the remains of a Renaissance *jubé* c. 1530, dismantled in 1804, and the organ case is of 1748.

Furnishings include two Renaissance bas-reliefs under the organ loft, the pulpit (18th century), tombs (19th century), elegant wrought ironwork around the choir by Charlut (18th century), and stalls (1690) by a member of the Tournier family from Gourdon (*see p. 173*), as well as wooden doors (18th century) at the end of the choir from the church of St-Bruno. On the floor of the choir is a Roman mosaic from Hippo, Algeria, sent here by the first archbishop of Algeria after its conquest in 1830; the episcopal chairs are 19th-century. In the Mont Carmel chapel, north of the choir, is an alabaster statue (14th century) of *Our Lady of the Nave*, typical of those imported from England at that period. The third chapel to the northeast contains the mausoleum in stone and marble (1562) of Antoine de Noailles, and two alabaster reliefs (15th century), reputed to be English, of the *Assumption* and *Resurrection*. Opposite the chapel, in the ambulatory, is a polychromed English alabaster of St Martial. The axial chapel has some fine carvings of the *Life of the Virgin* and the *Childhood of Christ* in the spandrels and wood panels (17th century). The southeast Ste-Anne chapel was found to have 15th-century paintings under 19th-century murals, and these have been restored. Opposite is the Gothic funerary niche or *enfeu* of Archbishop Arnaud de Canteloup (d. 1332). The statue of Joan of Arc in the ambulatory is by Antoine Bourdelle (*see p. 324*) and against the choir on the south is a rather lovely *St Anne and the Virgin* (early 16th century). In the St-Joseph chapel is a wooden reliquary (15th century), a Spanish *Crucifixion* in ivory (15th century), and a lectern in wrought iron (18th century).

There is little stained glass except in the south rose window, which has kept its original 16th-century iconography, whereas the glass in the north rose has been mixed up following several restorations.

There are several 17th- and 18th-century paintings, including a *Crucifixion* by Jacob Jordaens in a chapel on the south side.

Around the cathedral

The unmistakable **Tour Pey-Berland** (*open June–Sept 10–6; Oct–May 10–12.30 & 2–5.30; closed Mon*) is a stand-alone Flamboyant Gothic tower (1440–46) which takes its name from the archbishop at the time. It is 50m high and contains the great bell, Ferdinand-André, installed in 1869. Weighing in at 1150kg (8 tonnes), it is the fourth heaviest in France. In 1863 the over-emphatic gilded statue of Notre-Dame d'Aquitaine was placed on the highest pinnacle.

Opposite the north flank of the cathedral is the **Musée Jean Moulin** (*open Tues–Fri 11–6; Sat, Sun 2–6; closed Mon and holidays; T: 05 56 79 66 00*), dedicated to the Resistance, the Deportation and the Free French Army, and in particular to the great hero of the Resistance, Jean Moulin, whose secret office is re-created.

Since 1835 the **Hôtel de Ville** (*guided visits mid-June–mid-Sept, Wed at 2.30*) has occupied the Palais Rohan (1773–86), the former archbishops' residence built by Archbishop Ferdinand-Maximillien Mériadeck de Rohan which occupies a large area to the northwest of the cathedral. The building work was initially financed by the sale of neighbouring land, but the project became so expensive that the Archbishop had to dig in his own pockets. The first architect was Joseph Etienne but he displeased the prelate and was replaced by Bonfin, the city architect. The main building is separated from the square by an arcaded loggia which is linked to the main façade by low build-ings on both sides of the courtyard. The upper floors of the main elevation are spanned by giant Ionic pilasters on a rusticated base, and articulated by a central pavilion with rounded pediments. The rear façade has a triangular pediment and is prolonged on each side by two low pavilions with balustrades and garlands. The restrained lines and composition are undoubtedly influenced by Victor Louis, who was working on the Grand Théâtre at the time. The interior has conserved its monu-mental staircase by Bonfin, a suite of grand rooms on the ground floor with wood panels carved by Cabirol, and a dining room decorated with *trompe-l'oeil* figures. More examples of elegant 18th-century buildings are in Rue Bouffard, Cours d'Albret (nos 91, 29, and 17) and Place Pey-Berland.

Musée des Beaux-Arts

Open Wed–Mon 11–6, closed Tues and holidays; T: 05 56 10 20 56, www.culture.fr./cul-ture/bordeaux. The collections are housed in the two buildings flanking the Jardin de la Mairie, 20 Cours d'Albret. The main entrance is in the south building. Temporary exhibi-tions are held in the Galerie des Beaux-Arts, Place du Colonel Raynal, which runs off the Cours d'Albret; T: 05 56 96 51 60.

The Museum, which opened in 1801, was one of 15 established in France by Napoleon. The founder curators until 1859 were father and son Pierre Lacour, who did not benefit, as at some of the other museums, from collections being put at their disposal that had been seized during the Revolution. Even so, today its 3,000 works (not all on show at one time) constitute an excellent representative cross-section of the main currents of Western art from the Renaissance to the mid-20th century. There is a special emphasis, however, on the work of certain Bordelais artists, especially in

the modern section, with some revealing examples of work by Odilon Redon, Albert Marquet and André Lhote. The works are pleasantly and simply displayed in a series of continuous galleries.

South gallery: In the south gallery are Italian paintings from the Quattrocento to the Baroque (15th–18th centuries) including a large *Virgin and Child between Saints* by Perugino and studio; *Tarquin and Lucretia* by Titian (c. 1571); and Veronese's *Holy Family with St Dorothy* (c. 1560). Representative of followers of Caravaggio in 17th-century Europe are the *Lute Player* (1624) by the Dutch painter Hendrick ter Brugghen; and from France, *David holding Goliath's Head* by Aubin Vouet and *St Sebastian* by the Master of the Candle. Among the varied Northern European works are Davidsz. de Heem's *Still Life with a Rose* (1636); Rubens' the *Martyrdom of St George* (c. 1615); van Dyck's portrait of Marie de Medicis (c. 1631; *pictured opposite*); and Jan 'Velvet' Brueghel's *Wedding Dance* (c. 1600); as well as a little masterpiece of textures and surfaces by Chardin, *Still Life with Pieces of Meat* (1730). There are a number of British 18th-century portraits—reminders that many Britons settled here at the time—by such artists as Lawrence and Reynolds, and by Reynolds' Scottish counterpart, Allan Ramsay. Topographical engravings by Léo Drouyn record local historic monuments and moments, and a large painting by Pierre Lacour, the museum's first curator, records a view of the port and quays of Bordeaux in 1804.

North gallery: Here are displayed works from the 19th century onwards,

starting chronologically at the far end of the gallery. The most famous and Romantic of the five by Delacroix in the museum, *La Grèce sur les Ruines de Missolonghi* (1826), is a tribute to the heroism of the women and children who were taken hostage during the Greek battle for independence from the Ottoman Empire in 1821. Corot's *Diana Bathing* (1855) is the essence of discretion in a luminous dawn landscape whereas Henri Gervex's *Rollo*, inspired by a poem by Musset, is decidedly titillating and predictably drew the crowds when first exhibited in 1878. A small, intimate painting by Bonnard, *Les Bas Noirs* (1899), contrasts with a large and phantasmagorical painting by the Toulousain Henri Martin (*see p. 187*), *Chacun sa Chimère* (1891), inspired by Baudelaire.

Modern collection: This manages to be wide ranging but at the same time draws particular attention to three local artists, Redon, Lhote and Marquet. The Symbolist Odilon Redon was influenced by Delacroix's paintings in Bordeaux, as well as by Gustave Moreau and by Darwin's theories. He produced atmospheric works, often lithographs or pastels, with a dreamlike and metaphysical tendency, as in the enigmatic *Le Chevalier Mystique* (c. 1892). André Lhote produced a decorative version of Cubism in such works as *Baigneuses* (1935), *Pins à Arcachon* (1948) and

Portrait by van Dyck of Marie de Medicis (1631).

Entrée du Bassin à Flot de Bordeaux (1912). Lhote played an important role in diffusing 20th-century developments in painting through his teaching and writing. Albert Marquet, close friend and working colleague of Matisse, Manguin and Dufy, had a brief encounter with Fauvism, *Nu à Contre Jour* (c. 1909–11), but tended generally towards a subtler palette, understated but poetic, as in *Naples, le Voilier* (1909).

Guillaumin, Renoir, Morisot and Cassatt, the American painter of child portraits, are represented in the collection. There are also some early works by Matisse, *Belle Isle* (1896), a *Nature morte* (1898–99) and the small *Paysage Villars-sur-Ollon* (1901). Works by lesser-known adherents to the Fauve move-ment include *Paysage de Cagnes* (c. 1910) by Louis Valtat, from Dieppe, Jean Puy's *Nu aux Bas Roses* (c. 1924); and Othon Frièze's *Paysage—La Route* (c. 1907). Picasso's portrait of his wife reading, *Olga Lisant*, is a monochrome oil of 1920, monumental and serene, characteristic of his work after the First World War. The Lithuanian Chaim Soutine, who painted *L'Homme Bleu sur la Route* (la Montée de Cagnes, 1923/24), belonged to the School of Paris, and *L'Eglise Notre Dame* (1925) was painted by the Viennese Expressionist Oskar Kokoschka, who visited France in 1925 and spent 15 days in Bordeaux. Abstraction is repre-sented by Jean Harbin and Surrealism by André Masson.

Musée des Arts Décoratifs

39 Rue Bouffard; open Mon–Fri 11–6; Sat–Sun 2–6; closed Tues; T: 05 56 00 72 53.
North of the Beaux-Arts, the museum is housed in the Hotel de Lalande, an impres-sive 18th-century mansion with a vast courtyard, built by Etienne Laclotte for the Marquis of Lalande. The collections concentrate mainly on the decorative arts of the Bordeaux region in the 18th century: furniture, ceramics, glassware, the goldsmith's art and wrought ironwork are exhibited in a series of panelled rooms on three floors. Three period rooms evoke the opulence of bourgeois interiors in Bordeaux in the 18th and 19th centuries, and five small rooms are dedicated to a collection of Royalist sou-venirs from the Jeanvrot collection. In the upper rooms are pewter, arms and locks, as well as earlier works such as enamels and 16th–17th-century furnishings. Frequent temporary exhibitions are mounted. The tea room is to the left of the courtyard.

SAINT-MICHEL & SAINTE-CROIX DISTRICTS

South of Vieux Bordeaux and Cours Victor Hugo, Rue des Faures or Rue de la Fusterie lead to one of the city's great monuments, the Basilica of St-Michel, from which the lively and picturesque district takes its name. On Sunday mornings, the large Place Canteloup is busy with a fleamarket and on Monday and Saturday mornings, a local produce market. This was once the *quartier* of the craftsmen—such as carpenters (Rue Carpenteyre) and coopers (Rue de la Fusterie)—who worked the wood which arrived by river in *gabares*, and is now undergoing a revival. The square is surrounded by

Picasso: *Olga Lisant* (1920).

North African cafés where you can sip a good mint tea. A statue by Gaston Leroux to Ulysse Despaux (1844–1925), a local poet who composed in the local *bordeluche* dialect, stands on the square.

Built on a hillock sloping towards the river, the **Basilica of St-Michel** was begun in 1350, replacing an earlier one destroyed during the Hundred Years War, and took some 200 years to complete. The dominant style is Flamboyant with some early Renaissance influences. Following the collapse of the chancel vaults in 1693, there were a number of alterations and additions in the 18th century, more renovations in the 19th century, and in June 1940 the church suffered from bomb damage. The Flamboyant west door (incomplete), presents the *Adoration of the Shepherds* and of the Magi (16th century) in vertical panels which seem to be original. The north portal, considered the best of the entrances, shows the transition between late Gothic and early Renaissance in the carvings. The tympanum, divided vertically, contains the *Expulsion of Adam and Eve*, and the *Sacrifice of Abraham* (c. 1520). There are angels in the intrados of the arches and the prophets Abraham, Isaac, Jacob and David in the niches, and a *Trinity with the Virgin and St John* above. On the south portal, reworked in the 19th century, is the *Apparition of St Michael*.

The interior is all of the same height, giving a feeling of spaciousness similar to a hall church, with a stunning collection of modern stained glass. The choir and flat-ended apse, built in the 14th century, perhaps show English influence; the transept and aisles date from the 15th century, and most of the chapels were endowed by local merchants from the 16th century. The vaults to the west, where there are no capitals, were completed 1553–54. Wrought-iron screens were added in the 18th century to close off the chapels. The southwest chapel contains a 15th-century relief illustrating the legend of St Ursula protecting her Virgins. In the St Joseph chapel on the north, with lierne vaulting, is an 18th-century retable containing statues of the Virgin, St Catherine and St Barbara and 16th-century English alabasters, and on the pillar opposite this chapel is a late 18th-century *Pietà*, its pathos emphasised by the realistic approach. The carving of the *Descent from the Cross* or *Entombment* (1492) in the southeast is a characteristic group including the Virgin, Mary Magdalene and St John. The mahogany and marble pulpit (1753) shows St Michael overpowering the Dragon and the organ case (1760–64) is by Micot. A little 16th-century stained glass survived the bombing, but the bold and colourful 20th-century windows (1962–64) were created by Ingrand, Couturat, Godin and Lardeur.

To the west of the church on Place Canteloup stands a soaring hexagonal bell-tower known locally as **La Flèche** (*open daily in summer 2–7; in winter confirm with Tourist Office*). The tower was built 1472–86, with the financial help of Louis XI, fervent devotee of St Michael, and is detached from the church due to boggy ground. It contains 22 bells cast in the 19th century. Beneath it is a charnel house containing models of mummified corpses, popular but macabre curiosities. Between 1861 and 1869 Paul Abadie, a Historicist architect of eclectic tastes, better known as a restorer, practically rebuilt the steeple and the tower which, unsurprisingly, affords spectacular views.

Sainte-Croix

Rue Camille Sauvageau links St-Michel with Ste-Croix. From the 12th century until 1801 there was a royal mint in this area, hence Porte de la Monnaie (1752–58) and Quai de la Monnaie. In Rue Porte de la Monnaie are two restaurants of renown, La Tupina and Chez Greg. On Quai de la Grave is part of a Neoclassical fluted column incorporated in the Grave Fountain (1787).

A densely populated suburb developed extra-muros around the 11th–12th-century Benedictine **abbey of Ste-Croix**, enclosed within fortified walls in the 14th century. The first church was built in the 7th century on a Gallo-Roman necropolis. The 12th-century church was influenced by the architecture of the Saintonge or Poitou, former provinces of the Dukes of Aquitaine, but the west front was subjected to the heavy hand of Paul Abadie (*see p. 112*) in the 1860s, which left little of the original. The lower part, arranged like a triumphal arch, has remained essentially unchanged and the sculptures of *Avarice* and *Lust* in the intrados of the smaller arches, and the shafts and capitals, may be original. The same cannot be said for the level above, which has been drastically rearranged. The south tower is mainly 12th-century, but the north tower and the shorter adjacent elevation are fantasies of Abadie. The church has a tall apse and two smaller lateral chapels on a flat-ended choir.

Among surviving Romanesque decoration in the interior are several decorated capitals on the massive piers of the crossing, including three storiated ones, *Jesus among the Doctors* on the northeast, *Daniel in the Lions' Den* on the southeast and the *Sacrifice of Abraham* on the capital at the angle between the south aisle and transept; there are also eight medallions of the founders in the nave. The nave piers were adapted to carry sexpartite ribs in the 13th century and there are several Gothic capitals. There are a number of objects of interest in the church including the tomb of St Mommolin (643), first abbot during the reign of Dagobert, in the northwest chapel and, in the transept, the 14th-century tomb of an abbot. The main altar and choir enclosure in wrought iron are 18th-century and the organ case has been restored and painted in green and gold.

In the 17th century the monastery was affiliated to the Congregation of St-Maur, and a great building campaign was carried out. One of the remaining buildings now houses the Académie des Beaux-Arts. Behind the church is the Centre André Malraux and the fountain of Ste-Croix, constructed in 1735 against the 14th-century rampart, while no. 6 Place Pierre-Renaudel is the former 17th-century gate of the abbey. The Musée des Métiers de l'Imprimerie (Museum of Craft and Printing; *T: 05 56 91 61 17*) at 10 Rue Fort Louis, contains working machinery associated with the production of books under the headings of typography, lithography and bookbinding. Further south is the train station, Gare St-Jean (1888–1900).

Place de la Victoire and the west

Rue St-François runs past Place des Capucins to Place de la Victoire, with an 18th-century triumphal arch, Porte d'Aquitaine, opening onto Rue Ste-Catherine. This was the Jewish quarter, where Spanish and Portuguese refugees gathered in the 15th century. The **synagogue** is in Rue Grand Rabin J. Cohen, off Rue Ste-Catherine. Close by, at 54 Rue Magendi, is the former **Couvent de l'Annonciade** (*summer, guided visit Wed 4pm; winter check with Tourist Office*), one of several religious houses founded in this area in the 17th century. Now used by the DRAC (Regional Office for Cultural Affairs), the earlier cloister (c. 1530), and the chapel containing an Entombment group can be visited during office hours. Rue Magendie leads to the old parish church of Ste-Eulalie, where pilgrims congregated before setting out to Compostela. The church contains some fine wrought iron by the master of the craft, Blaise Charlut, and also a magnificent lectern.

Opposite is the Hôpital St-André (1826), and to the north, across Place de la République, is the Palais de Justice (1846) a Neoclassical building with a Doric colonnade. On the other side of this building are all that remains of the Fort du Hâ—two bulky towers, Tour de la Poudrière and Tour des Anglais—which Louis XI ordered built in 1456, at the same time as Château Trompette. In the 19th century the fort was partly demolished to make way for the Palais de Justice and the St-André Hospital and recently the surroundings have been improved. In glaring contrast are the Ecole Nationale de la Magistrature (1972) and Richard Rogers' Tribunal de Grande Instance (1994–98).

THE SAINT-SEURIN & MERIADECK DISTRICTS

Place des Martyrs de la Résistance is the heart of this ancient district, which developed around the former collegiate church of St-Seurin, and still retains an atmosphere apart. From the garden to the south is the entrance to the early Christian archaeological site (*crypt open daily in summer 2–7; in winter confirm with Tourist Office*). Excavated in the 20th century, it revealed the earliest known traces of civilisation in Bordeaux and consists of two ancient burial places with sarcophagi, amphorae and frescoes (4th–8th centuries).

Basilica of St-Seurin

This is one of the earliest Christian sites in Bordeaux and an important sanctuary, second only to the cathedral, which developed extra-muros in the 5th century. The first bishop of Bordeaux, Seurin, reputedly from Byzantium, is accredited with the foundation c. 410 of a monastery outside the walls of the town on the site of the Gallo-Roman necropolis. In the 6th century an oratory was built over what was probably a 4th-century place of worship, and as the church developed this became the crypt of the 11th-century church, to be refashioned again in the 16th century. During the Middle Ages the Collegiate Church contained relics (St Peter's staff, Roland's horn) venerated by pilgrims en route to Santiago de Compostela. By the 12th century much of the church was built and parts of the apse, choir, crossing, first bay of the nave and the west porch survive from this period. Henry III Plantagenet financed further work on the building in the 13th century, to complete the nave and narrow aisles. The south façade is 14th-century, and during the 18th century the belfries were raised.

The neo-Romanesque west end, with statues of St Seurin and St Amand, dates mainly from 1829. This and the southwest flank have recently been restored (2001).

Behind the 19th century mock-medieval west façade is a genuine Romanesque tunnel-vaulted porch with two storiated capitals, depicting the Death of St Seurin on the right, and opposite the Sacrifice of Abraham, the remaining capitals decorated with imaginary birds and beasts. A Renaissance porch protects the south portal (c. 1200) with a central trefoil door and a multitude of figures, several recarved in 1844. In the tympanum is a restored *Last Judgement* and statues in the jambs represent the Apostles, with the Church on the left and the Synagogue on the right.

The interior is fairly dark with somewhat garish glass (1875–89), and evidence of several additions and rebuildings. The wide nave is supported by massive pillars which were reinforced after the vaults collapsed in 1566 and 1700, and unusually buttressed by high aisles with transverse arches spanning wide bays. The square-ended apse contains stalls with lively 15th–16th-century misericords and end figures. Against the north pier of the chancel is the finely chiselled stone cathedra (15th century) with a decorative canopy, where the incoming prelates spent the night on the eve of their induction. Opposite is an alabaster altarpiece (c. 1400, but re-framed) consisting of 12 scenes from the Lives of St Martial and St Seurin and beautiful *Annunciation* and *Crucifixion* panels. It is unclear from the style and iconography whether these came from England or were made locally and influenced by English work.

To the south is a truncated transept with a small chapel but the north transept barely exists, becoming a large chapel dedicated to Notre-Dame de la Rose (1424–44), with carved pendant bosses. The chapel contains two of the treasures of the church. The English polychromed and gilded alabaster statue of the *Virgin of the Rose* (14th century) is considered one of the best of its kind in the region. A 15th-century retable, also alabaster, has panels depicting episodes from the Life of the Virgin, although the sequence was upset when they were reframed in the 19th century. The complicated 15th-century Sacré Coeur chapel off the north aisle, with three altars, contains another 14th-century alabaster statue of the Virgin, known as *Notre-Dame-de-Bonne-Nouvelle*, and a stone statue of St Martial holding a staff (c. 1500). Another statue of St Martial is in the St Etienne chapel. The baptismal font is 17th-century, and the organ is 18th-century. The entrance to the crypt is in the third bay of the nave (enquire at the Sacristy). This contains two marble Gallo-Roman or Merovingian sarcophagi, Carolingian chancel plates, and the 17th-century tomb of the semi-mythical St Fort.

On Place des Martyrs de la Résistance is **Hôtel Frugès** (*visits by appointment, 06 07 60 09 55*), an old city mansion revamped in the 1920s by Henry Frugès (*see p. 45*), with the input of architect Pierre Ferret. The dining room takes inspiration from Art Nouveau and oriental designs, and the living room and garden can also be visited.

Communauté Urbain Mériadeck

This modern district south of St-Seurin and west of the Hôtel de Ville is named after Archbishop Mériadeck. An earlier prelate, Archbishop Cardinal de Sourdis (*see p. 430*), was responsible initially for draining the desolate, plague-infested marshland outside the city at the beginning of the 17th century. The district remained pretty insalubrious until 1955 when the municipality decided to clean it up and after 17 years of construction and reconstruction it has become the administrative and business centre of Bordeaux. This pioneering exercise in mid-20th-century urban regeneration does not, admittedly, have much appeal to the visitor. Seven hectares is taken up by the Esplanade Charles de Gaulle, where green spaces and gardens suspended above the transport system (similar in concept to La Défense in Paris) are dotted with office buildings, but not a tower block in sight. The Caisse d'Epargne Mériadeck, on Rue Château d'Eau, is a characteristic building of the 1970s, a horizontally assembled series of curved and rectangular planes, clad in a brown stone effect.

The church of St-Bruno was originally the chapel of the charterhouse planned by Archbishop Cardinal Sourdis (*see p. 430*) on land which was levelled and planted, pre-empting the work of the Intendants in the 18th century. The church, begun in 1611, is a simple one-nave structure containing a stunning Baroque altarpiece boasting a painting of the *Assumption* by Philippe de Champaigne, and marble sculptures, of the Virgin and the Archangel Gabriel by the great Italian sculptor Gian Lorenzo Bernini, and his father Pietro, respectively. Despite the fact that the church was ransacked at the Revolution, it kept some good choir stalls (1619–20) and panelling in the choir (1668–74). The Cimetière de la Chartreuse is a 19th-century creation with an array of tombs and sculptures and was the first resting-place of the Spanish painter Goya.

THE CHARTRONS DISTRICT

The quartier of Les Chartrons, named after a 14th-century charterhouse (Carthusian monastery) north of the city centre has undergone the most radical regeneration as part of the project to improve the riverside. This was, until the 19th century, the real commercial centre of the city; during the 18th century English merchants, followed by other Europeans, traded here.

To the south is the gracious Cours Xavier-Arnozan, formerly the Pavé des Chartrons, which is lined with balconied houses (1770–88) built by Etienne Laclotte, the homes of the great wine-trading families. The former English church is now Evangelical and here traffic drives on the left, supposedly a hand-down from the area's former inhabitants. The Bourse Maritime (1921–25) on the quay is a copy of the central pavilion of Place de la Bourse, and opposite is the Hôtel Fenwick, which housed the first United States consulate. Built by a rich American in 1795, it has reliefs of ships' prows on the façade. On Quai des Chartrons at the end of Rue Latour are the 'Dutch houses' (c. 1680), the sole reminders of a continuous terrace of gabled houses built for a Dutch ship owner. Nearby Rue Notre-Dame, a street of antique dealers, with the old Turkish baths at no. 29 and the Temple des Chartrons, an exemplary Neoclassical edifice (1833–35). Between Rue Notre-Dame and the quay, on the Parvis des Chartrons, is the Cité Mondiale (1992), a modern office block with the Bar à Vins at its base. To the right is Place Langalerie and the neo-Gothic church of St-Louis des

Chartrons (1875). In the adjacent Place du Marché des Chartrons is the *Halle* or market place (1869), built in iron, stone and wood, now converted to host a variety of artistic activities.

Moored to the bank of the Garonne is *Croiseur Colbert* (opposite no. 60 Quai des Chartrons; *for opening times T: 05 56 44 96 11*), one of France's last great battleships, converted into a museum. Just beyond it is the Sunday market, Marché Colbert, and various restaurants and bars in the area are an opportunity for a half-dozen oysters and slurp of white wine. Alongside the Garonne were once kilometres of wine stores (there are still underground cellars). Now there are kilometres (5k) of cycle track, 900m of colourful facades, exhibition spaces, huge areas for shops, and back-to-back bars and restaurants in the converted warehouses (Hangars 14 to 19). The old commercial centre has been transformed into a new and fashionable commercial centre and leisure area. Inland from Hangar 14 is the new Rue du Faubourg des Arts, which has shops specialising in furnishings and decoration, open every day.

Vinorama at 12 Cour du Médoc (*T: 05 56 39 39 20*), is a waxworks which retraces the history of Bordeaux wine from the Gallo-Roman period to the 19th century. And beyond is Cap Sciences, at Hangar 20, Quai des Chartrons (*T: 05 56 01 07 07, www.cap-sciences.net*), a window on major scientific aspects of technical innovation in research and industry. Marinexpo is a centre for temporary exhibitions in an old touring barge, evoking the history of Bordeaux's maritime and river life, with model boats, figureheads and other naval decoration.

PESSAC

West of Bordeaux, near the Périphérique, in the direction of Arcachon, is the Cité Frugès. The Maison Municipale Frugès-Le Corbusier (*4 rue Le Corbusier, open Wed, Fri, Sun 2–6; Thurs 10–12 & 2–6; Sat 10–12 & 2–5; guided visits Thurs, Sun, 10 and 11; T: 05 56 36 56 46*). This fascinating group of buildings is part of a far-sighted project of 1924 promoted by industrialist Henry Frugès (*see p. 43*), who commissioned Le Corbusier (1887–1966) and his cousin Pierre Jeanneret to build low-cost, functional houses. The original concept was for 35 houses in four sections around a communal area with shop, café and fronton for pelote. True to Le Corbusier's ideals, the house design is ingenious, comprising a basic unit and standardised elements which could be variously assembled to create Styles Isolée, Quinconce, Arcade and Gratte-Ciel. Built 1924–27, but beset by many problems, some caused by the architect's high-handed dealing with the authorities, as well as escalating costs and lack of public transport, the project was abandoned half-way through. Altered, neglected and derided for many years, the houses are now sought-after and have been protected since 2000.

PRACTICAL INFORMATION

GETTING AROUND

• **Airport:** T: 05 56 34 50 00, www.bordeaux.aeroport.fr
Shuttle Bus every 45mins to town centre and St-Jean train station; stops at Barrière Judaïque, Pl. Gambetta, Grand Théâtre and Quai Richelieu
Taxis from airport to city centre, about €20
• **By train:** Main station Gare St-Jean, is 3km to the south of centre. T: 08 92 36 35 35. Shuttle buses to the city centre. Tram line C. Taxis €7–10
• **By bus and tram:** Day pass and passes for 2 to 6 days. Three tram lines operate: A: Mériadeck–Cenon-la Morlette/Lormont-Lauriers; B: Quinconces–Pessac-Bourgnard; C: Quinconces–St-Jean train station
The main bus stations are at Halte Routière de Carcan, T: 05 56 43 68 43; Réseau Trans-Gironde, Allées de Chartres, T: 05 56 81 16 82. From the Gare St-Jean, buses depart for coastal resorts such as Lacanau and Cap Ferret.
• **Traffic-free days:** On the first Sunday of each month the centre of the city is closed to vehicular traffic; that day, *calèches* (horse-drawn carriages) from the Tourist Office, and *vélos* (bikes) from the Hemicycle des Quinconces, are free.
• **By bike:** Le Vélo Parlant (the bike has a city plan and plays a recorded tour) from Bord'eaux Vélos Loisirs, Quai Louis XVIII, May–Oct 9.30–9 daily; Nov–April all day Wed, Sun and school holidays; Mon, Fri, Sat 2.30–6.30; closed Tues, Thur.

• **By boat:** Visits to the port and vineyards by boat depart all year round from Embarcadère des Quinconces, Quai Louis XVIII on the Ville de Bordeaux (T: 05 56 52 88 88) or the Alienor (T: 05 56 51 27 90), which both offer a variety of excursions; or from La Bastide, on the Burdigala (T: 05 56 86 64 59). All three boats have restaurants

TOURIST INFORMATION

12 Cours du XXX Juillet, T: 05 56 00 66 12/05 56 00 66 10, www.bordeaux-tourisme.com Open July–Aug, Mon–Sat 9–7.30, Sun, holidays 9.30–6.30; May–June, Sept–Oct, Mon–Sat 9–7, Sun, holidays 9.30–6.30; Nov–April, Mon–Sat 9–6.30, Sun, holidays 9.45–4.30.
Maison du Tourisme de la Gironde, 21Cours de l'Intendance, T: 05 56 52 61 40, www.tourisme-gironde.cg33.fr

TOURS OF THE OLD TOWN

On foot from the Tourist Office: 10am daily, 2-hour, bilingual tours.
By bike, first Sun of the month: 3 circuits, Bordeaux Art Deco, Bordeaux Art Nouveau, Bordeaux seen from the hillsides.
By 1900 omnibus, June–Sept; Horse-drawn carriage tours July–August; and tours by taxi.

ACCOMMODATION

€€€ **Le Grand Hôtel de Bordeaux**.
The re-opening of the magnificent 18th-

century Grand Hotel opposite the Opera House is anticipated at time of writing, shortly scheduled to re-open. A major renovation has been underway, the architectural work supervised by Michel Pétuaud-Létang and the interiors by Jacques Garcia. It promises 150 luxury rooms including 40 suites, a gourmet restaurant and bistro, pool, sauna, boutiques and the rest. Place de la Comédie.

€€€ **Hôtel Burdigala**. Elegantly modern and upmarket hotel in an old building, close to the business area, with irreproachable service and gourmet restaurant, Le Jardin de Burdigala, lit by a glass dome. The 68 rooms are varied in style and range, and of the utmost good taste and comfort. 115 Rue Georges Bonnac, T: 05 56 90 16 16, www.burdigala.com

€€€ **Petit Hôtel Labottière**. Ultra gorgeous *chambres d'hôtes* in an 18th-century mansion of great charm close to the Jardins Publics at the heart of the city. There are two beautifully kitted-out apartments with antique furniture and a brunch-style breakfast is served. 14 Rue Francis Martin, T 05 56 48 44 10, petithotellabottiere@chateauxcountry.com

€€ **Hôtel de Normandie**. A wonderfully situated hotel in a handsome 18th-century building opposite the Tourist Office and overlooking the Esplanade des Quinconces. Welcoming and well tended, the 100 bedrooms are charmingly understated, the best on the top floors with views of the river. No restaurant. 7–9 Cours du XXX Juillet, T: 05 56 52 16 80, www.hotel-de-normandie-bordeaux.com

€€ **Grand Hotel Français** (Best Western). An old coaching inn in Vieux Bordeaux with an elegant 18th-century staircase and period decoration, close to

Cours de l'Intendance and the best shops. 12 Rue du Temple, T: 05 56 48 10 35, www.bestwestern-grandhotelfrancais.com

€ **Hôtel Acanthe**. Totally renovated hotel in great situation on a small street at the edge of the old town and close to Place de la Bourse and the riverside. The reception is bright and a beautiful spiral staircase leads from it to 20 neat bedrooms which are relatively spacious. 12–14 Rue Saint-Rémi, T: 05 56 81 66 58, www.acanthe-hotel-bordeaux.com

€ **La Maison du Lierre**. This intimate hotel has the ambiance of a guest house. In the centre of the city not far from Pl. de Tourny, the renovated *maison bourgeoise* has a garden patio, and the quiet rooms, are pleasant but not large, are not expensive. Home-made breakfast; car parking. 57 Rue Huguerie, T: 05 56 51 92 71, www.maisondulierre.com

€ **Hôtel la Tour Intendance**. ▄ Tucked away in a small street close to the Cours de l'Intendance and Place Gambetta, the old building has been cleverly and attractively revamped to provide interesting, modern rooms incorporating the old stone and a spiral staircase. There is a small breakfast room, and helpful staff; also a garage. 14–16 Rue de la Vieille Tour, T: 05 56 44 56 56, www.hotel-tour-intendance.com

RESTAURANTS

€€€ **Le Chapon Fin**. Famous since the 19th century, it has become a Bordelais institution, and is remarkable for the grotto-like décor let alone the superb cuisine under the direction of Chef Nicolas Frion. Among the late and great who dined here are Sarah Bernhardt, Toulouse-Lautrec and Edward VII. Frion's CV is impressive, and his reputation is based on his talent for creative renditions of classic dishes based on the season. The wines are chosen with care to harmonise with the food. While expensive, there is a lunch menu around €30. Also a cookery school run by Frion. 5 Rue Montesquieu, T: 05 56 79 10 10, www.chapon-fin.com

€€€ **Le Pavillon des Boulevards**. Denis Franc's number one restaurant is Michelin starred. The food is thoughtful and very much Franc's own sure touch, combining flavours with care and attention. Although once a leader in nouvelle cuisine he doesn't bow to trendy concoctions. A *menu découvert* at around €60. The restaurant is west of the city centre towards the Barrière de Médoc. 120 Rue de la Croix-de-Seguey, T: 05 56 81 51 02.

€€ **L'Estaquade**. An upmarket, modern version of a *guinguette* on the right bank of the Gironde opposite Place de la Bourse, zen and atmospheric, its feet in the water. Chef Frederic Montemont's combines Mediterranean and Atlantic flavours with Japanese subtlety: try *Tartare de St-Jacques, milk shake à la Mangue* or *Gross Sole rôtie, beurre d'Anchois et Câpres*. Midi menu around €15, fully inclusive menu €50. Quai des Queries, La Bastide, T: 05 57 54 02 50, www.lestaquade.com

€€ **La Tupina**. ■ Chef Jean-Pierre Xiradakis is part of Bordelais gastronomic legend and his bistro has been described as the second best in the world. The food is resolutely of the southwest and the atmosphere is about

as authentic as it can be, with the *tupina* (Basque for cauldron), gently simmering over the fire diffusing aromas of soup. Xiradakis is to open a 5-room hotel opposite the restaurant above his shop, Au Comestible. Also possible to eat more simply there or in the Bar Cave. 6–8 Rue Porte de la Monnaie, T: 05 56 91 56 37, www.latupina.com

€€ **Le Café Gourmand**. A chic and fashionable restaurant within the Triangle with outdoor tables. The cuisine is varied and very good value, including local specialities, organic produce, and dishes with a more international flavour, or a combination of the two such as *Sushi de crevettes à la citronnelle* and *Lotte rôtie à la ventreche, coulis de Piquillos* (monkfish, pork belly and red pepper sauce). 3 Rue Buffon, T: 05 56 52 03 45.

€€ **Chez Greg**. Small smart restaurant at the heart of the old town with a great wine selection. There is a fireplace for winter and outdoor dining in summer. Varied choice, including regional, Japanese, seafood and fish; vegetarian also available. 30–31 Rue Porte de la Monnaie, T: 05 56 31 30 30, www.chezgreg.fr

€ **Le Café Maritime**, Hangar G2, Bassin à flots, 1 Quai A. Lalande, T 05 57 10 20 40, www.cafemaritime.com A converted warehouse in the Chartrons district that has adopted a slightly Asian setting with coloured lanterns, greenery and large mirrors. The reputation of the cuisine goes before it, and is based mainly of seafood.

€ **L'Olivier du Clavel**. A good restaurant opposite Gare St-Jean, serving regional and Mediterranean food. In the southern part of town, very convenient if travelling by train or exploring the Ste-Croix district; good-value lunchtime menu. 44 Rue Charles Domercq, T: 05 57 95 09 50.

€ **Restaurant Quai'Zaco**. A new restaurant opened by chef Denis Franc (of Le Pavillon des Boulevards), in an old wine warehouse on the quay. Southwest cooking, fish and seafood lead the menu and meals cooked on the spot in an open kitchen. 80 Quai des Chartrons, T: 05 57 87 67 72.

WINE

Visits to the vineyards: Guided tours (half-day) leave from Gare St-Jean, Arrivals, 15 April–15 Nov, 1.15 daily, from the Tourist Office at 1.30; 16 Nov–14 April, Wed, Sat only at the same times. Full-day tours leave from Gare St-Jean, Arrivals, 1 May–31 Oct, 9.15 Wed, Sat, from the Tourist Office at 9.30.

Introduction to wine tasting at the Tourist Office every Thur, also Sat in July, Aug. The Maison du Vin, 3 Cours du 30 Juillet (opposite the Tourist Office), T: 05 56 00 22 88, offers information on all the vineyards of the Bordeaux region, helps to plan visits, and runs courses at the *Ecole du Vin de Bordeaux* (School of Wine). Open Mon–Fri 9–5.30, closed Sat, Sun

MARKETS

Marché des Capucins daily covered market
Marché du Colbert Sunday on the quay
Marché St-Michel Saturday
Marché Biologique (organic) Thursday on the quay

FESTIVALS & EVENTS

January: *Salon des Antiquaires*, Antique Dealers' Fair, T: 05 56 81 80 88
February: *Le Jumping International*, International show jumping, T: 05 56 11 99 00
March: *Carnaval des Deux Rives*, Carnival on both banks, T: 05 56 94 43 43
April: *Brocante*, spring and autumn flea market, T: 05 56 06 24 91
Escale du Livre, book fair, T: 05 56 10 10 12
May: *Foire Internationale de Bordeaux*, regional crafts and buildings, T: 05 56 11 99 00
June: In alternating years:
Bordeaux Fête le Vin (even numbered), last weekend of June, international trade fair for wine, T: 05 56 00 66 17.
Bordeaux Fête le Fleuve, four days of celebrations and festivities on both banks of the Gironde, with historic boats, music and markets (odd numbered years) T: 05 56 00 66 00
August: *Musique d'Eté*, all types of music in a variety of historic venues
September: *Journée du Patrimoine*, national heritage day, T: 05 57 95 02 02
October: *Festival International du Cinéma au Féminin*, international women's film festival, T: 05 56 17 00 33
Le Bon Goût d'Aquitaine, food from all over the Aquitaine region, T: 05 56 32 94 00
La Fête du Vin Nouveau et de la Brocante, new wine and bric-à-brac with special events, T: 05 56 52 66 13
November: *Novart*, performing arts festival, T: 05 56 10 20 46

THE GIRONDE

THE MÉDOC PENINSULA

The Médoc Peninsula is a triangular headland northwest of Bordeaux, defined by the Atlantic Ocean and the Gironde Estuary. Two derivations of the name are suggested, either *pagus medulorum*, 'the middle territory', or *media aquae*, 'between the waters'. This flat, once marshy land, is indeed surrounded by water. The flat coastal plain along the Atlantic shore has long windswept beaches and sand dunes, tranquil inland seas and deserted pine forests. The most important of the inland seas in the area is the Bassin d' Arcachon. On the banks of the Gironde Estuary to the east are small villages with very famous names: they are set among mainly low vegetation dominated by the exceptionally well-disciplined vines of the celebrated vineyards of the Médoc.

THE MEDOC & ITS VINEYARDS

The world-famous Médoc vineyards, among the most celebrated in the Bordelais, are confined to a strip about 65km long and 10–15km wide on the west of the Gironde Estuary from Blanquefort Brook to the north of Bordeaux, almost to Pointe de la Grave. They cover 115,000 hectares and 57 Bordelais *appellations*. In the Médoc, a château is not just a building but describes a wine-producing estate (*domaine* or *cru* are also used). Here the mansions are mainly 18th/19th century, neo-this or neo-that, ranging from Classically elegant or Palladian practical to absurdly eclectic. Some of these great estates have been bought up by large public enterprises such as Chanel, AGF and GMF. A journey through this extraordinarily regimented landscape, with battalions of vines and immaculately turned-out properties, is fascinating even for non-wine buffs, but the best time to visit is during the *vendange*, which is mainly done by hand. The vineyards at times go almost to the waters of the Gironde and there are quiet spots on the banks where only the fishermen go.

Wines of the Médoc

The temperate climate and poor gravelly soil of the Médoc create perfect conditions for vines. Only red wines have the Médoc/Haut-Médoc label, and they represent more than 16% of Bordeaux reds. The wines are the result of a carefully balanced blend of authorised grape varieties: Cabernet Sauvignon, Cabernet Franc, Merlot Noir, Carmenère and Cot or Petit-Verdot. There are some delicious white wines produced here, sold under the Bordeaux label.

HISTORY OF THE MEDOC

The Médoc was, in Roman times and up to the Middle Ages, an empty region of marsh and moorland with a few vineyards owned by religious communities and feudal landlords. By the 16th century major estates were established on the alluvial plains, stretching to gravel ridges further inland in the early 17th century, when the understanding of viticulture expanded. Around this time the marshes to the north were drained by the Dutch for crops and pasture and English importers gave the name New French Claret to wines of the region in the early 18th century. By 1760 the Médoc vineyards were definitively established and the larger estates had been acquired by members of the Judiciary of Bordeaux. Techniques to improve and age wine continued to develop, and in the mid-18th century the designations *Grand Cru* and *Château* were introduced, inherent in which was a concern for the maintenance of vineyards and improvement of the wines. At the request of Napoleon III the classification Grand Cru was drawn up in 1855 by the Syndicate of Brokers on the Bordeaux Stock Exchange. It included five classes of Grand Crus in Médoc, and 61 châteaux, a hierarchy which was challenged only once, in 1973, when Chateau Mouton-Rothschild was elevated from second to Premier Grand Cru. However, nothing protected the Médoc from the phylloxera epidemic in the 1860s, which resulted in the restructuring of vineyards with American graft-stocks. The quality picked up again and there were four great vintages in 1921, 1924, 1928 and 1929. In the 1960s there were only 6,000ha of vineyards compared to 14,161ha currently under production.

Appellations d'Origine Controlées (AOC)

The Médoc peninsula is divided into eight AOC. The two regional *appellations* are Médoc in the north of the peninsula and Haut-Médoc to the south (*haut* meaning upstream on the Gironde). The division between it and Médoc was official only in 1935. Within Haut-Médoc are also six great local or *communale* appellations: Margaux, Moulis-en-Médoc, Listrac-Médoc, St-Julien, Pauillac and St-Estèphe. There are 60 great *Crus Classés* in Haut-Médoc. The whole Médoc region has 419 *Crus Bourgeois*, almost half the total production. There are also 335 *Crus Artisans*, a category recognised in August 1994, plus some 1,000 growers who are members of one of the 13 cooperatives.

The *appellation* regulations determine the minimum number of vines per hectare and the manner of cultivation; natural sugar content equivalent to 170g per litre for Médoc and Haut Médoc AOCs, and 178g for the local AOCs; natural minimum degree of wine at 10° and 10.5° respectively; chaptalization (addition of sucrose) limited to 2°; the final maximum degree, generally 12.5° for the Médoc and Haut-Médoc, and 13° for the local AOCs; and the earliest date of harvesting.

AOC Haut-Médoc and the Communal AOCs

As far back as 1815 a wine broker from the Chartrons district (*see p. 44*) referred to the high quality of wines in Haut-Médoc. It now stretches over 59 kilometres north to south, and over 4,200ha (28% of the Médoc vineyards) with 375 growers. Within the area are 26 zones which produce wines exclusively with the Haut-Médoc AOC, including five Crus Classés.

The six Communal AOCs within Haut-Médoc are all familiar names. In the area around Margaux vines were already cultivated during the Gallo-Roman era and now covers 1350ha, with 79 independent growers. Château Margaux was mentioned in 1705 and the classification, which recognised 21 Crus Classés in the Margaux appellation dates from 1855 at the time of Napoleon III. Margaux wines are described as 'feminine'; they age well, are subtle and elegant, characterised by a bouquet of fruity flavours.

Moulis-en-Médoc, once a region of windmills, is the smallest of the appellations, covering 600ha and 38 growers. Vineyards appeared here in the 13th century, but the reputation of its wines developed in the second half of the 19th with the policy of free trade and the privileged relationship between Napoleon III and Queen Victoria. While young these wines have great finesse, but are at their best after 7–10 years. The colour is intense, the bouquet elegant and complex, and they last long in the mouth.

Listrac-en-Médoc covers 670ha with 91 growers, 60 in cooperatives. It went into decline in the 1930s but picked up by 1957 when it became one of the six local appellations. The Listrac appellations fill the palate, and in time the wine takes on a ruby tint, and eventually blends to a velvety hue.

St-Julien has the largest concentration of Crus Classés in Médoc because of the soil's outstanding uniformity. Its fame can be dated to the 17th century and it covers 910ha with 25 growers. The two villages of Beychevelle and St-Julien account for over four fifths of the vineyards. The wines are a fine deep colour, harmonious and mild, but with plenty of body and a superb bouquet.

On the edge of the estuary Pauillac, around the town which was once an important wine port, covers 1200ha and 107 growers (80 in cooperatives). The velvet red wines are full-bodied, complex, vigorous and rich in tannin, with aromas of red fruits, violets or roses and deserve to be laid down for some time.

Although St-Estèphe had vines during the Roman occupation, the great estates date from the 19th century. It is the largest of the local appellations, with 1370 ha and 160 growers (100 in cooperatives). The wines are sturdy and robust, and can be laid down for a very long time while maintaining their youth and freshness.

AOC Médoc

The Médoc appellation is applied to wines produced on 5,300 ha in the north of the Médoc peninsula, where the great majority (33%) of Médoc wines originate. These newer vineyards of the peninsula have expanded more recently, giving rise to numerous small estates (658 growers), and precipitating the development of a powerful cooperative movement (460 cooperatives). The terrain is very varied and links

Garonne gravel, Pyrenees gravel and clayey limestone soils. Due to this variety the wines are distinct, round and well-balanced. Certain are full bodied with a good ruby colour and should be laid down for a long time to develop; others are elegant with a fine bouquet and can be drunk younger.

The Commanderie du Bontemps de Médoc et des Graves, created in 1950, found its roots in the Knights Templar (*see p. 288*). It brings together professionals in the wine trade in order to promote Médoc wines and holds three exclusive celebrations: St Vincent's Day in January, the Flower Festival in June, and the Harvest Banns in September.

Visits to the châteaux

Many châteaux receive visitors to their *chais* and for tastings, but it is essential to arrange visits well in advance. For more information, contact local tourist information centres or the Maisons du Vin, either in Bordeaux (*see p. 21*) or in the region:
Margaux: Maison du Vin, 7 Place Tremoille, 33460 Margaux, T: 05 57 88 70 82;
Moulis: Maison du Vin, 1137 Le Bourg, 33480 Moulis, T: 05 56 58 32 74;
Pauillac: Maison du Vin, La Verrerie, 33250 Pauillac, T: 05 56 59 03 08 (*see p.56*);
St-Estéphe: Maison du Vin, Place de l'Eglise, 33180 St-Estéphe, T: 05 56 59 30 59.
A *Guide Découverte* of the Médoc, is published by the Conseil des Vins du Médoc (*1 Cours du XXX Juillet, Bordeaux, T: 05 56 48 18 62, www.medoc-wines.com*). *Itinerary of an Art Lover in the Médoc*, reveals the art collections at wine châteaux; information from the Maison du Tourisme at Pauillac.

LA ROUTE DES VINS

From Blanquefort (north of Bordeaux) the Route des Vins (D2) passes many of the great *crus*. Macau, close to the estuary, where the church has an 11th-century belfry, is a typically simple Médoc village, as is Arsac, further inland, with a partly Romanesque church. Here the vineyards start in earnest. The roses at the end of rows of vines, which are traditional in the Médoc, were originally planted for the early detection of mildew, to which roses succumb before vines; they are now purely for decoration. At the Château d'Arsac (*visits by appointment; T: 05 56 58 83 90, www.chateau-arsac.com*), contemporary art and wine have gone hand-in-hand for 18 years.

The Margaux region

Labarde and Cantenac are villages in the Margaux AOC region. The châteaux are all Grand Cru Classé since 1855. Neoclassical Kirwan (*visits, T: 05 57 88 71 00, www.chateau-kirwan.com*), owned by the Schÿler family, has a rose-garden; Issan is a beautiful 17th-century building surrounded by a moat (*visits all year, T: 05 57 88 35 91, www.chateau-issan.com*); and Palmer, a pretty building not far from the estuary (*visits all year, T: 05 57 88 72 72*). Château Rauzan-Ségla (*T: 05 57 88 82 10*) belongs to the Chanel group; several châteaux are owned by commercial enterprises. Category Cru Bourgeois Exceptionnel, Château Siran (*T: 05 57 88 34 04, www.chateausiran.com*) is one of the few which can be visited without an appointment.

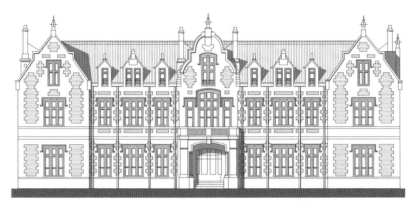

CHÂTEAU CANTENAC-BROWN

The red-and-white Cantenac-Brown, in English Queen Anne style (*visits by appointment, and meals for 4 people upwards, T: 05 57 88 81 81, infochato@cantenacbrown.com*) is one of the most handsome. Unusually for this region, there are a few vineyards surrounded by stone walls in Margaux.

A village within a village, the great Château Margaux, Premier Grand Cru Classé (*visits, T: 05 57 88 83 83, www.chateau-margaux.com*), built by Louis Combes (1810–16), is a masterful Neoclassical pile approached by an avenue of plane trees. It now belongs to Corinne Mentzelopoulos, daughter of the founder of the Felix Potin grocery chain. Its reds are blends of Cabernet Franc, Merlot and Cabernet Sauvignon; it also produces a white, labelled Bordeaux. In the village of Margaux is a Maison du Vin, also a good place to eat (*see p. 54*). Château Lascombes (near Margaux) can also be visited (*T: 05 57 88 70 66*). There are three very pleasant *chambres d'hôtes* at Château Giscours (*T: 05 57 97 09 09*) in Labarde.

Moulis and environs

Around Tayac the vines peter out for a while but across the Tiquetorte river are the vineyards of Moulis and Listrac AOCs to the west of Arcins. Moulis has a 12th–13th-century church and the vineyards of Listrac are the most elevated in the Médoc. Château Maucaillou, Cru Bourgeois Supérieur 2003 (*visits T: 05 56 58 01 23, www.chateau-maucaillou.com*), has a Musée des Arts et Métiers de la Vigne et du Vin, and runs wine courses and visits by helicopter; also *repas dégustations* by reservation, as well as *chambres* and *table d'hôtes*.

In Lamarque village there are places to eat, a small church with a huge 18th-century tower which resembles a lighthouse and a part 12th-century castle. There are practically no vines here because the land is too marshy. At the mini port of Lamarque you can take the ferry across the estuary to Blaye (*see p. 66*) or taste local shrimps. Nearby, at Cussac, Fort Médoc (*open May–Oct 9–8, Nov–April 10–5, closed Mon, T: 05 56 58 91 30*) was built in 1689 by Vauban (*see p. 67*) as part of a line of defence with

Blaye and Fort Pâté, to protect the estuary. Somewhat less impressive or restored than the citadel of Blaye, Fort Médoc is a different shape and smaller. It contains an interior courtyard with the former guardroom, bakery and powder store and there is a museum of the history of the village and regional objects. From the bastion is a view over the Gironde estuary and Blaye. Between Cussac and St-Julien less grand wines, the crus bourgeois, are produced. Cru Bourgeois Supérieur can be sampled at Château Lanessan at Cussac. The neo-Tudor château has a Museum of Horsemanship c. 1900 (*T: 05 56 58 94 80, www.lanessan.com*) with waxwork models.

St-Julien

Beychevelle, at the centre of the AOC St-Julien, has a yachting basin on the estuary. Among the best known châteaux in this region producing Grand Cru Classé are Château Talbot (*T: 05 56 73 21 50, chateau-talbot@chateau-talbot.com*); Château Leoville-Barton (*T: 05 56 59 06 05, chateau@leoville-barton.com*), originally owned by an Irish family, established here for three centuries; and Château de Beychevelle (*T: 05 56 73 20 70, www.beychevelle.com*), a magnificent 18th-century house and garden on the banks of the estuary, revamped in 1927. The name reputedly originates from *baisse voile*, at the time of the Duc d'Epernon, when boats passing his property lowered their sails in acknowledgement. Châteaux Ducru-Beaucaillou (*T: 05 56 73 16 73*) contains a reference in its name to the stony terrain (*caillou*, stone). Château Branaire-Ducru (*T: 05 56 59 25 86, branaire@branaire.com*) has an 18th-century orangery and *cuvier* which functions by gravity.

The Pauillac region

AOC Pauillac is named after a plain little town stretched out along the estuary, whose port dates back to 2000 BC for the shipment of bronze. Pauillac has an important Maison du Vin and Visitor Centre (*see p. 54*) with abundant information on the vineyards and châteaux. Overlooking the Gironde are Château Pichon-Longueville and Château Pichon-Longueville-Comtesse-de-Lalande, which produce both Pauillac and St-Julien AOCs and welcome visits by appointment. Château Pichon-Longueville-Château Comtesse-de-Lalande (*T: 05 56 59 19 40, www.pichon-lalande.com*), closest to the estuary, is a family-owned estate and in the orangery is a remarkable Glass Museum, the collection of the proprietor, May-Eliane de Lencquesaing, of some 700 items from the 18th century onwards including a Fabergé ewer. Château Pichon-Longueville (*T: 05 56 73 17 17, accueil@pichonlongueville.com*) on the other side of the road belongs to AXA, a French insurance company. Also falling within AOC Pauillac are Château Latour (*T: 05 56 73 19 80, www.chateau-latour.com*), with a wonderful 19th-century domed dovecote, and the great Rothschild châteaux, Mouton and Lafite, belonging to the English and French sides of the family. Château Mouton-Rothschild (*T: 05 56 73 21 29*), designated Premier Cru Classé in 1973, the only new entrant since 1855, can be visited only by appointment. It has video and slide shows, visits to the 100m cellars designed by Charles Siclis, and the Musée du Vin dans l'Art, with wine-related artworks spanning 6,000 years of wine production. The château is also famous for its labels, designed since 1924 by great artists, including Braque, Chagall, Baselitz, Motherwell and Balthus. The artists are paid in wine. Château Lafite-Rothschild (*visits strictly by appointment, T: 01 53 89 78 00, www.lafite.com*), has a circular wine store designed by Ricardo Bofill. Chateau Lynch-Bages, Cru Classé since 1855, welcomes visitors (*T: 05 56 73 24 00, www.lynchbages.com*). From 1749–1824 it belonged to the Lynch family, Irish who settled in Bordeaux. Since 1933 it has been owned by the Cazes family who have totally renovated the property and modernised the equipment although the 19th-century building has been conserved; temporary exhibitions are held here. In the renovated hamlet of Bages is a traditional bakers, Au Baba d'Andrea, set up by Thierry Marx, chef at Cordeillan-Bages.

St-Estèphe

Further north near the pretty village of St-Estèphe are the vineyards of AOC St-Estèphe, with one of the most eccentric mansions, Château Cos d'Estournel (*visits by appointment T: 05 56 73 15 50, www.estournel.com*), an early 19th-century building which blends Indian and Chinese elements and contains a museum and exhibition room. Here the landscape becomes slightly more undulating and varied with hedgerows. Château Phélan Ségur (*T: 05 56 59 74 00, phelan.segur@wanadoo.fr*) is a beautiful château with a lovely view, once Irish-owned, which produces a Cru Bourgeois Exceptionnel. Further inland the old abbey church at Vertheuil (11th–12th centuries) founded by Guillaume d'Aquitaine, was influenced by the churches of Saintonge and Poitou. It has a square tower and the remains of Romanesque sculpture, but needed rebuilding in the 18th century. Château Sociando Mallet, St-Seurin de Cadourne, Haut Médoc (*T: 05 56 73 38 80, scea-jean-gautreau@wanadoo.fr*) dominates the estuary and produces a Cru Bourgeois Exceptionnel as well as having an impressive cellar.

Bas Médoc and the Gironde Estuary

Beyond are oceans of Médoc AOC vineyards producing wine that is not Premier Cru Classé, but still of extremely good quality. The vineyards start around St-Yzans and continue until St-Vivien. Château Verdus at St-Seurin-de-Cadourne (*T: 05 56 73 17 31, www.chateau-verdus.com*) has a huge 14th-century dovecote and a Museum of the History of Médoc and can be visited, as can Château Loudenne (*T: 05 56 73 17 80, www.lafragette.com*). In a former religious establishment close to the Gironde, is a lovely building with little towers to keep watch over the vineyards, which also has *chambres d'hôtes* (*see p. 65*). The Bas Médoc is characterised by canals and dykes, although there are still vines.

The banks of the Gironde Estuary are very quiet in this area, peopled by fishermen and their shacks or *carrelets* and jetties with fishing nets like sails. Away from the vineyards there are isolated spots to picnic with your bottle of Médoc. Around St-Christoly the annual Marathon du Médoc is run in September among the vines. Punctuated by *dégustations*, this must be one of the toughest to survive but is an impeccable excuse to *faire la fête*.

ARCACHON, CAP FERRET
& THE ATLANTIC COAST

Some 5,000 years ago, the Atlantic coast had an irregular profile, with deep inlets or harbours that were gradually cut off from the sea by banks of sand to create huge inland lakes. In this area a constant battle is fought against wind and tidal erosion. Now the almost unbroken strip of beaches and dunes from Cap-Ferret to La Pointe de la Grave is unprotected from the Atlantic breakers. This is part of the 270km of the Côte d'Argent or Silver Coast (*see p. 62*). Among several seaside resorts are Le Porge, Lacanau-Océan, Hourtin Plage, Montalivet and at Soulac-sur-mer there are two huge *étangs*, Lacanau and Hourtin-Carcans (6,000ha), the largest in France. The population here is very sparse and the area is ideal for outdoor activities; a huge network of cycle tracks crisscrosses this part of the peninsula. The most popular and populated resort is, however, Arcachon in the southernmost part of the peninsula, which is protected by Cap Ferret, a sandy spur of land stabilised by pine forests.

Bassin d'Arcachon

An inland sea of 155 square km, the Bassin d'Arcachon enjoys endlessly changing seascapes and sandscapes and remarkable luminosity. It has remained linked to the sea, unlike the lakes of Lacanau and Hourtin to the north, because of strong currents and tides. The largest, and constantly shifting, sand deposit at the mouth of the lagoon, the Banc d'Arguin, is a wildlife reserve, as is the Ile aux Oiseaux, identified by two wooden hides on stilts known as *cabanes tchanquées*. Apart from tourism, the main industry of the basin is oyster farming. This is a determining factor on the environment and what appears as a partly submerged petrified forest in the lagoon is in fact posts or *pignots* marking the oyster beds. The basin is very crowded in the summer; less so in spring or autumn, when the climate is also pleasantly mild.

ARCACHON

The busy resort of Arcachon stands on a small peninsula southwest of the lagoon and offers sheltered beaches with the more volatile Atlantic coast nearby. Fashionable since the 19th century, it combines old and new fashions in architecture, and tourism with the oyster industry.

In the early 19th century the mild climate, pure sea air and the scent of pines led to the promotion of this small fishing community for the rehabilitation of tuberculosis sufferers. Later in the century the vogue for sea bathing attracted a stream of visitors, convalescents and developers. Arcachon became fashionable, receiving the royal seal of approval from Napoleon III and Eugénie in 1863, and the following year the railway chugged in. The Péreire brothers, main shareholders in the railroad, created the winter town, the Ville d'Hiver, and the artists Toulouse-Lautrec (*see p. 256*), Cézanne and Monet came to admire. Early on the town was endowed with splendid examples of 19th-century vernacular seaside architecture and later with promenades and jetties. The town's fishing industry is still active, although the modest sardine has been replaced as the main catch by more glamorous fish such as turbot, brill, monkfish and sea bass, while oysters are big business.

The Ville d'Hiver

For an idea of Arcachon in its heyday, stroll through the Ville d'Hiver. The highest part of the town, it was laid out from 1862 around the Parc Mauresque (Moorish Park), containing a grand casino inspired by the Alhambra in Granada (destroyed by fire in 1977). The area boasts a variety of stylishly designed houses. The earliest are wooden, like Swiss chalets, with verandas and decorative eaves; out-

The Hôtel Semiramis, formerly Villa Térésa.

standing among these are Villa Térésa, now the Hôtel Semiramis, and villas Tolédo, Montesquieu, Marguerite and Bremontier. The years 1870–1900 produced exotic, fanciful residences of Hispano-Moorish inspiration or Belle-Epoque ostentation, featuring bow windows, stained glass, turrets and other such ornament. Villas Faust, Graigcrostan, Dumas and Vincenette are notable examples. After 1914, charming but more modest single-storey houses were favoured. The Anglican church (now the Protestant church), consecrated in 1878, has some good stained glass.

The Villes d'Eté, Automne and Printemps

The sector of Arcachon described as the Ville d'Eté or Summer Town, encompasses the centre and promenade. This was the first part of Arcachon to be developed (the neo-Renaissance Château Deganne is in fact a casino), and it has been unsympathetically redeveloped since, although an effort was made in 1994 to improve the area along the Thiers Beach. Ferries to Cap-Ferret and boat trips leave from the jetties. The Ville d'Automne is the modest fishermen's district on the eastern side of town around the church of St-Ferdinand, which has a sculpture of the Sacred Heart on the spire.

Ascending the Dune du Pyla.

To the west is the younger Ville de Printemps, built around the 18th-century fishermen's church of Notre-Dame (restored in 1987), which contains a marble statue of the Virgin, some good furnishings and numerous *ex-votos*.

The Dune du Pyla and the oyster farms

Outside the shelter of the Bassin, south of Arcachon, is the area's most spectacular natural phenomenon, the **Dune du Pyla**. At 105m high, 500m wide and 2.7km long, it is the largest sand dune in Europe. Its formation began in the 18th century when wind carried sand from a bar in the channel, and sand continues to blow across from the Banc d'Arguin so that the great dune is shifting a staggering one metre per year towards the forest. Wooden steps facilitate the climb and protect the dune.

At Les Abatilles, south of the town centre, is the deepest still-water spring in France, exploited by Vittel, and beyond, in Le Moulleau, Notre-Dame-des-Passes is a brick and stone Byzantine/Tuscan-inspired church with some good glass.

The **oyster farming** at some 20 villages on the Bassin d'Arcachon has become a tourist attraction and it is possible to call in at a *cabane*, taste oysters and make a guided visit by land or water to see the *ostréiculteurs* at work. Gujan-Mestras is described as the oyster capital of the basin: it has seven small ports or inlets lined with the wooden huts and all the paraphernalia associated with the trade as well as traditional vessels, the flat-bottomed *chalande*, the narrow-hulled *pinasse* (9–10m long), navigated by sail, oar or motor, and the *pinassotte* (a smaller version of the *pinasse*), with sail. The name comes from the word *pin*, pine, from which wood the boats were originally built. The Maison de l'Huître at Port de Larros, Gujan-Mestras is all about oysters and the industry. (*For information on the Route de l'Huître et du Patrimoine Maritime, T: 05 57 52 74 94, www.route-huitre-bassin-arcachon.com.*)

In the southeast corner of the basin, where the salt water is diluted by the mouth of the Leyre River, is the ornithological **park of Le Teich** (*open 10–6, to 8 in summer; T: 05 56 22 80 93, www.parc-landes-de-gascogne.fr*). Covering 120ha of the Leyre Delta, this closely controlled natural environment has a network of dykes and locks and 6km of walks and hides to protect about 250 species of water fowl and migratory birds. The visitor centre, the Maison de la Nature, provides information on the park and its activities, including guided visits. The largest community on the north side of the basin is Andernos-les-Bains, an ancient site where two prehistoric settlements have been discovered; the remains of a 4th-century basilica are still standing. Adjacent to the archaeological site is a small 11th–12th-century Romanesque church, St-Eloi.

LÈGE-CAP FERRET

Lège-Cap Ferret, the playground of Parisians and Bordelais, is a different world from commercialised Arcachon. The peninsula, usually referred to as Cap Ferret, is a narrow spit of sand stretching for 25km between the Bassin d'Arcachon and the Atlantic, with the village of Lège to the northeast and the community of Cap Ferret to the south; the tip is called La Pointe. From around 1830, the huge sand dune was gradually transformed over some 50 years by the introduction of deep-rooted plants and then maritime pines which are now interspersed with February-flowering mimosas and small oaks. Cap Ferret also offers some excellent beaches and some 50km of cycle routes. The first road to Cap-Ferret was built in 1930.

One of the main features of the Cap are the fishing communities, or *villages ostréicoles*, where there are ample opportunities for tasting oysters. Fishermen have been coming to the peninsula since the 17th century. By the mid-19th century the *ostréiculteurs* began to build cabins for the *tri* (sorting) of oysters at the water's edge, and these gradually became homes as well as workplaces. They huddle together near the coastline, separated only by narrow alleyways. These little villages were legally acknowledged in 1878 and are now protected *sites classés*. Building control is strictly maintained and the exclusively wooden dwellings are roofed in tiles and painted in bright colours. Some are still inhabited by the oyster fishermen but others are now holiday homes.

Villages of the peninsula

Lège, at the north of the peninsula, was established in the mid-19th century on a canal built to drain the vast marshes, and further developed with the introduction of the railway and then the road to Cap Ferret. The Modernist architect Le Corbusier (*see p. 45*) designed the *cité ouvrière* in 1925. Just north of Claouey, at Jane-de-Boy, was the small port from which pine pit-props were once exported to England.

The picturesque villages stretch from Les Jacquets in the north, with a tiny, sheltered harbour, one of the first to be settled by the oyster farmers. Petit Piquey has smart villas and a sheltered beach, and from the dune of Grand Piquey is a great view of the Ile aux Oiseaux. In the 1930s the likes of Jean Cocteau, Le Corbusier, Jean Marais and André Lhote patronised the Hôtel Chantecler, next to the jetty. Further south are Piraillan and Le Canon (named after a cannon from the old Napoleonic fort), which were originally surrounded by sand dunes. One of the most characteristic villages is L'Herbe (cows once grazed here), a cluster of wooden *cabanes* close to the shore, in various states from pristine to nearly derelict. Hôtel de la Plage—offering good, simple fare—is typical of the large houses in Basco-Landais style, with attractive overhanging eaves and verandas.

The most southerly oyster-fishing village, Cap-Ferret, still exists but has grown into the largest community on the cape with some fine old villas around the Bélisaire jetty. The main curiosity is the lighthouse, Le Phare (1949), 52m high with 250 steps (*guided visits in summer, T: 05 56 03 94 49, www.lege-capferret.com*).

THE ATLANTIC COAST

Near the tip of the Silver Coast, between the ocean and the estuary, is the senior town, Soulac-sur-Mer. Settled by the Romans, it became a staging-post for English pilgrims travelling south (*see p. 11*), and has the best medieval building in the Médoc, a fine 11th–12th-century church, Notre-Dame-de-la-Fin-des-Terrres (*T: 05 56 09 86 61*), supposedly founded by St Veronica. The church was almost totally enveloped in sand in the 18th century and in 1859 work began to dig it out and renovate. It has three naves of equal height with a rounded apse and two chapels, a few good 12th century capitals and modern glass by Chicot (1954). The resort was first developed in 1849 by Antoine Trouche and was established as a garden city by 1900. It has a splendid assortment of villas and chalets (mid-19th century to 1936), fully exploiting the eclectic vocabulary of styles and decoration so beloved in seaside resorts.

The **Cordouan lighthouse** (*organised boat trips/visits—3hrs—from Le-Verdon-sur-Mer; June–Oct; T: 05 56 09 61 78; www.littoral33.com*) has directed sailors to the entrance of the Gironde Estuary for centuries and claims to be the oldest lighthouse in existence (there was one other on the French coast in the 15th century). Built in stone, it was begun in 1584 to replace a 14th-century structure. In 1593 Henri IV gave his approval to elaborate on it, and royal apartments, a chapel and elegant Renaissance windows were incorporated. It was completed in the early 17th century and Neoclassicised in the 18th century. The lighthouse rises about 66m and is topped with a lantern dome. Electricity was connected in 1950 to light a 6000 watt lamp.

La Pointe de Grave is the very tip of the Médoc peninsula, where sea defences against coastal erosion were erected in 1850.

PRACTICAL INFORMATION

GETTING AROUND

• **By train:** Routes are Bordeaux–Le Teich–Gujan-Mestras–La Teste–Arcachon; Bordeaux–Margaux–Pauillac–Lesparre–Soulac–Pointe de la Grave.

• **By bus:** Routes run from Bordeaux to Andernos-les-Bains, Pointe du Cap Ferret; Bordeaux to Pyla and Biscarosse.

• **By tram:** Bélisaire jetty at Cap-Ferret –l'Horizon beach (April–Sept).

• **Car ferries:** Pointe de la Grave–Royan; Blaye–Lamarque (car ferry).

• **Pedestrian/bike ferries:** Arcachon–Cap Ferret (various ports); Arcachon–Bank d'Arguin; Arcachon–east side of Basin (Ports: Arès, d'Andernos, de Taussat, de Cassy).

• **Bicycle hire:** Information from the Maison du Tourisme de la Gironde, 21 Cours de l'Intendance, Bordeaux, T: 05 56 62 61 40, www.tourisme-gironde.cg33.fr

TOURIST INFORMATION

Arcachon Esplanade G. Pompidou, BP 137, T: 05 57 52 97 97, www.arcachon. com

Arès Esplanade G. Dartiguelongue, T: 05 56 60 18 07, email office-tourism-ares@wanadoo.fr

Cussac-Fort Médoc T: 05 56 58 91 30, office.tourisme.cussac.medoc @wanadoo.fr

Lège-Cap-Ferret 1 Ave du Général-de-Gaulle, T 05 56 03 94 49, www.lege-capferret.com

Le Pyla Rond Point du Figuier, T: 05 56 54 02 22, www.pyla-sur-mer.com

Le Teich Hotel de Ville, T: 05 56 22 80 46, office-de-tourisme-le-teich @wanadoo.fr

Pauillac La Verrerie, T: 05 56 59 03 08, www.pauillac-medoc.com

St-Vivien de Médoc T: 05 56 09 58 50, www.littoral33.com

Soulac-sur-Mer BP2, 68 Rue de la Plage, T; 05 56 09 86 61, www.soulac.com

ACCOMMODATION & RESTAURANTS

Arcachon

€€€ **Arc-Hotel-sur-Mer.** The only 4-star hotel in Arcachon, it is in a peaceful spot right on the seafront and surrounded with greenery. The 30 rooms are comfortable, if slightly old fashioned, but many have really superb sea views. No restaurant. 89 boulevard de la Plage, T: 05 56 83 06 85, www.arc-hotel-sur-mer.com.

€ **Les Vagues.** This welcoming Logis de France hotel is on the seafront and has 30 rooms, each differently styled, some with terraces or large windows and great views. 9 Blvd de la Plage, T: 05 56 83 03 75, info@hotel-les-vagues.com

Blanquefort

€€€ **Château de Grattequina.** At the gateway to the Médoc, just north of Bordeaux and the airport, a very handsome and newly converted 19th-century house turned into a 4-star quality hotel. The grounds, with pool area, sweep down to the Gironde estuary which can be seen from the terraces and all 10 lovely bedrooms with great bathrooms. Av. de Labarde, T: 05 56 35 76 76, www.grattequina.com

Cap Ferret

€ Hôtel La Maison du Bassin. ■ A traditional fisherman's house has been converted into a pretty hotel with 7 charming bedrooms with an old-fashioned seaside feel to the décor. There are also 4 annexes and an apartment. The food in the bistrot is very reasonable with menus from €25 and €39.5 Rue des Pionniers, T: 05 56 60 60 63, www.lamaisondubassin.com

Gujan Mestras

€€ Restaurant la Guérinière. Uncluttered restaurant where the creative and beautifully presented cooking has earned Chef Thierry Renou the only Michelin star on the Basin. Also a hotel. 18 cours de Verdun, T: 05 56 66 08 78, www.laguerinere.com

L'Herbe

€ Restaurant Chez Magne. At the heart of an oyster-fishing village, fish and shell fish predominate, including *langoustines à la persillade, huîtres farcies, soupe blanche de pêcheur, moules grande-mère* and *cassoulette de chipirons* (baby squid), with menus at around €18 and €27. 1 Ave des Marins, T: 05 56 60 50 15.

Lamarque

€ Le Relais du Médoc. Close to where the ferry leaves for Blaye, and in a region of expensive restaurants, this is one place you can eat well and inexpensively. 70 Rue Principale, T: 05 56 58 92 27.

Lège-Cap-Ferret

€€ Restaurant Chez Hortense. At the Pointe du Cap, with a magnificent view from the terrace over the Arcachon Basin towards the Dune de Pyla. The cuisine is based on very fresh fish, including *maigre* (croaker) which is fished locally in certain seasons. Ave. du Sémaphore, T: 05 56 60 62 56.

€ Restaurant L'Escale. Jetée Bélisaire, 2 Ave de l'Océan, T: 05 56 60 68 17 and **€ Café Pinasse**, Jetée Bélisaire, 2 bis Ave de l'Océan, T: 05 56 03 77 87. Both these modest restaurants have terraces and are next to the jetty where the boats arrive from Arcachon; lunchtime menus around €15/25.

Le Taillan-Médoc

€ Chambres d'hôtes Château Le Lout. A friendly and peaceful ambiance pervades the beautiful and elegantly decorated 19th-century mansion, belonging to Colette and Olivier Salmon. Eight bedrooms and three suites overlook the grounds, which are the epitome of refined simplicity. There is also a pool. Good, simple, family-style home-cooked *table d'hôtes* (by reservation) is served in a pretty dining room. Ave de la Dame Blanche, T: 05 56 35 46 47, www.chateaulelout.com

Macau

€ Ferme Auberge Château Guittot-Fellonneau. On the edge of the Médoc vineyards, the winery has one *chambre d'hôtes* and a *gîte*. T: 05 57 88 47 81, guy.constantin@wanadoo.fr.

Margaux

€€€ Le Relais de Margaux. The original house, a hotel since 1985, has been extended horizontally into a large and swish establishment with 86 bedrooms in different categories and 14 suites. The 55 hectare property sweeps down to the estuary, has an outdoor pool and own vegetable garden supplying the gourmet restaurant run by Laurent Costes. Chemin de l'Ile Vincent, T: 05 57 88 38 30, www.relais-margaux.fr

€ Ferme Auberge Château Guittot-Fellonneau. On the edge of the Médoc vineyards, the winery is also a farm-auberge, run by Maryse and Guy Constantin, serving good local dishes including *entrecôte sur sarment*. There is one *chambre d'hôtes* and a *gîte*. T: 05 57 88 47 81, guy.constantin@wanadoo.fr.

Pauillac

€€€ **Château Cordeillan-Bages**. The ultimate in luxurious accommodation and food in an elegant 17th-century setting. There are 29 rooms which are bright and beautiful as are the lounges. Route des Châteaux, T: 05 56 59 24 24, www.relais.chateaux.fr

€ **Hôtel de France et de l'Angleterre** ■ and €€ **Hôtel le Vignoble and Restaurant**. Attractively renovated hotel where the 29 two-star rooms overlook the estuary, and the 20 more evolved three-star rooms are in the quiet garden annexe. The restaurant serves beautifully cooked local specialities and fish including sturgeon, lamprey and shad (*alose*), and dishes such as *Soupe d'orange au vin du Médoc, Cannelé fourré en surprise*. There is a sunny terrace, and initiations to wine tasting can be arranged. 3 Quai Albert Pichon, T: 05 56 59 01 20, www.hoteldefrance.angleterre.com

€€ **Château Cordeillan-Bages**. The sublime cooking matches the extensive wine selection and is based on local specialities such as Pauillac lamb, fish and freshly-grown vegetables. The Ecole de Bordeaux based here runs wine courses.. Route des Châteaux, T: 05 56 59 24 24, www.relais.chateaux.fr

St-Yzans-de-Medoc

€ **Chambres d'hôtes and Ecole du Vin Château Loudenne**. A magnificent pink-tinted 17th-century *chartreuse*, the only château with a private port on the Gironde estuary, which offers great hospitality in a tranquil and beautiful setting

with 62ha of vines running down to the water's edge. Both red and white wines are produced here, there is a museum of wine and 19th-century cellars. T: 05 56 73 17 80, www.lafragette.com

MARKET DAYS

Andernos Covered market Tuesday, Thursday, Friday, Saturday
Claouey Summer markets: Piraillan and **Cap Ferret**, every day; Arès Tuesday
Montalivet Sunday
Lacanau-Océan Wednesday
La Teste de Buch Covered market daily, and Thursday, Saturday, Sunday
Lesparre Tuesday, Friday, Saturday
Pauillac Saturday
St-Vivien de Médoc Wednesday
Soulac Covered market every day.

FESTIVALS & EVENTS

March–April: *Portes Ouvertes dans les Châteaux du Médoc*, open weekend for about 80 wineries, for buyers, collectors and all wine-lovers.
May: *Fête de l'Agneau de Pauillac*, 2-day celebration of local lamb, with replica sheepfold, ceremony marking departure to pastures, and sheepdog demonstrations, Pauillac; *La Médocaine*, cross-country bike race (3 courses) in the heart of the Margaux appellation vineyards for serious and not-so-serious, with street festivities and sports-related events
June: *Jumping des sables* Beach show-jumping, unique in the world, on Plage Péreire at low tide, Arcachon
July: *Les regates* Regattas, Arcachon
July–August: *Fête du Village de l'Herbe*, music and tastings in oyster villages, Lège-Cap Ferret

HAUTE GIRONDE

The Garonne and the Dordogne rivers merge at Bec d'Ambès, about 20km north of Bordeaux, to become the Gironde Estuary. Along the right—or east—bank of the estuary are the modest towns of Blaye and Bourg. Despite their historic roles as forts to protect the great port and city of Bordeaux vulnerable to attack from the sea, they have now become gently soporific, snuggled between pretty coastal views and undulating limestone plateaux sprinkled with vines and chequerboard fields. In contrast, further north, is a modern port and a nuclear power station. This outreach of the Gironde *département* was the old border between the Saintonge and Aquitaine, and thus the historic boundary between the language of *oc*, in the south, and *oïl*, in the north. In the vicinity are many small Romanesque churches, the remains of a Roman villa at Plassac, and the caves of Pair-non-Pair. As well as the wines of Blaye and Bourg and the fish of the Gironde, and at one time plentiful caviar, the area now produces strawberries and asparagus,

The Gironde Estuary

The water of the estuary is usually murky due to the mix of fresh and salt water. Particles of soil and vegetation that are suspended in fresh water clump together in salt water, creating silt on which the flora and fauna of the estuary depend. Some coastal land has been reclaimed, but there are still wetlands and wild, untamed marshes attracting thousands of birds including herons and egrets. The estuary fish include obscure species such as the lamprey, an eel-like creature which is in fact a parasite feeding on the blood of other fishes; eels and shad. Sturgeon, once plentiful and the mainstay of this region, is now rare and protected.

BLAYE & ENVIRONS

So strategically placed is Blaye that it has always been an important stronghold, and the small town on the banks of the Gironde is dominated by its huge fort. Now the fort has a peaceful role, and shelters crafts' workshops, museums, a hotel and a camp site and from it are the most majestic views of the estuary. Blaye is at the centre of an important wine-producing area, and although the name may not run off the tongue as would those of its neighbours Médoc or St-Emilion, the wines are of excellent quality and several wine châteaux also have *chambres d'hôtes*. There is a regular ferry service from Blaye across the Gironde to Lamarque in the Médoc. The town makes much of its local speciality, *Praslines de Blaye* (sugar-coated almonds), named in the 17th century after the Maréchal de Plesis-Praslin, whose cook it was that devised them.

Citadel of Blaye

The citadel is unique in Aquitaine, although the author, Vauban, did work in Bayonne (*p. 443*). It covers 33ha and its 40m-high ramparts have two gateways. The area inside the fortifications covers 17ha, large enough to contain a small working community.

The rock dominating the estuary was an obvious place for a defensive system. Vulgrin Rudel, descendent of the Counts of Angoulême, rebuilt the existing castle (1126–37) and its remains are inside the citadel. Blaye was part of English Aquitaine, and only returned to the French in 1451 under Dunois, Comte d'Orléans (1403–68), an officer in the army of Charles VII, who fought beside Joan of Arc against the English. In the 16th century the town was besieged twice during the Wars of Religion, and in the 17th century work was undertaken to strengthen the ramparts when the Fronde (*see p. 16*) underlined Blaye's importance as the key to Bordeaux, and therefore to all of Aquitaine.

Following a visit by Louis XIV in 1650, the construction of a larger and stronger fort was deemed necessary, to the detriment of the Rudel château, some 260 houses and eventually the church of St-Romain, yet this large undertaking was still not massive enough for the huge garrison. Two projects were submitted, by François Ferri and by Vauban (*see box below*). Vauban's plans were realised under Ferri's supervision (1686–89). His fortifications were characterised by their angular bastions. The citadel became part of a string of fortresses across the Gironde, with Fort Médoc on the west bank (*see p. 55*) and Fort Pâté on the island opposite Blaye. The latter was originally called Fort Saint-Simon after the governor of the Citadelle, but was changed at the Revolution to Fort Pâté as its shape resembles a mould for *pâté de campagne*. The Blaye citadel was in fact tested only once, by the British in 1814, in a siege lasting 14 days. In 1832 the Duchesse de Berry, Marie-Caroline of Naples, was imprisoned here following a conspiracy to topple her uncle, Louis-Philippe, from the throne of France. In 1841 the future city planner Baron Haussmann became *sous-Préfet* for Blaye; and the citadel continued to be used as a prison during the Second Empire (1852–70) and the First World War. It remained in the hands of the military authorities until 1954, when it was purchased by Blaye town council for the symbolic sum of 1 franc.

Maréchal de Vauban (1633–1707)

Born Sébastien Le Prestre, *seigneur* of the Château de Vauban, to a family of lesser nobility, Vauban is far better known for his contributions to military architecture at the time of Louis XIV than for his genius on the field of battle. His important socio-economic activities in his native Burgundy are also less feted. As an engineer, although not by training, he became Commissaire Général des Fortifications in 1678. While he did not invent the type of fortifications for which he is best known, he nevertheless brought them to a state of perfection and is credited with the construction or repair of a network of some 150 strongholds to protect France on all fronts, ranging from massive forts such as Blaye and Bayonne to monumental gateways. He was elevated to Maréchal de France when he was 70.

The entry on foot is via Porte Dauphine spanning the dry moat. Stone bridges replaced wooden ones in the 18th century. Inside the severe battlements is a pleasant village with around 15 residents; the garrison buildings have become workshops and boutiques for artists and craftspeople. There are also a museum and exhibition gallery, large open spaces and wonderful views. Among buildings which can be visited are the Manutention, or Musée de la Boulangerie (*open April–Oct daily 1.30–7; Nov–March, 1.30–5.30*), a solid 17th-century building used for exhibitions and containing old bread ovens where there is an exhibition of bread-making. The Pavillon de la Place, the Duchesse de Berry's prison, and Porte Liverneuf, are relics of the time when the upper town and the esplanade had a dividing wall.

The remains of the 12th-century Château des Rudel, incorporated into Vauban's fortress, were reduced to ruins in the 19th century. From the 12th to the 15th centuries, the Rudel family controlled Blaye and the castle was the birthplace of the famous troubadour and author of *Amours lointains*, Jaufré Rudel, who left for Tripoli in 1147 in pursuit of his beloved Melissande, only to expire in her arms.

Commanding the estuary is the Tour de l'Eguillette, looking across to Fort Pâté and the Médoc beyond. Further south is Place des Armes and the Hôtel de la Citadelle (*see p. 78*). The former gunpowder store, the Poudrière (1687) is used by the Syndicat Viticole de Blaye. Exhibitions are held in the remains of the 17th-century Couvent des Minimes. Outside the citadel walls, to the east, are the foundations of the Abbaye de St-Romain, a site of Christian worship since the 4th century. The Rudels were patrons of the abbey which was on the pilgrimage route, and legend has it that Roland, Charlemagne's chevalier (*see p. 476*), was buried here. It was badly damaged during the Wars of Religion.

THE WINES OF BLAYE & BOURG

The less-known wines of Bourg and Blaye, both red and white, are produced in an area between Bordeaux and the Charentes in an area of limestone plateaux sloping towards the Gironde, and a temperate climate. The history of wine here goes back to Roman times, but the *appellations* are fairly recent. The 3,900ha of the Bourgeais, including AOC Côtes de Bourg rouge and AOC Côtes de Bourg blanc, stretch over 15 communes close to the confluence of the Dordogne and Gironde. North of Bourg are the Blayais vineyards of over 5,500ha and including four *appellations*, Premières Côtes de Blaye, red and white, Côtes de Blaye white, and Blaye white. Crus Bourgeois was mentioned for the first time in 1868, but disappeared until revived in 1990, and now 12 producers adhere to the quality regulations laid down by the Syndicat des Premières Côtes de Blaye. The most recent *appellation* in Blaye was introduced in autumn 2002. There are some 71 châteaux which receive visitors either at fixed times or by appointment. Further information from the Offices de Tourisme in Blaye and Bourg, or the Maison du Vin, Cours Vauban, Blaye (*T: 05 57 42 91 19, www.premieres-cotes-blaye.com*)

Plassac Gallo-Roman villa and the Corniche Fleurie

Just south of Blaye, at Plassac, are the remains of an important Gallo-Roman villa and museum (*guided visits May–Sept 9–12 & 2–7; April, Oct daily 9–12 & 2–6; T: 05 57 42 84 80*). The modest museum is a reminder of the size and luxury of Gallo-Roman rural estates through the display of mosaics and fragments of superb wall paintings in the 3rd Pompeian style (c. 30–40 AD) found at Plassac, as well as smaller finds such as weights, coins, pottery and jewellery. Plans and reconstructions explain the evolution of the three successive villas erected between the 1st and 6th centuries on the domain of *Blacciacum*, each rebuild increasing in size and complexity. The first was an agricultural villa, but it eventually grew into an elegant estate with courtyards and gardens, covering 6,000 square metres. The archaeological site to the north of the church is almost entirely open to the elements, although there are fragments of 5th-century mosaics still in place but partly submerged under the church (and others being renovated). The villa opened onto the estuary but there are now houses standing on this part. To help distinguish the successive villas, they are indicated on the site by yellow pots for the first, pink for the second and mauve for the third.

The pretty coastal route between Blaye and Bourg has a magnificent panorama over the Gironde and is known as the Corniche Fleurie because master mariners built mansions along the river. The *corniche* is a viewing point for the Mascaret, or tidal bore. This occurs on the Dordogne at certain times of the year, caused when the rising tide surging up the Gironde estuary is as strong as the down current from the Dordogne. This especially happens during high tides and shallow water levels, between April and November, the optimum time being August–September. These conditions create a series of spectacularly powerful waves, spaced out over about 10m, the largest of them reaching around 2.5m in height. The phenomenon is best observed from the port of St-Pardon, west of Libourne, or from Podensac or Pont d'Arcins, and its time can be precisely calculated. The Mascaret is now the only example in France of a tidal bore—the others have disappeared due to environmental changes—and is enthusiastically awaited by surfers although in the past it was extremely hazardous for navigation.

Most of the dozen or so islands in the archipelago are deserted, although they were formerly inhabited, and some (Cazeau, North and Green islands) have fused as a result of the constant build-up of silt. These form the spit which protects Margaux island. The church at Bayon has a monumental apse on three levels with a series of superimposed blind arcades.

BOURG & ENVIRONS

Bourg-sur-Gironde is a stunning fortified village built on a rocky outcrop surrounded by medieval ramparts and set in the vineyards of Côtes-de-Bourg. Picturesque narrow streets descend to the port via the sea gate, La Gouttinière, or the Escalier du Roy (King's Steps). In the centre of the *cité* is the market hall, the Hôtel de la Jurade; the citadel, built originally by the English (rebuilt 1964); a 12th-century *chartreuse*; and a communal wash-house (1828). The Romanesque crypt of the ruined chapel of St-Saturnin-de-la-Libarde has 11th–12th-century carved capitals.

Among several rural Romanesque churches nearby is the 12th-century church at Tauriac, with some fine relief carvings on the façade and interesting capitals inside. A 12th-century Templar chapel of Magrigne (*T: 05 57 43 01 61*), St-Laurent d'Arce, has ancient murals. There is a superb example of Romanesque architecture at Peujard with a Saintonge-style portal and cupola on pendentives. In Cubnezais, the church has a Romanesque façade decorated with animals and figures. At Marcenais is a fortified Templar church. St-Gervais, close to St-André-de-Cubzac, has a 12th-century church.

The **Grotte de Pair-non-Pair** at Prignac-et-Marcamps, east of Bourg, is an important prehistoric site (*guided visits at 10, 10.45, 11.30, 2.30, 3.30 , 4.30; 15 June–15 Sept also 12.30, 1.30, 4.30; closed Mon, and 1/1, 1/5, 1/11, 11/11, 25/12; T: 05 57 68 33 40*) Discovered in 1881 when a cow fell through a hole, and excavated by the local archaeologist François Daleau, the cave is remarkable because unusually it was actually inhabited by prehistoric man. This was possible as there are natural openings in the rock letting in light and acting as a vent for smoke; there is also a source of water. The excavation of archaeological levels and the tools and animal bones found point to its being the habitat of Neanderthal and Cro-Magnon man from c. 80,000 to c. 20,000 BC. The engravings, from the Gravettian period (c. 30,000–27,000 BC), are among the earliest examples of cave art and include horses, ibex, deer, mammoths and other mammals.

The Château du Bouilh (*gardens open, guided visits to interior, 1 July–30 Sept, Thur, Sat, Sun and holidays 2.30–6.30; T: 05 57 43 01 45*), was the work of Victor Louis, author of the Grand Théâtre in Bordeaux (*see p. 21*). It was built for the Marquis de la Tour du Pin to receive Louis XVI and is set in a magnificent park overlooking the Dordogne. The park, graced with 200-year-old trees, is open most of the time. The château has a grand staircase and furnished reception rooms through which passed the Duchesse de Berry (*see p. 67*) and the Romantic poet Alphonse de Lamartine (1790–1869).

St-André-de-Cubzac on the right bank of the Dordogne was the birthplace of Jacques-Yves Cousteau, the underwater explorer who brought the aquatic world alive to millions via television. He was born at 83 Rue Nationale (now a pharmacy) in 1910, and returned to his native land at the end of his life. In the town is a 13th-century church with a military look, having been fortified in the 14th century.

The Pont Eiffel at Cubzac-les-Ponts has an impressive enfilade of stone piers c. 140m long which, viewed from below, gives the effect of a Gothic construction. The piers support an enclosed metal road and railway bridge built by Gustave Eiffel in 1883. The lower part is freely accessible from the port.

THE LIBOURNAIS & ST-EMILION

The Libournais, watered by the confluence of the Isle and Dordogne rivers, is an area of intense wine-production, notably around St-Emilion, Pomerol and Fronsac. Apart from the vineyards, the landscape is varied, and there is a wealth of châteaux and churches.

Libourne and Fronsac

The agreeable town of Libourne, the second largest in the Gironde, is strategically placed at the union of the Dordogne and the Isle rivers. Edward I planned a *bastide*-port here in 1268, and it was named after Roger de Leyburn who supervised the project in 1270. English until the end of the Hundred Years War, it was protected by walls with eight fortified entrances. The advantages of the position ensured a dynamic river port shipping local wine to England and northern Europe. It suffered the usual problems in the 17th–19th centuries, but has remained a major centre of the wine trade.

A few fragments of the ramparts still line the Isle, including the mid-14th-century Porte du Grand Port flanked by one complete round tower and part of another, but most of the walls have been replaced by tree-lined esplanades. The regular *bastide* layout has been maintained, and at the centre is Place Abel-Surchamp which is surrounded by *couverts* and enlivened by the Sunday markets. The former Hôtel de Ville dates from the 15th century (restored 1911–14) and houses the municipal library and the Musée des Beaux-Arts et d'Archéologie (*open Mon–Fri 10–12 & 2–6, closed Sat, Sun; T: 05 57 55 33 44*). It contains paintings by Jacopo Bassano, Philippe de Champaigne, Raoul Dufy and Leonard Fujita, and has a room devoted to René Princeteau, Toulouse-Lautrec's first drawing master (*see p. 257*), and other local artists.

THE WINES OF ST-EMILION & THE LIBOURNAIS

The St-Emilion *appellation* covers the area between the Dordogne and the little river Barbane. The St-Emilion and St-Emilion Grand Cru appellations (AOC) are spread over almost exactly the same area as the eight communes recognised in 1289 by Edward I of England and established under the ancient Jurisdiction of St-Emilion, although these communes were abolished in 1789. The vineyards then covered 7,800 hectares, whereas the present St-Emilion appellations cover 5,400 hectares. St-Emilion produces 5.5 per cent of the total Bordeaux AOC red wine and the predominant grape variety is Merlot, combined with Cabernet Franc and Cabernet Sauvignon. In 1999 the area of the old Jurisdiction was designated a World Heritage cultural landscape by UNESCO.

There are four further St-Emilion appellations towards the north: Montagne Saint-Emilion, Lussac St-Emilion, Puisseguin St-Emilion and St-Georges St-Emilion, covering another 3,800 hectares and 500 producers. The estates, therefore, are fairly small and the quality of the wines is jealously maintained. Châteaux Cheval-Blanc and Figeac are towards Pomerol. Other neighbouring appellations are Fronsac and Castillon. Among the 1,000 or so producers of St-Emilion and St-Emilion Grand Cru, Châteaux Ausone and Cheval-Blanc have enjoyed an outstanding reputation for some 50 years. Other châteaux producing high-quality wine are Beauséjour, Bélaire, Canon, Clos-Fourtet, Figeac and La Gaffelière. *For information on visits and tastings, see p. 79.*

SAINT-EMILION

The richly endowed town of St-Emilion stands confidently on a limestone escarpment surveying the vineyards on which it depends. Beautifully turned out, it has many interesting buildings solidly built in the local cream-coloured stone, and is well organised to manage the thousands of visitors. The biggest surprise is that it is not as solid as it looks because carved out of the rock below is a vast network of underground galleries and a huge monolithic church. In the air there is always a hint of the wine for which the town is so revered, and some 5,200 hectares of land and 1,000 vineyards of the appellation produce as much wine as the whole of Burgundy. Sweet specialities sold all over town include *cannelés de Bordeaux* (small doughy cakes, coated in caramel and baked in a fluted mould), and *macarons*. The tradition of making almond biscuits or macaroons started with the Ursuline nuns, who founded a community on the west of the town in 1630.

Place du Marché is the hub of the town, enlivened by café tables and wine boutiques. From here Tertre de la Fente leads uphill to the collegiate church (*described below*). The four sloping *tertres* (mounds) in the town are paved with granite which was used in the 12th century as ballast on ships returning from Cornwall or Brittany after offloading their cargoes of wine. *Escalettes* (narrow stepped paths) are similar and run west to east along the contours of the hill, linking the *tertres* with steps and terraces. These were the only way of getting around until Rue Guadet was built in the 19th century.

HISTORY OF SAINT-EMILION

The 4th-century Roman poet and proconsul Ausonius is connected with the vineyards, but the town took its name from Emilion (d. 6th January 767), a hermit from Brittany, who settled in a local cave and performed miracles. He was first mentioned in 12th-century texts, although by the end of the 11th century two religious buildings already existed, dedicated to Emilion and Mary Magdalene. The large collegiate church and monastery were begun early in the 12th century. In 1199, during the period of the Anglo-Gascon alliance, the future King John granted St-Emilion the status of commune and established a body of aldermen, called the Jurade, to supervise the town and vineyards. The Jurade lost its political role with the Revolution, and the town became a place of refuge for Elie Guadet, a member of the Girondins who met his end at the guillotine in Bordeaux (*see p. 25*). As elsewhere, the wine trade suffered from mildew and phylloxera outbreaks in the 19th century, but in 1884 a wine syndicate was formed, and the *appellation contrôlée* was defined in 1936. In 1948 a confraternity named after the old Jurade was created to promote the wine.

The town walls

A stroll around the perimeter following the old walls brings into focus the layout of the town and its relationship with the vineyards. The rocky outcrop forms a natural amphitheatre sloping downhill from north to south and St-Emilion is still contained within the walls erected between 1110 and 1224. Strangely isolated just outside the walls to the north are Les Grandes Murailles, all that remains of a 13th-century Dominican monastery, destroyed c 1340. Three bays of the nave wall, a perilous 26m high by 20m, with two slender Gothic openings and fine mouldings, seem to have no business still to be standing. The old Porte Bourgeoise was the main and most heavily fortified entrance to the town, but the walls and gate were demolished in the 18th–19th centuries. Built into the walls beyond is the Palais Cardinal, possibly named after the first dean and cardinal. The double round-headed windows were probably part of the defences. On the corner is a section of wall with massive corbels and from here the path runs between the vineyards and the ditch. The only gate more or less in its original 12th-century state is the Porte Brunet, with later fortifications, and this and the Tour Guetteur now look out over benign battalions of vines. The path descends to Place Bouqueyre, named after the gate to the lower town; the *guérite* (lookout), a strange isolated construction, is the only fragment left of the barbican. From Rue de la Porte Bouqueyre a flight of steps climbs to Rue de la Porte, leading from Porte Ste-Marie, which was walled up in the 16th century. The quarries of the old Hospice de la Madeleine have become an underground pottery museum, Musèe Souterrain de la Poterie, 21 Rue André Loiseau (*open daily; T: 05 57 55 51 65*), containing a collection of regional pottery dating from the 13th century onwards.

The Château du Roi (*open May–Oct 10–7; times can vary so check with the Tourist Office*), in which both Louis VIII and Henry III had a hand, was begun c. 1237. Protected by a dry ditch, the massive, square Gascon-style keep undoubtedly played a symbolic as well as a military role. Until 1720 it was used as the town hall, and in June and September the Jurade adds a dash of colour when its members gather at the top in their red and white outfits to pay homage to the wines of St-Emilion. From the terrace you can enjoy classic views over the town, uninterrupted by cables or aerials.

The west gate, Porte St-Martin, has completely disappeared, but the walls flanking it are still standing and in the thickness of the wall are steps which led to the *chemin de ronde* (path around the battlements). From here the route outside the walls reveals the best-conserved section of the ramparts (roofed over) and the rebuilt bridge. The path inside the ramparts leads past the entrances to the caves and former quarries. Something like 200km of quarries, on four or five levels, provided stone to build St-Emilion, Libourne and Bordeaux.

The collegiate church

The collegiate church, one of the finest in the Gironde, was established in 1110 with an independent chapter of Augustinian canons and was secularised by Bertrand de Got (*see p. 92*) in 1306 when his nephew, Gaillard de la Motte, was installed as dean. These associations were obviously relevant to the prestige of the church. The chapter was dissolved in 1790, and it became a parish church after the Revolution.

The church is an imposing but severe building, the long, low roof covered in red tiles interrupted only by the slightly truncated belfry over the narthex, and the gable and steep roof over the apse. Work began on the church and cloister before the mid-12th century and continued through the 13th century, and the Romanesque cloister was rebuilt in the late 13th century. The oldest part of the building is the nave; the west door is Romanesque with a succession of round-headed arches with a window above in the style of the Saintonge. The exterior decoration of the north door (c. 1306) is damaged and difficult to decipher but it is just possible to make out scenes of the *Last Judgement* on the tympanum, with *Christ in Majesty*, the *Virgin and St John* and, on the lintel, the *Separation of the Righteous from the Damned*. Either side of the door, very battered, are the *Crucifixion of St Peter* and the *Martyrdom of St Paul*.

Inside the narrow, three-bay, aisleless nave is part of the original 12th-century building with little decoration except for a mural (*see below*). The two east bays are spanned by domes on pendentives in the style of the Périgord but at some point the belfry over the west porch collapsed, bringing down the vaults (or dome) of the first bay where there is now a 13th-century ribbed vault. At the same time the original transept was demolished and replaced with a Gothic edifice, three bays wide and two deep, extended by a flat-ended chancel with large windows. The two chapels date from the 14th century, as does the sacristy above, which has a six-lobed rose window. After the Hundred Years War the Flamboyant polygonal apse with large windows was added, no doubt replacing an earlier one. The relics of St Emilion would have been conserved behind the main altar; the early 14th-century southeast chapel is dedicated to the saint.

There are a number of wall paintings but these are probably only a sample, as the remaining traces suggest a far more complete programme covering the transept and vaults. On the pilaster in the southeast of the nave is a 12th-century image of the Virgin standing on the World, and adjacent are four scenes, enclosed in circles, from the Legend of St Catherine. On the west wall are more murals, including a *Crucifixion*. Near the sacristy door is a 16th-century painted wooden statue of St Valéry, local saint and patron of wine-growers, dressed in the appropriate working outfit of the day. The late 15th–early 16th-century choir stalls have misericords with a variety of lively carvings. The pulpit is 19th century, and the organ is an excellent instrument from the end of the 19th century by Gabriel Cavaillé-Col, son of Aristide. There is 20th-century glass by Mirande.

The **cloister** is entered from the church or from the tourist office. Of the Romanesque version, only the east and south walls remain following rebuilding at the end of the 13th or early 14th centuries. The south wall has ten funerary niches (of the same period) decorated with trefoil arches and dragons, whereas the east wall has a series of Romanesque and Gothic niches with hints of early 14th-century painting, restored in 1997. The cloister is used in the summer for craft markets and other activities.

The rather smart **Maison du Vin** is installed in the old Logis de l'Abbé, part of the 18th-century conventual buildings, with a wrought-iron staircase ramp of 1744.

On Place des Créneaux is the great **belfry**, 133m high measured from Place du Marché below. The first two levels are 12th-century, the second and third 13th-century, and the spire was completed at the end of the 15th. In 1626 it had to be reinforced with extra buttresses. It stands directly above the monolithic church (*see below*) and the bell ropes originally connected with the underground building. From the top of the belfry, 187 steps above, marvellous views can be had over the town and vineyards.

The monolithic church

Guided tours every 45mins all year round, between 10 and 4.15; April–Oct until 5.45; T: 05 57 55 28 28.

The monolithic church, catacombs, hermitage and Trinity chapel, were all constructed in natural caves which have been modified and used since prehistoric times. The hermitage, St Emilion's rock shelter, which was originally open to the south, is 'furnished' with a stone table and bed, and had a miraculous source of water. The Trinity chapel, built over the hermitage c. 12th–13th centuries, was rebuilt in 1730. In 1995 the paintings between the ribs of the early Gothic apse (13th century) were discovered. The catacombs contain several sarcophagi, one with an epitaph dated 1014, and monolithic columns to support the roof, one decorated. The original entrance to the catacombs was the curious funnel-like opening with a spiral staircase supported by a dome cut into the rock. Around the base of the dome are three half-figures in relief, which seem to support the construction on their backs.

The badly damaged Gothic door of the church carries an incomplete *Last Judgement* in the tympanum, and the *Resurrection of the Dead* on the lintel. The monolithic church was carved from the rock, entailing the removal of some 15,000 cubic metres of rock to enlarge an existing natural cave under Place des Créneaux. Its astounding dimensions—38m long, 20m wide and 12m high—make it the largest of its kind in Europe. The church is thought to date from the end of the 11th century or beginning of the 12th. An inscription on the third pillar (south) of the nave may refer to the dedication, but gives only the day and month, not the year. The church reopened in 2003 after a lengthy programme of restoration revealing the true proportions of the beautiful, simple interior of this remarkable structure. Concrete pillars (38) installed in 1990 have been removed leaving just the ten original pillars, four of which, at the base of the church tower, are reinforced with a metal corset. The floor has been returned to the medieval level by removing layers of earth that had built up over the centuries as drains became blocked; some of these drains can be seen as well as ancient stone flags. Windows have been re-opened and the lighting improved as part of the renovations thus enhancing reliefs high on the pillars and the west wall of the nave. These are mainly of animals but on the vaults are two cherubim, halo to halo, surveying the scene. The church was pillaged in 1793, and wall paintings dating from the 14th century were neglected and badly damaged when saltpetre was scraped off the walls for the explosives industry in the 19th century. The altars are 16th- and 18th-century.

East to the Rue Guadet

The arcaded Halle du Marché on Rue de la Cadène has a staircase leading to a very fine ogee and the old *hôtel de ville* upstairs. In the street, a stone archway, Arceau de la Cadène, is the remains of a gateway across which a *cadena* or chain was supposedly thrown to separate the upper and lower towns. The picturesque old house on the right is possibly 12th century, but was altered in the 14th century and again in the 19th. Next door is the only timber-framed house (16th century) still surviving in St-Emilion. The upper road, Rue de la Porte-Brunet leads to Place du Cap-du-Pont where, on the corner, there is the so-called Templar commandery, a building with an *echaugette* and the outlines of some pretty Romanesque windows.

Almost opposite are the overgrown ruins of the **Couvent des Cordeliers** (*open daily March–Oct 10.30–7.30; Oct–March 2– 6. Guided visits to the chais in the afternoon; T: 05 57 24 72 07*). A branch of the Franciscan Order, the Cordeliers moved inside the walls in the 14th century and erected a chapel (15th century), cellars and residential buildings. Already run down, it was sold in 1791. What remains of the cloisters appears to be pre-14th century, and was perhaps transferred from the earlier building. The walls, but not the vaults, of the chapel are still standing. In the cloisters you can enjoy a tasting of Crémant de Bordeaux and visit the wine store.

On the 19th-century Rue Guadet, nearly opposite Rue des Girondins, is the Maison Gothique (15th–16th centuries), with two-light windows and numerous corbels, one of the best-preserved medieval houses in St-Emilion although disfigured in the 18th century. Further on is the former Couvent des Jacobins (or Dominicans), given permission to build *intra muros* on land abutting the Cordeliers convent. The gardens of the *Mairie* (18th century) are on the left; if they are open, see the restored wall on the right with a mixture of architectural elements. Place Mercadieu has two adjacent late-medieval buildings, one with a square tower.

Environs of St-Emilion

The undulating countryside around St-Emilion is densely packed with strictly regimented lines of vines. The dips and hollows are described as *combes*. Small churches and villages abound. Fronsac, northwest of St-Emilion, which gives its name to the local AOC (*see p. 52*), is between the Dordogne and the Isle rivers to the west of Libourne. A succession of hilltop forts, or *tertres*, was built and destroyed here by Gauls, Romans, Carolingians, Vikings and the English. In 1663 the Duc de Richelieu took possession of these territories and his great nephew, Arnaud de Plessis, built a folly on the ruins. In the town is a 12th–13th-century church with a *clocher pignon*.

The church of St-Pierre at **La Lande-de-Fronsac**, has naïve sculptures around the south porch accompanied by an inscription. The tympanum unusually presents the *Vision of the Apocalypse* inspired by the text of *Revelations*, where Christ reveals himself to St John with 'seven stars in his right hand, with a sword coming out of his mouth'. The arches and capitals are decorated with interlacing, monsters and old bearded men. In the restored interior are archaeological excavations under glass. The square belfry has a bell dated 1347, recast in 1855.

THE WINES OF POMEROL & FRONSAC

The wines of Pomerol and Fronsac abut St-Emilion. Pomerol is one of the smallest wine producing areas of Bordeaux along a slightly hilly plateau almost 5km long and just over 3km wide, northwest of St-Emilion, with only 780ha of vines. Its reds are easily recognisable for the subtle bouquet reminiscent of truffles which is accounted for by the iron oxide or 'dross' content of the soil here. The topsoil consists of gravel, more like the Gironde. These are such famous wines that they have never had to be formally classified but, like all Bordeaux wines, Pomerol is strictly monitored to guarantee the required degree of perfection. Outstanding are the wines of Château Petrus, but also representative are Châteaux Beauregard, le Caillou, Clos du Clocher, La Conseillante, Clos-l'Eglise, La Croix, Sergant and Borseau.

Fronsac and Canon-Fronsac, the two *appellations* of the Fronsac area, are much sought after. The great-nephew of Cardinal Richelieu, Duc de Fronsac, introduced the wines to the Court of Louis XV. The full-bodied, ruby-coloured wines are produced in about 170 wineries.

One of the best church façades in the Gironde is that of St-Pierre at **Petit-Palais** (northeast of St-Emilion), built in the late 12th century and partly rebuilt in the 16th. The tiered west end, richly ornamented over the whole elevation, exhibits the influence of the Saintonge. The first level is decorated with columns and carved capitals, and the central door and side niches have multi-foil decoration which is echoed on the next level. In the spandrels of the main entrance are statues. The second level, slightly laid back, is very ornate with blind niches around the central window, clustered columns, carved capitals and arches, and in the triangular pediment are four blind arcades on double columns. The interior is late Gothic

The name Castillon-la-Bataille gives a strong clue as to what happened here. Once a thriving town and stronghold on the Dordogne, the château and ramparts were destroyed during the Hundred Years War and the Wars of Religion, and there is not a great deal left to see. It overlooks the vineyards of the AOC Côtes de Castillon. In 1452 Castillon was controlled by the English, but Charles VII's army took Chalais and Gensac nearby, and marched on the town with 6,000 men. Castillon requested help from Bordeaux. General Talbot, Count of Shrewsbury, arrived with 8,000 men and met with some success but, led erroneously to believe that the French had abandoned camp, Talbot decided to continue attacking. The English army was decimated and abandoned the battle after Talbot's death, bringing the Hundred Years War and the English occupation of Aquitaine to an end. The French generals erected a chapel on the site, Notre-Dame-de-Talbot, where there is a procession around the feast of the Assumption (15th August). The battle is commemorated every summer (July/Aug) on the Coly plain (*T: 05 57 40 14 53*).

PRACTICAL INFORMATION

GETTING AROUND

• **By train:** TGV Paris–Bordeaux–St-Emilion; Paris–Libourne Bordeaux–St-André de Cubzac–St-Yzan-de-Soudiac–Saintes; Bordeaux–Périgueux –Libourne–Brive-la-Gaillarde
• **By bus:** Bordeaux–Libourne; Libourne–St-Emilion. Trans-Gironde network, T: 05 56 99 57 83.
• **Ferry:** Blaye–Lamarque, passing the islands of Pâté and Bouchaud-La Nouvelle (T: 05 57 42 04 49).

TOURIST INFORMATION

Blaye Allées Marines, T: 05 57 42 12 09, www.tourisme-blaye.com
Bourg-sur-Gironde Hôtel de la Jurade, T: 05 57 68 31 76, tourismebourg@wanadoo.fr
Castillon-la-Bataille Allée Marcel Paul, T: 05 57 40 27 58, otcastillonpujols@wanadoo.fr
Libourne 45 Allée Robert Boulin, T: 05 57 51 15 04, www.libourne-tourisme.com
Lussac 2 Rue Gambetta, T: 05 57 74 50 35, tourisme-lussac@wanadoo.fr
St-André-de-Cubzac 9 Allée du Champ de Foire, T: 05 57 43 64 80.
St-Emilion Le Doyenné, Pl. des Créneaux, T: 05 57 55 28 28, www.saint-emilion-tourisme.com
St-Savin Maison de Pays, BP 32, T: 05 57 58 47 79, cdc-st-savin@wanadoo.fr

ACCOMMODATION & RESTAURANTS

Blaye
€ **Hôtel/Restaurant La Citadelle**. Tucked inside the walls of the Vauban's Citadelle, this is to say the least an unusual setting for a hotel. It is next to the old convent where exhibitions are held and has 21 comfortable rooms, a gastronomic restaurant (menus €25–51), overlooking the Gironde estuary, a pool and a terrace.Pl. d'Armes, T: 05 57 42 17 10, www.hotel-la-citadelle.com

Bourg-sur-Gironde
€ **Restaurant Le Plaisance**. Close to the port in a triangular end-of-block building, this attractive, large, lively and relaxed restaurant and wine bar, open 7 to 2 a.m. every day, is a popular local place to eat and drink (menus €15–50). Au Port, T: 05 57 68 45 34.

Fronsac
€€ **Restaurant Le Bord'eau**. Perched right on the edge of the river, traditional and gastronomic dishes, featuring local fish such as lamprey and shad, when in season. Poinsonnet T: 05 57 51 99 91.

Juillac
€ **Le Belvédère**. A terrace overlooking the Dordogne, a traditional dining room, and the best quality ingredients. Or, according to your budget (minimum €39) and preferences, chef creates a personal menu accompanied by appropriate wines. Set menus at €25/39/56 and weekday lunch €18. 1 Côte de la Tourbeille, T: 05 57 47 40 33, le-belvedere@wanadoo.fr

Pessac-sur-Dordogne
€ **Chambres d'hôtes Château Carbonneau**. A 19th-century château with magnificent glass in the style of Napoleon III. Listed under Chambres d'hôtes Bacchus, it won the accommodation category award in 'Best Of' Wine

Tourism in 2004. This is born out by the six elegant rooms, one in the pigeonnier. Not only a winery which can be visited, but the owners also farm and breed dogs. There is a pool next to the vines and meals can be booked in advance. T: 05 57 47 46 46, www.chateau-carbonneau.com

St-Emilion

Note that hotel tariffs increase when the Jurade meets in June and September.

€€€ **Château/Restaurant Grand Barrail**. The beautifully restored 19th-century château with original stained glass and stucco, is set in a park surrounded by vineyards. It has 33 luxurious rooms and nine suites, some with balconies, in four unique properties. Of the three Dining Rooms, one has a Moorish ambiance; and a terrace in summer. Francis Giraud's cooking is impeccable and creative, and there is, of course, an extensive choice of St-Emilion wine. The hotel has also recently opened a spa. Route de Libourne (D243), T: 05 57 55 37 00 www.grand-barrail.com

€€ **Hôtel/Restaurant Palais Cardinal**. A calm retreat on the northern edge of the old town within the walls of the old residence of the Dean of the Collegiate Church in the 14th century, Gaillard de Lamothe, nephew of Pope Clement V. The restaurant serves regional specialities accompanied by the wine of the property, Château Clos de Sarpe. There is a pretty interior courtyard with swimming pool, and 17 comfortable rooms. Pl. du 11 Novembre 1918, T: 05 57 24 72 39, www.palais-cardinal.fr

€€€ **Restaurant Clos du Roy**. ■ 12 Rue Petite Fontaine, T: 05 57 74 41 55. Very tucked away and exclusive, and

mouth-watering food using fresh vegetables, cured ham, lobster and the like, and they make a super traditional apple tart. The wine list is a symphony of the best of Bordeaux.

€ **Restaurant Amelia Canta**. In a popular setting in the town centre, with two dining rooms and terrace, where the food is mainly based on regional specialities. Pl. du Marché, T: 05 57 74 48 03.

€ **Restaurant Chez Dominique**. Rue de la Petite Fontaine, T: 05 57 24 71 00. Good regional cooking and reasonably priced menus.

St-Palais-de-Blaye

€ **Chambres d'hôtes La Sauvageonne**. ■ This is a perfect stopping place in northern Gironde and you can be sure of a warm and enthusiastic welcome. The long, low elegant 18th century house is framed in trees, and beyond are vineyards. Inside are vast bedrooms and ensuite bathrooms, and spacious day rooms for guests. The pool is surrounded by carefully tended gardens with vines. M. Bienfait, pastry cook by profession, serves an excellent breakfast and *table d'hôtes*. There are also two gîtes, one a recent conversion. MM Bienfait and Rudat, T: 05 57 32 92 15, www.relax-inn-gironde.com

VINEYARD VISITS & TASTINGS

St-Emilion: The Tourist Office advises on planning vineyard tours and tastings. Daily wine tours depart from the tourist office, mid-May–mid-Sept, every afternoon; July–Aug twice a day; all visits in English and French. Also guided visits to vineyards by bike (2–3 hours). There is a booklet, *Cellars Open to the Public*. An initiation wine-tasting, mid–July to

mid–Sept, at the Maison du Vin, Pl.
Pierre-Meyrat, T: 05 57 55 50 55,
www.vins-saint-emilion.com
Town or vineyard visits by *petit train*
from Place Poincaré are probably one of
the best uses ever for this method of
transport. Easter to mid-Nov,
10.30–6.30; 10 departures a day lasting
35mins; T: 05 57 51 13 76,
www.visite-saint-emilion.com
Information for other vineyards in the
St-Emilion area from: Maison des Vins
de l'Union des Satellites de St-Emilion,
Montagne, T: 05 57 74 60 13,
www.montagnesaintemilion.com
Maison des Vins de Lalande-de-
Pomerol, T: 05 57 25 21 60,
www.lalande-pomerol.com
Maison des Vins de Fronsac, Canon
Fronsac, T: 05 57 51 80 51

MARKET DAYS

Blaye Wednesday, Saturday
Bourg-sur-Gironde Sunday
Castillon-la-Bataille Monday
Coutras Wednesday, Saturday
Gensac Friday
Libourne Tuesday, Friday, Sunday
Puissguin Wednesday
Rauzan Saturday
St-Christoly-de-Blaye Sunday
St-Emilion Sunday

FESTIVALS & EVENTS

May: *Portes Ouvertes en Côtes de Bourg*,
wine producers open up for tastings,
and meals and concerts, T: 05 57 94
80 20 or 05 57 68 22 28,

www.cotes-de-bourg.com *Portes
Ouvertes aux Châteaux*, St-Emilion
appellation wine châteaux open their
doors to the public, St-Emilion, T: 05
57 55 50 50 *Paroles en Bouche*, actors
take you through the St-Emilion
region, discovering its vineyards and
the history, St-Emilion, T: 05 57 55 28
28
June: *Fête de la Fleur*, at the moment
when the vines start to flower, the
Jurade processes through the town, St-
Emilion, T: 05 57 55 28 28
Fête du Printemps de la Jurade, spring
festival to announce the judging of new
wine, St-Emilion
June-September: *Jumping International
de Blaye*, international show-jumping,
Blaye, T: 05 57 41 12 09
Musique en Citadelle, wine and music by
international artists light up the citadel,
Blaye, T: 05 57 42 12 09
July–August: *Les Collégiades*, interna-
tionally famous musicians in the old
streets, St-Emilion, T: 05 57 55 28 28
August: *La Dordogne en Feu*, sail past of
boats, illuminations, festivities, music
at La Plage de Ste-Terre near Castillon,
T: 05 57 47 14 34
September: *Fête du Mascaret*, festival at
the time of the tidal bore (*see p. 69*) in
the estuary, St-Pardon-de-Vayres, T: 05
57 55 25 55
September/October: *Ban des Vendanges
de la Jurade* festival to mark the start of
the grape harvest proclaimed from the
Tour du Roy by the Jurade; guided
tours by torchlight. St-Emilion

ENTRE-DEUX-MERS & GRAVES

Entre-Deux-Mers and Graves are both names resonant of great wines from the Gironde. The vineyards follow the banks of the Garonne to the southeast of Bordeaux, a gentle landscape with numerous historic buildings and picturesque villages. The wines can be tasted at many of the great Châteaux and the lesser ones. In Entre-Deux-Mers, as well as the cooperatives, 132 properties receive visitors, and some 39 in Graves and Sauternes, although it is important to make a prior appointment.

THE WINES OF ENTRE-DEUX-MERS

These include all categories—red, rosé, dry and sweet whites—and are divided between several *appellations*. The AOC Premières Côtes-de-Bordeaux, is a thin strip 60 k long and 5 k wide, between Ste-Eulalie (north of Bordeaux) and St-Maixant on the right bank of the Garonne. These are quality reds blended from Merlot, Cabernet Sauvignon and Cabernet Franc grapes, combined with a small amount of Petit-Verdot, Malbec or Carmenère. The whites are produced principally from Sauvignon, Sémillon and Muscadelle. The AOC Entre-Deux-Mers refers exclusively to dry white wines produced in the large area spreading to the Dordogne. The AOC Entre-Deux-Mers-Haut-Benauge, and Bordeaux-Haut-Benauge refer to a pocket north of Langon, between Arbis and Targon, which produces sweet and dry whites as well as reds under Bordeaux or Bordeaux Supérieur regional *appellations*. Graves-de-Vayres, on the Dordogne left bank opposite Libourne at Vayres et d'Arveyres, where the soil is exceptionally gravelly, is a small AOC of dry whites and reds. Ste-Foy-Bordeaux in the northeast of the region produces sweet and dry whites and, increasingly reds, usually marketed as Bordeaux and Bordeaux Supérieur. The finest *blancs moelleux et liquoreux* are AOC Cadillac (producing also dry white and reds under the label AOC Premières Cotes de Bordeaux, Bordeaux Supérieur and Bordeaux), AOC Loupiac, and AOC Côtes de Bordeaux-St-Macaire, which includes some dry whites. For further information and visits, contact www.entredeuxmers.com or the individual Maisons des Vins (*see p. 98*).

ENTRE-DEUX-MERS

The area known as Entre-Deux-Mers is a triangular limestone plateau running east-west between the Garonne and the Dordogne whose Latin denomination was *inter duo maria*, referring to the rivers or 'seas' which are still tidal at this point. The geographic region is defined by the communities of Ste-Foy-La-Grande to the north, and La Réole to the south, trailing off to the west at Bec d'Ambès. The most elevated part of the *département* of the Gironde, although rarely rising over 100m, Entre-Deux-Mers represents the largest AOC territory in the Gironde, its vineyards covering the slopes. The region was also once known as the 'bread mill of Bordeaux' and is scattered with old water mills, frequently fortified.

ABBAYE DE LA SAUVE MAJEURE

From the hilltop site the church tower signals the magnificent ruins of the Abbaye de La Sauve Majeure, one of the highlights of the Bordelais. The abbey was laid out in the Benedictine manner with the cloister and monastic buildings south of the church. The cloister is now just a shadow and what is left of the abbey buildings is mainly 17th century. Gérard, Abbot of Cluny, came to the heart of the *sylva major* in 1079 where a simple oratory in the woods established at an earlier time by a hermit, stood near the ruins of a castle on the pilgrimage route to Spain. On 11th May 1080, Gérard, with Guillaume VII, Duke of Gascony, laid the first stone of the future Abbaye de La

Decorated capital (12th century) depicting Salome's dance in the Abbaye de La Sauve Majeure.

Sauve-Majeure. Well funded and well organised, by the time of Gérard's death in 1095 there were some 300 monks and many affiliated priories. In the safety of the shadow of the abbey, a secular community, now the village of La Sauve, developed around a parish church dedicated to St-Pierre, which was begun in 1083 by Gérard. The founder-abbot was canonised in 1197, and among those who came to venerate the relics of St Gérard were Henry II, Eleanor of Aquitaine and Thomas Becket. The abbey was attacked and badly damaged in 1179, but not repaired until 1219–31, and in 1369 it was fortified. The death knell for the abbey tolled in the 16th century, when it was placed *in commendam*. The Congregation of St-Maur (founded after the Reformation and religious wars to assist religious communities that had been passed to an absentee landlord) took it over in 1660 but ran out of funds. An earthquake caused further damage in 1759. The property was confiscated at the Revolution but the relics were saved and translated to Bordeaux. The building, used as a school, went up in flames in 1910 and was more or less neglected until 1952, when work began to consolidate the ruins.

Visiting the abbey

Open June–Sept 10–6; Oct–May 10.30–1 & 2–5.30, closed Mon; T: 05 56 23 01 55.
The visit begins in an elegant conventual building from the later transformations, with displays and a bookshop. Despite all the abuse, the remains of the abbey church resonate with the beauty of the original. The north transept and choir are the most complete parts, and much good Romanesque carving has survived. From the exterior the three parallel apses and transept chapels are remarkably intact, despite the lack of cornice and roof on the main chapel, which is divided into three by pillar buttresses. Each segment has three levels, plain base, round-headed window and blind arcade above. The side apses are much smaller and simpler than the central one. The fragments of the west façade suggest it was inspired by the Saintonge. Because the ruin is open to the sky the bell-tower (which can be climbed) is omnipresent. It stands unusually over the fourth bay of the south aisle, square in the lower level and octagonal above, the second level pierced on seven sides by large 13th-century twin windows with triple-moulded arches. The third level has single trefoil openings and is topped off with the remains of an open parapet, but the spire has gone. The aisled nave, open and uncovered, was higher in the central part and was no doubt enclosed to create an extended chancel, as at Albi (*see p. 253*) or Auch (*see p. 398*). The nave was preceded by a narthex.

The interior

In the interior, the eastern part of the church is the best conserved and the most decorated, and provides a pure illustration of Romanesque architecture. The large square choir is succeeded by a semi-circular apse. The choir vaults have disappeared, but part of the extreme eastern semi-dome has survived. The choir is on two levels. The ground level has small round-headed arcades linking the smaller side chapels to the choir, and the eastern bay rests on squat but enormously powerful round pillars. The twin bays of the upper choir are repeated in the transept. The apse has three large

Romanesque windows flanked by small columns with a very stylised acanthus-leaf motif extending into the string courses. The mass of masonry and clear-cut shapes convey a tremendous impression of solidity and the choir, when decked out in fine furnishings, must have been breathtaking. The south wall of the south arm of the transept has disappeared, but the north survives.

Of the 34 **Romanesque capitals** that have survived more or less intact, the iconography is varied, including five Old and two New Testament themes, fabulous creatures and foliage. The carvings may not be as masterly as those at Moissac or Conques, but are still memorable. The most celebrated of them, in the last bay of the south aisle on the corner of the south transept, are four scenes from the *Beheading of St John the Baptist* (*pictured on p. 82*). The scenes include *Salome's Dance*, where in a small space below the table the dancer's body is arched seductively while she hangs on to the table edge for support. The space is used skilfully, the expression acutely observed and the entire scene packed with anecdotal detail. *Episodes from the Life of Samson* are on the south of the first apsidal chapel in the south transept, including a nonchalant long-haired Samson carrying one of the gates of Gaza, Samson overcoming the Lion, animal larger than man, and *Samson with Delilah*, who is wielding what look like sheep shears. Opposite, on the north of the apsidal chapel, is *Daniel in the Lions' Den*, with the prophet meditating fearlessly between two snarling (or smiling) lions. On the north side of the first apsidal chapel in the north transept is *Adam and Eve*, or *Original Sin*, a less busy composition, with the tree and serpent on the extreme right, Eve tempting Adam, Eve after giving birth, and Adam looking sorrowful. In the southeast bay of the choir are scenes from the *Temptation of Christ*, including Christ emerging from a tower (which looks more like a chimney pot) and the Devil pointing down with the index finger. The *Sacrifice of Abraham* in the last bay of the nave, south, is a more naive work, with Sarah learning that she will have a child, Abraham grasping the sword and an angel clutching his arm, and another angel arriving with the sacrificial ram. The capitals of the round pillars carry fierce combats between fabulous beasts, and in the north chapel apse are two scenes from *Ulysses and the Sirens*. There are many wondrous animals, a variety of lions, and finely chiselled plant motifs. Note also the abaci beautifully carved with decorative motifs.

ALONG THE GARONNE

Cadillac

On the northeast bank of the Garonne, Cadillac is a small *bastide* with a massive château, which provides the best reason for a visit. The town, founded in 1280 by Edward I's man, Jean de Grailly, prospered from shipping, especially of wine. Of the fortifications, begun in 1315, two of the four gates and a substantial proportion of the triangular ramparts and round towers are still standing. Inside the town gates are several 15th- and 16th-century houses, as well as a 19th-century covered market. In the church of St-Blaise and St-Martin, the chapel of St-Blaise was built to contain the grandiose tomb commissioned from Pierre Biard in 1597 by Jean-Louis Nogaret de la

Valette for his wife, Marguerite de Foix Candale (d. 1593). The exterior of the chapel is dated 1606, probably the date of the completion of the work, but only the white stone and black marble screen still stands following the demolition of the mausoleum in 1793. The bronze winged figure that crowned the tomb, *Renommée* (Fame) by Pierre Biard (1606), was saved at the Revolution and resides in the Louvre,

Château des Ducs d'Epernon

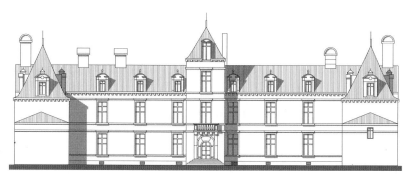

FAÇADE (C. 1635) OF THE CHÂTEAU DES DUCS D'EPERNON

Open June–Sept 10–1.15 & 2–6; Oct–May 10–12.30 & 2–5.30, closed Mon; T: 05 56 62 69 58.

In the north of Cadillac, the château is now a cavernous place spoilt by many transformations of its original 17th-century form. Nonetheless, it is of significant historical interest, and much is made of its dual role as a 17th-century palace and 19th-century prison. The old feudal castle was entirely rebuilt from 1599 by the Governor of Guyenne, Jean-Louis de Nogaret de la Valette (1554–1642), Duc d'Epernon and *mignon* (favourite) of Henri III. Epernon married Marguerite de Foix-Candale, and with her came Cadillac complete with its château. Epernon's meteoric rise to power was a thorn in the flesh to Henri IV, who encouraged him to invest his considerable fortune in a grand residence distanced from Paris. Construction began in 1598, possibly to plans by Pierre Biard, although Pierre Souffron directed the work at first (1599–1603) and Gilles de La Touche until 1616, but it was not completed until c. 1634. The new château was designed as a classic U-shaped block around a courtyard, closed by a screen wall and with a monumental gateway. The rear façade, facing away from the courtyard, overlooked a formal flower garden. Epernon died ruined, and the second duke had no heirs, so the property passed to the Preissac family, who partly demolished the building to transform it into something more fashionable. It was eviscerated at the Revolution and turned into a women's prison and house of correction (1819–22); more structural alterations were carried out in 1865. Its doors were finally closed in 1952.

The entrance gate and lodge were rebuilt to suit the needs of the prison, and in the 19th century the courtyard was planted with trees, now cleared. Around the courtyard, only the main building and the angle pavilions, notably the left-hand one with the tall roofs, are remotely as they were after the first building campaign. The right-hand one (c. 1635) is more severe. The extensions were rebuilt in the 19th century. The garden façade is the result of two building campaigns, of the late 16th century and early 17th century. Large pavilions which once framed the main block were destroyed in the 18th century leaving only the lower part and the stair block. The garden was restored in the 1980s.

The interior
The main block consists of series of apartments flanking the staircase on two levels. Inside, the main relics of the 17th-century décor are some of the 20 original fireplaces decorated in marble, stucco and gilt, the grandest with Michelangelesque figures. On the ground floor are the remains of beautiful 17th-century painted ceilings, some modern reproductions of painted décor, and monumental fireplaces in the Appartements de Madame. The Salle de la Reine on the other side of the stairs was transformed into a chapel for the prison inmates, although again the fire surrounds have survived here and in the adjacent antechamber. L'Appartement du Roi on the first floor was the most sumptuous of all, but the prison and a fire in 1928 did it no favours. The best of the decorated fire surrounds, in the antechamber, sculpted in 1606 by Jean Langlois and Jean and Joseph Richier, is still partly intact and depicts Fame surrounded by trophies, with damaged stuccoes featuring sculptures in the round of reclining and standing figures (inspired by the Pitti Palace, Florence). There is a display presenting the history of the prison. The basements were originally kitchens and possibly accommodated a tapestry workshop for Claude de Lapierre, who created a vast series of the life of Henri III (only two of 22 remain, one in Cadillac and one in the Louvre); they were reused as kitchens and refectory in the 19th century. There is a remarkable cantilevered spiral staircase. The garden can be visited and the château also hosts temporary exhibitions of contemporary art.

Downriver from Cadillac
The Gallo-Roman castrum *Riuncium* (built on the rock), on the northeast bank of the Garonne, became the tiny medieval fortified town of **Rions**. Its fortifications were destroyed in 1295, and Edward I encouraged their rebuilding which began in 1330. By 1379 Rions was affiliated to Bordeaux as part of a defensive league with Cadillac, St-Macaire and others and by the 15th century came under the control of the Albret family (*see p. 364*). It experienced more turmoil in the 16th–17th centuries, and in 1814, when the English were returning from the Napoleonic wars in Spain under Marshal Beresford, the Rionais defended themselves from within their ramparts. Later in the 19th century, there was a local campaign to save the old town, and most of the 14th-century fortifications are still standing.

Upriver from Cadillac

On the Garonne at **Loupiac** are interesting remains of a Gallo-Roman villa and baths (2nd–5th centuries), with mosaics (private property; *open Sun 2–6; at other times telephone in advance: T: 05 56 62 93 82*). The restored Romanesque church has a three-tier west façade in the Saintonge style and a chevet.

Nearby, **Ste-Croix-du-Mont** is a pretty village atop a hill which produces a super sweet white wine and has remarkable caves with fossilised oyster shells lining the walls, which have been made into cellars and a chapel. There is also a 13th/15th century church with a fine portal, and beautiful views.

The **Château de Malromé** (*no visits*) at St-André-du-Bois, built in the 14th century, was the home of Adèle de Toulouse-Lautrec, mother of the painter Henri de Toulouse-Lautrec (*p. 256*) who died here on 9th September 1901 and was buried at Verdelais. From 1883, while his mother lived here, the painter visited regularly, but spent the end of his life in Bordeaux and Arcachon. Adèle owned the château until her death in 1930. Malromé now has no connection with the family.

Back on the Garonne, at St-Maixant, the **Domaine de Malagar** (*open June–Sept 10–12.30 & 2–6; Oct–May Wed–Fri 2–6, Sat, Sun and holidays 10–12.30, 2–6; T: 05 57 98 17 17*), was the country home of the novelist François Mauriac (1885–1970). A charming, simple house overlooking vineyards, it was inherited by the writer in 1927, and is something of a shrine, kept as it was in his time. Mauriac enjoyed coming to Malagar and wrote *Le Noeud de Vipères* (1932) here; many of his novels are set in the landscapes of the Gironde and Landes. The visit also includes the gardens and *chais*.

ST-MACAIRE

With tightly packed houses and narrow streets, the little town of St-Macaire, set on a high point above the Garonne, is locked in a charming time warp. The story goes that a disciple of St Martin (d. 397), a Greek called Makarios, came to the ancient site of *Ligena* in the 4th or 5th centuries and settled here. In fact the town developed in the 11th century around a Benedictine community, grew very rich during the English occupation of Aquitaine and produced two consecutive fortified *faubourgs* (13th and 14th century), with the Mercadiou (market) at the core of the earlier development. Once an important river port, the landscape and the fortunes of St-Macaire changed radically in the 18th century when the course of the Garonne shifted, leaving the port high and dry. Rich merchants had already begun to abandon the town for Bordeaux in the 17th century and by the 19th it was practically deserted, relying on cooperage and stone quarrying for its livelihood.

Just inside the old fortified gate and town clock-tower, Porte de Benauge (14th century), is a crossroads with some fine Renaissance houses, to the left a hotel and to the right the *Maison du Pays* in a 16th-century shop. Straight ahead is Rue de l'Eglise leading to the church (described below). The street to the right of the church once led to the château. The road to the left brings you to the narrow rectangular Place du Mercadiou which has not been too prettified and retains its medieval allure, surrounded by diverse arcades and a variety of façades (13th–16th centuries). Notable is the mansion with a tower called the *relais de poste*. East of the Mercadiou is the Turon gate, part of the 14th-century barbican, near which is a 19th-century *lavoir*. This was the route to the river port, and the river once lapped the walls where now are gardens.

The priory, southwest of the Mercadiou, was founded in the 12th century. In the little garden to the south is a 12th-century colonnade which is all that remains of the rectangular cloister squeezed in between the 11th-century ramparts and the church. Part of the refectory is also standing, with cellars beneath and monks' cells above (restored in 1968).

The **church of St-Sauveur** is large and unusual and much altered since the 12th century. It has a tripartite Romanesque chevet with a little decoration. The 14th-century west front, with a 15th-century rose window, is decorated with angels around the door and *Christ, the Virgin and St John with the Apostles* in the tympanum. Either side are saints in trefoil arcades. The nave has four square bays and is covered by 17th-century vaults, whereas the apses are half-domed and the crossing has massive piers as if to receive a dome. There are some coloured Romanesque capitals and an extensive programme of painted decoration on the east vaults, carried out in the second half of the 13th century and indifferently restored in 1825. As they are now, they consist of a *Trinity* in the central mandorla, from which flows the *River of Life* between the *Ox of St Luke* and the *Lion of St Mark*. The left-hand mandorla contains *Celestial Jerusalem* and the right the *Lamb receiving the Book of Seven Seals* from *Revelations*, and the *Story of St Catherine* and the *Wise and Foolish Virgins*.

LA RÉOLE

La Réole is built on a slope on a cliff high above the Garonne. The place was called *Regula* in the 10th century, after the monks who adhered to the rule of St Benedict re-established a monastery here dependent on the abbey of Fleury-sur-Loire. The town was built around the monastery and received its charter in 977. On the Franco-English border, it prospered during the English occupation of Guyenne and was enclosed in a succession of protective walls (12th–13th and 15th centuries).

Exploring La Réole

The Benedictine priory (begun 1704) by Maurice Mazey took about 50 years to build. It is now occupied by the *services publics*. There is a library and small museum in the vaulted basement on the south side. A corridor running north to south alongside the cloister is closed at each end by very fine wrought-iron gates, the work of Charlut, who was also responsible for the balustrades on the south. The façade towards the Garonne is a fine example of Louis XIV style and is graced with a double flight of steps. Inside on the east–west corridor is a staircase with a balcony on which *Instruments of the Passion* are carved, and a wooden ceiling painted with *St Benedict in Ecstasy*. Another elegant monumental staircase in the east is lit by a lantern opening and there is an agreeable 17th-century garden court.

The parish **Church of St-Pierre** on Place Rigoulet, was built to the north for the priory at the end of the 12th century. It underwent some rebuilding during the 13th century and was damaged by the Protestants in 1577. Renovations were carried out in 1608 and c. 1687–90 the sexpartite vaults were introduced and the walls raised. The church was emptied out at the Revolution and many of the furnishings went to Bordelais churches, including much masterly ironwork by Blaise Charlut. The entrance is through the Flamboyant north transept door. Most of the church is Gothic, including the wide nave with no aisles and the five-sided apse with 17th-century alterations. Of the old church, there is one Romanesque capital re-used in the south of the chancel, while the south transept chapel and the southern rose window are 15th-century. The *Marriage of the Virgin* (1666) is signed by the Spanish painter from Seville, Valdès-Léal.

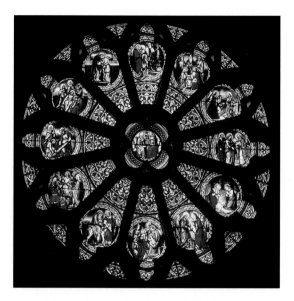

Rose window (15th century) in St-Pierre, La Réole.

GRAVES

Described as the cradle of Bordeaux wines, Graves, 60km long by 14.5km wide, is bounded by the Garonne to the east and the Landes to the west. This is the oldest and arguably the most prestigious wine-producing area of the Bordelais, and includes the AOCs of Sauterne and Barsac.

THE CHÂTEAUX OF GRAVES

Château La Brède
Guided visits: July–Sept 2–6, closed Tues; April–June Sat, Sun and holidays 2–6; Oct–mid-Nov Sat, Sun and holidays 2– 5.30; T: 05 56 20 20 49.
The birthplace of the writer, Montesquieu (*see box overleaf*), has barely changed since the great man's time. An austere building, it is the result of alterations made in 1419

to a fortress dating back to the 12th century. In the moat are reflected the reminders of the earlier fort: a 13th-century keep containing the library, pepper-pot towers and fortifications; footbridges replace three drawbridges. In 1404 Pope Boniface IX authorised a new chapel. The château passed as dowry to the Montesquieu family in 1686, when Marie-Françoise de Pesnel married Jacques de Secondat. The park was landscaped in the English manner by the writer in the 18th century.

From the entrance hall with fine wooden twisted columns, the visit takes you to the Grand Salon, with portraits of Montesquieu's relatives, and memorabilia. His study bedroom contains 17th-century furniture, notably his four-poster bed. On the floor above is the well-endowed library with some 7,000 books, and an impressive chestnut ceiling and mural. Montesquieu was also an enthusiastic wine producer.

MONTESQUIEU (1689–1755)

Charles Louis Secondat de Montesquieu, Baron de La Brède, deeply Gascon and a countryman at heart, is known universally as a writer and philosopher of the Age of Enlightenment. He was trained in law and appointed to the *parlement*, rising to the post of Président du Parlement in 1716. His boundless intellectual curiosity led him to carry out research at the Academy of Science, and in 1711 he began his first literary work, *Lettres persanes*, a satire on French society (completed in 1721). He was an ardent democrat, tireless traveller, frequent visitor to the court and literary salons in Paris, and especially liked England, perhaps because the wine from his vineyards was much appreciated in the British Empire. Jeanne de Lartigue, whom he married in 1715, brought a healthy dowry and property, enabling Montesquieu to abandon his legal work in favour of his vines and writing. His *L'Esprit des Lois* (1748) was the inspiration behind the Constitution of 1791.

Château de Mongenan

Guided visits, in English or French, July–mid-Sept 10–7; mid-Sept–Dec and mid-Feb–July Sat, Sun and holidays 2–6; check in advance. T: 05 56 67 18 11.

Mongenan was built in 1736 on the banks of the Garonne, east of La Brède. It is surrounded by remarkable formal gardens in 18th-century style. In front of the house is the *Jardin d'Ornement*, the *Jardin d'Utilité* (which includes 1,000 varieties of flowers), vegetables and medicinal plants), and a *Jardin d'Agrément* which is more of an informal park *à l'anglais*.

Inside the house is a museum of 18th-century traditional arts and costumes, with examples of fabrics, and three important *herbiers*. One of the herbariums is by writer-philosopher Jean-Jacques Rousseau, who spent time in the Gironde c. 1740. The other two are by his pupil, Valdec de Lessart, and by Balan de Balansee. There is also an 18th-century Masonic lodge.

THE WINES OF GRAVES

One of the best known *appellations* of Bordeaux, the region stretches from Blanquefort, just to the north of the city, southwards almost as far as Langon, on the southwest bank of the Garonne and dies out in the Landes forests to the west. The land became known as Graves because of the gravelly clay soil, its surface of white quartz pebbles and other debris deposited a long time ago by the Garonne. The sun's rays reflecting off the pebbles help the ripening process. The region prospered in the 14th century as the English passion for claret developed. Graves is more diversified than Médoc (*see p. 51*), producing red and dry white wines, as well as sweet (*liquoreux*) or medium sweet (*moelleux*) whites. There are three distinct AOCs: Graves and Pessac-Léognan, which produce both red and dry white wines, and Graves Supérieures, reserved for sweet whites.

In the north of the region, AOC Pessac-Léognan, created in 1987, small, isolated but prestigious vineyards in the middle of a spreading urban environment, include 16 Crus Classés. At the head of the list is Château Haut-Brion, which was named Premier Cru Classé in 1855. This area produces 60,000 hectolitres a year of reds and dry whites. From La Brède south to Langon is the land of AOC Graves: reds and dry whites. In the southern part of Graves the great sweet whites of Cérons, Barsac and Sauternes, are produced in a small area along the valley of the Ciron River. Here the early morning mists of autumn dispelled by warm sunshine are essential for producing *pourriture noble* (*see p. 123*). The most celebrated of the golden liquors comes from Château d'Yquem. The reds are blended from Cabernet Sauvignon, Cabernet Franc, Merlot, and lesser quantities of Malbec and Petit-Verdot grapes; the sweet white wines are produced from Sémillon, Sauvignon, and a small amount of Muscadelle.

Château de Malle

Guided visits and tasting of Sauternes: April–Oct 10–12 & 2–6; T: 05 56 62 36 86.
The Château de Malle, near Preignac, is a superbly elegant residence set in the midst of a park and vineyards built at the beginning of the 17th century by Jacques de Malle, a Bordelais magistrate. The main block consists of a central pavilion in the style of Louis XIV with a hipped roof and rounded pediments and low wings ending in round towers. There is a pronounced Italian influence in the succession of terraces leading to a small open-air theatre decorated with characters from the *commedia dell'arte*.

Langon and Château d'Yquem

Langon is the main town of southern Gironde, at the highest point that the river is tidal. The doyen of the wine châteaux of the Bordelais is Château d'Yquem, owned by the Lur-Saluces. The route to the château is indicated from Sauternes. This was the first wine to be classified as Premier Cru Supérieur in 1855. With 100 hectares, it produces only nine hectolitres per hectare, which represents about a third or a quarter of the yield in a Médoc estate. Applications to see the cellars (the château itself is private) should be made in writing three weeks in advance of the intended visit, giving a name, date, reason for the visit and the number of people (no more than 20); visits can be made Mon–Fri at 2pm and 3.30pm. Wine is not sold here directly but must be purchased through dealers (*www.chateau-Yquem.fr*).

Châteaux de Villandraut and de Budos

Guided visits: July–Aug 10–7; May–Sept, Oct–Apr 10–6; T: 05 56 25 87 57
The ruined Château de Villandraut was the prototype of the *châteaux Clémentins*. Begun in 1306 by Pope Clement V (*see box below*), it combined defence and comfort and was built by English masons who had worked for Edward I in Wales. It was systematically protected by towers and arrow slits at different levels. The walls marked out a large empty interior space, without a keep, in which the pontifical palace could develop. It has not, thankfully, been renovated and the visit to the ruins includes a climb to the top of one of the six towers, conserved on three floors, and the fortified walkway. Superb fireplaces and deep vaulted cellars have also survived. The influence on the castle at Roquetaillade is obvious, but Villandraut was larger, rectangular and more refined. On the edge of Sauternes, the ruined **Château de Budos**, built c. 1308 by Cardinal Gaillard de la Mothe, nephew of Clement V, was a refinement on Villandraut.

CHÂTEAUX CLÉMENTINS

Bertrand de Got (1264–1314) was born into the lesser nobility near Villandraut or Uzeste. He entered the priesthood in 1289 and rose rapidly, becoming Bishop of Comminges in 1294 (*see p. 539*), and was appointed to the bishopric in Bordeaux in 1299. With the backing of Philippe IV he was elected pope by the Sacred College on 5th June 1305, and took the name Clement V. Due to the volatile situation in Rome, he returned to Aquitaine and in February 1306 began the château at Villandraut. He gave permission for his nephews to build châteaux in the Bazadais, known as the *Châteaux Clémentins*, including Castets-en-Dorthe (private), Fargues (ruins), Budos (ruins), La Trave (ruins, near Préchac, which can be explored) and Roquetaillade. Philippe IV drew Clement V into the indictment of the Templars and in 1309 the proceedings took place in Avignon, a neutral territory belonging to the Holy See. Subsequently the Pope remained in Avignon and established a papal court there. The Templars were suppressed and burned at the stake (*see p. 288*), and it is said that as their Grand Master, Jacques de Molay, was about to die, he laid a curse on the King and the Pope that they would be dead within a year. Already a sick man, Clement V started the journey back to Bordeaux in 1314, but died before reaching his destination. He was buried at Uzeste (*see below*). The king died the same year.

Collegiate Church of Uzeste

Open 9–6. Guided visits Easter–Oct Sat, Sun, from 3pm onwards; guided visits outside these times can be arranged: in French T: 05 56 25 87 48, or English T: 05 56 65 22 47.

In the modest village of Uzeste, east of Villandraut, is the imposing collegiate church, dedicated to the Virgin, and selected by Pope Clement V to contain his tomb. Pilgrims had gathered here to venerate the Virgin since the 12th century, and it was suitably transformed in the 14th century to receive the Pope's remains. The belfry is 15th-century, although the steeple is 19th century, as are the stained-glass windows. Over the south door (entrance) is a worn image, once coloured, of the *Coronation of the Virgin*.

Inside, the wide nave is flanked by alternate piers and columns, with two massive cylindrical piers at the west, and a high choir precedes a fairly shallow five-sided apse with ambulatory. The Pope's tomb, now behind the altar, was damaged and his remains burned in 1572 during the Wars of Religion. The monument, scrupulously sculpted by Jehan de Bonneval from Orléans, was completed in 1359, the *gisant* (recumbent statue) in white Italian marble and the base in black marble from Denmark. It was originally decorated with alabaster and jasper columns.

CHÂTEAU DE ROQUETAILLADE

Open July-Aug 10.30–7; Easter–Oct every afternoon; Nov–Easter afternoons on Sun, holidays and school holidays; T: 05 56 76 14 16; www.roquetaillade.com.

The Château de Roquetaillade at Mazères, is a showpiece medieval castle which has been handed down for some 700 years through the same family. High and visible, Roquetaillade literally means 'carved from the rock'. Two separate medieval forts, it contains three magnificent 16th-century fireplaces. In the 19th century, the arch Gothicist, Viollet-le-Duc was persuaded to transform the interior. The grounds, which are open, consist of an English-style park and a delightful farm museum, with Bazardais cows, old farm equipment, and rooms typical of the 19th and 20th centuries.

History of the Chateau

The old castle, part of which is still standing, was built piecemeal between the 12th and 14th centuries. The adjacent later castle, begun in 1306 by Cardinal Gaillard de la Mothe, nephew of Pope Clement V, was conceived of as a whole and embraced innovations in fortified architecture introduced with the English, such as the central square keep, six round angle towers and crenellations. The new castle combined a degree of comfort and strong protection, and is the only complete survivor of the five Clementine fortress-palaces (*see box opposite*). The de la Mothe family supported the Anglo-Gascon alliance. In recognition, Gaillard de la Mothe received in 1313 the Archdeaconry of Oxford, but did not take it up and therefore did not receive the accompanying stipend. Lengthy proceedings over the non-payment ensued (1326–47), which ended when the French repossessed Aquitaine. The property was regularly transferred through the female line, and in 1552 Catherine de la Mothe married into the de Lansac family, who added Renaissance features. The property stayed in the family during the Revolution, and passed in 1807 to the de Mauvesin. By 1793 it was in a parlous state. The de Mauvesin, desiring a setting compatible with their status and considerable means, commissioned the celebrated Viollet-le-Duc. He accepted in collaboration with Edmond Duthoit, and two campaigns of work followed (1866–70 and 1874–78), during which the structure was consolidated and Gothic revivalist décor introduced. The work was never completed, but detailed preparatory drawings have survived. In 1882 the last of the de Mauvesin bequeathed Roquetaillade to a cousin, Hippolyte de Baritault, whose descendants are still in possession.

The exterior
Sections of the 12th-century walls and a gateway, which protected the village surrounding the castle until the end of the feudal era, still exist. The 12th-century chapel was restored and exotically decorated by Duthoit (1875–78) by combining Gothic, Arabic and Sicilian elements. The picturesque remains of the Château Vieux include the keep (13th century), gateway tower (12th-13th centuries) and the large hall (early 14th century). Although the layout of the Château Neuf has not essentially altered since the 14th century, the elevations were 'medievalised' in the 19th century with the addition of machicolations, merlons, extra crenellations, trefoil windows and the neo-Gothic loggia on the north side bearing family coats of arms. The drop bridge over the dry moat leads through the fortified doorway in the west elevation, virtually unaltered since the 14th century, with crenellations and latrines. The low arrow slits in *croix pattée* were an English innovation to accommodate crossbows.

The interior
Viollet-le-Duc's designs are the highlight of a visit to the interior. His ambition to create a monumental staircase was realised in Roquetaillade's keep in 1867, when he replaced original wooden steps with a stone flight. The headstops over the entrance carry the likenesses of the patrons, the architect, and Empress Eugénie. The dining room (1868), created from the old stables, uses metal decoratively and combines it with painted stylised trailing greenery. All the neo-Gothic furniture was designed by Viollet. The delightful bedrooms, the work of Duthoit under the supervision of Viollet, date from 1868–69, when painted décor was the height of fashion. Original fabrics in the Chambre Rose were replicated in Lyons some years ago. The hall has 14th-century vaulting and leads to the grand late 16th- or early 17th-century Salle Synodale. This room contains the most impressive chimneypiece of its period in southwest France, dating from 1599, which uses marble from the Pyrenees; it is similar to two in the Château des Ducs d' Epernon at Cadillac (*see p. 85*). The painting which was originally an integral part of the chimneypiece was recently re-discovered. Restored at the Louvre, it has been reinstalled above the fireplace and shows *Hercules Fighting the Hydra*. This room should have been the triumph of Viollet-Le-Duc's projects at Roquetaillade, but work was brought to a halt because in 1870 the de Mauvesin's fortunes melted away as phylloxera engulfed their vines.

EUGÈNE-EMANUEL VIOLLET-LE-DUC (1814–79)

Archaeologist, writer, theoretician, restorer and architect, Eugène-Emanuel Viollet-le-Duc began his career at 26 when he was put in charge of the restoration of the church of the Madeleine in Vézelay (Burgundy). He was given the job by Prosper Mérimée (1803–70), the first Inspecteur Général des Monuments Historiques, a post created in 1830 to safeguard the national heritage. Later, Viollet-le-Duc succeeded Mérimée in this role. He probably did more than anyone else in the 19th century to save France's heritage but, like George Gilbert Scott and others in England, he was much criticised in the 20th century for his creative restorations. Now that the tide of opinion has turned, his efforts are viewed more favourably. Largely self-taught, his revivalist tendencies were fired by Victor Hugo and the archaeologist Arcisse de Caumont. He was involved in a number of restoration assignments in Paris and in the southwest, notably at St-Sernin in Toulouse, St-André in Bordeaux, Moissac and the Château de Roquetaillade. He published learned works on Gothic architecture, the *Dictionnaire raisonné de l'architecture française* (1854–68) and *Entretiens* (in two volumes, 1863 and 1872).

BAZAS

Bazas stands on a cliff above the River Beuve, and developed into a major Roman settlement on an important road from Bordeaux to Toulouse. The first bishop was named in 506, and the Roman road became a pilgrimage route. Over the centuries it withstood many sieges, and was enclosed in walls in the 11th century, which were extended in the 13th century and had five gates. The power base gradually developed into joint control between Church and judiciary. The *présidial* (law courts) was instituted in 1551 and in the 18th century the town was at the head of a vast judicial district. Bazas is now the modest centre of an agricultural region known for Bazadais cattle and for several traditional *fêtes*.

The cathedral

The focus of the town centre is the triangular Place de la Cathédrale, dominated by the west front of the cathedral to the east. The Cathedral of St-Jean Baptiste was begun in 1233 to replace an 11th-century church, but was badly damaged by the Protestants in 1561. Remarkably, the astonishing west front survived Protestant iconoclasm and is almost complete, but the body of the church was virtually rebuilt (1583–1635). The belfry on the north is part 11th-century (up to the openings). The three-bay lower level of the west façade has three Gothic portals (13th century) and much of the original décor has survived. The iconography of the central door is dedicated to the *Last Judgement*, in which *Christ in Majesty* is surrounded by the Virgin, St John and angels, and Apostles and saints occupy the voussoir blocks of the five arches. The south door has scenes from the *Life of the Virgin* and the north the *Life of St Peter*, *Adam and Eve* and *Cain and Abel*. The single-bay second level dates from a new building campaign in 1537 which introduced the Flamboyant style in the magnificent rose window with a spiral surround, the flying buttresses and crocketed pinnacles. The 17th-century gable collapsed and was later replaced by the Neoclassical version. After the destruction of the 16th century, the interior was entirely rebuilt, apart from four bays near the choir, following the same layout with a long, aisled nave, a false transept and five radiating chapels around the east.

Around the cathedral

On the south side of Place de la Cathédrale is the Hôtel du Présidial (1730) which encompasses the market-hall (1890), the Hôtel de Ville and the Musée Municipal. Nearby in Rue Servière is Hôtel Bourriot (18th century), built by Pierre Bourriot, mayor of Bazas, who is credited with introducing the potato to the region. The Chapter Gardens by the south flank of the cathedral, overlooking the river, contain a few remains of the medieval ramparts on a Gallo-Roman base. The most eye-catching house is the Maison de l'Astronome (c. 1530), on the north side of the square, with a stepped gable and decorated with celestial bodies and an 'oriental' astronomer.

CHÂTEAU DE CAZENEUVE

Guided visits to the interior, June–Sept 2–6, park open from 11; May, Oct Sat, Sun and holidays 2–6, park open from 11; T: 05 56 25 48 16; www.chateaudecazeneuve.com
The Château de Cazeneuve is a splendid property, on the edge of the Landes' pine forests, which has been owned by descendants of the illustrious Albret dynasty since the 12th century, including King Henri IV and the present owners, the de Sabran-Pontevès. It is beautifully furnished and some ten rooms as well as the chapel and kitchens are open to the public.

History of the château

The first fort was built here in the 11th century and was enlarged towards the end of the 13th century. Propitious marriages ensured that the fortunes of the family, and consequently the château, continued to grow. In 1368 Armand Amanieu VIII married Marguerite de Bourbon (one of several Marguerites associated with Cazeneuve), linking the Albret to the royal family, and the union in 1484 of Jean d'Albret with Catherine de Foix added the title of King of Navarre. Henri II d'Albret, owner of the Château de Cazeneuve in the 16th century, married Marguerite d'Angoulême, sister of François I, and the title subsequently passed to their daughter, Jeanne (*see p. 364*). Her son, Henri III de Navarre, the future Henri IV, assigned Cazeneuve in 1583 to his then estranged wife, Marguerite de France (la Reine Margot; see *box opposite*). Cazeneuve was a favourite hunting retreat of Henri IV but the property suffered badly during the Wars of Religion as did the King's purse, and he bequeathed it to his wealthy cousin and close friend, Raymond de Vicose. Alterations were carried out early in the 17th century by de Vicose, and the medieval castle metamorphosed into an elegant and comfortable palace. In 1704 the property passed to the de Sabran-Pontevès family.

LA REINE MARGOT

Marguerite de Valois or Marguerite de France (1553–1615), also known as La Reine Margot, was the daughter of Henri II and Catherine de Medicis, sister of kings François II, Charles IX and Henri III. In 1572 she married Henri de Navarre. Delightful and outrageous, as well as beautiful, cultured and ambitious, her promiscuity was shocking even in that period of lax morals and her life was a series of barely credible episodes. Her wedding took place a few days before the appalling events of St Bartholomew's Eve. The union between these two individuals, who cared little for each other, turned out particularly ill-fated; nor did it produce an heir. In 1583, pending the annulment of their marriage, Henri installed Marguerite at Cazeneuve, which did not prevent her from continuing her amorous adventures. Her gravest and most deliberate error was to side with the Catholic League (*see p. 15*) against her husband, who consequently locked her away in the Château d'Usson in the Auvergne. She became Queen of France after Henri of Navarre's accession to the throne in 1589 as Henri IV until 1599 when the marriage was eventually annulled. Henri finally agreed a truce, and she spent the last ten years of her life in relative contentment in Paris. The novel *La Reine Margot* (1845) by Alexandre Dumas has been adapted for the screen many times, most recently in 1994.

Ground floor

Aross the dry moat, a 17th-century archway leads into the irregular five-sided courtyard, on two levels with the entrance on the right. On the ground floor are a vaulted gallery with Aubusson *verdure* tapestries and leather-backed chairs with the coat of arms of the de Sabran-Pontevès family. On the same level are the dining room, with porcelain and earthenware pieces, a gallery of hunting trophies, and the kitchen equipped with copper pans and salt chests. In the large fireplace are a pair of firedogs—male and female versions—traditionally presented by families of the bride and groom as a wedding gift.

First floor

A wide staircase leads to the first-floor gallery connecting the whole of the east wing, containing another Aubusson tapestry, paintings, a splendid clock and fine walnut chest with reliefs representing the four seasons. The luxurious drawing room of La Reine Margot contains a magnificent marble fireplace, on which is inscribed the last two lines of verse reputedly composed by her in response to being caught in *flagrante* by her husband. The portrait of the young Louis XIV (Henri IV's grandson) was presented by the King when he stopped here on his way to Pau, and the room is furnished mainly in Louis XV style (first half 18th century), whereas the Louis XVI bedroom is furnished in the style of that period with a bed draped *à la Polonaise*. It contains souvenirs of Delphine de Sabran, beloved aunt of Chateaubriand. Also on the first floor are the bedchambers of Margot and Henri, as well as a music room. The gallery ends at the chapel with Gothic vaulting (1680), containing a painting of two saintly members of the de Sabran family, Elzéar and Dauphine. The chapel received not only the family but also the people of the neighbourhood who entered via the *chemin de ronde* and this route now offers views over the courtyard and countryside, and leads back to the lower courtyard.

The most ancient parts of the château are the vaulted caves below the yard, the well with Gallo-Roman columns, and the prison. There is also a wine cellar, and the extensive grounds leading to the Ciron Valley can be visited.

PRACTICAL INFORMATION

GETTING AROUND

• **By train:** Bordeaux to Langon and Bazas. Bordeaux-St-Jean–Portets–Podensac–Barsac–Preignac –Langon–St-Macaire–La Réole–Agen

TOURIST INFORMATION

Bazas 1 Pl. de la Cathédrale, T: 05 56 25 25 84, www.ville-bazas.fr
Cadillac 9 Pl. de Libération, T: 05 56 62 12 92, www.entredeuxmers.com
Créon La Gare 65 Bl. Victor Hugo, T: 05 56 23 23 00, otcreon@wanadoo.fr
La Brède 3 Av. Charles de Gaulle, BP12, T: 05 56 78 47 72, www.graves-montesquieu.com
Langon 11 Allée Jean-Jaurès, T: 05 56 63 68 00, www.sauternais-graves-langon.com
Portets 31 Rue du 8 Mai 1945, T: 05 56 57 41 65.
La Réole Pl. du Col. Bouché, T: 05 56 61 13 55, lareole@entredeuxmers.com

Monségur 4 Rue Issartier, T: 05 56 61 82 73, www.entredeuxmers.com
St-Macaire Maison du Pays, T: 05 56 63 32 14, saintmacaire@entredeuxmers.com
Sauternes 11 Rue Principale, T: 05 56 76 69 13, www.sauternais-graves-langon.com
Sauveterre-de-Guyenne 2 Rue St-Roman, T: 05 56 71 53 45, email sauveterre@entredeuxmers.com
Targon 11 Pl. de l'Eglise, T: 05 56 3 63 69, email sitargon@aol.com
Villandraut Pl. du Général du Gaulle, T: 05 56 25 31 39.

WINERIES

For further information and visits contact: **Maison des Vins de Graves**, 61 Cours du Maréchal-Foch, Podensac, T: 05 56 27 09 25, www.vins-graves.com
Maison de Sauternes, Place de la Mairie, Sauternes, T: 05 56 76 69 83, www.sauternes.com

Maison de Barsac, Pl. de l'Eglise, Barsac, T: 05 56 27 15 44, www.maisondebarsac.fr

Maison des Bordeaux et Bordeaux Supérieur, Planète Bordeaux, Beychac-et-Caillau, RN89 (exit 5), T: 05 57 97 19 35, www.maisondesbordeaux.com

Maison des Vins des Premières Côtes de Bordeaux et Cadillac, La Closière, Cadillac, T: 05 57 98 19 20, www.premierescotesdebordeaux.com

Maison des Vins de l'Entre-deux-Mers, 4 Rue de l'Abbaye, BP 6, 33670, La Sauve, T: 05 57 34 32 12, www.vins-entre-deux-mers.com

Syndicat Viticole des Côtes de Bordeaux-St-Macaire, Maison du Pays de St-Macaire, 8 Rue du Canton, T: 05 56 63 32 14

Maison des Vins du Pays de Benauge, Château Les Vieilles Tuileries, Escoussans T: 05 56 23 61 70, www.bordeaux-haut-benauge.com

Maison du Sauveterrois, 4 Pl. de la République, Sauveterre-de-Guyenne, T: 05 56 71 61 28

Maison des Arts et du Vin, Pl. du Colonel Bouché, La Réole, T: 05 56 61 12 55

ACCOMMODATION & RESTAURANTS

Barsac
€ Chambres d'hôtes Les Vignes de Camperos. The handsome 18th-century *maison de maître* owned by Valerie Casasola has three large, restful rooms and a dining room for guests. The salon-veranda has views immediately onto vines, and the family wine producing Chateau Closiot can be visited. 8 Comperos, T: 05 56 17 15 47, www.lesvignesdecamperos.com

Beautiran
Chambres d'hôtes Chateau Couloumey. The vineyards were revived by by Pierre Bon in 1996, and more recently four guest rooms have been created in the 18th-century *chartreuse* which are unfussy and restful. Breakfast is served in the large kitchen/living room. 12 Rte. de Landes, BP2, T: 05 56 67 66 65, www.chateau-couloumey.com

Cadillac
€ Restaurant L'Entrée Jardin. Local cuisine served in an attractive blue-and-white setting; with a terrace. Near the château. 22 Rue de l'Oeuille, T: 05 56 76 96 96.

Castres-Gironde
€ Chambres d'hôtes Le Moulin de Pommarède. The 13th-century mill on the banks of the Gât Mort is a wine making property. It has been entirely restored by M. et Mme. Boussiers and the three rooms are uncluttered and a nice combination of colours. There is a bright and airy salon/dining room for guests as well as a pergola in the garden. Route de Pommarède T: 05 56 67 21 28, www.pommarede.com

Créon
€€ Hostellerie/Restaurant Château Camiac. There are 14 rooms in the romantic 19th-century chateau which is a *relais de silence* in a beautiful setting. Route de Branne D121, T: 05 56 23 20 85, www.chateau-camiac.com

Langon
€€ Hôtel/Restaurant Claude Darroze. Hotel-restaurant that is comfortingly traditional and three-star in every way: an 18th-century mansion where ancient trees shade the terrace. Under the experienced guidance of

Claude Darroze excellent food and service is assured. Three menus (*Saison, Saveur* and *Plaisir*) or à la carte offer such delights as *Brouillade d'œufs crémeuse aux Morilles fraîches, Filet de Boeuf grillé au foie gras sur fond de sauce bordelaise*, and *Croustillant aux fruits rouges sur coulis, quenelle de glace vanille*. The hotel has 16 rooms. 95 Cours du Gen.-Leclerc, T: 05 56 63 00 48, www.darroze.com

€ **Hôtel/Restaurant Horus**. A moderately priced Logis de France 9km from Sauternes in a green setting, with 33 standard rooms. The breakfast at €7 is copious and the food in the restaurant semi-gastronomic with a buffet for €11 at midday and in the evening. 2 Rue des Bruyeres, T: 05 56 62 36 37,

La Réole

€€ **Restaurant Les Fontaines**. A late 18th-century *maison bourgeoise* with a large park is the setting for an elegant restaurant where the cooking is based on the seasons. The chef, from the Cote d'Azur, assures there is always a fish dish, as well as more traditional dishes. Choices include *Fricassée d'escargot au pied de cochon, Gratin d'écrevisses aux légumes, et Pigeonneau en deux cuissons*. The exclusively set menus change at least four times a year, and range from €16 to the *menu dégustation* at €46. T: 05 56 61 15 25.

Martillac

€€€ *Les Sources de Caudalie*. This is a beautiful hotel set in vineyards, with fabulous food and a spa where 'vinothérapie' is on offer. The 49 suites in four different buildings, with four different themes. There are two gourmet restaurants, the elegant La Grande Vigne which picks up the style of an 18th century orangery with a terrace overlooking a small lake; and La Table du Lavoir is a more rustic setting. Chemin de Smith Haut-Lafitte, T: 05 57 83 83 83; spa T: 05 57 83 82 82, www.sources-caudalie.com

Monségur

€ **Chambres d'Hôtes and Restaurant Sous le Cep d'Antan**. A new guesthouse in a building of 1597 at the heart of a 13th-century *bastide* has benefitted from the sure touch of Catherine Maurel in combining old stone and pastels shades to make 5 charming rooms. The adjacent café, brasserie and restaurant is enveloped in a 300-year-old vine. Pl. Darniche, T: 05 56 61 60 28; restaurant 05 56 71 45 99, www.souslecep-danton.com

Ste-Radegonde

€ **Hotel/Restaurant Château de Sanse**. A slightly austere but handsome 18th-century building has become a comfortable and welcoming hotel with 16 cooly spacious rooms and suites some with terrace or balcony. On a lower level is a beautiful pool and sun terrace overlooking the vineyards. The new restaurant with glass walls benefits from views all round, and in summer meals are served on the terrace. The cuisine is creative and is accompanied by local and world wines. T: 05 57 56 41 10, www.chateaudesanse.com

St-Macaire

€€ **Hôtel/Restaurant Les Feuilles d'Acanthe**. ■ Two beautifully restored adjoining Renaissance houses at the heart of the town have been successfully adapted for modern comfort while keeping the characteristics of the old buildings. There is a pool and jacuzzi in the courtyard, and a charming restau-

rant. 5 Rue de l'Eglise/6 Rue du Carnot, T: 05 56 62 33 75, www.feuilles-dacanthe.com
€€ **Restaurant L'Abricotier**. Fresh local ingredients determine the seasonal dishes which are mainly traditional and are presented in a personal manner in this charming restaurant in an old house. There are several dining rooms and a garden, and menus from €20 to €38; à la carte around €40/45. L'Abricotier also has three large bedrooms with cooking area. (off the N113 east of St-Macaire), T: 05 56 76 83 63.
Sauternes
€€ **Le Saprien**. A gastronomic restaurant which has an excellent reputation with two attractive dining rooms and terrace overlooking the vineyards. The cuisine is based on regional and seasonal produce, and certain dishes incorporate the local wine, such as *Terrine de foie gras à la gelée de Sauternes, Lamproie au Sauternes* and *Ris de veau au Sauternes et au curry*, followed by *Gâteau coulant au chocolat*. Set menus at €23 and €35, and average à la carte, €50. T: 05 56 76 60 87.
€ **Relais du Château d'Arche**. This very beautiful 17th-century *chartreuse* seems to float in a sea of vines at the heart of a property which produces a Grand Cru Classé de Sauternes. T: 05 56 76 67 67, www.chateaudarche.fr

MARKET DAYS

Bazas Saturday, evening market in August
Cadillac Saturday
Coutras Wednesday, Saturday
Créon Wednesday, Saturday
Langon Friday, Saturday

La Réole Saturday
Sales Thursday
St-Seurin sur l'Isle Sunday
Sauveterre-de-Guyenne Tuesday

FESTIVALS & EVENTS

May: *Promenade des Boeufs Gras*, presentation and judging of prize beef cattle, traditional music, communal meal, Bazas
June: *Fete de la St-Jean et Hommage au Taureau*, festival of St-John and of the Bull, Bazas. *Festival des Fifres de Garonne*, Festival of fifes, St-Pierre d'Aurillac
July: *Les 24 heures du Swing*, three days of continuous jazz from international groups, Monségur
July–August: *Jumping national de Bazas*, Bazas. *Festival des Nuits Atypiques*, jazz, rock and world music, Langon. *Fête nautique,* floral floats and decorated canoes on the Ciron, Bommes. *Festival international Danses et Rythmes du monde*, Langon. *Les Journées de Villandraut*, French theatre and dance in the setting of Pope Clement V's château. *Les Nuits Macariennes*, medieval festival, St-Sauveur and St-Macaire. *Uzeste Musical*, jazz from Gascony and Occitan festival, Uzeste. *Les Rencontres Musicale Internationales des Graves*, classic music and talented performers, in the Graves wine châteaux
August: *Journées médiévales*, medieval celebrations in the villages of the Dropt valley. *Balades en Cadillac*, a weekend of music, cinema and street theatre, rides in Cadillac cars, and fireworks, Cadillac *Radofolies*, descent of the Garonne on rafts, from Marmande to La Réole

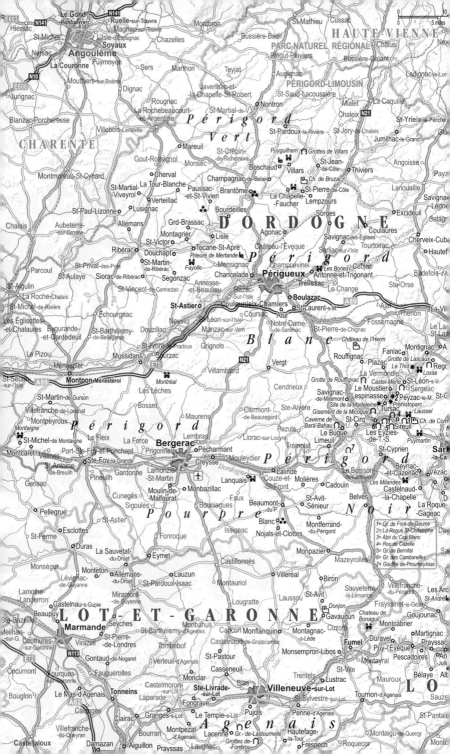

THE DORDOGNE

The name Dordogne is evocative of one of the best-loved rivers in France, whose formidable waters, like the other great rivers of the southwest, for centuries created both a barrier and a major highway. The river rises in the Massif Central and flows west for 472km, receiving the Cère, the Vézère and the Isle Rivers, until uniting with the Garonne near Bordeaux. Dordogne also designates a modern administrative *département*, which corresponds almost exactly to the former province of Périgord, and is associated with lush landscapes, intense Paleolithic activity and '1001 castles'. Those who inhabit the *département* of Dordogne are *Périgordiens* and the capital is Périgueux. Périgord is frequently divided into four parts, according to distinctive cultural and geological features, which are identified by colours: green, white, black (*see p. 129*) and purple.

PÉRIGORD VERT

The northern reach of Aquitaine, and therefore of the *département* of the Dordogne, is known as Périgord Vert. Well watered and densely wooded, the rounded foothills of the Massive Central in the east give way to a plateaux (350-400m) into which the rivers Dronne, Bandiat, Loue and Côle are deeply incised. The northeast is given over to the Parc Naturel Régional du Périgord-Limousin, created in 1998, which straddles the Dordogne and the Corrèze. In the west, La Double is a region of forest and lakes.

Château de Mareuil

Open summer 10–12.30 & 2–6; winter 10–12 & 2–6, closed Tues, Sun morning; closed Dec–Feb; T: 05 53 60 74 13.

Still inhabited, this somewhat eccentric pile with a dry moat goes back to the 12th century but has been thoroughly knocked about over the centuries. Damaged during the Hundred Years War, it was rebuilt in the 15th century integrating some earlier defensive elements into a more habitable Renaissance mansion. Just before the Revolution, the Duc de Montebello transformed it into a farm and gave considerable land to a hospice. The property was repurchased by the family in the 20th century who began to restore it about 40 years ago. The buildings, arranged around a courtyard include, in one of the towers, a splendid Flamboyant-style chapel with a 15th-century fireplace (now used as storage for mower and wheelbarrow). The visit includes the spaces two floors down, and rooms on the upper floors with extraordinary collections including 47 drawings in Chinese ink of the history of Chaumont-sur-Loire; memorabilia of Maréchal Lannes, Duc de Montebello, an ancestor of the present owner; Napoleonic letters; and an example of the first electric clock.

Vieux-Mareuil has an impressive, fortified 12th–13th-century church dedicated to

The Abbaye de Brantôme, with 11th-century bell-tower, on the Dronne.

St Pierre, and over the third bay is a large bell-tower crowned by a 15th- and 16th-century defence structure. The west front, in the style of the Saintonge, is fairly plain with six small arches on pillars, and inside are three cupolas on pendentives. The flat chevet has small lancet windows with glass mosaics. Between Vieux Mareuil and Brantôme is the Château de Richemont (*open mid-July to August, 10-6, T: 05 53 05 71 81*) which contains the funerary chapel of Pierre de Bordeilles, or Brantôme (*see below*).

BRANTÔME & ENVIRONS

A tight loop in the Dronne created an island site on which the small town of Brantôme developed next to its ancient abbey, creating an unforgettable ensemble. This little town was the home of soldier-satirist Pierre de Bordeilles (1540–1614), better known under his pen name Brantôme, and the author of *Les Vies des hommes illustres et des grands capitaines* and *Les Vies des dames galantes*. He was made titular abbot at the age of 16 but spent most of his time gallivanting through Europe. The two parts of the old town either side of the river are linked by a picturesque dog-leg bridge between the the Grand Jardin and the Abbey.

Abbaye de Brantôme

Open July–Aug 10–7; April–June, Sept, closed Tues, 10–12.30 & 2–6; Oct–Dec, Feb–March, closed Tues, 10–12 & 2–5; T: 05 53 05 80 63.

The most important monument in the town is the Abbey. Its oldest part is an eye-catching 11th- and 12th-century bell-tower. The former abbey, a collection of white-and-grey 17th–19th-century buildings, is now occupied by the *Mairie* and the Musée Fernand-Desmoulins, and behind the buildings are the Troglodyte Caves.

The abbey stands on a narrow shelf of rock between the cliff and river. It was founded by Wisbode, Count of Périgord, vassal of Charlemagne, early in the 9th century, and Charlemagne himself dedicated the relics of St Sicaire, one of Herod's slaves who converted after the Massacre of the Innocents. The abbey was destroyed by the Normans and rebuilt in the 11th century, restored in the following century, rebuilt in the 15th century and subjected to Paul Abadie's (*see p. 112*) enthusiastic attention in 1850.

The huge free-standing bell-tower has, against all the odds, survived since the 11th century and is considered the oldest of its kind; it served as the model for Romanesque belfries in the Limousin. It consists of four stepped levels with a series of round-headed arches of different rhythms and sizes, with an unusual gabled element linking the third and fourth levels, topped off by a pyramidal roof. The ground floor is domed and there is an interior staircase. The ruined cloister (1465-1539) is on the west of the church, situated there because of the constraints of the site: three galleries were eliminated at the time of Napoleon III by Abadie. The church, basically Romanesque, has been much altered. Under the porch is a 13th-century relief of the *Massacre of the Innocents*. Inside the door of the narthex a Romanesque capital is used as a holy water stoup and the domes over the two bays of the tall nave and the choir were replaced by Angevin-type Gothic vaults during later transformations.

The troglodytic caverns and man-made galleries behind the abbey provided shelter to hermits who first Christianised the rock, and have protected others during attacks at various times. The caves can be visited along the 'troglodyte trail', which has information panels in French and English. Everything is carved out of the rock, including the *chauffoir, lavoir* and pigeon house and there is a spring dedicated to St Sicaire. The highlight is the cave containing a carved relief of the *Last Judgement*.

The Musée Fernand-Desmoulins contains prehistoric objects. It also contains the work of local artist, Fernand Desmoulins, who worked from 1900–1902 through the mysterious intervention of a medium, evoked in a multi-media projection and other displays. At the exit of Brantôme towards Thiviers (D78) is a Neolithic tomb, the Dolmen de la Peyrelevade (or Pierre Levée) around 6,000-years-old.

BOURDEILLES

A pretty drive southwest along the Dronne brings you to Bourdeilles, another of the four medieval baronies of Périgord. The beautifully kept village contains the ancient house of the seneschals, with picturesque old bridge and *bâteau moulin*, and shelters beneath the overhanging cliff, on which stand two magnificent châteaux (*see overleaf*).

Châteaux de Bourdeilles

Open July–Aug 10–7; April–June, Sept–Oct 10–12.30 & 2–6, closed Tues; mid-Nov–Dec, Feb–March, 10–12.30 & 2–5.30, closed Tues, Fri, Sat; mid to end–Dec 10-12.30 & 2-5 closed Tues; closed Jan; T: 05 53 03 73 36.

In the 13th century a family rift occurred when the region was ceded to the English, the older generation of the Bourdeilles supporting the Plantagenets and the younger Maumonts backing the Capetians. Gérard de Maumont, endorsed by the French king (Philippe le Bel) took over the castle and fortified it. The property returned to the Bourdeilles at the beginning of the 16th century and after the Wars of Religion Jacquette de Montbron, widowed sister-in-law of Brantôme (*see above, p. 104*), decided to demolish the baronial castle and start again in the style of the day. Moreover, anticipating a visit from Catherine de Médicis, she furnished the palace accordingly. The queen never arrived, Jacquette died, and the project came to a halt.

The medieval castle, enclosed in a series of walls, has a severe 13th–14th-century main block with plate-tracery windows and a wooden ceiling while the massive octagonal keep (14th century) has star vaults above each floor.

The Renaissance château has fairly simple three-storey elevations displaying the correct use of the orders of architecture, and is flanked by projecting pavilions. The low roof is screened by a balustrade. Inside is an extraordinary collection of 16th–17th-century Spanish and Burgundian furnishings, including travelling chests, tapestries and Hispano-Mauresque *faïences*, an *Entombment* group from Burgundy and the tomb of Jean de Chabannes (d. 1498), Chamberlain of Charles VIII.

THE RIBÉRACOIS

The Ribéracois, on the edge of the Forêt de la Double, is exceptionally rich in small Romanesque churches, typically with flat buttresses, frequently domed and often adapted for defence, with crenellations or galleries atop stout walls. There are examples at St-Martin-de-Ribérac, Siorac-de-Ribérac, altered in the 14th and 16th centuries, and at Douchapt. Lisle, an unspoilt village on the Dronne, has a fortified and domed church and a market hall on columns.

Montagrier is a tiny village on a natural terrace above the Dronne, with a domed church with five 12th-century apsidal chapels with ancient re-sited sculptures including a 4th-century Chi-rho monogram of Christ.

The small fortified church on a cliff at **Grande Brassac** has an impressive crenellated belfry; a collage of sculptures with traces of colour, above the main (north) door, includes Christ, the Virgin and St John above, and in the arch the *Adoration of the Magi*. Inside, the nave has three domed bays (late 12th–early 13th century).

Northwest of Ribérac there are more 12th-century gems at Allemans and St-Paul Lizonne, and fragments of wall paintings at St-Martial-Viveyrol. The church of St-Martin at **Cherval**, in the canton of Verteillac, is the finest, with three early 12th-century domes over the nave, a fourth, more sophisticated, of the late 12th century, while the fifth is modern.

EAST OF BRANTÔME

Along the valley east of Brantôme, where the Trincou and Côle Rivers unite with the Dronne, is a cluster of interesting sites. On the Côle is the quiet community of **La-Chapelle-Faucher** gathered around a little Romanesque church with domes and carvings. Lempzours has a rustic Romanesque church. From St-Pierre-de-Côle, it is a pretty drive to **St-Jean-de-Côle**, which is an idyllic spot. This small village with russet roofs, picturesque 12th–14th-century restored houses and a hump-back bridge has at its centre an interesting church. Built in granite the church of St-Jean-Baptiste, originally the chapel of an Augustinian priory, was begun late in the 11th century under the auspices of Raymond de Thiviers, Bishop of Périgueux. On the exterior are storiated capitals, one of them sheltered by the market hall built on the east of the church, including an *Annunciation*, the *Drunkenness of Noah*, the *Creation of Man* and *Daniel in the Lions' Den*. The one-bay nave and chevet are the survivals of a larger church. The nave was originally covered with a dome 12m in diameter, the second largest in Périgord but, after collapsing several times, it was replaced in the 19th century by a wooden ceiling. The apse has two Rayonnant chapels, and the choir was endowed in the 17th century with carved stalls. Between the church and the river are the priory cloisters (16th century), with large arches, included in the visit to the châteaux. The **Châteaux de La Marthonie** (*guided visits July–Aug 10–12 & 2–6; low season 10-12; T: 05 53 62 30 25*), are made up of two distinct parts, one medieval with imposing 15th–16th-century square and round towers, the other a Classical wing at right angles to the first with arcades, mansard roofs and high dormers. There is an elegant interior staircase.

The **Grottes de Villars** (*guided visits July–Aug 10–7.30; April–June, Sept 10–12 & 2–7; Oct 2–6.30, closed Mon; T: 05 53 54 82 36*), west of St-Jean-de-Côle, are a double treat: some 10km of labyrinthine galleries are not only adorned with brilliantly white stalactites and other natural formations, but also with prehistoric paintings discovered in 1958. These date back to the Aurignacian period, some 30,000 years ago, and include bison and antelope and a rare human image called 'the sorcerer'.

Château de Puyguilhem

Open July–Aug 10–7; April–June, Sept to mid–Nov, 10–12.30 & 2–6, closed Mon; mid–Nov to mid–Dec, Feb–March 10–12.30 & 2–5.30, closed Mon, Fri, Sat; mid to end–Dec, 10–12.30 & 2–5, closed Mon; closed Jan; T: 05 53 54 82 18.

The Château de Puyguilhem near Villars is a delightful example of early Renaissance architecture (completed 1530), combining an exuberant interpretation of 15th-century Italian detail with a charming insouciance towards the Italian Renaissance ideals of harmony and balance. Mondot de La Marthonie, president of the *parlements* in Bordeaux and Paris, built Puyguilhem on the site of an earlier redoubt. It was taken over by the state in 1939 and is furnished from the national reserves. The main building is framed by two towers, the right-hand one round and chunky with ornate machicolations, a relic of the feudal castle updated with a high conical roof and fancy dormer. Tucked in behind it is an octagonal stair-tower. The left-hand tower is taller and angled, and altogether more convincingly Renaissance, with a finely sculpted balustrade and elaborate dormers which break into the pyramidal roof. The roofs are a mixture of cool grey slate over the towers and warm red on the main building, and over the centre of the main roof is a heavily embellished chimney stack. Above the main entrance are the initials of the builder and his wife, Anne de Vernon, and inside are monumental fireplaces, one with scenes of the Labours of Hercules, and a fine ceiling above the main staircase.

Just outside Villars in a beautiful and isolated spot are the picturesque remains of the Cistercian abbey of Boschaud (built 1154–59), devastated during the Hundred Years War and Wars of Religion. A wing of the cloister with unequal arches has survived, as well as the chapter house, and the ruined church is a unique example of sober Cistercian architecture combined with a succession of characteristically Périgordian domes.

PÉRIGORD BLANC

The White Périgord is a swathe across the middle of the *département* following the Isle River. It is described as white because of the limestone screes and numerous quarries producing typically pale masonry. Bordering the Corrèze to the east it is lush and green, but becomes increasingly industrial to the west beyond Périgueux. Périgueux itself is the ancient and modern capital of the Périgord and Dordogne, an attractive, lively town. It is also important for its Gallo-Roman museum and for the two domed churches which go back to the 12th century.

PÉRIGUEUX

The town of Périgueux occupies a prime position on the banks of the Isle. Emblematic of the city are the curiously exotic white cupolas and minaret-like steeple of the Cathedral of St-Front which stands on a knoll above the river with the medieval town clustered around it. Less conspicuous are the important Gallo-Roman remains enhanced by the new museum. Périgueux is first and foremost a place where real people live and work, not simply a tourist destination. It is large enough to absorb visitors, has plenty to see, wonderful old streets with distinguished medieval and Renaissance buildings, excellent shops and a particularly lively twice-weekly market. It is, in fact, a welcome contrast to the tourist-focused Sarlat, Les Eyzies or Domme. The city was made *préfecture* of the modern *département* of Dordogne in 1790.

La Cité
To the west of Place Francheville, laid out on the meeting point of the two ancient sections of the town, is the area once known as la Cité. This was the Gallo-Roman town and also in this quarter is the church of St-Etienne-de-la-Cité (*see overleaf*).

HISTORY OF PÉRIGUEUX

A Celtic tribe, the Petrucores, occupied the hills on the south bank of the Isle, and at the time of the creation of *Aquitania* by the Romans at the end of the 1st century BC, the territory became known as *Civitas Petrucoriorum*. The main *oppidum*, Vesunna (or *Vesona*), was named after a local god to whom a sacred spring was probably dedicated. A fine Roman town of some stature developed on the right bank, with forum, temples, amphitheatre, *thermae* and aqueducts, but this was attacked at the end of the 3rd century AD by the Alemani. The inhabitants of *Vesunna* rebuilt a smaller city within the walls, using the amphitheatre as a bastion of defence, and gradually the name *Vesunna* disappeared and the area became known as La Cité.

Legend has it that St Front brought Christianity to the Périgord; the first bishop recorded was Paternus in 360. The relics of St Front became crucially important and were placed in the first sanctuary on the hill, or *puy*, opposite La Cité. This developed into a monastic centre around which the suburb of Puy-St-Front grew up, eventually eclipsing the Cité where traditionally the nobles lived. The bourgeoisie, artisans and immigrants inhabited Puy-St-Front, which came under the protection of the King of France. By 1240 the two communities had come together as Périgueux, although unification was not necessarily harmonious. There were severe attacks during the Hundred Years War, and by the Treaty of Bretigny (1360) the town was subjected to English administration. Accounts vary, but either Count Archambaud V betrayed the English, or the French hero Bertrand du Guesclin liberated the town in 1369. Renewal during the relatively peaceful period 1550–1650 produced the handsome Renaissance buildings which enhance the old centre. During the Reformation, Périgueux remained Catholic until taken by the Protestants (1575–81), was torn apart by the Civil Wars, and divided during the Fronde.

By the 19th century, navigation on the Isle provided employment and the arrival of the railway in 1856 opened up even more opportunities for the development of industry. The town grew rapidly and spread beyond its medieval confines, necessitating new roads and public buildings. The start of the 20th century coincided with a downturn, and the First World War and lack of employment decimated the population.

During the Second World War some 25,000 refugees from Alsace swelled the numbers for a while. There was a strong Resistance network based in Périgueux which provoked the Germans to establish a garrison here for 21 months until Liberation in August 1944. The population is now around 60,000 and the suburbs are spreading. The largest employer is the French stamp print-shop, transferred here from Paris in 1970, but Périgueux is now best known as a gastronomic centre.

St Etienne-de-la-Cité, an austere building that until the 17th century was the cathedral of the Périgueux, was begun in the 11th century and originally consisted of a succession of four domed bays, but was damaged during the Wars of Religion and rebuilt (1625–47). The two domed units to the west then collapsed and only the east dome was rebuilt. During the Fronde, in 1652, the Prince of Condé's men used the church as a *manège* for training horses and riders; in 1669 the episcopal see was transferred to St-Front and at the Revolution the church was deconsecrated.

The exterior is sober and undecorated, with high wall arcades and few windows, while the scarred west front is the 17th-century infill of the former internal arch of the second bay, with evidence of the lost dome at the angles. The cavernous interior is sombre and awe-inspiring with just two bays and lateral wall walks. The oldest part is the first bay, and most impressive, with enormous pendentives (9m high) that make the transition from a square of 13m to a single span dome of 15m diameter (compare Cahors 16m, *see p. 178*; St-Front 13m, *see p. 112*); the apex is 22m from the floor. The east bay, originally mid-12th-century, is more decorative and lighter but this dome was rebuilt in the 17th century. Behind the choir organ is a *Table Pascale* dated 1163 for calculating the date of Easter up until 1253. On the north wall is the arcaded tomb of Bishop Jean d'Asside (d. 1168), with an inscription which includes the name of the stonemason, Constantine de Jarnac. The 17th-century Baroque altarpiece in wood features the Four Evangelists, and among the scenes on the lower part is one of St Front casting the Devil off the Gallo-Roman Vesunna Tower.

Rue Romaine leads south on the line of the old Roman town wall erected to protect *Civitas Petrucoriorum* at the end of the 3rd century AD. It leads to the Tour de Vésone or Vesunna Tower which is the most imposing Roman monument in the Périgord yet consists only of the central part, or *cella*, of a 2nd-century AD circular temple. The massive cylinder of brick, small stone blocks and rubble appears precariously thin-walled and is immensely tall (27m high and 20m in diameter), but has a dramatic rent at the point of the original entrance. It stands on the remains of a circular podium and would have been surrounded by a colonnade or peristyle with an entry vestibule, but only fragments of the base are visible. Undoubtedly once clad in marble and roofed, it has courses of large connecting blocks and narrow brick as well as brick arched openings. The temple was the focal point of the Roman city, at the convergence of important roads to the north of the forum. It was abandoned and left outside the reduced enclosure of the Roman town c. 270. Around it are fragments of columns found in digs.

Musée Gallo-Romain Vesunna

Open July-Aug 10–7; April–June, Sept–mid-Nov 10–12.30 & 2–6, closed Mon; mid-Nov–mid-Dec, Feb–March 10–12.30 & 2–5.30, closed Mon; mid- to end-Dec 10–12.30 & 2–5, closed Mon; T: 05 53 53 00 92.

The new museum, west of the Tour de Vésone, opened in July 2003. Designed by Jean Nouvel, who was born in the Southwest, responsible among other projects for the new museum on Quay Branly in Paris, the 4,000 square metre glass-walled building brings together archaeological remains excavated on site with a fine collection of

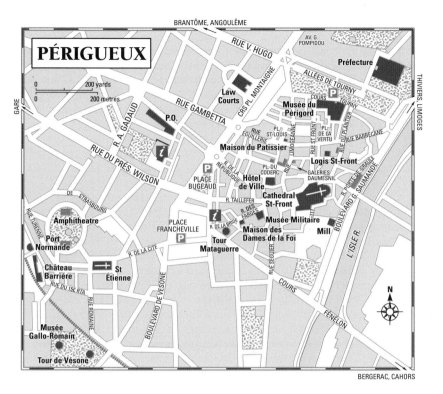

Gallo-Roman artefacts and objects. The 1st-century AD *domus* or Gallo-Roman house, is the main focus of the museum and is incorporated in the large new building. The excavations can be viewed from two levels of overhanging balconies or from walkways at ground level for a closer view of the structure of the domus.

In the balconies permanent exhibits are displayed according to two themes: 'The Town and Public Life of Vesunna' addresses the town and its inhabitants, the major monuments and architecture, death, religion and the economy and has sacrificial altars dedicated to Cybele (*see p. 373*) and architectural fragments. 'The House and Private Life' describes the construction and evolution of the house, beauty and adornment, food and heating with objects in pottery, glass and metal. Outstanding is the collection of mural paintings found *in situ*, many of which are still in place.

The amphitheatre

The medieval Château Barrière, on Rue Turenne, consists of a 12th-century keep and 15th-century stair-tower with Renaissance windows constructed on top of the Roman wall; it was damaged in 1575. Nearby is a single Roman arch, the Porte Normande, one of the three original 3rd-century town gates, damaged by Viking or Norman invaders in the 9th century. The Jardin des Arènes is the amphitheatre (1st century

AD), disguised as a public garden. On further investigation, sections of the substructure can be made out, including arches, *vomitoria,* and steps. With seating for some 20,000 it was slightly smaller than those at Arles or Nîmes. It served as an outer bastion during late antiquity, and as a fortress during Vandal attacks, and as fort and prison during the alliance between the Counts of Périgord and the English during the Hundred Years War, but much of what remained was demolished in 1391 and a convent was installed there from 1664 until the Revolution.

DOMED CHURCHES OF AQUITAINE

Of the 77 domed churches built in Aquitaine c. 1100, some 60 remain. Périgueux is thought to be one of the most important centres for the development of this system, inspired either directly by the 6th-century Justinian church of the Holy Apostles in Byzantium (destroyed) or via St Mark's, Venice (consecrated 1094). St-Etienne is often posited as the prototype domed church in the region. The dome was, of course, already used in smaller secular buildings, and as a centralising feature it is logical at a crossing; a half dome frequently covers an apse. The use of the dome to span a nave or transept, sometimes in a file of up to four, is particular to the Southwest. These are very strong constructions, supported by solid outer walls, using pointed arches with pendentives in the transition from square to circle. Aisles were usually avoided in domed churches and there was never an ambulatory. Important examples are Cahors (*see p. 178*) and Souillac (*see p. 164*).

Cathedral of St-Front

Closed 12–2.30.

The medieval *quartiers* of Le Puy St-Front are on a knoll, east of Place Francheville, which slopes away to the River Isle on the east On the site of an early monastic church, the cathedral is one of the largest and most eye-catching in southwest France. The great bulbous pile standing high above the Isle is a fanciful 19th-century neo-Byzantine silhouette of domes. Built in almost white ashlar, it contrasts strongly with the rustic stone of the rest of the town. It results from the fusion of two Romanesque churches, one 11th-century and the other 12th-century, and a radical rethink by Paul Abadie and Emile Boeswillwald between 1852 and 1908. While Abadie was working at Périgueux he was preparing to build Sacré-Coeur in Paris, and the cross-fertilisation is obvious.

The cathedral is named after the semi-legendary evangeliser of Périgueux around whose relics a chapel had existed since the 6th century. An earlier church (10th–11th

Cathedral of St-Front, Périgueux.

centuries) was replaced by a larger one consecrated in 1047. The tower-porch led in the 11th century to a domed sanctuary and high altar which contained the remarkable shrine of 1077 inspired by the St-Sepulchre in Jerusalem, and designed by the monk Guinamond from La Chaise-Dieu monastery. It was placed under a hollow turret with dome and gables and described by Aymery Picaud in his pilgrim's guide to Santiago (*see p. 11*). The church was damaged by fire in 1120; the next version was erected east of the previous church but incorporated part of it and was completed c. 1170. The shrine stayed in its original place and the church was extended beyond it, imposing a reverse orientation. Unlike the majority of domed churches in the west, St-Front was not designed with a file of domes with apse and apsidioles, but in the shape of a Greek cross.

The church was pillaged and the tomb of the saint destroyed by the Protestants in 1575. In 1669 the episcopal see was transferred from St-Etienne-de-la-Cité to St-Front. When Abadie took over the building in the 19th century it was in a poor way but served as the basis for the present cathedral although it was subjected to considerable alteration.

The interior

To understand the layout of the Romanesque church enter from the west: the modern entrance is through the porch on the north. The massive western elevation was originally preceded by a porch, now reduced to a single arch leading into an open forecourt or atrium formed from the nave walls after the fire in the 12th century. On the lateral walls are wall arcades similar to those of St-Etienne, and great corner pylons were constructed in the 12th century to sustain a dome over this space, seemingly never completed. To the south is the cloister (12th–15th centuries). The main entrance to the 12th-century church was beneath the extraordinary tower. This was one of the structures least altered by Boeswillwald in the 19th century. It consists of a succession of stepped levels decorated with pilasters, pediments and columns and topped off by a colonnaded drum with cone-shaped roof and imbrications.

From below the west tower, you pass through the narthex, covered with two sequential domes on squinches, flanked by aisles (part 11th century) and, to the east, a doorway with original Corinthian capitals. The multi-domed interior is cool, spacious and gravely majestic, composed of five equal-sized domed sections, except for the little apse bumps to the east. It is also smoothly colourless and, unlike Sacré-Coeur in Paris, has no paintings or mosaics. Over the body of the church the domes, all on pendentives, are equal in size (13m in diameter and 27m high) and supported by four-part piers detached from the walls with small round-headed windows (a 19th-century rebuild). The space under the west dome was the site of the medieval shrine and main altar, but the traditional orientation was restored by Abadie by grafting a neo-Romanesque apse and placing the high altar in the east (the main altar is now in a central position). The apsidal chapels in the transepts may be 12th-century and in the south transept is a tiny alcove with a medieval painting on the vault. On the north and south of the chancel are medieval paintings of the Life of St Front.

The magnificent 17th-century wooden altarpiece with twisted columns, in the east (coin-operated light), was designed for a Jesuit chapel and transferred to the cathedral via St-Etienne. It is dedicated to the Virgin of the Assumption, presented by a female donor. The pulpit (c. 1680) is also an outstanding piece with magnificent turned balusters; the stalls, also 17th-century, came from the abbey of Ligueux. The altar of 1762 originates from the abbey of Vauclaire. The unremarkable glass is 19th-century and the neo-Gothic light fittings were designed by Abadie and used at Notre-Dame in Paris for the wedding of Napoleon III.

Around the cathedral

The *quartier* immediately west of the Cathedral is a commercial battleground on market days, crowded with shoppers, the brightly coloured stalls setting up vivid contrasts with the white-grey of the cathedral on Place de la Clautre. The market is focussed around Place du Coderc with the covered market (1832) and spreads into the surrounding streets as well as into Place de l'Hôtel-de-Ville. Here the most important building is the Logis Gilles-Lagrange, and the 18th-century home of the Lagrange-Chancel family.

On Rue des Farges, the **Musée Militaire** displays a range of military equipment (*open April–Sept 1–6; Oct–Dec, 2–6; closed Sun; Jan–Mar, Wed, Sat 2–6; closed holidays; T: 05 53 53 47 36*), and Nos 4/6, the **Maison des Dames de la Foi**, is heralded as one of the oldest buildings in France. The mission of the faithful ladies, who occupied the building 1680-1792, was to bring Protestants back to the Catholic faith. The house is also said to have been the residence of Constable du Guesclin (*see p. 109*) during the Hundred Years War. At the end of the street is Tour Mataguerre, the last remnant of the 28 towers and ramparts that enclosed Le Puy. This survivor, with machicolated parapet and gun loops, was rebuilt in 1477 and the more recent *fleurs de lis* symbolise the alliance between king and consuls of the town back in 1204. In Rue Aubergerie the Hôtels Abzac de Ladouze (no. 16) and Saltgourde (no. 4–8) were fortified in the 15th century. The small square off Rue Séguier, Place de Navarre, has renovated buildings. The river can be accessed through the Jardin du Thouin—with 16th-century cannons—next to the cloister or Rue de Tourville to the east.

On the quay is the Vieux Moulin, built on a section of the ramparts, and a small garden. From the bridge is the best view of the cathedral and of a group of particularly attractive houses. These are the L-shaped 16th-century Maison Lambert (under restoration), with a wooden loggia, the Maison des Consuls (15th century) with Flamboyant dormers and a machicolated cornice, and the high-roofed Hôtel de Lur (17th century), also angled. Behind these buildings is Rue Porte-de-Graule, a somberly picturesque street which the passage of time has left untouched. A flight of steps links it with Rue Barbecane/Rue Notre-Dame leading back to the old town centre.

The area north of the cathedral is a labyrinth of streets lined with wonderful boutiques of epicurean delights and squares with interesting facades. Off Rue de la Miséricorde and Rue de la Clarté are passageways leading to the Galeries Daumesnil, a series of interior courtyards surrounded by a group of carefully restored buildings.

Rue de la Constitution contains the Logis St-Front, an elegant building with late Gothic and early Renaissance features around a courtyard and in Rue Limogeanne is the sophisticated Maison Estignard (16th century) with the salamander motif of François I over the interior courtyard door. In Place St-Louis there is a *marché au gras* in winter and café tables in summer. The handsome building with a tower, the Maison du Pâtissier (1518), has Renaissance features and is partly fortified. Other squares nearby are Place du-Marché-au-Bois and Place de la Vertu with renovated Renaissance buildings.

Musée du Périgord

Open April–Sept, Mon, Wed–Fri 10.30–5.30, Sat, Sun 1–6; Oct–March, Mon, Wed–Fri 10–5, Sat, Sun, 1–6; closed Tues and holidays; T: 05 53 06 40 70.

This museum on Cours Tourny has a little bit of everything, not necessarily connected with the Périgord, including some surprising exhibits. The museum took over an Augustinian monastery which was rebuilt, except for the 13th-century chapel, with a cloister, in 1895. The prehistoric section displays local finds. In the former there are both human remains and important engravings on stone and bone. The early Middle Ages are represented by certain religious pieces, and especially fragile masonry from the cathedral which was replicated for the restorations. Among a collection of sacred artefacts are a diptych on leather and an enamel pyx (both 13th century). There are paintings and sculpture from the 15th–20th centuries combined with furniture and other examples of the decorative arts. One of the most revered works of art in the museum is *The Rialto Bridge* by Canaletto (1697–1768). There are also works reflecting local personalities and events in the context of French art and rooms have been set aside for the sculptures of Gilbert Privat (1892–1967) and Etienne Hajdu (1907–1996).

ENVIRONS OF PÉRIGUEUX

Abbaye de Chancelade

Immediately northwest of Périgueux, is the Abbaye de Chancelade (*no visits to the interior*) one of the most delightful oases in Périgord. Cross the village to reach the abbey, set in lush surroundings and crossed by a little stream. The first community settled here, close to the spring, in 1096 and adopted the Augustinian rule. Construction of the abbey began in 1129 and it prospered until the Hundred Years War when the English took it over and turned it into a garrison. They were chased out by du Guesclin (*see p. 109*), but there was another hiatus during the Wars of Religion in the 16th century. The abbey took off again spiritually and physically during the time of Abbot Alain de Solminihac in the 17th century. Only the lower part of the church with a series of wall arches is 12th-century; above are Gothic-shaped windows of the 17th century. Over the crossing is a square three-tier Romanesque belfry, the first two levels decorated with arches and openings but the third consisting only of short blocks supporting a roof. The 12th-century entry door has decorative mouldings and a cornice supports an arcaded gallery in the manner of the Saintonge, with arcades and a small window. Next to the church are the remaining buildings of the abbey with the bare bones of the cloister and a Gothic church.

The pure Romanesque parish Church of St-Jean, on the other side of the road, has a lamb and cross on the west façade.

Further to the north of Périgueux, a priory was founded at **Merlande**, by monks of Chancelade in the 12th century and the chapel and prior's lodgings were restored in the 20th century. The chapel had two domes but one was destroyed in 1170 and replaced with a barrel vault, and it was fortified in the 16th century. The oldest part is the choir, decorated with arcades on small columns supporting magnificent Romanesque capitals with monsters, beasts and foliage.

The **Château des Bories** (*guided visits July–Sept 10–12 & 2–7; T: 05 53 06 00 01*), just northeast of Périgueux near Antonne, is a typical Périgordian structure begun in the late 15th century, combining medieval defensive elements with Renaissance luxury; it is privately owned. The interior is particularly splendid with a monumental stone staircase in the square tower leading to a private oratory, a guardroom vaulted from a central column, and a magnificent vaulted Gothic kitchen. The main gallery, furnished in Louis XIII style, has a fine Renaissance fireplace and Flemish tapestry, and there is a terrace overlooking the Isle.

THE ISLE VALLEY TO THE SOUTHWEST

Downstream from Périgueux to the southwest, the Isle Valley broadens out towards the confluence with the Dronne, with fertile basins between the Forêt de la Double to the north and the Forêt du Landais to the south. **St-Astier** has an industrial past in lime extraction, cement and white limestone. Its old underground quarries are open in summer (*T: 05 53 54 13 84*). The square belfry (16th century) of the Romanesque church dominates the small community and some good Renaissance houses surround it. In the 11th century a chapel was built above the primitive sanctuary of St-Astier, the massive piers were erected in the 12th century to carry the domes, and there were later additions in the 15th and 16th centuries.

Mussidan has had its quota of troubles. It was destroyed by Vikings in 849; it was an English stronghold during the Hundred Years War; took up the Reformation and incurred the wrath of the Catholics several times during the Religious Wars; and it was the theatre of a battle between the Resistance and German troops on 11th June 1944, resulting in the execution of 52 locals.

Southeast of Mussidan the **Château de Montréal** (*guided visits, July–Sept 2.30–6.30; T: 05 53 81 11 03*), is a hilltop castle built to stand guard over the road between Périgueux and Bordeaux. It combines parts of a medieval feudal castle and more elegant 16th-century Italianate elements, with windows framed between columns and sculpted medallions. This is the Montréal which gave its name to the Canadian city: Claude de Pontbriand, lord of Montréal, was on the banks of the St Laurence with the city's founder, Jacques Cartier, on that auspicious day in 1535.

THE AUVÉZÈRE & HAUTEFORT

The Auvézère river makes its tortuous way into the northeast of the Dordogne and flows southwest to join with the Isle about 10km east of Périgueux. There are picturesque drives or walks in the section between Sevignac-Lédrier, with a 15th-century forge, and Cherveix-Cubas which has a *lanterne des morts* in the cemetery similar to others in the region (*see p. 147*).

Château d'Hautefort

Guided visits daily, July–Aug 9.30–7; April–June 10–12 & 2–6; Sept 10–12 & 2–6, Oct–Nov, Feb–March 2–6, closed January; T: 05 53 50 51 23.

The château is a grand affair set on a prominence (231m), with tall slate roofs reminiscent of a Loire château. All around are commanding views and the terraces are planted with the most formal, and some of the most famous, of French parterres.

The Marquis of Hautefort, Jacques-François, though a miserly man, instructed the architect Nicolas Rambourg to build the present elegant residence (1630–70) in honour of his sister, Marie, unrequited favourite of Louis XIII. This courtly love was appropriate to Hautefort whose owners in the 12th century had been Constantin de Born and his troubadour brother Bertran, who dedicated verses to Eleanor of Aquitaine (*see p. 12*). Bertran managed to seize the estates of Hautefort from his elder brother, Constantin, who lodged his grievances with the Governor of Aquitaine, Richard the Lionheart. Bertran deployed his considerable skills in writing acerbic propagandist songs or *sirventes* to stir up the locals against Richard and consequently lost the château. He went on to influence Richard's elder brother, the young king, Henry Court Mantel (*see p. 167*) who died in 1183, eliciting an eloquent lament from Bertran, convincing Henry II to restore Hautefort to him. Bertran was eventually reconciled with Richard whom he nicknamed *Oc et No* (Yea and Nay), reflecting Richard's single-mindedness (the sobriquet *Coeur de Lion* only came into use later) but the unruly troubadour was relegated to Inferno by Dante.

In 1588 the fortress was modified and in the 17th century the lords of Hautefort were elevated to the title of *marquis*. Hautefort passed to the Damas family and was finally sold in the 19th century. Eugène Le Roy (*see p. 140*), author of *Jacquou le Croquant* (1899), a tale of the hardship of peasant life in the 17th century, was born here. In 1929 the property was acquired and renovated by the Baron and Baroness de Bastard, but in 1968 much of it was gutted by fire; the by-then widowed Baroness, undeterred, restored the building.

The visit to the interior is guided but the precisely trimmed box and yews of the formal gardens can be visited independently, as can the *parc à l'anglaise* to the west. The château is preceded by a wide esplanade and a drawbridge over the ditch, and the main entrance leads through a low building to the *cour d'honneur* with the main block to the north and open to the south. At the end of each of the flanking wings is a round tower with pepper-pot roof, the southeast tower 15th-century, the other a copy of 1670. The main residence has steep slate roofs, four-square windows and dormers with rounded pediments. At ground level is a gallery running the length of the building with basket-handle arches alternating with narrow rectangular bays, flanked by two forward pavilions with segmented domes and lanterns.

In the village, the large cruciform and domed Hospice d'Hautefort shelters the Musée de la Médecine (*open June–Sept 10–7, April and May 10–12 & 2–6 closed Tues; other times by appointment; T: 05 53 51 62 98*). The hospice was founded in 1680 to give shelter to 11 old men, 11 boys and 11 young women.

THE ISLE VALLEY TO THE NORTHEAST

In the extreme northeast corner of the Périgord Blanc, a remote and wooded area, is Jumilhac-le-Grand, a small town dominating the river. The **Château de Jumilhac** (*guided visits July–mid-Sept 10–7, July–Aug, Tues, Thur 9–11.30 pm, June, Sept, Tues 9–11.30 pm; mid-March–May, Oct–mid-Nov, weekends and holidays 2–6.30; T: 05 53 52 42 97*), sprouts towers and turrets of all sizes with tall slate roofs, their verticality emphasised by decorative spiky finials. The original medieval castle was subsumed in the present 16th-century version by Antoine Chapelle, the very wealthy Master of the King's Forges who was ennobled by Henri IV, hence the ironwork display on the roofs. The château comprises two large 17th-century wings enclosing a courtyard, and inside a large staircase leads to an immense, panelled room and chimney-piece with allegorical carvings. The church with an octagonal belfry was formerly the private chapel of the château. The Musée d'Or in the castle cellars (*open mid-June–mid-Sept daily 10.30–12.30 & 2.30–6.30; mid-Sept–mid-June, Sun and holidays 3–6; closed Dec–Mar; T: 05 53 52 55 43*), has a display pertaining to the Gallo-Roman mines at Fouilloux.

Thiviers is a dynamic little market town with some picturesque old streets leading to the market square. Above the church entrance is the date 1515, and while the nave is rib vaulted (14th century) the capitals indicate its Romanesque origins and that it was once domed. There is also later sculpture. Behind the church is an old, but heavily restored, fortified house, the former presbytery, and the château which has been much remodelled.

Excideuil on the valley of La Loue, is well known for its winter truffle market. The town developed at a strategic point on the old Périgord–Limousin road and vertiginous twin keeps are a reminder of the fortress built by the Viscounts of Limoges. Much renovated, the church is endowed with a Flamboyant porch thanks to Anne de Brétagne (daughter of François II, and wife of Charles VIII and Louis XII), a *pietà* and retable (both 17th century), and a statue of Maréchal Bugeaud, who conquered Algeria in the mid-19th century and donated a fountain to the town after his return. In Preyssac d'Excideuil there is a Romanesque church with an interesting belfry-gable.

Sorges, northeast of Périgueux, is on the map mainly for its status as an *étape gastronomique*. No detail in connection with the 'black diamond' is overlooked at the Ecomusée de la truffe (*open July, Aug daily 9.30–12.30 & 2–7; Sept–June, Tues–Sun 10–12 & 2–5, closed Mon; T: 05 53 05 90 11*). Sorges has a Romanesque church whose domes were rebuilt in the 16th century when a fine Renaissance doorway was added.

PÉRIGORD POURPRE

The Purple Périgord is the southwestern section of the *département* of the Dordogne. The colour coding is contrived here, having no traditional basis, being justified by the purply-red wines of Bergerac. The sweet wine of Monbazillac, on the other hand, is golden in colour. The vineyards are on both banks of the Dordogne around Bergerac; towards the Bordelais, mainly on the north.

BERGERAC

Bergerac, capital of Périgord until the Revolution, has always benefited from its position on the banks of the Dordogne. A great effort has been made to enhance the picturesque old quarters on the sloping north bank of the river where there are reminders of the town's former importance as a river port. The majority of the older buildings date from after the Wars of Religion. Wine is a flourishing industry in the region. It also a major tobacco producing area with a research laboratory, the Institut du Tabac, near Bergerac. The connection between the town and Edmond Rostand's Cyrano is extremely tenuous but has proved enduring.

HISTORY OF BERGERAC

By the end of the 12th century, the town already had the advantage of a bridge to link upper Périgord with the Bordelais. By the beginning of the 14th century, the town was protected by a brick enclosure and was at its most prosperous. Then from 1345 the full fury of the Anglo-French conflict reverberated through the town, bringing it three times under English control and three times under French. During the subsequent period of peace Bergerac again flourished but, around 1546, as part of the Kingdom of Navarre, it became solidly Protestant and another ten years of struggle ensued. In 1577 Bergerac had its own Peace Treaty, signed by Henri of Navarre and representatives of Henri III. The reign of Henri IV (1589–1610) and the Edict of Nantes (1598) allowed freedom of worship to Calvinists in denominated areas, but Louis XIII's army took the town in 1620 and ordered the demolition of the ramparts. Some Calvinists stayed on until 1681, but the Revocation of the Edict of Nantes resulted in the loss in 1685 of many rich merchants and tradesmen to England and Holland.

The town centre

The old town centre is Place de Dr Cayla with the Protestant Temple (19th century). The **Cloître des Récollets**, was rebuilt in the 17th century on a 12th-century base. This was taken over by the Pères Recollets in 1630: they established a mission in Bergerac at the wish of Louis XIII with the express aim of bringing locals back to the

Roman Catholic faith, sometimes by force. Arranged around a small, galleried court-yard it now houses the Maison des Vins de Bergerac (*open June–Aug 10–7; rest of year 10–1 & 2–6; closed Mon and Jan; T: 05 53 63 57 55*), with information and exhibitions concerning the *vignoble bergeracois* and its 12 *appellations*.

The rectangular Place de la Myrpe is surrounded by pretty 17th- and 18th-century houses, some timber and brick, and is dominated by the statue of Cyrano de Bergerac by Dorillac and Varoqueaux. The real Savinien Cyrano (1619–55), who was the basis for Rostand's character, was born in Paris, became a musketeer, adopted Gascony as his *pays*, and took the name Bergerac. He was a great duellist and also a poet, but the truth of his origins was only established in the early 20th century.

The Musée Régional de la Tonnellerie et Batellerie (*open 10–12 & 2–5.30, Sun 2.30-6.30; closed Sat, Mon; T: 05 53 57 80 92*) at the end of the square in a timbered 18th-century building which had been a sailors' tavern, describes the formerly very important local activity of river shipping, with models and tools. Bergerac was once one of the most important inland ports on the Dordogne.

In the small streets to the east, on Rue de l'Ancien Pont, is the Maison Peyrarède (1604), which has a small suspended watchtower on the angle. In the 17th century there were small shops and stabling at street level. Installed here is the Musée du Tabac (*open Tues–Fri 10–12 & 2–6; closed Sun, Mon and holidays; T: 05 53 63 04 13*), which has a remarkable collection of pipes and other objects associated with tobacco worldwide.

North from Place du Dr Cayla, on Rue des Fontaines, in the Maison Doublet Henri of Navarre and representatives of King Henri III met in 1577 to negotiate a ceasefire during the Wars of Religion. Framing Rue St-James off to the left are some fine bourgeois houses (17th–18th centuries), and the Font-Peyre, a fountain which ran with wine during festivities when King Charles IX visited the town in August 1565.

Facing the renovated Place Pélissière is the church of St-Jacques, which developed from a modest chapel in the 12th century to an important urban church in the 14th. Meetings were held here during the Hundred Years War. Damaged then and in the 16th century, it was almost completely rebuilt in the next century when the Catholics moved back.

Below the church, installed in the Catholic Mission of 1680, the Musée d'Art Sacré, (*open July, Aug, Tues–Sun 3.30–6, closed Mon; rest of year Sun only 3.30–6; T: 05 53 63 40 22*) has 17th–18th-century Counter-Reformation pieces.

The *marché couvert* (1885), is a metal structure built on the site of a Protestant church demolished in 1682. Behind it is the 15th-century Maison Charles IX, where the king stayed with his mother, Catherine de Médicis, in 1565. The Grand'Rue arrives at Rue de la Résistance and the newer part of town. Opposite is the neo-Gothic church of Notre-Dame (1856–65), built to initial plans by Viollet-le-Duc (*see p. 95*) and completed by Abadie (*see p. 112*).

ENVIRONS OF BERGERAC

Château de Tiregand
Open by appointment only: T: 05 53 23 21 08.
The Château de Tiregand stands at the heart of the Pécharmant vinyards east of Bergerac, on the north bank of the Dordogne (the Bergeracois) around Creysse on the D660. The château, rebuilt in the 17th century, and substantially altered many times since, belongs to the Saint-Exupéry family (*see p. 583*). It is set among working vineyards and produces a grand cru. The château, gardens and *chais* (wine cellars) can be visited, and tastings arranged.

Château de Monbazillac
Open June-Sept 10–7.30; rest of the year 10–12 & 2–6; April 10-12 & 2-6; closed Jan; T: 05 53 63 65 00/05 53 61 52 52.
High on a cliff facing towards Bergerac, the chateau stands at the end of an alley of vines and commands a sea of vineyards. The site offers both a visit to the château and

an opportunity for a *dégustation* in the smart Cave Coopérative. The property has 3000 hectares of vines, the majority (2,700 hectares) for whites—Sémillon, Sauvignon and Muscadet. It gives its name to the sweet, strong yellow wine for which it is renowned, which is produced from grapes which are heavy in sugar and left on the vine until they arrive at a state of *pourriture noble* (noble rot) and produce a fungus, *botrytis cinerea*.

The château dates from the mid-16th century and is a handsome combination of military might and domestic elegance, with sturdy angle towers, decorative machicolations, steep russet roofs and four-square windows. It was a Protestant stronghold but survived the Civil Wars and the Revolution virtually unscathed. The visit takes you to three levels. In the basement kitchens is a display of bottles and a wine museum. The ground floor combines a little local ethnology with the history of local Protestantism, and rooms furnished with rustic 17th-century furniture. On the level above is some extraordinary 19th-century neo-Baroque dining-room furniture, bedrooms and old photographs of about 100 Périgordian châteaux.

Cross-country to the west of Monbazillac (D17) is the Moulin de Malfourat, a group of wrecked windmills on a high ridge.

THE WINES OF BERGERAC

The Bergerac region is promoted as the 'Other Great Vineyard of Aquitaine', geographically close to and historically competing with Bordeaux. The wine has been much appreciated in the past (and the present) by the English, and from the 14th century a special mark of distinction was stamped on its barrels. During the Reformation, the Netherlands was the main customer for Bergerac wine and it is now exported throughout the world. There are 12 AOCs, and 12,000 hectares under cultivation, with a production of 52 per cent red and 48 per cent white.

The reds and rosés of Bergerac, supple and fruity, are produced from Cabernet Sauvignon, Cabernet Franc, Merlot Noir, Côt or Malbec; the dry whites are a blend of Sémillon, Sauvignon, Muscadelle, Ondenc and Chenin Blanc. Rosette is a sweet and subtle white wine, slightly straw-coloured. The Côtes-de-Bergerac produce reds, using the same grape varieties as the Bergerac red, and whites, divided between *demi-sec*, *moelleux* (mellow) and *doux*. Montravel is a dry white, Haut Montravel is mœlleux and Saussignac is another fruity sweet white. Monbazillac is probably the best known of the heavy *blancs liquoreux*, blending Sémillon, Sauvignon and Muscadelle which are harvested late and by hand; individual grapes are selected when they reach the correct degree of noble rot (*see above*). Pécharmant is the most famous of the reds, its distinctive taste coming from the sand and gravel of the banks of the Dordogne which cover a deep layer of ferruginous clay, called Tran. The Maison des Vins at Bergerac (*see p. 121*) supplies information on wines, tastings and routes.

WEST ALONG THE DORDOGNE

The section of the Dordogne between Gardonne and Castillon-la-Bataille marks the border between the Gironde and the Périgord. On the river banks, in countryside not totally made over to vines, is the busy commercial town of **Ste-Foy-la-Grande**. Ste-Foy has one of the best markets in the region as well as two annual fairs in March and November. This *bastide* was built in 1255 at the orders of Alphonse de Poitiers around an existing Benedictine monastery, dedicated to Ste Foy (St Faith; *see p. 218*). It became an important Protestant centre of erudite humanism where Henry of Navarre sought refuge in 1576. In the middle of the main square, Place Gambetta, is the 18th-century *Mairie* and around it some fairly attractive arcaded houses. The older houses are 16th- or 17th-century, including the tourist office. Rue Pasteur leads to the banks of the Dordogne where once there was a small harbour. In Rue des Frères-Reclus are some interesting houses, notably no. 27, and the church is a 19th-century remodelling of a succession of churches (13th and 17th centuries).

The village of **Montcaret** shelters the remains of a 1st- and 4th-century Gallo-Roman villa (*open daily July–Aug 9.30–1 & 2–6; rest of the year 10–12.30 & 2–4.30; T: 05 53 58 50 18*). The site was excavated in 1922–39, after the village cemetery was relocated. The remains are well conserved, partly sheltered and partly in the open, on both sides of the road and around the church that was built over the site. The discoveries include some particularly fine mosaics, and reception rooms with hypocausts have been exposed although the peristyle was partly obliterated by the church. Parts of some *thermae* (bath houses) can be seen to the south of church, with the *frigidarium* mosaic visible. Built in Graeco-Roman style, the villa at Montcaret is similar to those at Montmaurin (*see p. 547*) and Plassac (*see p. 69*). It was probably abandoned in the 6th century, and there is a leap of five centuries to the Romanesque church, which incorporates some Roman elements on the exterior. Inside there are some good capitals, some of them recycled Gallo-Roman and some 11th-century, one of which shows Daniel in the Lions' Den.

Nearby at St-Michel-de-Montaigne on the edge of the Périgord is the birthplace of Michel Eyquem de Montaigne, humanist and philosopher. The château cannot be visited but Montaigne's tower can, as can the gardens with their wonderful views.

Montaigne's Tower

Guided visits July–Aug 10–6.30; rest of the year 10–12 & 20–6.30, closed Tues; closed Jan to mid-Feb; T: 05 53 58 63 93.

The ancestral home was burned to the ground in 1885 and has been rebuilt in Renaissance style. Happily, the tower, standing apart, was spared and has remained shrine-like since Montaigne's time. On the ground floor is a small chapel, and on the floor above a bedroom linked to the chapel by a recess. On the top floor is the famous library, where the ceiling beams are decorated with maxims chosen by Montaigne to encourage meditation on the human condition. Several of Montaigne's family were buried in the village, but Montaigne himself is not.

MICHEL DE MONTAIGNE (1533–92)

Michel Eyquem took the name of his birthplace. He had a Classical education and then went into law. While a member of the *parlement* in Bordeaux he established a long and enduring friendship with the writer Etienne de la Boétie (*see p.146*). Elected mayor of Bordeaux in 1581, Montaigne held office for four years. Strongly attached to his native Périgord, in 1570 he began his best-known work, *Essais*, an extraordinarily frank and modern discussion of the difficulties inherent in the search for truth, justice and tolerance, published in Bordeaux in 1580. His travels across Europe in 1580–81 were the source of his *Journal*, which served to confirm his philosophy. At the age of 52 he gave up his official duties to dedicate himself entirely to study and meditation in his library in the tower at Montaigne. He continued to add to the *Essais* so that by 1588 it comprised three volumes. He judged that the art of living should be based on prudent wisdom and inspired by good sense and tolerance.

PRACTICAL INFORMATION

GETTING AROUND

• **By train:** Paris Austerlitz to Périgueux via Limoges. Bordeaux to Périgueux.
Bordeaux–Bergerac–Lalinde–Le Buisson–Sarlat.
Périgueux–Coutras–Mussidan–Neuvic–Les Ezies–Le Bugue–Villefranche-en-Périgord–Penne–Mussidan.
• **By bus:** Occasional buses Périgueux–Sarlat and Périgueux–Angoulême

TOURIST INFORMATION

Bourdeilles Pl. des Tilleuls, T: 05 53 03 42 96, www.bourdeilles.com
Bergerac 97 Rue Neuve d'Argenson, T: 05 53 57 03 11, www.bergerac-tourisme.com
Brantôme Abbey, T: 05 53 05 80 52, www.ville-brantome.fr
Excideuil Pl. du Château, T: 05 53 62 95 56, syndicat.initiative.excideuil@wanadoo.fr
Mareuil 4 Rue des Ecoles, T: 05 53 60 99 85, si.mareuil@perigord.tm.fr
Mussidan Pl. de la République, BP32, T: 05 53 81 73 87, www.chez.com/otmussidan
Nontron Rue de Verdun, T: 05 53 56 25 50, ot.nontron@wanadoo.fr
Périgueux 26 Pl. Francheville, T: 05 53 53 10 63, www.ville-perigueux.fr
Ribérac Pl. de Gaulle, T: 05 53 90 03 10, ot.riberac@perigord.tm.fr
St-Astier Pl. de la République, T: 05 53 54 13 85, www.ville-st-astier.fr
Ste-Foy-la-Grande 102 Rue de la République, T: 05 57 46 03 00, www.paysfoyen.com

St-Jean-de-Côle Pl. du Château, T: 05 53 62 14 15, www.ville-saint-jean-de-cole.fr
Thiviers Pl. du Maréchal Foch, T: 05 53 55 12 50, ot.thiviers@wanadoo.fr
Verteillac Ave d'Aquitaine, T: 05 53 90 37 78, si-verteillac@perigord.tm.fr

ACCOMMODATION & RESTAURANTS

Antonne-et-Trigonant
€€ **Hôtel/Restaurant L'Ecluse**. A largish hotel with a long veranda and 46 rooms; close to Perigueux but in a quiet position in extensive grounds next to the river. The cooking is an excellent example of what the Périgord can offer and the pretty restaurant has garden views. Rte de Limoges, T: 05 53 06 00 04, www.ecluse-perigord.com

Bergerac
€€ **Hôtel/Restaurant Bordeaux**. An authentic and welcoming oasis in the town, with a pool. Calm and good value. Hotel since 1855, it has always had a good reputation for its food and offers adventurous versions of local recipes. 38 Pl. Gambetta, T: 05 53 57 12 83 www.hotel-bordeaux-bergerac.com
€€ **Château de Lespinassat**. Marion and Christian Cales recently opened a select hotel in the former home of the Viscount of Monbazillac, an 18th-century château which stands on a terrace overlooking a lake. There is a discreet pool and a billiard room. Evening meals can be ordered in advance. Rte. d'Agen, T: 05 53 74 84 11
€€ **Chambres d'hôtes Château les Farcies du Pech**. An 18th-century wine-producing property owned by the Dubard family in the Pécharmant vineyards, has 5 guest rooms which are a real home-from-home experience (one a family room), with high quality décor, comfort and bathrooms. Marie Dubard serves breakfast in her picturesque kitchen or in the garden. Hameau de Pécharmant, T: 05 53 82 48 31, www.chambre-hote-bergerac.com

Bourdeilles
€ **Hostellerie Les Griffons**. This is a gorgeous spot and the welcome from Lucille and Bernard Lebrun is genuine. Set in a beautiful 16th-century building below the castle and next to the Dronne, it has a pretty garden terrace and the 10 rooms are charming, with rustic beams, others with views of the river and old mill. The food served is a light version of Perigordian cuisine; menus around €22–38. Le Bourg, T: 05 53 45 45 35, www.griffons.fr

Brantôme
€€€ **Hôtel/Restaurant Moulin de l'Abbaye**. The hotel comprises three stunningly picturesque ancient buildings, the Moulin de l'Abbaye, the Maison du Meunier, and the Maison de l'Abbé, all with views of the river and in the old town, each slightly different in character but all with delightful rooms. The seriously good food in the restaurant is the domain of experienced chef Bernard Villain and inventive pastry chef Pierre Hamard. Also a bistrot Au Fil de l'Eau, and rôtisserie, Au Fil du Temps. 1 Rte de Bourdeilles, T: 05 53 05 80 22, www.moulinabbaye.com
€€ **Domaine de la Roseraie**. A 300-year-old wine chartreuse prettily renovated and watched over by Denis and Eveylne, is surrounded by lovely gardens where there is a pool. 10 peaceful rooms of varying sizes. The dining room is extremely pretty: menus 42€ and 58€.

Route d'Angouleme, T: 05 53 05 84 74, www.domaine-la-roseraie.com

Champagnac de Belair

€€€ **Hôtel/Restaurant Le Moulin du Roc**. A 17th-century walnut oil mill has been transformed into a luxury hotel and restaurant by Alain and Maryse Gardillou. It is an idyllic and peaceful setting with a pretty garden and the 14 lovely rooms in three different parts of the mill overlooking the millstream. Alain's cooking is based on excellent local and home-grown produce and served in two dining rooms or on the terrace. There are various set menus. T: 05.53.02.86.00, www.moulinduroc.com

Chancelade/Périgueux

€€€ **Hôtel/Restaurant Château des Reynats and Restaurant**. A romantic 19th-century mansion with an orangery, set in a park with ancient trees and swimming pool. The 24 bedrooms and suites are agreeably spacious. The l'Oison restaurant has earned a Michelin rosette for its inventive, light and tasty cooking, especially seafood. Av. des Reynats, T: 05 53 03 53 59, www.chateau-hotel-perigord.com

Monbazillac

€€ **Restaurant La Tour des Vents.** ■ The cooking here is imaginative and not too heavy; in fact it is impossible to refuse a bite. Specialities include *Foie Gras de Canard en Pot au Feu* and *Duo de Bar et Homard* (white fish and lobster). The décor is unobtrusive, and the setting overlooking the vineyards of Monbazillac is lovely. It also has a terrace. Moulin de Malfourat, T: 05 53 58 30 10, www.tourdesvents.com

Périgueux

€€ **Hôtel/Restaurant Le Talleyrand-Perigord**. This is a traditional hotel of great charm in the heart of the old town, where the welcome is warm and friendly. There are 41 good bedrooms and a terrace overlooking the garden. 21 Pl. Francheville, T: 05 53 06 06 84, www.hoteltalleyrand.com

€€ **Le Clos Saint Front**. An elegant setting in a 15th-century building in the centre of the old town, there is also the added attraction of a delightful shady garden. The food is gastronomic and inventive. Various menus between €12 or €19 at midday, and €50. 5 Rue de la Vertu, T: 05 53 46 78 58.

€€ **Aux Berges de l'Isle**. This restaurant is the only one to benefit from a marvellous view across the river towards the cathedral. Menus are from €12.50 and the food served is traditional Périgordian, using duck and foie gras, wine sauces. 2 Rue Pierre-Magne, T: 05 53 09 51 50.

€ **L'Epicurien**. In the old quarter of Perigueux, this little restaurant has a rustic and welcoming atmosphere. The cooking varies according to the season and the specialities are based on duck foie gras: menus range from 15€ at midday to 35€. 1 Rue du Conseil, T: 05 53 09 88 04.

€ **Le Grain de Sel**. Situated in the central pedestrian area this is a pleasant and uncomplicated restaurant with reasonable priced menus (€11–14 at lunch, €18–27). The cooking is traditional regional based on the availability of produce at the market. 7 Rue Farges, T: 05 53 53 45 22.

Razac-sur-l'Isle

€€ **Hôtel/Restaurant Château de Lalande**. One of the Dordogne's many châteaux has become a splendid hotel run by Martie Rijhboek and Klaas

Touwen. It sits in 3 hectares of wooded park with a pool. The 15 bedrooms and 3 suites are each different with personalised touches, and the food served is a blend from all regions of France. 57 rte. de St-Astier, T: 05 53 54 52 30, www.chateau-lalande-perigord.com

Saussignac

€ **Chambres d'hôtes Domaine de la Queyssie**. In the vineyards west of Monbazillac the 18th-century farmhouse recently opened as a B&B with 4 rooms full of character and with independent entrance. *Table d'hôtes* is available on request taken *al fresco* in summer, and there is a lovely pool. T: 05 53 27 39 37, www.laqueyssie.com

Sourzac

€€ **Hôtel le Chaufourg**. An exceptionally lovely spot, the hotel stands in a loop in the Isle between Perigueux and St-Emilion, utterly romantic and original. Georges Dambier has transformed his birthplace into his ideal hotel. Delightful. T: 05 53 81 01 56, www.lechaufourg.com

Verteillac

€ **Chambres d'hôtes Domaine de Teinteillac**. Catherine and Jean-Yves Pin's ancient château between Mareuil and Riberac is surrounded by 150 hectares of land where goats and ducks are raised organically. Bourg des Maisons, T: 05.53.35.50.01, www.teinteillac.com

MARKET DAYS

Bergerac Wednesday and Saturday; covered market every day
Brantôme Friday; farmers market Tuesday
Périgueux Daily Place du Coderc; Wednesday, Saturday, Pl. de la Clautre/Pl. de l'Hôtel de Ville/Pl. du Coderc; Nov-March, Wednesday, Saturday, Truffle market; July-Aug Occasional evening markets
Ste-Foy-la-Grande Saturday

FESTIVALS & EVENTS

May: *Fête de St-Sicaire*, traditional fair, Brantôme
July: *Le Table de Cyrano*, annual food and wine festival, Bergerac
Itinéraire Baroque en Périgord Vert, Baroque choral and instrumental music over several days in exceptional locations in the region, T: 05 53 90 05 13
Festival Macadam Jazz, jazz in the streets Périgueux
Balades aux flambeaux/Visites nocturnes insolites, evening walks by torchlight in Périgueux
Truffe d'argent/Trophée Radio France, Radio France Silver truffle Award,
Musitinéraire, all types of music in all types of venues, and an evening market on the quays with street music, Ste-Foy-la-Grande
August: *MIMOS, Festival International du Mime*, Festival of contemporary mime, Périgueux, T: 05 53 53 18 71
MINOP, Musiques de la Nouvelle Orléans, New Orleans-style music Périgueux, T: 05 53 53 66 11
September: *Sinfonia en Périgord*, Festival of Renaissance and Baroque, choral and instrumental, at selected sites in and around Périgueux, T: 05 53 04 78 49

PÉRIGORD NOIR

Périgord Noir is a rather misleading description of this part of the Dordogne. It derives from its woodland, especially the pine and juniper and other scrub but also the dark bark of the small variety of oak found here, which loses its leaves in spring. At the beginning of the 19th century, much of this area (with the exception of the Dordogne Valley) was still covered in dense forests. In the summer especially, it is anything but black.

THE VÉZÈRE VALLEY

The southeast corner of the Dordogne has the greatest intensity of sites and monuments in the *département*, with a remarkable concentration of prehistoric caves and rock shelters, castles and *bastides* along the major river valleys. In the pretty and sometimes spectacular valley of the Vézère, remarkable overhanging rocks and cliffs provided prehistoric man with a profusion of *abris*. The porous limestone also contains numerous *grottes* and *gouffres*, some adorned by early man, some fascinating for their mineral concretions and formations. A quantity of archaeological sites have offered up *gisements* (layers of finds). Many of the 200 or so prehistoric sites along the Vézère (which are often open to the public) are clustered around the small village of Les Eyzies-de-Tayac, billed as *Capitale Mondiale de la Préhistoire* and home to the recently expanded Musée National de Préhistoire.

LES EYZIES-DE-TAYAC

Bounded on one side by the Vézère, the village (*pictured on p. 132*) creeps up the looming cliff which runs parallel to the river. Small troglodyte buildings and caves are visible on the cliff face, as well as the 16th-century Château des Eyzies built by the Barons of Beynac, which is now part of the Musée de Préhistoire. On the high terrace stands a fanciful sculpture (1930) of Neanderthal man, by Paul Dardé. It was at Les Eyzies in 1868, at the Abri de Cro-Magnon, that the first ever remains of *Homo sapiens sapiens* were discovered. The site was near the hotel of the same name behind the station, now with a commemorative plaque. Buried in a grave of the Aurignacian period were five skeletons, one of a man who had reached the then-remarkable age of 50.

Musée National de Préhistoire
Open July, Aug 9.30–6.30; June, Sept 9.30–6, closed Tues; Oct-May 9.30–12.30 & 2–5.50, closed Tues; T: 05 53 06 45 45.
The museum as originally conceived in 1913 by the prehistorian Denis Peyrony (1869-1954) was housed in the medieval castle, which itself clings to a rock shelter

PREHISTORY IN SOUTHWEST FRANCE

The limestone of southwest France is riddled with caves and galleries formed by natural fissures and erosion, and by underground rivers, millions of years ago. Surface rivers carved their way through the landscape, creating deep gorges and exposing high cliffs pitted with caves. The south-facing cliffs, especially along the rivers Vézère, Isle, Dordogne and Garonne, provided the ideal habitat for early man (500,000–10,000 BP) who built rudimentary protection with branches and skins and chose to live in the shelter of a south-facing rock face—an overhanging cliff or the opening of a cave—and rarely inside caves, which were dark, unwelcoming and soon filled with smoke.

Evidence of the existence of *Homo erectus* in Périgord was initially discovered at three sites. La Micoque, close to Les Eyzies, produced finds in the late 19th century which identified a stone industry characterised by the bifacial tool (a type of flint hand axe) and described as Acheulian, although no human remains of this period were discovered in Périgord. The Mousterian culture, identified at Le Moustier, with a more diverse stone industry than their predecessors, is found in a wide area of Périgord and is associated with Neanderthals (*Homo sapiens neandertalensis*), who buried their dead and surrounded or covered the remains with stones. The first Cro-Magnon remains (*Homo sapiens sapiens*), dating from the Upper Palaeolithic period, were named after the Cro-Magnon rock shelter at Les Eyzies-de-Tayac.

Sites in Périgord identified with the earliest Cro-Magnon culture, Aurignacian, are La Ferrassie, Castanet and Pataud. It was at this time that the climate became milder and more humid and the consequent increase in vegetation required an industry producing flint tools and thick blades, spear-points and bone implements. This culture was also notable for the first drawings and engraving, and use of colour, at Castanet and La Ferrassie (the Chauvet Cave, in the Ardèche, discovered in 1994, has proven the existence of similarly highly sophisticated paintings at quite possibly the same period in other areas). The Gravettian civilisation was widespread (sometimes referred to as Périgordian as most of its known sites are in the Périgord), and it produced more specialised flint tools, burins and straight-backed blades to fix to hunting weapons, as well as an increasing number of more recognisable figurative images on the rock face, identified at Pair-non-Pair in Gironde, Gargas, Le Pataud shelter, and the Abri du Poisson. They also produced human representations, and carvings in the round of females, or 'Venuses', including the celebrated Venus with the Horn (now in the Musée d'Aquitaine, *see p. 31*).

The Solutrean period (from Solutré, Saone-et-Loire), during a time of harsh climatic conditions, was relatively short. It was identified in 1869 and is characterised by the skilfully knapped, thin and sharp 'laurel leaf' tool, which could have served a wide variety of purposes, as well as fine engravings, reliefs and paintings, including the ibex at Abri Pataud and portable objects, such as incised stones and engraved horn. The period has also provided evidence of horse-butchery on a significant scale, a practice that continued well into the Magdalenian period. The hunting of reindeer seems to have been undertaken only between November and May. A huge area at Laugerie-Haute was occupied, where 42 strata and levels of occupation have been revealed. A number of decorated rock shelters of this period include Le Fourneau-du-Diable, near Bourdeilles, from which comes a superb sculpted block with relief images of aurochs, now at the Musée de la Préhistoire in Les Eyzies.

Then came the Magdalenians (c. 17,000 BP), named after La Madeleine Shelter, the most remarkable phase of the Upper Palaeolithic era and the one most closely associated with cave painting. The Early Magdalenians experienced a milder climate and were found mainly in southwest France and Spain, but gradually extended over most of Europe. They invented, or at least made greater use of, the stone tallow lamp, which provided the opportunity to access deeper recesses underground and to produce imagery of the most exquisite quality, such as the famous images at Lascaux. The single archaeological level at Lascaux, which gave up artists implements, flint and bone tools, jewellery, and lamps, as well as pollens and remains of food, has been vital in understanding the Early Magdalenians. The cave was decorated by outstandingly gifted and highly practised artists for some kind of ritualistic purpose, although exactly what remains open to conjecture. The entrance to the cave was blocked soon after the paintings were made.

The Middle Magdalenian period (c. 16,000 BP–13,000 BP) is characterised by bone and reindeer antler industries. Pieces, sometimes decorated, were used as smoothing tools and needles and prototype harpoons; an increase in engravings on a variety of materials is also recorded. Cap-Blanc revealed a unique monumental parietal frieze of horses in relief. The huge number of engravings at Les Combarelles have been associated with this period, as well as magnificent examples of polychrome work, signs and other animals at Font-de-Gaume, Bernifal, and Rouffignac. At the latter a depiction of a pair of mammoths has been the main attraction since their discovery in 1956.

The Upper Magdalenian period (c. 13,000–10,000 BP), during the last cold blast of glaciation followed by increasing humidity, saw impressive examples of carved bone and ivory, the development of the harpoon and engravings as at La Madeleine cave. The names associated with the first scientific descriptions of the discoveries in several of the caves in the Perigord region are Dr Louis Capitan, Denis Peyrony and the Abbé Henri Breuil. Capitan, Professor of Prehistory at the College de France, inspired Peyrony, who founded the museum and whose friend Breuil was one of the first to examine Lascaux.

The village of Les Eyzies-de-Tayac on the Vézère, and (right) the Musée National de Préhistoire.

inhabited by Magdalenian man some 12,000 years ago. In 2004 a state-of-the-art extension opened alongside the castle. Modern techniques, enhanced layout, subtle lighting, audio-visual and interactive displays, models and clear information have modernised and clarified the layman's journey through prehistory and makes for an enlightening visit. The extra space allows previously undisplayed collections and pieces from elsewhere to be included, with more than 18,000 objects representing prehistoric cultures in Périgord from c. 350,000–c.10,000 BP. In the Entrance Hall, the emergence of man from c. 3.5 to 1.8 million years ago is explained by an anthropological chart, with casts of skeletons of the first hominids in Africa, and rudimentary tools dating from 2.5 million BP. Casts of human footprints (c. 3.5 million BP) found in Tanzania, lead to the *Puits du Temps*, a large spiral staircase which illustrates time vertically through replicas of superimposed archaeological layers of man's presence in the Vézère Valley. It begins at the foot with Vaufrey, Cénac-St-Julien, c. 470,000–70,000 BP through to Laugerie-Basse, Les Eyzies, c.14,000 BP.

First level gallery

'Au fil du temps' sets out prehistory chronologically, 350,000–10,000 BP, using a variety of objects and presentations. 'Les Clés de Lecture' then introduces methods of dating that are used. There is also a model of a Megaloceros, which lived c. 2 million–c. 10,000 BP.

The earliest signs of man in Eurasia are represented by casts of a site at Dmanisi (Georgia), of c. 1.8 million BP including bones. And a video which shows the making of a bifacial tool, the industry which arrived in Europe c. 500,000 BP. A long display-case the full-length of the gallery, representing evolution, is divided into four superimposed levels: climatic variations; species of animals which were hunted; lithic or stone cultures; and major site finds. Transverse displays provide back-up information on early man's adaptation to environmental changes illustrated by examples of the evolution of stone and bone industry. During the Lower and Middle Palaeolithic periods the first signs of human life appeared in Southwest France, culminating in the Neanderthals. They are strikingly represented by models of a man and child reconstructed from skeletons, with evidence of their way of life until their mysterious disappearance. The appearance of modern man, the Cro-Magnons, during the Upper Palaeolithic period demonstrates the variation in the manufacture of tools and other objects which identify the main cultures, Chatelperronian, Aurignacian, Gravettian, Solutrean and Magdalenian. Evolution in the animal world is illustrated by the cast of a woolly Rhinoceros (c. 30,000 BP). The gallery ends at the Epipalaeolithic period, after the end of the last glaciation in Europe (c. 10,000 BP), with an evocation of Neolithic, Mesolithic and Bronze Age cultures, and a multi-media model.

The spiral to the second level has examples of uncut stone which may be touched into order to better appreciate the physiognomy of raw materials and to provide an introduction to the palaeoethnological displays.

Second level gallery

'Modes de vie et habitat' displays the museum's items of palaeoethnological interest. Casts and originals (c. 20,000-15,000 BP), from a number of archaeological sites, provide a vividly realistic reconstruction of early man's activities both inside and outside the habitat. The section addressing the collection of raw materials, hunting and fishing shows a pirogue (c. 5,000 BP), which was the type of simple dug-out used later. The work area was where raw materials, mineral or animal, were transformed into the tools involved in that industry. The domestic and social activities which took place inside, around the hearth, is represented by the cast of a vertical archaeological layer where fires were lit over some 2,000 years. The second part of the gallery has three sections. 'Les Vivants et les morts' (the living and the dead) is given expression through domestic objects and objects of adornment, such as beads, skin, and shells. Burial places are vividly illustrated by original finds: a richly adorned 30-year-old woman, from St-Germain-la-Rivière (Gironde); a two- to four-year-old child found at La Madeleine buried with some 1,500 objects; and a third person from Roc-de-Cave (Lot), all coated in ochre. 'Expression symbolique sur bloc' has examples of carved or engraved blocks found in rock shelters, the first forms of symbolic expression which are mainly schematic, but include silhouettes of animals and feminine symbols. Engravings from deeper inside caves are both geometric and figurative. The atmosphere of *Le sanctuaire* is recreated with dim lighting and includes examples of lamps, including the celebrated original from Lascaux, decorated objects and handprints.

ENVIRONS OF LES EYZIES

Grotte de Font-de-Gaume and Les Combarelles

Guided visits only to these two sites; visitor numbers are limited, making it essential to book at least a month in advance for either site; April–Sept 9–12 & 2–6; rest of the year 10–12 & 2–5; Jan–May, Nov closed Sat; opening times can vary; T: 05 53 06 86 00. Allow for the uphill walk (10mins) to the entrance of the cave.

Font-de-Gaume should not to be missed: one of the last caves with original coloured paintings that can still be visited, it is a high point of cave art with regard to painting technique, polychromy, expressiveness and the subtle use of the contours of the rock face. The paintings, on the sides of narrow galleries some 120m long, are quite superb. They date from the Magdalenian period, and consist mainly of groups of bison (*pictured below*), with some horses and other animals. Although the work has been defaced in places, it is of extremely high quality.

Les Combarelles is a cave with engravings (no paintings) discovered by Peyrony, Abbé Breuil and Louis Capitan in 1901. The engravings are dated from the same period as Font-de-Gaume and almost 200 have been identified. They are mainly of animals, with some anthropomorphic imagery as well as signs. They record the variety of fauna of the Magdalenian period, such as rhinoceros, bears, felines and wolves, but horses, bison, aurochs, bears, reindeer, mammoths and deer are favoured. The main gallery stretches for 240m and is narrow, excavated in places to ease visitor access.

Middle Magdalenian cave paintings in the Grotte de Font-de-Gaume.

PREHISTORIC ART

Prehistoric man developed extraordinary skills in a variety of techniques of carving, drawing and painting to create images, and had an innate ability to handle the limited palette available. He was capable of creating movement and perspective, and of cleverly using the rock face to give depth and animation, which has to be imagined in the flickering light of a tallow candle. In certain caves or shelters only one technique is found, in others a combination. This work was carried out in sites which were often difficult to access, suggesting extreme dedication; the period over which the same cave was decorated might span tens of thousands of years.

The pigments for painting were limited to natural ochre—ranging from yellow to brownish red oxides obtained from iron oxides or iron ore—or black from manganese dioxide or carbon. Colour was dabbed on with the finger, with some kind of rudimentary brush made of clumps of hair or moss, or applied with a 'pencil' of coloured rock. A technique of spray-painting involved projecting pigment either directly from the mouth or through a hollow bone, sometimes using a template to create a silhouette, typically the 'negatives' of hands as found in Pech Merle and Gargas, as well as to form the outline of images such as the horses at Lascaux. The period of the Middle Magdalenian is represented by a unique carved relief frieze of horses and other animals at the Cap Blanc rock shelter and by a mass of engravings at the cave of Les Combarelles, as well as the marvellous series of painted bisons at Font-de-Gaume (all in the Dordogne).

Subjects are usually limited to certain animals (bison, mammoths, horses, aurochs, antelope), although there are occasional representations of fish or human figures. The paintings are described as 'mythograms', with no immediately decipherable symbolism although it could be said that they are generally understood as icons or visual aids where the action is implicit. They are rarely explicitly anecdotal in our eyes although just occasionally some action is depicted, such as a man and an ox at Lascaux, Villars and Le Roc de Sers, mountain goats locked in combat at Lascaux, or one deer tenderly licking another at Font de Gaume.

Musée et Site de l'Abri Pataud

Guided visits July–Aug 10–7; April–June, Sept–mid-Nov, and late Dec 10–12.30 & 2–6, closed Fri, Sat; mid-Nov–mid-Dec, Feb–March 10–12.30 & 2–5.30, closed Fri–Sun; closed Jan; T: 05 53 06 92 46.

On the edge of Eyzies, downstream from the Cro-Magnon shelter, is the Musée et Site de l'Abri Pataud. This rock shelter was inhabited by Cro-Magnon man for the entire Upper Palaeolithic period, some 15,000 years embracing the Auginacian, Gravettian and Solutrean cultures. The shelter altered over the duration of its occupation, at first

*

shallow, by 27,000 BP it was considerably enlarged by erosion, and by 20,000 BP part of the shelter had collapsed. The archaeological dig which has been preserved and is part of the visit, is of world-wide importance for prehistory and the collections from the dig are kept here in the archives. Fourteen archaeological levels, dating from c. 35,000–20,000 BP, were excavated to a depth of 9.25m over an area of 84 square metres, between 1958 and 1964, by Professor Movius, in the area where the original rock shelter had collapsed. The visit is illustrated by two films. The museum is installed in a separate prehistoric shelter, the Abri Movius, which is still intact (although closed in the 18th century) but has been altered. Nevertheless, a beautiful relief (c. 19,000 BP), of an ibex has survived on the vault. The museum contains objects found in the shelter, including those made by human production, and human remains such as bones and teeth. Explanatory panels elucidate the prehistoric way of life, with models of huts of two different periods, as well as the methods of study used by modern archaeologists. A bronze sculpture here is based on the skeleton of a 16-year-old girl found in the Abri who probably died in childbirth.

Valley of the Beune

Close to Les Combarelles is the **Grotte de Bernifal** (*open by prior booking only July, Aug 9–7; June, Sept, Oct–May 9–12 & 2–6; T: 05 53 29 66 39*), on the left bank of the Petite Beune millstream. Bernifal, discovered by Peyrony in 1902, contains both paintings and engravings of horses, bovine creatures and an ass, but the favourite animal image is the mammoth, as at Rouffignac. It also contains what are known as tectiform signs, 12 engraved and one painted, unique to the Périgord. They look a bit like houses with gable roofs but their true significance remains a mystery. The cave is made up of two main galleries and a low, narrow linking corridor. On the same side of the Vézère, a small turning onto the D48 between Les Combarelles and Bernifal runs downhill to the **Abri du Cap Blanc** (*guided visits daily July–Aug 10–7; April–Oct 10–12 & 2–6; closed Nov–March; T: 05 53 59 21 74*). A path leads through the woods to the entrance in a building that protects the site and houses a small exhibition. This is another extraordinary work, but different from most and unique in Périgord (there is something similar in the Vienne), in that it consists of a stunning high-relief frieze of monumental proportions, beautifully executed 16,000–13,000 years ago. The site was carelessly excavated in 1909, damaging the lower part of the frieze carved on the surface of a rock shelter which had been obscured by the collapse of the overhang. What remains is the upper part of six horses facing to the right, except for the most dominant one which is 2m long and facing the other way. The images are cleverly superimposed to give the impression of depth. There are also small bison and some other animals, more difficult to see, and traces of red ochre which suggest that the work was once coloured.

Near Cap Blanc, at Sireuil, are the fairytale ruins of the **Château de Commarque** (*open July–Aug 10–8; May–June, Sept 10–7; April 10–6; T: 05 53 59 00 25*) which are the remains of a fortified or 'castral' village. Watched over by a magnificent 14th-century keep, it consisted of a Romanesque chapel, a 12th-century *maison-tour* and lodgings, with a defensive wall and ditch. During the Hundred Years War it twice fell into the hands of the English and it was fought over by Protestants and Catholics in the 16th century. By the early 18th century the property had been abandoned. In 1968 a descendent of the Commarque family purchased the ruin, ensuring its conservation. Opposite is the restored Château de Laussel; about 500m from here is the Grand Abri where the Horned Venus (*see p. 32*) was discovered.

Valley of the Manaurie

Leaving Les Eyzies on the Perigueux road brings you to **Les Jardins de la Licorne** (a sign marks the turning, and the track up is very steep; *pre-arranged visits only by reservation at the Tourist Office in Les Eyzies, T: 05 53 06 97 05*). For keen gardeners, the effort of visiting this remarkable site high among fields and woodland is well rewarded. In a clearing beside a delightful house is a fanciful and enthusiastic interpretation of a medieval garden—divided into 12, very small, interconnecting areas.

A cluster of prehistoric sites can be visited around the Gorge d'Enfer on the right bank of the Vézère on the road towards Périgueux. Here the **Musée de la Spéléologie** (*open June–Sept 11–6, closed Sat*) in the fort on the Roc du Tayac, covers the underground world of caves and potholing. High above the gorge, with great views, is the entrance to two sites, the **Grotte du Grand Roc** and **Laugerie Basse** (*guided visits July–Aug 9.30–7; March–June, Oct–mid-Nov, school holidays Dec, and Feb 10–6; closed mid-Nov–Jan; T: 05 53 06 92 70*). Grand Roc contains spectacular natural formations, the most special among them being the triangular crystals. Other sites which can be visited (*advance booking only, T: 05 53 06 86 00*) include the Abri du Poisson, a small rock shelter with a rare metre-long engraving of a salmon, and the oldest, Laugerie-Haute, a vast shelter with 42 sedimentary levels, home to man for thousands of years; and also La Micoque, a *gisement* which has provided information from 450,000–100,000 BP.

Further up the little valley of the Manaurie is Rouffignac, a pleasant and tranquil village. The church, rebuilt after the Second World War, has a belfry-porch (c.1530) displaying knowledge of Renaissance architectural vocabulary and a Flamboyant nave. The village is another important name in the annals of prehistory. The **Grotte de Rouffignac** (*guided visits in French only, daily July–Aug 9–11.30 & 2–6; March–June, Sept–Oct 10–11.30 & 2–5; closed Dec–Feb; T: 05 53 05 41 71*) is a dry cave on the banks of La Binche, a tiny tributary of the Manaurie, in a flint-rich limestone hill. It is described as 'the cave of a hundred mammoths' and visits along some 10km of tunnels are made on an electric train. It was first described by Francois Belleforest in 1575 but was only fully opened to the public after the work of Romain Robert and Louis-Rene Nougier in the late 1950s. The 226 animal images and four human representations in fact include 158 mammoths (some 70 per cent of the decoration), bison, horses, ibex, and one bear, but the 11 rhinoceros are the most unusual: the representations are drawn in black or engraved and, since no tools or other objects have been found, are dated stylistically to the Magdalenian period.

North of Rouffignac are the romantic ruins of the **Château de l'Herm** (*open April–11th Nov 10–7; at other times by appointment; T: 05 53 05 46 61*). Built 1485–1512 by the Calvimont family, members of the Parlement de Bordeaux, the site is identified by two robust defensive towers looming above the dark forest of Barade. A third hexagonal tower has a richly decorated Flamboyant doorway and contains a splendid spiral staircase ending in a star vault. Bizarrely superimposed monumental fireplaces decorated with the arms of the Calvimont family have been left suspended since the floors crumbled after the château was abandoned in the 17th century.

Le Bugue

Downriver from Eyzies, Le Bugue is a busy tourist village where the Vézère loops to create a natural amphitheatre. It exploits the prehistory trail with a wide range of different tourist attractions, including the Aquarium du Périgord Noir (*June–Aug 9–7; April–May, Sept 10–6; rest of year 10–5; closed mid-Nov to mid-Feb; T: 05 53 07 10 74*), an important freshwater aquarium with over 300 pools. Nearby, caves include the **Grotte de Bara-Bahau** (*guided visits July, Aug 9.30–7; Feb–June 10-12 & 2-5.30; Sept–Dec 10–12 & 2–5; closed Jan; T: 05 53 07 27 47*), with engravings of the Magdalenian period on the roof.

East of Le Bugue is the **Grotte de St-Cirq** (*guided visits June–Sept 10–6, closed Sat; Sept–May 12–4, closed Sat; T: 05 53 07 14 37*), which also has some engravings, one entitled the *Man or Sorcerer of St-Cirq*, and a small museum. **La Ferrassie** (*visits by advance booking only T: 05 53 06 86 00*) near Savignac-de-Miremont, to the north, consists of three prehistoric sites where Neanderthal graves and Mousterian tools came to light.

High in the cliff overlooking the river, south of Le Bugue near the village of Audrix, is the **Gouffre de Proumeyssac** (*open July–Aug 9–7; May-June 9.30–6.30; March- April, Sept–Oct 9.30–12 & 2–5.30; Feb, Nov-Dec 2–5; closed Jan; T: 05 53 07 27 47*), which has no prehistoric art but some wonderful stalactites and crystalline formations. It is in a spectacular position, accessed by a man-made tunnel.

ALONG THE VÉZÈRE

La Madeleine

The left bank of the Vézère from Les Eyzies to Peyzac provides a meandering, scenic drive through Tursac, where there is a Romanesque domed church with a large belfry, and where 'scenes of prehistoric life' can be explored in a pleasant setting at the Préhistoparc (*T: 05 53 50 73 17*). Crossing the river at Tursac leads to La Madeleine, where the 15th-century chapel is dedicated to Mary Magdalene. The prehistoric rock shelter of La Madeleine (*open July–Aug 9.30–7; Sept–June 10–6; T: 05 53 46 36 88*), is an attractively remote site at the base of a cliff at the water's edge on a particularly tight loop in the river. It stretches over 50m and is up to 15m wide. As well as sheltering prehistoric man, it was probably also occupied from the end of the 9th century—during Viking raids—until some time in the 19th century. The remains of a medieval troglodyte village are visible, complete with chapel and fort. The intangible significance of the site is even more impressive, making a visit here something of a pilgrimage for prehistorians. In 1863–64 a prehistoric *gisement* was identified close to the village. Excavations at this site prompted one of the most important phases in the study of prehistory and identified the Magdalenian culture. In May 1864 the discovery of a large piece of mammoth tusk engraved with an image of the animal proved that man had indeed had the living creature before his eyes. Many other works of art were also found here. Since 1872 the term Magdalenian has been applied to the most important period associated with Palaeolithic art. The large quantity of reindeer bones through the various levels excavated indicated the main diet of prehistoric man, and hundreds of decorated objects were also found which have all now been moved to museums.

La Roque St-Christophe, Le Moustier and environs

The most spectacular of all rock shelters is at La Roque St-Christophe (*open July–Aug 10–7; May–June, Sept 10–6.30; March–April, Oct 10–6; Nov–Feb 11–5; T: 05 53 50 70 45*). It dominates the left bank of the Vézère near Peyzac-le-Moustier from a height of 80m, on a sheer cliff following the curve of the river, with five horizontal terraces and hundreds of caves which afforded protection to man from prehistoric times to the 16th century. The earliest finds date from c. 25,000 years ago, and others prove the presence of man here through the Neolithic, Bronze and Iron Ages. The fortifications were destroyed after the Reformation in 1588. Nevertheless, evidence of man's occupation is still visible and there are reconstructions to assist the imagination. Steps hewn into the rock link the fourth and fifth levels some 60m above the river, and there are tremendous views of the valley along the length of the cliff.

The village of Le Moustier on the right bank is perched on a promontory at the meeting of the Vézère and Vimont valleys. The rock shelter (*visits by advance booking only, T: 05 53 06 86 00*) within the village was explored in 1863–64 and the evidence gathered in the upper shelter led to the identification of the Mousterian period. The lower shelter yielded up a Neanderthal skeleton.

St-Léon and Thonac

As a respite from prehistory, on the other side of the river at the pretty village of St-Léon-sur-Vézère is one of the most perfect Romanesque churches in the Périgord. A dependency of the abbey of Sarlat, it was built beside the river on the site of a Gallo-Roman villa. A Benedictine abbey was first mentioned here in 1155, but the foundations to the west seem to be Gallo-Roman. It has a square belfry with arcades on two levels and a *lauze* roof. The massive but simple interior has a vaulted nave and domed crossing while the apsidal chapels are connected to the apse by narrow passageways. In the cemetery is a 14th-century chapel.

The **Château de Chabans** (*guided visits July–Aug 2–8; May–June, Sept 2–7, closed Sat; Oct Sundays only 2–5.30; T: 05 53 51 70 60*) is an elegant edifice on high ground dating from the 16th–17th centuries which has undergone considerable restoration. It contains some fine furnishings and a rare collection of 15th–20th-century stained glass. One room is dedicated to the story of the restoration of the house. The gardens and parkland can be visited, and temporary exhibitions are mounted. To the north, following the Thonac valley, is the delightful village of Fanlac, typical of the Dordogne.

Back on the river, at Thonac, the **Château de Losse** (*guided visits Easter, June–Aug 10–7; April, May, Sept 11–6; closed Oct–March; independent visits to the grounds; T: 05 53 50 80 08*), is one of the most delightful small castles in Périgord, positioned right on the water's edge. The château was originally a medieval fort with a dry moat. The building was replaced in the 16th century with a more refined residence: the main L-shaped block with four-square windows has a round angle tower, crenellated walk-ways and machicolations under a soaring red roof. The property belonged to Jean II de Losse, preceptor of Henri IV and later Governor of Limousin and Guyenne. Carved over the entrance is the inscription: *L'homme fait ce que peut, La Fortune ce que veut* (Man does as he may, Fortune as she will). Inside there are interesting Italian and Louis XIII furniture and some good Flemish and Italian tapestries.

Le Thot Espace Cro-Magnon

Open July–Aug 10–7; April–June, Sept 10–6; Oct to mid-Nov 10–12.30 & 2–6; mid-Nov–Dec and Feb–March 10–12.30 & 2–5.30; closed Mon; closed Jan; combined ticket with Lascaux II available; site T: 05 53 50 70 44; semitour T: 05 53 05 65 65.
Le Thot is both a museum and animal park that has collected examples of species that are the same as, or similar to, those found in prehistoric imagery, including Przewalski horses. Animals that no longer exist have been replicated in models. The museum gives an overall view of Palaeolithic art, shows a fascinating film and exhibition on the making of Lascaux II, and provides the opportunity to create your own cave painting.

Montignac

The busy little town of Montignac, with a ruined castle, spans the Vézère and is the gateway to the most famous painted cave of all at Lascaux. In France, the town is also well known as the home of Eugène Le Roy, the author of *Jacquou le Croquant*. His most famous book, popularised by a French TV series in the 1960s, recounts the adventurous struggles of a young peasant boy against an evil Count in the early 19th century. Eugène Le Roy died in 1907 and a museum in the town is dedicated to him, the Musée Eugene Le Roy (*open July–Aug 9–7; rest of year 9–11.15 & 2–6, out of season by appointment, closed Sun; T: 05 53 51 82 60*).

LASCAUX II

Timed and guided tours (including English, about 40 minutes) July–Aug 9–8; Sept–Oct, April–June 9.30–6.30; Oct–mid-Nov 10–12.30 & 2–6; late Dec and Feb–March 10–12.30 & 2–5.30, closed Mon; closed Jan. Confirm times on T: 05 53 51 95 03 or 05 53 05 65 65. During the summer, tickets sold at Semitour Périgord ticket office in Montignac; in winter at the site.
Lascaux, south of Montignac, is the high spot of Palaeolithic painting in France, with images of intense beauty and careful observation; but the cave paintings were nearly lost because of over-enthusiasm when the cave was first discovered (*see box opposite*). As a result, the cave has been closed to the public since 1968, and since 1983 the general public has visited Lascaux II, a brilliant replica of the original cave about 200m

from the real thing on the same wooded hill. Everything about Lascaux has been reproduced as faithfully as possible, including the temperature, which is kept to an authentic 13°C. It is entered by a flight of steps leading to an outer cement bunker. At the start, diagrams and displays describe the original layout, tools and pigments used in Lascaux 17,000 years ago. The shape and contours of the two main chambers have been precisely reproduced. The paintings are quite outstanding, both in terms of their original appearance and in their painstaking recreation by a local artist, Monique Peytral, using the same methods and materials as Palaeolithic man. Lascaux II took ten years to complete. The Hall of the Bulls is dominated by huge aurochs, galloping over the walls; one, at 5.5m long, is the largest known prehistoric painting. In the narrow Axial Gallery are some of the most haunting images of horses and deer.

The majority of animals depicted in Lascaux are horses, aurochs (horned bovines which disappeared in the Middle Ages) and deer executed in a style peculiar to Lascaux. The confidence of the line, the emotive use of colour, the manipulation of form to express movement and create depth are quite remarkable and barely surpassed in the 20th century. The best known images of Lascaux are the horses, delicate creatures similar to the Przewalski horse found in Asia, with small heads and hooves and round bellies; they are also described as 'Chinese' because of the black outline and delicate ochre wash. The majestic auroch bulls are represented in part three-quarters view, whereas most of the animals are shown in profile. The deer are delicately and gracefully drawn, the stags displaying fine antlers. The animals appear in series or in friezes interspersed with a repertoire of repetitive enigmatic signs, ranging from a four-part rectangle to stick-like or jagged lines. The ochre pigments, varying from deep maroon to yellow, are used in combination with striking outlines of black manganese dioxide.

HISTORY OF LASCAUX

The entrance to Lascaux, in a limestone hill, was blocked shortly after it was decorated by the early Magdalenians. It was not reopened until 1940 when a local boy, Marcel Ravidat, was searching for his dog. By 1948 it had been made ready for the public and the hordes who visited the limited space—the cave is only 150m long—in uncontrolled numbers, did almost irrevocable damage. Green algae built up on the surfaces and, even worse, a deposit of opaque calcite crystals formed a coating over the paintings. By 1963 it was decided that the cave should be closed and since then careful monitoring of the site has brought it back almost to its original state. The cave floor had only one archaeological level but, despite careless removal in the 1940s, rich finds including the painters' tools, charcoal and pollens narrowed down the date of the works on the walls to c. 17,000 years ago, dating them among the oldest paintings, from the Early Magdalenian period. The quality of the work suggests that the cave had an important role in ritual or as a sanctuary.

Aerial view of the fortified church (12th–13th centuries) of St Amand-de-Coly.

St Amand-de-Coly

East of Montignac, at St-Amand-de-Coly, the fortified church towering over the village is one of the finest of its kind in the region, built in pale limestone and roofed in *lauze*. Dedicated to the 4th-century hermit, Amand, there has been a monastery here since 1048, which was soon attached to the Augustinian Order. The abbey declined during the Hundred Years War and the church (12th–13th centuries) was transformed into a powerful fort with a towering west front and enormously high belfry (21m). Protected by the belfry recess is the 14th-century west door flanked by slim colonettes supporting several arches. The interior, rising towards the east, is simple but stunning, with only a few decorative features in the east. The oldest part is the chapel in the north transept, dedicated to Abbot Guillaume who is remembered in an inscription. The nave has a single-span, slightly pointed barrel vault and high windows, while the crossing is domed. Eight steps lead up to the choir with early rib vaults. The apse is flat with a harmonious arrangement of windows. Defensive elements were also added inside, such as a high walkway around the choir and transepts and hidden stairs.

Terrason-la-Villedieu

On the border of the *departements* of Dordogne and Corèze is Terrasson-la-Villedieu, at the centre of a region famous for its walnuts and truffles. At the top of the town, which slopes down towards the valley, are attractive old houses above the market place. The only surviving part of the Benedictine abbey around which the town developed is the church. It was heavily repaired in 1889 in late-Gothic style but has some good 16th-century glass. There is also a 12th-century church with a Romanesque door, and another which is part 15th- and part 19th-century, with a *clocher-mur*. Two bridges span the Vézère here, one of them mediaeval and some 100m long.

Opposite the old town, making good use of natural terraces above the river, are the **Jardins de l'Imaginaire** (*guided tours July-Aug 9.50–11.50, visits 12.50, 1.50, 6.10; May–June, Sept 9.50-11.50 & 1.50-5.20, closed Tues; April–Oct 9.50–11.20 & 1.50–5.20, closed Tues; T: 05 53 50 86 82*). The idea of a terraced garden here on a naturally sloping and fertile site was born in 1990, and the project took shape under the direction of Kathryn Gustafson and architect Ian Ritchie, opening 7 years later. It covers 6 hectares and evokes different geographical, cultural and temporal environments using a wide variety of plants and themes. Inspiration is drawn from its proximity to the Vézère valley, cradle of humanity, and water, wind and perspectives are harnessed to create some outstanding contemporary water gardens.

SARLAT-LA-CANÉDA

Capital of the Périgord Noir and *Sous-Préfecture*, Sarlat-la-Canéda is a beguiling town which makes an excellent touring base, especially out of season, placed as it is 7km north of the Dordogne River. It has an extraordinary density of beautiful medieval and Renaissance buildings in golden limestone with grey *lauze* roofs which line attractive squares and narrow streets. This remarkable townscape attracts some 500,000 visitors a year, welcomed at numerous epicurean boutiques, souvenir shops and restaurants.

EXPLORING SARLAT

The town plan (*see p. 145*) shows clearly the irregular-shape of the old quarter, which is now ringed by an exterior boulevard that follows the line of the old defences, fragments of which remain. The main axis, Rue de la République, runs more-or-less north-south, dividing in half the town, which rises up the slopes either side. The open areas at either end, Place de la Petite Rigaudie (or Place du 11 Novembre), and Place de la Grande Rigaudie (or Place du 14 Juillet), are covered with stalls on market days; there is a small garden to the north, Square du 8 Mai, 1945, and the large Jardin Public du Plantier to the south.

Place de la Liberté and vicinity

Framed by 16th–18th-century houses, Place de la Liberté includes the 18th-century Hôtel de Ville. One Renaissance door (1615; on Rue Fénelon) is all that remains of the previous Hôtel de Ville, itself on the site of a 13th-century *maison communale*. After a fire in 1727, Place de la Liberté, which is at its liveliest and most mouth-watering during the Saturday morning market, was enlarged. Across from The Hôtel de Ville is the mutilated church of Ste-Marie (1368–1507) with a very steep stone roof

HISTORY OF SARLAT

Sarlat most probably developed around a Benedictine community which settled in this remote place in the early 9th century, safe from marauding Vikings. The church was placed under the protection of St Sauveur, but at some point it received the relics of a Bishop of Limoges who had died in 720, and the dedication was changed to St Sacerdos in the 12th century. The relics drew pilgrims who enriched the abbey, and the abbots controlled the town, provoking dangerous rivalry. The townsfolk, administered by consuls, struggled for emancipation from the stranglehold of the clergy and were eventually granted certain liberties by King Philippe IV in the late 13th century. In 1317 Sarlat was elevated by Pope John XXII (*see p. 179*), to the episcopal see of a newly formed diocese defined by the Vézère and Dordogne rivers, and the monks were replaced by canons. These developments introduced a new era of prosperity to the town and its population grew in the 15th and 16th centuries to around 6,000 (today 10,650). The cathedral was rebuilt from 1505 by Bishop Armand Gontaud-Biron. It is not known exactly when the town was first enclosed with walls, but these were reinforced c. 1340–50 during the Hundred Years War. Sarlat, on the Franco-English border, was ceded to the English by the Treaty of Brétigny in 1360, although the English were ousted in 1370 by Bernard du Guesclin (*see p. 109*). By the end of the war in 1453, Sarlat had flourished for some two-and-a-half centuries. The town was granted certain royal privileges including, in 1552, the creation of the *présidial* or judiciary, and business boomed, especially in linen cloth. The wealth was displayed in buildings as clerics, nobles and rich tradesmen vied to build the most distinguished residences. During the Wars of Religion, Sarlat took a Catholic stance and was punished in 1574 by pillaging Protestants under Geoffroy de Vivans, but resisted a siege by Protestants in 1587. During the 17th and 18th centuries urban development slowed, although Bishop François II de Salignac (*see p. 148*) restored the episcopal palace, completed the cathedral and laid out the Plantier gardens. There was little new construction because of the lack of space inside the city until the walls were dismantled in 1750. The Intendant of Guyenne, Tourny, created a tree-lined garden on the edge of the town, the Grande Rigaudie, with a statue of Etienne de La Boétie. Administrative reorganisation after the Revolution proved a disaster for Sarlat. It lost its clerical and legal prestige—ceasing to be a bishopric and returning to the control of Périgueux in 1790. Its commercial role diminished and the railway arrived late, in 1882. The only major construction in the 19th century was Rue de la République or La Traverse, cutting straight through the old town. Sarlat was one of the first towns to benefit from the pioneering Malraux Law of 1962 created by André Malraux (d. 1976), France's most celebrated Minister of Culture, to safeguard historic towns.

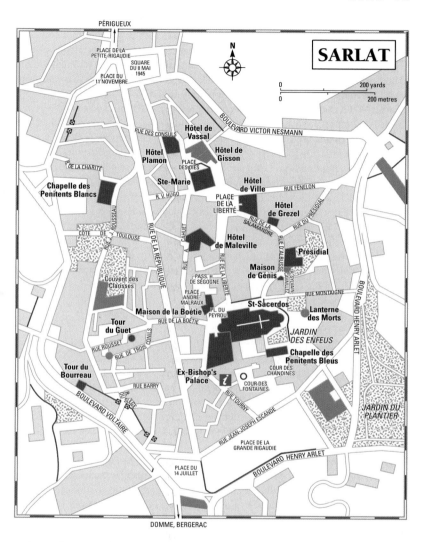

PÉRIGUEUX

PLACE DE LA
PETITE RIGAUDIE

SQUARE
DU 8 MAI
1945

PLACE DU
11 NOVEMBRE

N

SARLAT

0   200 yards
0   200 metres

BOULEVARD VICTOR NESMANN

RUE DES CONSULS

**Hôtel de
Vassal**

**Hôtel
Plamon**

**Hôtel de
Gisson**

PLACE
DESPOIES

R DE LA CHARITÉ

Ste-Marie

R. V. HUGO

**Hôtel
de Ville**

RUE FÉNELON

**Chapelle des
Penitents Blancs**

PLACE
DE LA
LIBERTÉ

**Hôtel
de Grezel**

RUE DE LA
SALAMANDRE

CÔTE   DE   TOULOUSE

RUE J. J. ROUSSEAU

RUE DE LA RÉPUBLIQUE

RUE A. CAHUET

RUE DE LA LIBERTÉ

**Hôtel
de Maleville**

RUE DU PRÉSIDIAL

RUE D'ALBUSSE

Présidial

RUE SYLVAIN CAVAILLEZ

**Couvent des
Clarisses**

PASS. H.
DE SÉGOGNE

PLACE
ANDRÉ
MALRAUX

**Maison
de Génis**

RUE MONTAIGNE

BOULEVARD HENRI ARLET

Maison de la Boétie

PL DU
PEYROU

RUE DE LA BOÉTIE

St-Sacerdos

**Lanterne
des Morts**

**Tour
du Guet**

RUE DES CONSULS

*JARDIN
DES ENFEUS*

RUE ROUSSET

RUE DE TROIS

**Chapelle des
Penitents Bleus**

**Tour du
Bourreau**

**Ex-Bishop's
Palace**

RUE BARRY

RUE DU SIÈGE

COUR DES
CHANOINES

COUR DES
FONTAINES

RUE TOURNY

*JARDIN DU
PLANTIER*

BOULEVARD VOLTAIRE

RUE JEAN-JOSEPH ESCANDE

PLACE DE LA
GRANDE RIGAUDIE

BOULEVARD HENRY ARLET

PLACE DU
14 JUILLET

DOMME, BERGERAC

and tiny dormers. The building was truncated at the chancel arch in 1915 and has recently been transformed into a modern covered market by the Parisian architect Jean Nouvel (*see p. 110*) with huge doors closing the chancel arch. At the west end are decorative gargoyles and a rose window, and on the north side a tower. Small streets inch up the slopes east and west of Place de la Liberté. To the north is Place du Marché-aux-Oies, the former goose market graced with three splendid bronze geese, overlooked by tall stone buildings, including the Hôtel de Gisson (Maison Chassaing) with plate-tracery windows (c. 1200) and a hexagonal stairtower (16th century) linking the two parts. Next door is the Hôtel de Vassal (15th century) with a corbelled turret and stair-tower. Opposite these is the magnificent façade of the Hôtel Selve de Plamon or des Consuls (14th–17th centuries) with sophisticated traceried Gothic windows, built by the merchant draper, Guillaume de Plamon, who was a consul from 1330. He transformed the shop of his forebears, adding a further floor in the 16th century. When the family was ennobled, they were granted the right to add a tower. Inside is an impressive courtyard with timber staircase and galleries, under which ran a stream, no doubt used for dyeing linen or treating flax. Opposite is the vaulted Fontaine Ste-Marie. On the angle of Rue des Consuls is an extraordinary squinch, and there are other tall buildings (15th and 17th centuries) and some good doorways.

From Place de la Liberté south along Rue de la Liberté are several half-timbered buildings, including the Hôtel de Maleville (or Hôtel de Vienne), created from three existing buildings in the 16th century. A Doric doorway leads to a stairtower, and flanking the 'M' for Maleville are busts in roundels, purported to be Henri IV with a lady—wife or favourite—who remains unidentified. The adjacent projecting façade with decorative gable and an original shopfront is early Renaissance. Next to the Maison de Maleville, Passage Henri de Ségogne leads to what were once courtyards of 13th-, 15th- and 17th-century houses, creating a maze of tiny streets lit with old-fashioned gas lamps, around Place André-Malraux.

Place du Peyrou and St-Sacerdos

On Place du Peyrou, opposite the west end of the cathedral, is the **Maison de La Boétie**, the show house of Sarlat, built by the magistrate Antoine de La Boétie in 1525. In characteristic first French Renaissance style, it has mullioned windows framed with decorative pilasters and a steep crocketed gable with just enough space for a third large window. Etienne de La Boétie (1530–63), writer and friend of Montaigne (*see p. 125*), was born here. His humanist ideas on freedom were to have a long-reaching effect, especially his *Discours de la servitude volontaire*. Written while a student at law in Orleans c. 1553, it examines the nature of tyranny, and was published posthumously, later inspiring Emerson and Tolstoy among others. On the opposite side of Place du Peyrou is the façade of the former bishops' palace, subjected to insensitive restoration at the beginning of the 20th century, with Flamboyant Gothic windows on the lower level and above a Renaissance loggia added by Cardinal Niccolo Gaddi, Bishop from 1533.

The **Church of St-Sacerdos**, originally Romanesque and part of the Benedictine abbey, became the cathedral when Sarlat was raised to the status of episcopal see in 1317. During the episcopate of Bishop Armand de Gontaud-Biron, most of the Romanesque church was demolished. The church as it now stands was begun c. 1504, and completed only in 1682–85, resulting in a confusion of architectural styles. Major restoration work was carried out in 2001–02. The Romanesque tower above the west door has three levels of blind arcades, two being 12th-century, the last level added in the 17th century, topped with an incongruous 18th-century cupola. On the west front are five late Romanesque sculptures, which seem to be figures on a balcony; the west door was altered in Classical style early in the 18th century. Despite being completed in the late 17th century, the majority of the exterior is Gothic. The nave has aisles and flying buttresses borrowed from northern churches, although the lateral chapels opening on aisles with interior buttresses are typically southern. The east end is the 14th-century cathedral of St-Sauveur, which is in the form of a Greek cross, and was absorbed into the later building.

The interior

Through the west door is the Romanesque narthex which has an original corbel table on the right. Beyond, the overriding impression is of workmanlike Gothic, probably because it was completed in the Neoclassical period. Only the first three bays of the nave are on a straight axis, and from there the church slopes gently off to the south to meet the earlier five-sided apse, adapted from the earlier church, which has haphazard stellar vaulting (15th century). The chancel (completed 1686), linked to it with five arches and an ambulatory, is pentagonal. In the chancel are 17th-century stalls with misericords. The nave piers are early and late 17th-century, some with slender spirals, and the nave was vaulted 1682–85, at the time of Bishop François II de Salignac de La Mothe-Fénelon. In the chapels are a selection of 17th- and 18th-century retables, some attributed to the Tournier workshop. The relics of St Sacerdos disappeared during the religious strife of the 16th century.

Around the cathedral

South of the cathedral is the site of the cloister. The east wall is decorated with arches made up of assorted fragments of Romanesque stonework from the old cloister. The Cour des Fontaines, where the first monks settled in the 9th century, is named after the pure spring water which gushes from three spouts. Further east is the Cour des Chanoines, closed to the south by the recently restored chapel of the Pénitents-Bleus or Chapelle St-Benoit, which is unadorned Romanesque inside. The 15th-century half-timbered house opposite was the residence of the chapter. East of the chapel is access to the old cemetery or Jardin des Enfeus, with Romanesque and Gothic funeral niches cut into rock, some containing sarcophagi. Steps lead up to a tiny garden with a view down onto the east end of the cathedral, and an enigmatic monument, the Lanterne des Morts (probably 12th century), also known as the Tower of St Bernard. It resembles an elongated stone beehive and has prompted many legends and interpretations including one involving St Bernard of Clairvaux. There are other examples in the region of this strange type of structure, with its conical stone roof. A small doorway leads into Rue Montaigne, named after La Boétie's friend, with one of the best views of the rooftops of Sarlat and some attractive houses. On the corner of Rue Sylvain-Cavaillez is a pretty balcony, and in Rue d'Albusse is the Maison de Génis (16th and 18th centuries) with a covered balcony and balustrade. The old Présidial or tribunal is set in a garden and has a fancy lantern on the roof. It is now a restaurant. Rue du Présidial was the legal quartier and runs into Rue Fénelon, recalling the Salignac-Fénelon family who dominated the episcopate in the 16th and 17th centuries. On this street is a group of 15th-century gabled houses and some other 16th-century buildings, not all entirely restored.

NORTH OF SARLAT

The village of **St-Geniès**, some 14km north of Sarlat, is a delightful ensemble of golden limestone and grey stone roofs. It has a small château (15th and 19th centuries). Next door is a little church with a partly Romanesque nave, but the Wars of Religion caused the belfry-porch to be rebuilt later and the apse redesigned. On a small hill east of the main road is the ruined keep of an earlier château, and next to it the Gothic Chapelle du Cheylard (1329) decorated inside with a series of frescoes contemporary with the building.

Northeast of Sarlat is the hilltop town of **Salignac-Eyvigues**. Off the main modern square is the old stone market hall surrounded by old buildings including the crumbling façade of a *hôtel noble*, sometimes erroneously called the Couvent des Croisiers (13th century). Rue Ste-Croix runs down to the rambling, partly ruined 12th–17th-century Château de Salignac (*guided visits to the exterior only in July–August; for information ask at the Tourist Office*). This was the home of the Salignac family who produced three archbishops, as well as nine bishops of Sarlat between 1359-1659, and one of Comminges. During the Hundred Years War, the château was ruined but rebuilt in the 15th century. Several rooms contain interesting 16th- and 17th-century furniture and a portrait of Louis de Salignac (d. 1598), who became Bishop of Sarlat, aged 22.

Jardins d'Eyrignac

Guided visits, lasting 1hr, daily June–Sept 9.30–7; April–May 10–12.30 & 2–7; Oct–March 10.30–12.30 & 2.30 until dusk; T: 05 53 28 99 71.

These gardens at Salignac were laid out in the 18th century by the Marquis de la Calprenède around a manor house dating from the previous century. Transformed in the 19th century into a more informal English style as was the fashion, the formal gardens were painstakingly recreated some 40 years ago by the father of the present owner. The sumptuous, carefully orchestrated landscapes of Eyrignac are made up of evergreen walks and vistas punctuated by elaborate topiary, pools and groves with perfectly manicured lawns. The regimented hornbeam, box, yew and cypress produce an architectonic setting articulated by variations of sunlight and shade.

Château de Puymartin

Guided visits July–Aug 10–12 & 2–6.30; April–June, Sept–Oct 10–12 & 2–6; rest of year by appointment, T: 05 53 59 29 97.

The Château de Puymartin at Marquay is a magical turreted place at the end of a steep, wooded drive. Part of the château is late medieval (15th–16th centuries) on the site of an earlier building (c. 1270) destroyed during the Hundred Years War, and a section was rebuilt c 1890. Since 1450 and its recapture by Radulphe de Saint-Clar, the property has passed through the de Montron family, which remained staunchly Catholic during the Wars of Religion.

Arranged around a three-storey central block, many original furnishings and decorations have been conserved. There are several painted ceilings and fireplaces. The main bedroom is adorned with green Aubusson tapestries and the *grande salle* contains six Oudenarde tapestries depicting the Trojan War. 17th- and 18th-century furniture includes a Louis XIII table and Louis XV desk, and the splendid timber roof structure can also be seen. One room, dating from the late 17th century, is painted with grisaille panels of mythological scenes. In the north tower is the room in which Thérèse de Saint-Clar, 'the White Lady', was imprisoned for some 15 years in the 1500s.

ALONG THE DORDOGNE VALLEY

From Sarlat to Lalinde, the Dordogne flows majestically past landscapes of walnut groves and fields of bright green tobacco, or below steep crags which have been peopled since time immemorial. Villages of golden stone developed in the shelter of the cliffs, at the foot of the castles which protected the frontier river in medieval times, or where important river ports shipped cargo destined for Bordeaux and beyond. The *gabares* which once carried these cargoes are now replicated for use as pleasure cruises. This is a particularly popular stretch of the Dordogne and the roads can become congested in midsummer.

CHÂTEAUX ON THE DORDOGNE

Château de Fénelon

Open daily July–Aug 9.30–7; March–June, Sept–Oct 10–12 & 2–6; Jan–Feb, Nov–Dec 2–5; T 05 53 29 81 45.

Between Sarlat and Souillac at Ste-Mondane, in a corner of Périgord Noir, the castle rises out of the woods of the Bouriane on the banks of the Dordogne. Most of the château is 15th or 16th century, although parts are older, and the site has been occupied since Merovingian times. Property of the de la Mothe family, one of whom was French Ambassador to Elizabeth I, birthplace of writer Fénelon (*see box p. 150*), it was altered in the 17th century and sold in 1780. Misused for some decades, it was restored in the mid-19th century. Three defensive baileys with towers dating from the 14th century present a severe front. The two-storey main block, with 15th-century machicolated towers, lauze roofs and late-Gothic dormers, adds a lighter touch. The main north façade welcomes visitors to the *cour d'honneur* via a fine double staircase which replaced the more formidable drawbridge. Inside the château are Fénelon's bedroom with a massive fireplace, the medieval kitchens carved out of the rock, and the chapel (13th–17th centuries). The upper rooms, in Louis XVI and Empire style, display a variety of 17th- and 18th-century furniture, Dutch and Chinese porcelain, and contain some good fireplaces, tapestries, and a collection of medieval military paraphernalia. In the grounds is a huge Cedar of Lebanon planted on 6th August, 1651, birth date of Fénelon. On the opposite bank of the river can be seen the pretty village of Carlux, which has a Gothic chimney and the remains of a castle.

FÉNELON (1651–1715)

François de Salignac de la Mothe-Fénelon, born at the Château de Fénelon, who became Archbishop of Cambrai at the end of his life, was appointed Abbot of Carennac (*see p. 167*) when the abbey was placed *in commendam*. An acknowledged writer as well as prelate, he was author of *Traité de l'éducation des filles*, and came to the notice of Madame de Maintenon, influential mistress of Louis XIV who was responsible for the education of the king's children. Fénelon was appointed tutor in 1689 to the Duke of Burgundy, the Dauphin, grandson of Louis XIV, who died young. Among Fénelon's other works were *Fables*, and the more subversive *Aventures de Télémaque* (1699) in which he indirectly criticised the politics of Louis XIV which ultimately led to his disgrace. While Abbot of Carennac, Fénelon resided at the priory and the town maintains that he returned there after becoming tutor to the prince to work on *Télémaque*, and consequently the Ile de Calypso in the Dordogne was named after the island in the book.

La Roque-Gageac

La Roque-Gageac is confined between the river and the cliff, and the buildings have been forced to creep up the rock face where they glow in the afternoon sun. At each end of the village there is a castle, the neo-Gothic Château de la Malartrie to the west and the 16th century Manoir Tarde to the east. A walk up the cliff brings you to troglodyte houses, the little church (16th–17th centuries) and sub-tropical gardens. River cruises on *gabares* leave from the quay, which was originally used for cargoes such as wood and wine.

Château de Beynac

Guided visits June–Sept 10–6.30; March–May 10–18; Oct–Nov 10–dusk; Dec–Feb, 12–dusk; closed 25 Dec, 1 Jan; T: 05 53 29 50 40.

Glowering from its high crag 150m above the Dordogne, this proud fortress is recognisable for miles around, and the village is huddled beneath on the riverbank. The château is a superb example of a medieval fortress with rare original 12th-century parts. It was altered in the 13th and 14th centuries, also during the Renaissance, and again in the 17th century. The parts that can be visited are heavily restored, painstakingly executed by the present owner, who is undertaking a 100-year recreation of the castle, adding an extra piece each year. Funding is raised through visitor admissions and frequent use as a film set.

History of the château

The fortress was occupied by Richard the Lionheart for about 10 years in the 12th century, and attacked by Simon de Montfort 1214–18 during the crusade against the Cathars of the Agenais and Périgord. During the Hundred Years War, Beynac changed hands on several occasions. When the border was fixed on the Dordogne, Beynac became French and Castelnaud opposite remained English, resulting in regular skirmishes across the river. At the close of the Wars of Religion, the military role of Beynac finally ended and the fort fell into disrepair, although one section was converted into a comfortable Renaissance habitation.

Visiting the château

Through the massive double entrance visitors arrive in the lower courtyard outside the castle itself, and then pass through a further entrance leading to an interior courtyard. Here, the stables on the right are 17th-century, while on the left are the 12th-century section of the castle and the original ramp up to the barbican and the castle door (now the exit). Another ramp leads to the terrace and panoramic views of the Dordogne and the castles of Marqueyssac, Fayrac and Castelnaud beyond. Immediately to the right is the former castle chapel, now used by the parish, with a fine *lauze* roof. Visitors enter the building through a doorway in the gabled façade flanked by the 12th- and 13th-century keeps, to arrive in the vast and bare guardroom, lit only with oil lamps to provide authentic medieval obscurity. The remains of stabling for the horses can be seen at one end. A skilfully crafted modern wooden spiral stair leads up to the more comfortable 13th-century rooms with latrines and *pisé* floors. On the same level is the meeting room of the four baronies of Périgord (Beynac, Biron, Boudeilles and Mareuil), their banners hanging on the wall. The room has a slightly pointed barrel-arched vault, Renaissance chimneypiece and chapel with 15th-century paintings. The battlements high above the valley afford yet another staggering view and also a rare opportunity to admire a *lauze* roof from above. A stone spiral descends to the courtyard over a 12th-century cistern still in use and the restored kitchens and barbican.

Jardins Suspendus de Marqueyssac

Open July, Aug 9–8; April–June, Sept 10–7; March, Oct–early Nov 10–6; mid-Nov–Feb 2–5; Thurs evenings in July and Aug candlelit walks; T: 05 53 31 36 36.

The 'hanging' gardens, which surround the Château of Marqueyssac at Vézac, draw huge numbers in the summer. The late 18th-century château takes second place, but a couple of rooms can be visited; the garden, however, has some 6km of walks and numerous attractions for all ages.

In 1692 the property was acquired by Bertrand Vernet de Marqueyssac who created the first gardens here, a great period in French formal gardens following the example of Le Nôtre. When Julien de Cerval (1818–93) inherited the property in 1861 the gardens had been neglected. A keen gardener, he had been impressed by the Italian gardens that he had seen while serving with the Roman legion. He dedicated the latter part of his life to creating an extravaganza of shaped box and cypress, relieved in winter by tiny Naples cyclamen. The sheer stone terraces, covering 22 hectares of the rock, take full advantage of the panorama high above the Dordogne. The 150,000 box shrubs are not restricted to straight lines and sharp edges, but disappear into the distance in undulating waves.

Château de Castelnaud

Open July, Aug 9–8 (historic visit 8.30); April–June, Sept 10–7; Feb–March, Oct to mid–Nov 10–6; mid–Nov–Jan, 2–5, Christmas vacation, 10–5; T: 05 53 31 30 00.

The Château de Castelnaud on the south bank of the Dordogne (cross at Vézac), has developed in a different direction from its old adversary across the river, Beynac, by capitalising on its picturesque semi-ruinous state. Soaring over the confluence of the Dordogne and the Céou, the fortress provides plenty of entertainment for all the family, including the Musée de la Guerre au Moyen Age featuring reconstructed medieval military apparatus. The dramatic site provides fine views over the Dordogne valley.

History of the château

Castelnaud, the 'new castle', was taken from Bernard de Casnac in 1214 by Simon de Montfort, who was forced out again after a year. The castle was subsequently destroyed but was ceded to the English and largely reconstructed after the Treaty of Paris in 1259. In 1273 it reverted to the Castelnaud barons, who were a constant thorn in the flesh to Beynac, although an unsteady peace held after 1317 when the pope authorised a marriage between the two families. The Hundred Years War began in 1337, renewing hostilities across the Dordogne, especially after 1368 when the heiress of Castelnaud married into the Caumont family, loyal to the English who took back the castle in 1405. In 1442 a three-week siege by the French finally drove them out, and after the war ended, repairs were carried out to the castle. François de Caumont built a pleasant Renaissance house called Milandes (*see p. 153*), and c.1520 the artillery tower was erected, more symbolic than practical. During the Reformation the castle came under the control of the feared and revered Huguenot, Geoffroy de Vivans, and such was his reputation that the castle was not attacked. It was gradually abandoned after his death, and after the Revolution it deteriorated further as building stone was scavenged from the site. A new lease of life was granted with the modern renovations (1967–98).

Visiting the château

A well-presented visitor attraction, the castle is dominated by a tall (30m) keep with a pointed roof, built by the English in the 13th century. Flanking it are 15th-century living quarters. Between the 16th-century round artillery tower on the right, with cannon ports—never used—in its thick walls, and the square tower to the left as you approach is the northern wall protecting an enclosure called a *chatêlet*. The barbican (15th century) inside this was the next defensive layer, designed to protect the entry to the castle at the weakest point. Beyond is the 15m-high curtain wall or *courtine* (13th century), punctuated by arrow loops, linking the keep with the main building but separating the lower courtyard (bailey) from the inner courtyard. In the keep are some original wall decorations and the museum of medieval weapons, arms and armour. Replicas of siege equipment and war engines can be seen, including a bombard, a primitive means of projecting 100kg cannon balls, an *arbalète à tour* (fixed crossbow) and a trebuchet, a massive catapult used for flinging missiles over high walls. The trebuchet is demonstrated on summer afternoons.

The Château des Milandes

Open July, Aug 9.30–7; mid–March–June, Sept–Oct 10–6; early–Nov 10–5; closed mid–Nov to mid-March; T: 05 53 59 31 21.

Les Milandes, famous later as the home of Josephine Baker, was begun in 1489 by François de Caumont for his bride as an alternative to the fortress of Castelnaud. Most of the late Gothic décor was destroyed by a zealous Protestant descendent of the family. The château was reborn in the 19th century as a largely neo-Gothic structure with show turrets. Josephine Baker (1906–75) made her name as a dancer in the Harlem cabaret La Revue Nègre and at the Folie Bergères in Paris in the 1920s. She worked for the French Resistance and lived at Les Milandes 1937–69 with her multi-racial group of 12 children, the 'Rainbow Tribe' until, in financial straits, Princess Grace of Monaco stepped in and offered them a home in Monaco.

Reminders of the old castle have survived in the shape of some fine fireplaces, panelling and stained glass. The kitchen and other rooms have been kept as they were during Josephine Baker's time, and contain memorabilia and a museum dedicated to her. The nearby private chapel, sometimes open, is in Flamboyant style but was emptied of its ornament and turned into a Protestant place of worship in the 16th century. There are pleasant grounds with formal gardens, views, and regular falconry demonstrations.

DOMME

The popular hilltop *bastide* of Domme was founded in the 13th century, extending an existing 12th-century fortress, Domme Vieille, which has now disappeared. The shape of the hilltop dictated the otherwise erratic layout of the *bastide*, although there are parallel streets around the traditional covered market place. There are also sections of well-preserved ramparts and fortified gates and the majority of the pretty stone houses have been beautifully restored.

Domme is much visited in the summer, which can make parking very difficult. There is a *petit train*, with commentary, from the bus-park at Le Pradal (*Easter–end Oct; T: 06 07 02 98 66*). In order to find Le Pradal, from Vitrac on the Sarlat to La Roque-Gageac road cross the Dordogne to 'Domme parking'.

Exploring Domme

It is the ensemble of Domme which makes it so engaging, more than any individual buildings. The village is built on the slope running down from the sheer cliff on the north, and was protected by ramparts and fortified gates. Sections of the wall and three gates—Portes Delbos, de la Combe and des Tours—are still standing. Porte Delbos, to the south, leads almost immediately into Place de la Rode with, on the left, the pretty medieval mint. Leading out of the square are the busy Grand'Rue and the quieter Rue M.-Mazet. Both lead to Place de la Halle, the main square where there is a rustic 18th-century covered market with stone pillars supporting a wooden gallery. This stands over the entrance to the Grottes de Domme (*open July–Aug 10–7; April–June, Sept 10–12 & 2–6; March, Oct to mid–Nov 2–6, closed Mon; closed mid–Nov* to Feb; T: 05 53 31 71 00), caves with natural formations, stalactites and stalagmites, illuminated to introduce an aspect of wonder, and a few animal bones. The exit is via panoramic elevator further west. The Maison du Gouverneur (16th century), opposite the *halle*, used by the tourist office, has a variety of roofs, dormers, and a huge tower with a corbelled turret. Behind the market is the Musée d'Arts et Traditions Populaires (*open July–Aug 10.30–7; May–June, Sept 10.30–12.30 & 2.30–6; April 2–6; closed Oct–March; T: 05 53 31 71 00*). The church is to the northeast of the market, and is a fairly severe building with a rustic belfry-gable above a sophisticated Classical west door with columns and broken pediment. Beyond the church is a shaded terrace and the Promenade de la Barre, with a bust of Jacques de Malleville and a breathtaking view over the valley, the patchwork of fields and distant hills. Further west in the town are the remains of an Augustinian abbey and public gardens, and beyond them the Moulin du Roy on the foundations of the old castle.

The *hôtel de ville* is in Rue des Consuls off the Grand'Rue. Rue Le Roy is where the writer lived. The finest individual structure is the Porte des Tours, a superb example of 13th-century fortification, best viewed from outside the walls. The gabled archway originally had a portcullis. It is flanked by powerful twin towers, square towards the town and rounded towards the countryside, of beautifully worked masonry, with arrow slits and machicolations. Inside are graffiti carved by Templars (*see p. 288*) imprisoned in 1307–18 after the suppression of the Order (guided visits from the tourist office). Inside the gate, the road or track follows the ramparts back to Port Delbos passing Porte de la Combe, the smallest gate and the route to water.

ST-CYPRIEN TO LIMEUIL & LALINDE

St-Cyprien, downriver from Beynac, stands on high ground against a backdrop of darkly wooded hills. The large church which dominates the town was part of an abbey and has retained its fortified Romanesque belfry. The rest of the building was altered later in the Gothic period and contains 17th-century furnishings, including retables, pulpit, stalls and organ.

South of the Dordogne, where the landscape is more wooded, **Belvès** emerges on high ground to create an attractive backdrop to the Nauze River. At the centre of the town in the Place des Armes stands the 15th-century market hall on 23 wooden pillars with stone bases. Beneath it is a series of rock shelters which were inhabited by prehistoric man during the Neolithic period, and then became troglodyte dwellings which were used intermittently from the 13th–18th centuries. The rock shelters (*guided tours from the tourist office, mid-June–mid-Sept 10–12 & 3–6*) lined the ancient city ditch, part of the medieval defences, and were forgotten about for some 200 years after the ditch was filled, only being rediscovered by chance in 1907. The eight dwellings, which consist of just one sombre room each, were excavated in 1989. Buildings of note in the town include the Maison des Consuls and the Renaissance Hôtel Bontemps. To the west is the church, built in the 12th–13th centuries as part of a Benedictine priory and reworked in the 15th century.

At the confluence of the Vézère and the Dordogne is **Limeuil**, a pretty village which tumbles down the hill to the water. It was once an important fishing community. Before the construction of the bridges in 1891 the rivers were forded here, preventing the heavy *gabares* from Bordeaux sailing further upriver. Merchandise was therefore forced to be trans-shipped onto lighter boats. The remains of the ramparts and fortified gates are still visible. The handsome 16th-century house near the Porte du Port was the headquarters of the boatmen. The uphill walk is steep at times and runs past attractive houses and two open squares. On Place des Ormeaux, an iron cross is the only reminder of the Protestant Temple. Higher up is the church of Ste-Catherine, part 19th-century, part much older, which shelters a statue of the Virgin (14th century) formerly venerated by boatmen. At the top of Limeuil is the Porte du Marquisat, beyond which is the chapel of St-Martin at Paunat. This sturdy little Romanesque chapel (restored) is dedicated to Saints Thomas, Martin and Catherine, and was jointly founded by Richard the Lionheart and Philippe Auguste as a chapel of atonement for the murder of Thomas Becket by Henry II in 1170. The exterior is very plain, with a Latin inscription over the door pleading for God's mercy. Inside there is a domed crossing and half-domed apse, a series of wall-paintings (14th and 15th centuries), and a consecration plaque on the north wall.

Lalinde was the first English *bastide* at the entry to the Dordogne and Vézère valleys, founded on the water's edge by Jean de la Linde for Henry III in 1267. This was a crucially important position at the ford across the Dordogne on the La Rochelle–Montpellier route. Although the regular layout has survived, practically all the old town has disappeared as a result of the struggle between the English and French in the 14th and 15th centuries, and the Catholic versus Protestant conflicts in the 16th and 17th centuries.

CADOUIN

The abbey church

An abbey was founded on this site in 1114/15 by Geraud de Salles, disciple of Robert d'Arbrissel, who founded Fontevraud in the Angevin. Around 1117 a cloth, said to be the *sudarium capitis*, part of the shroud that had enveloped Christ's head, came to Cadouin and around 1119 de Salles affiliated Cadouin to the Cistercian monastery of Pontigny in Burgundy. The shroud became a hugely important object of veneration and attracted pilgrims to Cadouin for eight centuries until it was de-authenticated in 1934. The monastic buildings have been greatly modified. The abbey church (1118–54) is severe and unadorned in the Cistercian manner. It remains essentially 12th-century and is the most important Cistercian work in Aquitaine. The west front, looking out on what was the abbey yard, is massive, relieved only by three large round-headed windows between buttresses and a simple triple-arched doorway. A small concession to the severity is the blind arcade above, which owes a debt to the Saintonge, and a small oculus. The façade seems to lack an upper level. The unusual tower over the crossing has a stone base with a two-tier chestnut shingle roof. The harmonious interior is uncluttered. It is in the shape of a Latin cross and, unusually for Périgord, has nave and side aisles. More typical is the cupola over the crossing. The four-bay nave has slightly pointed barrel vaults. Around the east end and transepts are some carved friezes and capitals, otherwise the decoration is kept to a minimum, as are the furnishings. There is a 13th-century sarcophagus, a statue of the Virgin (15th century), and the much-restored remains of a 15th–16th-century mural.

The Cloister of Cadouin

Open July–Aug 10–7; April–June, Sept to mid–Nov, 10–12.30 & 2–6, closed Tues; mid–Nov–mid–Dec, Feb–March 10–12.30 & 2–5.30, closed Tues, Fri, Sat; mid- to end–Dec 10–12.30 & 2–6, closed Tues; closed Jan; T: 05 53 63 36 28.

The cloister is a high point of Gothic art in the region, with exuberant Flamboyant tracery carved in glorious golden stone, an anachronism for a Cistercian monastery. It is a celebration of the late medieval style with an almost overwhelming array of niches, pendant bosses, corbels, tracery, lierne and tierceron vaults, curly kale, and carvings, in three galleries (north, east and south). The more sober west gallery is 16th-century, heavily restored in the early 20th century. There are 26 bays, and the best carvings—in the north and east galleries—present scenes of monastic life, vices and virtues, scenes from the Old and New Testaments, from antiquity, and from everyday life. In the south-facing gallery against the church, therefore sunny, is the finest group around the chair of Abbot Pierre de Gaing, which is decorated with the rebus of Cadouin, a quince tree (*cadoun* in Occitan). The engaged columns either side of the chair have been wittily transformed into turrets from which figures process. On the left are monks, their abbot and a kneeling Mary Magdalene and on the opposite side are scenes from the Passion including Mary and Christ carrying the Cross. The wealth of anecdotal detail includes little figures peeping around corners. In the northeast angle are two doors, one Gothic, decorated with the Order of St Michael, and the other, partly obscured by the 15th-century pier, a remnant of the Romanesque cloister. On the exterior of the chapter house (east gallery) are scenes from the parable of Lazarus and Dives, including *Dives' Feast* and the *Death of Lazarus*, and opposite, the *Death of Dives*. The southeast door is also elaborately decorated, with a *Crucifixion*, pelican and phoenix. There are close similarities to the cloister at Cahors (*see p. 182*), which fared worse during the Wars of Religion than Cadouin.

The *Saint Suaire*

In the chapter house is the *Saint Suaire*, still described as the holy shroud despite overwhelming proof to the contrary. Nevertheless, it remains an object of veneration for its age and quality of workmanship. This superb length of cotton muslin was made by Coptic weavers in Egypt at the time of the Fatimid Empire. At each end there are embroidered bands in coloured silk incorporating floral patterns and Arabic script. When the text was finally deciphered in 1934, it was discovered that it sings the praises of Emir El Moustali, who reigned over Lower Egypt 1094–1101, and his powerful vizir, El Afdal. The fabric was probably acquired during the First Crusade (1096–99).

THE COUZE VALLEY

St-Avit-Sénieur

South of Cadouin, on a rocky outcrop above the small river Couze, St-Avit-Sénieur is a little village, with a mighty abbey church, severe and fortified, reminiscent of Beaumont (*see below*). The relics of St Avitus, born locally c. 487 and persecuted at the time of Clovis, were translated into the new church in 1118. The community was fortified in the 13th century on the orders of Philippe III, and the abbey was ransacked and fired by the Huguenots in 1577, who demolished the great north belfry. Part of the 12th-century church collapsed at some point and had to be rebuilt. There have been many campaigns of restoration since the second half of the 19th century, in the 1960-70s, again in the 1990s, allowing the reopening of the whole church in 2000. The local community continues to make improvements to the furnishings.

The courtyard north of the church has remnants of the old fortifications, including the *maison des gardes* (1628), on the left. Southeast of the church is the monk's dormitory, and the old sacristy and chapter house, the latter vaulted in the 12th century. A porch leads to the remains of the cloister, destroyed in the 15th century and used as a cemetery. The 17th-century presbytery on an 11th-century base has arrow slits, and the south wall of the cloister seems to have been built using Gallo-Roman techniques.

There is also a small museum of geology and archaeology (*open in summer, T: 05 53 22 32 27 or 05 53 22 39 12*). Digs have uncovered the foundations of an earlier church and monastic buildings. Inside, it is likely that domes were intended although never constructed. Evidence of scorch marks may indicate attack during the Albigensian Crusades, and the present vaults date from the 13th–15th centuries. The round apse was replaced by a flat chevet in the 17th century. Inside, magnificent Gothic wall-paintings in the nave, both decorative and figurative, were uncovered during the last round of restorations. Modern additions are the subtle glass and the main altar with, north and south, scenes from the life of St Avit.

Monferrand-du-Périgord

Isolated in the small churchyard above the village of Monferrand-du-Périgord is the tiny church of St-Christophe (11th–12th centuries), a remnant of a larger sanctuary. The three little round-headed windows in the east are original but the church was altered later. The main interest lies in the painted decoration of the interior (sadly neglected), with a *Christ in Majesty at the Centre of the Universe* on the vault surrounded by the symbols of the four Evangelists (12th century), and in the east an *Annunciation* and St Christopher. The oldest Romanesque paintings are on the north of the choir and represent a *Miracle of St Leonard*, companion at arms of Clovis. On the north wall is *Hell* with the damned being consumed by Leviathan.

Beaumont-du-Périgord

The *bastide* of Beaumont-du-Périgord was the result of a *paréage* between Edward I and local landowners in 1272. Lucas de Thaney, the king's lieutenant, supervised its construction and laid it out in the form of an 'H' as a tribute to his father, Henry III. Beaumont remained English for most of the Hundred Years War, until 1442. It was attacked four times during the Religious Wars. The massive church (end-13th/early 14th century) looms above the town, still redolent of its protective role in the Middle Ages. There are large square twin towers at the west, and two more at the east. The west façade is fairly plain except for some foliate capitals and a gallery of animal faces. The flat Gothic east end is English. Inside, the cavernous single nave has a 19th-century vault. Under the northwest tower are some good carvings.

Dolmen de Blanc and Couze

Just before the village of Nojals-et-Clottes south of Beaumont is the Dolmen de Blanc, a splendid example of a megalith or neolithic burial chamber some 5,000 years old, although much altered over the millennia. A reminder of a local industry going back to the 15th century is the Moulin du Papier de la Rouzique at Couze (*open July–Aug 10–7; April–June, Sept 2–6.30, closed Sat, Sun morning; T: 05 53 24 36 16*). At the height of its production, there were 13 mills on the little River Couze, but these had all been closed down by the 20th century. This particular mill was running from 1530 until 1983 and is now working again.

Château de Lanquais

Open July–Aug 10–7; May–June, Sept 10.30–12 & 2.30–6.30, closed Tues; April, Oct 2.30–6, closed Tues; T: 05 53 61 24 24.
The château, which stands in a pretty valley west of Couze, south of the Dordogne, was grandly described by the art historian André Chastel as the *'Louvre inachevé du Périgord'*. This charming L-shaped building in golden stone is a textbook example of the evolution from defensive structure to comfortable residence and demonstrates clearly at least two campaigns of building: the medieval castle (14th–15th centuries) on the right, and a Renaissance palace (16th century) on the left. In addition there is a small neo-Gothic (19th century) building and chapel. Certainly Galhiot de la Tour, owner of Lanquais in the 16th century, was cousin of Catherine de Médicis and would have had knowledge of, even had access to, the best architects of the day, including Philibert de l'Orme and Pierre Lescot. Lanquais was on Protestant territory, and by extending it in 1533 in the style of the Louvre, Galhiot was using architecture to underline his Catholic and Royalist loyalties. Indeed, it provoked strong reaction from Huguenots and Henri de la Tour d'Auvergne besieged Lanquais in 1577, interrupting building works and leaving the low pavilion on the west unfinished.

Visiting the château

The visit starts in the tall octagonal tower, built in the 15th century to replace a 14th-century round tower; it stands on the original 12th-century base. The spiral staircase, acting as a spine to support the structure, which is not buttressed, ends in a sophisticated 'palm-tree' vault. The tower and 14th-century north block show the scars of the siege of 1577. The Renaissance angle pavilion in the style of Pierre Lescot's Cour

Carrée at the Louvre was added 1561–74; the elaborate upper windows are taken from Androuet du Cerceau's *Book of Architecture*. Several rooms, including two bedrooms, are decked out in the style of the Renaissance, with large windows and wooden bath tubs, and in Monsieur's Room, an outstanding carved fireplace and door surround (1601). The dining room was restored in the 19th century by Alexis de Gourgue, while the games and music room is in the taste of 1780–90, and has an English pianoforte (c. 1840). The Grand Salon is dominated by a Renaissance chimney-piece the width of the room, altered in the 19th century. The kitchens are also part of the visit.

PRACTICAL INFORMATION

GETTING AROUND

• **By train:** Périgueux–Le Bugue–Les Eyzies–Agen. Périgueux to Brive change at Condat-le-Lardin for Montignac Souillac–Sarlat; Bergerac–Sarlat; Le Buisson/Libourne–Sarlat

TOURIST INFORMATION

Beaumont Pl. Jean Moulin, T: 05 53 22 39 12, www.pays-beaumontais.com/tourisme
Belvès 1 Rue des Filhols, T: 05 53 29 10 20, www.perigord.com/belves
Beynac-et-Cazenac Rue de La Balme, T: 05 53 29 43 08, www.cc-perigord-noir.fr
Le Bugue Porte de la Vézère, Rue du Jardin Public, T: 05 53 07 20 48, bugue@perigord.com
Domme Pl. de la Halle, T: 05 53 31 71 00, www.domme-tourism.com
Les-Eyzies-de-Tayac 19 Ave de la Préhistoire, T: 05 53 06 97 05, www.leseyzies.com
Lalinde Jardin Public, T: 05 53 61 08 55, www.lalinde-perigord.com
Limeuil Annexe Mairie, T: 05 53 63 38 90, www.limeuil-perigord.com

Montignac Pl. Bertrand de Born, T: 05 53 51 82 60, www.bienvenue-montignac.com
La Roque-Gageac T: 05 53 29 17 01
Rouffignac Le Bourg, T: 05 53 05 39 03, www.multimania.com/rouffignac24
St-Amand-de-Coly, Mairie, T: 05 53 51 67 50
St-Cyprien Pl. Charles-de-Gaulle, T: 05 53 30 36 09, www.stcyprien-perigord.com
Salignac-Eyvigues Pl. du 19 Mars 1962, T: 05 53 28 81 93
Sarlat Rue Tourny, BP 114, T: 05 53 31 45 45, www.ot-sarlat-perigord.fr
Terrasson-la-Villedieu BP 37, Rue Jean Rouby, T: 05 53 50 37 56, www.ot-terrasson.fr

RIVER CRUISES

Beynac, Gabares de Beynac T: 05 53 28 51 15, www.gabarre-beynac.com
La Roque-Gageac: Gabares Norbert, April–Sept 10–6, Oct afternoons only; operated by T: 05 53 29 40 44, www.norbert.fr or Gabarres Caminade, Easter to Oct, 9.30-6, T: 05 53 29 40 95, vecchio@tiscali.fr

Belvès

€ **Hôtel Le Clément V**. In the centre
of the village, the hotel's unassuming
façade belies an interior with loads of
personality, picturesque nooks and
crannies, an 11th century vaulted cellar
and ancient beams. The 12 rooms are
shared between the main wing and the
stable block across the winter garden.
There is also a antiques boutique. T: 05
53 28 68 80 www.clement5.com

Le Bugue

€ **Royal Vézère**. This largish hotel with
48 reasonably priced rooms and 4 suites,
21 with river views, has a pool with
solarium. The restaurant, l'Oustalou,
which overlooks the Vezere River. Closed
October to April. Pl. de l'Hôtel-de-Ville,
T: 05 53 07 20 01, www.hotels-restau-
dordogne.org/royal-vezere

€€ **Domaine de la Barde**. A superb
complex dating back to the 13th century and amended up to the 18th century.
Close to the town in beautiful grounds,
with formal gardens, a trout stream,
pool and tennis court. The 18 gorgeous,
large rooms with unusual features–sloping roofs or stone fireplaces–are divided
between the main house, the old mill
and the 16th-century forge; wide price
range. The very pretty restaurant with
large terrace, Le Velo Rouge, serves
excellent food with a menu around
36€. T: 05 53 07 16 54,
www.domainedelabarde.com

Le Buisson de Cadouin

€€€ **Le Manoir de Bellerive**. In a
superb position on the banks of the
Dordogne surrounded by informal gardens, the hotel occupies a handsome
19th-century house and guarantees the
highest standards and atmosphere of
well-being both in its 22 rooms, and in
the restaurant. Cooks Marcel Clevenot
and Eric Barbe have been awarded a
Michelin rosette. Meals are served in the
dining room or on the pretty terrace
and there is also a pool, jacuzzi and
tennis court. Route de Siorac, T: 05 53
22 16 16, www.bellerivehotel.com

Campagne

€ **Le Château**. A quiet and attractive
setting in an L-shaped building with 16
reasonably-priced rooms and traditional
restaurant in an excellent location
between Les Eyzies and Le Bugue. (east
of Le Bugue, D703), T: 05 53 07 23 50,
www.hotels-sarlat-perigord.com

Les Eyzies-de-Tayac-Sireuil

€€ **Hotel/Restaurant du Centenaire**.
A smart address with personal service
and beautiful setting with gardens and a
discreet pool. Raymond Mazère's cooking is an original slant on Périgordian
cooking which aims to please the eye
and the palate in superb combinations.
Wide ranging luxuriously modern
accommodation includes 20 rooms and
4 suites with beautiful bathrooms. Le
Rocher de la Penne, T: 05 53 06 68 68,
www.hotelducentenaire.com

€€ **Hotel/Restaurant Les Glycines**.
An old *relais de poste* at an upmarket
address in a lovely setting, with pool,
against a backdrop of cliffs. The 19
rooms are freshly renovated in restful
colours and the cooking, under the
direction of Pascal Lombard, uses
home-grown vegetables and local produce; samples are *Crème d'orties au cap-
pucino samoussa de langoustines,
Escalopes de foie gras frais au citron vert,
Côte de veau rôtie au jambon du pay et sa
polenta à la truffe*, and *Le biscuit coulant*

au chocolat chaud, sauce caramel. T: 05 53 06 97 07, www.les-glycines-dordogne.com

€€ **Moulin de la Beune/Restaurant Au Vieux Moulin**. An old mill, with the mill wheel still in place, has been transformed into a delightful hotel in a leafy setting. On the edge of the village, it is close to the museum. It has a quite small and picturesque restaurant with interesting and unconventional food, impeccably served. In summer meals are served on the terrace overlooking the mill stream. T: 05 53 06 94 33, www.moulindelabeune.com

€€ **Hotel/Restaurant Cro-Magnon**. Literally built into the cliff, this is about as close as you can get to the Cro-Magnon rock shelter. In charming surroundings with a pretty garden/terrace, the unassuming rooms have all been renovated. The restaurant is traditional with beams and fireplace and the cooking thoughtful; menus €15 (lunch) to €39. T: 05 53 06 97 06, www.hostellerie-cro-magnon.com

€ **Hôtel/Restaurant Le Passeur**. The charming old house is on the riverside. It has 19 pleasant rooms of varying quality and price. Especially renowned for their foie gras, chefs Gérard Brun and his son Franck, experts in Périgordian cuisine, create dishes such as *Lapin confit dans son jus de truffes, Soufflé chaud à l'orange et chocolat*. Meals are served in the comfortable restaurant, in the covered terrace or in the garden with river view; menus from €22. T: 05 53 06 97 13, www.hostellerie-du-passeur.com

Domme

€€ **Hôtel/Restaurant L'Esplanade**. At the heart of the *bastide*, this hotel/restaurant is in a spectacular position with panoramic views towards the Dordogne. It is furnished with antiques and the 15 rooms are prettily presented; also 2 apartments and 1 suite. The regional cuisine served in the restaurant is carefully prepared. T: 05 53 28 81 41, esplanade@chateauxhotels.com

Meyrals

€ **Hôtel La Ferme de Lamy**. Close to Sarlat, Christine and Michel Duneau's country hotel occupies a farmhouse partly dating to 1650, with red tile roof and stone walls. It has 12 delightful rooms, all different, and furnished with antique pieces. Some rooms have exposed beams and original features, others open onto the lovely garden and superb pool. Demi-pension can be provided. Between Sarlat and Les Eyzies, T: 05 53 29 62 46, www.ferme-lamy.com

€ **Chambres d'hôtes La Bélie**. Monique and Roger Baltzer's renovated 16th-century farmhouse has been completely renovated to a very high standard. The hosts offer 3 interesting and attractive guest rooms for guests with beautiful fabrics. There are 12 hectares of woodland and meadows, and it is possible to order *table d'hôtes*. Equally charming in summer on the terraces or in winter at the fireside. L'Abeille, T: 05 53 35 50 01, www.perigord-labelie.com

Monpazier

€ **Bar-Restaurant de la Bastide**. A traditional restaurant with a large dining room with beams and game trophies. The food is good, fairly rustic but reliable. 52 Rue St-Jacques, T: 05 53 22 60 59.

Montignac

€€ **Hostellerie/Restaurant La Roseraie**. The charming 19th-century building overlooks a beautiful square and backs onto the river. It has 14 cosy rooms and a panelled restaurant overlooking the garden; also a pool. The cooking specialises in foie gras and truffles (but there are other choices). Pl. d'Armes, T: 05 53 50 53 92, www.laroseraie.fr.st

€ **Relais du Soleil d'Or**. Close to Lascaux and in the town of Montignac, the medieval post house has a long tradition of hospitality and offers a gentle pace of life. It has 28 rooms and outside is a lovely pool. Regional menu at 33€. 16 Rue du IV Septembre, T: 05 53 52 80 22, www.le-soleil-dor.com

La Roque-Gageac

€€ **Hôtel/Restaurant La Belle Etoile**. Modest hotel with 16 rooms in this lovely village on the Dordogne. The restaurant, which has a terrace, serves traditional fare with subtle innovations; menus around 23€, 28€ and 37€. T: 05 53 29 51 44, hotel.belle-etoile@wanadoo.fr

€€ **Restaurant/Auberge La Plume D'Oie**. In a glorious setting overlooking the Dordogne, the auberge is owned by a Dutch-British couple who guarantee that everything is home-cooked (including the bread), and very inventive. Dinners only are served, except for Sunday lunch, and there are menus at €45 and €58. Covers are limited to 12, and only advance bookings are accepted. There are four rooms, let only with a dinner reservation. T: 05 53 29 57 05, laplumedoie@wanadoo.fr

Rouffignac

Chambres d'hôtes Château de Fleurac. A 19th century pile comfortably transformed has beautiful interiors with period furnishings and is surrounded by 600 hectares of parkland and vines. Five bedrooms and two large, extremely elegant honeymoon suites. T: 05 53 05 95 01, www.fleurac.com

Salignac-Eyvigues

€ **Chambres d'hôtes Le bois de l'Ange, Cacavon**. This is a spacious, bright building with pool and three simple, but bright, new rooms as well as a suite. *Table d'hotes* with the family when home-produced dairy products and fresh vegetables are served. T: 05 53 28 89 08, du-bois-de-lange@wanadoo.fr

Sarlat-la-Canéda

€€ **Hôtel/Restaurant La Madeleine.** ■ An attractive building with blue shutters and mansard roof close to the town centre, this reliable and friendly hotel has 39 comfortable rooms. The dining room and lounge have been attractively revamped, and chef-owner Philippe Melot cooks with care and pride. Typical dishes include La crème de *lentilles vertes et blondes aux truffes du Périgord, Le medaillon de lotte rôtie à l'orange*; menus €26, €34, €44. 1 Pl. de la Petite-Rigaudie, T: 05 53 59 10 41, www.hoteldelamadeleine-sarlat.com

€€ **Hôtel/Restaurant La Hoirie, rue Marcel-Cerdan**. The building goes back to the 13th century and is set among woodland, it has a pool and are 19 charming and quiet rooms, including two apartments. The service is efficient and the cuisine typical unpretentious Périgordian; meals are served in the old *rôtisserie* or in the gardens. T: 05 53 59 05 62, www.lahoirie.com

€ **Hôtel des Récollets**. A nice little hotel in a building which was once part of the 17th-century Récollets Convent on the quiet western side of town. It has a pretty cloister/courtyard and attractive rooms. 4 Rue J.J.-Rousseau, T: 05 53 31 36 00, www.hôtel-recollets-sarlat.com

€ **Hôtel La Mas de Castel**. A wonderfully quiet spot with restful rooms in an old Périgordian house with a tower, in which is one of the 13 rooms. In a rural setting, it is surrounded by a woodland and there are also a garden and pool. The décor is a mixture of old and modern. No restaurant. It can be found 3km south of Sarlat on the D704, T: 05 53 59 02 59, castalian@wanadoo.fr

Vézac

€€ **Relais des Cinq Châteaux**. Good, hearty traditional Périgordian cooking with plenty of duck and foie gras, but the restaurant also specialises in seafood. The building, typical of the area, has a large dining room and popular terrace overlooking open countryside towards Domme. A popular place with locals for Sunday lunch. (D57), T: 05 53 30 30 72, 5chateaux@perigord.com

Vitrac

€€€ **Hôtel/Restaurant Domaine de Rochebois**. A grand affair, this hotel-restaurant occupies a superb position on the Dordogne with its own 9-hole golf course and splendid pool. The 19th-century chateau has 10 rooms, with 24 more rooms in annexes and 4 apartments with terraces. The elegant restaurant has a reputation for excellence using produce from Aquitaine, such as caviar and sturgeon, foie gras and truffles. Rte de Montfort, 6k from Sarlat, T: 05 53 31 52 52, www.rochebois.com

MARKET DAYS

Beaumont Tuesday, Saturday
Belvès Saturday
Beynac Monday
Le Bugue Tuesday and Saturday
Domme Thursday
Les Eyzies Monday
Lalinde Thursday
Montignac Wednesday, Saturday
La Roque Gageac Friday
St-Cyprien Sunday
St-Geniès Sunday
Salignac Tuesday
Sarlat Saturday and Wednesday
Terrasson-la-Villedieu Thursday

FESTIVALS & EVENTS

May–June: *La Ringueta*, traditional games held in alternate years, Sarlat
July: *Festival Bach*, Belvès
Festival de Montignac, Dances et Musiques du Monde, World Music and Dance, Montignac
Les Chemins de l'Imaginaire, Street theatre, Terrasson, T: 05 53 50 13 80
July and August: *Festival du Périgord Noir*, combines exceptional sites throughout Périgord Noir with masterpieces of baroque music performed by international artists, T: 05 53 53 18 71
Festival des Jeux du Théâtre, Sarlat, T: 05 53 31 10 83
August–September: *Musique en Périgord*, All types of music in concerts indoors and out, T: 05 53 30 36 09
November: *Festival du Film*, Sarlat, T: 05 53 29 18 13

THE LOT

The *département* of the Lot corresponds to much of the old province of Quercy, the name of which is derived from the Gaullish tribe, the Cadourques, who once inhabited the area. The east and centre of the Quercy has a rugged and desolate charm, in contrast to the lush valleys of the Dordogne to the north (Haut Quercy) and the Lot valley further south (*see p. 178*), with its tributaries the Célé and Vers (*see p. 192*). Rainfall and rivers disappear rapidly through the porous limestone plateaux called *causses* which at their highest, are only about 360m above sea-level, where caves and caverns are formed. In this stone-rich land, early man built dolmens (2500–1500 BC) with great slabs of stone, some 500 of which can be identified in the Lot; and the country is brindled with dry-stone walls and shelters called *cabanes*, *cazelles* or *gariottes*.

HAUT QUERCY

SOUILLAC

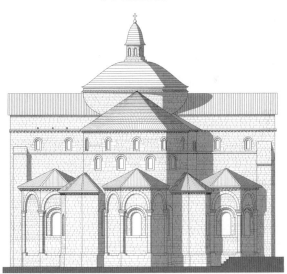

EAST ELEVATION OF THE CHURCH OF SAINTE-MARIE

Souillac is situated on the Borrèze, a tributary of the Dordogne River, and this corner of the Lot is still often described by its old name, Haut Quercy. The main monument of the town is the domed Romanesque church of Sainte-Marie.

Church of Sainte-Marie

The church was part of a Benedictine abbey built between 1075 and the mid-12th century and survived the destruction wreaked by the Protestants in the 16th century, although most of the original monastic buildings were lost. They were rebuilt and the church repaired from the 17th to 19th centuries. The exterior of the church is coolly beautiful in crisp white stone, with polygonal radiating chapels opening off the apse in a multi-tiered arrangement culminating in the lauze-covered cupola and lantern, one of three. The tower in the west is the remainder of the 10th-century belfry. The foundations of an earlier church and elements of the Carolingian chancel as well as 11th –13th-century sarcophagi were discovered in the crypt in 1948.

The interior

Inside, the cavernous two-bay nave is covered by two cupolas on pendentives supported by massive interior buttresses, and above the crossing is a third cupola. The interior is harmonious and unornamented, except for some interesting carved capitals in the capacious east end. The furnishings include a 16th-century retable of the *Mystery of the Rosary*, a painting of Christ's Agony on the Mount by Chassériau (19th century), and 18th-century choir stalls.

The most thrilling feature of the church is a group of **Romanesque reliefs** on the reverse of the west door, possibly moved here in the 17th century, with many stylistic similarities to those at Moissac. The tympanum is a complicated illustration, framed by three arches, of the dream of the monk Theophilus, who, having sold his soul to the Devil, begged for the Virgin's intercession for its recovery. Heavenly forces, represented by the Virgin descending from the clouds accompanied by angels, oppose the Devil, shown as half-man, half-beast. This animated scene is framed by the figures of St Peter and St Benedict. The trumeau on the north is a masterpiece of tumbling and intertwined figures of men and monsters representing, right and centre, various sins and their punishments. The left face shows the *Sacrifice of Abraham*, an extraordinarily vital and cleverly composed version in the narrow perpendicular space. The Prophet Isaiah on the right door jamb, a graceful figure with crossed legs, flowing beard and hair, and swirling drapes which cling to his limbs, is a more vigorous version of Moissac's Jeremiah (*see p. 332*) and fills a larger space. The rather less wonderful figure on the opposite jamb is the patriarch Joseph or Josea.

Musée de l'Automate

Open July–Aug 10–7; June, Sept, 10–12 & 3–6; April–May, Oct 10–12 & 3–6, closed Mon; Jan–Mar, Nov–Dec 2.30–5.30, closed Mon, Tues; T: 05 65 37 07 07.

In Place de l'Abbaye, in striking contrast to the serenity of the church, the Musée d'l'Automate is installed in the 17th-century monastic buildings adjacent to the church. This is a wonderland of mechanised dolls and models arranged thematically and activated in rotation to perform all sorts of acrobatics and contortions. It claims to be the most comprehensive collection of its kind in Europe with more than 1,000 pieces, dating from 1862 to 1960.

ALONG THE DORDOGNE

Lacave

The **Grottes de Lacave** (*guided visits Aug 9.30–6; July 9.30–12.30 & 1.30–6; April–June 9.30–12 & 2–6; Sept 9.30–12 & 2–5.30, Oct-Nov and Easter, 10–12 & 2–5 T: 05 65 37 87 03, www.grottes-de-lacave.com*) make a magical visit and include an electric train ride, underground lakes and spectacular concretions. Further upriver, there is stunning scenery around St-Sozy and Creysse, which has a Romanesque chapel, and there is a semi-troglodyte church at Gluges. The road follows the high cliffs overlooking the Cirque de Monvalent, a natural amphitheatre carved out by waters of the Dordogne.

Martel

Famous for its 7 towers, Martel was supposedly founded by Charles Martel (c. 685–741), grandfather of Charlemagne, best known for defeating the Arabs at Poitiers in 732. It is more likely that the name is a derivation of an Occitan word associated with workers in stone, metal and wood, as represented by the three *marteaux* (hammers) on the coat of arms. As the ancient capital of the Viscounty of Turenne it became a free town in 1219 and has retained much of its medieval character.

The Palais de la Raymondie at the centre of the old town (13th–14th centuries but altered later) has interesting late-Gothic windows. It contains the Musée d'Uxellodunum (*open by appointment, July-Aug, Tues–Thurs, Sat, 10–12 & 3–6; T: 05 65 37 30 03*), a small museum with an eclectic collection including prehistoric and Gallo-Romain and later objects. Nearby are the Hotel de la Monnaie (13th century, formerly the mint) and the Tour d'Henri Court Mantel. Curtmantel, the name sometimes used for Henry II, is associated locally with the king's eldest son, known as the Young King Henry, elder brother of Richard the Lionheart, who was destined to inherit Aquitaine. South of the market is the late medieval Maison Fabri with a round tower, built on the site of the house where the Young King Henry died of dysentery in 1183, predeceasing his father by 6 years.

Puy-d'Issolud

Puy-d'Issolud, 14km east of Martel on high ground limited by steep escarpments, is the site of a Celtic fort excavated during the mid-19th century and one of three sites (the others being Murcens, on the Causse de Gramat, and Capdenac-le-Haut east of Figeac) that claim to be *Uxellodunum,* where Vercingetorix and the Cadurci suffered their last defeat before Caesar in 51 BC.

Carennac

At Carennac, on a backwater of the Dordogne, there is an ancient priory which, despite periods of abuse, has retained a certain charm. A dependent of Cluny dedicated to St Peter, it was probably begun towards the end of the 11th century. In the 15th century, the cloister and chapter house were rebuilt. Even before the Revolution the monastery was in a lamentable state and most of its possessions were sold soon after. The priory buildings were remodelled in the 16th and 17th centuries and incorporate the façade facing the river known as the château (c. 15th century) which contains a museum of local history.

The Romanesque sculpted tympanum above the church porch is impressive. Protected by a deep arch and supported by a cluster of four pillars in the centre and two at each side, it is a finely chiselled but rigorous composition of great clarity, reminiscent of the north porch at Cahors (*see p. 180*). The centre panel is filled by the hieratic figure of Christ in a mandorla, his hand raised in blessing. In the spandrels are the symbols of the four Evangelists. The space on either side is divided horizontally into two registers containing the Apostles, with small crouching figures in the extreme corners. A delicately carved vegetal *rinceau* outlines the composition and the narrow lintel has a regular pattern of alternating pearls and little animals.

To the east an 11th-century door with a double arch and four decorated capitals is signed by the mason, Girbertus. The modest 12th-century church has a barrel-vaulted nave and some interesting capitals. There is a shallow transept and a cupola on pendentives above the crossing and a few touches of colour in the vaults.

The Cloister of Carennac (*open July–Aug 10–12 & 2-7; April–June, Sept 10–12 & 2–6, closed Sun; Oct–March 10–12 & 2–5, closed Sun; T: 06 65 10 51 22*), has one surviving Romanesque gallery on the south whereas the rest was rebuilt in Flamboyant style in the 16th century, also reminiscent of Cahors. In the restored chapter house is a 16th-century *Entombment*, a moving ensemble of sculptures with a hint of the original polychrome. Gathered around the Christ are the life-sized figures of Nicodemus and Joseph of Arimathaea, with Mary in the centre, on her right St John, Mary Magdalene holding the ointment jar, and two other Maries.

The Chateau de Carennac (*open July–Sept Tues–Sun 10–12 & 2–6; Easter–June, Oct, Tues–Fri 10–12 & 2–6; for other times T: 05 65 33 81 36*) was the Residence of the Deans of Carennac, and contains the *Espace Patrimoine*, with an exhibition of the Pays d'Art et d'Histoire de la Vallée de la Dordogne.

Château de Castelnau-Bretenoux

Open July–Aug 9.30–7; May–June 9.30–12.30 & 2–6.30; Sept–April 10–12.30 & 2–5.30, Oct–April closed Tues; T: 05 65 10 98 00.

The hamlet of Prudhomat-Castelnau, between Carennac and St-Céré, cowers in the shadow of the Château de Castelnau-Bretenoux. This is a truly impressive example of feudal architecture, emphasised by the blood-red colour of the ferruginous limestone of its construction and its position on a plateau overlooking the borders between the old provinces of Périgord, Limousin, Auvergne and Quercy. The Barons of Castelnau go back to the 11th century, and the castle remained in the hands of their descendants or a branch of the family for 38 generations until 1830. The last of the line, Albert de Luynes, was forced at the Revolution to demolish the upper part of the towers and fill in the ditches. In 1851, a fire caused extensive damage. Jean Mouliérat, a well known member of the Opéra Comique and the castle's last private owner (1896–1932), partially restored it before donating it to the State.

The castle follows the triangular form of the plateau and has a massive tower at each angle, a semi-circular one in each side and a square keep on the southwest. The earliest section of the building dates from the turn of the 12th century, with two-light round-arched windows. Major programmes of enlargement and fortification were carried out in the following two centuries assuring its defence during the Hundred Years War, but by the 16th–17th centuries it was transformed into a more hospitable residence. It contains, among other things, a collection of medieval sculpture and Jean Mouliérat's collection of religious art.

In the village the Collegiate Church, built in the 15th century by Jean de Castelnau, still has its 16th-century carved wooden stalls, similar to those in the Cathedral of Auch (*see p. 398*), and several statues including a polychrome *Baptism of Christ* (15th century). In the treasury is a 14th-century arm-shaped reliquary, *le Bras de St Louis*.

ST-CÉRÉ & ENVIRONS

St-Céré, is a lively and cultured town that holds an important summer music festival. In the centre of town, around Rue de la République, the main street, and Rue du Mazel, are some 15th–17th-century houses with medieval and Renaissance features. The Quai des Récollets, on the bank of La Bave, has pretty views onto the river, with old houses and bridges. The artist Jean Lurçat (1892–1966) lived in St-Céré for over 20 years and his work can be seen in two places. In town, off Place du Mercadial, the Casino contains the **Gallery d'Art Exposition Jean Lurçat** (*open Mon–Sat 9.30–12 & 2.30–6.30; Oct–June closed Tues; May–Sept also open Sun 11–7; T: 05 65 38 19 60, www.le-casino.fr*), which combines an art gallery for temporary exhibitions, a shop and café, and a permanent collection of Lurçat's tapestries and ceramics.

The two towers high above St-Céré mark the 14th-century château purchased in 1945 by Lurçat, St-Laurent-les-Tours. The **Atelier-Musée Jean Lurçat** (*open Easter, and mid-July–Sept 9.30–12 & 2.30–6.30; T: 05 65 38 28 21*) is a fascinating insight into Lurçat's later work. He started his career as a painter and was influenced by the important artistic movements of the early 20th century but he is best known as a tapestry designer, the most prolific of his generation. He began experimenting with the medium in 1917. The large rooms of St-Laurent-les-Tours, decorated in his own inimitable style, make the perfect setting for his highly idiosyncratic and vividly coloured tapestries. There are also tapestry cartoons, a large number of paintings, sketches, ceramics, fabrics and furniture, demonstrating the full range of the artist's work. Mme Simone Lurçat, the painter's widow, donated the collection to the *département*.

Château de Montal
Open April–Oct 9.30–12 & 2.30-6, closed Sat; T: 05 65 38 13 72.
West of St-Céré at St-Jean-Lespinasse, this perfect French Renaissance château has a sorry history. It was built by Jeanne de Balzac, who in 1503 had inherited a fortune from her father, Robert de Balzac d'Entragues, Governor of Pisa during the French occupation of Northern Italy. Widowed in 1511, she began the construction of Montal for her son Robert, killed six months after his departure for Italy in 1523. The house

is a testament to Jeanne de Balzac's enthusiasm for Italian Renaissance architecture and demonstrates the alacrity with which innovations introduced into France from Italy were taken up in the early 16th century. In the rugged Quercy, Montal must have been an oasis of refinement. The exterior façades retain all the characteristics of a feudal fortress, while the interior courtyard elevations are luxuriously decorated with an Italianate vocabulary of friezes, pilasters, candelabra, allegorical subjects, statues in niches, and high-relief busts commemorating Jeanne de Balzac's family. There is also a very grand straight-flight staircase, sculpted on the underside. Montal was stripped of all its decoration in the late 19th century and the items were sold off in job lots. It was purchased just before the First World War by the wealthy industrialist and enlightened patron, Maurice Fenaille (*see p. 214*). After years of patient searching, Fenaille recovered many of the original pieces or had copies of them commissioned, returning the château to something approaching its original appearance. During the Second World War, Montal was the last hiding place of the *Mona Lisa* (*see p. 238*).

ROCAMADOUR

Rocamadour, the principal attraction in this part of the Midi-Pyrénées, shelters at its heart a group of sanctuaries which have been the object of pilgrimage for hundreds of years and to which pilgrims are still drawn on the first Sunday of each September. The magnetism of the place is hard to define, but in the Middle Ages the challenging aspect of this inhospitable ravine and the difficulties of access probably contributed to the penance of a pilgrimage. The drama of the *cité* clinging to the rock above the Alzou Valley is best viewed from the hamlet of l'Hospitalet on the plateau above. Today the site has been fully developed to make life much easier for visitors. Lifts run in two stages from the village to the sanctuaries (March-15 Nov) and from the sanctuaries to the château (all year). The Cité Réligieuse and the centre of the Cité Médiévale are pedestrianised and there are night-time visits by little train (T: 05 65 38 33 94) around the illuminated site, starting at Porte du Figuier. At L'Hospitalet, La Féérie autour du Rail (performances throughout the day April-Nov, T: 05 65 33 71 06, www.la-feerie.com) is a model *Son et Lumière* in an enchanted miniature kingdom. When it comes to the edible specialities of the area, the most renowned are the small disks of soft goats' milk cheese that carry the AOC 'Rocamadour'.

CITÉ MÉDIÉVALE

Pilgrims have always gathered at Porte de l'Hospitalet, at the top of the cliff, where fragments of the chapel of the old pilgrim hospital of St-Jean have survived, incorporated into the 19th-century chapel. The pilgrimage *voie sainte* leads down the cliff to the village which clings precariously to the rock-face suspended just above the valley of the tiny Alzou river. The buildings, some genuinely old, nearly all now eateries or boutiques, are strung out along one main street which runs under four fortified medieval gateways. Between the first, Porte du Figuier, and the most picturesque, Porte Salmon, is the lift to the sanctuaries of the Cité Religieuse.

The 15th-century Hôtel de Ville contains tapestries by Jean Lurçat (*see p. 169*) and nearby are the 216 steps of the Grand Escalier to the Cité Réligieuse. From here the road slopes downhill under Porte Hugon, the penultimate of the four gates, to arrive at Porte Basse at the end of the village.

CITÉ RELIGIEUSE

The Cité Religieuse, sadly lacking in spiritual warmth on non-pilgrimage days, consists of a number of sanctuaries or churches, some open only from July to September. The sanctuaries were massively restored and rebuilt in the 19th century, the best features being fragments of 12th- and 15th-century frescoes. The churches are on different levels but all lead off a common parvis centred on the first rocky resting-place of St Amadour where, so the story goes, his body was exhumed intact in 1166, centuries after his death. Picturesque legends are associated with the saint. One proposes that he was Zacchaeus, the Jew, former tax collector of Jericho, who climbed a maple to see Christ and who, after his conversion to Christianity, distributed half his wealth to the poor. He was said to have become the servant of the Virgin, but eventually he left for Gaul and there led the life of a hermit. Another legend suggests that he and his wife, St Veronica (of the cloth with the image of Christ), sailed away up the Gironde and, after Veronica's death, Amadour lived in the caves above the Alzou.

Church of Notre-Dame

Open April–Oct 8.30–6; Jan–March 9–5.30; Nov–Dec 9-6.30.

The main sanctuary, the Church of Notre-Dame, was rebuilt after a rock fall in 1479 and damaged in the 16th century. It was restored and enlarged in the 19th century. To the right of the entrance is a fragment of a 15th-century wall-painting of ghoulish skeletons, The Three Dead and the Three Living. Inside, above the altar (1889) stands the famous 12th-century *Black Virgin*, one of a series of enigmatic black Madonnas. The 'blackness' of this Madonna was

The entrance to the church of Notre-Dame with (right) traces of 15th-century wall paintings.

first mentioned in the 17th century. Originally a reliquary statue, it has suffered over the centuries and both Madonna and Child acquired crowns in the 19th century. Rocamadour has connections with the sea, represented by *ex-voto* models of boats. But the most phoney of all the accoutrements associated with the place has to be the replica of Roland's faithful sword Durandal, embedded in the cliff above the Notre-Dame chapel, the original of which was offered by Charlemagne's companion to Our Lady of Rocamadour. In June 1183 Young King Henry (*see p. 167*) and his brother Geoffrey, their allowances cut off by their father, went looting and plundering through the region, and snatched Roland's sword from Rocamadour.

HISTORY OF ROCAMADOUR

The first mention of a church at 'Roc-Amadour' comes in the 11th century when the two Benedictine abbeys of Marcilhac and Tulle disputed the site. The monks of Tulle won the day and it was at this time that a Marian cult associated with Rocamadour was first recorded. Its reputation was enhanced by the *Book of Miracles of Our Lady of Rocamadour* written in 1172. Pilgrimages by such notables as St Bernard de Clairvaux (c. 1147) and Henry (II) Plantagenet (1170) put the site securely on the map, and other pious grandees followed in their wake. At its apogee in the 14th century, Rocamadour was quite probably as busy as it is today, but the troubles of the Reformation started a decline until, by the 19th century, the town had been all but forgotten. In 1829 a group of enthusiastic ecclesiastics instigated the physical and spiritual revival of the site and reinstated an annual pilgrimage in 1835. Evening candlelight processions take place from 14th August–8th September each year.

Other sanctuaries and the Musée d'Art Sacrée

On the exterior wall of the 12th-century chapel of St-Michel (opposite Notre-Dame) are some remarkable but damaged late 12th- and 13th-century frescoes of the *Annunciation* and *Visitation*. Beyond, a terrace offers good views over the village. On the northeastern side of the terrace, next to Notre-Dame, the Basilica of St-Sauveur (*same opening times as Notre-Dame*), originally 12th-century, is the largest sanctuary, its west end built into the cliff face and supporting a wooden gallery. A rectangular space divided into equal naves by two piers with eight columns from which spring diagonal ribs, it is lit by diffused light from the five windows in the east. Confusingly it has been reorientated so that the altar is in the north. Steps from St-Sauveur lead down to the church of St-Amadour underneath, the least altered of the medieval buildings with heavy squared ribs similar to the narthex at Moissac. The sacristy was created later from the cistern of the keep. The three further sanctuaries of St-Blaise, St-Jean and St-Anne (*only accessible during religious festivals or guided visits June to September, 10.30–2.30*), containing the 17th-century altar from the Notre-Dame chapel, close the terrace to the east.

The 'abbey palace' (mainly 19th century) houses the **Musée d'Art Sacrée** (*open July–Aug 9–7; Sept–June 9.30–12 & 2-6; T: 05 65 33 23 23*), dedicated to Francis Poulenc (1899–1963), who composed the Litanies to the Black Virgin. Born in Paris to a family who originated in neighbouring Rouergue, the composer experienced a religious reconversion before the Virgin of Rocamadour in 1936. The museum has a wide and interesting range of religious objects (11th–20th centuries) including reliquaries, statues, stained glass and paintings. An exterior glass-sided lift with great views of the valley serves the different floors.

THE BOURIANE

GOURDON & ENVIRONS

Gourdon, situated on a limestone mound typical of the landscape, is the main town of the Bouriane, the wooded area south of the Dordogne river, west of Rocamadour. A circular boulevard surrounds the mound with buildings whose colour and quality are reminiscent of Sarlat, some 20km to the northwest across the valley of the Dordogne. The old main street, Rue Majou (Mayor), starts at a 13th-century chapel and climbs up to the arcaded main square between attractive old buildings. The unadorned but surprisingly large **Church of St-Pierre**, which was built in the 14th century, has some late medieval and 16th-century stained glass. It also contains gilded 17th-century works by the Tournier family, three generations (Raymond, Jean and François) of master-sculptors from Gourdon. They turned out elaborate altarpieces to a certain standard format in line with the recommendations of the Council of Trent during the period of the Counter-Reformation (1660–1720). Their work can be found over a fairly wide area in southwest France. From the church, steps lead up to the summit where the castle once stood, now an open space with an all-round view and orientation table.

Just north of Gourdon, the **Grottes de Cougnac** (*guided visits April–June 10–11.30 & 2.30–5; July–Aug 10–6; Sept 10–11.30 & 2.30–5; Oct 2–4 closed Sun; T: 05 65 41 47 54*) are in fact two separate caves, one with fantastic concretions and the other with important prehistoric paintings of animals and also human figures in black and red.

At **Les Prades**, 3.5km from the centre of Le Vigan, in a delightful rural setting is the Musée Henri Giron (*open July–Aug 10–6; June, Sept 10–12.15 & 3–6; closed Mon; open Sundays only in winter; restaurant and museum T: 05 65 41 33 78*). Created in 1991 around a private art collection, Henri Giron, born 1914 near Lyons, now lives in Brussels. Self-taught, he almost always paints women and has developed a very distinctive figurative style. There is an excellent little restaurant at the museum, open on Friday evenings and Sunday (for a seven-course feast) at midday only, which must be booked in advance.

Some 20km southwest of Gourdon at **Les Arques** is a virtually unaltered 11th-century Romanesque church with unique Mozarabic-inspired capitals and a crypt. The tiny village, with about 170 inhabitants, made a huge impact on the Russian sculptor, Ossip Zadkine (1890–1967), who had an on-going love affair with the Midi-Pyrénées from the 1920s and bought a house in Les Arques in 1934. Intellectual, musician and poet as well as sculptor, his arrival in this bucolic village must have caused quite a stir.

The **Musée Zadkine** (*open April–Sept 10–1 & 2–7, Dec–Jan 2–5; T: 05 65 22 83 37*), opened in 1988 in the sculptor's former studio which has been converted into an attractive gallery. The work here shows his range, including sculpture, prints, photographs and tapestries. Stylistically his work owes a particularly heavy debt to Cubism and primitive sculpture but emotionally it is Expressionist. The exhibits are on loan from the Musée Zadkine in Paris but several of the large wooden sculptures were conceived in Les Arques: *Daphne* (1939), hewn from a massive trunk; *Diane* (1941) in poplar and painted, a work he always kept in his home; and the stark, highly charged *Pietà* (1939–40) in the church. In the museum are the project for his first major monument, for Rotterdam, *The Destroyed City* (1947), and bronzes of his most successful work, *Orpheus* (1948), the dynamic *Arlequin Hurlant* (1956), *Arbre des Grâces* (1962) and the compact and polished *Pomone* (1960).

Zadkine also participated in the restoration of the Romanesque church of **St-André-des-Arques**, and in 1954 discovered some remarkable 15th-century murals which have, unfortunately, been allowed to deteriorate.

PRACTICAL INFORMATION

GETTING AROUND

• **By train:** Paris Austerlitz to Toulouse via Souillac, Gourdon, Cahors, Lalbenque, Caussade. From Brive to Toulouse via Rocamadour-Padirac, Gramat, Flaujac, Assier, Figeac, Capdenac; also Brive to Aurillac via Vayrac, Bétaille, Puybrun, Bretenoux, Laval-de-Cère; Aurillac to Capdenac via Figeac.

• **By bus:** Cahors to Libos, serves the Lot valley west of Cahors; and Cahors to Capdenac to the east. Timetable: Conseil Général du Lot, Hôtel du Département, Pl. Chapou, BP 291, 46005 Cahors, T: 05 65 23 27 50

TOURIST INFORMATION

Carennac Cour de Prieuré, T: 05 65 10 97 01, www.tourisme-carennac.com
Gourdon 24 Rue du Majou, T: 05 65 27 52 50, www.quercy-tourisme.com/gourdon
Martel Pl. des Consuls, T: 05 65 37 43 44, www.martel.fr
Rocamadour l'Hospitalet, T: 05 65 33 22 00, Hôtel de Ville, Pilgrimage information, T: 05 65 33 23 23. www.rocamadour.com .
St-Céré Pl. de la République, T: 05 65 38 11 85, www.quercy-tourisme.com/saint-cere
Souillac Blvd L.J.-Malvy, T: 05 65 37 81 56, www.tourisme-souillac.com

Alvignac

€ Hôtel/Restaurant du Château. On the foundations of an ancient château within a large park in the northern Lot, this hotel has a flowery terrace and shady courtyard. Run by Valérie et Jean-Philippe Perrier, there is a friendly welcome and good service. Rte de Rocamadour, T: 05 65 33 60 14, www.hotelduchateaualvignac.com

Bretenoux

€ Hostellerie Belle Rive Dumont, Port du Gagnac. On the banks of the Cère, 14 pleasant individualised rooms, a shady terrace, and delicious traditional cooking, listed among *Bonnes Tables du Lot*, with menus €22–38.

Calès

€ Le Petit Relais. In a pretty *bastide* this comfortable little hotel has 15 recently renovated rooms. It has a terrace and sizeable restaurant where the food is very good with menus from €15–55 serving traditional dishes. T: 05 65 37 96 09, www.le-petit-relais.fr.

Gourdon

€€ Hôtel/Restaurant Domaine du Berthiol. Very attractive hotel in a leafy setting with pool just outside the pretty town of Gourdon. The dining room has a luminous quality and the dishes are colourful and easy on the eye and palate; menus €24–46. The 29 rooms are pleasantly light and the décor understated. (on the D704) T: 05 65 41 33 33, www.hotelperigord.com

Lacave

€€€ Château de la Treyne. This medieval château set in elegant gardens and 120 hectares of forest above the Dordogne has glorious views. It is run by Michèle Gombert and son Philippe. The spacious rooms are full of character - one in the old chapel and another in the 14th century tower - with luxury modern bathrooms. The restaurant, under the watchful eye of Stéphane Andrieux, was awarded a Michelin rosette in 2001, and meals are served in the Louis XIII salon or on the riverside terrace. A62 from Souillac, D43, T: 05 65 27 60 60, www.chateaudelatreyne.com

€€ Le Pont de l'Ouysse. Discreet elegance is the hallmark of Marinette and Daniel Chambon's establishment in a gorgeous setting on the south bank of the Dordogne. The 11 bedrooms combine beautiful wooden floors and graceful modern decor; there is a heated pool. Dishes cooked with simplicity and guile have earned the restaurant a Michelin rosette. They are based on the excellent fish, game, fruit and vegetables of the region, and served on the riverside terrace in summer. T: 05 65 37 87 04, www.lepontdelouysse.fr.

Les Arques

€€€ Restaurant La Récréation. Jacques Ratier's table is considered one of the best for local traditional cooking but his personal flair has been expanded through his training in some of the great kitchens of France and from experience abroad. He and his wife Noelle run an establishment which is equally appreciated locally and by visitors from all over the world. T: 05 65 22 88 08.

Martel

€ Relais Ste-Anne. This charming small hotel occupies in a former nuns' residence complete with chapel. The elegantly modern and bright rooms overlook a walled garden with heated pool and sauna. Breakfast is served in front of a large fireplace or outside. No restaurant. Rue Pourtanel, T: 05 65 37 40 56, www.relais-sainte-anne.com.

Meyronne

€€ **Hotel/Restaurant La Terrasse**. The splendid old castle was converted by the Liebus family into a hotel in the 1920s. Inside and out are beautiful spaces, a pool under the walls, views of the Espérance Valley and elegant bed-rooms. Regional gastronomy reigns supreme. Menus €20–49. T: 05 65 32 21 60, www.hotel-la-terrasse.com

Padirac

€ **L'Auberge de Mathieu**. This is a small and charming auberge in green surroundings with just 7 comfortable rooms. Meals are served in the restau-rant, on the veranda or on the terrace, where you can appreciate the cooking of Christian Pinquie who specialises in ingredients from the region. Lieu-dit Mathieu, T: 05 65 33 64 68, http://perso-wanadoo.fr/ auberge.matheiu

Prudhomat

€€ **Restaurant Les Remparts 'Castelnau'**. At the foot of the Château de Castelnau benefitting from a magnif-icent view, the restaurant serves regional specialities in an inventive and appetis-ing manner. T: 05 65 38 52 88.

€ **Chambres d'hôte Relais du Seuil de la Dordogne**. The old stone house dates from 1600 and stands in 2 hectares of grounds with a view of the Chateau de Castelnau-Bretenoux. Calm, restful, close to the Dordogne, there are 7 rooms and a studio. No *table d'hôte* but a terrace, barbecue and small kitchen for guests' use. M. et Mme. de

la Barrière, Vayssières, T: 05 65 38 50 22, email jean.de.labarriere@wanadoo.fr

Rocamadour

€€ **Le Beau Site**. Hotel and restaurant are opposite sides of the main street at the heart of the *cité*. The hotel has been carefully restored and the bedrooms are fresh and contemporary with views either onto the sanctuaries or the valley. The bright, airy restaurant overlooks the Alzou gorge and Franck Laubadere's cooking is based on local ingredients. T: 05 65 33 63 08, www.bw-beausite.com.

€€ **Le Troubadour**. This small, restored farmhouse combines conven-ience with tranquillity very close to the village. There are ten bedrooms, five of them with balcony, as well as a billiard room and pool. Marie José cooks good traditional Quercynois dishes such as *foie gras au torchon*, or *magret de canard au vin de Cahors*. Belveyre (on the Padirac road/D673), T: 05 65 33 70 27, www.rocamadour.com/fr/hotels/Troubad our/index.htm

St-Céré

€ **Hôtel/Restaurant Le France**. A good value hotel with 22 rooms in the town centre, set in gardens, with a pool, with a recommended restaurant.181 Ave F. de Maynard, T: 05 65 38 02 16, www.lefrance-hotel.com

€ **Hôtel/Restaurant Villa Ric**. This green oasis above the town shelters an intimate hotel with five charming rooms and a lovely pool and terrace with superb views. The owner/chef Jean-Pierre is known for his inventive cook-ing. Route de Leyme, T: 05 65 38 04 08, www.jpric.com

St-Jean-Lespinasse

€€ **Hôtel/Restaurant Les Trois Soleils de Montal**. A relatively new establishment surrounded by 4 hectares of park, elegant and well-equipped, with a pool, 2 restaurants and terrace with panoramic views. The exceptional cuisine offers dishes using the local produce such as foie gras and truffles, lamb and veal and well deserves its Michelin rosette. Dishes range from hearty-rustic to very refined; menus €35–50. Route de Gramat, Montal, T: 05 65 10 16 16, www.lestroissoleils.fr.st

Souillac

€ La Vieille Auberge. Excellent traditional dining under the direction of Robert Veril, in the restaurant decorated in pastel shades (menus €25–35); comfortable but unexciting rooms, pool, sauna. 1 Rue de Recège, T: 05 65 32 79 43, www.la-vieille-auberge.com

€€ Les Granges Vieilles. A 19th-century mansion full of character set in a 3 hectare park with 11 rooms. On fine days, meals served outside near the pool. For 20 years Gérard Cayre has concocted delights from regional produce as well as specialities such as *ragoût d'escargots a la crème d'ail en feuilleté*, and is famous for his *soufflés*. Route de Sarlat, T: 05 65 37 80 92, www.lesgrangesvieilles.com

St Médard

€€€ Restaurant Le Gindreau. At St Médard near Catus, Alexis Pélissou has transformed the old village school into a gastronomic destination. His cooking is traditional and inventive. It calls on local and seasonal produce—melons, walnuts, truffles—which he blends with the carefully calibrated spices to create fresh and colourful dishes with hints of the Orient. Meals served on the terrace or in the comfortable dining room. (Michelin star) T: 05 65 36 22 27, http://perso.wanadoo.fr/le.gindreau/

MARKET DAYS

Carennac Tuesday afternoon (July and August)
Bretenoux Tuesday, Saturday
Gourdon Tuesday, Saturday; *foire* 1st/3rd Tuesday of month
Lacave Monday, Thursday afternoon July-August
Martel Wednesday, Saturday; Truffle market December-January
St-Céré Saturday; *foire* 1st/3rd Sunday of month
Souillac Friday; Wednesday afternoon July-August ; *foire* 1st/3rd Friday

FESTIVALS & EVENTS

July: *Les Trétaux de la chanson Française*, French song festival, Gourdon, T: 05 65 41 17 17
Festival du jazz Sim Copans, annual jazz festival, Souillac, T: 05 65 37 81 56
Festival de la Bande Dessinée, celebrating the comic-strip, Martel, T: 05 65 37 43 44
July and August: *Les Mercredis de Rocamadour*, open-air concerts and cinema, Rocamadour, T: 05 65 33 22 00
Festival Lyrique de St-Céré, operas and concers, St-Céré, T: 05 65 38 29 08
August: *Festival du Mime Automate*, celebration of silent automata, Souillac, T: 05 65 37 07 07
Rencontres Cinéma, open-air cinema, Gindou, T: 05 65 22 89 99
Divergences s'exportent à Gindou, festival of contemporary dance, Gindou, T: 05 65 22 86 41
September: *Rassemblement européen de montgolfières*, hot-air balloons, Rocamadour, T: 05 65 33 22 00.

THE LOT VALLEY

The Lot River creates an extraordinarily beautiful valley, although less celebrated than the Dordogne Valley or Tarn Gorges. To the east of Cahors, the Lot flows through countryside which is at times untamed and the population sparse, passing beneath the cliff-top village of St-Cirq-Lapopie; to the west, the valley is wider and gentler, scattered with small communities such as Puy l'Eveque, and dominated by the vineyards which produce the robust red wines of Cahors. Parts of the river are navigable and a peaceful time can be spent on a river boat.

CAHORS

Cahors, situated on a peninsula formed by a tight bend in the river Lot and protected by rocky cliffs, is a small town at ease with its historic past and equally comfortable in the 21st century. The town is divided unequally in two by the post-Revolution Boulevard Gambetta, a shaded avenue running north–south and lined by 19th century institutions. The two most important monuments of the town are the medieval Pont Valentré to the west, bridging the Lot; and the domed Cathedral of St-Etienne in the old town to the east. Here the streets are crammed with interesting buildings and secret courtyards, which have been the focus of much careful restoration. Three further bridges span the river, Pont Cabessut to the east, Pont Louis-Philippe to the south, and the most recent, Pont des Ramparts, built in the 1990s, some way north of the Pont Valentré. In the past few years, Cahors has also capitalised on its green spaces, linking them along a route marked out with studs bearing an acanthus leaf design and described in the leaflet *Les Jardins Secrets* available from the Tourist Office.

EXPLORING CAHORS

St-Etienne Cathedral
A veritable textbook of architecture from the 12th to the 18th centuries, the cathedral was begun c 1109–12 to replace an earlier building. Work went on almost continuously until the 13th century. Major modifications were carried out at the end of that century and also in the 14th. The cloister was altered in the 15th century. Further changes in the 18th century were followed by restoration in the 19th.

The west front
The main west door was created during a grand scheme of renovation and Gothicisation from 1280 to 1324. This was a propitious moment both politically and spiritually and a time of great prosperity. It coincided with the urban reorganisation and the reaffirmation of the orthodox Church after the Cathar heresies. In a desire to

harmonise the building, the cupolas were covered by a single roof and the east end was raised. The west end was added at the end of the 13th century, re-orientating the building, originally facing the town with the Romanesque north portal (*pictured overleaf*). The decorative features of the west front are emphasised by a barely articulated surface. The elevation is divided horizontally by two moulded string courses supporting high-relief sculptures and, apart from these and the hood mouldings carrying sculptures, all the decoration—made up of blind arcades organised into a square—is concentrated around the Rayonnant rose window, innovative for the period. The upper parts of the belfry-porch were completed in the 17th century.

HISTORY OF CAHORS

The ancient city of Cahors, known by the 1st century BC as *Divona* and from the 3rd century as *Civitas Caducorum*, was capital of the Cadurci people and the site of a shrine linked with the cult of water. Gallo-Roman *Divona* occupied most of the peninsula for some centuries but Frankish invasions in the 6th century brought this culture to an end and barely a stone of the old city remains. Cahors had already been Christianised in the previous century, and the rebirth of the town is attributed to St Didier (bishop 630–55). In the 12th century, a new cathedral and cloister replaced an earlier building, and when the troubles of the Cathar heresies (*see p. 251*) had passed, the town expanded into an important banking centre. In his *Divine Comedy* (1321) Dante condemned Cahors' bankers or moneylenders to hell and *Caorsin* became synonymous with usurer.

In 1316 the town prospered further when Jacques Duèze, from a local family, was elected second pope at Avignon. As John XXII (1316–34) he bestowed many favours on his town including, in 1332, a university which enjoyed a wide reputation for three centuries. A vast programme of urban renewal was launched around this time. In 1360 the Treaty of Brétigny placed Cahors, as part of Aquitaine, under English control but the town managed to break away after only 10 years. During the conflicts of the Reformation, extremely divisive in the Quercy, Cahors remained Catholic resulting in two attacks by the Protestants. By the 17th century Cahors' zenith had passed and it settled down as a legal and academic centre with lawyers, magistrates and, with the foundation in 1627 of an Académie de Lettres, intellectuals. In 1674 the Collège des Jesuits was built, and by 1680 the population began to spread beyond the ramparts which were by then redundant, initiating their demolition. It was not until the 19th century, when remaining defences were taken down and ditches filled, that the town began to grow, with the construction of Allées Fénelon and Blvd Gambetta, the introduction of the railway, and erection of civic buildings such as Hôtel de Ville (1837–47), the theatre (1832–42) and the Palais de Justice (1857). Only in the 1950s did Cahors begin to spread beyond the natural confines of the peninsula.

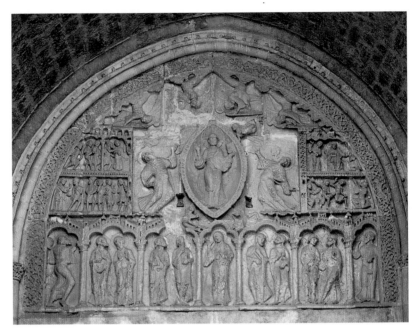

The tympanum (c. 1140–50) of the north portal of St-Etienne cathedral.

The north portal

The Romanesque north portal, one of the masterpieces of Romanesque sculpture in the Midi-Pyrénées, disappeared from view in the 18th century. It was rediscovered in 1840 and for some time mistakenly thought to have been moved from the west front. During the 12th century, the orientation of the streets around the cathedral had a different emphasis, the main north–south route through the medieval town corresponding to the present Rue Clément Marot running perpendicular to the north door. In the 1990s this approach to the door was lowered to return the porch to its original proportions.

A deep, slightly pointed arch protects the sculpted tympanum, generally thought to date c. 1140–50. The main theme of the relief is the Ascension of Christ, but unusual emphasis is given to the patron saint of the cathedral, the protomartyr St Stephen. There are stylistic links with Moissac, and although there is a serious attempt to introduce variety to the individual figures and a certain animation to the composition, the arrangement is more rigidly compartmentalised and less free-flowing. Christ, isolated in an oval mandorla, is flanked by two dancing or gesturing angels who emphasise his upright figure and form a link to the other parts of the composition. To either side of the Virgin below, her hand raised towards Christ, are the eleven Apostles present before Pentecost (when Judas was replaced by Matthias) framed in trilobed arches. It is not easy to make out the eleventh apostle who is squeezed into the left-hand corner beside the back view of the tenth. Unlike Moissac, there is a striking uniformity in the size of the main protagonists.

The anecdotal scenes of St Stephen's martyrdom in the spandrels are in a different mood and tempo. On the left, Stephen professes his faith to the Sanhedrin, the supreme court of Ancient Israel, some of whom wear bonnets. On the opposite side, present at the stoning of Stephen is Saul, at whose feet the false witnesses place their mantles in readiness to cast the first stones. One of Stephen's persecutors can be seen sheltering in the foliage of the extrados. The hand of God linking the upper register to the lower refers to Stephen's blessed vision before his execution: 'I see the heaven's opened, and the Son of man standing on the right hand of God'.

Banal scenes of hunting and fighting fill the outer arch. The cornice above the portal, however, is peopled by a series of witty little figures whose torsos extend into the billet moulding and whose legs appear in the medallions on the underside. The rosette decoration was extended into the upper part of the portal in the early 20th century.

On the opposite side of the cathedral, the third entrance to the cathedral is the small south door (c. 1130; *open*), by a narrow margin the oldest of the three entrances. It is a pretty trilobed construction under a double round-headed arch in which the points of the lobes are divided and rolled. The brick arcades above are a later addition.

The interior

The west porch or narthex is linked to the nave by a descending flight of steps. Around the upper section are murals (1316–24) with 12 scenes from the *Creation* to the *Expulsion*, restored in 1988; the organ (1702–06), placed in the porch in 1722, was moved forward to its present position in order to expose the murals. The surprisingly vast (20m wide) aisleless nave, probably begun c. 1120, was one of a group of 12th-century domed churches in the southwest (*see p. 112*). The cupolas at Cahors, on pendentives and carried by massive arches and six strong piers, are the most audacious, 16m in diameter and 32m above ground. The western cupola is embellished with a rare monumental Gothic mural representing in the corolla, the Prophets, and in the apex, the *Martyrdom of St Stephen*.

The walls of the east end were raised in 1280—just two Romanesque capitals survive on the north—bringing it to a height commensurate with the nave and making feasible the insertion of tall windows. The St Anthony chapel was added in 1491, and the more original Notre-Dame chapel (also called the Chapelle Profonde) was consecrated in 1484 by Bishop Antoine d'Alamand. The decoration introduces the Cadurcien rose motif, with *bâtons écotés* (resembling pruned branches) and suns with undulating rays. These motifs also became very popular on secular buildings in and around Cahors until the beginning of the 16th century. The polychrome relief panel of the *Immaculate Conception* in the chapel was almost completely destroyed after the Wars of Religion but the vaults still have their original 16th-century painted decoration. The retable (1679–81) dedicated to the Virgin was designed by Gervais Drouet of Toulouse and made in Cahors. Drouet, a student of Bernini's in Rome, was one of the more brilliant sculptors in southwest France during the reign of Louis XIV.

Surviving features from a revamp of the interior during the 18th century are the main altar (1702–06) in red marble from Caunes in the Languedoc; the red-marble north gallery (1734), which resulted in the disappearance of the north portal; and the pulpit which was installed in 1738. The walls were plastered in white to set off the marble. Fragments of 14th-century paintings discovered in the apse during restoration work in the 19th century led to the repainting, or reinterpreting, of all the painted decoration. This was completed in 1874 and coincided with the introduction of stained glass commissioned in 1872 by Bishop Grimardias from Joseph Villiet of Bordeaux. The iconography is based on cycles of the lives of Christ, the Virgin and local saints as well as St Stephen. The glass is of very high quality, being among the best in the Lot.

The cloister

The Flamboyant cloister, which replaced the 12th-century cloister, is linked to the church by a door in the south of the choir. Work began in the east gallery and continued through two building campaigns (1497–1509 and 1514–53), as is demonstrated by the complicated lierne vaults and variation in the doorways carrying the coats of arms of successive bishops, and discrepancies in the height and decoration of the arcades. A few tantalising samples of late Gothic sculpture survived the Reformation, notably the glorious *Virgin of the Annunciation* on the angle pillar in the northwest, with long wavy hair falling on her shoulders. The pendant boss above is decorated with *Christ and Angel musicians* and there is more carving on the door opposite. The cloister garden has been planted with box and rosemary bushes.

The St-Gausbert chapel off the east gallery was the former chapter house (*open June–Sept 10–12.30 & 3–6, closed Sun; T: 05 65 53 20 65*). It houses a small collection of religious artefacts and has late 15th- and early 16th-century murals.

When the cloister is closed, it can be glimpsed from the enclosed courtyard southeast of the Cathedral entered through a vaulted passageway from Rue de la Chantrerie. The courtyard is enclosed by the former archdeacon's residence to the south and west, an engaging building made up of two Gothic houses around a stairwell which were re-done during the Renaissance (c. 1520–40) with mullioned windows, *rinceaux*, busts in medallions, pilasters and candelabras.

Place Jean-Jacques Chapou

Place J.-J. Chapou, the cathedral forecourt, was named after a hero of the Resistance, Jean-Jacques Chapou (1909–44), a bust of whom can be seen near the south door. In one of their first theatrical gestures of defiance, on November 11th, 1943, Armistice Day, Chapou's group of *maquis* briefly occupied the village of Marcilhac (*see p. 203*) in order to lay a wreath at the war memorial. This space was first created at the beginning of the 14th century, as was the former episcopal palace on the north side, but the latter was almost totally rebuilt and altered in the 17th and 19th centuries and is now occupied by the *Préfecture* of the Lot. On the west side of Place Chapou, the sign *Gambetta Jeune et Cie, bazar génois* was discovered when a bank took over the premises (*see box below*). On Wednesday and Saturday mornings, one of the best open-air markets in the Lot fills Place Chapou, a sensual experience of sight, taste and smell, bringing together regional and seasonal produce such as strawberries, Rocamadour cheese and *cèpes*. There is a flower market on Sunday mornings and a market every day in the market hall (1869) to the south. Two of the many superb delicacies to be found in Cahors are *pruneaux fourrés* (stuffed prunes) and *noix enrobés de chocolat* (chocolate-covered walnuts).

LÉON GAMBETTA

Born in Cahors in 1838, Gambetta was the son of an Italian grocer. He went into the legal profession before embarking on a complex career in politics. A vociferous defender of the French Republic, during the siege of Paris by Prussia in 1870 he escaped in a hot air balloon and organised resistance from the provinces with the help of the young Charles de Freycinet. Elected President of the Chamber of Deputies in 1879, where he pleaded for clemency to be shown the *communards*, he was made *Conseil de Cabinet* in 1881. He died in an accident with a revolver at his home in Sèvres in 1882, aged 44, shortly after his lifelong lover Léonie Leon had agreed to their marriage. His funeral was attended by crowds of devoted mourners and prompted nationwide outpourings of grief.

La Chantrerie and Place Champollion

Behind the cathedral, at no. 36 Rue de la Chantrerie (off Place Champollion) a complex 14th-century building, called La Chantrerie, was used from the 17th century by the cathedral chapter to store their wine presses or vats. It was so called because of its proximity to the old residential quarters of the cathedral cantors. An exemplary restoration, the façade has two two-light windows with columns flanking a vast overhanging chimney breast above four Gothic arcades. It now houses the Musée du Vin et de la Truffe (*open July–Aug 9.30–1 & 2.30–7, closed Sun and Mon; T: 05 65 23 99 70*), a cultural centre for temporary exhibitions.

At 27 Rue St-James part of the old choir school, Le Grenier du Chapitre, exists in the courtyard, a 12th–13th-century construction with 13th-century doors and windows. Maison Manhol at no. 18 has a characteristically symmetrical 17th-century façade with mirandes at the top, and just before the corner with Place Chapou is a late medieval façade.

The riverbank, Quai Champollion, leads to Place Champollion, where there is a colourful 19th-century monument by Turcan, Denys Puech (*see p. 214*) and Olivier Merson, to Clément Marot (1495–1544), poet, statesman and sympathiser with the

Reformation. A detour over Pont Cabessut is worth making for the views back across the river to the old town. North of Place Champollion is the pretty Parc Olivier-de-Magny, built on the old cemetery of the church of la Daurade, of which there are scant reminders, and the adjacent 17th-century Benedictine convent. On the south side of the square are two beautiful facades: the restored house with a tower dates from two periods, c. 1250 and c. 1310; and of a similar period is the angle building, with stone arcades supporting a timber-framed and brick upper floor. The 17th-century house at 12 Rue Clément Marot, on the west side of the square, is on the site of the birthplace of Olivier de Magny (1530–c. 1561), lyric poet and sonneteer, contemporary of Ronsard, lover of Louise *La Belle Cordière* Labé, and secretary to Henri II.

To the north, Place de la Libération also has a variety of interesting buildings including no. 44, with three symmetrical bays (rebuilt in 1633). The small streets northwest of the square are worth exploring: no. 3 Rue St-Pierre has a group of 16th- and 17th-century sculpted heads while no. 40 Rue du Portail Alban has a stair-tower with a 16th-century door decorated with *bâtons écotés* and a Neoclassical portal.

Quartier des Soubirous

North of Place de la Libération is the Quartier des Soubirous, served by Rue du Château du Roi and its continuation Rue des Soubirous, leading gently uphill. In this district were built the principal urban palaces of the gentry and nobility. No. 58 displays a mixture of styles, and no. 43 has one of the few remaining exterior timber staircases in the courtyard of the 13th- and 14th-century mansion. In Rue du Four Ste-Catherine is a late 15th-century battlemented stair-tower with a splendid profusion of *bâtons écotés* around the door, one of the best examples of Cadurcien sculpture. Behind is the only remaining, and somewhat disfigured, building of the university, Collège Pélegry. The college, founded in 1368 by Raimond and Hugues de Pélegry for 13 poor students, survived until 1751, when it was suppressed. The Château du Roi, part of a modern block next door, was the temporary residence of the king's representative in the Quercy in the 15th century, but it had previously belonged to relatives of Pope John XXII, the De Via family, who were probably responsible for its construction. By the 19th century it was being used as a prison.

The most remarkable medieval building in Cahors is the 14th-century **Palais Duèze**, attributed to Pierre Duèze, brother of John XXII. The vast urban palace was arranged around a square courtyard. What is left can best be seen from Rue Albe and Place Thiers. The tower (34m high) on Boulevard Gambetta was the tallest in the town, a certain mark of prestige, and favoured the style of the preceding century with two-light Romanesque windows. The palace was subsequently taken over by Edward, the Black Prince, in 1364, but the main wing was demolished in 1405. The church of St-Barthélémy, enclosed within the same walls as the Duèze palace, was partly rebuilt in the 14th century. Orientated north–south, it has a monumental entrance at the base of the belfry similar in style to that of the cathedral and to St-Urcisse (*see p. 186*). The upper part of the imposing belfry-tower has blind arcades in brick. Inside is a plaque commemorating the baptism of the Pope in 1245, and some 15th-century murals.

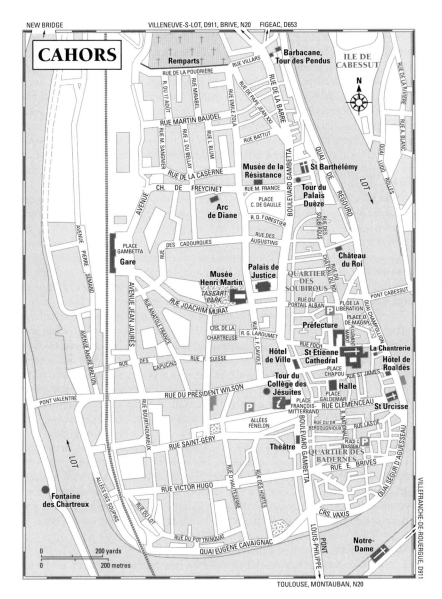

CAHORS

NEW BRIDGE — VILLENEUVE-S-LOT, D911, BRIVE, N20 — FIGEAC, D653

Remparts — Barbacane, Tour des Pendus — ILE DE CABESSUT

RUE DE LA POUDRIÈRE — RUE VILLARS

N

RUE DU 17 AOÛT — RUE MIRABEL — RUE EMILE ZOLA — RUE DE PAPE JEAN XXI — RUE DE LA BARRE — RUE DE LA RIVIÈRE

RUE MARTIN BAUDEL — RUE A. BLANC

RUE M. SANGNIER — RUE J. DU BELLAY — RUE L. BLUM — RUE BATTUT — QUAI LUDO. ROLLÈS

RUE DE LA CASERNE — BOULEVARD GAMBETTA — St Barthélémy — QUAI DE REGOUR

CH. DE FREYCINET — Musée de la Résistance — LOT

RUE M. FRANCE — Tour du Palais Duèze

AVENUE — PLACE C. DE GAULLE

Arc de Diane — R. D. FORESTIER — RUE DES SOUBIROUS

RUE DES AUGUSTINS — Château du Roi

DES CADOURQUES — RUE DU ROI — CHÂTEAU DU ROI

PLACE GAMBETTA — Gare — RUE — PONT CABESSUT

AVENUE PIERRE SÉMARD — Musée Henri Martin — Palais de Justice — QUARTIER DES SOUBIROUS

TASSART PARK — RUE DU PORTAIL ALBAN — PL DE LA LIBÉRATION — QUAI CHAMPOLLION

AVENUE JEAN JAURÈS — RUE JOACHIM MURAT — PLACE O. DE MAGNY

RUE ANATOLE FRANCE — CRS. DE LA CHARTREUSE — R. G. LAROUMET — Préfecture — PLACE R. CLÉMENT

AVENUE ANDRÉ BRETON — RUE DES CAPUCINS — RUE F. SUISSE — RUE J. F. CAVIOLE — RUE FOCH — La Chantrerie

PONT VALENTRÉ — Hôtel de Ville — St Etienne Cathedral — Hôtel de Roaldès

Tour du Collège des Jésuites — PLACE CHAPOU — RUE ST JAMES

RUE DU PRÉSIDENT WILSON — Halle — PLACE GALDEMAR

RUE BOURTHOUMIEUX — PLACE FRANÇOIS-MITTERRAND — RUE CLEMENCEAU — St Urcisse

ALLÉES FÉNELON — BOULEVARD GAMBETTA — RUE DU DR. BERGOUGNIOUX — PLACE C. ROUSSEAU — RUE LASTIÉ

RUE SAINT-GÉRY — Théâtre — QUARTIER DES BADERNES — RUE E. BRIVES

LOT — ALLÉES DES SOUPIRS — RUE DES HORTES — QUAI SÉGUR D'AGUESSEAU

Fontaine des Chartreux — RUE VICTOR HUGO — RUE DU LOT

RUE DU POT TRINQUAT — CRS. VAXIS

0 — 200 yards
0 — 200 metres — QUAI EUGÈNE CAVAIGNAC — PONT LOUIS-PHILIPPE — Notre-Dame

TOULOUSE, MONTAUBAN, N20

VILLEFRANCHE-DE-ROUERGUE, D911

Quartier des Badernes

The area south of the cathedral is called the Quartier des Badernes, the lower (down-hill) area where the rich bourgeoisie built their houses. The grander houses are concentrated around the Rue Nationale, the old Rue Droite, and at the end of the street is the emplacement of the original bridge, the Pont-Vieux. No. 116 has Cahors' most voluptuous Baroque entrance with volutes, an oculus and a heavy panelled door carved with luscious fruit and flowers. No. 128 is early 13th-century, with squat arcades and the outlines of a gallery with three three-light round-headed bays.

On Rue du Dr. Bergougnioux is a 17th-century doorway; the tower on the right has damaged mullioned windows. The 16th-century *hôtel* at no. 40 is a charming if dilapidated example of the arbitrary juxtaposition of successive decorative modes without regard to overall harmony: next to Cadurcien Gothic windows (1480–1500) with *bâtons écotés* is a triple bay of more Italianate design (c. 1530), exploiting the idiom of the early Renaissance. The mid-16th-century rear façade is altogether more disciplined, displaying a deeper understanding of the use of the Classical orders.

Where Rue Nationale runs out of Place Claude Rousseau are a variety of interesting details in doors and windows, and in the street elevation of the Résidence du Lavoir (no. 321) are restored 13th-century windows and gargoyles of a dog and a bear. Rue Lastié also has a number of beautiful buildings. On the left, no. 35 has a fine 14th-century window with bar tracery. On Place St-Priest is a restored 17th-century Toulousain-style open staircase. To the right is a medieval house with the outline of a pointed gable above 14th-century windows. No. 117 is a particularly fine 14th-century jettied house with three Gothic windows above and a low 16th-century arch to the shop below.

There are restaurants behind several of the attractively restored late-medieval half-timbered façades in Place St-Urcisse. The early 13th-century church of **St-Urcisse** was altered in the following century but has retained its late Romanesque door and Gothic capitals around the south door (in the garden of the neighbouring restaurant), whereas the west porch is contemporary with the west façade of the cathedral, c. 1320, and similarly has a large rose window above the portal. On the central pillar is a standing Virgin and Child protected by a carved baldaquin. If you can get inside (usually closed) you will see storiated capitals of Original Sin and the Life of Christ.

Further north, the Romanesque house, 62 Rue St-Urcisse, has a restored early-13th century brick façade, and the adjacent one a timber gallery or soleilho. One of the best-known houses in Cahors is, however, the Hôtel de Roaldès on Place Henri IV. Heavily restored, it changed hands many times but in 1636 passed to a family of magistrates, the Roaldès. At its core is a 13th-century tower in brick and facing the river is a beautiful soleilho. The façade on Place Henri IV is richly decorated with the Quercynois idiom of the early 16th century: roses, *bâtons écotés* and flaming suns.

Pont Valentré

The tree-lined Quai Cavaignac, which follows the river round the southern perimeter of the town, is a pleasant route to the Pont Valentré, emblem of Cahors and the most famous medieval fortified bridge in France. When construction of the bridge began in 1308, it was the third in the town after the Pont Vieux to the south and the Pont Neuf to the east, built between 1254 and 1291. The slow progress of the Pont Valentré was traditionally blamed on satanic forces, but the problems were as much financial as technical, despite a grant from the king in 1312. The bridge was in use by 1335 but not completed. As hostilities with the English increased in 1345 and the defences of the town were being improved and extended there was an added impetus to complete the bridge, although work continued until 1378. Restoration began in 1879 under the supervision of Paul Gout who, in tribute to the legendary diabolic intervention, sculpted a little devil clinging to the angle at the top of the central tower.

The bridge's six wide arches and the three high towers (40m above the river) are a magnificent sight. The arches at each end once had a portcullis and there was a barbican on the eastern bank. The bridge, which is pedestrianised, is narrow but has passing bays. Below the bridge a dam, which has existed since the 14th century, links the lock (1808) to the 16th-century Périé mill downstream.

Just upstream on the east bank is the old pumping station (1853). Above that is the site of the ancient Fontaine des Chartreux, supposedly the source of the sacred fountain, *Divona*, around which the Gallo-Roman town developed. The fountain springs from a natural reservoir under the Causse de Limogne about 20km to the east and still carries drinking water to the town.

West of Boulevard Gambetta

Behind the tourist information centre on Allées Fénelon is the eye-catching tower of the Jesuit college (1674) and around Place François Mitterand at the centre of town, with a large fountain and a statue of Léon Gambetta, is the 19th-century Hôtel de Ville which was rebuilt in 1840, but in the passageway which cuts the building (Rue Fondude) are the remains of the old residence of the seneschal.

At 792 Rue Emile Zola, is the municipal museum, **Musée Henri-Martin** (*open 11–6, Sun 2–6, closed Tues; T: 05 65 30 15 13)*, occupying the former bishops' palace since 1906. It contains Gallic and Roman archaeology, pre-Romanesque, Romanesque and Gothic elements from lost buildings, and 14th- to 16th-century religious art. The Henri Martin gallery has a collection of works given to the town by the Toulousain painter and his son, Martin Ferrères. Henri Martin (1860–1943) studied in Toulouse and Paris under J.P. Laurens and started out as a Salon painter. In 1889 he adopted neo-Impressionism and in the 1890s became known for his decorative work. The 18 paintings exhibited in Cahors are from this period when he was increasingly concerned with idealised scenes of contemporary life and idyllic pastorals. He was influenced by the work of the Italian Divisionist painter, Giovanni Segantini, and owes a debt to Pierre Puvis de Chavannes.

A scrap of the antique baths (*thermae*), the Arc de Diane, stands in an incongruous setting on Avenue de Freycinet behind Place de Gaulle. North of the place in Espace Bessières is the Musée de la Résistance (*open daily 2–6; T: 05 65 22 14 25)*. The remaining fortifications are at the north end of the town; they were extended in the mid-14th century to protect the entire peninsula and to incorporate religious communities outside the walls of the *cité*. There were two fortified gates and 11 square towers. Four survive—Tour St-Jean dominating the east bank, Tour Morlas and St-Mary in the centre, and Tour du Pal on the west. Of the gates, the Porte St-Michel opening on to the cemetery can still be seen and the barbican, which once protected the eastern Porte de la Barre, still stands high above the river.

WEST ALONG THE LOT

Along the Lot's meandering route west of Cahors are vineyards which reach down to the water's edge, many providing opportunities for tastings of the exclusively red wines produced in the region. The route crosses and recrosses the river through varied scenery and picturesque communities with remnants of castles and old churches. The potential of transport on the Lot River was exploited as early as the 13th century and became the main means for exporting overseas via the Garonne and the port of Bordeaux. The cargo most closely associated with the river was wine. By the 17th century navigation had improved with numerous locks and by the 19th century up to 300,000 tonnes of freight was carried each year. Then the railway took over; for 60–70 years the locks and weirs were neglected and traffic on the Lot ceased. At the end of the 20th century, 70km was made navigable again and pleasure boats now offer a variety of excursions between Luzech, Cahors and St-Cirq Lapopie.

Douelle, a once-important river port on the left bank of the Lot, is used by pleasure boats in the summer. An attractive little place, it has a 15th-century church, heavily restored in the 19th century, with a model of a boat suspended from the nave vaults. There are also the remains of the medieval fortress of Cessac, and a modern fresco by Chamizo on the quay wall along the river.

The village of **Mercuès** on the right bank, is an ancient *bastide* entirely dominated by the Château, favourite residence of the bishops of Cahors from 1212 and now a luxury hotel and restaurant (*see p. 196*). The owner, Georges Vigouroux, is a wine dealer and the cellars can be visited. On the right bank of the Lot the vineyards start in earnest.

At **Caillac**, the church of St-Pierre and St-Paul was built in the 11th or 12th centuries although the only Romanesque elements to survive are on the south entrance. Resulting from a rebuild at the beginning of the 16th century is the delicately sculpted Renaissance doorway with Adam and Eve (lower right).

From the high ground on the Col de Crayssac (D23), there is a great view down to the loop in the river encompassing the vineyards of **Parnac**, which has been known as the capital of Cahors wine since the cooperative of the Côtes d'Olt was installed there. **Caïx**, a boating centre on the Lot, has an immaculately tended *domaine* belonging to the Danish royal family, a small partially 12th-century church and a sculpted cross (1772).

LUZECH & ENVIRONS

Protecting a particularly tight meander in the Lot are the small town and great 12th-century keep of Luzech. After the Albigensian Crusades, both the bishops and barons of Cardaillac had a castle here, the episcopal fort on the higher ground and the seigneurial one lower down. Richard the Lionheart was overlord in the 12th century. The medieval town clustered around the castle is still enclosed in part of its protective walls.

In Rue de la Ville, the restored 13th-century Maison des Consuls houses the tourist office and the small Musée Armand Viré of local archaeology (*open July–Aug, Mon–Sat*

10–1 & 3–8, Sun 10–12; telephone for other times, T: 05 65 20 17 27). Further along is Ichnospace (*open July–Aug, Mon–Sat 2–7; T: 05 65 30 58 47*), which the village proudly claims as the first European museum of dinosaur footsteps and other fossilized remains. Place du Canal, now the main street, was originally a canal or moat dividing the medieval town from the *barri* (suburb), which itself has existed since the 13th century. An important market is held here on Wednesdays.

A path leads from the château up to the plateau above the isthmus, called the Impernal, a prehistoric and Gallo-Roman site which is the source of most of the exhibits in the museum. At the opposite extremity of the peninsula is the Flamboyant chapel, Notre-Dame-de-l'Île, submerged in vineyards. Built by Bishop Antoine de Luzech c 1505, in a style reminiscent of the cloisters at Cahors, it was a pilgrimage chapel for sailors and still hosts a pilgrimage in September.

THE WINE OF CAHORS

The Romans were cultivating wines here by the 3rd century and Pope John XXII took Quercynois wine-growers to Avignon where they produced Châteauneuf du Pape. The Bordelais resented the competition and did what they could to block exports but the strong dark wine of Cahors was carried to Northern Europe and became the communion wine in Russia. The final death-knell to the wine trade and river transport was phylloxera, which destroyed the vineyards in the 1880s. In 1961 new vinestock of traditional types, Auxerrois and Merlot, was planted in the valley and production and quality was gradually built up until 45 communes qualified for the AOC in 1971. Like many of the smaller wine-growing areas, Cahors is putting an emphasis on improving quality and it is possible to buy excellent wine at a reasonable price. Many of the vineyards offer a *dégustation. Le Livret du Vin de Cahors*, published by the Maison du Vin de Cahors, can be obtained from the tourist office or by post from the Maison du Vin de Cahors, 430 Av. Jean-Jaurès, BP 61, 46002 Cahors.

ALBAS TO DURAVEL

NB: This section is covered by the map on p. 102.

Albas, south of the Lot, is spectacularly perched on top of a cliff. This was a wine port and another favourite watering hole of the bishops of Cahors, especially in the 16th century. The episcopal residence was restored by Antoine d'Alamand c. 1485 and is decorated with Cadurcien roses. There is just one medieval gateway standing. On the other bank of the Lot is the *bastide* of Castelfranc surrounded by hills: the 14th-century church with a splendid belfry-tower helped defend the town against the English in 1355.

Anglars-Juillac, standing in the middle of vineyards, has a restored Romanesque church (remodelled in the 16th century) with a belfry-gable, and around the upper part of the apse is a motif special to the valley, consisting of pierced metopes.

Bélaye, a picturesque castrum around a castle on a narrow spur above the river, was acquired by the bishops of Cahors c. 1236. It has a 15th-century church and castle, parts of the old city walls, and stunning views towards Prayssac on the opposite bank. Small but lively, **Prayssac** is one of the starting points for the Dolmen Circuit—others are Castelfranc (across the Lot) or Les Junies—a walk indicated by arrows.

On the opposite bank is the church of St-Pierre-ès-Liens at **Pescadoires**, a priory founded in 1037 and attached to Moissac. It has lost its apse, but is still interesting for its squat square belfry supported by a cupola and for the exterior decoration.

Puy-l'Évêque is a small, ancient town built on an escarpment on the right bank of the Lot, descending in terraces to the river where there used to be a major port. A stronghold of the bishops, it was occupied by the English during the Hundred Years War, who reinforced the defences so well that the town withstood attack during the Religious Wars. At the highest point, the square keep, c.1230, is the only part of the episcopal fort still standing and the Esplanade de la Truffière at its base is a good vantage point. One level down, enclosed in a second *enceinte*, the Château de Bovila has a late Gothic door decorated with *bâtons écotés*.

The 14th-century fortified church of **St-Sauveur** was remodelled in the late 15th century by Antoine d'Alamand who added the superb porch belfry with a Flamboyant portal and above it a Crucifixion with the Virgin and St John.

A detour north takes in the Romanesque church at **Martignac**, with 15th- and 16th-century murals of *Christ in Majesty*, the *Entombment*, *Deadly Sins*, the *Virtues* symbolised by angels, and the *Saved received into Paradise by St Michael*.

One of the major Romanesque churches in the Quercy is at **Duravel**. The church has kept many of its Romanesque elements, despite radical restoration in the 19th century, and has a 15th-century west entrance and 14th-century square belfry. The lateral door is 12th-century and around the east end are decorated corbels and a frieze of palmettes; the pierced metope motif appears here as at Anglars-Juillac. The church was part of an important priory, founded in 1055 and affiliated to Moissac, which acquired the relics of three oriental hermits, Agathon, Poémon and Hilarion, guaranteed to attract pilgrims. Their relics are in a red sandstone sarcophagus behind the altar. Storiated capitals recount the martyrdom of St Peter, and offer reminders of Hell and the Archangel Michael; in the nave are a Gothic holy-water stoup and a Gallo-Roman relief decorated with vines. The small, square Merovingian crypt, built to contain the relics, has four pillars and ten engaged columns supporting the groin vaults. Two of the decorated capitals are exceptional, one with a peacock, its tail spread, standing above a serpent and the other with an inscription recording the consecration of the sanctuary.

Montcabrier, to the north, is a 13th-century *bastide* with the Gothic church of St-Louis (King Louis IX). It has a 14th-century Rayonnant rose window in the west, a fine doorway and a stunning belfry-gable with six arcades. Inside is a statue of a bearded St Louis. Nearby, on the border of the *département* with Lot-et-Garonne, is the Château de Bonaguil (*see p. 352*).

EAST ALONG THE LOT

The character of the Lot Valley east of Cahors is very different from downstream. Here there are very few vines, and in places this is a wide, fertile valley, lined with walnut trees and poplars, where tobacco, sunflowers and strawberries are cultivated; in other parts it is confined within high cliffs. There are picturesque villages clinging to the river bank, numerous castles, and always beautiful scenery.

TO ST-CIRQ-LAPOPIE & CAPDENAC-LE-HAUT

Laroque-des-Arcs was founded in the 12th century to protect the Roman aqueduct, built on three levels, which carried water some 30km to Cahors. In 1370, during the Hundred Years War, both aqueduct and castle were destroyed to prevent them falling into the hands of the English and only small sections have survived. The most eye-

The village of St-Cirq-Lapopie perched above the Lot.

catching of the village's four churches is the tiny chapel of St-Roch (1842) perched on Pech Clary. Further upstream, **Vers** is named after the river that cascades through the village the source of which, Font-Polémie, provided water for Cahors and here also are tiny fragments of the Gallo-Roman aqueduct. On the banks of the Lot is the little 12th-century sailors' church of Notre-Dame-de-Velles.

Bouziès is divided by the river into two communities. The cliffs of the right bank have caves. The largest of them, used as a castle by the English in the Middle Ages, has a battlemented wall. Further up the the valley of the Célé is the Grotte de Pech-Merle (*see p. 204*). On the other side of the Lot is the port of Bouziès-Haut, from where you can take river boats. A spectacular walk to St-Cirq-Lapopie along the old towpath of Ganil (built in 1877) is carved out of the overhanging cliff in places and decorated with stone sculptures and carvings from the late 1980s by Daniel Monnier.

The curious name **St-Cirq-Lapopie** comes from the patronymic Pompeius, which became La Popia. It is a memorable sight (*pictured on previous page*) stretched out on a ridge overlooking the valley. This is the most famous attraction on this part of the Lot and has developed into a well-manicured village full of artists, boutiques, cafés and tourists. Dominating the scene is the 16th-century church but it has little of interest. At the highest point, next to the church, are the remains of a feudal castle. At the extreme east is the Porte de la Pélissaria leading to the river where there were once tanneries. The attractions of St-Cirq did not go unnoticed even by that most sceptical of men, André Breton, leader of the Surrealist Movement, who stayed here during the 1940s with artist colleagues; his widow continued to visit St-Cirq until her 90th year. There are two museums in the village. The Musée Rignault (*open July–Sept 10–12.30 & 2.30-7; March–June 10–12.30 & 2.30–6; closed Tues; T: 05 65 31 23 22*) is in an old *auberge* purchased by the art collector Emile Joseph Rignault (d. 1966) in 1922 and dominating the valley. Rignault gave the property to the *département* in 1946. A charming place, regular exhibitions, spring and summer, of contemporary art are put on here, and the garden is frequently used for displaying sculptures. The other is the little Musée de la Mémoire du Village (*open mid-May–Aug 2–7; Sept–mid-Nov and mid-March–mid-May 2–6; closed Mon; T: 05 65 31 21 51*), of local archeology and memorabilia, featuring a wood turner's workshop.

Some 8km east of St-Cirq-Lapopie, the **Château de Cénevières** (*open April–Sept 10–12 & 2–6; Oct 2–5; closed Sun; T: 05 65 31 27 33*) stands high on a cliff, a 13th-century privately owned building, but in the 16th century the fortress was transformed into a Renaissance residence. There are painted decorations on the walls of the so-called Alchemist's Room.

Across the river is the small town of **Cajarc**, birthplace of the writer Françoise Sagan (1935–2004) and a favourite watering hole of George Pompidou, President of France 1969–74, who frequently visited the Quercy. The Centre d'Art Contemporain Georges Pompidou (*open July–Sept 1–7, Sun 2–7; Feb–June, Tues–Sun 2–7; check in advance, T: 05 65 40 63 97*), at 134 Av Germain Canet, stages temporary exhibitions by eminent contemporary artists. Cajarc is a pleasant old town enclosed within a circular boulevard with many interesting buildings, such as the 13th-century Maison de l'Hébrardie and the remains of a fortified mill. The Musée Ferroviaire (*open July–Sept 3–6; T: 06 81 74 16 47*) contains a collection of objects associated with the railway.

On the right bank at **Larroque-Toirac** is an impressive château (*guided tours, 9th July–15th Sept 10–12 & 2–6; T: 06 12 37 48 39*) which is built into the rock. Occupied several times by the English during the 14th century, it still has its medieval defenses intact as well as Gothic fireplaces and 16th-century wall paintings. The terraces are planted with some exotic plants.

Nearby **St-Pierre-Toirac** is a tumble-down place with old houses with *bolets*. At the centre is an austere Romanesque church with carved corbels, raised and fortified in the 14th century, which contains numerous decorated capitals, many of them storiated. Merovingian sarcophagi are laid out to the south of the church. The Musée Rural de l'Autrefois Quercynois (*open July–Aug 2.30–6.30; closed Sat; T: 05 65 34 26 07*), at St-Pierre-Toirac-Bas, has a gathering of *Mouniques* or lifesize mannequins in traditional costumes, items of witchcraft, and three medieval themed gardens. The road from here continues to Figeac via Frontenac and the historic and picturesque village of Faycelles.

Staying close to the Lot, which here forms the border with the *département* of the Aveyron, this winding route ends at Capdenac Gare, a 19th-century conurbation whose raison d'être was the arrival of the railway (1856). Above Capdenac Gare is **Capdenac-le-Haut**, a village in a key defensive position high on the north bank above a tight loop in the river. It is optimistically promoted as the site of ancient *Uxellodunum*, the Celtic oppidum taken by Caesar in 51 BC and the symbol of the resistance of the Gauls. Often besieged, it has ramparts, two Gothic gateways with a barbican, and a 14th-century square keep which houses the Musée de Capdenac-le-Haut (*open July–Aug 9.30–12.30 & 2.30-6.30; Sept– June Tues–Sat 2-6; T: 05 65 50 01 45*). This small collection includes prehistoric, Gallo-Roman and medieval objects as well as as well as what is described as 'Caesar's fountain'.

THE CAUSSE DE LIMOGNE

A visit to **Lalbenque** in the winter can provide a fine opportunity to snuffle a truffle (*see box overleaf*). This small town southeast of Cahors, on the Causse de Limogne south of the Lot, has the most important truffle market in the Midi-Pyrénées; the optimum time to buy is January. Near the crossroads of D19 and D6 north, is a superb carved stone cross.

North of Lalbenque (on the D10), **Aujols** has an impressive *lac-lavoir*, a village pond surrounded by old washstones, and houses with *bolets*. There are more such typical houses at Concots, which has an old tower called the Tour de l'Horloge.

Limogne-en-Quercy, capital of the Causse, has a Sunday market and truffles are sold here on Fridays in the winter. There are several dolmens nearby and at Promilhanès to the west there is a restored working windmill, Moulin de la Bosse (*open Sun July–Aug 4–7, June 3–6; T: 05 65 31 52 71*).

Further west, at **Laramière**, is another windmill (without sails) and, next to the church with three bells, the privately owned Prieuré (*open July–Aug 2–7*) which has seen better days. An Augustinian priory was founded here in 1148 on a rocky site above the stream. The Wars of Religion destroyed a great deal of the building and the Jesuits altered it in the mid-17th century. Despite all the abuse, there are still interesting elements, including the 13th-century chapel, divided in two horizontally in the 17th century, the Romanesque pilgrim hostel, and above all the chapter house painted with geometric designs and carved capitals representing Blanche of Castille and Louis IX.

TRUFFLES

The slightly bitter aroma of truffles is very distinctive and the odour wafts down the street at market time. There you are likely to find them enveloped in a napkin in a small basket on trestles. The contents of a basket are sold as one lot. The price is completely dependent on supply: a kilo can fetch anything between €400 and €700. At Lalbenque, trading begins when a whistle is blown. The prospective purchaser writes a price on a slip of paper and if the vendor keeps it, the price is acceptable.

Truffles are a type of underground mushroom. The only variety sold is the *Tuber melanosporum*. Perhaps the most surprising discovery for the uninitiated is that they are rock hard and resemble lumps of coal. The spores begin to grow in July and do best in a warm, humid season. Pigs were once used to snuffle them out but now the *trufficulteur* is more likely to use a dog. Since the beginning of the 20th century there has been a huge decline in production, from more than 200 tonnes of truffles a year in the Lot c. 1900 to between 5 and 20 tonnes today. The main truffle markets are at Lalbenque and Limogne-en-Quercy.

PRACTICAL INFORMATION

GETTING AROUND

• **By train:** Cahors is on the Paris to Toulouse line, linked with Capdenac, Souillac, Gourdon, Montauban, Sarlat and Bordeaux via Bergerac
• **By bus:** Cahors to Libos, serving the Lot Valley west of Cahors via Luzech and Puy l'Evêque; and Cahors to Capdenac for the Valley east of Cahors.

TOURIST INFORMATION

Cajarc Pl. du Foirail, T: 05 65 40 72 89
Capdenac-le-Haut Pl. Lucter, T: 05 65 50 01 45, www.capdenac.net
Cahors Pl. F-Mitterrand, T: 05 65 53 20 65, www.mairie-cahors.fr
Duravel T: 05 65 24 65 50, www.duravel-tourisme.com
Luzech Maison des Consuls, T: 05 65

20 17 27, www.ville-luzech.fr
Prayssac Pl. d'Istrie, T: 05 65 22 40 57, www.quercy-tourisme.com/prayssac
Puy-l'Évêque Pl. de la Truffière, T: 05 65 21 37 63, www.puy-leveque.fr
St-Cirq-Lapopie Pl. du Sombral, T: 05 65 31 29 06,
www.saint-cirqlapopie.com
Lalbenque T: 05 65 31 50 08,
www.lalbenque.net
Limogne-en-Quercy T: 05 65 24 34 28, www.tourisme-limogne.com
Wine: Maison du Vin de Cahors, 430 Av. Jean Jaurès, 46000 Cahors, T: 05 65 23 22 21

RIVER CRUISES

Cahors and Bouziès (April–Oct): Les Bateaux Safaraid, T: 05 65 35 98 88, bateaux.safaraid@club-internet.fr
Reservation only: Le Lot eau rail (train and boat)
Cahors (April–Nov) or **Luzech** (rest of the year): Les Croisières Fénelon, T: 05 65 30 16 55 05,
bateaufenelon@wanadoo.fr
Cajarc (July–Aug): Le Schmilblic, Jean-Luc Forestier, T: 06 03 02 08 04.
Caïx–Douelle (April–Sept): Navilot, T: 05 65 20 18 19, www.ville.luzech.fr

ACCOMMODATION & RESTAURANTS

Capdenac le Haut
€ **Hôtel/Restaurant le Relais de la Tour**. A pretty pink façade with arched windows on ground level in the centre of this ancient town. The 11 rooms are a cheerful mix of old and modern and the breakfast buffet is taken either inside the original café or on the terrace. The restaurant offers a good variety of regional dishes. T: 06 76 29 59 38.
Cahors
€€ **Hotel Le Terminus/Restaurant Le Balandre**. ■ A friendly, family-run establishment: Chef Gilles Marre is in charge of the cuisine, his brother Laurent sommelier. The care given to all aspects has earned them a Michelin rosette and meals are served in the dining room graced by original 19th-century stained glass. The rooms are spacious and simple, furnished with handsome period pieces. 5 Av. Charles-de-Freycinet, T: 05 65 53 32 00, www.balandre.com
€€ **Restaurant Au Fil des Douceurs**. Floating restaurant on a barge on the Lot, looking across to the cathedral and old town, which specialises in fish dishes and cooking to a high standard under the watchful eye of Philippe Larguille. 90 Quai de la Verrerie, T: 05 65 22 13 04.
€€ **Restaurant La Garenne**. Just outside Cahors, this restaurant is enveloped in exotic flowers in summer. Michel Carrendier draws on his experiences in Luxembourg, Alsace and Lorraine and eastern Europe to produce delicate and tasty food using local produce. St-Henri, RN 20 (direction Brive), T: 05 65 35 40 67, www.lot-tourisme.com
€ **Restaurant L'Ô à la Bouche**. Jean-François Dive gained world-wide experience working on a luxury catamaran, learning to improvise from unknown products and the voyage continues in his Cahors restaurant. 134 Rue St-Urcisse, T: 05 65 35 65 69.
€ **Marie Colline**. A small and inexpensive vegetarian restaurant which is very popular at lunchtime; especially good

puddings. 173 Rue Clémenceau, T: 05 65 35 59 96.

Cajarc

€ Hotel/Restaurant La Ségalière. The pleasant establishment just outside Cajarc, is run by Virginia and Alain Massabie. There are 23 renovated rooms (one with disabled access), a good pool, and buffet breakfast. The excellent cooking is based on traditional local ingredients such as foie gras, truffles, saffron, and duck; menus €22–50. Rte de Cadrieu, T: 05 65 40 65 35; www.lasegaliere.com

Douelle

€ L'Auberge du Vieux Douelle. ▪ A popular restaurant in a delightful riverside village serving a range of down-to-earth food, such as parcels of *cabecou* with honey and walnut or fresh young venison in generous portions. The rooms are ordinary. T: 05 65 20 02 03, aubergededouelle@aol.com.

Lamagdalene

€€€ Hôtel/Restaurant Claude Marco. In the Lot valley, father and son team, Claude and Richard Marco, produce nouvelle cuisine with a Franco-Spanish touch, combining southern flavours and superb ingredients. The setting is an old winery surrounded by greenery and the restaurant is a delightful old vaulted cellar. There are five uniquely decorated guest rooms (one has disabled access) with views of the garden, terrace and pool. T: 05 65 35 30 64, www.restaurantmarco.com

Luzech

€ Restaurant Le Capitan. On the banks of the Lot, in a lush but simple setting, Yves Safourcade's cooking combines the best of the Quercy with a hint of the Mediterranean. Les Berges de Caïx, T: 05

65 20 18 19, www.ville-luzech.fr

Mauroux

€ Hôstellerie le Vert. Eva and Bernard Philippe's 17th-century domaine, a haven of peace, has 7 beautiful rooms (one in the vaulted cellar). There is also a spacious terrace with views over the countryside and a pool. Chef Bernard is Belgian, his wife German, and his cooking draws on his origins and vast experience to create dishes using juniper perhaps, or characteristic dishes such as *l'épaule d'agneau confite aux épices, citron confit et tomate sechée*. South of the Lot, southeast of Fumel D65/D5 from Touzac; T: 05 65 36 51 36, www.hotellevert.com

Mercuès

€€€ Hôtel/Restaurant Le Château de Mercuès. A superb and prestigious hotel/restaurant disguised as a medieval castle high above the Lot Valley. It has 30 beautifully turned out rooms, while in the vast wine cellar Georges Vigouroux's vintage Cahors gently matures. Surrounded by terrace gardens and wonderful views, in the elegant dining room local specialities such as foie gras and truffles are cooked to perfection by Philippe Combet. T: 05 65 20 00 01, www.chateaudemercues

€ Chambres d'hôtes Mas d'Azémar. A charming 18th-century country house in the vineyards, with six high-quality rooms, terrace, garden and pool. M. Patrolin, T: 05 65 30 96 85.

St-Cirq-Lapopie

€ Hotel la Pélissaria. A 13th-century listed building, tastefully decorated, and a reputable, small restaurant. T: 05 65 31 25 14, lapelissariahotel@minitel.net

€ Auberge du Sombral. Perfectly restored house at the heart of this most

picturesque of villages. No restaurant.
T: 05 65 31 26 08.

St-Pierre-Lafeuille

€ **Hotel/Restaurant La Bergerie**. An
upmarket establishment in the *causse*
under the direction of chef Joël Gilbert,
with an exclusive hotel with ten rooms
and a highly reputed restaurant, very
pretty and airy with a shady terrace and
careful cooking. 8km north of Cahors
on the N20; T: 05 65 36 82 82,
www.labergerie-lot.com

Touzac

€ **Hôtel La Source Bleue/Restaurant
La Source Enchantée**. Three medieval
watermills converted into a place of
total calm, with Zen gardens, a bamboo
forest, pool and sauna. The 16 bedrooms are equally restful. Intimate
restaurant in an old barn; booking
essential. Moulin de Leygues, between
Grézels and Fumel; T: 05 65 36 52 01,
www.sourcebleue.com

MARKET DAYS

Capdenac-le-Haut Wednesday (July
and August)
Cajarc Saturday afternoon, *Foire* 2nd
and 4th Wednesday of month
Cahors Wednesday, Saturday; *foire*
1st/3rd Saturday of month; Foie gras
market November–March
Douelle Sunday
Duravel Saturday
Lalbenque Truffle market Tuesday
afternoon, December-March; *foire* last
Tuesday of each month
Limogne-en-Quercy Sunday; Truffle
market Friday morning
December–March; summer truffles

Sunday morning June–August
Luzech Wednesday; *foire* 1st
Wednesday of the month
Mercuès Thursday
Prayssac Friday; Sunday July-August;
foire 16th of month (Sat if 16th falls on
Sunday) 22 January, 23 August
Puy-l'Évêque Tuesday, Saturday
St-Cirq-Lapopie Wednesday (July and
August)

FESTIVALS & EVENTS

Un Eté Culturel dans le Lot supplies
information on arts festivals in the Lot,
obtainable from ADDA, 115 rue de l'Ile,
46000 Cahors, www.tourisme-lot.com,
or from local Tourist Offices
May: *Festival Régional de Théâtre ama-
teur*, Cahors, T: 05 65 35 47 15
Le Bon Air est dans les caves, Cahors
wine festival, Albas, T: 05 65 20 18 54
Fêtes Médiévales, medieval celebrations,
Puy l'Evêque, T: 05 65 21 37 63
June: *Les Chantiers de l'acteur, Théâtre de
l'Oeil du Silence*, theatre workshops
Anglars-Juillac T: 05 65 36 23 75
July: *Cahors Blues Festival*, Cahors, T:
05 65 35 99 99
July and August: *Les Estivales*, Cultural
activities, entertainment, exhibitions,
Cahors, T: 05 65 53 20 65
August: *Festival mondial de Folklore*,
World folklore festival, Prayssac, T: 05
65 22 40 57
Rencontres de violoncelle de Bélaye, semi-
nars and concerts in the churches of the
Lot valley, Bélaye, T: 05 65 29 18 75
September: *Salon du livre ancien*,
Antique book fair, Cahors, T: 05 65 53
20 65

THE CÉLÉ & CAUSSE DE GRAMAT

The Célé, tributary of the Lot, rises in the Cantal and flows southwest through the Causse de Gramat, eventually to meet the Lot just south of Cabrerets. At the level of Figeac the two rivers are just under 4km apart. The Causse de Gramat is a dramatic landscape, wild and remote, which is part of the Parc Naturel Régional des Causses de Quercy. Here the empty rugged spaces are unexpectedly softened by lush valleys watered by small streams. Dotted about the landscape are simple dolmens, and also some surprisingly sophisticated villages and châteaux.

FIGEAC

On the sloping north bank of the small river Célé, Figeac is the second largest town in the Lot after Cahors, and parts of the medieval ramparts are still standing. It has an almost intact medieval centre with a variety of beautiful houses from the 12th century onwards, combining stone, brick and timber. Figeac can also boast a superb little museum dedicated to the Egyptologist, Champollion.

HISTORY OF FIGEAC

The town developed around an abbey founded in the 9th century, enriched by pilgrims on their way to Rocamadour and Santiago da Compostela. On the major north–south route from Marseilles to Champagne, it grew into a large mercantile centre with a wealthy merchant class who had trade links from the Levant to Northern Europe. The merchants grew powerful enough to challenge the abbots and town councillors were elected from among them. Their prosperity ensured a brilliant period in Figeac's architectural history from the late 12th century to the mid-14th century. So prestigious was the town that by then it had been placed under the direct guardianship of the king through his representative, the *Viguier*. After the onset of the Hundred Years War (1337) and the plague, the town only recovered late in the 15th century, shortly before the religious fervour of the Reformation took its toll. The Protestant Calvinists made the hill or *Puy*, their citadel and the church of Notre-Dame-du-Puy their Temple. The abbey church of St-Sauveur was set ablaze by the reformers. Once the town had been designated a Protestant place of safety in 1598 (under the terms of the Edict of Nantes), it flourished again until the fall of Montauban to the troops of Louis XIII. The 17th and 18th centuries barely altered the medieval layout of the town. In the 19th and 20th centuries, the canal was filled and Place Vigal opened up, but since the 1980s, Figeac has made considerable efforts to conserve its past.

JEAN-FRANÇOIS CHAMPOLLION (1790–1832)

Champollion began studying Egyptian hieroglyphics when he was at the Lycée in Grenoble. His major work was to decipher the inscriptions on the Rosetta Stone, discovered in Rosetta (Rashid) during Napoleonic expeditions in Egypt in 1799

but held in England after its capture in 1801, when the British took Alexandria. In a letter dated 27th September 1822, Champollion announced that he had solved the mystery of hieroglyphics by comparing the picture images with known scripts. The stone bears three versions—in Egyptian hieroglyphics, in Greek and in demotic script—of the same decree, drawn up by Egyptian priests at Memphis on 27th March 196 BC. Champollion did not visit Egypt itself until 1828 when he was already Curator of the Egyptology Department at the Louvre. He returned to Figeac in 1816–17, and made his last visit in 1831.

An oversize copy (1991) of the Rosetta Stone, created in the Place des Ecritures by Joseph Kosuth in celebration of the bicentenary of Champollion's birth.

EXPLORING FIGEAC

Place Champollion and environs

At the heart of the old town, the triangular Place Champollion, formerly the Place Haute, is surrounded by picturesque buildings. The Romanesque (12th century) house at no. 4, the Maison du Griffon, is considered to be the oldest in Figeac. It has obscured arcades at ground level and three-light windows with sculpted elements on the first floor. South of Place Champollion is a restored 14th-century house with a series of superb traceried windows on a deep moulded course and a battlemented soleilho. From here narrow roads lead out in several directions.

The little Rue des Frères Champollion leads to the **Musée Champollion** (*closed for renovation at time of writing; T: 05 65 50 31 08*). This small museum of Egyptology occupies the 14th- and 16th-century house where Jean-François Champollion was born. The museum has three rooms devoted to the Egyptologist, arranged thematically. The first contains a documented account of his life and career. The Salle des Ecritures Egyptiennes contains a cast of the Rosetta Stone given by the British Museum in the 1950s and the room is devoted to Champollion's research. The gallery contains few, but good, pieces including examples of scripts on different types of materials such as papyrus parchment, and on different supports—stelae, fragments of architecture—and also has instruments used by scribes. The third room is concerned with the illustrations of the afterlife—pantheons, divinities, mummies and several sarcophagi. Temporary exhibitions are regularly mounted on the top floor.

The Egyptian theme does not end with the museum. The courtyard at the end of the cul-de-sac, La Place des Ecritures, opened in 1990 to mark the bicentenary of the birth of Champollion. It is enclosed by beautiful medieval façades and on the ground is a giant version of the Rosetta Stone (*see box on previous page*), the creation of the American artist, Joseph Kosuth. The text, enlarged nearly 100 times, is engraved on black Zimbabwe granite arranged on several levels to follow the contours of the site and to symbolise the passage from one language to another. The courtyard is used for summer concerts. A French version of the hieroglyphics is engraved on the glass door of a vaulted cellar just off the courtyard but, because of the transparent surface, is intentionally as difficult to decipher as the original.

There is an exit from the courtyard to Rue Séguier. Alternatively, steps lead up through the terraced gardens, from which there is a wonderful birds-eye view over the rooftops. If it is open, there is a route through the 17th-century Hôtel de Colomb, 5 rue de Colombe, to the Espace Patrimoine and the exhibition *Portrait d'une ville, Figeac* (*open mid-July–mid-Sept 10–12.30 & 3–7; April–June mid-Sept–Oct, Tues–Sun 2–6, closed Mon; T: 05 65 50 05 40, www.ville.figeac.fr*).

Leading southwest out of Place Champollion is Rue Emile Zola (formerly Rue Droite or Rue Drecha), the oldest street in Figeac, with a number of wonderful medieval houses, restored and unrestored. The whole street is worth exploring. The most outstanding, the 14th-century Château du Viguier du Roi (*now a hotel, see p. 207*) at nos 48–50 and 3 rue Delzhens, comprises a group of houses dating from the 12th, 14th and 18th centuries around a series of courtyards and was the residence of the *Viguier* from 1302 to the Revolution. The oldest part has characteristic ground-floor arcades and on the *étage noble* a magnificent Romanesque window of two-light bays divided by carved piers and subdivided by columns. Although partly reconstructed and restored, it contains original carved detail, and there is a the sculpted head of a man on the 14th-century façade. At the end of the street is a medieval jet-tied house which was the watchman's house near one of the city gates. Rue du Canal carried water into town for the tanning industry.

Place Carnot and Rue Gambetta

Place Carnot (originally Place du Froment), has a covered market of 1900 which replaced the 13th-century market hall knocked down in 1888. Around the square are reminders of earlier times, with soleilhos from the 16th to 19th centuries in a variety of forms on the upper levels of the houses. One of the most eye-catching is the Maison Cisteron, at the junction with Rue Séguier, which has a colonnaded soleilho. The lower floor with arcades is medieval, the angle turrets are 16th-century, and the wrought-iron 18th century. On the narrow north façade of the building at the corner of Place Carnot and Rue de la République is a Romanesque relief sculpture of a green man. At no. 30 Rue Caviale is the Hôtel de Marroncles, a fine and rare example in Figeac of an early 16th-century house with mullioned and transomed windows, and

View over the rooftops of Figeac towards the church of St-Sauveur.

further along on the left is the 18th-century Hôtel de Salgues, the sous-préfecture, with an angled entrance and courtyard.

Rue Gambetta, the main shopping street running north–south, and continuing over the Célé, is interesting for the variety of façades characteristic of the medieval houses in Figeac with large arches at street level, intended for storage and workshops: during the medieval period their basic shape did not change but the profiles of the arcade mouldings grew more pronounced. The older, modest houses have tall, narrow doorways at the side with a staircase immediately behind, necessitating an outward-opening door. No 34–43 is a beautiful 14th-century *hôtel particulier* with an inner courtyard and a diversity of windows on the street façade, while the Crédit Lyonnais building, reconstructed in 1900, has a series of Romanesque three-light windows. Nos 28 and 27 have 16th-century timber and brick façades and at no. 13, Hôtel de Livernon, was built in 1367 with the earliest rectangular windows in the town, one still in place on the tower.

Place Vival

In the southwest of the town centre, Place Vival was opened up in 1920. On the south side is the seemingly medieval Hôtel de la Monnaie containing the Tourist Office and the Musée du Vieux Figeac, a small museum of life in the Quercy with a collection of stone carvings including a monumental Renaissance doorway, prehistoric objects, furniture, and the 13th-century matrix of the town seal. It is a pretty building but disappointingly only the back elevation is authentically 13th-century, and it had nothing to do with minting money; the front was reconstructed in the 1900s with windows from elsewhere. It has large arcades on the ground floor and more ornate openings on the first with two-light windows (12th century) and a variety of tracery. Under the eaves is a soleilho. In Rue Balène, close to the river, the angle block is given over to the Château de Balène, a large urban palace built in the 14th century; it was partly dismantled in 1900 but the windows with late Gothic tracery and mouldings are original. .

Church of St-Sauveur

The church of St-Sauveur formerly belonged to the Abbey of Figeac, rival to the Abbey of Conques, which was affiliated to Cluny in 1047. Its entry into the Cluniac domain precipitated the building of a new church towards the end of the 11th century. The partly completed building was consecrated in 1093 and work continued from the 12th to 14th centuries. From 1623, after the Protestants were expelled from the town, repair and consolidation work were necessary, but during the 18th and 19th centuries the cloisters and monastic buildings were lost. Saddest of all was the demolition of the abundantly carved west end, known as La Grotte, and its replacement by the present unspectacular west entrance in 1823. The only relics of La Grotte are the upturned capitals used as bases for holy water stoups. The rectangular tower (*pictured on previous page*) is 17th-century. Today St-Sauveur does not match up to its old rival Ste-Foy (Conques), but there are a few details which attest to its former glory such as the traces of the Romanesque building on the north and east, which are juxtaposed with Gothic extensions and 17th-century alterations. To the south the façade is more regular, but with the addition of a chapter house in the 13th century.

The interior

Steps lead down from the narthex into the nave, which took its present form in the 17th century while retaining the general layout of a Benedictine pilgrimage church, with aisles and ambulatory. The 12th-century engaged columns on square piers support the 17th-century groin vaults of the seven-bay nave. The south elevation has a blind triforium and 14th-century clerestory whereas the north was rebuilt 300 years later, when the vaults were replaced, and has no triforium. The crossing vaults date from 1920 and were built after the 18th-century dome collapsed in 1917, but the transepts have their original 13th-century decorated rib vaults, some of the oldest in France, a deep cornice supported by a carved corbel table and rose windows. The mock-Gothic choir and most of the ambulatory were built in the late 17th to early 18th centuries, although the radiating chapels are late 12th-century, as are the carved capitals including a *Christ in Majesty* and *Martyrdom of St Stephen*. The best of the stained glass (all 19th century) is in the clerestory. In the last bay of the south aisle is a wooden relief of the *Dream of St Martin*. Opening on the south side is the 13th-century former chapter house (light switch on left by curtains) with 17th-century carved and painted wooden décor. The violently coloured glass dates from 1883.

North of the cathedral, the crenellated soleilho in Rue Roquefort identifies the 16th-century town house of Galiot de Genouillac, builder of the Château d'Assier (*see p. 206*).

Le Puy (Mont Viguier)

Both Rue Boutaric or Rue Delzhens climb from Rue Emile Zola up to le Puy (Mont Viguier), a commanding position over the red-tiled rooftops and beyond, and the church of **Notre-Dame-du-Puy** which was recently restored. It stands on the site of an ancient cemetery and the first Christian sanctuary, dedicated to Notre-Dame-la-Fleurie. In 1372 the Romanesque church was destroyed by *routiers* (road builders) but was rebuilt and enlarged. Most of the exterior decoration, now damaged, is concentrated around the projecting west front (c. 1345). The Protestants turned it into their temple in 1576 and the area into a citadel, and the Catholics took their revenge on the building on the Protestants departure in 1622. It was repaired between 1666 and 1693, keeping as close to the original as possible. Nevertheless, the three naves were transformed into a single wide nave, only the first bay retaining the earlier nave and four aisle layout. In the east end, four Romanesque storiated capitals have survived. The monumental retable, carved in walnut, was made locally in 1696, and has a profusion of columns, vines, putti, reliefs and statues and a painting of the *Assumption*. There is an 18th-century wooden sculpture of St James and an early 19th-century altar with a clothed *Virgin and Child* dedicated to Notre-Dame-la-Fleurie who, according to a legend, caused roses to open in the snow one Christmas Day. An alternative and picturesque route between the lower town and Notre-Dame (probably easier going downhill) is via Rue St-Jacques, a cobbled, twisting alleyway, Rue de Colomb, and Rue Malleville, spanned by a vaulted passageway belonging to the 15th century Hôtel de Laporte. Rue St-Thomas is linked by steps with Rue de Crussol where the 16th- and 17th-century Hôtel du Crussol stands on the right (now a restaurant with an elegant galleried courtyard), external staircase and colonnaded soleilho.

THE VALLEY OF THE CÉLÉ

The beautiful drive west from Figeac following the Célé River winds first through a lush, tamed landscape, now planted with maize or sunflowers, and occasional vines and tobacco, although from the 14th to the 18th centuries saffron was a major crop.

Marcilhac-sur-Célé

The outstanding sight of the valley is Marcilhac-sur-Célé. Surrounded by cliffs in shades of white, grey, ochre and pink, the village runs down to the river's edge and at its heart lie the ruins of the once important Abbaye St-Pierre (*open July, Aug 10–12 & 2–6.30; April–May 10–12 & 2–5; Sept 10–12 & 2–6; closed Mon; T: 05 65 40 68 44*), attached to Moissac. Dating from the 11th and 12th centuries, it was pillaged during the Hundred Years War, and from 1461 the abbots attempted to revive and rebuild the church and the protective walls around the village. Damaged again by the Protestants in 1659, it received its final blow in the 19th century, but the ruins of the church still give an idea of its former grandeur. The west portal, flanked by the bases of towers and the ruined first bays of the nave, with massive cruciform pillars, is reminiscent of Conques. Above the entrance are five primitive Romanesque reliefs, possibly re-used, of a *Christ in Majesty* flanked by the sun and the moon, and two angels, with St Peter and St Paul below. The present church, now used by the parish, incorporates the remains of the earlier one of the 15th century. The chancel is protected by a narrow ambulatory and it has conserved its 17th-century stalls and pulpit. The best preserved Romanesque building is the late 12th-century chapter house which contains some beautiful capitals framing the door and early rectangular rib vaults. North of the chapter house are more sculpted capitals. The monastic buildings have almost entirely disappeared although two of the five defensive towers are still in place.

Grotte de Pech-Merle

Guided visits Easter–Oct 9.30–12 & 1.30–5; T: 05 65 31 27 05 or 05 65 31 23 33, www.pechmerle.com. Number of visitors limited to 700 per day; booking advisable in July 203and August.

The site combines the A.-Lemozi prehistory museum and the caves discovered in 1922, which are some of the most interesting in the region for their natural formations and for the range and beauty of the images they contain. Discovered by two teenage boys, the caves and were soon explored and studied by Father Amédée Lemozi. The museum provides an introduction to the region from Paleolithic times to the Iron Age, and there is an audio-visual presentation. The underground visit covers some 1.2km and numerous galleries, not difficult to negotiate but sometimes damp; there are 48

'Dappled horses' and stencilled hand prints (c. 25,000 BC) in the Grotte de Pech-Merle.

steps down. The natural formations include the usual stalagmites and stalactites, but also upright calcite discs and white 'cave pearls'. Yet far and away the most awe-inspiring features are the marks left by man. The images are mainly executed in black (carbon), and red (iron oxide) and date from 20,000 to 15,000 BC, the Solutrean to the Magdalenian periods. The majority of the nearly 80 representations are of animals, the most beautiful frieze being the famous 'dappled horses' (c. 25,000 BC), one of several using or inspired by the natural contours of the rock.

THE CAUSSE DE GRAMAT

At the heart of the Causses de Quercy, between Labastide-Murat, Livernon, Gramat and Sauliac-sur-Célé, the skies are the least polluted in mainland France. This area northeast of Figeac and south of Rocamadour has been designated *Triangle Noir*, as it provides a phenomenal opportunity for star gazing and attracts astrologers and other visitors from far and wide. The Triangle is protected and there are observation posts in the *communes* of Sauliac-sur-Célé and Reilhac: information can be obtained from the relevant *Mairies* or from the Astronomy Club at Gigouzac.

GRAMAT & ENVIRONS

Gramat is surrounded by the Parc Régional, and indeed the area around the town has more attractions than the place itself, which is crossed by the busy N140 although Gramat is a good place to stop and taste the precious truffle at the excellent Lion d'Or (*see p. 208*). On the edge of the Alzou (the ruined Moulin du Saut on its banks) and always an important trade route which led pilgrims towards Rocamadour, today the most interesting sites are the market hall, the 16th-century Tour de l'Horloge and the old houses in Rue St- Roch. A new innovation is Les Jardins du Grand Couvent, 33 Av. Louis Mazet (*open July–Aug 10-7; May–June Sept–Oct 2–6; T: 05 65 38 73 60*). These peaceful gardens covering 1.2 square kilometres feature flower gardens, a biblical path, a meadow with donkeys, an old bread-oven and wash-house, and a teashop and boutique among other things. Just outside the town to the east, relics of the neolithic occupation are the huge tumulus on the racecourse and the dolmen in the area, especially at Les Plassous. On the Route de Cajarc is the Parc Animalier (*open April–Sept 9.30–7, Oct–April 2–6; T: 05 65 38 81 22, www.grand-parc-animalier.com*) with both wild and domestic animals.

LACAPELLE-MARIVAL TO LABASTIDE-MURAT

The well-kept village of Lacapelle-Marival is built in local stone whose colour ranges from pinkish gold to grey. It has a small rectangular market hall (15th century) with a tile roof supported by stone pillars. The tall keep of the castle, 13th-, 15th- and 18th-century (*open July–Aug 10–12 & 3–7; 1st–15th Sept 3–7; T: 05 65 40 80 24*) dominates the village and shelters a grand staircase and wall paintings. Nearby is the tiny *bastide* of **Rudelle** with an ancient ford and bridge, founded in 1250 on the Figeac–Rocamadour road. It has an impressive fortified church complete with crenellations and machicolations, though the upper part owes much to 20th-century restoration.

Château d'Assier

Open July–early Sept 10–12.30 & 2-6.45; May–June 10–12.30 & 2–5.45, closed Tues; Sept–April 10–12.30 & 2–5.30, closed Tues; T: 05 65 40 40 99.

A proud, ambitious and flamboyant soldier and administrator under three kings—Charles VIII, Louis XII and François I—Galiot de Genouillac, Seigneur d'Assier (1465–1546) became Seneschal of Quercy in 1526 and Grand Ecuyer (equerry) de France. He began to build the Château d'Assier in 1525 after his return from the Italian campaigns. At the battle of Marignano (1515), he had been master of the French artillery of Francois I, commanding 60 bronze cannons and making a significant contribution to the defeat of the 'invincible' Swiss infantry fighting in support of Milan.

The castle is more reminiscent of the Loire Valley than the Quercy, built around four sides of a vast rectangular courtyard. It was sold off piecemeal by its owners, descendants of Galiot, in 1768. The little that remains conveys the grandeur of the project and the exuberant but empirical use of knowledge acquired in Italy or in the Loire. The church, Gothic in essence but Renaissance in detail, was built by Galiot in 1540: his coat of arms is in the pediment. A continuous frieze around the church is concerned with military exploits and techniques, constituting a catalogue of artillery and fortifications. Inside the church is the funerary chapel Galiot built for himself, with an accomplished stellar vault and two effigies of the First Master of the Artillery, standing in armour and recumbent in court dress. Galiot also introduced the wine of Cahors to Francois I.

Cardaillac

Here the feudal Barons of Cardaillac were once one of the most powerful dynasties in the region: with 20 parishes under their control by 1300 they dominated the Haut Quercy. The original community was divided between the village and the fort to the southwest—the ruins can be visited—which existed by 1064 of which two towers, de l'Horloge and de Sagnes (11th and 12th century) are standing. To the east was the priory and church of St-Julien, established by 1146, rebuilt in the 17th century. Le Musée Eclaté (*guided visits mid-July–Aug 3, 4.30; first-half July and first-half Sept 3; closed Sat; T: 05 65 40 10 63*), is an accompanied visit along a discovery trail through local traditions and history.

Labastide-Murat

Labastide-Murat, originally called Fortanière, was re-named in memory of the brother-in-law of Napoleon I, Joachim Murat (1767–1815), King of Naples from 1808–1815. A vain and dashing cavalry commander, outstanding at the battle of Marengo, he famously asked the firing squad of King Ferdinand IV of Naples to 'save his face and aim at his chest'. The Musée Murat (*open July–Sept 9–12 & 3–6; closed Tues; T: 05 65 21 19 23*), created with gifts from the family is the house of his birth.

PRACTICAL INFORMATION

GETTING AROUND

• **By train:** There are trains between Paris Austerlitz and Figeac via Brive; between Aurillac and Figeac; and between Toulouse and Brive to Capdenac Gare, Figeac, Assier, Flaujac, Rocamadour-Padirac

TOURIST INFORMATION

Assier Pl. de l'Eglise, T: 05 65 40 50 60, www.quercy-tourisme.com/assier/visite.html
Capdenac-Gare T: 05 65 64 74 87, office.detourisme.du.capdenacois@wanadoo.fr
Figeac Hôtel de la Monnaie, BP 600, Pl. Vival 46100, T: 05 65 34 06 25, www.quercy-tourisme.com/figeac
Gramat Pl. de la République, T: 05 65 38 73 60, www.tourisme-gramat.com
Labastide-Murat (Parc natural régional des Causses du Quercy) T: 05 65 21 11 39, labastide-murat@wanadoo.fr
Lacapelle-Marival T: 05 65 40 81 11, ot.pays.lacapellemarival@wanadoo.fr
Marcilhac-sur-Célé T: 05 65 40 68 44

ACCOMMODATION & RESTAURANTS

Boussac
€ **Chambres d'hôtes Domaine des Villedieu**. In the beautiful Célé Valley, far from the madding crowd, Martine and Michel's web-site must be one of the more original, describing themselves as *neo-ruraux*, with a working duck farm. The five ensuite rooms are in the dry-stone 18th-century house and there is home-produced and cooked *table d'hôtes*.

Martine and Michel Villedieu, T: 05 65 40 06 63, www.villedieu.com
Cardaillac
€ **Chez Marcel**. Delicious regional dishes served in the village restaurant. Friendly atmosphere and small, good-value bedrooms. Picturesque village. Rue du 11 Mai 1944, T: 05 65 40 11 16.
Camboulit
€ **Restaurant La Belle Epoque**. Chef Pierre Sowinski's restaurant is close to Figeac and the Célé Valley in a delightful old house. Meals are served in the dining room or on the terrace with a view of the pool and dishes include *Ravioles de langoustine de légumes d'automne, Filet de boeuf, crêpe de potiron et cèpes* with menus €15–39. There are also three little *gîtes* and a camp site. T: 05 65 40 04 42, www.restaurantlabelleepoque.com
Faycelles
€ **La Forge**. Combination of Quercynois and Provençal recipes, and themed menus which change monthly. There is a view over the Lot Valley from the terrace. Le Bourg, T: 05 65 34 65 09, www.promenades-gourmandes.com.
Figeac
€€ **Hôtel du Château du Viguier du Roy**. ■ The hotel occupies an exquisitely restored medieval building in the town centre, with courtyard garden, pool and jacuzzi, and some outstanding old features. The 21 impeccable rooms and suites are all individual and the 14th-century tower which overlooks the courtyard and town contains an apartment. 48–50 Rue Emile-Zola, T: 05 65 50 05 05, www.chateau-viguier-figeac.com
€€€ **La Dinée du Viguier**. Adjoining the Hotel Château du Viguier in the old

guard room with painted beams, is the restaurant under the direction of Daniel Authié and Bernard Badia. The cuisine is high-quality and attractive, based on the best of regional traditions. Menus €21–72. 4 Rue Boutaric, T: 05 65 50 08 08.

€€ La Cuisine du Marché. An attractive and spacious modern restaurant in an old house in the town centre. The carefully considered offerings include fish dishes as well as more traditional local fare and the service is very attentive. 15 Rue Clermont, T: 05 65 50 18 55.

€ AC'Hostellerie de l'Europe. There is a warm welcome at this old coaching inn on the banks of the Célé which has been colourfully renovated. It has 30 rooms and pool. 51, Allées Victor Hugo, T: 05 65 34 10 16, www.inter-hotel.com

€ Restaurant La Table de Marinette. ▬ It is possible to eat exceptionally well at this charming restaurant run by Marinette Baldy, whose *foie gras aux épices orientales* is 'a voyage in time'. There is an exotic interior garden; plat du jour/menus €14–45. 51B Allées Victor Hugo, T: 05 65 14 12 82, www.latabledemarinette.com

Gorses
€ Hotel-Restaurant Colombié. Friendly family-run auberge in green surroundings with a pool. It has 13 inexpensive but comfortable rooms, some refurbished, and excellent value menu. Close to St-Céré. Le Bourg, T: 05 65 40 28 02, www.hotel-colombie.com

Gramat
€ Le Relais des Gourmands.
Refurbished with pool and shady terrace. Gérard Curtet's cooking will be appreciated by lovers of good food. 2 Av de la

Gare, T: 05 65 38 83 92, www.relais-des-gourmands.com

€€ Hotel/Restaurant Le Lion d'Or. A well-established hostelry, with 15 aircon-ditioned and elegant rooms. The top class meals are served in the attractive restaurant or on the vine-shaded terrace. The cooking changes with the seasons–a great place to eat an *Omelette aux truffes* on a winter's day, or *Homard Breton rôti* and *tarte aux framboises* in the summer. In fact generally excellent cooking by René Mommejac at any time with menus €22–60. Pl. de la République, T: 05 65 38 73 18, www.liondorhotel.com

Lacapelle-Marival
€ Hotel/Restaurant La Terrasse.
Inventive chef Stéphane Amalric's restaurant is near the castle in one of the prettiest villages in the Southwest. If you want something unusual to eat, this is the place. Stéphane's influences are widespread; he uses local produce–wild mushrooms, truffles, strawberries–and has also created a novel version of traditional Chinese rolls: *nem de mangue au coulis de coco*. T: 05 65 40 80 07, www.hotel-restaurant-la-terrasse-lot.fr

MARKET DAYS

Figeac Saturday; *foire* 2nd/last Saturday of the month
Brengues Thursday evenings
Gramat Tuesday, Friday
Labastide-Murat Sunday (July and August); *foire* 2nd/4th Monday of month
Lacapelle-Marival Sunday (July and August); *foire* 2nd/4th Monday of month
Marcilhac-sur-Célé Tuesday afternoon, July–August

THE AVEYRON-ROUERGUE

The modern *département* of the Aveyron, the largest in the Midi-Pyrénées, is often referred to by the region's old name of Rouergue, and the people as the Rouergats. The modern name is taken from the river that rises in the east near Sévérac-le-Château. The landscapes of the northern Aveyron embrace the high empty spaces of the Monts d'Aubrac on the edge of the Massif Central, a landscape that lends itself to outdoor pursuits and is also rich in flora and fauna. To the northwest, the gentler side of the Rouergue is characterised by the rivers and gorges of the Olt (Lot) Rouergat and the Dourdou, peppered with castles and Romanesque churches, the most spectacular of which is the Abbey Church of Conques. South of both is the main town of the Rouergue, Rodez, marked out on its hill by a massive Gothic cathedral and tower.

RODEZ

Rodez is a bustling town stacked up above the Aveyron river. The attractive old centre, concentrated around the great roseate pile of the cathedral at the highest point, has been spruced up, well worth the climb from the ungainly sprawl at the foot of the hill. At the top is not only the cathedral but also the renovated Musée Fenaille.

HISTORY OF RODEZ

Called *Segodunum* by the Romans, the town became an important Gallo-Roman oppidum of the local tribe of the Ruteni, hence Rodez, extending until the 3rd century almost to the base of the hill. During the Middle Ages, the counts and bishops maintained a fierce rivalry that divided the community in two, Bourg and Cité, separated by a wall and gates. From the 13th century the Comté of Rodez passed to the d'Armagnac family who made a great impact on the town in terms of culture and construction, and withstood English domination in the 14th century. Notre-Dame was the last great cathedral begun in the Midi during the 13th century and took 300 years to build during the episcopate of 20 bishops. The Wars of Religion had little impact on Rodez. In more recent times, Rodez was a refuge for the surrealist writer and poet, Antonin Artaud (1896-1948), who was treated at the psychiatric hospital here and subsequently published *Letters from Rodez* in 1946. Today the town, Préfecture of the Aveyron Department, has spread all the way down the hill and beyond. Greater Rodez has a population of around 53,000, mainly employed in the service industries, and in the production of automobile parts and agricultural seeds. Some few make rustic-style furniture.

EXPLORING RODEZ

Cathedral of Notre-Dame

Open summer 8–7; winter 8–6.30; T: 05 65 75 76 77.

The cathedral is the major monument of the town. In May 1277 the first stone of a new cathedral was laid following the collapse of the belfry of the old church in 1276, which took with it the choir and part of the 10th-century nave. The new building, modelled on the great Gothic cathedrals of northern France, continued in fits and starts until Bishop Georges d'Armagnac (1530–62) brought it largely to the state in which it now stands. Despite the span of years, there is little sense of hiatus in the architecture.

The chevet was completed between 1277 and 1300. Five pentagonal radiating chapels are separated by large, sparsely decorated rectangular buttresses. Flying buttresses, rare in the Midi, help to take the thrust of the ambulatory vaults. The pride of the Rouergats is the free-standing belfry tower, on the north flank of the cathedral (*visit by appointment at the Tourist Office, July–Aug Sun 3–5, T: 05 65 75 76 77*). At 87m it is the highest flat-topped belfry in France. Begun in 1513 at the time of Bishop François d'Estaing (d. 1526), under the supervision of the master-mason Antoine Salvanh (1476–1554), it was completed by 1529. It is made up of three progressively more elaborate stratified octagonals and around the top are angels with censers, saints and apostles, culminating in the figure of the *Virgin of the Assumption*. In 1793–94, when irreparable damage was done to the cathedral, the belfry was saved.

On ground level, the Flamboyant doors on the transepts (c. 1440–end 15th century) are executed in fragile limestone and lost most of their figures during the Revolution. The iconographic portal represents the *Incarnation* on the north, and the *Redemption* on the south. The great west elevation, dominating the Place d'Armes, was completed c. 1562. This part is more typical of the region: sheer and massive with little decoration, and no west door, having been incorporated into the city walls. The austerity is relieved by the elegant Rayonnant rose window, in place by 1529. Work continued on the southern tower during the episcopate of the humanist, Georges d'Armagnac (1500–85), and his secretary and archdeacon, Guillaume Philandrier, pupil of Serlio in Venice and editor of Vitruvius, who introduced new concepts of architecture into the Rouergue. The upper part of the southwest tower is constructed in the style of a classical temple, and above the central bay, incongruously placed between the two crocketed Gothic pinnacles, is a Renaissance gable, a tribute to Philandrier's knowledge.

The interior

This is a large, essentially Rayonnant cathedral, with aisles and ambulatory but very little integral ornament, typical of meridional Gothic. The shallow undulations on the piers of the main arcades are atypical of Rayonnant Gothic except in southern France, for example at Narbonne, as is the same smooth elision from the piers to the finely moulded ribs and arcade arches. Another trait of the Midi is to reduce the glazed section of the clerestory to only part of each bay. The 11 pentagonal chapels in the east were completed 1277–1300 but the Romanesque nave was still in existence until the 15th century. The last bays of the nave and the façade towers brought the building near completion at the beginning of the 16th century.

The plain interior is a setting for a number of interesting elements which have survived. The Flamboyant *jubé* avoided destruction at the end of the 17th century but was damaged after the Revolution and lost all 38 statues. It was finally removed and re-sited in 1872 inside the south door. Some choir stalls (1478–88) were damaged when the *jubé* was removed but the elaborate episcopal throne plus 62 stalls on the upper level and 14 on the lower are original. The remainder are 17th-century, as is the balustrade above. On the exterior of the choir enclosure a 15th-century mural was discovered, with scenes from the life of St Eligius (588–659). The late 14th-century statue of Notre-Dame-de-Grace is still delightful despite the loss most of its colour and all of its precious stones.

In the 27 chapels is a variety of furnishings. The oldest piece is the 10th-century marble altar table on the north wall of the axial chapel (there is a light). The main altar until 1525, it has an inscription recording that Deusdedit the Bishop (961–1004) ordered it to be made. In 1662 it was painted with an *Annunciation* and used as a retable. In the chapel vault are 14th-century frescoes, probably part of a cycle originally covering the whole chapel, discovered under plaster in 1986. There are more frescoes (1340–50) in the northeast chapel of the choir which resemble stained glass: 18 of the 24 original figures are identified by their symbols or by an inscription. Others were discovered in 1994 in the southeast choir chapel. Unusually there is a painting of Notre-Dame de Guadeloupe in the north-east chapel, brought back from the island by a monk.

The most important late Gothic carved retables are found in the two central chapels on the south of the nave. The *Mount of Olives* (last quarter 15th century?) has delicately sculpted and polychromed limestone figures in a richly decorated surround. The adjacent St-Sepulchre chapel is closed by an elaborate openwork Gothic screen, but of the 12 statues only five on the interior, four *sybils* and an *Ecce Homo*, are original. The vast altarpiece in three registers inside the chapel (1523) introduces elements of Renaissance decoration into a late Gothic context. The lower register contains a polychromed *Entombment* characteristic of many in the region, but in addition are three small reliefs, and crowning the ensemble is Christ stepping out of his sarcophagus. The most important painting in the cathedral is on the wall opposite: *Tobias and the Angel* (1715) by Antoine Coypel.

The entrance to the sacristy (c. 1525) is finely sculpted, as is the screen of the St-Raphael chapel opposite, part of the stone choir enclosure of c. 1526–27. It contains one superb openwork panel carved with a vase, garlands and cherubs. The 16th-century canons' tribune is above the St-Sacrament chapel in the northwest. Relics were displayed in the chapel, which has remarkable coffered vaults. There is a very fine carved walnut organ case (1628) in the north transept, and the organ itself has 3,155 pipes.

Around the cathedral

The **Evêché** (Bishops' Palace) north of the cathedral, built in 1694 but partly reconstructed in the 19th century, derives much inspiration from Fontainebleau. From inside the courtyard there is a good view of the 15th-century Tour Corbières in the city walls. In the southeast corner of Place d'Estaing, east of the cathedral, a vaulted passageway leads to an elegant late medieval courtyard in the 15th-century **Maison de Benoît**. Typical of the transition between Gothic and Renaissance, it has a Flamboyant gallery and a tower decorated in the idiom of the early Renaissance. Rue de Bonald on the northeast leads to Place des Embergues, an imaginatively reinvented area, and Rue Cusset, south of Place d'Estaing, leads to something similar called Place des Maçons (*see plan on p. 216*). Place Raynaldy, further east, which was the site of the Roman Forum (1st–5th centuries), has been renovated and restored.

Musée Fenaille

Open Tues, Thur, Fri, 10–12 & 2–6; Wed, Sat 1–7; Sun 2–6; closed Mon; T: 05 65 73 84 30; www.musee-fenaille.com.

At 14 Place Raynaldy, the archaeological and history museum of Rodez and the Rouergue from pre-history, c. 400,000 BC, to the 17th century, is housed in two adjoining buildings, one of them the oldest in the city. The museum spaces have been completely overhauled and the galleries on four levels are now light and modern. To follow the presentation chronologically, a visit begins on the top floor.

Level 3: Displays trace the story of mankind from hunter-gatherer to farmer, from pre-history to c. 3500BC. A small but moving direct human reference are the four milk teeth of a Neanderthal child (c. 115,000-80,000 BC) which make a striking contrast in scale with the museum's most celebrated exhibit, the collection of monumental statues menhirs. These ancient standing stones from the end of the Neolithic period, c. 4000 BC, carry rudimentary anthropomorphic carved reliefs, male and female, the most famous of them, about 1.5m high, called *La Dame de Saint-Sernin (pictured opposite)*. They are the oldest known sculpted representation of humanity on such a scale, some more than 2m tall. Their importance was recognised only in

1880 and the museum now has 19 of the 120 examples identified in France. Associated exhibits relate to daily life, with models of dolmen, tools, and the beginnings of bronze working.

Level 2: A vast stretch of time, from 2200 BC to the 16th century, is covered in nine rooms around two courtyards. The exhibits range from the Bronze Age, via Gallo-Roman *Segodunum*, the introduction of Christianity in the region and medieval *Ruteni*, right through to the development of the Church and bourgeois life in Rodez. Displays include part of a Bronze Age horse bit made from bone; a maquette of the Gallo-Roman Forum (now Place Raynaldy, just outside the window); a

Carved menhir (c. 4000 BC) known as the 'Dame de Saint-Sernin', in the Musée Fenaille.

The courtyard of Hotel Jouéry (12th century), restored (1929) by Maurice Fenaille.

Roman capital in bronze; a superb collection of sigillated pottery; a Gallo-Roman altar Christianised around the 8th century; coins that were minted in the 12th to 14th centuries by the Counts of Rouergue; Romanesque carvings; fragments of the *jubé* from the Gothic cathedral; splendid red silk liturgical gloves with gold embroidery; some 15th-century wood panels from bourgeois houses; and a pair of medieval leather shoes.

Level 1: Exhibits on this level concentrate on the 16th and 17th centuries.

The Hotel Jouéry, built in the 12th century, with 14th-century murals, is built around a Renaissance-style courtyard (*pictured above*) remade by the originator of the collection, oil magnate Maurice Fenaille (*see p. 170*). A maquette shows the building in the early 17th century. The collection includes some graceful religious statuary, such as the early 16th-century *Virgin of the Annunciation* from the Couvent des Annonciades in Rodez; a 16th-century wooden Head of Christ from the Abbaye de Bonnecombe; Flemish tapestries; and 16th-century *jaune d'argent* glass.

Musée des Beaux-Arts Denys Puech

Open Wed–Sat 10–12 & 2–6; Tues, Sun and holidays 2–6; T: 05 65 77 89 60.
East of the Musée Fenaille, in Place G. Clemenceau, is the Musée des Beaux-Arts Denys Puech. Aveyronnais sculptor Denys Puech (1854–1942) promoted the idea of a museum for Aveyronnais artists leading to the museum's inauguration in 1910. A campaign of renovation (1984–89) created an attractive installation in the building

designed by André Boyer for the contents of Puech's studio and work by his contemporaries, including the painter Maurice Bompard (1857–1935) and the engraver Eugène Viala (1858–1913). The upper floor and basement are given over to temporary exhibitions from the museum's collections. Puech's work, displayed on the ground floor, is a technical *tour de force* with a tendency towards sleek, sentimentalised and mildly erotic female or hermaphrodite nudes in mythological or allegorical guises. It makes no apologies for ignoring any attempt at psychological insight. Works here include a portrait bust of his wife, Princesse Gargarine Stourdza (1908), and *Mézence blessé*, which won him the *Prix de Rome* for sculpture in 1884. The head of the *Muse d'André Chenier* is a portrait of the singer Emma Calvé, born in Decazeville, but we are not told who was used as model for the deliciously rounded bottom and soles of the feet. Several works were commissioned from Puech for the town, and for the Cathedral. Also on the ground floor are works by Bompard and Viala. On the first floor, a collection of contemporary works (from the last three decades of the 20th century) is exhibited in rotation. It includes the work of sculptors Bernard Pagès (b. 1940 in Cahors), a New Realist working in natural materials, and Carmen Perrin, a Swiss-based artist born in Bolivia, and a collection of abstract paintings by Michel Cure (b. 1958), who works in Bozouls in the Aveyron.

Place du Bourg

The medieval commercial centre, Place du Bourg, is framed by some interesting jettied and half-timbered houses. In the middle of the square is a bust (1900) of a local benefactor, A. Blazy Bou (1778–1846) by Puech. The elegant 16th-century Maison de l'Annonciation is named after the relief sculpted on the corner and the *Préfecture* occupies the Hôtel d'Ayssènes (1716), on Place Charles de Gaulle, more reminiscent of the *châteaux* of the Loire Valley than the Rouergue. A bronze plaque near the entrance was erected to the memory of Jean Moulin (1899–1944), *sous-préfect* of the Aveyron and Resistance hero (*see p. 35*). The cinema opposite the *Préfecture* was formerly a convent. Maison Trouillet is a late 15th-century house with some fine decoration, as is the late Gothic Maison d'Armagnac (1525–31) on Place de l'Olmet. A rib-vaulted passage leads to a tiny Italianate courtyard with three miniature galleries and a stair-tower with Renaissance windows.

Further south is the **Church of St-Amans** on the Place des Toiles, a little square with a fountain, the site of a Gallo-Roman necropolis. Reputed to be the oldest church in the Rouergue, most likely 11th- or 12th-century, it once contained the relics of St Amans, first Bishop of Rodez, buried here in the 4th century, and of his deacon Naamas and another Bishop, St Dalmas (the 6th-century sarcophagi are in the cathedral). In 1758, after being closed for some 150 years and in danger of collapse, the Romanesque church was re-built. Much of the old building material was salvaged and reused, including the Romanesque capitals. The result is a Baroque exterior in dark pinkish-red sandstone with an impressive west façade reminiscent of Venice, in contrast with the pure Romanesque style inside. The cupola was painted by a local artist, Alexis Salinier II (c. 1763), with scenes from the *Life of St Amans*, and 16th-century

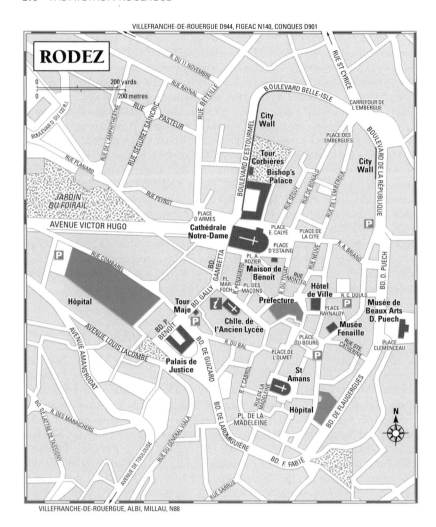

VILLEFRANCHE-DE-ROUERGUE D944, FIGEAC N140, CONQUES D901

RODEZ

0   200 yards
0   200 metres

R. DU 11 NOVEMBRE
RUE RAYNAL
RUE BÉTEILLE
BOULEVARD BELLE-ISLE
RUE ST CYRICE
CARREFOUR DE L'EMBERGUE
RUE PASTEUR
RUE SÉGURET SAINCRIC
RUE DE L'AMPHITHEATRE
BOULEVARD DU YZR.I
BOULEVARD D'ESTOURMEL
City Wall
PLACE DES EMBERGUES
BOULEVARD DE LA RÉPUBLIQUE
RUE PLÁNARD
Tour Corbières
Bishop's Palace
City Wall
RUE SEGUY
RUE DE BONAD
RUE DE L'EMBERGUE
JARDIN DU FOIRAIL
RUE PEYROT
PLACE D'ARMES
AVENUE VICTOR HUGO
Cathédrale Notre-Dame
PLACE E. CALVÉ
PLACE DE LA CITÉ
R. A. BRIAND
PUECH
BD. D. PUECH
PLACE D'ESTAING
RUE NEUVE
RUE COMBAREL
BD. GAMBETTA
PL. A. ROZIER
Maison de Benoît
PL. DES MAÇONS
RUE DU TOUAT
RUE MONTEIL
Hôtel de Ville
PL. MAR. FOCH
Hôpital
Tour Maje
BD. GALLY
Préfecture
R. C. DOULS
PLACE RAYNALDY
Musée de Beaux Arts D. Puech
Chlle. de l'Ancien Lycée
BD. P. BENOÎT
BD. DE GUIZARD
R. DU BAL
PLACE DU BOURG
Musée Fénaille
RUE STE CATHERINE
PLACE CLEMENCEAU
AVENUE LOUIS LACOMBE
AVENUE AMANSRODAT
Palais de Justice
R. F. CABROL
RUE DE LA MADELEINE
PLACE DE L'OLMET
St Amans
BD. DE FLAUGERGUES
R. DES MARAICHERS
BD. DE LATTRE DE TASSIGNY
AVENUE DE TOULOUSE
RUE DU GÉNÉRAL VIALA
BD. DE LAROMIGUIÈRE
Hôpital
PL. DE LA MADELEINE
BD. F. FABIE
N
RUE SARRUS

VILLEFRANCHE-DE-ROUERGUE, ALBI, MILLAU, N88

tapestries have the same iconography. There is a 15th-century *Pietà*, a curious 16th-century statue of the *Trinity*, and the reliquary bust of Amans.

Place Foch is a large open square with a white marble statue, *Naïade de Vors* (Puech, 1859) symbolising the Gallo-Roman supply of water from the Vors. The chapel of the former Jesuit college, Lycée Foch (*open July–mid-Sept 9-1 & 2-7*) is a sober 17th-century Baroque building now used for concerts. The attractive galleried interior has conserved the original Louis XIII painted woodwork, pink and grey stone architectural elements and rendered walls decorated with portraits of Ignatius Loyola (c. 1491–1556), who founded the Order in Paris in 1534, and other leading Jesuits. A bust of Loyola can also be seen outside. To the west of Place Foch is the Tour Maje, the most important of the 30 fortified towers which once protected the town. Just before the end of Rue Penavayre, close to the cathedral, there is a pretty Gothic courtyard with a well, in a former canonical residence. The bishops of Rodez lived in Salles-Curan (*see p. 284*).

CONQUES

Conques occupies a magnificent but isolated site north of Rodez, clinging to the side of a natural amphitheatre or *concha* at the confluence of the narrow Ouche Gorge and the Dourdou Valley. The village, built entirely in silvery-yellow schist, the steep roofs clad in gradated fish-scale tiles, forms a protective terraced semi-circle above the Romanesque Abbaye de Ste-Foy. Over the west door of the church is a superb 12th-century sculpted tympanum, and the museum holds a unique and priceless collection of religious artefacts. The route to the site winds up from the Dourdou Valley past the west (exit only) of Conques, above and behind the village and finally down to the main car park to the east. From the highest point you will be rewarded with a view onto the schist rooftops of quaint houses clustered around the ancient church. The walk downhill from the car park towards the village is accompanied by the gurgling of the unseen Ouche deep in the leafy gorge. On the way, a terrace overlooks the east end of the church.

ABBAYE DE STE-FOY

Open April–Sept 9.30–12.30 & 2–6.30; Oct–March 10–12 & 2–6.
The terrace above the east end of the church provides a rare view down onto a perfect example of a Romanesque chevet, made up of abutting sections rising in a pyramid to support the octagonal lantern-tower (15th and 19th century). The clerestory of the choir has six blind arches alternating with glazed windows and supported by carved capitals. On the lower level, superimposed engaged columns flank the windows of the chapels and support the cornice. The church was begun in red sandstone in the 11th century, which can be clearly identified, and continued in yellowish limestone with schist infill. Further along the street a narrow flight of steps descends to the base of the church walls at the level of the nave, and from here the considerable height of this satisfying building comes into perspective. The oldest door, in the north transept, has small, finely carved capitals with interlacing and palmettes, as does the south door. A walk around the east end reveals vaulted cavities between the chapels for tombs, the most important of which, the tomb of Bégon III, is in a deep recess on the south. An inscription celebrates the accomplishments of the abbot as benefactor of the cloister, and a relief panel represents Christ enthroned between the abbot and Ste Foy (St Faith). The figures have characteristics—little ears, pierced eyes, centrally parted hair—typical of the work of the Master of the Abbot Bégon. As you climb the incline you pass on your right (below the parvis) the Fontaine de Plô, the hermit Dadon's source of water.

HISTORY OF SAINTE-FOY

It is said that in the 8th century a hermit called Dadon settled in this place and gathered a pious community around him, which eventually adopted the Benedictine Rule. The abbey's reputation was firmly secured in 866 when the relics of the young Christian girl, Foy (Faith), martyred at the age of 12 in the 3rd century, were furtively translated from Agen to Conques. A church existed to house the relics by c. 980, and St Faith's first miracle was reputedly performed in 983. Books of miracles in the 11th century enhanced her reputation for curing eye maladies and liberating prisoners. The cult spread throughout Europe and Conques became a major stage on the *Via Podiensis* to Santiago de Compostela. A larger church dedicated to St Faith was begun by Abbot Odolric (1030–65), and continued by his successors, Etienne II (1065–87), Bégon III (1087–1107) and Boniface (1107–25). The result was a remarkably fine example of a pilgrimage church sheltered by an abbey so powerful that, unlike many on the pilgrim route, it remained independent of Cluny. As time went on the abbey inevitably suffered and declined and, at the Revolution, the chapter was dissolved, the property sold and most of the 12th-century cloister disappeared. Help was desperately sought in the 19th century as the church threatened collapse. Salvation came in 1837, thanks to Prosper Mérimée, the newly appointed Inspector of Historic Monuments, who visited Conques accompanied by the writer Stendhal. Repair work began in 1839 and continued through the 20th century. The Pilgrimage of St Faith is celebrated on the second Sunday in October. *Little Saint*, by the American author Hannah Green, is an involving study of the town, its church and the cult of St Faith.

The tympanum

The mainly severe west front was probably built during the abbacy of Boniface (1107–25). It is buttressed by two tall square towers culminating in 19th-century belfries, and between them are an oculus, two round-headed windows and polychrome stone rose motifs. A deep arched hood protects the celebrated tympanum (*pictured opposite*). Endearingly anecdotal, its 120 figures, in a style more Auvergnat and rustic than elegant Languedocian, are arranged, like a strip cartoon, in compartments. The visual message is clear, nevertheless reinforced with numerous Latin inscriptions. The subject is the Last Judgement, based on *Matthew 25*, a didactic warning of reward or punishment. On the left as you face the tympanum is an orderly composition appropriate to Heaven, contrasting with the confusion of Hell on the right. Christ enthroned at the centre is pivotal, symbolically and artistically. His hands extend beyond the mandorla, establishing a link with mankind—with the right he shows the way of the chosen and with the left indicates the path of the damned—and at the same time orchestrating the composition. Angels above support a cross, others sound the horn and carry

Detail of scenes of the Last Judgement carved on the tympanum (12th century).

the instruments of the Passion, and on Christ's left four more carry the book of life and a censer to ward off evil. Opposite, the blessed line up, the Virgin first, the blue of her cloak still visible, followed by St Peter and Dadon. Next is an abbot, leading Charlemagne by the hand, with members of the Carolingian royal family. The last four figures with halos, one female, are not securely identified. The three arcades below represent the abbey church and the suspended manacles symbolise *ex-voto* offerings by Christian prisoners saved from the Moors by St Faith, prostrate before the hand of God. Next to her the dead rise from their earthly tombs. Framed in a series of arches in the lowest register is Abraham flanked by the Wise Virgins, martyrs and prophets, all about to be received into Paradise by way of an open door, whose hinges and lock are carved with infinite care. During the weighing of souls a sly demon attempts, unsuccessfully, to bring the scales down on his side, watched by the Archangel Michael. Juxtaposed with the Gates of Paradise are the jaws of Leviathan, into which the damned are being stuffed by a hairy demon. All of the deadly sins and a few more are represented with their appropriate punishments: spiritual laxity, heresy, pride, lust, greed, gluttony, envy, anger and fornication. The scandalmonger has his tongue cut out; the poacher is roasted by a hare; and in the upper corner a money-forger, surrounded by his equipment, is forced to swallow molten metal. The inscription on the lintel reminds us: 'Sinners, if you do not reform your morals, know that you face a terrible judgement.'

The interior

The narrow **nave** (22.1m high) is impressive and yet modest, with just six bays: the total length of the church is 56m, with alternate round and square piers with attached shafts and barrel vaults. The aisles are groin vaulted. The half-barrel vaulted gallery takes the thrust of the high vault and enriches the overall design of the interior with elegant double openings divided by pairs of slender columns. Indirect light falls on the nave from the aisles and the galleries and directly from the windows in the west façade. There is one deep and one very small chapel on each arm of the ample transept. In the tradition of pilgrimage churches, it was designed with an enclosed choir where the clergy could worship undisturbed while the flock filed past the relics.

At the **crossing** four piers rise to arches supporting the octagonal Gothic lantern (15th century) by which it is lit. In 1982 the crossing had to be underpinned and the lantern reconstructed. A semi-circle of columns, rebuilt in the 19th century, marks off the choir from the ambulatory, presumably built on the foundations of the earlier church. Around the choir are 12th- and 13th-century wrought iron screens.

The sculptures in an *Annunciation* scene high on the **north transept** wall are of the same period as the tympanum but where they originally stood remains a mystery. The Virgin, who is employed in spinning, and the Angel Gabriel are framed in separate arches and in the angles to either side of the main group are St John the Baptist and Isaiah. There is a total of 250 carved capitals, 212 of them inside the church, most with decorative motifs and some elegantly simple. Storiated capitals are infrequent but on the fourth pier north is a *Last Supper* (south face) and the *Martyrdom of St Faith* (east face) and south of the choir is the *Sacrifice of Abraham*, a symbol of the Eucharist. The earliest of these, in the **south transept**, have scenes from the *Life of St Peter*. The chapel dedicated to St Faith contains the only incongruous element, a 17th-century gilded reredos. On the south wall of the nave is a rather damaged 15th-century fresco of scenes from the saint's martyrdom. In 1993 a complete set of new windows was installed, designed by the artist Pierre Soulages after lengthy research to perfect the manufacture of glass with varying luminosity, recalling the quality of alabaster.

The cloister

On a lower level than the church, Abbot Bégon's cloister remains only in spirit, delineated by a low wall. The sole relic is the beautiful serpentine stone pool, made at the same time as the cloister, reassembled and restored, which is skillfully decorated in miniature with 18 columns and capitals with alternate masks and atlantes. The two small arches to the east were part of the entrance to the chapter house, and from the southeast corner is the entrance to a little cemetery suspended above the Ouche gorge.

On the west side are six bays of the façade of the **refectory**. About 30 capitals of the cloister, in pale-coloured limestone from the Causse, have been conserved and reused here or exhibited in the museum. At the entrance to the gallery is a capital which shows eight monkish builders who seem to be constructing a wall, although one is holding a horn, and probably refers to the construction of the cloister.

Trésor de Conques

Open April–Sept 9.30–12.30 & 2–6.30; Oct–March 10–12 & 2–6.

In the refectory gallery is the entrance to 'Trésor I', a unique collection which remarkably evaded iconoclasts and treasure seekers The centrepiece is the reliquary statue known as *St Faith in Majesty*, a curious and disturbing work, a cult image of a type now rare but traditional in central France in the Middle Ages. It was created to contain the skull relic of the young martyr, and its chilling gaze drove pilgrims to part with money or jewels, some of the latter being added to the statue over the centuries. At its core is a basic wooden frame of two roughly sculpted pieces of wood, to which was fixed the hollow gold head from a pre-9th-century bust. The reliquary was assembled in the second half of the 9th century and the relic was placed in the wooden body, not in the head. The wooden support was covered with embossed sheets of precious metals, filigree, precious and semi-precious stones and enamels. A second casket reliquary of St Faith was found under a flagstone in the choir in 1875. Other reliquaries and treasures include the lantern-shaped Pepin's shrine (9th–10th century); a triangular reliquary with a large rock crystal in the apex called the 'A of Charlemagne'; the portable altar of St Faith (early 12th century); and Bégon's altar (dated 26 June 1100), in porphyry with niello and silver-gilt ornament. From the goldsmiths of Villefranche-de-Rouergue are a charming small silver statue of St Faith (presented in 1497) and a magnificent processional cross (c. 1503) which also bears an image of the child-saint which came from the silver workshops in Villefranche-de-Rouergue.

The Musée Joseph Fau or 'Trésor II' is next to the tourist office. It contains Romanesque capitals, mainly from the cloister, and a collection of religious carvings, furniture and tapestries, including a series of four 16th-century Aubusson tapestries describing the events leading to St Faith's martyrdom.

Exploring the village

The village of Conques is small. The main street, Rue du Abbé Floran, runs the length of the village, east–west. Rue Haute (Rue Emile-Roudié), as its name suggests, runs along the top of the village above rooftops and alongside some picturesque houses. To the west of Rue Haute is Rue du Château, named after the 15th- and 16th-century Château d'Humières, the grandest house in the village. Round the corner, Porte de la Vinzelle, with a 17th-century polychrome statue of the Virgin, straddles the route the pilgrims usually took on the next stage of their journey, passing the 17th-century Capelette oratory.

Rue Charlemagne, on the lowest level, takes you under the Porte du Barry, one of the 11th-century gateways, past the Romanesque Fontaine du Barry, and eventually to the Pont Romain (not Roman but derived from the Arab word for pilgrims, *roumis*), over the Dourdou in the lower village. Just as the path leaves the upper village, however, a left fork goes to the tiny 16th-century chapel of St-Roch where there is a beautiful view of the village. The best place for distant views of Conques is the Site de Bancerel across the Ouche. On the Rodez road, a left turn opposite the Pont Romain leads to the viewpoint, which can also be reached by a climb on foot from the bridge.

THE DOURDOU

CONQUES TO RODEZ

Near the Pont de Coursavy, just north of Conques, where the Dourdou river runs into the Lot, is **Grand-Vabre**, the reputed resting place of Dadon (*see p. 218*), marked by the chapel Notre-Dame-de-la-Nativité, restored in 1978. The 15th-century parish church has a relief with a *Pietà* with St Faith and St Catherine.

Nearby St-Parthem is a stunning village, as is La Vinzelle standing sentinel over the Lot valley. This is the region in which to taste a hearty *estofinado* in the winter, the local dish made from stockfish. The drive from here following the Lot Valley takes you through a fairly wild and sparsely inhabited countryside, wooded with oaks, silver birch and box, to Entraygues.

Further downstream in the Lot valley is **Decazeville**, a town with a very different history from Conques. One of the few coal mining towns in the region, the open-cast mines have now closed and one has become a museum, La Découverte (*open 10–12 & 2–5; T: 05 65 43 18 36*). A wealthy mining benefactor endowed the Church of Notre-Dame here with 14 Stations of the Cross by Gustave Moreau (1826–98), an early religious work (1863) by the Symbolist painter, and the town's greatest artistic treasure. Unsigned, they were 'discovered' by Marcel Proust, who described the paintings in his novel *Jean Santeuil*. Moreau was an intensely individualist and Romantic artist, reclusive and drawn to mysticism, but much admired in his own lifetime. In later life he was an inspirational tutor to Matisse and Rouault among many others, at the Ecole des Beaux Arts in Paris.

The drive between Conques and Rodez follows the **Gorges du Dourdou** at the end of which is the Moulin de Sagnes, a 17th-century mill built in deep red stone which once belonged to the Abbey of Conques. To the east is the Causse Comtal. The route south continues through the *vallon* or *rougier* of **Marcillac**, a valley washed in the purplish-red of the local sandstone. Vines, cultivated on the south-facing terraced slopes, were introduced by the monks of Conques in the 11th century. Today's producers of the local wine, red only, have made great strides in improving its quality in recent years. The results can be tasted at the Caves des Vignerons du Vallon, Valady (*open 9–12 & 2–6; closed Sun; T: 05 65 72 70 21*). The village of Marcillac, almost entirely of the same purple-red colour, is extraordinarily picturesque, with several fine old houses grouped around the 14th–15th-century church, south of the road. A seemingly disproportionate number of these houses are attractively refurbished as *maisons de retraite* (retirement homes).

Salles-la-Source, in truth three villages on three levels niched in a south-facing hollow on the flank of the Causse Comtal, has a 20m waterfall on the highest level. In the 12th century there were five *châteaux* and three churches here. The ruins of the 10th-century St-Laurent can be seen in the north-west sector. St-Loup, at the top of the village, was rebuilt in 1880. St-Paul on the lower level has survived almost intact, and harbours eight decorated capitals and a large Romanesque *Christ on the Cross*. On the upper level is the Musée du Rouergue Arts et Métiers (*open July–Aug 10–12 & 2–7, closed Sat morning; May–June, Sept 2–6, closed Sat; Oct Wed, Sun 2–6; T: 05 65 67 28 96*), an important museum of local industry and agriculture in a fine old industrial building arranged over four levels, each treating a different theme: old machinery; skills used in working with the mineral environment; man's role in the world of plants — agriculture, woodworking; and products associated with the animal world. Hands-on activities and a planetarium enhance the museum's subject matter.

Near Rodez, the Romanesque church at Souyri was fortified in the 15th century. The castle (14th–16th centuries) at Onet-le-Château, on the outskirts of the town, was formerly the residence of the chapter of Rodez, and faces towards the cathedral.

CAUSSE COMTAL

The remote and scenic region southeast of Conques, via St-Cyprien-sur-Dourdou, with a 15th-century church and belfry, is described as the Causse Comtal. The Pic du Kaymard (707m) is the highest point in the *canton* of Conques. At this point various geological strata come together: the granite of the plateau, the red sandstone of the valley, and the yellow limestone (used in the church of Ste-Foy) of the *causse*.

Château de la Servayrie

Guided/audio guided visits July–Aug 10.30–6; spring hols, May–June, Sept–Oct Tues–Thurs 2.30–5; Easter–Nov, Sun and holidays 2.30–6; T: 05 65 72 82 97; www.chateau-servayrie.fr
In a green hollow in the tiny village of Mouret, La Servayrie has been superbly restored through the dedication of the owners, who have made it their home. The architecture of the 21st-century reincarnation illustrates the evolution of the castle from the 12th to 17th centuries, enhanced by furnishings and objets d'art of the appropriate periods, as well as some understated modern glass. The oldest part of the château is the beautifully constructed medieval keep. It can be explored in all its levels, from the 12th-century base to the 14th-century parapets, via a series of steps and ladders, revealing how medieval towers were once used. Until the Revolution, the château was one of a *co-seigneurie*, not uncommon in the Southwest, consisting of four *seigneurs*, each with his own castle. The four shared control over the tiny *domain* of Mouret. Abbot Bégon of Conques issued from one of the families. The only reminder of the other three castles is a solitary ruined tower.

Château de Pruines

Open July–Aug 10–1 & 2.30–7; Sept 3–6.30; April–June, Oct, Sun and holidays 3–6.30; T: 05 65 72 91 64; www.chateau-de-pruines.com
Close to La Servayrie is another example of a local red sandstone château, dating from the 15th to 18th centuries. The fairly severe exterior of the living quarters, which abut a tower, gives way to interiors of traditional elegance approached via a handsome 18th-century entrance and grand staircase, the former apartments of the Barons de Bancalis. Eleven rooms over three floors are open to visitors including the outstanding vaulted

kitchens with monumental fireplaces. Renovated several years ago to make a 21st-century home, the present owners continue to add to their unique and colourful collection of some 800 pieces of 17th- to 20th-century pottery from southern France.

Villecomtal to Bozouls

Villecomtal, a 13th-century *bastide* in sandstone and slate, has old fortifications and a church (14th–15th centuries) with a small polychrome *Pietà* (15th century) and a finely carved altar rail and pulpit. The Château de Villecomtal (*guided visits July–Aug 3–6, closed Mon and holidays; rest of year by appointment; T: 05 65 51 40 64*) dominates the village. It was built on the banks of the Dourdou by the Counts of Rodez and offers panoramic views from the 15th-century keep.

Rodelle (little Rodez) is perched above the left bank of the Dourdou. A Carolingian site, the church is part Romanesque, part 15th-century, and has a very touching and unusual late Gothic polychrome *Pietà*, with Christ's head supported by St John, and Mary Magdalene at his feet. Just outside Rodelle is the Grotte des Meules and a modern chapel, Ste-Tarcisse (15th century), with a monument to the local sculptor, Denys Puech (1854–1942), born in Bozouls (*see p. 214*).

Bozouls, between the Causse du Comtal and the Lot Valley, is a remarkable natural site carved by the Dourdou about 700m deep into the tender rock. The newer part of town on the right bank has a small square with a monument to the war dead designed by Denys Puech. Across the bottom of the ravine is a bridge reached by Rue de l'Hospitalet, passing near two old towers, and the road leads up to the medieval village on the opposite bank through a fragment of the old outer walls. The restored Romanesque church of Ste-Fauste, with Gothic chapels to the south, has some interesting storiated capitals and 15th-century sculptures of the Virgin, St Peter and St Anthony in the porch.

THE OLT ROUERGAT

In Occitan the Lot was known as the *Olt*, and *Olt* frequently appears in the toponymy. This section of the river across the northern Aveyron runs north-westwards from St-Laurent to Entraygues, in the last part through a gorge. It marks the southern boundary of the Monts d'Aubrac (*see p. 228*) and was of strategic importance in the Middle Ages when a line of castles was built to protect each crossing point.

ENTRAYGUES TO ST-CÔME D'OLT

The terraced slopes either side of the valley west of Entraygues are reminders of the many abandoned vineyards of the Pays d'Olt, although some have been revived between Le Fel and Espalion. The best part of the town is close to the 13th–14th-century bridge over the Truyère, restored in the 17th century and claiming to be the oldest bridge in the Rouergue. Spanning the Lot is the Pont Notre-Dame. Between the two is the old town with jettied houses and covered passageways called *cantous*. Two towers of the 13th-century château still stand, the remainder being 17th-century.

Upriver, on another loop, where the Coussane meets the Lot, is **Estaing**, a very picturesque small town, its tall castle creating an impressive silhouette. The elegant 16th-century bridge is protected by a chapel and decorated with a wrought iron cross and a statue of Bishop François d'Estaing (1460–1529) whose family built the castle, the **Château d'Estaing** (*guided visits July–Aug 9.30–12.30 & 2.30–7 closed Mon and holidays; June 9.30–12.30 & 2.30–7, closed Sun, Mon and holidays; Sept–Dec 9–12 & 2–6 closed Sat, Sun and holidays; Jan–May 9–12 & 2–6, closed Sat, Sun and holidays; T: 05 65 44 72 24*). The interior was modernised when occupied by a religious group who left in 2000, and will be restored. The château, first mentioned in 850 and rebuilt in the 16th century, was owned by the Estaing family until 1794 when the last, Jean-Baptiste, victor over the English in the West Indies and hero in the American Wars, was guillotined for attempting to save the royal family during the Revolution. The 15th-century church behind the château has a belfry and a pretty clock-tower with a bell, and outside the Flamboyant porch are two very weathered carved crosses. The narrow streets around the church are worth exploring for the fine schist houses and for the tanneries on the Coussane, some storiated capitals, an ancient altar, and a chapel dedicated to St-Michael in the 12th-century tower.

Espalion and environs

Another ancient community on the Lot, Espalion, straddles the old Languedoc–Auvergne route, midway between Rodez and Laguiole. Attractive houses in typical Aveyronnais red sandstone with slate roofs line the river, crossed here by an ancient triple-arched bridge. The 15th-century church of St-Jean is occupied by the Musée d'Arts et Traditions Populaires et du Scaphandre (*T: 05 65 44 09 18*). This museum holds a famous collection of holy water stoups and, curiously, one room devoted to the history of the diving suit, an apparatus pioneered by two Espalionais. A branch of the Musée de Rouergue, Moeurs et Coutumes (*T: 05 65 73 80 50 or 05 65 44 10 63*), is established in the 19th-century Neoclassical prison, displaying a collection related to local customs and costumes, as the name suggests, such as clothes, headgear, implements used in cottage industries and an old wine press.

Just outside Espalion is the ruined **Château de Calmont d'Olt** (*open July–Aug 9–7; May–June, Sept 10–12 & 2–6, closed Thur, Fri; April, Oct 2–6, closed Thur, Fri; T: 05 65 44 15 89*). Dating from the 11th and 15th centuries, the castle stands high above the Lot Valley. It specialises in medieval war machinery and has set up an adventure trail for children. At Bessuéjouls (west of Espalion) is the little Romanesque church of St-Pierre with an elevated chapel dedicated to St Michael. This, and the small Church of **Perse** (southeast of Espalion), were on the pilgrimage route to Compostela in Spain (*see p. 11*). The latter is part 11th- and part 12th-century with two 15th-century chapels, all that is left of the priory of St-Hilarion, which came under the protection of Conques. Built in reddish regional stone, it has a stunning belfry gable and a south portal of note with a sculpted tympanum in a direct and naïve style of *Pentecost*. On the lintel is an animated scene of the *Apocalypse* and the *Last Judgement*. In the west spandrel little figures represent the *Magi* and *Virgin and Child*. North of Espalion, off the D921, the 12th-century Abbey of Bonneval is occupied by Trappist nuns who sell their own chocolate (*closed Sun; T: 05 65 44 01 22*).

St-Côme d'Olt is an exceptionally pretty town on the Lot. The bridge, decorated with a cross, existed in the 14th century but has been frequently rebuilt. The medieval *château* (now the *Mairie*) opposite the church was built inside the walled *cité* in the 12th century, the towers added in the 14th century, and restored in the 15th century. The town fortifications have all but disappeared. There are several beautiful silvery-grey stone medieval houses, which encircle the church and *château*, as well as grand 17th- to 18th-century mansions, some with pavilion roofs. The most original roof, however, is the steeple of the Church of St-Côme and St-Damien, a tall witch's hat with a twist, intentional or otherwise, the ultimate flame on the Flamboyant church (1522–32). It is attributed to Antoine Salvanh, master mason of the belfry of Rodez (*see p. 210*). The carved portal has a pair of particularly splendid Renaissance doors (1523) in oak with panels containing busts, animals and linenfold; each door is studded with 365 star-shaped nails. The wooden *Christ* (16th century) is carved in walnut, the *Pietà* is 18th-century, and the remainder of the furnishings are 19th-century. To the north is the first church in St-Côme, dedicated to St-Bouïsse, which has kept its Romanesque features although the porch was added in the 18th century when it was used by the Pénitents Blancs (1756–1935) and is known as the Chapelle des Pénitents.

STE-EULALIE D'OLT & ST-GENIEZ D'OLT

South of the river a pretty drive leads to the beautiful village of Ste-Eulalie d'Olt whose 16th- and 17th-century houses were built by wealthy weavers. The 15th-century Château des Curières de Castelnau is well preserved, and an old mill has been transformed into an *hôtel-restaurant*. The church has an 11th-century east end and a pre-Romanesque altar recording the consecration of an earlier church c. 1000. In the 12th century the church doubled as a citadel and c. 1530 it was enlarged by two bays to the west. The successive alterations can be clearly made out on the exterior.

St-Geniez d'Olt was an important town in the 19th century and has some fine 18th- and 19th-century *hôtels particuliers*. Whereas its former wealth was due to cloth and leather, today it is renowned for its strawberries. In Rue de l'Hôtel de Ville is the cloister of an Augustinian convent founded in the 14th century and rebuilt in the 17th century, now housing the *Mairie*. The adjacent church of the Pénitents-Blancs harbours a precious small late 15th-century triptych, with the *Epiphany* represented by ten gilded wooden statues; and painted panels of the *Circumcision* and *Nativity*. Through the cloister and across Place de la Mairie is the Tourist Office, installed in the Baroque chapel of the Pénitents-Noirs. The chapel, completed in 1705, has a painted wooden ceiling and a magnificent altarpiece. On the riverbanks are the old tanners' houses; on the other side of the river, the 12th-century parish church of St-Geniez underwent a Baroque transformation in the early 18th century, and is graced with a stately double staircase. It contains the marble tomb of Mgr. Frassinous (1765–1841), tutor to the Count of Chambord, grandson of Charles V, sculpted by a local artist, Gayrard. The steps south of the church climb to the Monument to Madame Talabot, partly realised by Denys Puech (*see p. 214*).

THE AUBRAC AVEYRONNAIS

The Aubrac is a beautiful high plateau at the opposite end of the Southwest to the Pyrenees, and less well known. Part of the southern Massif Central, it is shared between the Aveyron, the Cantal and the Lozère. Although its highest point is 1400m, there are no abrupt peaks but soft reliefs scattered with strange rock formations, smoothed and rounded in the Ice Age and eroded by time. It is particularly attractive to those who enjoy outdoor pursuits, the natural world and plant spotting The landscape is broken up by drystone walls and stone shelters called *burons*, once used by the shepherds or cheese-makers. In 1900 there were some 300 working *burons* but all have since been abandoned (one, near Marvejols in neighbouring Lozère, is up and running again). Cattle and sheep reign supreme, but the gentle Aubrac breed of cattle is the champion. The race was revived in the 1980s and has proved its worth both for beef and milk production. When the traditional transhumance—the seasonal moving of livestock to mountain pastures—is celebrated on the Sunday nearest 25th May (St-Urbain's Day) the cattle are beribboned and garlanded and make their stately way towards the higher ground. The villages and sturdy churches are in dark granite or basalt, as are the roofs, sombre in winter against the snow, and there are frequent carved *croix de chemin* in the same dark stone, marking the old pilgrim route or standing outside a church.

THE FLORA OF THE AUBRAC

The ardent Aubracophile will claim that the region has more varieties of flower in bloom in early summer than the Pyrenees: 1,300 species have been identified here. There are fields of narcissi; tall spiky yellow gentian; wild geraniums (cranesbill); calamint or 'tea of the Aubrac', with a tiny pink flower; digitalis; euphorbia; anemones; campanulas; German and English types of broom; and wild orchids of all varieties, some resembling bees and spiders, little spiral ones, and some that smell of goat. One of the most fascinating of all must be the carnivorous plant of the peat bogs, *Drosera rotundifolia*. There are also prehistoric plants such as Ligulaire de Sibérie (asphodel) and an orchid called *Malaxis paludosa*. For those who enjoy gathering there are wild raspberries, juniper and bilberries. The pastures are occasionally interrupted by patches of woodland: beech in the northeast, at their best in autumn, sweet chestnut to the west, and pubescent oaks in the valley.

LAGUIOLE & ENVIRONS

Laguiole, the small but dynamic capital of the Monts d'Aubrac, is held up as a shining example of the exploitation of local resources. The town's economy is built on the Aubrac cattle, celebrated in the marketplace by a bronze sculpture of a bull by Georges Guyot (1947); on its cheese, called Laguiole, produced since the 12th century but now vigorously marketed and made into a dish called *aligot*; and on its famous knives with bone handles, 'couteaux de Laguiole', invented by Pierre-Jean Calmels in 1829 and revived in the 1980s. Several workshops and boutiques sell knives of varying quality and part-industrial production, often sporting a motif resembling a winged insect. The cutlery made at the Forge de Laguiole (*Route de l'Aubrac, open summer 9–5, closed Sun in winter; T: 05 65 48 43 34, www.forge-de-laguiole.com*), established in 1987, carries the logo 'Laguiole' bisected by a half-opened knife. It is manufactured from start to finish in the long low building designed by Philippe Starck with an eyecatching knife blade emerging from the roof. The Forge produces elegant designer tableware, as well as a completely handmade range. On the corner of Place du Forail the local history museum of the Haut-Rouergue and Mountain Life (*T: 05 65 44 35 94*) includes a reconstructed *buron*.

Château du Bousquet

Guided visits 2.30–6.30, closed Tues; T: 05 65 48 41 13
http://perso.wanadoo.fr/chateau.du.bousquet
The Château du Bousquet at Montpeyroux is privately owned by Pierre and Marine Dijols, who also give tours. The origins of the château are uncertain, but it may have been built by the Hospitallers on the Montpeyroux family's fief to protect the oldest and most direct pilgrimage route from Le Puy-en-Velay to Conques, the *Route de Godescalc*. In the late 1680s this fortress became the residence of the Roquefeuil family, who owned it until 1900, and made several alterations, notably to the windows. It stands on a small hill, constructed mainly in basalt, and is a remarkably well-preserved example of 14th-century military architecture.

Solid and compact, with four round angle towers and two square ones, the tower orientated east towards the rising sun encloses a small chapel; all six have high roofs. There are almost unbroken machicolations and a two-level parapet walk around the upper part. In the Gothic chapel, containing statues and a life-size *Crucifixion* which survived the Revolution, the Roquefeuils' coat of arms appears on the painted ceiling. The *grande salle* is richly furnished and the kitchen features a smoke-blackened ceiling, vast fireplace and bread oven.

Aubrac and the mountains

Southeast of Laguiole is the tiny village of Aubrac (1307m), once a centre for tuberculosis sufferers, now the perfect destination from which to hike and see the wildlife and flora of the high plateau. A remote and fearsomely exposed place on a winter's day, it stands at the crossroads for several ski centres in the eastern Aveyron. The

Dômerie d'Aubrac, a pilgrim hospice founded c. 1120, had a battalion of knights, monks, nuns and *donats* (lay brothers) under the control of the *Dom*, who protected travellers, and such was its reputation that it attracted large numbers of pilgrims. It was disbanded at the Revolution and many of the buildings demolished: still standing are the hospital, rebuilt in the 15th century and now private property; part of the *enceinte* called the tour des Anglais; and the church of Notre-Dame, built in the late 12th and early 13th centuries, sombre and unadorned inside and out, with a belfry dating from 1457. Pilgrims still pass through. The Maison de l'Aubrac (*open July–Aug 10–7; May–June, Sept 10–6.30; April, Oct–Nov 10–6, closed Mon; T: 05 65 44 67 90, email maisondelaubrac@wanadoo.fr*) opened recently and provides information about the area.

The granite village of **St-Chély-d'Aubrac** was developed around a stage on the route to Santiago da Compostela, a reminder being the sculpted pilgrims' cross on the ancient bridge over the Boralde. On the road from Aubrac, le Neck de Belvezet is a high volcanic peak created from a solidified lava lake which, due to erosion, resembles organ pipes. South of St-Chély, the small community of **Prades d'Aubrac** (925m) is built in dark basaltic stone and dominated by the silhouette of the octagonal belfry and spire of the church built in 1540. Unusually for the Rouergue the vaults have pendant bosses and shelter a 15th-century polychrome stone *Pietà*.

PRACTICAL INFORMATION

GETTING AROUND

• **By air:** Ryanair London-Stansted to Rodez
• **By train:** Paris to Rodez, Villefranche-de-Rouergue and Millau Toulouse to Rodez, Séverac-le-Château and Millau
• **By bus:** Rodez to Conques, once daily Mon–Fri; to Laguiole, Entraygues/Mur-de-Barrez; Espalion Rodez to Mur-de-Barrez (for Entraygues, Ste-Geneviève), once daily. Rodez to Espalion three daily during term time, two daily rest of year. Rodez to Lagiuole, once daily.

TOURIST INFORMATION

Aubrac Maison de l'Aubrac, T: 05 65 44 67 90, maisondelaubrac@wanadoo.fr
Bozouls Pl. de la Mairie, T: 05 65 48 50 52, www.bozouls.com
Conques Pl. de l'Abbatiale, T: 0820 820 803, www.conques.fr
Decazeville BP 48, T: 05 65 43 18 36, www.decazeville-tourisme.com
Entraygues 30 Tour de Ville, T: 05 65 44 56 10, www.nord-aveyron.com
Espalion 2 Rue St-Antoine, BP 52, T: 05 65 44 10 63, www.ot-espalion.fr
Estaing 24 Rue François d'Estaing, T: 05 65 44 03 22, syndicatinitiative.estaing@wanadoo.fr
Laguiole Pl. de l'Ancien Forail, T: 05 65 44 35 94, www.laguiole-online.com
Montbazens T: 05 65 53 77 94, www.plateau-de-montbazens.com
Mur-de-Barrez T: 05 65 66 10 16,

www.carladez.net
Rodez Pl. Foch, BP 511, T: 05 65 75
76 77, www.ot-rodez.fr
St-Amans-des-Côts T: 05 65 44 81 61,
http://perso.wanadoo.fr/ot-stamansde-
cots/
St-Chély-d'Aubrac/Condom T: 05 65
44 21 15, www.stchelydaubrac.com
St-Geniez /Campagnac 4 rue du
Cours, T: 05 65 70 43 42,
www.st-geniez-dolt.com

ACCOMMODATION & RESTAURANTS

Aubrac
€€ **Hôtel de la Domerie.** ■ The
David family has been running this
hotel for several generations and the
welcome is warm and personal. Deeply
rooted in this beautiful area, they have
endless knowledge to impart about the
region, its walks and local flora. The 27
rooms in restful tones have colour photos of the plants of the Aubrac, and the
bathrooms are very good. The restaurant also has the family touch with
excellent home-cooked food using local
produce. T: 05 65 44 28 42.
€€ **Chambres d'hôtes de l'Aubrac.**
Whacky, original, ethnic, eclectic.
Painvin, creator of the childrens' clothes
range Tartine & Chocolat, has let her fertile imagination run riot to produce a
unique guesthouse. The two spacious
19th-century buildings have 5 generous
sized bedrooms, bathrooms and salons
where she blends local timber and stone
with exotic Asian and African fabrics and
furnishings. There is a boutique, garden,
library, *salon de thé*, massage parlour and
cookery courses. Catherine Painvin,
Comptoir d'Aubrac, T: 05 65 48 79 02,
www.catherinepainvincouture.com

Bozouls
€ **Chambres d'hôtes Les Brunes**. A
18th- and 19th-century house surrounded by wooded landscapes, in a
hamlet close to the extraordinary site of
Bouzouls and a perfect situation for
exploring the northern Aveyron. The 5
bedrooms, each with local names, are
accessed by the stone staircase in an old
tower with a pointed roof. One room is
under eaves and has an old fireplace.
Monique Philipponnat, T: 05 65 48 50
11 or 06 80 07 95 96,
www.lesbrunes.com /monique.philip-
ponnat@libertysurf.fr

Conques
€€ **Grand Hôtel Ste-Foy**. ■ Practically
on top of the Abbey Church of St-Foy,
this is a charming hotel around a small
interior courtyard, and a terrace overlooking the main street. The traditionally elegant restaurant sets the tone for
French cooking at its best, well balance
and refined; menus arround €35–60.
There are 14 very comfortable but
unostentatious bedrooms and 2 suites.
A wonderful village to wake up in. T:
05 65 69 84 03,
www.hotelsaintefoy.fr
€ **Hostellerie de l'Abbaye**. A beautiful
position close to the abbey church, and
with a garden above the Gorges, the
hotel is watched over by an occasionally
rather fearsome owner. The building is
charming and the rustic restaurant has
old beams. The eight bedrooms are simple and have wonderful views. Rue
Charlemagne, T: 05 65 72 80 30
www.hostellerie-de-l-abbaye.fr
€ **Moulin de Cambelong**. A converted
watermill on the banks of the Dourdou,
with terrace and pool. The rooms are
individually furnished and some over-

look the river. The restaurant décor, like Chef Hervé Busset's creative dishes using local produce such as truffles, foie gras, fillet of duck, mushrooms, trout and crayfish, successfully combines traditional and modern. Rue Charlemagne, T: 05 65 72 80 30, www.hostellerie-de-l-abbaye.fr

€ **Auberge St-Jacques**. In the centre of the village, this modest hotel has a terrace-restaurant overlooking the village and serves dishes such as *ris de veau* and *sandre* in curry sauce, as well as snacks in the brasserie. T: 05 65 72 86 36, Fax 05 65 72 82 47, www.aubergestjacques.fr.

Entraygues-sur-Truyère

€ **Chambres d'hôtes Le Clos St-Georges**. The property has long belonged to a wine grower and has a splendid cellar to prove it. It is close to that part of the Lot valley where wine is still produced. In the upper part of the village there are great views and behind the large stone house is a kitchen garden. The interior decoration has maintained the rustic character of the house and there are 4 bedrooms for guests. Catherine Rethore, T: 05 65 48 68 22.

Espalion

€ **Chambres d'hôtes Domaine d'Armagnac**. Comfort and tranquility is offered to guests in this 18th-century convent which has two *chambres d'hotes* as well as *gites* and a suite. The bedrooms are large with wood floors and pale colours. The house has an Art Gallery with exhibitions all year round. St-Pierre is on the old pilgrimage road to Compostela and one of the main hiking routes today (GR65). An excellent position on the Lot Valley. M. et Mme. Calixte Calsat, St-Pierre-de-Bessuéjouls,

T: 05 65 48 20 71, www.domaine-armagnac.com

St-Geniez d'Olt

€€ **Hotel de France** Pleasant hotel with restaurant and and terrace, and 1km away its own *parc de loisirs* on the river, with pool and activities. The cuisine incorporates regional produce in an original way. Local dishes are based on the cheeses and meats of the Aubrac, as well as fresh-water fish. Pl. du Général-de-Gaulle, T: 05 65 70 42 20, Fax 05 65 47 41 38, www.hotels-circuits-france.com

Laguiole

€€€ **Hotel/Restaurant Michel Bras, Route de l'Aubrac.** ■ A modern hotel disguised as part of the landscape, with 15 rooms looking out over the Monts d'Aubrac. But it is Michel Bras's cooking, which has earned him three Michelin rosettes, that really draws lovers of exquisite food. With 20 chefs for 60 couverts, the cooking is impeccable and beautiful to look at: the landscape of the Aubrac or a still life on your plate. Michel Bras is deeply rooted in the Aubrac and combines the very best of local traditions with carefully selected produce: unusual vegetables such as ancient variety of beetroot; or local meat cooked to perfection; or the rich variety of local cheeses. From the *amuses bouches* to the mouthwatering desserts, dishes are served with minute attention to detail: tiny truncated spoonfuls of calves jelly, a small blossom from the Aubrac, some displayed on slabs of black granite. Expect to pay around €52–150 for the menus. T: 05 65 51 18 20, www.michel-bras.fr.

€€ **Grand Hôtel Auguy.** ■ This is a family run hotel, each room in a different style. The restaurant is noted for its blend of traditional and seasonal best. Isabelle Auguy, who grew up here, and who received a Michelin rosette in 2000, runs the business with her Jean-Marc Muylaert. Isabelle blends her lifetime knowledge of the region with her own innovative style. Her menu '*Découvertes du terroir de l'Aubrac*' proposes a taste of the Aubrac with *crépinettes de joues de porc confites à la crème de lentilles* or *filet de truite du Gagnot en croustillant de lard.* The welcome is warm and welcoming and the desserts especially mouthwatering. 2 Allée de l'Amicale; T: 05 65 44 31 11, www.hotel-auguy.fr

€ **Le Relais de Laguiole**. Youthful and fresh décor with lots of checked fabrics. Modern rooms with comfortable armchairs. A real bonus is the indoor pool, sauna, garden, and among other local specialities served in the restaurant is *aligot*. Espace Les Cayres, T: 05 65 54 19 66, www.relais-laguiole.com.

Livinhac-le-Haut

€ **Chambres d'hôtes Château de Marcenac**. This ancient property, close to the River Lot and standing in an ornamental park, with Renaissance features, offers two wonderfully elegant and romantic rooms, the Gironde Room overlooking the river and the Evangeline Room with an 18th-century bed alcove. There is a *salon*-cum-billiard room for the use of guests. The dinning room with oak beams and floors is the setting for breakfast and dinner. The evening meal taken with the owners and cooked by Fiona, is an important ritual. Tony Archibold and Fiona Cantwell, T: 05 65 64 53 38,www.charteaumarcenac.com

Loupiac

€ **Hôtel/Gîte Le Mûrier de Viels**. Set in 6 hectare grounds on the banks of

the Lot, the property is close to Capdenac Gare. The park has gardens embellished with modern sculptures, a salt water pool and the whole atmosphere is designed for calm. Each of the seven bedrooms has its particular character, and everywhere there is a beautiful blend of old stone and soft colours. There is a pleasant restaurant, and a *gîte* which sleeps up to 5 people. T: 05 65 80 89 82, www.le-murier.com

Onet-le-Château

€ **l'Hostellerie de Fontanges**. A 16th- and 17th-century château-hotel with a superb dining room, pool, and multitude of amenities. The restaurant serves local meats, home-made desserts and pastries, and local and regional dishes based on duck. The bedrooms are comfortable and spacious. Rte de Conques (D901 close to Rodez), T: 05 65 77 76 00, www.hostellerie-fontanges.com.

Rodez

€ **Hôtel le Biney**. In the centre of the city, a hotel Biney has existed since 1863, but has now been completely renovated and has pretty, cleverly arranged modern rooms, a garden, a bright and cheerful breakfast room and a Provençal-style bar. (No restaurant.) 7 Blvd Gambetta, rue Victoire-Massol, T: 05 65 68 01 24, www.chateauxhotels.com/biney

€€ **Restaurant Goûts et Couleurs**. Just as colourful in every way as the name suggests, the chef, Jean-Luc Fau, is also a painter. This is a top quality restaurant with one Michelin rosette. The décor is modern and dishes are creative and delicious. Suggestions include *soupe au pistou* served *avec une a boule de sorbe aux fruits, poitrine et cuisse de pigeon cuit rosé, sautéed foie gras*, and a 'chocolate garden' dessert. There is a range of menus. 38

Rue de Bonald, T: 05 65 42 75 10.

€ **La Taverne**. A restaurant with lots of atmosphere and friendly service. Its specialities are robust, such as *Picancel*, a terrine made with pork, spinach and prunes; *petits farçous*; or *tartinette de foie gras frais à la ciboulette*, grilled fois gras on toast. Match these dishes with the best of their wines from Marcillac–surprisingly good. 20 Rue de l'Embergue, T: 05 65 41 14 51, www.tavernerodez.com.

MARKET DAYS

Bozouls Thursday
Decazeville Tuesday, Friday
Espalion Tuesday, Friday; Summer occasional Wednesday evenings
Estaing Thursday evenings (July and August)
Entraygues Friday; Tuesday in summer; Wednesday evenings (July and August)
Marcillac Sunday
Mur-de-Barrez July and August, Thursday
Onet-le-Chateau Friday
Rieupeyroux mid-June to mid-September, Sunday
Rodez Wednesday, Saturday; Friday pm
St-Chély d'Aubrac mid-July to mid-Aug Sunday, Wednesday; Summer occasional Thursday afternoons/evenings
St-Geniez-d'Olt Saturday
St-Parthem July and August, Wednesday evening
Valady July and Aug Saturday evening
Villecomtal July–Sept Wednesday

FESTIVALS & EVENTS

Easter
Festival des Boeufsgras de Pâques, prize cattle show, Laguiole

May
Fête de la Transhumance, movement of cattle to the summer pastures, Sunday nearest to 25 May, Aubrac (*see p. 227*) T: 05 65 44 21 15

July
L'Estivada, Occitan Festival and medieval market, Rodez, T: 05 65 75 76 77
Festival du Musique de Chambre en Pays d'Olt, chamber music
Festival Intercontinental Pyrotechnique, Site de la Découverte, Decazeville, T: 05 65 70 43 42
Festival de la Sainte-Epine, religious festival, St-Eulalie-d'Olt

July and August
Festival de folk international du Rouergue, international folk music festival throughout the Aveyron
Festival de Musique 'La Lumière du Roman', concerts in the Abbey Church at Conques, T 05 65 71 24 00
Hier un village, living tableau of early 20th-century life Flagnac, near Decazeville, T: 05 65 64 09 92/05 65 43 18 36

July–September
Son et lumières du château et de la famille d'Estaing, the history of the Château, Estaing, T: 05 65 44 03 22

August
Festival lyrique 'Bel Canto', festival of song, Bouzouls, T: 05 65 99 81 50
Festival de la Terre, discovery and understanding of the geological site of Bozouls, T: 05 65 48 50 52

October
Atelier de l'Ecole Boulle à Conques, demonstrations by pupils at the Boulle workshops, Centre Européen d'Art et de Civilisation Médiévale, Conques
Fête de Ste-Foy, Conques

THE AVEYRON VALLEY

The Aveyron, whose source is near Séverac-le-Château (*see p. 285*) in the east of the *département*, flows westwards past Rodez. Sometimes visible, sometimes hidden, at Villefranche-de-Rouergue, one of the most attractive towns on the river, it turns towards the south-west to carve out lush valleys and spectacular rocky gorges. Along the riverbanks are some of the most appealing *bastides* and towns of the Rouergue. It reaches the plain at Montricoux and finally flows into the Tarn near Moissac.

VILLEFRANCHE-DE-ROUERGUE

Villefranche is a delightful market town beside the Aveyron at the centre of an important agricultural region. At its heart is a 13th-century *bastide* whose importance was measured by its markets and *foires,* which are still active. The weekly markets, held on Place Notre-Dame, have colourful and fragrant stalls, and the *foires* are still held monthly on the leafy avenues outside the bounds of the former city walls.

The Church of Notre-Dame, and Chapelle des Pénitents-Noir (right) in Villefranche-de-Rouergue

HISTORY OF VILLEFRANCHE-DE-ROUERGUE

Alphonse de Poitiers (c. 1220–71), brother of King Louis IX, chose the strategically advantageous position at the crossroads between Montauban, Cahors, Figeac, Rodez and Albi, to found this *bastide* in 1252. Privileges granted in 1256 drew peasants and rich merchants alike, and in 1342–43 the town was enclosed within walls. When, in 1369, Villefranche became the headquarters of the *Sénéchaussée de Rouergue* it took on the role of administrative and judiciary capital of the province, thus reducing Rodez's authority to religious and feudal capital. Villefranche continued to prosper and develop to become, by the end of the century, one of the main *bastides* of the southwest and with the re-opening of the ancient bronze and silver mines in the surrounding hills, it was granted (c 1370) the right to mint coins. Handsome religious artefacts in silver, such as the processional cross at Conques (*see p. 221*) were also created here. As a result of the wealth that ensued, many buildings were refashioned in the 15th century. The ideas of the Reformation penetrated Villefranche in the mid-16th century but, suppressed by Monluc (*see p. 243*), the Protestants fled to St-Antonin-Noble-Val. In 1643, a short-lived peasant uprising (*révolte des croquants*) against heavy taxation and appalling conditions, met with harsh reprisals (*see p. 16*). With the creation of the *Département de l'Aveyron* at the Revolution, Villefranche lost its prestige as provincial capital.

Collegiate Church of Notre-Dame

The overpowering and huge belfry-porch of the Collegiate Church of Notre-Dame straddles the northeast corner of Place Notre-Dame, at the centre of the town. The first stone of the church was laid in 1260, shortly after the foundation of the *bastide*; the vaults were completed in 1480, and it was consecrated in 1519. The building takes the traditional form of Gothic churches in the Midi: a single nave, without aisles, and with tall windows between the buttresses. The east end of the church is Rayonnant, the west Flamboyant. The Flamboyant belfry was completed c. 1560, although the spire was never built. Instead it is topped off with a demeaningly inadequate structure. Inside the elegant choir has heavily restored 15th-century glass, a gift of Charles VII and a 19th-century *Virgin and Child* in wood covered in silver leaf. The stalls, although badly damaged at some point, have interesting carvings and amusing misericords (c. 1480) by André Sulpice, a gifted local wood carver. The pulpit is also 15th-century. The Baroque medallion of the altar in the north transept is attributed to Pierre Puget from Provençe.

Around Place Notre-Dame

Among the tall arcaded houses surrounding the square is the Hôtel de Raynal on the south, an attractive early Renaissance façade with *baton écoté* mouldings around the door and first-floor windows, and carved label-stops including an *Annunciation*. Rue de la République runs between the church and the old bridge and crosses the Aveyron by the Pont des Consuls, now pedestrianised. The side streets south of the church are worth exploring, notably Rue Guillaume-de-Garrigues and Rue Polier, both lined with interesting old buildings. Rue du Sénéchal crosses Rue de la République and meets a small square, Place de la Fontaine, sporting the only fountain in town, Le Griffoul (1336), and also the Musée Urbain Cabrol (*open July–Aug 10–12 & 3-6.30, closed Sun, Mon; June, Sept 3–6, closed Sun, Mon; April–May 3–6, closed Sun, Mon–Wed and holidays; T: 05 65 45 44 37*) a small museum of archaeology and local history in an 18th-century residence. Near the junction of Rue du Sergent Bories and Rue Marcellin Fabre is, at the foot of a stair-tower on the left, a finely carved doorway (c. 1490); close by on the north side of Rue M. Fabre is another stair-tower with a splendid late Gothic door.

Chapelle des Pénitents-Noir

Open July–Sept 10–12 & 2–6; T: 05 65 45 13 18.
Rues Flassadiers and Campmas run north from Place Notre-Dame to the Chapelle des Pénitents-Noirs, one of the finest Baroque churches in the Midi-Pyrénées, begun in 1641. Soberly Classical from the exterior, but with a curious octagonal lantern, the restored interior adds another dimension. In the shape of a quadrangle with mitred corners, its eight main ribs support the wooden lantern. The walls and timber ceiling were painted in the 17th century. The ceiling, completed in 1701, includes scenes from the *Legend of the True Cross*. The overall effect was altered when the pilasters were marbled (1784) and stucco reliefs added but some of the marbling effect has been removed and the paintings underneath revealed. In 1709 the gilded retable was installed with *Scenes of the Passion* on four panels. Outside, on Place St-Jacques, the door marked Hôtel de la Charité is on the site of the old pilgrim *hôpital*, and in Rue St-Jacques is the façade of the 15th-century chapel of St-Jacques. Rue Halle stands on the site of the old grain market.

Chartreuse St-Sauveur

Open June–Sept 10–12 & 2–6.30; at other times enquire at Tourist Office; the charterhouse is about 1km south of the town centre on the D922 towards Cordes-sur-Ciel.
This rare surviving charterhouse was begun in the 15th century, when Villefranche-de-Rouergue was a flourishing commercial town with some 8,000 inhabitants. It was built with the fortune bequeathed by a rich draper, Vézian Valette, who died in Rome in 1450; his widow, Catherine Garnier, took over the task, which began in 1451. Such was the size of the donation that the church, the large cloister and the chapter house were completed in seven years, the small cloister between 1458 and 1460, and a chapel was added in 1528. Apart from a few outbuildings and the development of the agricultural annexes in the 17th century, it was not altered until the community was dispersed in 1790, when it was bought by the town. It was used by the hospital until a few years ago. The Carthusian order, founded by St Bruno in 1086, was strict but

The large cloister (1458) of the Chartreuse St-Sauveur.

not as strict as the Cistercian rule. The monks lived according to the rules of solitude, silence and devotion while fulfilling the needs of a communal life. To accomplish this they lived in hermitages, small self-contained maisonettes on two floors with gardens, opening on to the large cloister (*pictured above*).

The architecture and decoration is uniformly Flamboyant and has been subjected to very few restorations. The large west porch of the church protects carved door panels with two monks holding the coats of arms of Vézian Valette and Catherine Garnier. Inside is a simple space, the nave and polygonal choir divided by a screen. The choir contains 30 stalls (c. 1461) with decorated armrests and misericords and beautiful carved panels, from the workshop of André Sulpice. North of the altar is a memorial to the founders and their tomb with engraved effigies; also some original glass, richly carved bosses and brackets, and a 16th-century chapel on the north.

The vestibule, between the church and the chapter house, has 15th-century glass. The chapter house has a polygonal apse and three admirable windows with a *Nativity*, a choir of angels, St George and St Catherine, and carved capitals and bosses. The refectory, which has a beautiful pulpit, is usually closed. The magnificent but soberly uniform great Gothic cloister (60m by 40m) has remained intact. Around it are 12 hermitages, two of them original. The small cloister is more ornate and quite outstanding with 20 bays decorated with pendant bosses sculpted with the arms of the founders, 16 different adaptations of the reticulated tracery, and crocketed pinnacles and gargoyles on the piers. In the southwest, near the refectory, the *lavabo* has a carved relief of the *Washing of the Disciples' Feet*.

ENVIRONS OF VILLEFRANCHE-DE-ROUERGUE

East of Villefranche, **La Bastide-L'Evêque** on the Ségala (*see p. 269*) is a modest *bastide* founded in 1280 by the Bishop of Rodez in competition with its powerful neighbour, Villefranche. It has a 14th- and 15th-century church and several *martinets* (tilt hammers) attest to a local copper working industry.

Abbaye de Loc Dieu

Open July–Sept 10–12 & 2–6, closed Tues; T: 05 65 29 51 17.
West of Villefranche at Martiel is the Abbaye de Loc Dieu, a former Cistercian monastery, confusing at first sight as the ancient remains are camouflaged by a 19th-century pastiche of a Loire château and a landscaped park. The church, chapter house and cloister can be visited. Monks from the Limousin founded the abbey in 1123, and a stone to the right of the church door records two dates, 1124, the beginning of the abbey, and 1159, the start of the last church, completed 30 years later. The abbey eventually suffered the fate of many religious foundations—decline, destruction and dismemberment—but at its lowest ebb, in 1812, it was purchased by the Cibiel family who have restored and renewed the buildings.

The pure and simple exterior of the church has been straightforwardly renovated. A large part of the nave is 12th-century, the transepts shallow with square chapels, and a pentagonal apse. The walls were heightened in the second half of the 13th century and the apse c. 1300, explaining the tall, narrow two-light plate-tracery windows and another in the west end, and the rib vaults (the aisles are barrel vaulted). Above the crossing is a square tower with three bays of two-light openings and a steep roof. It is generally free of decoration or ornament, according to the rules of St Bernard, and the drama of the interior depends greatly on the play of light and shade with an occasional carved element.

The late Gothic cloisters with low wide arches and vaults springing from decorated imposts belong to the third stage of rebuilding, begun in 1470, as does the chapter house, which has three openings and three equal naves, the vaults supported by two slender clustered columns. The rest of the abbey was turned into a comfortable home in the Romantic manner of the 19th century. In 1940, when France's art treasures were at risk, this small château in the Rouergue became the repository, for a short time, for Leonardo's *Mona Lisa* and *La Belle Ferronière*.

Villeneuve-d'Aveyron

To the north of Villefranche-de-Rouergue is the attractive small town of Villeneuve-d'Aveyron. It acquired the status and privileges of *bastide* in 1271 after the *sauveté* that had grown around an 11th-century monastery had been acquired by Raymond VII, Count of Toulouse in 1231. In 1272 it was designated a royal *bastide* and was fortified in 1359. Four gateways still exist, the Tour Savignac or Cardaillac, built in 1359, Porte Manhanenque and Porte Isaurenque, which lost their towers in the 18th century, and Porte Haute, integrated into the fortifications in 1486. Villeneuve has preserved much of interest from its past, including a number of 15th- and 16th-century houses, with traceried or mullioned windows, notably around Place des Conques and Rue Pavie, lined with arcades. The church is made up of two parts. The 11th-century chapel of St-Sépulcre has a ribbed dome centred upon an oculus and supported by four columns. It was extended by the Church of St-Pierre and St-Paul—the nave and polygonal apse—in the 13th century. In the north apsidiole are medieval frescoes of a *Christ in Majesty* with the symbol of the Evangelists and scenes of pilgrimage.

The road north of Villeneuve brings you to the Grotte de Foissac (*guided visit July–Aug 10–6; June, Sept 10–11.30 & 2–6, closed Sat; April–May, Oct 2–6, closed Sat; T: 05 65 64 77 04 or 05 65 64 60 52, www.grotte-de-foissac.com*). This series of caves and underground quarries with a river running through it has colourful calcite concretions, and traces of occupation by prehistoric man and animals. There is also a small museum of objects relating to the caves and a park.

NORTH & EAST OF VILLEFRANCHE

Between Capdenac-Gare and Montbazens, Peyrusse-le-Roc was an important fort belonging to the Counts of Toulouse, abandoned in the 17th century in favour of Villefranche-de-Rouergue. Access to what remains—12th- and 13th-century towers and the remnants of the *cité* clinging to a steep rock—is possible although not easy, but it is very picturesque. The village church contains late 20th-century works by Hervé Vernhes, a local artist, which are lit automatically as you enter and include the altar which is in solid elm, a *Crucifixion* in walnut behind it, and a series of paintings on canvas.

Near the town of Montbazens is **Château de Bournazel** (*guided visits to exterior courtyards and outbuildings, Easter vacation and July–Aug 2–6, closed Thurs; T: 05 65 64 16 60*) a château that is considered a high point in the development of Renaissance architecture in the Rouergue. Two massive round towers of the medieval château mark the entrance but on the other side is a complete change of style. Presumed to have been built in 1545, the date found on the north wing, it displays a highly individual interpretation of the influences of antiquity and of Italy, with a disciplined use of the Classical orders. It was damaged by fire in 1790 and is now a retirement home.

Lugan and Clairvaux d'Aveyron

Closer to Montbazens is the Hospitallers Commandery at Lugan, also a retirement home. The main building which originally had four round towers–two remain standing–was administered from 1180–1623 by the Commandery at Auzits. The church and kitchens can be visited (*guided tours July–Aug 3-7, closed Mon, T: 05 65 80 46 59*) and there is an exhibition on the Order of Malta.

The little Romanesque Church of St-Blaise at Clairvaux d'Aveyron, with three bays, square piers and some carved capitals, was built by the monks of Conques and has some features in common with the Abbaye de Ste-Foy. It contains a number of post-Reformation gilded altarpieces. The tower was rebuilt in 1704 after a collapse some 6 years earlier.

Belcastel

One of the most beautiful villages in the area, Belcastel, south of Rignac, on the banks of the Aveyron, is something of a sham, but a very good one. By the early 1970s the village had all but disappeared. The enthusiasm of the architect Fernand Pouillon for the castle proved contagious and a concerted effort has now created something rather magical. The village climbs the slope up to the Château de Belcastel (*temporarily closed; T: 05 65 64 42 16, www.chateau-belcastel.com*) which has an austere 9th-century chapel encased in modern reconstructions. A superb old bridge leads to the 15th-century church of St-Mary-Magdalene, extended in 1891. It contains an altar found under the flagstones, and on the left the mausoleum and tomb of Alzias de Saunhac, Seigneur de Belcastel, builder of the church and bridge. Nearby are three 15th-century statues, the *Virgin and Child*, *St Anthony Hermit* and *Mary Magdalene* and a 15th-century St Christopher with the infant Christ on his shoulders in the north transept.

GORGES DE L'AVEYRON

NB: This section is covered by the map on p. 248.

South of Villefranche-de-Rouergue, the Aveyron carves a deep course through the limestone plateaux on the borders of the Rouergue and the Quercy. It is swelled by the Bonnet at St-Antonin-Noble-Val and joins with the Tarn near Moissac. The scenery is varied, with sensational villages huddled on the riverbank or perched on high cliffs.

Najac

Between Villefranche and Laguépie, Najac is stretched out precariously along a clifftop ridge above a loop in the Aveyron. It can be pinpointed from a distance by the ruins of the château on the highest point of the town. The *cité* or *bourg* developed lower down, and was separated by a wall and gateway from the *faubourg* or *barry* to the east until the 18th century.

Place du Faubourg is the only part that still shows the recognisable characteristics of a *bastide*, with its variety of houses shoulder to shoulder, and is known to have existed in 1258. More a wide street than a square, it has a fountain and *couverts* on the south. The buildings close in as the street descends into the *bourg*, framing a view of the castle, beside an ancient fountain (1344) carved from a single block of granite.

Rue du Château marks the entrance to the *cité* and climbs up to the Forteresse Royale at the west (*open July 10–1 & 3–7; Aug 10–1.30 & 2.30–7; June 10–12.30 & 3–6.30; April, May, Sept 10–12.30 & 3–5.30; closed Oct–Mar and holidays; T: 05 65 29 71 65*). Alphonse de Poitiers (*see p. 358*) incorporated a 12th-century castle, including the Tour Carrée, into his fort of 1253, adding four linked towers and a tall keep with three floors. The castle is surrounded by a wall with a square tower and the *salle*

The bridge (late 15th century; restored) and castle (15th century; restored) at Belcastel.

de justice with two fine windows. Despite many periods of destruction by rival lords, Cathars, English, Protestants and *croquants,* the château was finally ruined only in the 19th century when it was used as a quarry. A large model of the medieval castle illustrates the original defences.

Further east still is the 13th-century church of St-Jean-l'Evangéliste, built after the Albigensian heresies by the Cathar community (*see box on p. 251*), who were forced by the Inquisition to replace the 12th-century church of St-Martin. Erected 1258–75, it was one of the first Gothic churches in the Rouergue. Severe but well built, it is without aisles and has a flat east end; the plate-tracery windows of 1320 have mid-19th-century glass. Among the furnishings are the original altar, used as a doorstep for 150 years and returned to its rightful place in 1966, and a 15th-century *Crucifixion* with a 16th-century *Virgin and St John.*

Varen

It would be easy to pass through Varen without noticing its treasures. The Romanesque church (second half 11th century) whose west end is directly on the main road, was originally part of a Benedictine monastery dedicated to Notre-Dame-et-St-Pierre, which became the collegiate, then parish, Church of St-Serge. The simple west entrance opens into an austere 11-bay nave with a continuous tunnel vault, flat apse and windows only on the south. There is no transept and the nave is buttressed by narrow aisles ending in semi-circular apses over crypts. The interesting capitals are concentrated around the choir and apses, inside and outside. The interlace motif in the south chapel is the oldest (c. 1070–80). Others have vegetal and animal elements and are even storiated, including *Daniel in the Lions' Den*, and archangels Raphael and Gabriel. The most accomplished capitals in the choir may be as late as the early 12th century, and some carry traces of polychromy. Over the choir is a domical vault supporting the belfry. The flat apse is a mystery: altered in the 14th century—there are Romanesque capitals on the exterior (*St Michael and the Dragon*, *Samson and the Lion*)—it was possibly transformed from a semi-circle at some point to create access, then closed again when circumstances changed.

Abbaye de Beaulieu-en-Rouergue

Open July–Aug 10–12 & 2–6; Apr–June, Sept–Nov 10–12 & 2–6.30, closed Tues; closed Nov–March; T: 05 63 24 50 10.
Like most Cistercian abbeys, the Abbaye de Beaulieu-en-Rouergue was established near water and woodland, in a remote and serene place. The temporary exhibitions of contemporary art, held here since 1974 in what was once the lay brothers' dormitory, are an added bonus. The church is a rigorous structure, begun c. 1275 and completed in the 14th century, rhythmically articulated by tall buttresses, narrow lancets and seven plate-tracery rose windows. It has been heavily restored. The chapter house, with three open bays and traces of coloured wall paintings, is a superb piece of 13th-century architecture. Most of the monastic buildings were repaired and amended in the 17th and 18th centuries.

St-Antonin-Noble-Val

St-Antonin lays claim, among its many fine buildings, to one of France's oldest civic edifices, on Place de la Halle, the ancient Hôtel de Ville or **Maison Romane**, also called *palais vicomtal*. This is a magnificent example of Romanesque secular architecture, realised 1150–55. The three-bay façade abuts a tower on the south and on street level are four large archways. The main elevation has an open gallery, its full length divided by piers into three four-light bays. The piers carry some remarkable sculpture. On the right are Adam and Eve, and on the left a figure holding a book and a sceptre with an eagle, the Emperor Justinian. Justinian I, Christian Emperor of Byzantium (527–65), pioneered legislative justice in his time and was considered during the Middle Ages to be the first judge, the symbol of justice. Such iconography suggests that the large room on this floor originally had a judicial function. Each bay is divided by paired columns with carved capitals, seven of them figurative, representing the Vices, and eleven vegetal. On the top floor are three two-light bays with round arches under a continuous moulding. Indentations in the façade once contained coloured enamelled ceramic discs (the museum has some fragments). The building is now the Musée du Vieux St-Antonin (*open July–Aug 10–1 & 3–6, closed Tues; other times by appointment; T: 05 63 68 23 52*), which contains archaeological finds from the Grotte de Bosc to the northeast.

Caylus and environs

North of St-Antonin, in the valley of the Bonnette, Caylus has an old centre hidden in a hollow beside the main road, its whereabouts betrayed by the tall spire of the church. Rue Droite, which runs the length of the village from the church to the Place de la Mairie, and the quaint alleyways which intersect it, have examples of Gothic or Renaissance houses, most notably the Maison des Loups (13th century) with Gothic windows and high-relief carvings. In the market place is a 15th-century market hall with 18 octagonal pillars protecting the old grain measures (1714). Further west on a terrace overlooking the valley is the 13th-century *donjon* of the ruined castle.

The church of St-Jean-Baptiste (14th and 15th centuries) has a stone steeple (15th century) and steep slate-covered roof with tiny dormers. The entrance on the northwest is decorated with a continuous frieze, a *Virgin and Child* on the right of the door and animals on the left. The elegant seven-sided apse dates from 1470 and the tall lancets contain stained glass of the same date, mixed with glass added during restoration in 1868. Hidden away, despite its monumental size, is an anguished *Christ* (1954), arms upstretched, pinned to the wall by one hand. It was carved from the trunk of an elm by Ossip Zadkine (*see p. 174*) who made Caylus his home in the 1950s.

BRUNIQUEL & ENVIRONS

Bruniquel sits between the Aveyron and the Vère Rivers. On the threshhold of the Quercy, the Albigeois and the Rouergue, the village grew wealthy from important medieval fairs dealing in flax, hemp and saffron. The main street leading up the hill from the church (17th and 19th centuries) passes under one of the three remaining gateways of the old ramparts and 14th–16th-century houses. To the left is the Maison Payrol (*open July–Aug 10–7; April–June, Sept 10–6; T: 05 63 67 26 42*), named after an important local family, a fascinating sample of civil architecture (14th–17th centuries), built above an ancient vaulted cellar. It includes a room for receiving pilgrims or travellers, medieval wall paintings, fireplaces, a variety of windows, and a remarkable 15th-century sculpted ceiling over what was once a granary.

Chateaux de Bruniquel

Open July–Aug 10–7; April–June, Sept 10–12.30 & 2–6; Oct, Sun 10–12.30 & 2–6; Nov school hols 10–12.30 & 2–5; T: 05 63 67 27 67.

At the top of the hill are the two Châteaux de Bruniquel. The property originally belonged to the Counts of Toulouse in the 12th century and was divided between two branches of the family in the 14th century. The Château Vieux still has its original 13th–14th-century ramparts as well as its keep, called the Tour de la Reine Brunehaut after the colourful Merovingian queen who reigned over the Quercy c. 600 and supposed founder of the castle. Brunehaut (534–613), whom some have attempted to establish as the model for the Brynhildr of Norse mythology and hence Wagner's Brunhilde, married Sigebert, grandson of Clovis, in 567 and converted to Christianity. The main part of the Château Vieux was extensively altered in the 18th and 19th centuries with the addition of an arcaded terrace looking out towards the Aveyron Valley. Changes were made in the 17th and 18th centuries to the Château Jeune, built between 1485 and 1510.

Montricoux

Montricoux, to the west of Bruniquel, is a small unspoilt town remarkable for the number of 15th- and 16th-century timber-framed houses constructed with mud brick or wattle-and-daub infill. To the west of the village the 13th–16th-century Church of St-Pierre was once the chapel of a Templar commandery (*see p. 288*); one of the vault bosses is carved with a tau-cross, a T-shaped cross—sometimes shown as one of the attributes of St Anthony the Great or Hermit, along with a pig and a bell. The tall octagonal brick belfry was added c. 1549 to a massive stone base. The church has a narrow nave and pentagonal apse decorated with a mural of the *Annunciation* by Marcel Lenoir and modern glass in the windows. The Counts of Montricoux had a funerary chapel here. Among the fittings are an ancient stoup and font, a 12th-century statue of St Peter, and diverse retables. Opposite the church is a large square tower with shallow buttresses.

The keep of the commandery has been integrated into an 18th century château which houses the Musée Marcel-Lenoir (*open July–Aug 10–12.30 & 2.30–7; April–mid-Oct 10–12.30 & 2–6; T: 05 63 67 26 48*). This private collection of the paintings of Marcel Lenoir, who was born in Montauban in 1872 and died in Montricoux in 1931, is displayed in an elegantly colourful setting. The 121 exhibits, among them many portraits, demonstrate the influence of the Nabis and Maurice Denis as well as Lenoir's interest in fresco technique and his mystic tendencies. The visit also includes the 12th-century Templar *salle de garde*. Works by the artist can also be seen in Montauban (*see p. 321*).

PRACTICAL INFORMATION

GETTING AROUND

• **By train:** Paris to Caussade; Brive to Toulouse via Capdenac, Villefranche-de-Rouergue, Laguepie, Lexos, Najac.
• **By bus:** Six per day between Rodez and Villefranche-de-Rouergue.

TOURIST INFORMATION

Belcastel Mairie de Belcastel, T: 05 65 64 46 11, www.mairie-belcastel.fr
Bruniquel Promenade du Ravelin, T: 05 63 67 29 84,www.bruniquel.fr.sm
Caylus Rue Droite, T: 05 63 67 00 28, www.caylus.com
Laguépie-Varen-Verfeil Pl. du Foirail, T: 05 63 30 20 34
Monclar-de-Quercy Pl. des Capitouls, T: 05 63 30 31 72
Najac Pl. du Faubourg, T: 05 65 29 72 05, otsi.najac@wanadoo.fr
81140 Penne Le Bourg, T: 05 63 56 36 68, ot@vaour.net
Rignac T: 05 65 80 26 04, www.pays-rignacois.com
St-Antonin-Noble-Val Pl. de la Mairie, T: 05 63 30 63 47, www.saint-antonin-noble-val.com
Varen Place de l'Eglise T: 05 63 65 45 09
Villefranche-de-Rouergue Promenade de Guiraudet, BP 239, T: 05 65 45 13 18, www.villefranche.com
Villeneuve-d'Aveyron Pl. des Conques, T: 05 65 81 79 61, ot.villeneuve@wanadoo.fr

ACCOMMODATION & RESTAURANTS

Belcastel
€€ **Vieux Pont.** ■ A small and exclu-sive restaurant and hotel in a heavenly spot. The cooking is under the direction of Nicole Fagegaltier who, with her sister Michèle and her husband Bruno Rouquier, create sublime food which has earned the restaurant a Michelin star. The restaurant is simplicity itself, the village providing the scenery. Everything is exceptional from the *amuses-gueles* to the succulent desserts, a festival of colours and scents. The excellent produce of the Aveyron, such as pigs trotters and lentils, or poultry and Aubrac beef, are combined with aromatic herbs and unusual vegetables. The presentation is not over-complicated, and doesn't distract from the quality of the cooking. Menus range from €26 to €75. The seven rooms are on the opposite bank, a short walk across the bridge, in a happily converted old building with riverside gardens.
T: 05 65 64 52 29, www.hotelbelcastel.com.
Bioule
€ **Hôtel des Boissiers**. Close to the Gorges de l'Aveyron and in a brilliant position for exploring the Quercy, the hotel occupies a handsome old stone and brick building. It has 10 bedrooms with contemporary décor and is surrounded by a partly landscaped park with a fountain. The restaurant looks out onto the greenery and the cooking is refined and tasty. T: 05 63 24 50 02, http: lesboissiers.free.fr
Monteils
€ **Le Close Gourmand**. A very charming hotel in a beautiful *maison de maître*, with a garden and terrace. The cooking is good and specialities includes

Fricassée d'Ecrevisses (crayfish) and *salade de fois gras de canard frais poëlé* (cooked in its own juices).
T: 05 65 29 63 15.

Maleville

€ **Montbressous**. A country restaurant, and one of the few restaurants still specialising in the local salt-fish dish, *Estofinado*. Other rustic dishes include *poitrine de veau farci, chou farci* (stuffed cabbage), *coq au vin* and the good old-fashioned *ile flottante*.
T: 05 65 19 30 46.

€ **Chambres d'hôtes La Maison du Cordonnier**. A former cobbler's house in the middle of this gorgeous village close to the Aveyron Valley, in the entrance are the tools of the shoemaker's trade. The two bedrooms prettily combine modern and traditional fittings and overlook a flower-filled courtyard. High standard *table d'hôte* and *après-midi confitures*. Christiane Linas, Rue du Ravelin, T: 05 63 67 25 02 or 05 84 57 43 99.

Najac

€ **La Belle-Rive**. In the valley 2km from the centre of Najac (very handy for the train station), is this friendly family (and family-run) hotel offering reasonable rates. It also has a pool and activities for kids. The cooking is not overly fussy but good and hearty with good quality ingredients, such as *contre-filet de veau à chair rose* (pink veal, from calves which have been raised in the open). The shady terrace is very popular for al fresco eating. Au Roc du Pont, T: 05 65 29 73 90, www.najac.com/lebellerive/

€ **L'Oustal del Barry.** ◼ Corinne and Rémy Simon run this popular hotel-restaurant at the heart of the village.

The restaurant is appreciated for its gourmet cooking which blends the best of the region and home-grown vegetables with the more exotic. Dishes include *cannelloni de tourteaux* (crab) *braisés au fromage de Laguiole; aïoli safrané et rizotto à l'encre de seiche* (squid ink); *délice de framboises en chibouste* (meringue) *et vanille sorbet menthe*. Place du Bourg, T: 05 65 29 74 32, www.oustaldelbarry.com.

€ **La Salamandre**. The little café run by Michèle and Philippe is so in demand it is essential to reserve in advance. All home-made food and excellent value for money, there is always a *plat du jour* or reasonable fixed-price menus as well as enormous salads. Rue du Barriou, T: 05 65 29 74 09.

€ **Chambres d'hôtes Maison Authesserre**. Susan and Frédéric Maurau-Hanrion, have two airy, spacious rooms for guests in their large old house in the middle of Najac. Place du Faubourg, T: 05 65 29 73 47.

€ **Chambres d'hôtes La Prade Basse**. Jean-Pierre et Maïté Verdier have extended their modern home with three guest rooms. This is a working farm 3km from Najac. There is also the possibility of enjoying their excellent quality *table d'hôte* dinners. La Prade, T: 05 65 29 71 51.

Villefranche-de-Rouergue

€ **L'Epicurien**. Good quality refined cooking at a reasonable price. Specialities include fish, grilled meat, and *foie gras aux pommes et au vin de noix*. Av. Raymond de St-Gilles (close to the bridge), T: 05 65 45 01 12.

€ **L'Assiette Gourmande**.

Wholehearted local dishes such as *aligot, tripous, foie gras frais de canard poëlé aux pommes*. In the centre near Pl. Notre-Dame. Pl. A. Lescure, T: 05 65 45 25 95.

€ **Auberge de la Poste**. The 23 simple rooms are reasonably priced and the food good but inexpensive featuring the usual local specialities, such as *poule farcie* and *confit de canard*. 45 Rue Prestat, T: 05 65 45 13 91.

€ **La Bellevue**. Unsophisticated and inexpensive hotel/restaurant near the charterhouse. Local dishes include fish and *civet de canard*. 3 Av. du Ségala, T: 05 65 45 23 17.

€ **Relais de Farrou**. A modern hotel (just outside Villefranche-de-Rouergue in St-Remy) with a good pool and a shady park with tennis court and mini golf. The 26 rooms are fresh and bright. Meals are served in the pleasant restaurant or on the terrace and the excellent cooking is based versions of local dishes such as *magret de canard au miel et aux épices* (duck with honey and spices). Route de Figeac, T: 05 65 45 18 11, www.villefranche.com/relais_farrou/

St-Antonin-Noble-Val

€ **Le Lys Bleu**. Opposite the old market place at the heart of this enchanting village on the Aveyron River, the hotel is created from three ancient buildings. The 11 bedrooms are pretty and very comfortable. 29 Pl. de la Halle, T: 05 63 68 21 00 or 05 63 30 65 06.

Vaissac

€ **Terrassier**. A peaceful setting in a little bourg, with a deservedly popular restaurant using local produce. Pool. Le Bourg (near Montricoux), T: 05 63 30 94 60, F: 05 63 30 87 40, hotel-rest.terrassier@wanadoo.fr

MARKET DAYS

Belcastel occasional Fridays in summer
Caylus Tuesday Saturday
Laguepie Wednesday, Thursday
Monbazens July–Aug Wednesday morning
Najac 15 June–15 September Sunday
Negrepelisse Tuesday
Rignac Tuesday July-August 2 evenings
St-Antonin-Noble-Val Sunday
Varen Thursday
Villefranche-de-Rouergue Thursday; monthly *foires*
Villeneuve-d'Aveyron Sunday

FESTIVALS & EVENTS

April
Le Salon du Site Remarquable du Gout, a celebration and discovery of the gourmet specialties of the region, Najac T: 05 65 29 72 05

July
Festival de la Chanson Francophone, Festival of songs from French speaking countries, Villefranche-de-Rouergue, T: 05 65 45 41 12
Les Nuits Musicales, chamber music in the monuments of Villefranche-de-Rouergue
Son et lumière Roche d'Oc, sound and light, Penne

July–August
Musique classique dans la Cour d'honneur illuminée du Château de Bournazel, T: 05 65 44 56 10

August
Festival en Bastides, street theatre and other entertainment performed in turn in the *bastide* towns of Villefranche-de-Rouergue, Villeneuve-d'Aveyron, Najac and Bastide-l'Evêque, T: 05 65 45 13 18

THE TARN

The river Tarn carves a wide and, in most places, peaceful valley across the *départe-ment* which has taken its name, and was for several centuries crucial for carrying wine from the Gaillac vineyards to Bordeaux via the Garonne. On its banks stands the elegant brick town of Albi, *préfecture* of the Tarn, with its picturesque ensemble of Gothic cathedral and bishops' palace, while Castres on the Agout is built mainly in stone and is the main industrial centre of the southern Tarn. The Tarn also boasts one of the most celebrated *bastides* in the southwest, Cordes-sur-Ciel which, since the 13th century, has gradually encased the hill of Mordagne to the west of Albi.

ALBI

Albi is the best-known and most decorative of the brick towns of the Tarn valley, elic-iting many comparisons with Tuscany, and the ochres, roses, reds and purples do not disappoint. The cathedral, on a spur above the Tarn, dominates the town beneath and is visible from miles around. Albi's most famous son was Henri-Marie-Raymond de Toulouse-Lautrec Monfa whose work is represented in the museum installed in the former bishops' palace.

HISTORY OF ALBI

Settled by the 4th century BC, *Civitas Albigensium* was mentioned for the first time c. 400 and was head of a diocese in the 5th century. By the 7th century the *cité* was taking shape under the shared power of the Church and the nobility. At the break-up of the Carolingian Empire, the Counts of Albi became vassals of the infamous Trencavel dynasty, self-styled Counts of Béziers, Carcassonne and Albi, and protectors of Cathars, rivalling them in the 13th century until the Albigensian Crusade (*see box on p. 251*). Some half-century after the Crusade, the Orthodox bishops undertook the rebuilding of the cathedral as a symbol of their sovereignty. The town's prosperity increased during the late 15th and 16th cen-turies thanks largely to the production of of blue dye from the pastel plant (*see p. 315*). At about the same time two bishops of Albi, uncle and nephew Louis I (1474–1503) and Louis II (1504–10) of Amboise, great patrons of the arts, dec-orated the interior of the cathedral. Some fine Renaissance houses were built in the town and the Bishops' Palace went through various renovations. The metal-lurgical, mining and glass industries, which developed in the 19th century, have now largely ceased.

Cathedral of Ste-Cécile

Open June–Sept 9–6.30; Oct–May 9–12 & 2–6.30; T: 05 63 43 23 43. Tickets to enter the choir are sold inside.

The austere and inscrutable fortress of faith, the cathedral of Ste-Cécile, totally dominates the town and towers over the Place Ste-Cécile. It has stood isolated like a beached ship since the houses that surrounded it were cleared away in the 18th–19th centuries and a small market square (the market is still held here) transformed into a huge car park which has thankfully now been relocated underground.

History of the cathedral

The cathedral took about 100 years to build, replacing a more modest Romanesque church, at a time of spiritual renewal and pecuniary rigour between 1282 and 1383. Reconstruction began in the apse and the south side of the choir. Basically a skeletal structure supported by buttressing with non load-bearing walls, its originality is due both to the brick, a cheaper and faster means of building, and to the massive rounded buttresses which echo, and were probably inspired by, the fortifications of the adjacent bishops' palace. The seriousness of the building reflects the objective of its main champion, Chief Inquisitor Bernard de Castanet, Bishop of Albi (1277–1307), to reaffirm the authority of the Roman Catholic Church following the subversive Cathar heresies in the 12th century (*see box opposite*). Indeed the church resembles a massive fort.

The exterior

A great undulating pile of brick that looks as if it had been tipped all of a piece from a celestial mould, it epitomises southern or meridional Gothic, having none of the fractured restlessness of the High Gothic of northern France. There are no walls of glass, simply modest lancets; the lower windows were added in the 15th century. The silhouette of the cathedral was altered in the 19th century during work to solve the problem of water infiltration when the roof, which originally had wide overhanging eaves and rested directly on the vaults, was raised by the architect César Daly (1811–94), a disciple of Viollet-le-Duc. The 19th-century work is demarcated by the gargoyles and the lighter brick. Daly also began prettifying the roofline with small belfries to match the one already existing. Local disapproval eventually led to their demolition.

The 78m tiered cathedral belfry was built between 1355 and 1366. The tower is articulated by quarter-circle relieving arches between great rounded buttresses but the rhythm changes to octagonal in the upper level (1485–92).

The main entrance to the cathedral is on the south, approached from Place Ste-Cécile through the archway built by Bishop Dominique de Florence (1397–1410), which incorporates a round tower that was part of the fortifications of the episcopal city. Steps ascend to the ornate entrance under the early 16th-century crocketed Flamboyant baldaquin and filigree tympanum. The sculptures of the entrance were remade by Daly between 1865 and 1870, when the baldaquin vaults were filled in.

THE ALBIGENSIAN CRUSADES

The problem of the heretics or Cathars (*see p. 13*) in the southwest had been rumbling for some time before forcible repression was first suggested by the Church in 1177. The Counts of Toulouse were either ineffectual or reluctant to be heavy handed and Church-organised preaching missions met with little success in stemming the heretical tide. The incident that triggered the first crusade against a Christian country was the assassination in 1208 of the Papal Legate, Peter of Castelnau, in Languedoc, by a servant of the Count of Toulouse, Raymond VII. This gave the Church (Pope Innocent III, backed by the Cistercians) the excuse to encourage the French barons, with the promise of plenary indulgences, to appropriate the land of the Counts of Toulouse. It also gave the French king, Philippe-Auguste, the opportunity to gain control over evasive Languedoc. In June 1209 the crusading army gathered at Lyon, first besieging Béziers and Carcassonne. It was at the latter that Simon de Montfort took command. By 1210 the crusaders had spread into the Albigeois and Toulouse was attacked for the first time in 1211. There was an important battle at Muret in 1213 and fighting went on intermittently, spreading across the Quercy, Rouergue, Périgord and Agenais in 1214, when King John became involved. Simon de Montfort died in 1218 during another siege of Toulouse. The need for peace was not recognised until much later. On 12th April 1229 the Treaty of Paris was signed: Raymond VII undertook, among many things, to marry his daughter Jeanne to Alphonse de Poitiers, brother of Louis IX. Paris had got its hold on the Languedoc, but the heresies were not subdued. Pope Gregory IX ordered the Inquisition in southern France in 1233 and entrusted the task to the Dominicans. Persecution was severe throughout the 1240s. It is unclear why the label Albigensian was adopted for this episode in history, but it is possibly because the Albigeois (the area around Albi) was the scene of attempts at reconciliation between the Church and the 'heretics', or because there were intense military operations here early in the crusades. Only in the 1960s did the term Cathar begin to be widely used.

The interior

The Flamboyant vestibule (c. 1510–20) offers a hint of what is to come but nothing quite prepares the visitor for the contrast between the severe exterior and the extravagance of the interior. The cathedral was transformed in the calm years of nascent humanism before the Reformation. It is an essentially simple, unified space, without aisles, where the interior buttresses form the lateral chapels and support a rib vault rising to a height of 30m. The coherence of this space was disrupted before the end of the 15th century by the elaborate choir enclosure. Two bishops, Louis I and Louis II of Amboise, were responsible for the metamorphosis—powerful men from a great family of prelates and ambassadors, who were influenced by the artistic currents of the time in the Loire, in Burgundy and in Italy. There is no written documentation extant relating to the work as all the archives were destroyed during the Revolution. The all-over *trompe-l'oeil* pattern of the chapels and walls, conceived c. 1509–20, has been subjected to numerous restorations, especially in the 19th century.

The nave

The *Last Judgement* on the west wall is thought to date from the time of Louis I (late 15th century), whose gold and red heraldic colours fill the lower space. This is the largest surviving wall painting of the period in France and was probably executed by Franco-Flemish artists contemporaneous with Hieronymous Bosch. Applied directly to the brick, it covers some 200 square metres. The composition is organised according to tradition but there is one disturbing omission: the key figure of *Christ in Judgement*. In the 17th century different priorities permitted the piercing of an opening through the wall to the chapel where the relics of St Clair, first Bishop of Albi, lie and consequently the work is arranged around a void.

The composition is divided vertically, the blessed on the left, lined up in orderly fashion on a calm blue ground, and opposite, a murky *Hell* in all its confusion. It is also divided horizontally into three main registers: *Heaven* is subdivided into three hierarchies, of angels, the 12 Apostles, and a line-up of the saved with St Louis, Charlemagne and others now unidentifiable. Below is the theatre of the *Resurrection* where those mortals already judged hold the *Book of Life* open on their chests. Opposite them sinners are thrown back to the underworld. The lowest register is *Hell*, depicted in as much horror as the artists could muster and compartmentalised into scenes representing each of the Seven Deadly Sins, which are annotated in Old French: from left to right, Pride, Envy, Anger or Wrath, Avarice or Greed, Gluttony and Lust (Sloth is missing), each with appropriately grisly punishments.

In quite a different artistic timbre, high above this didactic message, is the splendid Baroque Moucherel organ (1734–36) supported by two muscular atlantes. The carved case is mainly in oak, and the figures, including St Cecilia (*see box opposite*) holding her small organ with tin pipes and the joyful angel musicians, are in lime. Restored in 1981, it is frequently used for recitals. A chapel on the south contains a highly sentimental statue of St Cecilia reclining, inspired by the work in Santa-Cecilia Trastevere, Rome, representing the saint as she was reputedly found in her tomb in 1599.

To meet a need to accommodate large congregations in the 19th century after the destruction of several parish churches at the Revolution, and to avoid having to dismantle the precious Gothic choir enclosure, the main altar was placed at the west. The black marble altar with enamels was made by two Parisian artists, Jean-Paul Froidevaux and his wife, Marie-Josephe Tournon-Froidevaux (1980).

The magnificent Flamboyant *jubé* (c. 1474–84) that divides the nave from the chancel, a profusion of ogees and lacework, pinnacles and broccoli leaves, was carved in tender limestone which has hardened over the centuries. The cutting of this scintillating work is a tribute to the virtuosity of French stonecarvers. The original 75 statues in the niches have disappeared; those present are replacements.

ST CECILIA

The mainly apocryphal story of the young Christian girl, Cecilia, tells that she avowed chastity when she married the pagan Valerius. He agreed, provided that the angel who watched over his wife appeared to him. The angel duly appeared and crowned the couple with roses. Valerius accepted baptism, along with his brother Tibertius, together with another called Maximus, but all were executed for their Faith. Cecilia was condemned to death by suffocation in a steam bath, but she did not die immediately, and following three blows from the sword she survived another three days. It was not until the later Middle Ages that she became patron saint of music. This is thought to derive from her *Passion* which tells of the sound of musical instruments (*cantatibus organis*) on her wedding day. *Organum* became associated with organ, and her attribute is often a small, portable organ. St Cecilia is represented several times both inside and outside the cathedral. The early 20th-century statue places gruesome emphasis on the wounds on her neck.

The choir is the most spectacular part of this amazing building. The entrance to the ambulatory is in the south section of the *jubé*. Inside, around the outside of the choir screen, is a procession of magnificent polychromed statues (c. 1480). They represent Old Testament prophets, priests and kings, those who have not yet seen the light but predict or prefigure the Coming of Christ. Above the entrance is an affecting *Virgin of the Annunciation*. Long-haired, She is sculpted with her hand on the Bible, as She receives the message of the Angel Gabriel to her left (on the choir screen). Of the 48 large-format sculptures over 30 are around the ambulatory and are in excellent condition; it is not known if their colour is original and, if not, when they were repainted. The figures stand in ornate niches, most carry a banderole and several are identified by name. The image-makers, who undoubtedly included Flemish masters, had a penchant for the anecdotal and descriptive use of costume and fashion, but also the expressive quality of each individual. Isaiah is presented as a prosperous bourgeois merchant, and Jeremiah appears appropriately grave. Simeon, the High Priest of the Temple, at the axis, is the linchpin between the Ancient and the New Law. His importance places him on the opposite side of the screen from the *Virgin and Child* (below Simeon is a plaque commemorating the quick action of a local official to save many of the 254 original carvings from destruction at the Revolution). The only female Old Testament figures are Esther and Judith, the latter wearing a rich red brocade dress hanging in heavy folds and a bejewelled headdress. The two great Christian Emperors, Charlemagne and Constantine, stand sentinel opposite each other over the north and south entrances to the choir. Inside the choir (entrance on north) are the Apostles, those who have seen the light, but they are less glorious artistically. At the west, on

the reverse of the roodscreen, is a small but voluptuous *St Cecilia* with her attributes, a crown of roses and lilies, a portative organ and a martyr's palm. All around the western part of the chancel, above the 120 oak stalls, are 70 delicately sculpted child angels, each holding a musical instrument or scroll, and above them are the arms of Louis of Amboise. The canopy of the episcopal throne is a *tour de force* of undercutting, whereas the modern altar table of white marble is a refreshingly simple piece.

What little medieval glass (c. 1320–25) there is can be found in the high windows at the east. Works in the chapels include a fresco of the *Resurrection* and the *Legend of the True Cross* (c. 1460–70), both heavily restored. In the east chapel are four paintings sent from Rome by Cardinal de Bernis in the 18th century.

The vaults

The vaults, best seen from the choir, were painted between 1509 and 1513 by Bolognese artists who worked suspended in baskets. The iconographic programme, like the chancel statues, unites the Old and New Testaments. The New Testament figures are painted in gold, the others in silver, on a deep blue ground, and have hardly been touched since they were painted. The scenes are arranged in the form of a triumphal procession from west to east with St Cecilia in the centre, and tell of the return of man to God under the guidance of the Church, culminating in the *Christ of the Second Coming* surrounded by the symbols of the four Evangelists. On the boss nearest to the organ are the multiple *fleur-de-lis* of France as they appeared before the mid-14th century (*see p. 361*). Among the scenes most easily recognisable are, reading from west to east, the *Last Supper*, the *Transfiguration*, the *Coronation of the Virgin*, St Cecilia and Valerian, the *Annunciation*, then Cecilia and Valerian again at each extremity of the next bay, the parable of the *Wise and Foolish Virgins*, the *Coronation of the Virgin* again, and the *Tree of Life*. Adam and Eve are easy to recognise in the east bay. This significant work was the first major example of Italian Renaissance art in the Midi, and compares very closely to the decoration of churches near Pavia in Northern Italy.

Gardens of the Palais de la Berbie

One of the loveliest places in Albi is the garden of the Palais de la Berbie. Steps lead down from Place Ste-Cécile and there is also an entrance from Place de l'Archêveché. The path runs past the entrance to the Musée Toulouse-Lautrec (*see p. 257*), up a slight incline, to arrive on a terrace high above the Tarn with a marvellous view of the river, spanned by the old and new bridges to the right. Beyond are the brick façades of the old suburb of La Madeleine and, on the horizon, the building that appears to be a miniature of the cathedral is the 19th-century church of Notre-Dame-de-la-Drèche (*see p. 269*). The formal garden below was installed by Archbishop Hyacinthe Serroni (1678–87), who was also responsible for the vine-shaded walk on the old ramparts, with 18th-century statues in the alcoves. The formal garden cannot be entered, but the rampart walk is reached via the steps in the southwest corner of the terrace.

The garden (late 17th century) of the Palais de la Berbie overlooking the Tarn in Albi.

Henri de Toulouse-Lautrec (1864–1901)

Lautrec is a legendary figure, a direct descendant of one of the oldest and most prestigious dynasties in southwest France, the Counts of Toulouse, but through a tragic quirk of fate also misshapen and ugly. Most importantly he was a dedicated painter caught up in the social debates of his time. He was also revered and protected by his family. He was born within sight of the cathedral, to Adèle Tapié de Celeyran and her first cousin Alphonse de Toulouse-Lautrec. The main occupation of the eccentric count and his family was hunting, but they all had a gift for drawing. In 1878, at the age of 14, Henri slipped from a chair when playing in the Albi house, and fractured his left leg; the following year, he broke the other leg while recuperating in Barèges in the Pyrenees with his mother. The bones did not knit and he remained just over five feet tall, so he took up drawing instead of riding. Until 1881, when he went to Paris to become a professional artist, his time was divided between the different family estates in the southwest. In 1882 he moved to Léon Bonnat's studio and then to Fernand Cormon in Montmartre. By 1884 he was established there and pursued his profession among the Parisian avant-garde. He evoked the sub-culture of Montmartre in all its gaiety and squalor. He travelled prodigiously but not far; he knew Van Gogh, the Pont-Aven Group, and Degas, whose work he admired most; he also knew Oscar Wilde, James Whistler and Aubrey Beardsley and was heavily influenced by Japanese prints; he made use of the effects of theatrical lighting; he assimilated Art Nouveau tendencies; and the popular illustrations of the 1880s were possibly the single most tangible influence on his art. Lautrec's *annus mirabilis* was 1892, when he produced his first colour posters. They brought fame to him and to the people he portrayed and were his main contribution to 20th-century art, but in fact he only made 32 lithographs for posters in the last ten years of his life. He died near Bordeaux in 1901 at Château de Malromé (*see p. 87*).

Toulouse-Lautrec: *La Buveuse* or *Gueule de bois* (1889).

Palais de la Berbie and Musée Toulouse-Lautrec

Open July–Aug 9–6; June, Sept 9–12 & 2–6; April, May 10–12 & 2–6; March, Oct,
10–12 & 2–5.30, closed Tues; Nov–Feb, 10–12 & 2–5, closed Tues; T: 05 63 49 48 70,
www.musee-toulouse-lautrec.com.

The great mass of the Palais de la Berbie, the name derived the from the old Occitan word *bisbia*, meaning bishops' palace, overlooks the garden. The Berbie fortress-palace is a powerful building of disparate parts, begun in the second half of the 13th century by Bishop Durand de Beaucaire and completed towards the end of the century by Bernard de Castanet, to protect the Church's authority over Albi and as part of the town's defences. Built entirely in brick, tamed and modified over the centuries, its architecture complements the cathedral. The oldest part is the Tour Notre-Dame on the east overlooking Place de l'Archevêché. The Chapelle Notre-Dame (13th century) dates from a similar period and the mighty Tour St-Michel on the west was completed by 1277. Only a stump remains of the largest tower, Ste-Catherine, built facing the river before 1300 and dismantled in the early 17th century. The bastions along the Tarn were probably constructed during the Hundred Years War. The Bishops of Amboise amended the east wing and Bishop Gaspard Daillon de Lude added the *salon doré* in the 17th century, with a ceiling *à la française*, and the monumental staircase in the style of the Loire. By 1790 the building was taken over by the state although the episcopal see was reinstated in 1823.

The museum

The main function of the Berbie since 1922 has been to house the largest single collection of works by Toulouse-Lautrec in existence, some 1,000 items, including paintings, drawings, lithographs and posters. The majority were donated by his mother, Comtesse Adèle, encouraged by Gabriel Tapié de Céleyran (*see p. 259*) and Lautrec's oldest friend and supporter, the art dealer Maurice Joyant. It also has a small collection of Regional Archaeology; two superb authenticated paintings by Georges de la Tour (1593–1652) *St Jude* and *St James Minor*, commissioned for the cathedral; and *Notre-Dame de la Salute, Venice*, by Francesco Guardi (1712–93). There is also a vast group of 19th- and 20th-century works by well-known artists and local painters. At time of writing the museum was undergoing extensive remodelling scheduled until 2010; the new entrance off the courtyard and three new galleries have been completed.

Ground floor

The three new brick-vaulted rooms are dedicated to the different aspects of Toulouse-Lautrec. To introduce the man and his environment are self-portraits, paintings of him by his friends, including a small full-length study of 1898 by Vuillard, and drawings by members of his family. Lautrec's earlier paintings reflect the influence of his first teacher, René Princeteau (1839–1914), painter of horses (*see p. 71*). There is a tiny, rather inept, portrait, c. 1879, of his father on horseback in Caucasian costume wearing a turban, with a falcon on his wrist (he was one of the last falconers in France). A form of diluted Impressionism is used to record family retainers and family

Toulouse-Lautrec: *Comtesse Adèle de Toulouse-Lautrec* (c. 1881).

properties, such as Céleyran, near Narbonne. He made two portraits of his mother, Comtesse Adèle de Toulouse-Lautrec (c. 1881, *pictured above*; and 1887), which show her seated and alone.

In the same room is a large painting *Maurice Joyant en baie de Somme* (1900), showing his life-long friend dressed in the yellow oilskins and sou'wester that Lautrec had acquired from the USA and wanted to paint; despite its seeming spontaneity, it took 75 sittings. His cousin, and faithful and discreet companion in Paris, Gabriel Tapié de Céleyran (1869–1930), featured in the silhouettes with Lautrec in some of his works.

Tour Ste-Catherine

The Impressionist influence gives way to linear studies of figures and interiors later on. By 1885 his work was becoming far more experimental and his social conscience was stirred by a totally different milieu and life in Paris. It is interesting to compare the quiet dignity of the portraits of his mother with the dejection of *La Buveuse* or *Gueule de bois* (Drinking woman, or Hangover, 1889; *pictured on p. 256*), a comment on isolation and self-destruction, for which his mistress Suzanne Valadon posed shortly before they separated. There are dandies and women with complicated coiffures, in a style he developed after 1889, in thin oils on board with a breathtaking fluidity and economy of line.

Tour St-Michel

The hard-core Montmartre works—sensual, erotic, funny, tender or wickedly satirical, with a straightforward realism that was considered outrageous at the time—are the moment where Lautrec's critical observation and technical prowess come together. Representative of his work are the two famous versions of *Au Salon de la Rue des Moulins* (1894), one a pastel study in preparation for the oil painting. A studied and carefully orchestrated piece in large format (111.5cm by 132.5cm), it is the culmination of his studies and sketches of *maisons closes* (brothels) and their occupants, made from 1891 to 1895. In these galleries are all the music-hall stars found in the posters, Yvette Guilbert, Jane Avril, La Goulue and Loïe Fuller (1893), a swirl of veils and graceful arabesques.

Second floor

The poster section contains original lithograph stones, which Lautrec prepared himself, and the posters. Lautrec's earlier work and experiments are synthesised in this flattened decorative formula which projected the art of the poster into the 20th century. He was a man with a foot in two camps, the establishment and Parisian sub-culture and this dichotomy is interestingly brought into perspective in the museum.

Third floor

The 19th–20th-century collection is an eclectic group of works from Corot to Cubism, not exhibited to best advantage but demonstrating the background to the influences on Lautrec. An added bonus are the views over the river and gardens. Many major painters are represented by just one work. There is a Degas pastel *Man in an Opera Hat*, a Matisse, a Vlaminck, a Marquet and a Dufy. There are paintings by members of the Pont Aven group, Emile Bernard and Paul Sérusier, and some small bronzes by Gauguin. There are examples of Intimisme by Bonnard, Félix Valloton and Edouard Vuillard; Cubism by André Lhote; and Expressionism by Georges Rouault. Yves Brayer is the most important of the group of local artists, and there are sculptures by Rodin, Bourdelle, Aristide Maillol and Paul Belmondo (father of Jean-Paul the filmstar).

EXPLORING ALBI

West of the cathedral

The Bondidou River, which now runs underground to the west of the cathedral, is the reason for the unusual lack of a west portal to the cathedral. Immediately west of the cathedral is Place du Château and the ancient quarter of Castelviel, the highest part of town, with its minuscule *places*. Rue du Castelviel is overwhelmed by the huge brick belfry of the Cathedral. From Place de la Trébaille there are steps down to the Berges du Tarn (riverbank). There is a small north door from the cathedral into Rue de la Temporalité, which links Place du Château and Place Ste-Cécile.

South of the cathedral

The area immediately to the south of Place Ste-Cécile is largely pedestrianised and upmarket, with restaurants and chic boutiques among the carefully restored medieval, Renaissance, 18th- and 19th-century houses.

In the area between Rue Ste-Cécile and Rue Mariès is the collegiate **Church of St-Salvy**, the oldest church in Albi. The three-tiered belfry, the Tour de la Gâche on Rue Mariès, signals its presence. A textbook example of evolving styles of architecture, the tower proves that Albi was once more white than red. The Romanesque base (c. 1080) with Lombard-style blind arches and the second stage (c. 1220–40), both in white stone, are topped off with a late 14th-century brick crown and watchtower. At the top of the flight of steps is the church's north door, originally Romanesque but almost obliterated by a pedimented version. The old sculpted capitals are still in place.

Despite successive modifications from the 12th to 18th centuries, the dim interior is quite harmonious. Behind the ornate Baroque altar with a baldaquin (1721) is a replica of the 12th-century wooden image of St Salvy who was made Bishop in the late 6th century. In 943 his relics were translated to this site and the cult of St Salvy was widely venerated in this region during the early Middle Ages. The lower parts of the four east bays (completed c. 1100) are heavily restored. Lateral chapels were added during the 14th and 15th centuries, and the chancel and two preceding bays, rebuilt in the 15th century, are Flamboyant. Louis I d'Amboise consecrated a new altar in 1490. The clerestory was added in the 18th century, as was the rose window. The early 16th-century organ was transferred from the cathedral in 1737 by master carpenter Christophe Moucherel, and is used for concerts. Behind a wrought-iron screen (light switch on the right) is a group of polychrome figures (c. 15th century), an *Ecce Homo* and the *Sanhedrin*, but not of the standard of those in the cathedral. From the north door are accessed the modest and secret cloistral remains, with just one gallery left standing, transitional Romanesque/Gothic (begun 1270). The tomb of Vidal de Malvési, creator of the cloister, and his brother, is against the church. From the exterior the alterations to the church are more evident, with the lower part and one 12th- century chapel in stone, and a thrusting 15th-century brick structure above. A flight of steps lead into Rue Ste-Cécile. Following the cloister aisle and turning left into a passageway leads eventually into the slightly run-down but picturesque Place du Cloître east of the church.

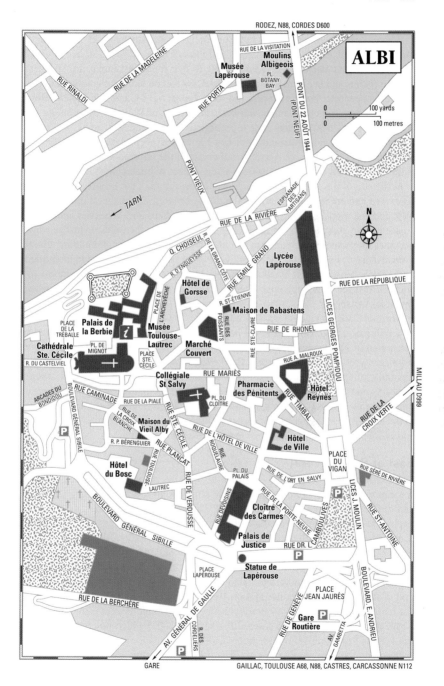

RODEZ, N88, CORDES D600

RUE DE LA VISITATION

ALBI

Musée
Lapérouse

Moulins
Albigeois

PL. BOTANY BAY

RUE PORTA

RUE DE LA MADELEINE

RUE RINALDI

PONT DU 22 AOÛT 1944 (PONT NEUF)

0   100 yards
0   100 metres

N

TARN

PONT VIEUX

RUE DE LA RIVIÈRE

ESPLANADE DES PARTISANS

Q. CHOISEUL

R. DE LA GRAND CÔTE

R. D'ENGUEYSSE

RUE ÉMILE GRAND

Lycée
Lapérouse

RUE DE LA RÉPUBLIQUE

PLACE DE L'ARCHEVÊCHÉ

Hôtel de
Gorsse

R. ST-ÉTIENNE

Maison de Rabastens

RUE DES POISSANTS

RUE STE-CLAIRE

RUE DE RHONEL

LICES GEORGES POMPIDOU

PLACE DE LA TRÉBALLE

Palais de
la Berbie

Musée
Toulouse-
Lautrec

Marché
Couvert

Cathédrale
Ste. Cécile

PL. DE MIGNOT

PLACE STE. CÉCILE

R. DU CASTELVIEL

RUE A. MALROUX

RUE MARIÈS

Collégiale
St Salvy

Pharmacie
des Pénitents

Hôtel
Reynès

RUE TIMBAL

RUE DE LA CROIX VERTE

MILLAU D999

ARCADES DU BONDIDOU

BOULEVARD GÉNÉRAL SIBILLE

RUE CAMINADE

RUE DE LA PIALE

RUE DE LA CROIX BLANCHE

Maison du
Vieil Alby

R. P. BÉRENGUIER

RUE STE. CÉCILE

PL. DU CLOÎTRE

RUE DE L'HÔTEL DE VILLE

RUE RIQUELAURE

Hôtel
de Ville

RUE PLANCAT

RUE TOULOUSE

Hôtel
du Bosc

LAUTREC

RUE DE VERDUSSE

PL. DU PALAIS

RUE DE L'ORT EN SALVY

RUE DEVOISINS

PLACE DU VIGAN

RUE SÉRÉ DE RIVIÈRE

RUE DE LA PORTE NEUVE

Cloître
des Carmes

CAMBOULIVES

LICES J. MOULIN

RUE ST-ANTOINE

BOULEVARD GÉNÉRAL SIBILLE

Palais de
Justice

RUE DR. L.

PLACE
LAPÉROUSE

Statue de
Lapérouse

RUE DE LA BERCHÈRE

AV. GÉNÉRAL DE GAULLE

R. DES CORDELIERS

RUE DE GENÈVE

Gare
Routière

PLACE
JEAN JAURÈS

BOULEVARD E. ANDRIEU

AV. GAMBETTA

GARE

GAILLAC, TOULOUSE A68, N88, CASTRES, CARCASSONNE N112

Where Rue Puech-Bérenguier and Rue de la Croix-Blanche meet is the pretty **Maison du Vieil Alby**, used for regional exhibitions (*open 10.30–12.30 & 3–7; closed Sun, Mon, holidays and Jan; T: 05 63 54 96 38*). In Rue Toulouse-Lautrec, no. 10 has an attractively restored late Renaissance courtyard. Further on to the right are a waxworks museum, the former home of Lapérouse (*see p. 263*) at no. 14, and next to it the **Hôtel du Bosc**, where Toulouse-Lautrec was born and where, in 1878, he broke his leg.

Rue de l'Hôtel-de-Ville was once a prestigious street lined with some of the best noble houses, the most outstanding at nos 13, 14 and 17, and no. 16, the Hôtel de Ville since the 18th century. Above the doorway of the restored 17th-century façade is the coat of arms of Albi and inside is a very attractive brick courtyard.

At the end of the street is Place du Vigan, created in the 18th century and recently renovated and embellished, marking the divide between the medieval quarter to the west and the modern town. Around two sides are shops and brasseries, and in the adjacent open area markets are held. On Place du Palais is the Palais de Justice which occupies the former Carmelite convent, an early 17th-century brick building around a small cloister. Its south façade looks over Place Lapérouse and the large monument to the explorer (*see p. 263*) by Nicolas Bernard Raggi (erected 1853) with cannon and anchors salvaged from Lapérouse's ships wrecked at Vanikorou, Solomon Isles, where the sailor perished.

North of Place du Vigan at no. 14 Rue Timbal is the Hôtel de Reynès (c. 1520), built by a rich pastel merchant. The small Italianate courtyard is the most sophisticated of the period in Albi, combining a stair-tower in the tradition of Gothic buildings with the elegance of a Renaissance loggia. On the south façade are two busts in medallions, reputedly of François I and probably his second queen, Eléonore of Austria. Almost opposite, on the corner of Rue des Pénitents, is the 16th-century Maison Enjalbert or Pharmacie des Pénitents, an outstanding timber-framed house using the vocabulary of the Renaissance, triangular pediments and Ionic and Corinthian pilasters. From the end of Rue Mariès is an interesting view towards the Cathedral.

East of the cathedral

The *quartier de la rivière* on the slopes of the Tarn has many beautiful old buildings, the majority faithfully restored. In Place de l'Archeveché are 16th-century slate roofs and dormers on the southeast of the Berbie. Between Rue Emile-Grand, the river and Esplanade des Partisans, is a tangle of narrow, sloping streets. Rue d'Engueysse has some jettied houses with open galleries or soleilhos (sometimes called *galetas*), origi-nally used for drying crops, including pastel. Rue de la Grand'Côte was one of the most important before the 18th century. The best house nearby is the 16th-century Hôtel de Gorsse, in a courtyard at the top of the steps north of the market. At the top end of Rue Emile-Grand is the Maison Pierre-Raimond de Rabastens, incorporating the remains of the oldest house in Albi (12th century), built in stone. Quite a contrast is the spruce, brick and steel covered market (1901–02) which functions every day but is at its busiest on Saturdays. At no. 16 Rue St-Julien is a fine soleilho.

Spanning the Tarn are two bridges. The pointed arches indicate the oldest part (c.

1220) of the much-modified Pont-Vieux and the brick sections indicate the enlargements made after 1820 to allow carts carrying coal and glass to pass. River trips on a replica *gabare* depart from Quai Choiseul. Up stream, the Pont Neuf (1866), was renamed Pont-du-22-août-1944 to commemorate a combat between members of the Resistance and a German column. On Lices Georges Pompidou is the 19th-century **Lycée Lapérouse** where Jean Jaurès (*see p. 308*), local champion of the working classes who became socialist deputy for Carmaux from 1893-98, taught philosophy 1881–83. He played a key role in encouraging local glassmakers to form the Verrerie Ouvrière d'Albi in 1896, one of the first worker-managed enterprises in France. George Pompidou, President of France 1969–74, was a pupil here 1919–28.

North of the river

Across the river is the Faubourg du Bout-du-Pont which developed in the 11th century, and Rue Porta has a terrace overlooking the river. In Place Botany Bay is the entrance to the **Musée Lapérouse** (*open July–Aug Mon–Fri 9–12 & 2–6, Sat, Sun until 7; March–June, Sept–Oct 9–12 & 2–6, closed Mon; Nov–Feb 10–12 & 2–5, closed Mon; T: 05 63 46 01 87*). The museum is devoted to the life and times of Jean-François Galaup de Lapérouse (1741–88), a sailor and explorer of the Age of Enlightenment, born near Albi, who was active at Hudson Bay against the English during the American Wars of Independence and followed the wake of Bougainville and Cook at Louis XVI's behest to the south seas. The old mills of Albi were below here and in the little garden in front of the museum are *isatis tinctoria* or pastel plants (*see p. 315*).

THE ALBIGEOIS

This area in the northwest of the Tarn is crossed by the little valley of the Cérou, a tributary of the Aveyron, which flows through beautiful fertile landscapes scattered with particularly fine hilltop towns and *bastides*, including Cordes-sur-Ciel. In nearby Monestiés is a unique group of Gothic sculptures.

CORDES-SUR-CIEL

Cordes-sur-Ciel, described locally as the *perle des bastides*, is the showpiece of the northern Tarn. One of the oldest and most picturesque *bastides* in the region, its charter was granted by Raymond VII of Toulouse in 1222. The suffix *sur-Ciel* ('in the sky') was officially recognised in 1990 to distinguish it from Cordes in the Vaucluse. Just after dawn on a clear autumn day, the mists are likely to gather in the Cérou Valley and swirl around the base of the hill on which the *bastide* stands. As well as a spectacular site, the town is graced with a unique group of Gothic houses. Unsurprisingly, Cordes has attracted a number of artists and artisans and there are some good shops as well as a few less good ones. The best way to get to the top of the hill is to walk, not in fact as daunting as it looks. A shuttle bus also runs from the foot of the hill.

Exploring Cordes

Cordes is made up of four concentric enclosures, the first two dating from the *bastide* built in 1222, the others later. The suburb of La Boutellerie on the eastern side remained outside the protected perimeter. On foot, from Place de la Boutellerie take the no-entry to cars road, past the chapel of the old Hôpital St-Jacques, to the junction with the Escalier du Pater-Noster on your left—with as many steps as there are words in the Latin version of the Lord's Prayer. On the right is the Porte de l'Horloge, with a clock and a round tower. This was the eastern entrance to the fourth *enceinte*, built in the 16th century to enclose the four *faubourgs* that had surrounded the medieval fort since the 14th century. The route gets steeper here on.

There was never a feudal castle at Cordes, but around the next bend the mighty barbican looms up on a cliff-like base which was part of the third enclosure, built at a time of great prosperity and population explosion at the end of the 13th century or early in the 14th century, when the first enclosures were outgrown. The road bends to arrive at Porte du Vainqueur (or Planol, 1222–29; *pictured below*), parallel with the wall, with a semi-circular tower engulfed by the buildings around it. Opposite is the late 15th-century Maison Gorsse, with early Renaissance windows. The street then turns left to pass through the barely altered Portail Peint (13th century), which originally had two portcullises and a wooden door, to the heart of the upper town. Immediately on the right is the entrance to the Musée Charles Portal (*open July–Aug 11.30–1 & 4–7; June, Sun 3.30–6.30; Sept–April Sun 3–6; T: 05 63 56 00 52*), a private museum of local archaeology and history with a remarkable and eclectic collection. On the Grand Rue are the best of the outstanding group of Gothic houses. On the

Porte du Vainqueur (1222–29) in Cordes.

south side, the Maison Carrié-Boyer, is considered to be among the earliest built (1295–1320). On three floors, the façade aggressively altered, it remains an example of how most of the houses were left in the 19th century. Next door is Maison Prunet, of about the same date, with three arcades on the ground floor and three two-light windows with a circular oculus outlined by deep mouldings, and carvings at the apex. It houses the Musée de l'Art du Sucre (*open July–Aug 9–7; Feb–June, Sept–Dec 10–12.30 & 2.30–6.30*), containing sugar fantasies conjured up by local restaurateur and master pastry cook Yves Thuriès (*see p. 277*). The next house, Maison du Grand Fauconnier, is one of the three masterpieces, probably dating from the first half of the 14th century.

Two of the original birds of prey from the façade are in the Musée Charles Portal. This is one of the most carefully executed façades, with five arcades at ground level and series of traceried windows on the first and second floors, arranged in different rhythms with high-relief carvings.

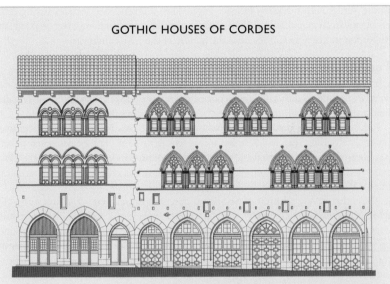

GOTHIC HOUSES OF CORDES

FAÇADES OF THE MAISON PRUNET & MAISON DU GRAND FAUCONNIER

This unique group of *hôtels particuliers* was begun nearly a century after the foundation of the *bastide* with fortunes made from linen and leather. At that time the population could have been around 5,000. The best are on the south, built into the hill, with an average of three floors on the town side but up to five or six facing out. On the ground floor are large arches of varying size giving access to the courtyard, stables or boutiques. The first floor is the most ornate, corresponding to a large room the width of the building lit by a series of sophisticated traceried windows. The sculpted decoration is usually concentrated around the windows and on the string courses linking the bays. The rhythm of the bays and the carvings are slightly different for each house. As the population decreased the occupants moved to the lower floors, partitioned the interior, blocked doors and windows (especially when windows were taxed in the 17th century), and sliced off the relief carvings to hang shutters, leaving the upper floors unmolested. When the time came to restore the houses, the second floor often served as a model for the lower one. The names are an invention of the 19th century, inspired by nothing more than the decoration on the façade.

Yves Brayer Museum

Open 10.30–12.30 & 3.30–6; closed Jan; T: 05 63 56 00 40 or 05 63 56 14 79.
The Yves Brayer Museum is on the first floor of the Maison du Grand Fauconnier (*see p. 264*). Brayer, best known for his landscapes of Provençe, lived here 1940–42 and donated 17 paintings. The museum includes a room dedicated to him, and the Espace André Verdet with works by Picasso, Léger, Miró, Prévert, Klee, Arman among others, as well as regional artists. There is also a permanent exhibition of lace-making, an important industry in Cordes until the middle of the 20th century.

Further along the Grande Rue

Opposite is Place de la Bride, where an open square with chestnut trees and a terrace overlooking the countryside have replaced the former public buildings of the *bastide*. Below the terrace wall, steep steps can be seen connecting the different levels.

Further west, the market hall is built between the two major streets. There was probably a market here in 1276, but it was rebuilt in 1358. The 24 octagonal pillars have been frequently repaired and the chestnut roof timbers were replaced in the 19th century. The depth of the well (85m) indicates that it was only used for emergencies; in any case there were other wells and cisterns.

The rather severe **Church of St-Michel** downhill to the west, was built 1263–87 when the community outgrew the old church outside the village. The nave was enlarged in 1345, and again between 1460 and 1485. The constant amendments are only too clear at the west end, a model of asymmetry: the belfry (1369–74), square at the base and octagonal above, doubled as a look-out post; it is supported by a relieving arch containing a rose window. Filling the rest of the façade is a walled-up Flamboyant portal suspended high above the present level of the small place. Above the south door is a polychrome wooden sculpture of the Virgin. The interior is typical of Gothic churches in the Midi, although little of the original building remains. The organ came from Notre-Dame in Paris in 1849.

The Maison du Grand Veneur on the Grande Rue is named after the huntsman in the narrative frieze running across the façade. It is the only house with the third floor still intact and is similar to the Grand Fauconnier but without the rhythmical arrangement of the bays. The first-floor windows are a reconstruction modelled on the second floor. Its special charm is the anecdotal nature of the high-relief carvings. Birds perch, dogs play and crouching figures inhabit the mouldings. The figures of the huntsmen, their hounds and their prey fill the spandrels on the second floor. The Maison Fontpeyrouse, on the opposite corner, houses the Tourist Office and Cultural Centre. Heavily restored, it is arranged around a large courtyard with a wooden staircase and galleries serving the floors. The Maison du Grand Ecuyer (Great Equerry), now synonymous with its restaurant (*see p. 277*), has a most accomplished façade, with simpler tracery, heavily foliate capitals and discreet carvings in the deep recesses of the window mouldings.

The two cobbled streets descend to the Porte des Ormeaux on the west. Two semicircular bastions flank the gate but the upper parts of the archway and towers were rebuilt at a very early stage. Around the tight bend to the right is Porte de la Jane, also between two semi-circular towers, but badly damaged during the Wars of Religion. Further downhill is the Jardin des Paradis (*open July–Aug 10–7; May, June 11–6; May, Sept, Sun and holidays 2–6. T: 05 63 56 29 77*), an intimate, modern garden with some unusual concepts in landscaping and garden design inspired by medieval and eastern ideas. Simple ornaments and materials are combined with flowers and vegetables.

MONESTIÉS

The peaceful valley of the Cérou east of Cordes leads to Monestiés. En route, the pretty village of **Salles**, famous for its stone quarries in the Middle Ages, has a part Romanesque, part Gothic church containing four 16th-century painted wooden statues. Monestiés is a charming village which shelters a group of magnificent late-Gothic sculptures, housed in the little chapel of St-Jacques on Le Barry, the street across the main road from the fountain in the village centre.

The *Entombment*

Open July–Aug 10–1 & 2–7; mid-March to June, Sept–Oct 10–12 & 2–6; Nov–mid–March 2–5; T: 05 63 76 41 63, www.monesties.com

In 1992 the sculptures were restored, perhaps too vigorously (reducing the original quite strong colours to very delicate shades) and rearranged to what is considered to be their original layout. The chapel was renovated at the same time and is the perfect foil for this deeply moving group of polychromed stone statues, which has been here for two centuries. The work was originally commissioned c. 1490 by the Bishop of Albi, Louis I of Amboise, for the chapel of the bishops' residence, the 13th-century Château of Combefa 3km south of Monestiés. It was designed as the retable of the main altar, although the iconography is unusual for that role. The plastic and expressive qualities of the carving compare with the finest produced in France at the end of the 15th century, marking the transitional period between Gothic spirituality and humanist naturalism. This monumental

Detail of the statue of Nicodemus from the *Entombment* at Monestiés.

The *Pietà* (c. 1490) at Monestiés.

work represents three episodes of the Passion, *Crucifixion*, *Pietà* and *Entombment*, in a vast triangular composition. At the apex is the *Crucifixion* whose Christ has passed through suffering to a state of compassion; below is the *Pietà* where the five Maries and St John, who supports the head of Christ, accompany the Virgin, a rare grouping. The *Entombment*, forming the base of the triangle, which expands on the Pietà group with additional figures, is a masterpiece of medieval art conveying a deep sense of tenderness and grief. This is another unique arrangement, with five male and five female figures standing either side of the tomb to include the donor prelate, Louis I of Amboise, who holds the shroud at Christ's head thus displacing Joseph of Arimathaea. Next is St James, holding a book, a rare participant in an *Entombment*, followed by St John and finally the 'weeping woman'. On the opposite side, behind Nicodemus, are the Virgin Mary, Mary Cleophas, Mary Magdalene and the 'praying woman'. The chapel also contains the stalls and some floor tiles recovered from Combefa and recent glass in the windows.

The village

Monestiés is a pretty village with medieval houses, an old market place shaded by trees and popular with petanque players, the church of St-Pierre and a particularly attractive old bridge. The Centre Bajén-Vega (*open July–Aug 10–1 & 2–7; mid–March–June, Sept–Oct, 10–12 & 2–6; Nov–mid–March 2–5; T: 05 63 76 19 17*), in a restored mansion on Place de la Mairie exhibits the work of two Spanish painters who took up residence in the Albigeois, Francisco Bajén and Martine Véga.

THE SÉGALA & THE VIAUR VALLEY

The Ségala is a generic term which here applies to the area directly due north of Albi. In general it describes regions where the soil was poor and only rye, or *sèigle*, and chestnuts would grow until lime dressing was brought to the region by the newly built railway in the 19th century. The Viaur Valley is a little known area with some dramatic vistas and an easy walk to a hidden chapel. The visits in this wild countryside have a rural charm and include the Mining and Glass Museums, the bastide of Sauveterre-de-Rouergue, and the former home of Toulouse-Lautrec, the Château du Bosc. There are also magnificent examples of barns with ramps for horse and cart still intact, and ancient churches at Boussac, La Savetat Peyralès and Quins.

Five km north of Albi is the mainly 19th-century brick church of **Notre-Dame-de-la-Drèche**. On the site of a 13th-century church, it comprises an octagonal rotunda (19.5m high and equally wide) over a nave with six chapels begun in 1861; the old east end is encased in a brick carapace. An ancient place of pilgrimage, the sanctuary shelters the 12th-century statue of the *Madonna de la Drèche* and the interior has a series of 81 murals completed in 1894 on the theme of Our Lady. In the spandrels she is represented by 16 women of the Old Testament; higher, flanking the windows, are 14 scenes of the *Life of the Virgin Mary*; and on the vault of the nave against a background of blue with gold stars is *Mary Glorified by the Saints*. The four paintings of the choir record events associated with the statue of the Madonna, including the homage paid to it by St Dominic, founder of the Dominicans (*see p. 593*).

Around Carmaux two major industries, now defunct, are reflected in museums. Relics of open cast-mines have been conserved at **Cagnac-les-Mines** at the Musée de la Mine (*open June–Sept 10–12.30 & 1.30–7; Oct–May Tues–Fri 10–12 & 2–5, Sat, Sun 10–12 & 2–6; closed Mon; T: 05 63 53 91 70*). Mining began in Carmaux in the mid-19th century and provided wealth to some, but in 1892 there was a general miners' strike for nearly three months and the mines gradually closed during the 20th century. At **Blaye les Mines**, the Musée du Verre at (*open June–Sept Mon–Fri 10–12 & 2–6.30, Sat, Sun 3-8; Oct–May Mon–Fri 10–12 & 2–6, Sun 3-6; T: 05 63 36 30 83*), is dedicated to the glass industry, once widespread in the area. The social conflicts and the role of Jean Jaurès, Deputy for Carmaux (*see p. 308*), are explored here, and there are glassmaking demonstrations in the summer.

In the woods above the Viaur Gorges, just south of Tanus off the D53 is a track to the magical site of **Las Planques**, where the only relic of a once active village is the stark and dramatic 11th-century church built in dark gneiss (*key at Syndicat d'Initiative or Mairie, Tanus; T: 05 63 76 31 11*). Further downstream, Pampelonne is a pleasant place founded in 1290 by a famous founder of *bastides*, Eustache de Beaumarchais. Heading north from Tanus a new road spans the Viaur ravine, the boundary between the *départements* of Tarn and Aveyron, on a dramatic new road bridge (2000) on stilts high above the valley. It dwarfs the elegant Viaduc de Viaur (1895–1902), a railway bridge on the Carmaux–Rodez line slightly further upstream. To view it, there is a parking area on the right of the old road going north as it rises out of the valley. The old viaduct was no mean feat at the time, poised 116m above the river with a span of 460m, and is still one of the most impressive constructions of its kind in France. It was built by a local engineer, Paul Bodin, who won the competition held in 1887.

Château du Bosc

Guided visits Feb–Nov 9–7; Dec 9–5; T: 05 65 69 20 83, www.toulouselautreclebosc.com.
At Camjac, the Château du Bosc is one of the properties still belonging to descendants of the family of Toulouse-Lautrec and where the painter spent much of his childhood. Quite apart from this connection, it is salutary to spend an hour or so in a property that has not been sold since the 12th century and in a setting that epitomises *la France profonde*. The visit takes you through the library, dining room, private chapel and drawing room which are richly furnished. The bedroom of Adèle, Countess Toulouse-Lautrec, the painter's mother, contains memorabilia such as English books, crayons and Punch and Judy that belonged to little Henri. There are also works by other members of the family and fascinating photos of the painter at the Château. A visit to the Bosc offers an important insight to Toulouse-Lautrec's background and the family's attitude to him, and complements a visit to the museum in Albi (*see p. 257*).

Not far across country from the Bosc, at Centres, is the 13th–14th-century **Château de Taurines** (*open July-Aug 3–7; Sept Sat, Sun 3–7; T: 05 65 74 28 47, www.chateau-de-taurines.fr.st*) where the restoration has been carried out with enthusiasm by local people and exhibitions of contemporary art and also concerts are now staged.

Sauveterre-de-Rouergue

A pristine example of a *bastide*, Sauveterre-de-Rouergue, was founded in 1281 by Guillaume de Mâcon, Seneschal of Rouergue in the name of Philippe (III) le Hardi, as a means of controlling the region. Its name, however, gives a clue to the fact that even before 1281 it was a safe haven (*sauvété*) under the protection of the Church via the Abbey of Bonnecombe. With a rectangular plan, the large central square, with an iron cross (1782), is overlooked by a variety of well-restored 15th- and 16th-century houses, shoulder to shoulder and extended in the 15th century to form continuous *couverts* or *chitats* around the square. From 1320 the *bastide* was enclosed within protective walls (initially wooden). Sections of the wall and two original fortified gateways, Portes St Christophe and St-Vital, still exist as does part of the moat. When the Rouergue came under English domination (1362-69), Sauveterre was one of their most resistant strongholds. Always somewhat isolated and in a poor agricultural region, the town developed trades such as knife making at the end of the 14th century (and which has been revived today). The nave of the church (1313; restored) was demolished and rebuilt to the west of the belfry to make way for the 14th-century town walls. Across the square is the 16th-century *Mairie*, built during the final period of prosperity for the town. A stone-flagged corridor leads to a small courtyard showing Italianate influences. Sauveterre is home to a small but thriving community of artisans, including a milliner.

WEST & SOUTH OF CORDES-SUR-CIEL

The **Forêt de la Grésigne**, on a knoll (300–500m) between the high plateaus of the Quercy and the Albigeois, was an ancient possession of the Counts of Toulouse which passed to the royal domain in 1271. Its oaks were used for shipbuilding in the 17th century and until the mid-19th century this was an important glass-producing area. Sections of the old walls still survive that once enclosed the forest which now covers some 3,500 hectares.

There is a route around the perimeter of the Forêt de Grésigne passing Vaour and Puycelsi and close to other picturesque villages. At a high point between the D91 and D15 near **Vaour** is a dolmen and far reaching views across the Quercy; closer to Vaour (D33), are the ruins of a Templar Commandery (*see p. 288*).

On a small hill, **Puycelsi** is an impressive sight as you drive up to the plateau. Close to where the cars are parked at the top, is a terrace which was the site of the old château, and on it is the tiny Baroque chapel of St-Roch (now used by the Tourist Office). Built in 1703, it contains a vine-entwined gilded retable. The village is still enclosed within the boundaries of its 15th-century walls. Beyond the chapel is a fortified gate, Porte d'Irrissou, the 15th-century Château du Petit St-Roch, and various other fortifications, including a 17th-century tower and the prison tower. In Place de la Mairie are the old *maison commune* and good 15th- and 16th-century façades. The church of St-Corneille, part 14th-, part 15th-century with an 18th-century belfry, is a simple structure with one or two amusing carvings around the porch.

Between Bruniquel (*see p. 243*) and Gaillac (*see p. 272*), **Larroque** is a mainly 17th-century village built into the cliffs below the Grésigne forest which has been much restored in recent years.

Castelnau-de-Montmiral is, like Cordes, a veritable *bastide*, but in miniature, also on a hill and founded in 1222. At its heart is a tiny arcaded square. A plaque on the south side commemorates a visit here by Jean-Paul Sartre and Simone de Beauvoir; on the northwest stands a post which was the village pillory. In the church, protected behind bars in a chapel in the northeast (timed light switch on right), is a remarkable 13th-century wooden reliquary cross, 96cm tall, covered in silver and gilt, decorated with filigree and studded with semi-precious stones, containing a relic of the True Cross.

The **Château du Cayla** at Andillac near Vieux (*open May–Sept 10–12 & 2–6, closed Tues; Oct–April 2–6, closed Mon, Tues; T: 05 63 33 90 30*), a 14th- and 18th-century house, was the idyllic birthplace of the Romantic writers Eugénie de Guérin (1805–48) and her poet brother Maurice (1810–39), preserved as a peaceful shrine.

At Senouillac, near Cahuzac-sur-Vère, is the **Château de Mauriac** (*open May–Oct daily 3–6; Nov–April Sun only 3–6; T: 05 63 41 71 18, www.bistes.com*), an uncompromising medieval fortress from the exterior, with an the interior domesticated during the Renaissance. It belongs to the painter Bernard Bistes (b. 1941). Many years of dedicated renovation, including several murals and ceiling paintings by the painter and his wife, have turned it into a beautiful setting for Bistes' works.

ALONG THE TARN WEST OF ALBI

There are several towns of rustic pink brick on the banks of the Tarn southwest of Albi in a landscape that has been patchworked with vineyards for about a thousand years.

GAILLAC

The town which gives its name to the vineyards has some interesting brick buildings in the old town on the south side and an attractive riverscape. The economy of this small town has revolved around the wine trade despite the crises of the 19th century, and is at its liveliest at the beginning of August during La Fête des Vins de Gaillac.

THE WINES OF GAILLAC

Gaillac is promoted, like most wine-producing areas, as one of the oldest in France; the cultivation of vines on the banks of the Tarn is thought to go back to the 6th century BC. The Benedictine monks of the abbey of St-Michel, who settled here in 972, were the prime movers in the development and perfection of viticulture and vinification and as early as 1271 a charter was granted guaranteeing the quality of Gaillac wine. The wine was carried via the Tarn and the Garonne to Bordeaux, and shipped to northern Europe. In the 1920s there was a strong revival after the phylloxera epidemics of the 1870s, and by 1938 the Gaillac whites received an AOC, followed in 1970 by the reds. There are 400 producers and three cooperatives over an area of more than 2,000 hectares between Cordes, Rabastens, Graulhet and Castelnau-de-Levis on the banks of the parallel valleys of the Tarn and the Vère, where the microclimate and soils are suited to vines. The local grape varieties are Mauzac and Len de l'El plus Sauvignon and Muscadelle for whites; the basis of the red appellation is Duras and Braucol complemented by Syrah, Gamay, Merlot and Cabernet. The cooperatives are at Labastide-de-Levis, Rabastens and Técou, the latter producing an excellent and typical red provocatively named Passion. The characteristic of the Gaillac reds is a flavour of blackcurrants or raspberries and the whites are slightly appley. Most of the 400 producers and the cooperatives are happy to give a tasting.

Exploring Gaillac

From the shady Place de la Libération, Rue Portal leads past the old church of St-Pierre with a 13th-century doorway. The Hôtel de Brens, just off Rue Portal on the right, is a pretty 13th–15th-century building in timber and brick with two overhanging turrets and a pentagonal gallery. At the end of Rue Portal is Place Thiers with arcades and *Le Griffoul* fountain in the middle. This is the heart of the old town. On the southeast side is Place St-Michel, the forecourt of the sheer brick face of the old **Abbey Church of St-Michel**. The gabled west end is flanked by a tower (13th and 14th century) and the portal was added in 1847. The single vessel of the nave, typical of the Midi, is huge (47.5m by 17m) and was painted in *trompe l'oeil* in the 19th century. The oldest part of the church is the 13th-century east end, profoundly modified in 1869 when pillars and arcades were substituted for a semi-circular wall around the choir. Between the interior buttresses are chapels, except on the third and fourth bays south where the abbey abuts the church. The chapel in the second bay on the north, with decorated capitals, was built in the late 14th century, possibly as a funerary chapel, by Abbot Roger de Latour whose coat of arms is on the boss. There are some fittings and furnishings of note, including a polychromed wooden statue of the Virgin and Child (early 14th century); a holy water stoup (13th century?) on the left of the entrance, decorated with birds and flowers; a Baroque retable with a painting by Antoine Rivalz; and on the wall of the southeast chapel a high-relief panel the *Resurrected Christ appearing to Mary Magdalene* (15th century). The main altar is of 1785–90 and the elaborate pulpit was made in 1883–85. The organ above the west door was made by Dominique Cavaillé-Col, from the dynasty of organ-builders who originated from Gaillac.

Beside the bridge is the attractive brick **Maison du Vin** (*open July–Aug 10–12.45 & 2–6.45; Sept–June 10–12 & 2–6; closed holidays; T: 05 63 57 15 40*), with a wealth of information on the local wines; also tastings and wine-tasting courses. The Tourist Office is in the same building, as is the **Musée de l'Abbaye, de la Vigne et du Vin** (*open 10-12 & 2-6; T: 05 63 41 03 81, www.ville-gaillac-fr*), with an exhibition of archaeology, navigation, wine and local history.

East of the church are the park and Château de Foucaud, built in 1647 on the edge of the Tarn. The building shows its most elegant face to the river, with double flights of steps leading to a formal garden and terraces to the river bank. In the château is the **Musée des Beaux Arts** (*open May–Oct 10–12 & 2–6, closed Tues; Nov–April Fri–Sun 10–12 & 2–6; T: 05 63 57 18 25*), which contains works mainly by regional artists of the 19th and 20th centuries.

MONTANS & LISLE-SUR-TARN

Southwest of Gaillac is Montans, today a tiny community of about 200 inhabitants, but once the site of a huge Gallo-Roman pottery works. Archéosite (*open April–Oct 10–12 & 2–6; Sat, Sun and holidays 2–6; T: 05 63 57 59 16, www.archeosite.com*) is a fascinating museum of local finds with a 'Gallo-Roman street' and exhibitions. The display of the techniques, tools and periods of production from 100 bc to the early 4th century is very comprehensive. The most creative period was 20–75 AD, after which production became more utilitarian. Much of the work is signed. At the height of production there could have been as many as 40 or 50 kilns at one time and only a part of the huge area used by the potteries has been excavated. An important find of 40 gold pieces was also made here.

Lisle-sur-Tarn

On the north bank of the river among vineyards, Lisle-sur-Tarn is a warm and sleepy brick *bastide* founded in the 13th century. It boasts the largest square in the Southwest, surrounded by *cornières* and *couverts* and a variety of façades, some half-timbered, some rebuilt from the 17th–19th centuries entirely in brick. A fairly recent innovation is the Musée Art du Chocolat (*open 10–12.30 & 2–7, closed Mon; T: 05 63 33 69 79*) at 143 Place Saissac. Former master *chocolatier* from Albi, Miche Thomaso-Defos, has opened a museum of chocolate sculptures, alongside other works of art, with a video on the history of *cacao*, and courses in how to work with chocolate. The Musée Raymond Lafage (*open April to mid–Oct 10–12 & 2–6, closed Tues; T: 05 63 40 45 45*), exhibits drawings and engravings by the local 17th-century artist who spent time in Rome, examples of glass made in the Grésigne (*see p. 271*) and archaeology.

RABASTENS

Towards the middle of the 12th century, Moissac founded a priory here where the old Roman road crossed the river and it became an important stage for medieval pilgrims between Rodez and Toulouse.

Notre-Dame-du-Bourg

The priory church of Notre-Dame-du-Bourg (*T: 05 63 33 56 90*) was rebuilt at the end of the Albigensian period. Eight capitals (1190–1200) with their slender marble columns were re-used in the recessed west porch. The capitals have scenes from the *Childhood of Christ* and the *Temptation in the Wilderness*. The church was conceived in the Gothic style of the southwest, with a cliff-like, angular west end pierced by a small rose window and two turrets flanking a rectangular gable belfry, the upper part completed in the 19th century. The dim interior is heavily ornate, reminiscent of Albi, with an unaisled nave. The 13th-century church was built with a flat east end, but in the 14th century this was opened and extended to make a large choir and polygonal chevet with chapels between the buttresses. An unusual Romanesque-style arcaded triforium was built above. The remodelled east end was consecrated in 1318. The vaults, walls and most of the chapels have painted decoration from different periods which disappeared under plaster after the Reformation. With few exceptions they were rediscovered c. 1859 and almost entirely repainted 1860–63 by Joseph Engalières.

The murals on the vaults of the nave are thought to originate from the second half of the 13th century, and include *St James* on the first crossing arch and *St Christopher* on the second, and also knights, possibly participating in a pilgrimage or in a crusade. On the walls of the nave are two cycles: on the south scenes from the *Childhood of Christ*, but in the fourth bay the original mural was replaced by the *Expulsion of Adam and Eve* in the 15th century; on the north are the *Resurrection*, *Crucifixion* and *Ascension*. Five chapels were built between the nave buttresses between 1374 and the end of the 15th century. The chapel of St-Roch on the north was painted in 1520–30, re-discovered in 1972 and subsequently restored.

PRACTICAL INFORMATION

GETTING AROUND

• **By train:** From Toulouse and Rodez to Albi. From Brive and Toulouse to Vindrac-Cordes (one night train direct to/from Paris stops at Vindrac-Cordes). Cordes station is about 6km from village and taxis are scarce. Between Rodez and Toulouse via Marssac, Gaillac, Lisle-sur-Tarn, Rabastens-Couffouleux. Between Clermont-Ferrand and Toulouse via Gaillac. Also via Naucelle-Gare, Tanus, Carmaux.
• **By bus:** Buses between Montauban and Albi via Gaillac and Marssac-Tarn. Gare routière (bus station), Pl. Jean Jaurès, Albi T: 05 63 54 58 61.

TOURIST INFORMATION

Albi Pl. Ste-Cécile, T: 05 63 49 48 80, accueil@albitourisme.com www.tourisme-tarn.com
Blaye-les-Mines Cap'Découverte, BP 20, T: 0825 08 1234, www.capdecouverte.com
Cordes-sur-Ciel Maison Fontpeyrouse, Grande Rue (at the top of the hill), T: 05 63 56 00 52, www.cordes-sur-ciel.org
Monestiés Pl. de la Mairie, T: 05 63 76 19 17, www.monesties.com
Castelnau-de-Montmiral Pl. des Arcades, T: 05 63 33 15 11, tourisme.bastide. castelnaugresigne@wanadoo.fr
Gaillac Pl. St-Michel, T: 05 63 57 14 65, www.ville-gaillac.fr
Lisle-sur-Tarn Pl. Paul Saissac, T: 05 63 40 31 85, www.ville-lisle-sur-tarn.fr.
Naucelle Pl. St-Martin, T: 05 65 67 82 96, www.naucellois.com

Puycelsi-Grésigne Chapelle St-Roch, T: 05 63 33 19 25, perso.wanadoo.fr/ot-puycelsigresigne
Rabastens (Pays de) 12 Rue du Pont de Pâ, T: 05 63 33 56 90, ot-rabastens@wanadoo.fr
Sauveterre-de-Rouergue Pl. des Arcades, T: 05 65 72 02 52, sauveterre.office@free.fr
Tanus Mairie, Av. P. Bodin, T: 05 63 76 36 71, tourisme.tanus@wanadoo.fr
Vaour (Pays de) Le Bourg, Penne-du-Tarn, T: 05 63 56 36 68, ot@vaour.net

ACCOMMODATION & RESTAURANTS

Albi

€€ **Hostellerie St-Antoine.** One of the oldest auberges in France, the advantage to the St-Antoine is its proximity to the town centre. The rooms are uniformly comfortable and attractive in a slightly old-fashioned way, and vary in size, and some overlook the garden. 17 Rue St-Antoine, T: 05 63 54 04 04, www.saint-antoine-albi.com
€€ **Hôtel La Réserve.** This is a gorgeous setting, in extensive grounds on the banks of the Tarn on the outskirts of Albi. The restaurant extends onto a delightful terrace with a view of the river. The 23 rooms are of a very high standard, some with balconies. Dining here is also a pleasure, with specialities based on good local produce (truffles, wild mushrooms, free-range duck). Route de Cordes, T: 05 63 60 80 80, www.relaischateaux.fr/reservealbi
€ **Hôtel St-Clair.** A modest, well-kept hotel around a tiny flower-filled courtyard right in the middle of the old

town. The rooms have been refurbished and those in the new annexe opposite are fresh and light with views of the old town. 8 Rue St-Clair, T: 05 63 54 25 66, http://andrieu.michele.free.fr.

€ L'Epicurien. ■ A modern brasserie in subdued colours and clean lines, and despite the open kitchen, not too noisy. The cooking is both adventurous and thoughtful combining oriental and traditional French, such as the cheese course, and some inventive desserts. A reasonably priced midday menu. 42 Pl Jean Jaures, T: 05 63 53 10 70.

€ L'Esprit du Vin. Below the Berbie, this intimate restaurant has recently changed hands and the new chef David Enjalran from Carmaux is coming up with some sophisticated ideas and a judicious use of spices and sauces. Typical dishes are *pigeon du Mont Royal désossé farci aux trompettes de la mort et pistaches* (boned and served in a glass jar), and *fish and chips de lotte accompagné d'une émulsion d'avocat au wasabi*, served in a paper cone. 11 Quai Choiseul, T: 05 65 54 60 44.

€ La Table du Sommelier. Across the river from the Berbie is Daniel Pestre's popular *bistro à vin*/restaurant (also in Gaillac and Castres) concentrating on local wine and dishes with a light touch. The €25 *Menu autour des Vins* has a choice of appropriate dishes to accompany 3 different wines; similarly the *Menu Vin Passion* at €30. The game is to identify the wines. A glass of Gaillac and lunch is good value and draws in the local business fraternity. Not large, so essential to book. 20 Rue Porta, T: 05 63 46 20 10

Castelnau de Levis
€ Chambres d'hôtes Au Bouquet de Roose. A restful spot close to Albi and the Gaillac vineyards, the village overlooks the Tarn. The large mansion has a flower-packed garden, the three rooms are restfully and simply decorated with plenty of space, and *table d'hotes*. Michèle and Serge Roose, T: 05 63 45 59 75, michele.roose@wanadoo.fr

Castelnau-de-Montmiral
€ Hôtel Les Consuls. At the heart of this wonderful medieval *bastide* on a hill is a small, straightforward hotel with 9 rooms, some with original features, some modern. It occupies a renovated 17th-century building with arcades on the little central square. Meals are served under the arcades in summer. Le Bourg, T: 05 63 33 17 44, hoteldesconsuls@aol.com

€ Chambres d'hôtes Château de Mayragues. ■ The château and vineyards are owned by a French-Scots couple who have won prizes for their wines and have restored the beautiful Renaissance château and *pigeonnier*. The *chambres d'hotes* have an exceptional position at the top of the house, surrounded by the *chemin de ronde* looking out over the most beautiful countryside and very attractively kitted out. There is also an independent *gîte*. Laurence and Alan Geddes, T: 05 63 33 94 08, www.chateau-de-mayragues.com

Cahuzac-sur-Vère
€€ Château de Salettes. ■ The chateau-hotel, in pale gold stone with red tile roofs, stands on a rocky outcrop in the middle of the Gaillac vineyards. The elegant conversion dates from 1994 and successfully combines medieval and modern. The 13 rooms and 5 suites are uncluttered with contemporary furnishings and colour schemes. Each is shaped by the old walls and every win-

dow frames a perfect view. The cooking is very refined, beautifully presented, and based on excellent local produce. There are two dining rooms and a courtyard; menus €29–65. A the foot of the rock the swimming pool, submerged in the vines, benefits from spectacular views. T: 05 63 33 60 60, www.chateaudesalettes.com

Cordes

€€ **Le Grand Ecuyer**. This well-known hotel and restaurant (one Michelin star) in a beautiful medieval house at the top of the village is the most upmarket of the Thuriès' empire in Cordes. Reassuringly old-fashioned, the comfortable public rooms and restaurant maintain the medieval theme, genuine and mock. The cooking is sumptuous. Also modern-medieval are the 12 luxury bedrooms featuring four-poster beds, exposed beams and parquet floors with huge windows and glorious views. 79 Grand Rue Raymond VII, T: 05 63 53 79 50, www.thuries.fr

€ **Hostellerie du Vieux-Cordes**. On the south side of old Cordes, the Hostellerie, also owned by Yves Thuries, has much charm, with a wisteria-covered courtyard, spiral staircase and pleasant bedrooms looking out on the Cérou valley. The restaurant specialises in main dishes based exclusively on duck or salmon. The décor, however, is old-fashioned. 21 Rue St-Michel, T: 05 63 53 79 20, www.thuries.fr

€ **La Cité**. This is a small hotel with just 8 rooms, with views to the south. No restaurant. 19 Rue de la République, T: 05 63 56 03 53, www.thuries.fr.

€ **Hostellerie du Parc**. At the foot of the old town, the cooking here is reliable. A rustic setting, with a terrace/garden. Les Cabannes (D600 west of Cordes), T: 05 63 56 02 59, www.hostellerie-du-parc.com

Gaillac

€ **La Verrerie**. A Logis de France in a town not well-endowed with hotels, this was a glassworks in a typical local building in brick and river-pebble. It is set in a green oasis with pool in a leafy setting among old bamboos. The 14 well appointed bedrooms are bright and light, and the restaurant has a choice of three 'tasting' menus of local specialities accompanied, naturally, by a good bottle of Gaillac. 1 Rue de l'Égalité, T: 05 63 57 32 77, www.la-verrerie.com

€€ *La Table du Sommelier*, Pl. Thiers, T: 05 63 41 20 10 (*see* La Table du Sommelier, Albi).

Monestiés

€ **Chambres d'hôtes Le Manoir de Raynaudes**. ■ Spacious and gracious, here is the best of English hospitality in a French setting. Surrounded by peaceful meadows and views of the Ségala, the buildings form a large courtyard. Outside is a peaceful garden, where Orlando nurtures home-grown vegetables and fruit which go into the gourmet meals he creates from scratch. Also has a pool. Among the happenings are informal cookery demonstrations on Tuesdays and regular musical evenings. The two carefully considered bedrooms are composed around cream tones: calm but not minimalist. There are also four split-level apartments. Orlando Murrin and Peter Steggall, T: 05 63 36 91 90, www.raynaudes.com

Puycelsi

€ **L'Ancienne Auberge**. A smart hotel-restaurant in a medieval house in this most beautiful hilltop town surrounded by forest. The German-Australian owners extend a very warm welcome. There are just eight attractive bedrooms. Pl. de l'Eglise, T: 05 63 33 65 90, www.ancienne-auberge.com

Vaour

Chambres et table d'hôtes Serene. Rustic outbuildings which are part of a working farm going back to Templar times have been converted, cleverly integrating old stone found on the farm. There are four bedrooms (including a family suite) and attractive dining room/lounge with fireplace Between the *bastides* and the forest, it is situated in beautiful rural surroundings and there are also a pool, activities, and farm animals. Brigitte and Francis Bessières, T: 05 63 56 39 34, francis.bessieres@freesbee.fr

Sauveterre-de-Rouergue

€€ **Auberge le Sénéchal**. ■ Small and fairly modern, on the edge of the peaceful village, the hotel/restaurant is run by Michel and Chantal Truchon who give a very personal service. Truchon's cooking is quietly excellent, and fully deserves its Michelin star. Truchon combines the best of local product in dishes such as *Le pigeon 'Bastidols' en moutarde de fruits, purée d'amandes fraiches au citron et thé du jardin*. Menus run from 25-110 €. There are 11 spacious rooms with some slightly quirky fittings; also an indoor pool. T: 05 65 71 29 00, fax 05 65 71 29 09, www.senechal.net

MARKET DAYS

Albi Covered market daily except Monday; general market Saturday; July, August evening market; flea market Saturday, Place du Castelviel
Cahuzac-sur-Vère Wednesday
Carmaux Friday (or Thur if a holiday)
Castelnau-de-Montmiral Tuesday
Cordes-sur-Ciel Saturday
Gaillac Thursday, Friday and Sunday; July, August evening market
Lisle-sur-Tarn Sunday
Monestiés Sunday June–Sept
Puylaurens Wednesday
Rabastens Saturday
St-Paul Cap de Joux Tuesday
Vaour Thursday

FESTIVALS & EVENTS

April: *Fête des Responchons*, celebration of a local delicacy described as wild asparagus, Cordes-sur-Ciel
May: *Fête des Croquants*, celebration of almond biscuits, Cordes-sur-Ciel
June and July: *Musique sur Ciel*, music festival, Cordes-sur-Ciel
Festival Pause Guitare, French and international guitar music, Monestiés
July: *Festifolie de Cabanès* cultural and sporting event Cabanès, near Naucelle
August: *Un été à Albi*, classical music performed at various prestigious sites
Fête du Vin, Gaillac. L'été de Vaour, international comedy festival, Vaour
Fête de la Saint-Privat, Carmaux's most important festival when 'Miss St-Privat' is crowned
September: *Fête de la Pâtisserie*, traditional pastries by the river, made by local pâtissiers, Albi

THE GRANDS CAUSSES

With the town of Millau on the Tarn at its centre, the Parc Naturel Régional des Grands Causses is a series of spectacular limestone plateaux on the edge of the Cévennes. This southern part of the Département de l'Aveyron acts as the pivot between the rigours of the Massif Central and the gentler Mediterranean and much of it is protected, embracing the agricultural Causse of Sévérac to the north, the strange rocky outcrops of the Causse Noir in the east, and the Causse de Larzac in the south east. West is the Lévézou with its lakes, and an area of red sandstone known as the Rougier lies to the southwest. The rivers Tarn, Jonte and Dourbie create beautiful gorges, and there are deep caves and caverns to explore. Fine leather and Roquefort cheese are products of the region. The sturdy villages and medieval Templar commanderies now vie for attention with the most spectacular construction of the 21st century in France, the great Millau Viaduct (*see p. 283*), to the west of the town.

MILLAU

Millau, at the south-eastern extremity of Midi-Pyrénées, the vibrant and active *sous-préfecture* of the Aveyron, stands on the right bank of the Tarn close to where it is swelled by the Dourbie. Millau is well positioned for exploring this wonderful rugged countryside. It is also a good starting point for a visit to the Gorges du Tarn.

Roofscape of Millau beneath the limestone plateaux of the *causses*.

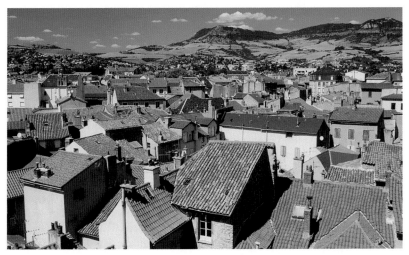

HISTORY OF MILLAU

Ancient civilisations (c. 2500–1500 BC) inhabited the caves in the region and erected dolmens and menhirs, but it was not until around the 2nd century BC that people came down from the hills. The Celtic tribe, the Rutenes, called their settlement *Condatomagos*, 'market-town on the confluence'. The Romans established an important pottery manufactory here from 10 BC to AD 150, and throughout the Middle Ages it was a major commercial centre, trading leather, cloth and copper with goods from the Languedocian seaports. By the 8th century the town was known as *Amiliavum*, and Millau achieved autonomous rule in the 12th century by an oligarchy of consuls, but lost its independence in 1361 when it came under English domination. It prospered again during the period of peace following the Hundred Years War and then, unlike most of the Rouergue, embraced the Reformation in the 16th century. The leather trade, and especially glove-making using the pelts of lambs sacrificed to assure sufficient milk for cheese production, was already well established and expanded with the town through the 18th and 19th centuries and flourished until the 1930s—everyone wore gloves in Millau. The two traditional industries, pottery and glove-making, are also represented at the museum. There are still *gantiers* at work in Millau, among them Maison Fabre, 18–20 Boulevard Gambetta (*www.maisonfabre.com*). Most of the medieval buildings were destroyed at the Reformation but the town has retained its medieval layout. The construction of the massive viaduct across the Tarn has brought Millau into the 21st century with some panache, dwarfing all around save its setting, the *causses*.

EXPLORING MILLAU

Rue Droite

At the centre of Millau is Place du Mandarous, a half-circle where four large boulevards meet. The old town is to the south, enclosed by wide boulevards forming an oval, which replaced the city walls. From Place du Mandarous, the narrow Rue du Mandarous leads south onto Rue Droite, the former main street, a pleasant, pedestrianised street of small shops. A left turn arrives beneath the ancient landmark of Millau, **le Beffroi** (12th–17th centuries) on the corner of Rue Droite and Rue du Beffroi, towering 42m over the old town (*open July-Aug 10–12 & 2.30–6, mid to end-June, Sept 2.30–6; T: 05 65 59 01 08*). The lower square section is all that remains of the original tower which was part of the city defences and represented seigneurial power. It was bought by the town in 1613 and subsequently became a symbol of municipal authority; the upper octagonal section was built to contain a bell and the town clock. Opposite, the Tourist Office on Place des Consuls occupies one of the best buildings in the old town, close to no. 21 Rue Droite, home to the **Atelier du Gantier** (*open 9–12 & 2–7, closed Sun and holidays; T: 05 65 60 81 50*) demonstrating the traditional work of the glover. Beyond Place des Consuls, the large Place Emma Calvé is named after an Aveyronnaise opera singer (1858–1942), heralded locally as *notre Carmen*, a role she sang 1389 times. The church of St-Martin, on the south side of the square, is a small simple church containing a large Baroque painting of the *Descent from the Cross* attributed to the 17th-century Flemish painter Gaspar de Crayer.

Further along Rue Droite, on the left, Place du Marché has a large covered market, a huge metal-and-brick construction with cellars, which was erected in 1899 and renovated in 1984–85, when Boulevard Sadi-Carnot and Rue Coussergues were created. At the end of Rue Droite is Place du Maréchal Foch

Place du Maréchal-Foch

The prettiest and oldest square in Millau is Place du Maréchal-Foch, originally the only public space in the old town. On Fridays the covered market overflows into the square and adjacent streets. Along one side are arcades with a colonnade of cylindrical piers which, according to popular tradition, come from cloisters destroyed during the Religious Wars. However, the capital above the stone table in the northwest, possibly part of the old pillory, has an inscription in Occitan: *gara que faras enant que comences*, the salutary message that you should give a thought to what you are about to do before you begin. The oldest houses on the north are 15th–16th-century; in the centre is a cooling fountain (1835) with silhouetted sphinxes; and the old grain market of 1836 is now occupied by a school.

North of the square is the church of **Notre-Dame-de-l'Espinasse**, mainly post-Reformation. From the time it reopened in 1646 until 1828 it was the only parish church in Millau. Little remains of the church consecrated in 1095 except perhaps the lower walls of the heavily buttressed east end and the base of the belfry (also 17th century), which is Toulousain in style. The west façade is pure Baroque. The interior space is straightforward, without aisles but with the addition of a gallery on three sides, and a seven-sided apse with murals by Jean Bernard (1940); the glass, blues to the north and pinks to the south, was made by Claude Baillon (1984). Place Grégoire, which has interesting 17th-century façades, doorways and a corbelled angle tower, links Place du Maréchal-Foch with Rue Droite.

The **Musée de Millau** (*open July–Aug 10–6; May–June, Sept 10–12 & 2–6; Oct–April 10–12 & 2–6, closed Sun and holidays; T: 05 65 59 01 08*), on Place Foch, is housed in the 18th-century Hôtel de Pégayrolles. Sober and genteel, the building is arranged around a U-shaped courtyard and has a fine staircase inside. The museum is divided between archaeology on the left and gloves to the right. The archaeological section has an area devoted to local palaeontology with the fossilised footprint of a dinosaur. The Bronze Age is also represented. The Gallo-Roman period (1st–4th centuries) is explored through objects from the site of Graufesenque (*see p. 282*) and includes lamps, *fibulae* (brooches), money, figurines in white and in terracotta pottery, bronze statuettes, mosaics, glass, and a multitude of pots. The potters of Graufesenque were expert in sigillated pottery (red with an embossed decoration) and the techniques, stages and periods of production from 10 BC to 250 AD are explained. Ceramics from Graufesenque were a major industry and exported as far as Scotland, North Africa, even India. There is one room devoted to 10th–18th-century Millau and another to a week in the life of an everyday Rutene. Up the stairs on the right of the entrance is a pretty octagonal room with a coffered vault and Millau-made gloves of all kinds and for all purposes, including a pair from Buffalo Bill's last show in Paris. Glove-making is fully explored here, from the tanning of skins (*mégisserie*) to glove design, backed up by films. There is also an exhibition of dolls, inevitably featuring mini-gloves.

Quartier du Voultre

Outside the museum, a covered passageway leads via Rue Guilhem-Estève and Rue Haute to the Quartier du Voultre. The Dominican convent was destroyed by the Calvinists who took over the 16th-century church, and eventually a new Protestant Temple was built in 1869. The Porte du Voultre was probably part of the old fortifications and gave its name to the leather-workers' quarter. Rue du Voultre continues southwest, coming out onto Boulevard de l'Ayrolle, built on the old city ditches. To the left is the Tarn with Rue de la Tannerie running parallel, leading to Pont Lerouge (1821). Next to the bridge are two arches of the 12th-century bridge and a 15th-century mill. Turning right at the end of Rue du Voultre reveals on the left a small elegant colonnaded building, a very grand *lavoir* or public laundry. Built in 1749 as part of a larger urbanisation scheme, it takes the form of a Neoclassical semi-circular pavilion with arcades.

ENVIRONS OF MILLAU

Site Archéologique de Graufesenque

Open May–Sept 9–12 & 2–6.30; Oct–April 9.30–12 & 2–6; T: 05 65 60 11 37.

The archaeological site of the Gallo-Roman potteries is east of the town on the plain where the Tarn and the Dourbie converge, reached via the Pont du Larzac to the south. The pottery covered some 10 hectares of which 4,000 square metres have been excavated. Excavations from 1973–81 uncovered traces of three successive periods of habitation: in the Celtic and early Gallo-Roman period (2nd–1st centuries BC) there was intense commercial activity with the Mediterranean; from the 1st century AD to the first half of the 2nd century, the workshops of the Gallo-Roman potters attest to a massive production of pots for export; later, 150–300 AD, there was a marked deterioration in the quality of the dwellings. The variety of buildings demonstrates the organisation of the community, and includes the modest homes of the potters and others, as well as two sanctuaries. The remains of roads, gutters, drains, baths and hypocausts can also be seen, although most interesting are the buildings related to the enormous production of pottery—workshops, wells, clay-storage areas, and kilns. Three kilns have been uncovered: the largest (6.8m by 11.3m) could have held between 10,000 and 40,000 vessels at one firing. At the height of production, some 500 potters worked at Graufesenque.

The Millau Viaduct (2004) seen from the east.

Millau Viaduct

Guided visits by appointment all year Sat, Sun and holidays; T: 05 65 60 02 42, www.ot-millau.fr; www.viaducdemillaueiffage.com. Information and viewing centre at Aire des Cazoulous (D992) open daily; film in English every 15 minutes.

Almost 2.5 km long and in places 343m tall, the Millau Viaduct is the highest bridge in the world and arguably one of the most beautiful. The English architect, Sir Norman Foster, beat 30 competitors for the €310-million project to produce a virtuoso triumph of engineering. As part of the Parc Naturel Régional the construction demanded a sensitive approach to the environment and its preservation, providing the solution to spanning the deep Tarn gorge in order to carry the A75 uninterrupted from Clermont-Ferrand to Montpellier, Perpignan and Spain. It was opened in December 2004, by President Chirac after 1,096 days under construction. The seven great pylons, the highest of them 19m higher than the Eiffel Tower, which rise out of the valley, divide to embrace the road, meeting again above. Graceful steel-cable 'sails' which fan out from the pillars seem to be the most delicate and decorative part of the structure, but in fact support the road. The bridge rises slightly toward the south (Béziers) and is slightly curved. From a distance it appears as light as a flight of arrows aimed at the stars. Travelling on it, the impression is one of a tall ship under full sail. There is also a particularly good view of the bridge from Peyre (*see p. 297*).

THE LÉVÉZOU

The Lévézou is a high plateau between the Tarn and the Aveyron, separating the two main towns of the *département* of the Aveyron, Millau and Rodez, dividing the wetter, wooded western Rouergue from the dryer more Mediterranean east. At 1000m above sea-level, it is exposed and relatively inhospitable but the numerous artificial lakes attract visitors looking for outdoor pursuits and watersports such as windsurfing, sailing, canoeing and fishing.

SALLES-CURAN TO RODEZ

Salles-Curan presents a curious mixture of old and new. It has become an important centre for tourism, benefiting from the lake. The town has narrow streets and old houses, and a piece of 19th-century kitsch in the form of a polychromed statue of the Virgin with a rakish starry halo. The bishops of Rodez resided here in the 15th century and the 15th-century church has some fine carved choir stalls adorned with a range of mythical beasts and vegetal motifs. The human figures have fared less well, and there is some restored 15th-century glass. The bishops' residence, also 15th-century, is now a hotel. The Renaissance house below the church has a corner window where *dimes* (tithes) were collected.

Close by is the vast Lac de Pareloup (1,300 hectares), into which thousands of streams pour their contents to supply the hydro-electric stations on the Tarn River.

East of Rodez at **Ste-Radegonde** there is an impressive little fortified church with an arcaded belfry and a pointed roof on top of the machicolated tower.

Another similar fortified church at the charming village of **Inières** further south protects a superb *Annunciation* group (c. 1470), which reputedly comes from the cathedral at Rodez.

PLATEAU DU LÉVÉZOU

Southeast of Salles-Curan, **Les Canabières** is a hilltop village constructed in severe dark schist. The first Templar commandery (*see box on p. 288*) in the Rouergue was established here and the church made over to the Knights in 1120. Unlike the village, the church porch is in pinkish sandstone, and the tympanum has carved reliefs.

Montjaux clings to the side of a high escarpment looking out over the Grands Causses and the Muse Valley. Washed in red, the houses are arranged in tiers stretching out along the hillside, with a stocky Romanesque church at the far end. The ruins of an old château, supposedly on the site of a temple dedicated to Jupiter, look down on the church, and another château (16th–17th centuries) stands below. The delightful church, in pink sandstone with blue-grey slate roofs, shows the stylistic influence of the Auvergne. It is mainly 12th-century, with some 15th-century amendments and a façade and belfry rebuilt in 1856.

Above the River Muse is the fortress-like **Castelnau-Pégayrolles**, a sensational red sandstone village, with several notable monuments: a castle, two Romanesque churches, a medieval hydraulic system and an old forge. Clustered around these are 15th–16th-century houses, with interesting windows and the occasional sculpted cornice. The Château de Castelnau-Pégayrolles (*open June–July 2.30–6.30, closed Tues; T: 05 65 62 00 94 or 01 46 33 72 73*) is one of the oldest castles in the Rouergue and suitably forbidding. The visit takes you through a vaulted seigneurial hall, an 18th-century style suite of apartments and fortified terraces and gardens. The 12th-century hydraulic system includes an aqueduct, reservoirs, the castle cistern, irrigation system and the mills that it powered. The system also provided water to the castle, the village and for agricultural purposes. The churches date from the 11th century (*open July–Aug, 10–12 & 2–5; March–June and Sept–Nov by appointment; T: 05 65 52 05 05*). The larger, the parish church of St-Michel, was subsequently modified in the 13th and 15th centuries. The Priory Church of Notre-Dame (11th–12th centuries) in the cemetery, contains some wall paintings.

Micropolis Cité des Insectes

Open July–Aug 10–7; June, Sept, 10–6, closed Mon except holidays; March–May, Oct–Nov, Mon–Fri 11–5, Sat–Sun 10–6; Feb daily 10–6; closed Dec–Jan; T: 05 65 58 50 50, www.micropolis.biz

This is a major attraction, in the village of St-Léons, which combines museum, research centre and theme park. Multi-lingual audioguides are available. It is made up of two sites, one inside and one outdoors. Inside, *La Cité des Insectes*, has 15 themed interactive exhibitions presented as a voyage into the world of insects in their natural environment with state-of-the-art models, giant beehives, a butterfly house and vivaria for observing insect life in close to natural conditions. Most engaging are the views of the industry inside the beehive and the ants nests. Outside, *Les Pavillons de la Cité*, is a carnaval of giant model insects. The eminent entomologist, Jean-Henri Fabre (1823–1915), was born in St-Léons. His house can also be visited (*open July–Aug 10-7; June, Sept 10–12.30 & 1.30-6, closed Mon; Feb–May, Oct–Dec, 11–12.30 & 1.30–5, closed Mon; T: 05 65 58 80 54, www. musee-jeanhenrifabre.com*). Fabre started out as a mathematician and scientist, but his interest in the natural world developed from 1851 in Corsica. He was a born teacher, his studies wide-ranging, and he acquired great academic honours. His numerous writings and theses ranged from hunter wasps and agricultural chemistry, *hymenopteras* or the order of highly specialised insects such as ants, wasps and bees, to a book of stories.

SÉVÉRAC-LE-CHÂTEAU

Small and ancient, Sévérac-le-Château, 32 km north of Millau, near the source of the Aveyron, seems to have changed little over the centuries. On the slopes below the ruins of a large feudal castle, the village still has two of the original four gateways. At the centre is Place de la Fontaine, named after the *fontaine romane*, where spring water was protected under a vaulted covering. There are numerous interesting buildings:

the oldest house is reputed to be the Maison de Jeanne which, with the Maison des Consuls and Musée Archaéologique, is open to visitors (combined ticket with Château). The Consuls House is close to the covered market, some of the smaller streets pass under vaulted alleys, and the church of St Sauveur is part 12th century including its square belfry. The Château (*open July–Aug 10–12 & 2–6; other times exterior of the ruins; T: 05 65 47 67 31 or 05 65 47 62 63, www.severac-le-chateau.com*) bears witness to frequent conflicts and subsequent restorations. The few remaining buildings date from the late Middle Ages with major alterations made in the 17th century. At the Revolution parts of the castle were demolished and it was in total ruins by the 20th century. Nevertheless, the site is magnificent (*son et lumière* in August).

THE DOURBIE & CAUSSE DU LARZAC

The river Dourbie, having carved a route through the Causse Noir to the north and the Causse du Larzac to the south, unites with the Tarn at Millau. A popular excursion from Millau towards the Causse Noir, which is defined to the north by the Gorges de la Jonte, includes the extraordinary natural phenomena of Montpellier le Vieux (*open June–Aug 9.30–7.30; March–May, Sept–mid-Nov 10–5.30; T: 05 65 60 66 30, www.aven-armand.com*) consisting of groups of rocks resembling ruined and deserted villages. Roquesaltes has similar formations, and Aven Armand (Lozère) is a vast cavern accessible by funicular.

VALLEY OF THE DOURBIE

East of Millau, the valley of the Dourbie almost immediately closes in, becoming a deep and magnificent rift between the limestone cliffs. At **Massebiau**, on a tight loop in the river, are the remains of castles that once protected access to the Causse Noir. The scenery becomes progressively more rugged while the villages scattered along the valley are the inheritors of the medieval forts that defended the territory. **La Roque-Ste-Marguerite** is a small community with a château (rebuilt in the 17th century) and church (11th and 18th centuries) picturesquely clamped to the cliff. Beyond Ste-Marguerite the road crosses the Dourbie, and high above are tiny villages, some saved from total abandon, such as **St-Véran**, the village where the family Montcalm de St-Véran originated, a descendant of which, Louis-Joseph, died defending Quebec in 1759; and **Cantobre**, in a vertiginous and spectacular spot where the dolomitic rock and buildings seem to merge into one craggy mass. The valley then widens out, becomes gentler, and fulfils its description as the *Jardin du Rouergue*. On the edge of the route is the church of Notre-Dame-des-Cuns, the most complete Romanesque church in the area. In golden limestone, it is compact and sturdy, with a polygonal apse, the only later addition being a chapel in the 15th century. Like many Romanesque churches in this vicinity with similar characteristics, it was affiliated to St-Victor at Marseilles.

Nant

On the banks of the Dourbie, Nant has a graceful 14th-century bridge, an arcaded 16th-century market with huge stone pillars and vaults (no longer used), and a *Mairie* in an elegant 18th-century building with a grand staircase and stucco. There is also a notable church with a massive, fortified west end. The church of **St-Pierre** is all that remains of a once-important Benedictine abbey. The pentagonal east end has conserved many of its 12th-century elements but the narthex was amended two centuries later with the addition of a Gothic door and tower. The nave chapels are 14th- and 19th-century, and the windows 19th-century. The interior is impressive and subtly lit. The nave has pointed barrel vaults supported by pairs of engaged columns and the short transept has apsidal chapels. The crossing is domed and the apse is semi-circular from the interior with three windows and simple decorations. There are 121 sculpted capitals altogether, mainly cubic in form, with stylised vegetal or geometric designs; they seem to be the work of several sculptors and some probably came from an earlier church.

CAUSSE DE LARZAC

The desolate Causse or Plateau de Larzac is a vast territory of some 1,000 square kilometres grazed by large flocks of sheep. Once covered in forest, it was cleared for agricultural purposes over the course of many centuries and evolved into its present grassland state in the 18th century. Donations of land in the Rouergue were made to the Templars (*see box p. 288*) from the mid-12th century, but the acquisition of the church of Ste-Eulalie in 1151 was the watershed. Gradually, by fair means or foul, the Templars became the principal landowners of the Larzac, at times coming into conflict with their neighbours. An important link between the Mediterranean and the Massif Central, there was land aplenty here for crops and horses. The Knights Hospitaller later added fortifications to many of the properties.

La Cavalerie and Ste-Eulalie-de-Cernon

The Templar and Hospitaller *cité* of La Cavalerie (*guided visits July–Aug 10-7; rest of year by appointment; T: 05 65 52 78 73, pointacceuil.cavalerie@wanadoo.fr*) is now submerged in a small town on the edge of a main road, consequently with less appeal than St-Eulalie (*see below*) or La Couvertoirade (*see p. 289*). Nevertheless, more than half the 15th-century fortifications survive, recently renovated, distinguished by three huge towers at two corners and over the main gateway. Along the old streets inside the walls are 15th–17th-century houses. The church, begun in the 12th century, was almost entirely rebuilt 1760–61, although inside a few fragments of the old building are visible.

Ste-Eulalie-de-Cernon (*church and castle open July–Aug 10–7; May–June 10–12 & 2–6; March–April, Sept–Nov, 10–12 & 2–6, closed Sat, Sun and holidays; T: 05 65 52 79 98*) is a distinctive sight, with its five defensive towers and belfry standing proud above the red roofs. It became the operational centre for the Larzac in 1153. The

Grande Rue leads up to a large open square with a 17th-century fountain. This was the cemetery until 1641 and marks the divide between the fortified town, enclosed in walls by the Hospitallers in the 15th century, and the earlier Templar castle. The present church, on the site of one made over to the Templars in 1151, has little ornament and was reorientated in 1648. A new main door, with broken pediment and statue of the Virgin, was constructed in the former apse, to either side of which are the remaining old chapels (13th century). The château was built (1187-1249) around a courtyard but has suffered many vicissitudes and alterations. The oldest part is the façade facing the square, and only one of four original square towers remain. A wing was added in 1648 to provide an upper floor with a grand staircase, murals and mullioned windows.

THE TEMPLARS

The religious and military Order of the Knights Templar was founded in 1119. As the Order of Poor Chevaliers of Christ, they supported and protected pilgrims in the Holy Land. King Badouin II of Jerusalem gave them a wing of his palace on the site of the old Temple of Solomon. They adopted the Rules of St Benedict and took their vows before the Patriarch of Jerusalem in 1128. Recognised by the Papacy as the Order of the Temple, in 1139 Innocent II granted them certain exemptions from tithes and episcopal jurisdiction. They became a permanent military presence in the Holy Land and in 1190, with the Hospitallers (founded 1113), backed Philippe II of France and Richard I of England during the third crusade. Donations and gifts of property flowed in from pilgrims and crusaders and the Templars eventually became bankers to kings, popes and merchants. They built great castles in the Holy Land and huge estates, or commanderies, in France farmed grain, wine, oil, wool and cattle for the military. By the 13th century, they owned more than 9,000 houses (fortresses and commanderies) in the West and the Middle East. After sustaining disastrous losses in the Holy Land, the Templars moved with the Hospitallers to Malta. The Order had become too rich and powerful for its own good, inciting jealousy, and began to lose sight of its original mission. The Grand Master, Jacques de Molay, refused to unite with the Hospitallers. King Philippe IV, in desperate need of revenue, took diverse measures to raise funds in 1306, the most unexpected and extreme was the simultaneous arrest of all Templars in France and the confiscation of their property, on Friday 13th October, 1307, on trumped-up charges including responsibility for losing the Holy Land. Between 1307 and 1314, most members of the Order were tortured, imprisoned and finally burned at the stake. In 1312, Pope Clement V (*see p. 92*) under the influence of the king, suppressed the Order and made over their property to the Order of Hospitallers of St John of Jerusalem.

La Couvertoirade commandery constructed by the Knights Templar and Hospitaller 1249–1439.

La Couvertoirade

Guided visits/audio guides, T: 05 65 58 55 59; www.lacouvertoirade.com
Isolated in a hollow of the rugged *causse*, the best of the Templar/Hospitaller towns is La Couvertoirade. Truly impressive and happily conserved, the little community is enclosed in 15th-century walls. The only entrance is through the Porte du Haut (the Porte du Bas collapsed in 1917). It is likely that the Templars took control of an existing community here some time towards the end of the 12th century and by 1249 they had built the castle. La Couvertoirade remained a dependence of the commandery of Ste-Eulalie until made over to the Hospitallers in the 14th century. The series of fortified towers and curtain walls follows the irregular shape of the rock on which La Couvertoirade is built, and from the ramparts is an overall view of the village. The 17th- and 18th-century Hôtel de la Scipione contains a permanent exhibition but the castle, incorporated into the enceinte in 1439, is now a ruin. The church opposite, a simple vaulted building with a tall tower that looks little different from the military buildings, was built by the Hospitallers in the 14th century. Near the church is the communal oven, and below the flight of steps is a public reservoir, Les Conques, supplied by rainwater from the church roof. There are a number of delightful houses, particularly along Rue Droite on the south, which formerly linked the two entrances, lined with 16th- and 17th-century buildings with exterior steps up to the doors and vaulted cellars beneath.

Viala-du-Pas-de-Jaux

West of Ste-Eulalie, the ensemble of tower (1430) and massive fortified barn (14th century) built by the Knights Hospitallers of St John of Jerusalem at Viala-du-Pas-de-Jaux, as a place of refuge for local people in time of war and as a place to store valuable crops, illustrates the agricultural importance of the Larzac since the 15th century. The five-storey tower has recently been restored and is open most of the year for temporary exhibitions (*T: 05 65 58 91 89*) and offers views over the *causse* towards Ste-Eulalie (*see p. 287*).

East of St-Affrique (*see below*) are the harmoniously restored buildings of St-Jean-d'Alcas, formerly the property of the Cistercian Abbey of Nonenque, which was fortified in the 15th century. The central block of handsome buildings is surrounded by the ramparts into which more superb houses have been built.

St-Rome-de-Cernon is the Château de Mélac (*open Aug–Sept Fri–Sun 10–12 & 2–6, T: 05 65 52 31 38*), a 14th–16th-century fortified house around a large, galleried courtyard, where the kitchen and vaulted hall are included in the visit.

Roquefort

Probably the most familiar name associated with the Aveyron is Roquefort-sur-Soulzon, famous for its blue cheese, which is the explanation for all those sheep on the *causse*. Milk from some 800,000 sheep owned by 2,500 farmers produce the cheese to which *Penicillium Roqueforti* is introduced. It is then wrapped and left to mature in cold, damp and draughty natural caves on long trestles, row upon row, to acquiring its blue veining and distinctive flavour. Only around the end of March is there much activity in the cellars. Otherwise, except for being turned regularly, the cheeses are left undisturbed. Three producers offer visits to the cellars or caves where the cheese matures: Roquefort Société (*T: 05 65 58 58 58, www.roquefort-societe.com*); Roquefort Papillon (*T: 05 65 58 50 08, www.roquefort-papillon.com*); and Roquefort Gabriel Coulet, Pl. de l'Eglise (*T: 05 65 59 90 21, www.gabriel-coulet.fr*)

St-Affrique and environs

St-Affrique is the major town in this part of the Aveyron, with a 14th-century bridge over the Sorgue. A recent innovation here is Pastoralia (*open May–Sept 10–6; Sept–April 10–12 & 2–6, closed Sat, Sun and holidays; T: 05 65 98 10 23*), a window on the farming of sheep and the production of milk in the Roquefort region, with an interactive exhibition and live sheep. The Maison de la Mémoire du pays St-Affricain (*open Wed 8.30–1; Tues, Thurs 2–6; T: 05 65 49 07 31*) is a collection of information on local history .

At Rebourguil the **Château d'Esplas** (*July-Aug 2–7, closed Fri; T: 05 65 99 87 96/05 65 58 91 89*) is a medieval fortified château (13th-18th centuries) on the top of a hill with a 20m keep, three angle towers and cistern carved from the rock. Inside are 16th-century monumental fireplaces and furnished 17th- and 18th-century *salons*.

Lapeyre has an 11th-century church. In the churchyard is the tomb of Medora Leigh (d. 1849), who married her brother-in-law and claimed to be the bastard daughter of Lord Byron by his half-sister Augusta Leigh (1783–1851).

PRACTICAL INFORMATION

GETTING AROUND

• **By train:** from Paris to Béziers via
Sévérac-le-Château, Millau. From
Clermont-Ferrand to Toulouse via
Sévérac-le-Château and Millau.From
Rodez to Séverac-le-Château via Laissac.
• **By bus:** regular services from Millau
to St-Affrique, St-Jean-du-Bruel, and
Montpellier l'Hospitalet du Larzac. In
summer, Gorges du Tarn via Aguessac,
Rivière-sur-Tarn, Le Rozier. From Millau
regular service to St-Jean-du-Bruel, via
La Mona, La Roque, Ste-Marguerite;
and to Montpellier regular service via
La Cavalerie, l'Hospitalet du Larzac, le
Caylar.

TOURIST INFORMATION

Millau 1 Pl. du Beffroi, BP 331,
T: 05 65 60 02 42, www.ot-millau.fr
Nant/Vallée de la Dourbie/Causses
Chapelle des Pénitents
T: 05 65 62 24 21, www.ot-nant.fr
Pont-de-Salars/Pareloup-Lévézou Pl.
de la Mairie, T: 05 65 46 89 90,
www.levezou-viaur.com
Réquista Pl. du Gl. De Gaulle,
T: 05 65 46 11 79,
www.tourisme-requistanais.com
Rivière-sur-Tarn Route des Gorges du
Tarn, T: 05 65 59 74 28
www.ot-gorgesdutarn.com
Roquefort Av. de Lauras, T: 05 65 58
56 00, www.roquefort.com
Salles-Curan-Pareloup Pl. de la Vierge,
T: 05 65 46 31 73
Sévérac-le-Château 5 rue des Douves,
T: 05 65 47 67 31,
www.severac-le-chateau.com

St-Affrique Blvd. de Verdun,
T: 05 65 98 12 40,
info.st-affrique@ roquefort.com

ACCOMMODATION & RESTAURANTS

Castelnau-Pégayrols
€ **Chambres d'hôtes Rouviac.** Part of
an old farm, the core of which is 16th-
century, with rooms in the converted
bergerie, two decked out in modern
colour and decorations, the vaulted living room with a huge fireplace and
original flagstones, and an old stone
sink. T: 05 65 62 09 17,
www.rouviac.fr.st
Luzençon
€ **Chambres d'hôtes La Saisonneraie.**
Claude and Bruno have carefully
restored their 11th-century listed stone
house situated on a south-facing slope
close to the hamlet of Luzençon near
Millau with a view towards the viaduct.
Table d'hôtes by prior reservation.
T: 05 65 52 58 86/06 84 47 18 72,
www.lasaisonneraie.com
Millau
€€ **La Musardière.** 14 bedrooms in a
stately 18th-century house in the centre
of Millau. The rooms and bathrooms
are spacious and comfortable. There is a
pretty dining room where a choice of
set menus is served. 34 Av. de la
République, T: 05 65 60 20 63,
email hotel-lamusardiere@wanadoo.fr
€ **Château de Creissels.** 2km from
Millau, the château is part 12th- and
part 19th-century, transformed into a
hotel in 1960. The 30 elegant bedrooms
have a view either of the Viaduc de
Millau or the grounds. The cooking is

based on local ingredients, served in the magnificent vaulted cellars or on the terrace. Rte de St-Affrique, Creissels, on D922, T: 05 65 60 16 59, www.chateau-de-creissels.com
€€ Chambres d'hôtes La Cadenède. The property goes back to the 13th century and was originally a fortified farm typical of the Rouergue. It was remodelled in 1660 around a Renaissance courtyard and this magnificent house is now set in a park with great vistas. There is a pool, billiards and fitness rooms. Les Hauts de la Croix Vieille, T: 05 61 23 98 00, www.cadenede.com.
€ La Braconne. ■ A traditional restaurant tucked under the arcades just opposite the museum. On the menu you might find *crèpes soufflées au roquefort* or *beignets de foie gras*; rabbit, hare and mutton basted in lard from a traditional long-handled utensil called a *flambadou*. 7 Place du Marechel-Foch, T: 05 65 60 30 93.
Salles-Curan
€ Hostellerie du Lévézou. An impressive 14th-century chateau with pleasant rooms. The dining room is stone vaulted and there is also a terrace. Rue du Château, T: 05 65 46 34 16, Fax 05 65 46 01 19, www.hostelleriedulevezou.com
Sévérac-le-Château
€ Chambres d'hôtes La Caussenarde. Conveniently close to the A75, yet in a wonderfully rural setting. The interiors combine the rugged charm of stone and original features with plain modern decoration. The bedrooms are each themed around a different colour scheme and are pleasantly unfussy. M. et Mme. Michel, Altès,

T: 05 65 47 80 19, http:perso.wanadoo.fr/catherinemichel
Versols et Lapeyre
€ Chambres d'hôtes Château de Montalègre. An impressive chateau dominating the Sorques Valley and set in extensive grounds with great vistas. The beautiful interior with has 4 charming rooms and 1 suite and a warm welcome on hand from Katy and Eric. The swimming pool is dramatically situated beneath the castle rock and there are plenty of activities. Also a *gîte* or rent the whole castle. T: 05 65 97 58 06, www.chateaudemontalegre.com

MARKET DAYS

Laissac Occasional summer markets
Millau Wednesday, Friday; Monday evenings in summer
Sévérac-le-Château Thursday
St-Jean-du-Bruel Thursday
St-Léons July/August Friday evenings

FESTIVALS & EVENTS

May: *Festival du conte,* storytelling, St-Affrique, T: 05 65 98 12 40
July: *Millau en Jazz,* Jazz concerts, T: 05 65 60 82 47
July/August: *Lundis en fete a Millau,* Monday evening markets, concerts and street entertainment, T: 05 65 60 02 42
Les Estivals du Larzac, medieval-style events in the Templar sites of the Larzac, at La Couvertoirade, La Cavalerie, St-Jean-d'Alcas and Viala du Pas de Jaux, T: 05 65 59 12 22
Spectacle son et lumière in the Templar sites of the Larzac, T: 05 65 59 12 22

SOUTHERN AVEYRON

The southern Aveyron and valley of the Tarn, from the district around Millau towards Albi, is a quieter, less frequented alternative to the famous Gorges du Tarn upstream. It is a wild, predominantly dry landscape with formidable villages still untamed and unprettified, as well as picturesque castles and stunning river scenery. The area between the Grand Causses and the Monts de Lacaune further south, at the eastern end of the *département* of the Tarn, it includes the peaceful valley of the River Rance on the edge of the Lacaune and the strange landscape of the Rougier de Camarès.

THE ROUGIER DE CAMARÈS

The Rougier de Camarès, south of St-Affrique (*see p. 290*), is an area of dark red soil, a mixture of sandstone and marl, where the villages built in the local materials reflect the warm red tones.

Château de Montaigut

Open July–Aug 10–6.30; Feb–June, Sept–mid-Dec 10–12 & 2.30– 6.30; T: 05 65 99 81 50.
Directly due south of St-Affrique, on the perilous but spectacular small road to Gissac, the Château de Montaigut sits atop a conical hill. The views over the Rougier de Camarès and the Grauzou Valley are marvellous. The château, which has retained its early medieval layout, possibly 11th-century, originally controlled the route between St-Affrique to the north and Camarès and has been saved by a long programme of restoration. Frequent cultural events are held here. The huge château-keep, a massive and simple construction, is protected to the south by an *enceinte* around a courtyard with stables and outhouses. In the lower vaulted rooms are a deep cistern and cellar carved out of the rock—safeguards against siege. The transformation from severe fortress to comfortable residence began in the 15th century with the addition of a large fireplace and ogee doorway, and was carried further in the 17th century with the insertion of large windows, more fireplaces and sophisticated decoration in stucco (gypseries). The plaster, or gypsum, used for the stucco was quarried and milled to the northwest of Montaigut and these sites can be visited on foot; ask for the pamphlet *Sentier du Plâtre*. At the end of the track to the Château of Montaigut is a small farmhouse which has been turned into a geological museum with a reconstructed farm interior of 1914.

The small road between Montaigut and Gissac follows an amazingly empty, furrowed valley, typical of the Rougier, with dark red soil and bright green vegetation. A sinuous route follows the Rance gorge west of **Camarès** where the *ville haute* and the lower town are divided by the Rance, spanned by a picturesque bridge with one very high and two smaller arches. This is a popular tourism centre.

Abbaye de Sylvanès

Open Feb–Nov 9–12.30 & 2–6; Jan, Dec, 9–12.30 & 2–6, closed Sat, Sun, and holidays; T: 05 65 98 20 20; www.sylvanes.com

In the green and wooded valley of the Cabot, Sylvanès is today an important centre for culture, art and spirituality, where courses are held nearly all year round. The abbey was founded in 1132 by a repentant brigand of noble birth, Pons de Léras, and four years later adopted the rule of Cîteaux. It was the first Cistercian abbey in the Rouergue and the church, begun c. 1151, is a good example of the style. Its construction lasted nearly a century, resulting in an interesting juxtaposition of Romanesque and Gothic building techniques. The church was left almost untouched by the Calvinists during the Reformation, and was hardly affected by the Revolution, although the monastic buildings fared less well during both periods.

The exterior of the west end of the church is plain with just two small doors (for the deceased to the north and the lay brothers to the south), with a Rayonnant window with glass from the end of the 13th to early 14th centuries. There is a small arcaded belfry over the crossing. The exterior of the east end is more inspiring, the flat chevet pierced with four rose and three lancet windows, and a cornice of small arcades running around the exterior. Some of the wrought iron is 12th-century. Even more uplifting is the interior, with the play of light from the many windows and uncluttered, beautifully proportioned elevations. The five-bay Cistercian-style nave is a paradigm for aisleless Gothic churches in the Midi. Nave, transepts and choir have pointed barrel vaults, whereas primitive rib vaults are introduced at the crossing and in the first bay of the nave. A door in the nave opened into the cloister and two doors in the south transept gave access to the monastic buildings.

Of the monastery only the east wing has survived, plus an incomplete gallery of the cloister, probably built later, towards the end of the 13th century. The rectangular sacristy with a low vault has a decorated tympanum over the door to the cloister and the chapter house has one single bay of vaulting with rectangular ribs springing from carved imposts in the angles. The walls were stuccoed in the 18th century. Finest of all is the monks' room or *scriptorium*, saved from near-ruin by an impressive programme of restoration, and used as a refectory or for concerts. Four central columns divide it into ten vaulted bays with rounded ribs similar to the chapter houses at Escaladieu (*see p. 524*) and Flaran (*see p. 383*), although probably pre-dating both, being built c. 1160–80. The mineral waters of Bains-de-Sylvanès were exploited in the 17th and 18th centuries.

Château de Fayet

Open April–Nov 10–12 & 2–6, closed Sun morning and holidays; T: 05 65 49 59 15; http://chateaufayet.free.fr

The Château de Fayet, east of Camarès, opened to the public relatively recently. This fine Renaissance mansion, in which Henri IV stayed, with a fairly rigorous exterior softened by a verdant setting, was conceived by Guy de Castelnau-Bretenoux. It comprises three wings around a *cour d'honneur* each angle marked by a round tower with pointed roof, while a fifth tower in the centre of the main façade contains a spiral staircase. A handsome 16th-century fountain and an old well (1564) with a sculpted coat of arms adorn the courtyard. The house was embellished in the 17th century by d'Arpajon, with elegantly painted ceilings *à la française* and stucco decoration. Descendants of the duke stayed until the eve of the Revolution. In 1999 the present owners moved in and began restoration work, ultimately bringing the château back to life with numerous events, exhibitions and concerts.

THE LACAUNE

The Lacaune is famous for charcuterie and *salaisons* (sausage, cured and dried meats) and for the bottled water of Mont Roucous. The boundary of the *départements* of the Tarn and the Aveyron, it is wooded country with great views: one of the most spectacular panoramas is at **Laval-Roquecézière** (900m), dominated by a monumental statue of the Virgin. Nearby, there is a small folk museum at **St-Crépin** (*open mid-April–mid-Sept 2–6, mid-Sept–mid-April 2–5, T: 05 65 99 61 57*), containing examples of menhir statues (*see box on p. 296*) from the St-Sernin region.

THE RANCE

Notre-Dame-d'Orient, tucked away north of Laval-Roquecézière, near St-Sernin-sur-Rance (*see p. 299*), is a beautiful hamlet close to the River Rance, tributary of the Tarn. The houses are gathered around a large red sandstone church (*open 8–12 & 2–7; T: 05 65 99 60 88*). The austere and unadorned exterior has the date 1666 on the southwest gable above a huge sundial, and a disproportionately small belfry on the east. At the beginning of the 17th century, after the Religious Wars, Franciscan friars re-established a community here and built a model Counter-Reformation church. The uncomplicated interior space bursts with Baroque exuberance on a predominantly blue background. The walls are covered with *trompe l'oeil* pilasters, candelabra, *rinceaux* and, behind the retable, draperies. The curved ceiling is the most original part, covered in wood panels in a herringbone pattern. The altar is decorated with paintings in medallions and the retable is splendid with a *Virgin and Child*, crowned in gold, in the centre. The middle section is set off by pairs of Corinthian columns and flanking it are statues of St Francis and St Clare, the whole decorated with angels. The polychromed relief medallions portray saints important to the Franciscan order. There are more Baroque altarpieces in the nave chapels, that of Ste-Marguerite with a fine worked leather antependium.

Before reaching here the River Rance runs through gentle pastures, tiny villages and deserted farmsteads, passing through **Combret-sur-Rance**. A typical once-fortified medieval village of the southern Aveyron in an impressive site.

An ancient bridge spans the river further upstream outside **Belmont-sur-Rance**, which overlooks the river and dominates the countryside with its celebrated crocketed spire (75m tall) of the Gothic collegiate church (1515–24). The church has an ornate Flamboyant tympanum and Renaissance and Gothic fenestration in the tower.

STATUE-MENHIRS

In the region of the Monts de Lacaune are a number of menhirs, monolithic blocks of flat stone standing in the earth, with parallel sides and rounded top. The surface is carved or engraved in low-relief, on one or both faces, with rudimentary features. The figures are represented full length, with straight legs, the waist indicated by a belt and folded arms and sometimes the body is covered in a cloak. The facial features are simple, the eyes and nose are indicated, but the mouth rarely, and there are often parallel marks on the cheeks. Females have breasts like buttons and wear necklaces with the hair pulled back; the males carry weapons, and wear straps or other accessories. The statue menhirs probably date from the transitional period between the Stone and Bronze Ages (c. 4000–2200 BC, as old as or slightly older than the pyramids). Their symbolism and significance are still wreathed in mystery although it has been suggested that they were devotional objects representing some kind of deity. Careful research is usually required to pinpoint their location, although the easiest to find are those in the Musée Fenaille, Rodez (*see p. 212*) and the Musée St-Crépin (*see p. 295*); more information on their whereabouts can be obtained at Lacaune Tourist Office.

MONTS DE LACAUNE

Murat-sur-Vèbre is a typical town of the Lacaune mountains, where the houses, huddled together shoulder-to-shoulder, are not only roofed in slate but have overlapping slate shingles on exposed walls. There is an 11th-century church here and all around are magnificent beech forests, glorious until late autumn. Between Murat and Lacaune, are menhirs (*see above*), some signposted.

Lacaune and environs

Lacaune is a small unpretentious spa nestling under slate roofs on the edge of the Monts de Lacaune in the Haut Languedoc regional park. At an altitude of 800m, it is dominated by the peak of Montalet (1260m). The town's main monument is the Fontaine des Pisseurs in Place du Griffoul, erected in 1559 by four consuls. In the same square is the Musée du Vieux Lacaune (*open July–Aug 10–12 & 2–6; June, Sept 3–6, closed Mon; T: 05 63 37 25 38*), a small museum of local pre-1940 history, and the spa in the 19th century; it also has three rooms dedicated to the 'Enfant Sauvage' (*see p. 299*). The church, built in 1668, has modern windows and a new organ which is used for recitals in the summer. There is a statue-menhir outside the tourist office. The Maison de la Charcuterie (*open mid-June–mid-Sept 10–12 & 2.30–6.30; T: 05 63 37 46 31*) is a very professional exhibition of the business of making the ham and sausages, a speciality of the region. The large lakes to the south of Lacaune offer beautiful scenery, water sports, and another chance to go menhir hunting.

ALONG THE TARN

ABOVE MILLAU

Le Rozier, upstream from Millau, is an attractive spot where the Gorges du Tarn and the Gorges de la Jonte converge. From here to Millau is a scenic drive between strange outcrops of rock. In the field beside the river near **Mostuéjouls** is the little church of Notre-Dame-des-Champs, with a *clocher-peigne* (a comb-like belfry). The **Château de Peyrelade** (*guided visit, July–Aug 10–12 & 2.30–6.30; mid-June, Sept 2.30–6, closed Sat; T: 05 65 59 74 28/05 65 59 81 37, www.ot-gorgesdutarn.com/peyrelade.html*) was once one of the most important castles in the Rouergue. It clings precariously to a rock which stretches out over the valley. A major programme of restoration has been completed. The visit introduces the castle's turbulent past, its architecture and its restoration and includes the natural rock keep. **Compeyre** is a high village downstream from Rivière, where the old hospital has become the Maison des artisans (craftsmen) and the Presbetery the Maison de la Vigne (wine).

BELOW MILLAU

The troglodytic village of **Peyre**, overlooking the Tarn a few kilometres west of Millau, is classed among the most beautiful villages of France and is now often cited as the epitome of old meeting new, thanks to the fine view towards the Millau Viaduct (*see p. 283*). Many of the tall, pale stone houses with lauze roofs emerge from the rock face, as does the church with a 17th-century doorway. The whole village, which looks down on the river, has been almost perfectly restored, including the medieval communal bread oven. Peyre and Comprégnac were once wine producing villages, but the terraced slopes now show little sign of cultivation.

St-Rome-de-Tarn, on the left bank of the Tarn, is surrounded by old vineyards. For a boat trip on the Raspes, close to St-Rome, an idyllic section of the Tarn flowing through steep wooded cliffs, depart from Mas de la Nauc on the right bank (*June–Sept daily; April–Nov check times; T: 05 65 62 59 12 or 05 65 62 52 49*). The two former industries of the area mining and wine-making, are addressed at a small museum in St-Rome, Musée de la Mine et de la Vigne (*T: 05 65 62 54 11 or 05 65 62 55 40*). In the church at St-Victor et Melvieu are neo-Byzantine murals by Nicholas Greschny (*see box p. 299*).

On the south bank close to where the Dourdou meets the Tarn are some beautiful *pigeonniers*. **St-Izaire** is an impressive site that was chosen by the bishops of Vabres for their episcopal château, towering above the reddish-stone houses arranged in terraces above the valley. The Château de St-Izaire (*open July–Aug 10–7; April–June, Sept–Oct 2–7; March 10–12, 2–4; closed Wed, Sat, Sun and holidays; T: 05 65 99 42 27*) is a large square building, built between the 14th and 17th centuries, with a little look-out tower on the angle towards the village and a variety of fenestration. Inside is a chapel with 14th-century frescoes and a marquetry ceiling.

BROUSSE-LE-CHÂTEAU

Brousse-le-Château is the site of a formidable castle with ramparts and towers cling-ing to a high rocky spur between the Tarn and the Alrance Rivers. The ancient hump-backed stone bridge in the village reputedly dates from 1366. The Château de Brousse (*open July–Aug 10–7; Feb–June, Sept–Oct 2–6; Nov 2–5; Dec by appointment; closed Jan; T: 05 65 99 45 40, www.brousse.le.chateau.free.fr*) was first mentioned in the 10th cen-tury and the considerable fortifications have been consolidated and restored. Inside the 13th-century gateway is a grassy area, and the whole is enclosed in a 15th-centu-ry *enceinte* incorporating earlier constructions. Almost totally intact, the ramparts fol-low the contours of the rock to make an irregular polygon, narrower at the southeast than the northwest, with a multitude of openings for a variety of weapons. The high-est tower, La Picardie, was dismantled in the 17th century and only the base is left as a reminder; the oldest complete tower, built towards the village, is 14th-century. Some of the towers were used as lodgings or for imprisonment. The château remained in the hands of the d'Arpajon family from the 13th century until 1700, and some time after the 15th century they converted the main lodgings into something more habit-able. These buildings contain the well, a bread oven (restored in the 19th century), stables, large rooms with fireplaces and a 17th-century staircase.

COUPIAC

Château de Coupiac

Open July–Aug 10–7; other times by appointment, T: 05 65 99 79 45.
On high ground at Coupiac at the heart of an area known as the Pays des Sept Vallons (comprising seven valleys and seven communities) west of the Parc Naturel Régional des Grands Causses, is another restored castle. The imposing Château de Coupiac is the last castle of the Counts of Rodez to remain intact. Different in character from Brousse-le-Château, it was built in the 15th century on a rock in the middle of the vil-lage, with three high round towers. The châtelain, Louis de Panat, was forced to dis-mantle a quarter of his castle by Louis XI after participating in a local revolt in 1465; the section between the north towers was rebuilt in the 16th century and amend-ments continued until the 18th century. A *chemin de ronde* and machicolations for defence, ogee and mullioned windows, Renaissance doorways, and a vaulted kitchen attest to its role as both fortification and stately residence.

The town

For almost five centuries Coupiac has owned an authentic relic of the Saint-Voile (Holy Veil), hidden during the Wars of Religion then forgotten, until it happened to be uncovered by a bull. In 1968 an oratory was built behind the castle to display the relic, which is still venerated, and there is a pilgrimage at Assumption. The neo-Byzantine painted décor of the oratory is by Nicolas Greschny (*see box on p. 299*). Another relic is the beautiful 11th-century tympanum from the first church, Notre-

Dame-de-Massiliergues, now under the archway west of the 19th-century parish church. It is semi-circular and has a monogram of Christ, or chrism, with a cabled outline inscribed in a tilted square. On either side are angels and small flowers or stars. Around Coupiac and nearby Martrin are menhirs dating from 3000-2500 BC.

Nicolas Greschny (1912–85)
Born in Estonia in 1912, during the Russian Revolution, Nicolas Greschny travelled through northern Europe and finally settled in the Tarn. From a long line of icon painters, he decorated many churches in the region in a modern version of traditional Byzantine murals, the figures hieratic and simplified. He wholeheartedly supported the improvement and conservation of churches and religious objects and at his former home at La Maurinié (between Albi and Ambialet) is a small museum. He worked in innumerable churches including Gabriac east of Bouzouls (Aveyron), in the Tarn at Fréjéville and Lacabarède east of Mazamet. His son Michael maintains the family tradition at the Atelier Greschny, Marsal (*T: 05 63 45 40 69; greschny@wanadoo.fr*)

ST-SERNIN TO AMBIALET

St-Sernin-sur-Rance, on a spur high above the confluence of the Rance and the Merdanson, has a fine 16th- and 17th-century bridge and was an important medieval stronghold. In the older part of town to the south are the 15th-century Hôtel de Ville, and church with a square rustic belfry and a small bell. In the south wall of the church, above a sundial is a pretty stone rose window. Inside the church is a lierne-vaulted chapel with Christ and the four Evangelists on the bosses, carved brackets and varied window tracery. St-Sernin is famous for *gimblettes*, a small hard cake with caraway seed, and also for the statue, on Place du Fort, of the wild boy of the Aveyron, who is thought to have been raised by wolves. Known as Victor, after the hero of Rene Gilbert Pixerecourt's play *Victor ou L' Enfant du Forêt* (1798), he first came to light in the district of Lacaune in 1798, walking out of the woods aged 12. In 1800 he spent a few days at a house in St-Sernin-sur-Rance before being taken to Paris to be paraded in front of society and examined by scientists. His story was brought to the screen by François Truffaut in *L'Enfant Sauvage* (1970).

The charming village of **Plaisance** is also on the River Rance. At the top of the little hill in the village is a small church (part 12th, part 15th and 16th centuries). Steps lead up to an entrance with deep roll-mouldings and bulbous capitals and bases. The exterior of the apse is also decorated, and above the south transept door is an ancient re-used tympanum with a chrism similar to that at Coupiac, flanked by two lions and daisies. Inside are storiated capitals, including *Daniel in the Lions' Den* at the crossing and leaping lions in the northwest transept. The crossing is covered by a lantern on pendentives supporting the heavy belfry.

Alban is not a particularly inspiring town but the modern Church of Notre-Dame has an interesting mixture of decoration and fittings. The west façade has modern abstract coloured glass by Bruno Schmeltz and an old balustrade. The door is late 18th-century in style and the interior is decorated with murals of the *Passion of Christ* (1957/58 and 1967) by Nicolas Greschny (*see box on p. 299*). A crowned *Madonna and Child*, possibly 16th-century, stand on the main altar and against the north wall is the most outstanding piece, a 16th-century wayside cross sculpted on three sides with *Scenes of the Passion*. It was found in 1927 and is considered the best of its kind in the Tarn.

Approaching **Ambialet** from the east there is an excellent view of the dramatic site where the Tarn forces its way through high cliffs to form a tight loop and a narrow isthmus. At the top of the cliff is a priory which can be reached either by road or by following the Stations of the Cross up a footpath. At the summit is a wide terrace with spectacular views and a long flight of steps leading up to the west end of the little 11th-century church of Notre-Dame-de-l'Oder. A religious community occupies the priory but the much-restored church can be visited. The deep porch has four carved capitals supporting a square belfry. The interior is very plain and simple with huge square pillars and exposed stone. The three-bay nave is barrel vaulted and the aisles have half-barrel vaults. There are shallow transepts and a trilobed east end.

ABOVE ALBI

East of Albi stands **St-Juéry** whose bridge across the Tarn overlooks the Saut du Tarn or Saut du Sabo, an 18m cascade in the river harnessed to create hydro-electric power. The Musée du Saut-du-Tarn (*open mid-April–Oct 2–7, closed Sat; Nov–mid-April, Wed, Sun, and holidays, 2–6; T: 05 63 45 91 01*), is a former metal foundry and workshop which once processed every stage from raw material to finished product. The introduction of hydro-electricity revolutionised the process and at its most productive it employed 3,800 workers, closing in 1983. In the 19th-century building, some 200 years of industrial history are retraced through original working machinery and animated models.

Lescure has a 12th-century church, St-Michel-de-Lescure (*open during exhibitions; T: 05 63 60 76 73*). Once part of a Benedictine abbey, it has the best Romanesque sculptures in the Albigeois. The west door has a wealth of sculpted decoration including four elaborately carved archivolts, mouldings, corbels and cornice, and capitals reminiscent of the Porte des Comtes at St-Sernin in Toulouse. The inner capitals have eagles and lions, and the outer ones the *Sacrifice of Abraham*, the *Temptation of Adam and Eve, Lazarus and Dives*, and the *Punishment of the Sinful*. The east end is also richly decorated. The nave has three bays with cruciform pillars and aisles. The belfry collapsed at some point, bringing down the cupola, and was rebuilt, as was the apse. There are a number of carved capitals of varying degrees of sophistication: at the entrance to the choir are two storiated capitals, *Jacob and Esau* and *Daniel in the Lions' Den*; at the crossing, a rare floral motif, eagles, and lions rampant, influenced by Moissac. Several of the nave capitals are of a more traditional design, and include dragons with crossed tails and the *Sacrifice of Abraham*.

PRACTICAL INFORMATION

• **By train:** Millau to St-Affrique.
• **By bus:** Millau to St-Affrique, regular service via St-Rome-du-Tarn, St-Rome-de-Cernon.

Alban 21 Pl. des Tilleuls, T: 05 63 55 93 90/out of season: Maison des Monts d'Alban, 2 Grand'rue,
T: 05 63 79 26 70
Ambialet Le Bourg, T: 05 63 55 39 14, www.si-ambialet.fr
Coupiac, Syndicat d'Initiative des Sept Vallons, Le Château, T: 05 65 99 78 82, email: 7vallons@wanadoo.fr
Lacaune Pl. Général-de-Gaulle,
T: 05 63 37 04 98, www.lacaune.com
Lacaze, T: 05 63 37 27 18
Lac du Laouzas Ferme de Rieumontagné, Nages, T: 05 63 37 06 01, www.lac-du-laouzas.com
Murat-sur-Vèbre Pl. de la Mairie,
T: 05 63 37 47 47,
mairie.murat81@wanadoo.fr
Rivière-sur-Tarn, T: 05 65 59 74 28, www.ot-gorgesdutarn.com
St-Juéry Plateau du Saut-du-Tarn, 26 Rue Germain-Téqui, T: 05 63 45 97 07, si-saintjuery@wanadoo.fr
St-Pierre de Trivisy Pl. de la Carriérasse, T: 05 63 50 48 69, otstpierretrivisy@free.fr

Ambialet
€ **Hôtel Du Pont**. A tried and trusted hotel-restaurant in the same family for more than two centuries, overlooking the Tarn at the entrance to this charming village. The rooms are not expensive and have river views. Meals are served in the dining room around the fireplace in winter, or on the terrace overlooking the Tarn in summer and the cooking is based on local ingredients, such as *Gigot et côtes d'Agneau, compotée provençale et ail rose de Lautrec*; menus range from €20–50. Pont d'Ambialet, T: 05 63 55 32 07, www.hotel-du-pont.com

Brousse-le-Château
€ **Relays du Chasteau**. On the banks of the Tarn at the foot of the castle is this modest but comfortable hotel. The restaurant offers a very reasonably priced set menu of local fare, rustic and satisfying. T: 05 65 99 40 15.

Compeyre
€ **Chambres d'hôtes ferme-auberge de Quiers**. The farmhouse clings to the cliffs in a tranquil spot on the edge of the Causses. The six rooms, in the converted barn have direct access to the exterior. The *table d'hôtes* is served in a rustic dining room. T: 05 65 59 85 10, www.ifrance.com/quiers

Gissac
€ **Hôtel Château de Gissac**. Splendid medieval château on the Rougier de Camarès, converted into a reasonably comfortable hotel, and in a spectacular position surrounded by wooded grounds with formal gardens and a large heated pool. Near Sylvanès, T: 05 65 98 14 60, www.chateau.gissac.com

Peyreleau
€ **Hôtel La Muse et du Rozier**. The site is tremendous, perched on wooded cliffs above the Tarn. Interior spaces are

calm, clear and light, themed around black and white with 35 uncluttered rooms. There is a spacious restaurant and vast terraces take advantage of the panoramas. The food served is as stylish as the rest of the hotel, a synthesis of modern and traditional, such as *confit de canard laqué au citron* or *petit* or *soufflé de truite rose et son jus de crustacés*. T: 05 65 52 60 01, www.hotel-delamuse.com

€ **Chambres d'hôtes la Grange Templière**. This is a handsome house of 1900 with a fine stone staircase, restored to maintain its character. The 4 pretty rooms have double beds; three of them have additional single beds. The convivial *table d'hôtes* is part of the pleasure of this house; the meals are prepared from good produce and cooked with care. Leslie Linarès, T: 05 65 61 82 09, http://leslie.linares.free.fr//

Plaisance

€ **Hôtel Les Magnolias**. ■ This delightful 14th-century house was once the home of Paul Valéry (1871-1945), poet turned mathematician and art and music critic. There are 22 bedrooms, slightly old-fashioned, but the setting is very pretty with a garden and pool. In the stone-vaulted restaurant the chef, William Nivoliez, proposes light and simple food which combines Aveyronnais, Mediterranean and Asian cooking. There is also a brasserie and terrace. A full English breakfast is available. T: 05 65 99 48 70, www.hostellerie-les-magnolias.com

St-Sernin-sur-Rance

€ **Hôtel Carayon**. Hotel-restaurant set in a park with a pool. Half the 60 quietly pleasant rooms have balconies overlooking the gardens. There are plenty of activities in and around the hotel. Pl. du Fort, T: 05 65 98 19 19, www.hotel-carayon.fr

Villeneuve-sur-Tarn

€ **Hostellerie des Lauriers**. In the village with grounds which stretch to the Tarn, the bar is part of local life and in the garden is a covered pool and jacuzzi. The nine bedrooms have recently been redecorated and the food is good simple fare including river fish and wild mushrooms. T: 05 63 55 84 23, www.host.des.lauriers.free.fr

MARKET DAYS

Alban 1st Tuesday of month; July-August, evening market
Ambialet July-August Wednesday; July, August evening market
Camarès July-August, Wednesday
Coupiac July-August Wednesday, Monday evening
Lacaune Sunday July-August Friday
Murat-sur-Vèbre 2nd Saturday of the month
St-Juéry Thursday
St-Pierre de Trivisy Last Monday of month
St-Rome de Tarn Tuesday

FESTIVALS & EVENTS

July–August: *Festival de la Vallée et les Gorges du Tarn*, Music festival, T: 05 65 52 60 99
Festival International de Musique Sacrée, Sylvanès, T: 05 65 98 20 20
Festival des 'Conteurs de Païs', Local Legends, Wednesdays, Pays des Sept Vallons (around Coupiac), T: 05 65 99 78 82

SOUTHERN TARN

The Agout, a tributary of the Tarn, crosses the southern part of the *département* linking the towns of Castres, built in stone, and Lavaur, mainly a brick town. The vineyards of Gaillac (*see p. 272*), north of Lavaur, give way to arable crops of maize, sunflowers and, around Lautrec and Réalmont, garlic in undulating landscapes encompassing the strange granite outcrop the Sidobre. The southern Tarn is under the spell of the densely wooded Montagne Noire that forms a barrier with the more Mediterranean Languedoc-Roussillon. The Park Régional du Haut Languedoc spans the two *départements* of the Tarn and the Aude.

CASTRES

Castres is a pleasant, leafy, prosperous town on the banks of the Agout River. Comparable in size to Albi, it is less exciting visually but has a charm and character of its own and a friendly market. The town also owns an important collection of Spanish art exhibited in the Goya museum. An international arts festival is held here during August.

HISTORY OF CASTRES

A vital stage on the *Via Tolosane* to Santiago (*see p. 11*), holding relics of St Vincent of Saragossa in an 11th-century basilica, Castres had a major Cathar community at the end of the 12th century but avoided major damage during the Albigensian crusades by submitting to the crusading armies (*see p. 251*). The town came under the control of the de Montforts in 1229 and was elevated to a bishopric by Pope John XXII in 1317, a status it maintained until 1801. The town enthusiastically embraced Calvinism to become a Protestant place of safety second only in the region to Montauban. In 1576 Henri IV helped the peaceful return of the Catholics with the institution of the Chambre de l'Edit to legislate over sectarian disputes. Between the Edict of Alès (1629) and the Revocation of the Edict of Nantes (1685) Castres enjoyed its most brilliant period: the population increased, monasteries were reinstated and most of the town was rebuilt. Architects from the Ile de France were introduced to build a new episcopal palace and design a garden typical of the Grand Siècle. In the mid-19th century, Castres was the birthplace of the influential socialist politician and pacifist, Jean Jaurès (*see box on p. 308*).

EXPLORING CASTRES

Bishop's Palace

The former Bishops' Palace is used by the Hôtel de Ville and the Goya museum. Jules Hardouin-Mansart (1646–1708), architect to Louis XIV, drew up the plans for this soberly Classical building, inaugurated in 1675. Around three sides of a courtyard with a monumental staircase, the unadorned façade serves as a backdrop to the dark greens of the yew trees and box hedges of the formal garden designed by the king's gardener, André Le Nôtre (1613–1700). Planted on the site of the southern ramparts and ditch, the garden began to take shape in 1696. The knot-gardens nearest the palace have box hedges trimmed into a *fleur-de-lis* pattern and the yews have a variety of designs. The avenue of limes along the river had to be replanted to replace the originals a few years ago; the chestnuts are some 95 years old. The municipal theatre, close to the museum, opened in 1904 and is an imposing Belle-Epoque building designed by Joseph Galinier of Toulouse, a pupil of Garnier, designer of the Paris Opéra; it was restored in 1982.

Musée Goya

Open July, Aug 10-6; April–June, Sept, 9–12 & 2–6, closed Mon; Oct–March 9–12 & 2–5, Sun 10–12 & 2–5, closed Mon; T: 05 63 71 59 30,
www.ville-castres.fr/www.goya.castres.museum.
On the first floor of the bishops' palace, overlooking Le Notre's garden, this tranquil museum has an excellent collection of Spanish works, arranged chronologically. Inspired by the donation in 1893 of three paintings and complete sets of etchings by Goya which had belonged to the local painter Marcel Briguiboul (1837–92), the museum has concentrated on Spanish works since 1947. Regional funding since 1972 has helped to make this one of the most important Spanish collections in France and the museum often holds temporary exhibitions with a Spanish emphasis.

I: Works by the Spanish primitives (14th–15th centuries) are among some of the most beautiful in the museum, and testify to a variety of influences. Among them, the *Crucifixion and Transfiguration of Christ on Mount Tabor between Moses and Elijah* showing Flemish influence, is attributed to Joan Rexach, who worked in Valencia 1431–84; in the style of International Gothic is the *Flagellation of Christ,* attributed to the Catalan artist Luis Borassa (c. 1360–1425); a small, expressive work, *St John the Evangelist on the Island of Patmos* (1431; *pictured on p. 307*), is a panel from a triptych (the central panel is in the Thyssen collection in Madrid). It is a late work by Joan Mates (fl. 1391–c. 1431) who worked in Barcelona cathedral and was influenced by Franco-Flemish manuscript illumination; and a later, more

Murillo: *Virgin Mary with a Rosary* (c. 1650) in the Musée Goya.

sophisticated painting *The Adoration of the Magi* (c. 1508–20) by Alejo Fernandez, a German who settled in Saville, which shows the influence of northern Europe. It has been suggested that one of the kneeling figures may be a portrait of Christopher Columbus.

II: A large part of the collection is devoted to the 'Golden Age' of Spanish painting in the 17th century, and includes a replica of the Prado *Portrait of Philip IV* (1634–36) attributed to Velázquez, and a sweetly gentle *Virgin Mary with a Rosary* (c. 1650; *pictured opposite*) by Murillo, who specialised in child portraits as well as paintings of the Virgin Mary. His work became very popular in 18th-century England, most notably influencing Thomas Gainsborough and Joshua Reynolds among others. Also here is Francisco de Zurbaran's *Carthusian Martyr* (c. 1636), as well as a large work by Francisco Pacheco, *Christ Served by the Angels in*

the Desert (1615–16). There are also works by Claudio Coello, Juan de Valdés and Alonso Cano.

III: The room dedicated to Goya has three of his works and also paintings inspired by him. The masterpiece is the calm, self-assured *Self-Portrait with Glasses* (c. 1797–1800), painted some years after the illness that left him deaf; the second portrait is of Don Francisco del Mazo (c. 1815). Filling the whole of the end wall of the gallery is the huge *Session of the Royal Company of the Philippines* (1815), an atmospheric work with a veiled criticism of bureaucracy.

IV: The museum also owns original prints by Goya from his series *Los Capricos*, the *Disasters of War*, and *Los Proverbios*, as well as the *Tauromaquia*. Among the modern Spanish works is a small drawing (1903) by Picasso and his *Portrait of a Man Writing* (1971).

The cathedral

The courtyard behind the Bishop's Palace and museum contains the Tour St-Benoit (c. 1100) on the northwest side, the last remaining fragment of the abbey of St-Benoit, with a 17th-century roof. Opposite is the large and ordered south flank of the Baroque Cathedral St-Benoit. Begun in 1678 and consecrated in 1718, the project was never completed to the specifications originally envisaged by the architect Guillaume Caillau. The interior is rather dull despite the *trompe l'oeil* decoration, although there is some good woodwork and a number of large 18th-century paintings by local artists, François Cammas, Le Chevalier de Rivalz, and Jean-Baptiste Despax. The coloured marble altar of 1763 is covered by a grandiose baldaquin made in 1768 by the Cailhive workshop.

At the east end of the exterior of the cathedral the space is enhanced by an elegant 19th-century colonnade made from columns salvaged from the old abbey and a small square, Place du 8-Mai-1945, which was the only sizeable square in the town centre before the Revolution. Passage St-Vincent opens into one of the main commercial streets, Rue Alquier-Bouffand, which was almost entirely rebuilt after a fire in 1724.

Joan Mates: *St John the Evangelist on the Island of Patmos* (1431) in the Musée Goya.

Pont Neuf to Place Pélisson

The Pont Neuf is the best place to enjoy the famous view of the colourful craftsmen's houses on the banks of the Agout, the painted timber façades creating the most original and emblematic feature of the town. They stand on large arcaded stone cellars (perhaps 14th century) opening directly into the river. In a region where the economy was based on leather and textiles, these houses were once the homes and workshops of tanners, weavers and dyers and their restoration began in 1979. The Quai des Jacobins, north of the Pont Neuf, also offers another good view of them, and there are short boat rides from across the Pont Vieux.

The market is held on Place Jean-Jaurès, a tree-lined square created in the medieval heart of Castres in 1872, graced with a pretty fountain with angels at one end and a statue of Jaurès (*see box on p. 308*) at the other.

One of the finest houses in Castres is the **Hôtel de Nayrac** (now belonging to a Société Générale) on Rue Frédérick-Thomas. It was built in 1620 by a wealthy draper, Jean Oulès, using brick and stone in the manner of the Renaissance mansions of Toulouse or Albi. The three linked façades have elegantly decorated dormers, and the main entrance, flanked by paired Doric pilasters with a huge coat of arms, is on the right. The plaster has been removed from the 17th-century façades of no. 14 uncovering the timber frame, known in Castres as *corondat*.

Place Pélisson is a small, smart junction close to the Hôtel de Nayrac decorated with a fountain. Attractively installed here in an old printing works since 1988 is the **Musée Jean-Jaurès** (*open 9–12 & 2–6; Oct–March open until 5; closed Mon except July, Aug, and Sun from Nov–March; T: 05 63 72 01 01, www.jaures.fr.fm*). The museum has a permanent exhibition of the life and work of Jaurès (*see box below*), contains a documentation centre, and holds temporary exhibitions.

JEAN JAURÈS (1859–1914)

Socialist leader, parliamentary orator, journalist and historian, Jean Jaurès was born in Castres on 3rd September 1859. Republican Deputy (member of the Chambres des Députés, now the Assemblée Nationale) for the Tarn in 1885, in 1889–93 he turned to socialism and championed causes such as the miners' strikes in Carmaux, the independence of the glassworkers in Albi (*see p. 263*), and Alfred Dreyfus, falsely accused of spying for Germany in 1894. He was described as the apostle of peace but his pacifist ideals led to his assassination on the eve of the First World War, on 31st July 1914. Although buried in Albi, his remains were transferred to the Panthéon in Paris in 1924, the only native of the Tarn to be buried there.

Eglise de la Platé

On Rue des Boursiers, behind Hôtel de Nayrac, there is a string of 16th- and 17th-century façades between nos 4 and 14; no. 1 has a late Gothic doorway. Rue de l'Hôtel-de-Ville and the parallel Rue Emile Zola are linked by another old street, Rue Victor-Hugo, site of Castres' second religious monument, the Eglise de la Platé, rebuilt in 1743 by the Jesuits. The accomplished Italianate façade on Rue Victor-Hugo superimposes Doric and Ionic orders and the Florentine-style campanile can best be seen from Rue de la Platé. The Baroque interior has a grandiose main altar flanked by six red marble columns supporting a canopy and the retable in Carrara marble of an *Assumption of the Virgin* by Italian artists (1754). There are paintings by the Despax, of the *Visitation* and *Annunciation*. The superb organ, with a sumptuous gilded case supported by atlantes and adorned with angel musicians, was installed in 1764 and decorated by a local artist called Chabbert. It was restored in 1980 and is used for concerts.

Opposite, in Rue de la Chambre de l'Edit, is the Hôtel de Viviès (1585), considered one of the finest pieces of late Renaissance architecture in the town, although with Baroque additions. It now serves as the Centre d'Art Contemporain (*open July–Aug 10–1 & 2–6; Sept–June Tues–Fri 10–12 & 2–5.30, Sat, Sun, 3–6; closed Mon and holidays; T: 05 63 59 30 20*). Rue Tolosane, at the west end of Rue de la Chambre-de-l'Edit, is flanked by two piers of the old Porte Tolosane. .

Notre-Dame de l'Esperance

On the eastern edge of town, in the Lardaille district (direction Sidobre) on Blvd Giraud, is the church of Notre-Dame de l'Esperance, which contains a monumental (12m) modern work of the *Apocalypse of St John at Patmos* (from 1970) by Gaston-Louis Marchal, a follower of Ossip Zadkine (*see p. 174*), in 84 panels executed in pen and ink and watercolour crayons.

THE SIDOBRE

Immediately northeast of Castres is the granite plateau of the Sidobre (600–700m), on the edge of the Massif Central. Wooded in places, with scrubby moorland or marsh elsewhere, it is characterised by strange biomorphic rock formations: giant granite boulders, smoothed and rounded by time, isolated or in a tumbled confusion called a *chaos*, have acquired descriptive names such as *Roc de l'Oie* (Goose), *Trois Fromages*, or *Chapeau du Curé*. These natural phenomena of the Sidobre are best seen along the D30 and D58.

Burlats

In a wooded area beside the Agout is Burlats. The church of St-Pierre, once part of a large Benedictine priory founded c. 1160, was wrecked during the Wars of Religion. The sacristy on the north is occupied by the *Mairie* and the remains of the Romanesque cloisters are now the schoolyard. The east end of the Romanesque church is mainly intact, as is the north transept door in the form of a triumphal arch with the remains of two carved capitals, one with birds, the other peopled. The west door has a similar but more elaborate arrangement with a triple portal and seven vigorously sculpted capitals. The skeletal ruin of the nave is separated from the chancel by a double transverse arch and some of the capitals, decorated with heads and volutes, have survived.

Standing isolated near the river is the ravishing **Pavillon de Adélaïde** (*open July-Aug, 2.30-6.30, closed Tues; T:: 05 63 35 07 83, www.burlats.com*), a rare masterpiece of Romanesque secular architecture, named after a legendary lady remembered in the songs of troubadours. A simple rectangular stone building carefully restored, its outstanding features are the beautiful two-light windows on the upper floor—four on the south façade and one on the west—carved with a variety of motifs. The floors are divided by string courses on which the upper windows rest. The first floor has large and small openings, and at ground level are three arched openings (as found at Figeac or Cordes). The Bistoure tower to the east was part of the Gothic ramparts, and near the bridge is the 12th-century Maison d'Adam with the outlines of one Romanesque window.

Vabre

A winding route along the Agout runs through wooded gorges for 21km to the little schist town of Vabre overlooking the Gijou, once an important textile centre, its medieval bridge revised in the 19th century. A few kilometres beyond is the château at Ferrières, the grandiose home of the Calvinist leader, Guillaume Guilhot, governor of Castres in 1562. The medieval castle was revamped over several centuries and brought up-to-date in the early Renaissance. Opposite is the **Musée du Protestantisme en Haut-Languedoc** (*open July–mid–Sept 10–12 & 3–7, closed Tues, Sun; April–June, mid-Sept–Nov, Sun and holidays 2–6; T: 05 63 74 05 49*), which follows the history of the Huguenots from the beginning of the Reformation in the Haut Languedoc, where the Reform took a strong hold, and despite tremendous persecution after the Revocation of the Edict of Nantes, pockets of Calvinism have survived in the region. The museum owns an important library.

THE MONTAGNE NOIRE

The Montagne Noire creates a barrier between the Atlantic and Mediterranean landscapes, and the boundary between the regions of Midi-Pyrénées and Languedoc-Roussillon; and its rocky outcrops were a place of refuge for the Cathars (*see p. 13*). From the Pic de Nore (1210m) you can see the Monts de Lacaune (*see p. 296*) to the north and the Pyrenees to the south. Mazamet is the gateway to the Parc Régionale du Haut-Languedoc, which encompasses the Montagne Noire. The park comprises 145,000 hectares of great natural beauty and is a walking centre *par excellence* with 1800km of signposted paths. The force of the mountain torrents of this beautiful landscape was soon harnessed to run mills, forges and pressing machines. By the 17th century, paper milling and textiles were major industries in the Thoré and Sor valleys, and many relics of the industrial past are still visible.

MAZAMET

The main conurbation of the area, tucked under the Montagne Noire, is Mazamet. It developed on the banks of the Arnette and is an essentially 19th- and 20th-century town where the roads from Narbonne and Carcassonne meet. Much influenced by the ideas of the Reformation, it still has a Protestant community: the Protestant Temple is indicated by the medieval tower of St-Jacques. The Catholic church of St-Sauveur was built in 1740. Maison Fuzier, Rue des Casernes, which contains the Tourist Office, is also the Maison des Mémoires. A typical 19th-century Mazamet house, two rooms on the ground floor are decorated in the style of the period. Upstairs is the the Musée du Catharisme Occitan (*open June–Sept 2.30–7; March–April, Oct–Dec Wed, Sat, Sun 2.30–6.30; T: 05 63 61 27 07*), a new permanent exhibition which approaches the controversial history of Catharism over three centuries. It presents the form in which this version of Christianity took hold, the daily life of Good Men and Women, and their persecution, using evidence discovered at Hautpoul (*see p. 311*).

Mazamet's wealth in the 19th and early 20th centuries is reflected in numerous mansions set in gardens and protected by high walls to the south of Place de l'Hôtel-de-Ville; some have a little house for the concièrge at the gate. The owners, often Protestant, had made their fortunes from *délainage*, which involved detaching the fleece from hides bought cheaply and imported from as far away as Argentina and

Australia. The town was already experienced in textiles, and this complicated process benefited from the pure water and hydraulic power available from the Arnette. The hides were either tanned locally or sold to Graulhet (*see p. 315*). The production of textiles was bolstered by orders for army uniforms, and such was the quality of the wool that the export trade soon flourished. Mazamet's population grew c.1815–50 from 3,000 to some 7,000 and workers' housing was built in Les Centenaires on the way up to Hautpoul. A branch of the Banque de France was opened here in 1902. In time mechanisation was introduced and production shifted to modern textiles. Entrepreneurs built their factories close to their houses, some of which still stand; the last factory closed in 2001.

ENVIRONS OF MAZAMET

Beyond Mazamet towards Béziers at **Labastide Rouairoux**, the Musée du Textile (*open May–Oct 10–12 & 2–6, closed Tues; Nov–April 2–6, closed Mon, Tues; closed Jan; T: 05 63 98 08 60*) attests to the importance of textiles to the Vallée du Thoré from the 19th century to the present day and the evolution of technology; there are demonstrations of old skills by former employees, as well as computer aided design.

Two roads climb steeply out of Mazamet into the forest to reach **Hautpoul**, a picturesque village along one street on the side of the hill. The vertiginous site above the Arnette Valley is typical of Cathar strongholds. It was fortified by Pierre Raymond d'Hautpoul in the 12th century, besieged by Simon de Montfort in 1212 (*see p. 251*), then ravaged during the Wars of Religion; parts have since been salvaged and houses are gradually being restored. In recent years it has been reanimated by the presence of a number of wood carvers whose workshops can be visited. The Maison du Bois et du Jouet (*open July–Aug 2–6; Jan–June, Oct–Dec 2–6 Wed, Sat, Sun; T: 05 63 61 42 70*), has a remarkable collection of wooden games and toys and activities for children.

Labruguière,

Labruguière, an industrial centre between Castres and Mazamet, has at its heart an ancient town built in concentric circles. It is also home to the **Musée Arthur Batut** (*open Wed–Sat 3–6.30; closed Tues; T: 05 63 50 22 18*), dedicated to the inventor of kite aerial photography

Arthur Batut (1846–1918): Self-Portrait

The town of Labruguière, photographed from the air by Arthur Batut using a kite in 1896.

(in 1888) who was born in Castres in 1846. A polymath and autodidact, Batut was a keen archaeologist, associated with the Lumière brothers, the founders of the cinema, and took colour photographs in 1887. He also developed the super-imposition of multiple images into 'portrait-types', anticipating modern morphing techniques. His pioneering experiments with aerial photography made him the leading specialist in the field by the turn of the century. Memorabilia on display here includes his photographic equipment and the kites to which he attached his heavy cameras, complete with a slow-burning fuse designed to trip the shutter.

SORÈZE & ENVIRONS

Sorèze, enclosed within avenues of plane trees, is a prosperous small town with jettied houses. The crenellated tower and octagonal belfry of St-Martin, towering above the college and the village, are all that remains of the 15th-century parish church except for the fragment of the apse below, open and unprotected since the church disappeared, exposing the Flamboyant decoration in the interior. The parish Church of Notre-Dame de la Paix is 19th-century and contains Lacordaire's tomb (*see below*). On Allée de la Liberation, the Maison du Parc (*open summer 2.30–6.30, closed Tues; winter Sun and holidays 2–6; T: 05 63 74 11 58*), is an archaeological museum and temporary exhibition space. The most important monument in Sorèze is the **Abbaye Ecole de Sorèze** (*open April–Sept 10–12 & 2–6, guided visits 3 and 4.30; Oct–March 10–12 & 2–6; audio guides available all year; T: 05 63 50 86 38, www.abbayeecoledesoreze.com*), a prestigious private school from 1682 until 1991, on the site of a Benedictine abbey founded early in the 9th century. Affiliated to Moissac in 1119, and totally destroyed during the Wars of Religion, it was rebuilt by the Congregation of St-Maur in 1637. By 1757 it had gained a solid reputation for the Benedictine teaching methods and was consequently elevated to royal military establishment in 1776. During the Revolution the monastery was dissolved, but secular schooling continued. Henri-Dominique Lacordaire (1802–61), priest, journalist and educator from Paris, who revived the Dominican Order in France after its dissolution in 1790, took over the academy in 1854. His leadership added to the institution's reputation, attracting pupils from all over the world. It remained in the hands of the Dominicans until 1978. Of the old school buildings, 9 rooms, exterior spaces and the park, can be visited. The Salle des Illustres contains busts of alumini and was used for special gatherings. The very simple 19th-century chapel, Lacordaire's apartment, a dormitory and a museum of architecture can also be visited. A music festival is held here in the summer.

Dourgne and Les Cammazes

Dourgne, a small town with a large fountain and arcades, has two working Benedictine abbeys, Ste-Scholastique (1895 and 1927) and St-Benoît-d'En-Calcat (1890–1936). A former member of the community here, Dom Robert (1907–97), was well-known for his designs for tapestries and murals (one can be seen in the church at Massaguel nearby) throughout France and also at the French church in London. A winding route goes up from here to the little mountain village of Arfons (660m) on the pilgrimage route.

Large reservoirs at Cammazes and St-Ferréol supply water to the Canal du Midi (*see p. 555*). At **Les Cammazes** is an exceptional structure known as the Voute de Vauban which spans one of the *rigoles* carrying water from the lake to the canal. The whole system is now a UNESCO World Heritage site.

THE AGOUT

The triangle between Albi, Toulouse and Castres, bisected by the River Agout, is the edge of the old Lauragais which runs south to Revel. The history of the area is marked by the religious strife of the Albigensian crusades and the Reformation, and the phenomenal commercial success of the blue dye from a plant known here as *pastel* (*see box on p. 315*) in the 15th and 16th centuries. Although no longer cultivated on a large scale, varieties of the plant can still be seen. The fertile land and warm, humid climate now benefit the cultivation of garlic, maize, sunflowers and oil seed rape.

LAVAUR

Lavaur is a small town, built in brick like Albi and Gaillac, and still in the throes of regeneration. The most outstanding monument here is the Gothic cathedral on a sheer cliff above the Agout, surrounded by pleasant gardens and a high terrace overlooking the river and the old port. The town was a Cathar stronghold and suffered the wrath of the crusaders in the 12th century (*see p. 251*).

Cathedral of St-Alain

The Cathedral of St-Alain replaced an earlier church all but destroyed by Simon de Montfort (*see p. 251*). In 1255, the city fathers, in the presence of the Inquisitors, undertook to build a new church and five bays had been completed by 1317 when the town was elevated to episcopal see. The exterior walls between the buttresses were added in the 14th century and the two southeast chapels in 1450. The massive west end closely resembles Albi cathedral, although more squared, and it has a truncated octagonal tower added at the end of the 15th century. The disproportionately small east end, sheer above the river, has two undistinguished little turrets. On the small south belfry is a famous *jacquemart*, who hits his bell with a hammer every hour. There has been one here since 1604, but the present oak figure dates from 1922, the bell from 1523.

The interior

The simple interior has a single nave with shallow chapels on the north, extended on the south in the 15th century. It was damaged at the Revolution and restored 1843–47 when the grisaille and coloured *trompe l'oeil* decoration was added by Italian painters called Ceroni. Importantly the cathedral has salvaged the 12th-century altar table, a relic of the first church, sculpted with a eucharistic theme on the chamfer, notably similar to the altar table at St-Sernin in Toulouse (*see p. 589*) and the capitals of Moissac (*see p. 333*). Also from the first church is the Romanesque porch, conserved in the first chapel on the right; the carved capitals show scenes from the *Childhood of Christ* (the first and last are 19th-century plaster replicas). An organ was installed in 1523 and the magnificent organ case has been restored. When the instrument was remade by Aristide Cavaillé-Col in 1874, certain elements were added, notably the volutes, vases and balustrade, as well as a coating of dark varnish which has now been removed to reveal the original 16th-century colours. Other fittings in the Cathedral include the mausoleum of Bishop Simon de Beausoleil (d. 1531); a wooden painted and gilded *Pietà* (17th century); six paintings of *Scenes of the Passion* (18th century), attributed to Pierre Subleyras; the main altar in polychrome marble; the wrought-iron lectern signed by Bernard Ortet (1778), who worked at the cathedral of St-Etienne in Toulouse (*see p. 603*); and the 19th-century pulpit. The stained glass of the choir is dated 1853–54.

The town

From the handsome Mairie west of the church, Rue Villeneuve takes you past Le Plô, the site of the old castle which fell to Simon de Montfort in 1211. A wiggly route through the small streets beside the Maison Occitane on Rue Père-Colin and left across Place du Vieux Marché, comes out at the Tour des Rondes, a sturdy brick and stone bastion (1250) now housing the Tourist Office, in a section of the old fortifications. The modern market hall is on the edge of the old town south of the Tour des Rondes. Rue Viel will bring you back to the Grand' Rue and the Cordelier Church of St-François, built in the 14th century and restored in the 19th century.

ENVIRONS OF LAVAUR

Giroussens, downstream on the Agout northeast of Lavaur, began in the 12th century as a fort defending the castle of the Viscounts of Albi in a strategic position overlooking the river. It was granted the privileges of a *bastide* in the 13th century, and became a pottery town. Ceramicists are still working here, at the Maison de la Céramique Contemporaine (*open July, Aug 10–12 & 2–7; Sept–June 2–6, closed Mon; closed mid-Jan–mid-Feb; T: 05 63 41 68 22*). The 15th-century church was repaired and amended in the 17th century, and contains two retables of that period; and the main retable in wood (18th century), sumptuously decorated and gilded, has a painting of the Crucifixion.

On the opposite left bank, at **St-Lieux-les-Lavaur**, a *Petit Train Touristique* with steam and diesel engines chugs 7km a round trip (*open 2.30–5.30, departures every hour; 1st to 15th Aug daily; mid to end-July, and mid to end-Aug, Sat, Sun, Mon, and holidays; Easter to mid-July, Sun; T: 05 61 47 44 52*).

Southwest of St-Paul-Cap-de-Joux, upstream of Lavour, is the Renaissance **Château de Magrin**, at the heart of the Pays de Cocagne housing the Musée du Pastel (*open July–Aug 10.30–12 & 3–6; Sept 3–6; check opening times on T: 05 63 70 63 82*), which tells the story of the blue dye, its cultivation, production and use. It also has rare examples of a drying rack and grinding mill.

PASTEL

Isatis tinctoria (also known as Persian blue or Dyer's woad, and in French as pastel) is a cruciferous plant producing a very high-quality blue or indigo dye. From the 15th century it was cultivated intensively in the damp valleys of the Lauragais, east of Toulouse. Its use was extremely labour intensive and involved harvesting the leaves, not the yellow flowers, of the plant, twice a year. They were reduced to a pulp, dried, and compressed into balls called *coques* (which gave rise to the expression in this region *le pays de cocagne* or 'land of plenty'). The *coques* could remain drying in this form for up to a year and then the cycle continued, with crushing, reduction, and fermentation for another 4–5 months. The raw material was exported all over Northern Europe for the dyeing trade and was in such demand that it brought enormous wealth to the region until the mid-16th century. The combination of a market crash in London and Anvers in 1561, the Wars of Religion, and the importation of indigo from the Americas, caused the bottom to fall out of the pastel industry by the end of the century.

Graulhet, Réalmont and Teillet

Between Gaillac and Lautrec is Graulhet, which at one time was an important leather-producing centre. The skills of the industry are revealed at the Maison des Métiers du Cuir (*guided visit and temporary exhibitions; July–Aug 10–12 & 2-6; May–June, Sept–Oct*

2–6, closed Sat, Sun; T: 05 63 42 16 04). Further east, half-way between Albi and Castres, Réalmont is a 13th-century *bastide* with an arcaded square. To the northeast at Teillet is the curiously romantic vision of the ruins of the Château de Grandval, half-submerged when the Rassise dam was constructed.

Lautrec

There is a stunning view of the hilltop village of Lautrec from the D92—when approaching from the south—and panoramas on all sides including the Montagne Noire to the south. There may also be a hint of garlic in the air. The region's 380 producers grow pink garlic with an AOC at the rate of 4,000 tonnes a year from 1,000 hectares here, one-tenth of the production of France. Kept in a cool place, it will last up to a year. Inside the village the streets are lined with some well-maintained 16th- and 17th-century timber-framed houses with jetties or arcades and, still intact, on the east side of the town are parts of the old ramparts and one of the eight original gateways, Porte de la Caussade. The church of St-Rémy was begun in the 15th century, vaulted in 1769, and is decorated with 19th-century *trompe l'oeil* and false marbling. Behind the church in Rue de St-Esprit, off the Grande Rue, are the steps up to one of the main attractions of Lautrec, the still-turning 17th-century Moulin à vent de la Salette (*open July, Aug 2.30–7; Sept–June, Sun and holidays only 3–5; T: 05 63 75 31 40*).

PRACTICAL INFORMATION

GETTING AROUND

• **By train:** Between Toulouse and Mazamet via St-Sulpice, Lavaur, Castres; between Albi and Castres via Lautrec.
• **By bus:** Rodez to Carcassonne via Castres and Revel; Toulouse to Mazamet via Castres; Mazamet to St-Pons; Sorèze to Castelnaudary (Aude) via Revel.

TOURIST INFORMATION

Agout (Val de) Rue de Strasbourg, St-Paul Cap de Joux, T: 05 63 70 52 10
Anglès Chalet, Route de St-Pons, T: 05 63 74 59 13
Brassac Hôtel de Ville, Le Bourg, T: 05 63 74 56 97
Les Cammazes 25 rue de la Fontaine, T: 05 63 74 17 17
Castres Rue Milhau-Ducommun, T: 05 63 62 63 62, www.ville-castres.fr
Dourgne 1 Av. du Maquis, T: 05 63 74 27 19, www.paysdedourgne-tourisme.com
Graulhet 1 Sq. Maréchal Foch, T: 05 63 34 75 09, graulhet.ot@wanadoo.fr
Labastide Rouairoux 47 ter Blvd Carnot, BP 43, T: 05 63 98 07 58, www.labastide-rouairoux.com
Labruguière Pl. de l'Europe, T: 05 63 50 17 21, www.ville-labruguiere.com
Lautrec Rue du Mercadial, T: 05 63 75 31 40, http://lautrec.free.fr

Lavaur Tour des Rondes,
T: 05 63 58 02 00, www.ville-lavaur.fr
Mazamet Rue des Casernes,
T: 05 63 61 27 07,
www.ville-mazamet.com
Montredon Labessonnié 21 Grand
Rue, BP 3, T: 05 63 75 18 65/05 63 75
14 18, syndicatdinitiative
2004@yahoo.fr
Puylaurens 2 Rue de la Mairie,
T: 05 63 75 28 98,
puylaurens.tourisme@wanadoo.fr
Réalmont 8 Pl.de la République,
T: 05 63 79 05 45, email office-
tourisme-realmont@wanadoo.fr
St-Sulpice la Pointe Parc George
Spénale, T: 05 63 41 89 50,
www.ville-saint-sulpice-81.fr
Sidobre Paysage Sculpté, Maison du
Sidobre, Vialavert, T: 05 63 74 63 38,
sidobreOT@aol.com
Sorèze Rue St-Martin, BP 18, T: 05 63
74 16 28, www.ville-soreze.fr

ACCOMMODATION & RESTAURANTS

Burlats
€ **Le Castel de Burlats**. In the village
of Burlats on a turbulent stretch of the
Adour in the Sidobre, the hotel occupies a small 14th- and 15th-century
château set in a 3 hectare park. The 10
rooms are attractively furnished. There
is also a *salon de thé*. 8 Pl. du 8-Mai-
1945, T: 05 63 35 29 20,
www.lecasteldeburlats.fr.st
Castres
€ **Hôtel l'Europe**. Italian Baroque
decor in a 17th-century building in the
town centre with an abundance of
beams and exposed stone walls around
an interior patio; lots of staircases but
no lift. The 30 bedrooms have distinctive modern décor; some bathrooms
need renovation. The annexe, Le
Renaissance, at No 17, T: 05 63 59 30
42, is in an 18th-century building with
nicely furnished rooms featuring
exposed brick. 5 Rue Victor-Hugo, T:
05 63 59 00 33,
www.hotel-renaissance.fr
€ **La Table du Sommelier**. The wine
bar/restaurant has 250 wines and offers
cuisine du marché with menus from
€10–30. 6 Pl. Pélisson, T: 05 63 82 20
10. (*See also Albi, p. 276*).
Cuq-Toulza
€ **Cuq-en-Terrasses**. ■ The old house
on a terraced west-facing ridge has been
stunningly restored to provide 8 very
pretty bedrooms where no detail is
overlooked. Equal care and attention is
paid to the cooking (restaurant exclusively for hotel residents), which is light
and imaginative, incorporating seasonal
produce and introducing local specialities with a Greek twist, such as
Moussaka au canard. Meals in the garden
or in the atmospheric dining room.
Cuq-le-Château, T: 05 63 82 54 00,
www.cuqenterrasses.com.
Dourgne
€ **Hostellerie de la Montagne Noire**.
Member of the *cuisinières gourmandes*,
you can be sure of the quality of the
cooking '*entre montagne et campagne*'
ranging from charcuterie to fresh water
fish. A typical menu might be *Tourte
aux gésiers*, *Suprême de caille en croûte*,
Gratin de fraises à la crème. Menus from
€18–31 served in the restaurant or
under the plane trees on the terrace.
There are also 9 rooms. 15 Pl. des
Promenades, T: 05 63 50 31 12,
www. montagnenoire.net
€ **Chambres d'hôtes Les Peyrounels**.

A low house with a red-tiled roof in open countryside, with 3 hectares of meadows and endless vistas from the covered terrace and garden. Inside the emphasis is on white with touches of black or colour against exposed stone and old beams enhanced by the owner's souvenirs of ancient China. Three large bedrooms, for 2, 3 or 4 people, continue the restful colour scheme. Alpacas, horses and dogs on the property. Françoise Corcelle, T: 05 63 74 29 87, www.lespeyrounels.com

Lacrouzette
€ **Auberge de Cremaussel**. ■ Gilbert Houles cooks the most wonderful *soupe au chou*, and the rest of his cooking likewise is straightforward, simple and hearty with menus priced €15–22. The rustic auberge is deep in the Sidobre, perfect for hikers and has five *chambres d'hôtes*. Closed in January. T: 05 63 50 61 33.

Labessière-Candeil
€ **Le Pigeonnier**. Marc Ferrand run this restaurant in a restored *pigeonnier* in a lovely setting on the edge of a lake. The menus €16–56 offer inventive and varied dishes such as *Râble de lapin désossé puis confit, gaufrette de campagne; Canon d'Agneau rôti au beurre, fleur de thym et douce moutarde de Brive*; and *Petit chèvre au miel et poivre de Széchuan*. La Ginestarié (3km north of Graulhet), T: 05 63 4 08 04, www.pigeonnier-restaurant.fr

Lautrec
Chambres d'hôtes La Terrasse de Lautrec. High in this lovely hilltop village is Philippe and Dominique's house, which offers 3 rooms facing west overlooking the village and a suite with a garden view. The guests' living room on the first floor is decorated with murals and looks out onto the surrounding countryside. From the formal garden built on the town walls is a view down to the village. Al fresco meals on the terrace when appropriate. Rue de l'Eglise, T: 05 63 75 84 22, www.laterrassedelautrec.com

Lombers
Chambres d'hôtes Le Moulin d'Ambrozy. An authentic, recently restored mill, on the bank of the River Assou, has three spacious bedrooms, each restfully decorated. The *Cathédrale* room has an independent entrance and can be connected with a second bedroom to create a suite. One room opens onto the shady garden and pool in the shelter of the house. Breakfast is served in the pretty salon. Jacques and Annick Novak, T: 05 63 79 17 12, http://moulin.ambrozy.free.fr

Mazamet
€ **Chambres d'hôtes Les Pierres Bleues**. A handsome 19th-century house close to the centre of town with three large rooms each with their own entrance and TV; two have a sitting area; fridge, kettle and microwave also available. The continental breakfast includes cheese and cold meats and is served on the terrace in summer overlooking the leafy garden. Erica Tricon, 3bis Rue de la Republique, T: 05 63 98 88 62, www.pierre-bleues.com

Pont-de-l'Arn
€ **Hôtel La Métairie Neuve**. An old fortified farm in the Montagne Noire. In the main house 14 rooms look out on cedars and mimosas as well as roses and hortensias and a smaller annexe has 3 rooms and an independent lounge.

The two dining rooms or terrace when warm offer menus from €16–32 and dishes such as *filet de rouget à la crème d'ail doux*, or *coquilles St-Jacques à la vanille, filet de boeuf au Reblochon*, and *soufflé au poire* combine local and not-so-local cuisine. Av. Jean Marty, T: 05 63 97 73 50; www.metairieneuve.com

St-Avit
€ Restaurant Les Saveurs de Saint Avit. An old farm and an ultra modern restaurant which opened in 2002 run by the English-born chef, Simon Scott, who trained at the Savoy in London, and his French wife Marie-Hélène. Simon believes in using ultra fresh produce chosen from local markets to determine the distinctly defined flavours, colours and textures of his cuisine. The presentation is stunning: light, airy montages of perfectly cooked ingredients and the dining room is simple, and summer meals served under the arcades. La Baraque (north of Dourgne), T: 05 63 50 11 45, www.les-saveurs-tarn.com

Sorèze
€ L'Hotellerie de l'Abbaye-Ecole. ■ Fresh and attractive renovations have created two unusual modern hotels, under the same management, in part of the old academy (*see p. 312*). Le Logis des Pères occupies a wing of the old abbey with wide corridors and elegant staircase. It has 52 well-appointed rooms created from the former monks' cells with an appropriately understated décor overlooking the park, the cloister or the old town. With a view of the large interior patio is the Gaillac bar and Les Collets Rouges restaurant which occupies the old refectory, where traditional southwestern cuisine is

based on high quality seasonal vegetables and fruit, and local poultry or meat as well as fish dishes. Le Pavillon des Hôtes has 17 pretty rooms in what were once the girls' dormitories around a central patio with a view of the park. 18 Rue Lacordaire, T: 05 63 74 44 80, www.hotelfp-soreze.com

MARKET DAYS

Anglès Wednesday
Castres every day except Monday
Graulhet Tuesday, Thursday, Sunday
Labastide Rouairoux Thursday
Labruguière Friday
Lautrec Friday
Mazamet Tuesday, Saturday, Sunday
Roquecourbe Friday
St-Sulpice La Pointe Wednesday
Sorèze Friday

FESTIVALS & EVENTS

April: *Marché de Potiers*, Pottery market, Giroussens
July: *Extravadance*, a wide range of music and dance, Castres
Fanfares sans Frontières, music, marches and festivities, Mazamet
July and August: *Histoires d'un Soir*, evening street festival, stories and theatre with a historic theme, *Musique des Lumières*, Baroque and Classic concerts and Opera, in the Cours des Collets Rouges, at the Abbaye-Ecole, Sorèze
Kermesse Médiévale, reenactment of the seige of Hautpoul, medieval repast, Hautpoul 05 63 61 4270
Castres and Mazamet (and Albi)
August: *Fête de l'ail rose*, celebration of pink garlic, Lautrec

TARN-ET-GARONNE

The Département du Tarn-et-Garonne was created only in 1808, rather than in 1790 like most others, with its *Préfecture* at Montauban. It encompasses the Bas Quercy, part of the Lomagne (which it shares with the Agenais and Gascony) and a slice of the Rouergue. It takes its name from the major rivers which run almost parallel just south of Montauban. The Tarn, swelled by the Aveyron, then turns west to meet the Garonne between St-Nicolas-de-la-Grave and Moissac. This was a wide and dangerous confluence in the Middle Ages but is now transformed into a tranquil boating lake.

MONTAUBAN

Montauban, a pink brick town on the banks of the Tarn, is an attractive, lively, and slightly dusty place with a number of museums and gardens and big markets. At the heart of the town is the old Place Nationale. From river level, alongside the Tarn south of the Pont-Vieux, there are steps or a lift up to the town centre and the Musée Ingres. At the head of the bridge is Bourdelle's epic *Monument to the Dead of 1870* (1893–1902), at first considered too controversial for a public monument (*see below, p. 324*).

The Pont-Vieux (1304–35) and Bourdelle's *Monument*, beneath the tower of St-Jacques, and (right) the Musée Ingres, Montauban.

Jean-Auguste-Dominique Ingres (1780–1867)
Born in Montauban in 1780, Jean-Auguste-Dominique Ingres studied in Toulouse, then in Paris in 1797 at Jacques-Louis David's studio. He won the *Grand Prix de Rome* in 1801, but only got to Italy in 1806, where he remained for 18 years. Exposure to the works of the Italian masters, especially Raphael, had a profound influence on his work. During the early years in Rome he painted his first large turbanned nude, *Bather of Valpinçon* (1806–10) and established the portrait style for which he became acclaimed. *The Vow of Louis XIII* (*see p. 326*) was well received at the Salon of 1824 which proved a turning point. It also established him as the last of the great history painters; he went on to open an extremely well-patronised studio in Paris and by 1826 was Director of Museums of France. A consummate draughtsman, he maintained that 'drawing is the proberty of art' and Montauban regularly mounts exhibitions of his drawings. Ingres' idiomatic linear style combined with formal composition gives an impression of surface calm that belies a disturbing underlying tension. He returned frequently to the same subject or even the same painting. He barely modified his style during his successful career, adhering to a strict Neoclassicism

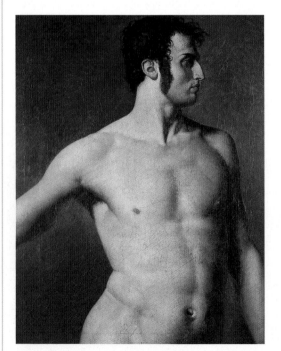

which has been seen as making its own distinctive contribution to the course of French Romanticism. In 1851 Ingres donated 54 paintings and antique vases to the museum, and at his death in 1867 more than 4,000 drawings, his personal collection of paintings and memorabilia. Here his pupil Armand Cambon was the first curator, and there are several quite charming works of his own on display.

Ingres: *Male Torso* (1800).

Jean Alaux: *Ingres' Studio in Rome* (1818).

Musée Ingres

Open July, Aug 9.30–6; mid-April–June, Sept–mid-Oct 10–12 & 2-6, closed Mon; mid-Oct–mid-April 10–12 & 2-6, closed Mon and Sun morning; T: 05 63 22 12 91.

The Museum is installed in the former episcopal palace, a brick building of 1664, on the site of Alphonse Jourdain's castle. In 1360 the English started to build their garrison here, and it was incorporated in the defences during the Wars of Religion: the English guardroom is the lower basement of the museum.

First floor: Ingres' work is exhibited here in six elegant rooms with painted ceilings (1868). His art represents a constant balancing act between Classicism and Romanticism and the works at Montauban demonstrate his range. Two small landscapes, rare in Ingres' repertoire, were probably painted in Rome before summer 1807. Among the best of the portraits is that of his friend, the Italian sculptor Lorenzo Bartolini (1806), who persuaded him to move to Florence between 1820 and 1824, and the *Portrait of Madame Gonse* (1852; *pictured opposite*), the sort of accomplished work, meticulously objective and intimate at the same time, for which the painter is best known. Such portraits were Ingres' chief source of income. *The Dream of Ossian* (1812–13 and 1835), as Romantic a work as you could wish for, was commissioned by Napoleon for the ceiling of his bedroom at the Quirinale Palace, which he never got around to sleeping in. Based on the greatest literary hoax of the 18th century, the supposed discovery of the poems of Ossian by James Macpherson (1736–96), the painting was originally oval but Ingres repurchased it and squared it up with the help of assistants. The Gobelins tapestry version of the most classical of subjects, the *Apotheosis of Homer* (1867), is based on a commission for a ceiling decoration at the Louvre of 1826. *Roger freeing Angelica* (1841) is one of four paintings derived from Aristo's epic poem *Orlando Furioso*. There are a number of works and studies which demonstrate Ingres' great debt to Raphael. Among his possessions are a delightful little painting of *Ingres' Studio in Rome* (1818; *pictured on previous page*) by Jean Alaux and the *Portrait of a Spanish Girl* by Claudio Coello. The huge collection of drawings is rotated thematically. There are also paintings by Ingres' followers Hippolyte Flandrin and Théodore Chassériau, and on the top floor are French and European paintings from the 15th to 18th centuries, including a number of fine Italian works donated by Ingres.

Ground floor: Antoine Bourdelle was born in Montauban in 1861 and died at Le Vésinet in 1929. Works by him here were donated by his daughter. Bourdelle was from a poor background and studied first at Toulouse. At 18 he experienced a close identification with Beethoven and the museum owns a bronze head by him of the composer. In Paris, Bourdelle studied with Jules Dalou, then worked in Rodin's studio between 1893 and 1906. His career divides into two phases, the first described as Dionysian, with works of an explosive, unrestrained nature, as in the *Monument to the Dead of 1870* (1895). The dynamic *Hercules the Archer* (1909) is a pivotal work, before he moved to the synthetic approach expressed in the *Head of Apollo* (c. 1900), bringing him into line with the early 20th century. His constant concern was the relationship of sculpture to architecture and in 1911 he worked on the reliefs for the Théâtre des Champs-Elysées. Montauban is graced with several fine examples of his work. Other local painters are François Desnoyer, a Fauve, Marcel Lenoir and Lucien Andrieu.

First and lower basements: The first basement, with particularly beautiful brick vaults, contains a collection of 18th- and 19th-century regional ceramics. Local Gallo-Roman and medieval exhibits are displayed in the lower basement.

Ingres: *Portrait of Madame Gonse* (1852).

Cathedral of Notre-Dame

The grandiose bleached face of the Neoclassical Cathedral of Notre-Dame from Rue de l'Hôtel de Ville (*see plan overleaf*) makes precisely the contrast with the rest of the town that was intended. Louis XIV's architects conceived a church which would symbolise the Counter-Reformation and celebrate the power of the monarchy. Its design and materials played an important psychological role. It was begun in 1692 to plans by François d'Orbay, son-in-law of Le Vau, modified by Robert de Cotte, and was consecrated in 1739. The façade has a Doric peristyle of four columns and the Ionic order above. The interior is imposing and austere, taking the form of a Greek cross with 16 arcades; it is 87m long in total, the nave barely longer than the choir, the Doric order used throughout. The pitted originals of statues of the four Evangelists (1719) made by Marc Arcis for the façade have been brought inside and replaced by reproductions. The pendentives of the dome are decorated with the *Four Virtues*. The most important work is Ingres' painting of the *Vow of Louis XIII* (1824) (timer light switch on the wall left of the altar). It was commissioned in 1820 and carried out in Florence. It shows Louis XIII placing France under the protection of the Virgin of the Assumption. The result is an eclectic work which bears out the duality of the theme. Ingres borrowed heavily from Raphael for the Virgin, but she is a worldly creature, imperious and sensuous, bathed in a diffused light and framed by drapes held back by voluptuous angels. The king, with up-stretched arms, is painted in harsher tones and in direct light. Also worthy of note in the Cathedral is some fine late 18th- and 19th-century wrought iron, a monumental candlestick with dolphins and a vast lectern; and 18th-century choir stalls. A 15th-century console with Bruniquel marble is used as an altar with a 16th-century statue placed on it. The organ, built in 1675, came from the Church of St-Jacques and has kept its original case. In one of the chapels on the left of the choir are gilded stucco sacred ornaments by Ingres' father.

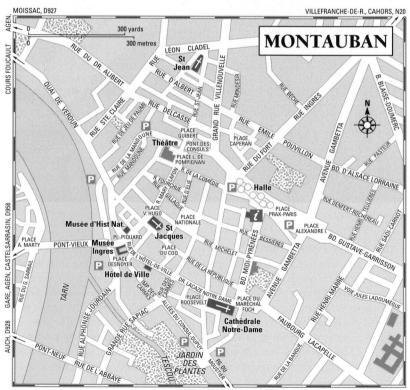

HISTORY OF MONTAUBAN

Always a major town in the southwest, Montauban lost its status as *chef-lieu* (main town) of a huge *généralité* (administrative district) in 1790 and became part of the Lot. Negotiations during a visit by Napoleon in 1808 resulted in its reinstatement at the head of the *département* of Tarn-et-Garonne, which acquired choice parts of Quercy, Gascony, Rouergue and Languedoc. Montauban is famous as the second Protestant stronghold in France after La Rochelle but, in common with most Protestant towns in the southwest, it has few pre-Reformation buildings. Less obvious today is that Montauban was one of the first *bastides* in the region, founded in 1144 by the Count of Toulouse, Alphonse Jourdain. The town enjoyed tremendous prosperity as a commercial centre after the Albigensian crisis, benefiting from its position between two navigable rivers, the Tarn and the Aveyron. Access and defence were improved by the Pont-Vieux across the Tarn, erected 1304–35, the foundation stone being laid by King Philip the Fair. During the Hundred Years War, the town was taken by Captain John Chandos for the English in the name of the Black Prince, and became the last frontier between Guyenne and the Languedoc until 1368. The recovery of the town's commercial status at the end of the 15th century engendered a brilliant cultural life in the early 16th century and resulted in the establishment of numerous schools which were a breeding ground for humanist ideas and the support of Calvinism. The first of the Wars of Religion had a profound effect on the town: Protestant zealots set fire to the cathedral in 1561 and destroyed all the churches except St-Jacques, which became their temple. Montauban was already a Protestant place of safety in 1570, following the Peace of St-Germain, reconfirmed by the Edict of Nantes in 1598. This situation lasted until 1621 when Louis XIII and his constable, de Luynes, marched on Montauban with an army of 25,000 and laid siege for three months, but despite terrible damage the locals held on. However, after the fall of La Rochelle in 1629, Richelieu succeeded politically where the king had failed militarily, and the fortifications of Montauban were destroyed. In the same year, more than 6,000 inhabitants died of the plague. As a powerful administrative centre Montauban continued to trade and prosper, particularly with the construction of major roads across the southwest. This wealth was converted into elegant, brick townhouses. The most obvious symbol of the Counter-Reformation is the Neoclassical cathedral built partly in stone. Prior to the Revolution, the economy slowed down and the few new buildings followed the pattern of the 18th century, resulting in an extraordinarily unified architecture. Montauban was the birthplace of two eminent artists, the painter Ingres and the sculptor Antoine Bourdelle (*see above, p. 324*). Ingres' father was *un petit ornemaniste*, who made models in clay, busts and ornaments in stucco for churches and for sale at country fairs.

The old town

Northwest of the cathedral, between Rue de l'Hôtel-de-Ville and Boulevard Midi-Pyrénées, is the old town. At the end of Boulevard Midi-Pyrénées is the tourist office in the former Jesuit College, a large 17th-century brick building with *mirandes*. Outside, Bourdelle's graceful bronze statue *Penelope* (1912) overlooks Place Prax-Paris where the markets are held. Rue de la Comédie, behind the tourist office, leads to Place L. de Pompignan in front of the theatre, and another Bourdelle sculpture, *Sappho* (1925). From the square, the Pont des Consuls flies over the Vallon de la Mandoune.

Around **Place Nationale**, in keeping with the rest of the town but unusual in the realms of *bastides*, are buildings entirely in brick, of different types and qualities incorporated with great subtlety, some parts possibly designed to be plastered over, some purely decorative. Also unusual is a double arcade following the layout of the original square, with arches at each angle. Two sides were destroyed by fire in 1614 and plans by Pierre Levesville were drawn up and carried out; but in 1649, the two remaining sides were consumed by flames and a new building campaign, led by Charles Pacot but following the original design, was carried through. Some houses were not completed until 1708.

West of Place Nationale is the **Church of St-Jacques**, the only church spared by the Calvinists. It was built for the parish and dedicated to St James of Compostela; the fortified west end is 13th-century, but after the Hundred Years War major repairs were carried out and the chevet dates from 1481. The octagonal Toulousain-style belfry has three levels of openings and was restored in the 18th century. It still carries scars inflicted by royalist bullets during the siege of 1621. Above the west door is an ugly ceramic reproduction of Raphael's *Vision of Ezekiel*. The characteristic aisleless nave with chapels was extended in the 15th century and revaulted in the 18th century. The chapel of St-Jacques (south) has gilded stucco work by Ingres' father.

South of St-Jacques is the municipal library in a grand building overlooking Rue du Général-Piquart, with Bourdelle's *Dying Centaur* (1914). Lower down on Place A.-Bourdelle is the Musée d'Histoire Naturelle (*open Tues–Sat 10–12 & 2–6, Sun 2–6; closed Mon; T: 05 63 22 13 85*). In the same building is the very small local history Musée du Terroir (*open 10–12 & 2–6; closed Sun, Mon; T: 05 63 66 46 34*).

The **Pont-Vieux**, a very strong construction in brick and stone and originally fortified, was begun in 1304. Straight rather than hump-backed, because of the difference in the levels of the two banks, it has seven high arches. The extremity of each triangular cutwater is in stone as are the bases of the piers, which helped it withstand the exceptional floods of 1441, 1766 and 1930. On the banks of the Tarn in the square close to the steps or lift next to the Ingres museum is a memorial to Ingres by Antoine Etex (1868). In the refreshing Jardin des Plantes, created in 1860 where the Tescou meets the Tarn, is a bust of Auguste Quercy (d. 1899), a local poet who wrote in Occitan, by Bourdelle (1911). To the north, on the banks of the Tarn in Cours Foucault, laid out in the late 17th century by Intendant Foucault, is Bourdelle's great memorial to the dead of the First World War, *France watching over her Dead*, a contrast in style to his Franco-Prussian war monument (*see p. 321*).

THE QUERCY BLANC

The chalk plateaux north of Montauban which characterise the Quercy Blanc, the most southerly part of the Quercy, and stretch into the Pays de Serres in the Lot-et-Garonne (*see p. 347*), are carved by several small rivers creating fertile valleys running down into the Garonne, with white or grey stone villages. To the northeast of Montauban, **Montpezat-de-Quercy** is a lovely medieval stone and timber village with Gothic and Renaissance houses. The church of St-Martin, completed by 1339 and consecrated in 1343, was designed by an architect from the papal court at Avignon, with a simple nave and no aisles, and with one rose window.

The main interest of the church is its furnishings and fittings (coins required for the lights). In the choir are the famous made-to-measure tapestries, of Flemish origin, which have been here since 1520 when Jean IV des Près presented them to the church on the occasion of his elevation to Bishop of Montauban. They are stitched, not woven, and are made up of five panels with 15 scenes of the *Legend of St Martin of Tours*. Above each scene is an explanatory octosyllabic quatrain in Old French verse. They read from left to right. The first panel shows St Martin in the town of Amiens, about to share his cloak with a beggar. Other, less well-known, episodes in Martin's life follow—his dream, his journey across the Alps when he is stopped by robbers, his ordination as Bishop of Tours and chasing away pagan beliefs. He is shown effecting conversions and cures in Germany. The last tapestries change emphasis and are concerned with the battle between good and evil. Finally there is a reminder to attend mass.

Left and right of the entrance to the choir are two funerary effigies of the benefactors, Cardinal Pierre des Près (1288–1361) in Carrara marble and his nephew Jean, Bishop of Coïmbra in Portugal then of Castres (1338–53) in Quercy stone, formerly coloured. The painting (16th century) above the dean's stall represents Jacques des Près (d. 1589), the last bishop in the family. Other artefacts include *Notre-Dame de-Pitié-de-Montpezat* (1475), sculpted in sandstone in Villefranche-de-Rouergue and polychromed in the 19th century, in the first chapel south. It was an object of veneration in the 16th century and there is still a pilgrimage on the third Sunday in September.

A detour of about 5km (D20, Cahors direction, signposted at Saux) takes you to the little chapel of **Notre-Dame-de-Saux**. The charming rural church with a belfry is in the middle of woods and serves as the frame for some precious 14th-century murals. Ask for the key at the presbytery or at the Hôtel de Ville, Montpezat.

En route to Montpezat from Montauban is Caussade, famous for its straw hats and markets. Beyond is **Puylaroque**, a village of great character, undoubtedly an important agricultural centre in the 13th and 14th centuries, with several Gothic houses reminiscent of Cordes or Lauzerte.

Some way west, **Lauzerte**, northwest of Montauban, justly deserves its reputation as one of the most beautiful villages in France. Clinging to a rock dominating the Cahors–Moissac road and the land from which it derived its wealth, it has a profusion of fine old houses, carefully restored, an arcaded square, and an interesting Gothic church enlarged in the 17th century.

MOISSAC

Moissac is a modest town but contains one of the major Romanesque sites of France in the shape of the Abbaye de St-Pierre. The town is situated in a fertile valley, the market garden of the region, producing some 200,000 tonnes of fruit annually, including kiwis and the unique Chasselas, a small sweet dessert grape.

HISTORY OF THE ABBAYE DE ST-PIERRE

Legend attributes the foundation at Moissac to Clovis in 506, although the Benedictine monastery was most probably founded by Bishop Didier of Cahors (630–655) at the time of Clovis II (639–657). It received gifts of land from rich benefactors, Nizezius and Ermintrude, in 680, and more gifts arrived in the 9th century from the Carolingian monarchs and the bishops of Cahors. Later, the abbey came under the protection of the Counts of Toulouse as a valuable source of revenue. The consequent decline was recorded in the chronicles of Abbot Aymeric de Peyrac (1377–1406). By 1030 part of the church had collapsed and in 1042 a fire destroyed the remainder. Abbot Odilon added Moissac to Cluny's chain of staging-posts on the *Via Podiensis* to Santiago. A Cluniac monk, Durand de Bredon, was named Abbot of Moissac in 1048, maintaining its status despite subordination to Cluny. The abbey grew into one of the richest, most influential in France, with sculpture transcending any other of the period. De Bredon (1048–71) and then Hunaud de Gavaret (1072–85) re-established the *scriptorium*: illuminated manuscripts were undoubtedly a source of iconographic and stylistic inspiration to the sculptors. A Romanesque church, constructed on the apse of the earlier building, was consecrated in 1063 and the monastic buildings blessed by Urban II in 1096. The cloister, completed in 1100, was created during the time of Abbot Ansquitil (1085–1115) who also added the massive porch and belfry at the west end of the church. Abbot Roger de Sorèze (1115–31) fortified the west end and was responsible for the monumental portal and tympanum. Attacked by Simon de Montfort during the Albigensian crusades in 1212, the cloisters and church suffered. A long period of stagnation was interrupted by the abbacy of Bertrand de Montaigut (1260–95) who restored the cloisters. After the Hundred Years War, the church was reconstructed in Gothic style and the brick part of the belfry was added. The church as we now see it dates from this period. In 1626 secular canons replaced the monks, and the library of some 120 manuscripts, already neglected, was sold to Louis XIV's chief minister, Jean-Baptiste Colbert. After the Revolution, a small seminary was returned to the parish in the early 19th century and now houses the Centre d'Art Roman Marcel Durliat. Disastrously, c. 1845 the refectory was replaced by a section of the Bordeaux–Sète railway. In the 1850s Viollet-le-Duc (*see p. 95*) and Théodore Olivier worked on the porch and belfry.

CHURCH & CLOISTER OF THE ABBAYE DE ST-PIERRE

The approach to the abbey church is most dramatic along Rue de la République from the market place, Place des Récollets. The church is a mixture of Romanesque and Gothic, a testament to successive building campaigns which transformed the late 11th–12th-century stone church into a 15th-century Gothic church of brick. The Romanesque bays, identified from the windows, were arbitrarily divided and submerged by the buttresses to support the higher levels. The belfry was amended in the 15th and 17th centuries. In 1985 the paving immediately in front of the portal and tympanum was dug out to counteract damp problems, revealing a paving of brick and pebbles dated 1611, and below that the two 12th-century steps flanking the entrance were uncovered. Thus the portal was finally restored to its original proportions.

The south portal and tympanum

On the engaged column on the east of the porch is the effigy of Abbot Roger de Sorèze (1115–31), responsible for its construction. Note the horn player on one of the merlons. The remarkable south door was executed between 1120 and 1125; the influence of Cluny is evident in the vaulting of the narthex, the cusping of the jambs and the plate drapery of the sculptures. Hints of colour suggest that it was originally polychromed. The whole ensemble presents a developing theme, part narrative and moralising, part visionary and inspirational, from the *Incarnation* to the *Last Judgement*, climaxing with the *Christ of the Parousia* (the Second Coming). It is impossible to take in the whole programme at one glance. Simultaneously enthralling and profoundly moving, its impact never diminishes. The semi-circular tympanum (*pictured overleaf*) is composed of 31 figures on separate blocks and presents an apocalyptic vision based on the text of *Revelations 4: 2–11*. The image of Christ in Majesty, enthroned, with one hand raised in blessing and the other on a book, dominates and focuses the composition. On his head is a crown surrounded by a large, richly decorated cruciform halo. The gaze is immobile, beard and hair highly stylised. The rest of the composition flows around him. Swooping in and out are the four Apocalyptic beasts, symbols of the four Evangelists (*Rev. 4: 7*), and flanking them are two seraphim. Around the throne are the Four and Twenty Elders (*Rev. 4: 4*), each crowned and carrying a musical instrument (rebec or viol), goblet or perfume flask, who represent the twelve prophets of the Old Testament and the twelve Apostles of the New Testament. The figures are meticulously detailed and in varied poses, craning their necks as they listen attentively. The horizontal lines which structure the composition lose their rigidity behind the undulations which evoke the 'sea of glass like unto crystal' (*Rev. 4: 6*) and around the outer edge a beautifully carved ribbon ornament adds to the mobility of the composition. The conceptual originality of this creation, by an unknown individual of undoubted creative genius, is matched by the skill and subtlety of its execution. The tympanum rests on a lintel decorated with eight large thistles and foliage spewing out of the mouths of beasts at each end (this is a block of reused marble with an earlier frieze on the under edge). Three pairs of lions and

The tympanum (1120–25) of the south portal of the Abbaye de St-Pierre, Moissac.

lionesses on a floral background appear to move restlessly on the supporting trumeau. Unseen when facing the portal straight on is the Prophet Jeremiah, on the right face of the trumeau. This is the single most moving figure at Moissac. Head inclined, hair and beard flowing, attenuated to blend with the narrow space, he exudes gentleness and sorrow, and there is also a suppressed dynamism in the crossed legs and floating drapery. His opposite number on the west face is St Paul, presenting the same plastic virtues as Jeremiah but a different character, more tense and alert but acquiescent and receptive. On the left jamb is a strangely contorted St Peter with the key of the Holy Kingdom. The only works comparable with these are at Souillac (*see p. 166*).

The left (west) side of the porch carries the parable of *Lazarus and Dives*. In the top register, Dives the rich man is at his table while, at his gate, Lazarus lies dying, the dogs licking his sores. An angel gathers up Lazarus's soul, represented by a little nude body (only the feet remain), and delivers it into the bosom of Abraham. St Luke, seated on the left, unrolls the text of his gospel. Below is the *Death of Dives*, whose soul is shown departing with demons (the angel arrived too late) and mourned by his widow, and in the lower register are almost illegible punishments for lust and avarice.

On the right-hand jamb the figure of the Prophet Isaiah balances that of St Peter, and like Jeremiah he carries his prophesy on a scroll. To his left his prophesy is confirmed in an *Annunciation* (badly worn, the angel poorly remade in the 19th century) and *Visitation* (also a copy) and above, scenes of the *Nativity and Epiphany*.

The interior

In the square, dark narthex (c. 1110–15), everything is on a massive scale to support the belfry tower. From solid pillars with engaged columns spring heavy primitive square ribs. Some of the huge capitals have foliate or decorative motifs, and the others show *Samson slaying the Lion* and lambs in the jaws of wolves. The painted decor in luminous yellow on the walls and ochres on the vaults, is a modern (1963) restoration of its 15th-century appearance. Romanesque walls and massive piers exist in the west bay, but the second bay was rebuilt towards the end of the 13th century and the polygonal, straight-sided east end dates from the 15th century, when it replaced the apse of 1063. The rib vaults were completed later in the 15th century. There are shallow chapels between the buttresses. Among venerable furnishings are a wooden *Christ on the Cross* (1130–40), contemporary with the portal sculptures and very close stylistically. There are three Gothic polychromed groups: a *Flight into Egypt* in wood (15th century; the figure of Joseph is 17th-century); a stone *Pietà* flanked by Mary Magdalene and St John (1476), with donor figures; and an *Entombment* (15th century; restored in 1985) in walnut with eight figures arranged around the body of Christ. Through the screen on the left on the north wall can be seen the plaque recording the dedication of the church of 1063.

The cloister

Open Jul, Aug 9–7; April–June, Sept 9–12 & 2–6, Sat, Sun 10–12 & 2–6; Oct–March 10–12 & 2–7, Sat, Sun 2–5; T: 05 63 04 01 85.

The almost square cloister on the north side of the church is on a grand scale. On a continuous low wall stand 116 slender columns, alternately paired and single, supporting capitals of a dramatic form which widen out from a narrow base, emphasised by a deep cut-away abacus above. All the faces of the capitals and the impost blocks are carved. This is the oldest and largest collection of Romanesque carved capitals which are still in their original place and represents a defining moment in Romanesque art. The date of the original cloister, 1100, is recorded on the central pillar of the west gallery. In the southwest corner is the stairway to the gallery above the narthex, with a domed vault supported by 12 heavy ribs centred on a compression ring, overlooking the church and the forecourt. The angle pillars of the cloister have carved reliefs on reused Pyrenean marble sarcophagi representing eight of the Apostles, each identified by an inscription. Despite damage, the capitals are still remarkably intact. The drums and the abacii are carved on all faces and each face is worthy of close examination for the artistic and anecdotal detail. Some 46 of the 76 capitals have narrative themes with inscriptions and were intended as contemplative visual aids designed to affirm faith. The iconography is based on both the Old and New Testaments, with an emphasis on episodes from the life of Christ, from the *Incarnation* to the *Last Supper*, but no scenes of the *Passion*. The capital (no. 40 on the plan; *see overleaf*), at the southeast corner, in a prominent position between the church and the chapter house, portrays the *Martyrdom of St Peter*, patron of the abbey, and the *Martyrdom of St Paul*, with an inscription in mock Kufic script. Palmettes or entwined stems are deeply incised, some inspired by Mozarab work.

MOISSAC CLOISTER

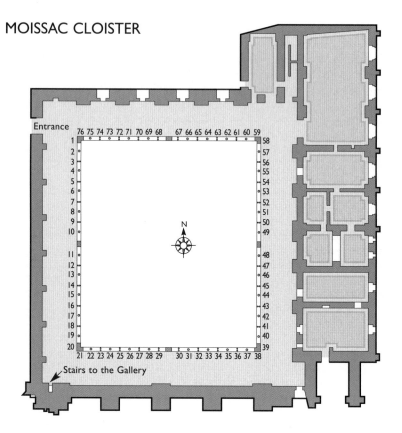

Iconography of the Pillar Reliefs and Capitals

Western Gallery
Northwest pillar (west face), St Philip
1. Sacrifice of Abraham
2. Glorification of the Cross
3. Acanthus leaves
4. Birds and lions
5. Daniel in the Lions' Den/Christ's Birth announced to the Shepherds
6. Acanthus leaves
7. The Devil Unleashed
8. Raising of Lazarus
9. Palm leaves
10. Fantastic figures and animals

Central pillar inscribed: 'In the year 1100 of the Incarnation of the Lord Eternal, this cloister was constructed, at the time of Dom Ansquitil, Abbot. Amen.' St-Simon on the east face

11. David anointed by the Prophet Samuel
12. Vegetal design
13. Birds and animals
14. Acanthus leaves
15. Eight Beatitudes from the Sermon on the Mount
16. Lions rampant
17. Cain and Abel
18. Vegetal design

19. Ascension of Alexander
20. David's Victory over Goliath
Southwest pillar (west face), St Bartholomew

Southern Gallery
Southwest pillar (south face), St Matthew
21. Herod's Feast
22. Birds among plants
23. City of Babylon
24. Birds
25. Dream of Nebuchadnezzar
26. Martyrdom of St Stephen
27. Acanthus leaves
28. David and his Musicians
29. Holy City of Jerusalem
Central pillar, red marble panel, with no decoration
30. The Well of the Abyss
31. Symbols of the four Evangelists
32. Canaanite Woman and the Centurion
33. Good Samaritan
34. Temptation of Christ in the Desert
35. Revelation of St John at Patmos
36. Transfiguration
37. Imprisonment and release of St Peter
38. Baptism of Christ
Southeast pillar (south face), St Paul

Eastern Gallery
Southeast pillar (east face), St Peter
39. Samson wrestling with the Lion
40. Two Martyrdoms: St Peter and St Paul
41. Vegetal design
42. Adam and Eve and the Fall
43. Acanthus leaves
44. Martyrdom of St Laurence
45. Christ washing the Disciples' Feet
46. Palm leaves
47. Lazarus and Dives
48. Eight eagles or dragons and human heads
Central pillar, Durand de Bredon, Abbot of Moissac (1047–71), Bishop of Toulouse (1059–71)

49. Four figures seizing eagles by the neck
50. Wedding at Cana
51. Vegetal design
52. Epiphany/Massacre of the Innocents/Herod at the Gates of Jerusalem
53. Palmettes and animals' muzzles
54. Acanthus leaves
55. Martyrdom of St Saturnin
56. Acanthus leaves
57. Martyrdoms of St Fructuosus, St Augurious and St Euologius
58. Annunciation and Visitation
Northeast pillar (east face), St James

Northern Gallery
Northeast pillar (north face), St John
59. Angels wrestling with Dragons
60. Eagles
61. Vegetal design
62. Two Miracles of St Benedict
63. Birds
64. St Peter healing the Paralytic
65. Vegetal design
66. Celestial Kingdom
67. Miraculous Draught of Fishes
Central pillar with grey marble slab decorated with wavy lines and imbrications
68. Daniel in Prayer in the Lions' Den/Prophet Habakkuk bringing Food to Daniel
69. Procession, possibly the crusade to Jerusalem
70. Vegetal design of Mozarabic influence
71. Symbols of the four Evangelists
72. Birds
73. Meshach, Shadrach and Abednego in the Fiery Furnace
74. Scenes from the Life of St Martin
75. Scrolling design of Mozarabic influence
76. Jesus and the Good Samaritan
Northwest pillar (north face), St Andrew

ENVIRONS OF MOISSAC

St-Nicolas-de-la-Grave is a small town to the southwest of Moissac. Its most famous son was Antoine Laumet de Lamothe-Cadillac (b. 1658), coloniser and founder of Louisiana and Detroit (1701), whose name was selected by General Motors to mark their luxury range of cars. His birthplace, now the Musée de Lamothe-Cadillac (*open all year but times vary; enquire at the tourist office*), is in a small street of the same name near the market hall. St-Nicolas is close to the great confluence of the Tarn and the Garonne, where medieval pilgrims crossed by ferry. It is now spanned by a mighty 19th-century suspension bridge.

South of Castelsarrasin, near Cordes-Tolosain, the former **Abbaye de Belleperche** (*open July–Aug 10–6; June, Sept 10–12 & 2–6; closed Mon; also closed Sun morning June and Sept; Oct–May by appointment only; T: 05 63 95 62 75 or 05 63 95 68 34*) founded c. 1143–44 and largely rebuilt in the 13th century, was one of the largest and richest Cistercian monasteries in the south. The vast church, with a belfry recalling that of St-Sernin in Toulouse, dates from 1230–63.

PRACTICAL INFORMATION

GETTING AROUND

• **By train:** Between Paris and Toulouse stop at Montauban and Caussade; between Montauban and Agen trains stop at Moissac; between Brive and Toulouse stop at Laguépie, Lexos, Najac; occasional trains between Cahors and Montauban at Montpezat de Quercy (station 5km from town).

TOURIST INFORMATION

Lauzerte Pl. des Cornières, T: 05 63 94 61 94, www.quercy.blanc.net
Moissac 6 Pl. Durand-de-Bredon, T: 05 63 04 01 85, www.moissac.fr
Monclar-de-Quercy Pl. des Capitouls, T: 05 63 30 31 72
Montaigu-de-Quercy Pl. du Mercadiel, T: 05 63 94 48 50
Montauban Pl. Prax-Paris, T: 05 63 63

60 60, fax 05 63 63 65 12, http://montauban-tourisme.com
Montpezat-de-Quercy Blvd. des Fossés, T: 05 63 02 05 55
St-Nicholas-de-la-Grave Pl. du Château, T: 05 63 94 82 81, www.stniolasdelag.online.fr

ACCOMMODATION & RESTAURANTS

Cazes-Mondenard
€ L'Atre. At the heart of a small village, east of Lauzerte on the D34, the modest hotel with 10 rooms has a charming rustic restaurant with large fireplace where you can try such traditional recipes and specialities as *Tarte flambée au foie gras, Pot au feu de canard,* or *Foie gras poêlé.* Pl. de l'Hôtel-de-Ville, T: 05 63 95 81 61.
€ **Chambres d'hôtes Grange.** The Maurel family has created three spa-

cious bedrooms, a lounge and dining room for guests, in this sturdy brick Quercynois house. Family souvenirs give it a special character, the *table d'hôtes* is generous. Also a pool. Grange Martissan, T: 05 63 95 83 71, www.montauban.cci.fr/grange/index.htm

Escatalens
€ **Chambres d'hôtes La Maison de Chevaliers**. An 18th-century mansion around a courtyard and in shady grounds with a pool which has four large and comfortable rooms. The graceful staircase is still in place, and there is a rustic salon, a music room and games for kids in the cellars. The *table d'hôtes* is cooked by the owner who is cordon bleu trained. Claude and Claudine Choux, Pl. de la Mairie, T: 05 63 68 71 23. www.maisondeschevaliers.com

Lafrancaise
€ **Au Fin Gourmet Hôtel Belvédère**. The hotel is in a little community in a green valley, and has 7 pleasant rooms and views over the countryside. Excellent inventive cooking served in the restaurant, and at midday also in the brasserie. Comfortable, pretty rooms. 16 Rue Mary Lafon, T: 05 63 65 89 55, fingourmet@oreka.com

Meauzac
€ **Chambres d'hôtes La Manoir des Chanterelles**. East of Moissac among the fruit orchards is this grand 19th-century house stands in a large park with tennis court. The two suites and three bed-rooms, as is the fashion, have different characters and names to suit: Zen, Romantique, Cocon, Oriental—with exotic drapes—and Louis XVI in tones of blue. Bernon Boutounelle, T: 05 63 24 60 70, www.manoirdeschanterelles.com

Moissac
€€ **Hôtel/Restaurant Le Moulin de Moissac**. In a prime location on the banks of the Tarn, the hotel opened in 2003 in a handsomely restored old mill whose history goes back to 1474. All is light, simple and colourful and accom-modation falls into three categories and three colour schemes, all with river views. The chef is top class and serves beautiful creative dishes in the restaurant decorated with appropriate murals by Stépane Hascoët. Esplanade du Moulin, T: 05 63 32 88 88, www.lemoulindemoissac.com

€ **Le Chapon Fin**. A comfortable hotel in the town centre which offers a warm welcome. The food served in the restau-rant is traditional, specialising in foie gras, fish dishes and good desserts. 3 Pl. des Récollets. T: 05 63 04 04 22, www.lechaponfin-moissac.com

€ **Le Pont Napoléon**. A small hotel on the banks of the Tarn next to the old bridge. Of 'retro charm', the accommo-dation has all mod coms and generous continental breakfasts. Michel Dussau uses the duck, foie gras, chasselas grapes and melons, apples and artichokes, nuts and cheeses and of course truffles, from the area in his refined cooking of repute. Menus €35–70. 2 Allées Montebello, T: 05 63 04 01 55, www.le-pont-napoleon.com

€ **Bistrot du Cloître**. Tucked away in the corner of a pretty square, this restau-rant is a good place to slip into for lunch during a visit to the cloister and church at Moissac. Pl. Durand-de-Bredon, T: 05 63 04 37 50

Montpezat-de-Quercy
€ **Chambres d'hôtes Domaine de Lafon, Pech de Lafon**. The pale pink

house is owned by artist and theatrical designer Bernard Perrone, whose works decorate the house and who runs a workshop for painting and stage design (up to 6 participants). The house is surrounded by gardens and has two rooms, Indian and Parakeets, as well as a *gîte*. *Table d'hôtes* by reservation. T: 05 63 02 05 09, www.domaindelafon.com

Montauban

€ **Mercure**. The hotel occupies an entirely renovated 18th-century mansion in the heart of the old town. 12 Rue Notre-Dame, T: 05 63 63 17 23, mercure.montauban@wanadoo.fr.

€ **La cuisine d'Alain/Hotel d'Orsay**. ■ Recommended as one of the best family-run restaurants in the Tarn-et-Garonne, Alain Blanc's cooking is a delight. Dishes using local produce combined with unusual accompaniments, include *foie poêlé aux fruits du Tarn et Garonne*, and the dessert trolley is not to be missed. There is a pretty flowery terrace and comfortable dining room. Also bedrooms, some sound-proofed and air-conditioned. 31 Rue Salengro (opposite the train station), T: 05 63 66 06 66, cuisinedalain@wandoo.fr

St-Beauzeil

€ **Château de l'Hoste**. Not far from Montaigu-de-Quercy, this 17th-century chateau in typical white limestone of the region is set is in a beautiful park with 100 year old trees. The food is good, served either in the restaurant, with large fireplace, or on the terrace. There are plenty of outdoor activities, including a pool. l'Hoste, T: 05 63 95 25 61. chateaudelhoste@wanadoo.fr.

St Paul d'Espis

€€ **Le Manoir Saint Jean**. Just 9 km from Moissac, the Neoclassical chateau has been transformed by Anne-Marie Morgadès. Beautiful clean lines and understatement epitomize the four categories of rooms: suite, luxury, classic or mansardees (under the roof) with names such as Ingres, Explorateur, Art Deco and Matin Calme. The dishes served are edible works of art, with a *dégustation* menu at €40. T: 05 63 05 02 34, www.chateaudelhoste.com

MARKET DAYS

Lauzerte Wednesday, Saturday; farmers' market Wednesday
Lavit de Lomagne Friday
Moissac Saturday, Sunday
Montaigu-de-Quercy Saturday
Montauban Wednesday and Saturday.
Montpezat de Quercy Tuesday
St-Nicholas de la Grave Monday

FESTIVALS & EVENTS

May: *Alors chante!*, French song festival
July: *Jazz à Montauban*, in several venues around town, some free
Festival Art Vivant, performing arts, Lauzerte
July and August: *Festival du Quercy Blanc*, classical music at Lauzerte, Montpezat-de-Quercy and Cazes-Modenard
Estivales du chapeau de Caussade et Septfonds, celebrating all types of hats
Fêtes des 400 coups in memory of the siege of Montauban in 1621.
Castelsarras' in Louisane New Orleans, Cajun and jazz in the streets of
September: (3rd weekend) *Fête des Fruits et des Legumes*, celebration of the Chasselas grape and other fruits

LOT-ET-GARONNE

The mighty Garonne was, for several centuries, the frontier between French Gascony to the south and English Guyenne (*see p. 354*) to the north. The Garonne is swelled by the Lot arriving from the east just below Aiguillon (*see p. 363*), and further downstream by two lesser tributaries, the Baïse and the Dropt. To the east of the *département* these rivers flow through rolling hills and gentle valleys, a landscape of lush pastures and plum orchards. Shipping on the rivers was dangerous and the volatile Garonne was finally supplanted as a means of transporting cargoes in 1856 by the more controllable *Canal latéral à la Garonne*. There are now nearly 200km of navigable waterways in the Lot-et-Garonne.

AGEN

Agen, *préfecture* of the *département* of Lot-et-Garonne, on the banks of the Garonne with some 30,000 inhabitants. With interesting half-timbered buildings and an excellent fine art museum, Agen is also well known as the guarantee of quality of French prunes.

HISTORY OF AGEN

The city of the Nitiobriges people became a Roman administrative district, *civitas Agennensium*, which developed as the prosperous city of *Aginnum* with its own theatre and amphitheatre in the 1st–2nd centuries AD on the heights above present-day Agen. By the 4th century the town had relocated to the banks of the Garonne: one of the most revered local martyrs, St Faith (*see p. 218*) was persecuted here. By the 5th century there was a small protected enclosure around the cathedral. By the 13th century the commune was strong enough to proclaim a degree of independence from the prelates. With the accession of Henry Plantagenet in 1154, Agen found itself in the position of border town between the territories of England and France: until 1370 the town changed hands no fewer than 11 times. The Renaissance period was a brilliant one for the Agenais. The area received a series of Italian bishops, encouraging an influx of Italian scholars and artists, including the humanist Giulio-Cesare Scaliger (1484–1558). His son, the Protestant philosopher Joseph-Juste Scaliger (1540–1609), was born in Agen. A new, extended enclosure was built incorporating the church of St-Caprais. The river port on the Garonne, and in the 19th century the Canal, were great assets until the introduction of the railway, and contributed to a flourishing fabrics industry from the 17th century.

EXPLORING AGEN

The cathedral and vicinity

The old town is between the canal to the north, and streets running perpendicular to it, Av. du Général de Gaulle and the modern Blvd. Président Carnot, with shops, banks and the Tourist Office. In the north of the old town, the 11th-century Tour Chapelet is the oldest monument in Agen, built on Roman foundations and incorporated into the first medieval fortifications. The twin towers are later, and the 16th–17th-century monastery was rebuilt in the 19th century. At the end of Rue Arago is the Cathedral of St-Caprais (*open 8–12 & 2–6; Sun 8–12; guided visits July-Aug, 2 and 5 p.m, enquire at the tourist office*). Built originally as a collegiate church to receive St Caprais' relics in the 6th century, it was elevated to cathedral only in 1803. The building was begun in the 12th century, but badly damaged by the Huguenots in 1591 and the cloister was destroyed during the Revolution. A major rebuild in the 19th century resulted in the construction of the belfry. The best part of the church is the Romanesque east end with apse and radiating chapels, sculpted corbels and capitals; the west door is Gothic. Enter by the south door. The interior is unremarkable. It was left unfinished in the Romanesque period and the large square piers with restored capitals suggest that a dome was originally intended. The shallow transept was vaulted in the 13th century and the nave completed in the 16th century. The decoration is outlandishly 19th century. The chapter house contains the best surviving Romanesque work and the relics of Agen's martyrs. In Rue des Martyrs behind the cathedral the 18th century Martrou is the purported resting place of St Caprais, beheaded in the 3rd century at the time of Diocletian. The site of the chapel dedicated to the girl saint, Faith (*see p. 218*), who was martyred at the same time as Caprais, is marked by a 19th-century tower at the end of Boulevard Carnot.

The old town centre

Between the Cathedral and the town's other major sight, the Musée des Beaux-Arts (*see below, p. 342*), is the lively historic centre. Place des Laitiers which, until Boulevard de la République sliced the town in two, led straight into Rue des Cornières, which means 'street of arcades', the main commercial district since the 13th century. The arcades of various designs on both the square and the street have undergone steady renovation. Rue Floirac, off Rue des Cornières, has some good 16th–19th-century doorways, and the severely Classical Hôtel Amblard (1773), built by the local banking brothers Pélissier. Rue Puits de Saumon has one of the best examples of medieval domestic architecture in Agen, the 14th-century Maison du Sénéchal, with pointed arches on the ground floor and an open loggia above with trefoil tracery. Ruelle des Juifs is the narrowest alley in town, where the money-lenders operated until the end of the 14th century. **Place Dr Pierre-Esquirol**, named after a local mayor, was the site of the Gallo-Roman town whose walls were absorbed by the buildings now containing the museum. Other buildings on the square are the 17th-century Hôtel de Ville and the Théâtre Ducourneau by Guillaume Tronchet (begun 1906),

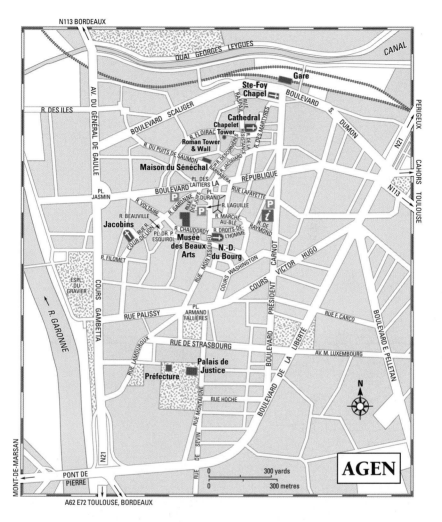

the first theatre in France to use reinforced concrete. Rue Beauville leads to a cluster of remarkable half-timbered houses grouped on an island plot. These picturesque properties, sensitively restored, have intricate timber designs, brick nogging, deep overhanging jetties and fine windows. Off Rue Chaudordy, which runs alongside the museum, is a Renaissance courtyard and on the corner of Rue Montesquieu and Rue Droits-de-l'Homme is a small space in front of the little 13th-century Church of Notre-Dame-du-Bourg. The church is a mixture of brick and stone, and over the porch is a tower with an open belfry. Damaged by Protestants, the interior is devoid of decoration, and has simple lancet windows.

Goya: *The Balloon* (1792), in the Musée des Beaux-Arts, Agen.

Musée des Beaux-Arts

Open May–Sept 10–6; Oct–April 10–12.30 & 1.30–6; T: 05 53 69 47 23.

The Musée des Beaux-Arts ranks among the best of the provincial galleries in the southwest. It occupies a series of four 16th–17th-century *hôtels particuliers* of rich interest in themselves, with elegant staircases and panelled décor. The entrance is in the Hôtel d'Estrades (c. 1600 and 19th century), of alternate brick and stone under a steep roof. It belonged to the Count d'Estrades (1607–86), ambassador and Maréchal de France during the reigns of Louis XIII and XIV. The Hôtel de Vaurs has an Italianate façade on the Rue des Juifs and played host to Scaliger and Nostradamus. The Hôtel de Vergès has an interior courtyard and Hôtel de Monluc was the town house of the Catholic leader Blaise de Monluc (*see p. 386*) during the Wars of Religion. The space in this labyrinthine but charming setting is well used and the exhibits are presented with care. The collection includes items from prehistory through to the 20th century and is presented chronologically. Like the museums at Bayonne and Castres, it is remarkably well endowed with Spanish paintings.

Archaeological and historical collections: These contain objects discovered during excavations in Lot-et-Garonne since the end of the 19th century. Iron Age finds include a superb bronze helmet and a stunning Horse's Head in bronze (5th century BC). Among Roman works are the 1st century BC marble *Venus* from Mas-d'Agenais, in the style of the Greek sculptor Praxiteles; the smaller alabaster *Venus of Tayrac* (2nd century AD); a bronze *Horse* (2nd century AD) discovered at Aubiac; and two early Christian sarcophagi (6th century) in white Pyrenean marble. Prehistoric finds are shown in the basement and include tools, engraved bones and other objects from the Palaeolithic to Neolithic periods. The medieval room contains capitals from the lost Romanesque cloister of St-Caprais and from the Augustinian monastery founded in 1287, both of which disappeared during the Revolution. There are also gold and silverwork, and enamels.

Paintings (16th and 17th centuries): Among paintings on display on the upper floors are some 100 out of a diverse group of 600 paintings acquired mainly through donation or bequest. Works of the 16th century include a Flemish triptych of the *Crucifixion*; five portraits of men by Corneille de Lyon; and a painting of Rinaldo and Armida illustrating Tasso's epic poem *Gerusalemme Liberata*, restored in 1997 and attributed to Tintoretto. Representative of 17th-century French paintings are a *Madonna and Child* and *Portrait of Etienne Delafons*, both by Philippe de Champaigne; and the Classical-style *Daedalus and Pasiphaë* from the Cretan myth of the minotaur. Among the still lifes are Jan Davidsz de Heem's *Still Life with Fruit* (1650) and *Still Life with Apricots and Plums* by Pierre Dupuis, both skilfully evoking contrasting textures.

18th century: The 18th-century paintings are dominated by the pictures confiscated from the estate of the Dukes of Aiguillon at the Revolution. They include works by J.-F. de Troy, F.-H. Drouais, Jean-Baptiste Oudry, François Jouvenet, and small gouaches of the *Aigullon Château at Veretz* (1771) by H.-J. van Blarenberghe, crammed with topographical details. Spanish art centres on five fine works by Goya: *Self-Portrait* (1783), a confident statement of the artist as young man; *The Balloon* (1792; *pictured opposite*), showing a hot-air balloon float-

Alfred Sisley: *September Morning* (1888).

ing above a milling group of people, demonstrating Goya's extraordinarily varied technique; also *Sketch for the Equestrian Portrait of Ferdinand VII* (1808), *Capricho* (1818–19), which echoes his engravings of the same title, and *The Churching* (c. 1819).

19th century: The museum has a rich collection of 19th-century paintings. From the earlier part of the century they include paintings by Millet, Corot and Boudin. Later works include a delightful pastel by Gustave Caillebotte of *The Diver* (1877); bursts of colour in Alfred Sisley's *September Morning* (1888; *pictured above*); and Francis Picabia's *Banks of the Loing at Moret* (1904). The Romanian artist, Nicolae Grigorescu, who regularly visited France between 1862 and 1887, is represented by two appealing portraits of young women.

20th century: The modern collection focuses on a small group of artists: there are about 38 works by a local painter, Roger Bissière (1886–1964), born in Villeréal, who was influenced by Cubism and Abstraction, but also designed stained glass; and sculptures by François-Xavier and Claude Lalanne.

Decorative arts: collections include sculpture, *faïence*, porcelain, crystal and tapestries from France and elsewhere. Among them is a sample of the ceramic creations of Bernard Palissy, born at St-Avit (*see p. 352*) near Agen. There are also collections of Middle Eastern art and Asian sculpture.

Towards the Garonne

On Rue R. Coeur-de-Lion is the great brick Church of the Jacobins (*open during exhibitions*). The Dominican order was established here in Agen in 1249 and although the monastery buildings have disappeared the church still stands. Laid out on similar lines to the church of the Jacobins in Toulouse (*see p. 593*), the large empty interior designed for preaching is divided by central columns supporting 'palm' vaults, but unlike Toulouse, Agen's church has a flat apse. It is decorated with Gothic *trompe l'oeil* designs and has 14th-century windows with trefoil tracery. Close by at number 55 is a sophisticated 18th-century house, the Hôtel Montesquieu-Suffolk.

Place des Laitiers is linked westwards to Place Jasmin and the Garonne River by Blvd de la République, off which is Rue Voltaire, popular for the numerous eating places. Esplanade du Gravier was created in the 19th century from an island in the river, and the footbridge was built (1833–40) at the spot where piers were erected at the time of Richard the Lionheart. South is the Pont de Pierre, begun in 1812 following a visit by Napoleon in 1808, and to the north the Pont Canal spectacularly carries the Canal latéral à la Garonne on 23 arches over the river.

Place Armand-Fallières

In the southern part of the town on the vast Place Armand-Fallières, the Neoclassical *préfecture* is one of the finest in France, housed in the 18th-century bishops' palace designed by Julien-David Leroy, who was one of the first academic architects to travel to Greece, infusing his work with Enlightenment ideals. The Palais de Justice (1869) is by Juste Lisch, also responsible for the Elysée Palace in Paris, in Second Empire style.

THE AGENAIS

AGEN TO AUVILLAR

Aubiac

The area southeast of Agen towards Moissac is rich in Romanesque churches. The tiny community of Aubiac nestles at the foot of sloping vineyards in the shelter of the sturdy fortified church of Ste-Marie (12th century), its west façade flanked by two square towers and a round turret. To the east, around the apse roofed in stepped lauze stone tiles, are carved corbels. The west door is round-headed and inside is a single nave with barrel vaults and a narrow apse with two chapels. There is a square lantern dome on crossed arches, in Carolingian style, with billet mouldings and palmettes. Adjacent is an 18th-century château, with cellars where exhibitions are held.

Abbaye de Moirax

A Cluniac priory was founded here in 1045 by Guillaume-Arnaud de Moirax. The little town, huddled around the church, still has remnants of the walled enclosure and a tower. The abbey church (c. 1070–1140) is the Romanesque high spot in the

Agenais and introduces local characteristics to the Cluniac formula. The harmonious tripartite west façade (restored) has a large decorated door, echoed by a round-headed window above inscribed in an arch, and arcades and windows either side. Above is a small belfry with a disproportionately large roof. The exterior of the nave and transepts is sober, but the choir has a scallop design and three high windows, and the apse is enlivened with much-restored carvings. The conical dome is topped with a mini campanile and pepper-pot roof.

The interior

The interior is breathtaking, with a rhythmical pattern of columns and arches dividing up the space, and some 100 carved capitals, 17 of them with a lion motif and 13 storiated. The church is built on a basilical plan, the nave covered with slightly pointed barrel vaults (remade in the 19th century) and flanked by aisles. There is no tribune as in Toulouse or Conques, but the transition from the nave to chancel is made with massive piers supporting an arch which encompasses both the aisle entry and a twin-arched opening above, suggesting a tribune was originally intended. The square crossing has capitals with primitive carvings, including *Adam and Eve* and *Daniel in the Lions' Den*, some with touches of colour. The transepts are rib-vaulted (15th century) and the chapels are decorated with capitals and wall arches which interconnect. Above the chancel is a cupola supported by squinches, rebuilt in the 17th century. In the north and south walls are three round-headed bays above wall arcades, all with capitals. The apse is covered by a half-dome. In the nave are late 17th-century walnut stalls, which have acquired a subtle patina, and carved panels by Jean Tournier.

Layrac

The Romans chose to settle on the bluff near the confluence of the Gers and the Garonne, which is now occupied by Layrac, an impressive silhouette. In the village centre is a pleasant square with arcades and a 17th-century *fontaine-lavoir*. This town, like Moirax, developed around a Cluniac priory, a dependent of Moissac, consecrated by Pope Urban II in 1096. The priory church is the focal point of a visit. The west end is partly obscured by later cladding, and in the style of the Saintonge the portal is flanked by two blind arcades. Blind arcades also articulate the exterior of the nave and the large apse and there are damaged Romanesque capitals on the south transept chapel. Over the crossing is a huge cupola. The large entrance opens into a wonderfully luminous interior. The aisleless nave has a pointed barrel vault and transverse arches on half-shafts and the crossing is domed (18th century). There are Romanesque carved capitals on the crossing piers and the barrel vault of the chancel continues without a hiatus into the half-domed apse decorated with foliate capitals. The transept chapels have little space, and on the west walls of the transept are large blind arcades with windows set unevenly. In the chancel are 12th-century mosaics representing the *Triumph of Samson*, and there is an elaborate Neoclassical altarpiece.

Auvillar

A small brick town, Auvillar stands on an escarpment above the Garonne. The attractive Porte de l'Horloge, the old city gate with a clock-tower rebuilt in brick and stone in the 17th century, is all that is left of the city defences demolished in 1572. In the town centre is a small triangular arcaded place surrounded by quite grand 17th- and 18th-century brick houses and

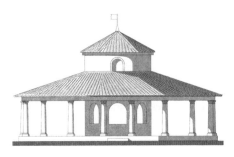

THE ROUND MARKET AT AUVILLAR

one 16th-century building. Justly famous is the circular market hall, its roof radiating out from a small central drum to rest on a Tuscan colonnade. It was built in 1825 and under its skirts are ancient grain measures. Auvillar reached its commercial high-point in the 18th century, thanks to its port on the Garonne, now a *base de loisirs*, and to the manufacture of pottery. There is a collection of faïence in the Musée du Vieil-Auvillar.

The château, north of the marketplace, disappeared in the 16th century but the Place du Château offers a tremendous vantage-point over the vast Garonne Valley as far as the slopes of the Quercy. The church of St-Pierre has an extraordinary ruined west tower, with two turrets and a belfry, built in the 16th century but almost entirely demolished in 1794, and then restored in 1862. The church also has a curiously disjointed exterior, the result of damage and rebuilds during the Hundred Years War and the Wars of Religion. It is strikingly large (43m long), the older parts in stone while the rest is in brick. The north apsidal chapel is all that is left of the earlier 11th–12th-century church, with some carved capitals of that period. The apse is Flamboyant and the nave dates from the 15th and 17th centuries. There is a Counter-Reformation retable behind the main altar.

PAYS DE SERRES

The Pays de Serres, an area northwest of Agen between the Garonne and the Lot, is a jagged, rocky landscape harbouring small delights in the shape of isolated churches and tiny *bastides*. There are also caves with remarkable natural formations, the Grottes de Fontirou at Castella (*open July, Aug 10–12 & 2–6; May–mid-June, Sun and holidays only 2–5.30; 15th–30th June, 1st–15th Sept 2–5.30; T: 05 53 41 73 97*) and the Grottes de Lastournelle at Ste-Colombe-de-Villeneuve (*open July, Aug 10–12 & 2–6.30; rest of year Sun or by appointment; T: 05 53 40 08 09*).

Further west, in an area where the sweet Chasselas grape is cultivated, **Prayssas** is a circular 13th-century *bastide* with four gates and a 12th-century chancel and tower on the church. Between Villeneuve and Prayssas (signposted) is the **Château de Madaillan** (*guided visits, Aug daily; for other times, T: 05 53 87 56 23*). A 13th–15th century stronghold, it resisted several sieges by Blaise de Monluc against the Protestants who had taken it over in 1575. **Monpezat d'Agenais** was the only English *bastide* in this region and the last Huguenot stronghold in the Agenais to surrender at the accession of Henri IV. A footpath leads to the churches of St-Jean de la Balerme, St-Vincent-de-Pérignac, St-Médard and Floirac.

Northeast of Agen are attractive villages such as **Laroque-Timbaut**, with a 12th-century market hall (restored) and, in the valley, a church and fountain which, legend has it, cured Roland's army of a contagious illness; **Hautefage-la-Tour**, which has a Renaissance tower and a 15th-century church under which is a spring that supposedly cures sterility in women—Anne de Neaujeu, daughter of Louis XI, visited and conceived a daughter; **Frespech**, a minuscule fortified village within the remains of 11th–14th-century walls, with an 11th-century chapel and a museum of foie gras; and further east, true to its name, **Beauville**, a pretty *bastide* set high above the Séoune Valley.

Puymirol

Puymirol, east of Agen, was the first *bastide* in the Agenais. It was established in 1246 by Raymond VII, Count of Toulouse, on a ridge overlooking the valley at a strategic point close to the Clermont–Agen route which had already been occupied in Roman times. Strongly fortified and supposedly impregnable, in 1574 it was taken by the Protestants, who remained until 1589. As a consequence, in the 17th century the ancient town received harsh treatment from Louis XIII, who destroyed much of the ramparts, although worse followed in the end of the 19th and early 20th centuries when the inhabitants used the stone from the walls to build their houses. In the town centre an 18th-century house has been transformed into an unusual and elegant hotel-restaurant (*see p. 369*).

ALONG THE VALLEYS OF THE LOT & THE LÈDE

NB: the following sections (to p. 364) are covered by the map on p. 102.

The Lot rises in the Cévennes and is one of the longest and most beautiful rivers in France, flowing from the east into the Garonne just north of Aguillon. During the English occupation of Guyenne (*see p. 354*), these lower reaches of the river were border territory, explaining the intense concentration of *bastides*, founded for defence by both the French and the English. The river flows gently across a wide, open valley that is also plum country, where the famous *pruneaux d'Agen* (*see box on opposite page*) are produced. The main town today is Villeneuve-sur-Lot, just above the confluence of the Lot and its tributary the Lède, a much smaller river but also fortified during the Middle Ages with a succession of impressive hilltop towns such as Monflanquin.

Clairac

Clairac, situated on the right bank of the Lot northeast of Aiguillon, is a little town steeped in history. It began life around a Benedictine abbey in the 8th century. The monks are credited with the introduction of the *prune d'Ente*, the particular type of plum used in the production of prunes; also of tobacco, and the region has benefited ever since. Clairac is best viewed from the river. The life of the abbey is celebrated in the Village des Automates (*open April–Oct 10–6.30; Jan–March, Oct–Nov Wed, Sat, Sun and holidays 10–6.30; also open during school holidays; T: 05 53 79 34 81*). The museum consists of tableaux with automated models of benign monks going about their daily devotions and amusingly conveys a quantity of information (French commentary, English text) on monastery life and the history of Aquitaine. It also introduces celebrated personalities associated with the town, such as Montesquieu (*see p. 90*), who wrote *Lettres persanes* (1721), a satirical description of French society, at Clairac.

PLUMS & PRUNES

The succulent *pruneaux d'Agen* are quite the best prunes in the world, and the Lot-et-Garonne is responsible for 65 per cent of national production. It all began when the Templars brought the plum back from Damascus in the 11th century but it was not until the 15th and 16th centuries that the transformation of plums into prunes began in earnest. From 1815, the fruit of the *prunier d'Ente* (from Old French *enter*, to graft) was the main variety. The prunes originally received the stamp of the Port of Agen when shipped out on the Garonne, and the label has stuck. The plums are harvested between 15th August and 25th September. In 1856 Pierre Pellier took plum scions embedded in potatoes to his brother in California where they grafted the first plums and so began the prune industry on the US west coast, although still nothing beats the veritable *pruneaux d'Agen*. A remarkable number of *prumandises* have been devised, including creams, juices and concentrates, prunes in syrup, in Armagnac, in *eau de vie*, and preparations which include chocolate. The most exotic are *pruneaux fourrés*, the stone replaced by a *crème d'Armagnac* or some other filling. But these top-quality prunes are really best eaten simply as they are.

Granges-sur-Lot to Casseneuil

The countryside is densely cultivated with vines, plums and maize all along the valley to Granges-sur-Lot and the Atelier-Musée, Au Pruneau Gourmand (*open March-Nov 9–12 & 2–7, Sun and holidays 3-7; Nov–March until 6.30; closed last 2 weeks of Jan; T: 05 53 84 00 69*). This museum is well presented and offers not only all kinds of historic details about the life and times of the prune, including an audio-visual display, but also the opportunity to buy and sample the remarkable number of *prumandises* that have been devised.

At **Le Temple-sur-Lot** are the handsome remains of the Templar commandery and chapel founded in the 12th century and rebuilt in brick in the 15th century by the Knights of Malta, with round towers and mullioned windows.

Nearby (off the D911) is the waterlily garden of **Latour-Marliac** (*open mid-March–Sept 10–6; T: 05 53 01 08 05*), the oldest waterlily nursery in the world, founded in 1875. Hardy varieties were developed here by Joseph Bory Latour-Marliac and the fame of his work was such that Claude Monet purchased the lilies for his own garden at Giverny from here. There are some 100 varieties of waterlilies and other water plants, mainly in outdoor tanks, as well as gardens with a statue of the founder.

The church at **Fongrave** north of the river was once part of a priory dependent on the Abbey of Fontevraud in the Loire, from which it acquired an elaborate wooden retable, an excessive but magnificent piece in Counter-Reformation style, with twisted columns framing a painting of the *Adoration of the Magi*. **Ste-Livrade-sur-Lot**, whose church was once part of a priory, was founded by the English, whose church was once part of a priory. The chevet is a Romanesque classic decorated with arcades, storiated capitals and billet mouldings. The remainder was rebuilt (15th century) in brick. Inside, the apse is covered in a half-dome and there is a recumbent marble statue of a bishop, finely carved but damaged. **Casseneuil**, at the confluence of the Lot and the Lède, was a little river port. It has pretty riverside façades, and a 12th–16th-century brick church with a series of early 16th-century murals (*key at the Tourist Office*).

Pujols

On a hill covered with fruit orchards above Villeneuve-sur-Lot, Pujols has been occupied since time immemorial. A Roman *castrum* protected the route between the Pyrenees and the Landes forest, called La Tenarèze (*see p. 377*). It became one of the most important fortifications in the Agenais by the 7th century and later a fiefdom of Raymond VI of Toulouse. It was not besieged during the Albigensian crusades but following the Treaty of Meaux in 1228 the stronghold was razed and the inhabitants moved to Villeneuve in the valley. Later in the 13th century the hill was substantially re-fortified with ramparts, towers, deep ditches and a castle enveloping the community. During the Religious Wars and the Fronde (*see p. 16*), Royalist Pujols stood firm against rebellious Villeneuve but suffered badly. After the Revolution the fortifications were abandoned, the ramparts demolished, and the château sold for its building materials. Some of the 13th-century ramparts are still in place though and a round tower to the east is a reminder of the castle. The entrance to the village is under the church belfry and leads to the Place du Marché with a wooden market hall (1860). The 15th-century church of St-Nicolas, Gothic Flamboyant and Renaissance, has tribunes equipped with fireplaces where the baronial families kept warm during mass. The other church, Ste-Foy-La-Jeune (15th century) to the south of the town, is now an exhibition space and contains some splendid murals (end 15th century) including the *Martyrdom of St Faith* (*see p. 218*) in three bays of the nave and choir.

Villeneuve-sur-Lot

The small town of Villeneuve-sur-Lot originated in another *bastide* founded by Alphonse after the Albigensian crusade in 1264 (*see p. 251*). The remains of the old defences consist in the Porte de Pujols to the southwest and the Porte de Paris to the northeast of the river, each with a stone base, brick above and steep roof. These demarcate the extent of the old town. Linking the old gates is the 13th-century Pont Vieux, built by the English (part rebuilt in 1642) and from it are picturesque views of dilapidated houses on the river. On the north side of the bridge is the chapel of Notre-Dame-du-Bout-du-Pont (rebuilt in the 16th century) curiously suspended over the river and containing *ex-votos*. Villeneuve has two churches: Ste-Catherine, a neo-Romano-Byzantine pile by Corroyer, begun in 1898, of appalling starkness in bright red brick, white stone and granite, with a tall octagonal belfry. The interior is decorated with mosaics representing different St Catherines (of Alexandria, Bologna, Siena, Sweden for example). In the chapels are 23 precious stained-glass windows (15th–early 16th centuries) saved from the Gothic church and similar to those in Auch (*see p. 396*) but less sophisticated. St-Etienne on the south bank is Gothic redesigned in the 17th century.

MONFLANQUIN & THE LÈDE

The meandering valley of the Lède River leads to Monflanquin, an important *bastide* which follows the shape of the hilltop. Alphonse de Poitiers acquired the 'mountain of Monflanquin' in 1252, and the *bastide* received its charter in 1256. When the Agenais passed to Edward I, Monflanquin, on border territory, was fortified with ramparts and towers; seconded by the French in 1346, it went back to the English again ten years later. The Château de Roquefère (13th–16th century) to the north was part of the defensive system. Monflanquin was an active Protestant town from 1562 and its fortifications played a part during the Reformation and Catholic attacks. It was subsequently recognised as a Protestant place of safety in 1598. After the accession of Louis XIII the ramparts were dismantled and in their place is the exterior boulevard.

Exploring Monflanquin

The Place des Arcades at the centre, is defined by the two parallel streets, Ste-Marie and St-Pierre, and enhanced by harmonious but not uniform *cornières*. A 13th-century house has a timber-and-brick façade supported by one main beam; the pillars of a 15th-century house supported the grain measures; and the so-called Black Prince's house (14th century) is distinguished by its height, the quality of the masonry and window tracery. The Tourist Office houses the **Musée des Bastides** (*open July, Aug 10–12.30 & 2.30-7; rest of year 10–12.30 & 2.30–6.30, Sun 3–5; visits in English in July, Aug, Tues, Fri at 5*), a comprehensive exhibition and explanation of the history and creation of the planned towns, using models, sculptures, audio-visual and scenographic displays (English translations). The smaller streets, or *carrerots*, which subdivide the space, are occasionally spanned by bridge-like *pontets* built in timber with brick or cob infill. Between the Carrerots Cabannes and Augustins, is the former Protestant Temple and the library. When open, the terrace of the latter affords panoramic views over the rooftops and beyond. The Church of Notre-Dame, on a diagonal with the main square, dates from the same time as the *bastide* but was rebuilt in the 18th century and more radically altered in the 19th century; some of the 13th-century base survives. The glass for the upper windows comes from Bordeaux and for the three lower ones from the Benedictine Abbey d'En Calcat in the Tarn.

Montagnac and St-Avit

At Montagnac there is a fortified church and old mill, the Moulin de Cros (*open July, Aug, Tues–Thurs 3–6; T: 05 53 36 44 78*), and further upstream, a huge six-storey keep rises out of the vertical cliff overhanging a narrow gorge. This is the only substantial reminder of the 12th–14th-century Château of Gavaudun (*open July, Aug 10–6; June, Sept 10–1 & 2–6; T: 05 53 40 04 16 or 05 05 40 82 29*).

At **St-Avit** is the Musée Bernard Palissy (*open July–Aug 11–5, May–Sept 2.30–5; Oct, Sun and holidays 2.30–5, closed Tues; T: 05 53 40 98 22*), dedicated to the Renaissance ceramicist, scholar and writer (1510–c. 1589). He perfected his art at Saintes, where he researched the technique of enamelled pottery. His strange, rustic ceramics decorated with high relief flora and fauna brought him fame at Court, but he was persecuted for his Protestant beliefs and died in the Bastille.

EAST OF VILLENEUVE-SUR-LOT

Back on the Lot, but high above the valley, is **Penne d'Agenais**, its steep-sided streets and medieval houses reminiscent of Provence. When Richard Lionheart became Duke of Guyenne in 1169 he fortified the small fort of Penne which had probably existed since the 11th century. A pilgrimage site since 1373, the most recent in a succession of churches (1897–1947) is a white neo-Byzantine basilica at the summit recalling St-Front at Périgueux. **Lustrac** has a 13th-century fortified mill and southeast, **Tournon d'Agenais** is a high *bastide* fortified by Edward I. It has some delightful half-timbered buildings including the 13th-century Maison de l'Abescat, arcades, and a clock tower with sundial. The *chemin de ronde* looks out over gentle countryside. North of the Lot, looking down into the valley, **Monsempron-Libos** has a sturdy church with a square tower, built in the 11th and 12th centuries on the site of a temple dedicated to Cybele, ancient Phrygian earth mother; a large choir was added in the 16th century. It is decorated with pierced metopes on the exterior, and the nave vaults and domed crossing are Romanesque. **Fumel** is an industrial town on the north bank of the Lot. At its heart is a handsome 18th-century château housing the *Mairie* which has an attractive river frontage, the Gardens and Château de Fumel (*guided tours June 10–12 & 2–5; July, Aug 10-5.45; Feb–Apr, Sept–Nov 10-12 & 2.30-4.30; closed Jan*). There are marvellous views from the terrace and interesting collection of trees and shrubs in the gardens.

Château de Bonaguil

Open June–Aug 10–6; Feb–March 11–1 & 2.30–5.30; Apr–May, Sept 10.30–1 & 2.30–5.30; Oct 11–1 & 2.30–5; Nov Sunday and holidays 11–1 & 2.30–5; Dec school vacations 2.30–5; Closed Jan; last entry 30 mins before closing; guided visits in English in July, Aug; T: 05 53 71 13 70.

The route to the magnificent Château de Bonaguil twists and turns through lush countryside before its towering turrets suddenly rise before you. It was the last of the great fortified castles to be built in France, standing on a rocky promontory with 13 towers and turrets, and military architecture ranging from the 13th to the 18th cen-

Château de Bonaguil (16th century).

tury. Bonaguil spans the style of military architecture at the end of the Middle Ages and the beginning of the Renaissance. It is organised concentrically, with a very strong exterior enclosure including bastions and barbican. The interior enclosure has five towers, one with exceptionally thick walls, and at the very centre is the superb keep topped with a slender look-out tower.

History of the castle

It is known that a castle existed here in the 13th century on land belonging to Jeanne de Toulouse. At her death in 1271 it became the property of the king, Philippe III, and some time later passed to the powerful House of Roquefeuil. Jean de Roquefeuil reconstructed it in the 15th century but the present version, which incorporates some earlier elements, dates from 1480–1520, the work of the long-lived Béranger de Roquefeuil (1448–1530). He vowed to build a castle which neither his 'brutish subjects, nor the English if they had the cheek to return, nor even the most powerful soldiers of the King of France, could seize …' Béranger's stronghold was somewhat of an anachronism at the beginning of the 16th century, a time when most *chatelains* were building fortified palaces rather than feudal castles, but it is also adapted to contemporary advances in military technology. Lawrence of Arabia visited in 1908 and was impressed with the provision for artillery and with the 'perfect' state of the ruin. There is no documented evidence of attacks, although there is evidence of damage during the Wars of Religion. At the Revolution, the château was declared national property and was partly demolished. Taken over by the Commune of Fumel in 1860, restoration work, sometimes brutal, was carried out in late 19th century, in 1949–50 and 1977.

Visiting the castle

The entrance is through the massive semicircular barbican on the vulnerable northern side, which leads into a courtyard overlooked by the prow of the vast central *donjon* to the left and the great tower, huge but truncated, to the right. Between the barbican and the inner enclosure there was originally a drawbridge, now a fixed one, leading to the main entrance to either side of which are *cannonières* (cannon loops). The slope to the left leads past the dovecote to *la cour basse* in the shadow of the keep, from where it is obvious how its shape was determined by the rock that it stands on. On the lower level are the remains of outbuildings and beyond are the curtain walls of the outer enclosure. The entrance to the underground gallery is to the right, ending close to the great tower (La Grosse Tour), originally 40m high (now 29m). Within its huge walls was a self-contained living unit and defences (similar to towers at Aigues Mortes and Carcassonne). The remains of the *chemin de ronde* is supported by corbels in the shape of inverted pyramids and pierced with round machicolations. The esplanade to the south is 18th-century and ends in a *chicane* or carefully designed trap. The square tower had its own drawbridge, and beyond is the red tower (La Tour Rouge); both have cannon loops. The square tower leads to the main courtyard (La Cour d'Honneur), with a well and the main apartments (Le Logis Seigneurial) including the great room. The doorway to the main living area has an elegant ogee arch and inside are rooms with monumental fireplaces (late 15th century) and 16th–18th-century graffiti. A steep flight of 22 steps and a spiral staircase of 68 steps in the look-out turret climbs to the terrace on top of the keep. Eighteen more steps (108 altogether) take you up the turret. In the keep, two rooms are set up as a small museum.

GUYENNE

Guyenne, thought to be a popular phonetic deformation of Aquitaine, was the name given to that English province from the mid-13th century until the end of the Hundred Years War in 1453. Until the 15th century it was a vague area of fluctuating boundaries, determined more by natural constraints, language and religion than by administrative concerns: it stretched from the Gironde estuary along the Garonne to Valence d'Agen and north to Monpazier and the Périgord. It ended to the east at the Quercy. Eventually it was absorbed into the modern *département* of Lot-et-Garonne

THE DROPT VALLEY

The Dropt River rises near Monpazier (Dordogne) and flows some 120km, linking Périgord with Guyenne, until it meets the Garonne west of La Réole. In the 13th century this was the boundary between English Guyenne and French Agenais, and to protect their territories both sides built *bastides* (*see box on p. 358*). The rolling countryside is a patchwork of vineyards, woodland and fields of maize, and is dotted in places with the remains of windmills, and a number of small, simple Romanesque churches.

Château de Duras

Open daily July–Aug 10–7; June, Sept 10– 12.30, 2–7; March, April, May, Oct and winter hols 10–12, 2–6; Nov–Feb 10–12, 2–6; T: 05 53 83 77 32.

Duras is a popular and attractive *bastide* built on a ridge overlooking the Dropt and surrounded by the vineyards of Côtes-de-Duras abutting those of Bordeaux. Duras claims the oldest AOC in the Guyenne (compared to Côtes-de-Buzet and Côtes-de-Marmandais) and produces the whites, reds and rosé to a good quality. The writer, Marguerite Duras, née Donnadieu (1914–96), adopted her professional name from the area where her father owned a property. At its western extremity is the elegant 17th-century château, much restored, and often used for theatrical performances.

History of the château

The first castle was begun in the 12th century but rebuilt in 1308 by Bertrand de Got, a member of one of the most powerful local families and nephew of Pope Clement V (another Bertrand) from Villandraut. In 1324, the strongly fortified property with eight towers passed to the Durfort family who fought with the English during the Hundred Years War and remained steadfastly English until Charles V made an all-out bid to regain the Guyenne in 1376. A powerful army led by Bernard du Guesclin laid siege to Duras, which capitulated after eight days; all therein were executed. After the English defeat at Castillon in 1453, the lords of Duras fled to England. By 1689 the Durfort became Dukes of Duras for services rendered to Louis XIV and built the pres-

The Château de Duras (17th century).

tigious 17th-century residence that stands today. After the Revolution all the towers but the largest were truncated, the place was sold and left to deteriorate until the commune took over and began restoration in 1973.

The interior
Protecting the Château de Duras is a medieval fortified gateway and on the left is the 18th-century *petit château*. Inside is a large courtyard with a double flight of monumental steps to the entrance, which leads into the vast Salle des Maréchaux and the adjacent Chambre de la Duchesse on the ground floor. Beyond is an inner courtyard with Italianate peristyle on the east and view of the park to the west. On the next floor is the Salle de la Charpente with a fine wooden ceiling; originally there were 11 fireplaces. From here you gain access to the large south tower, with a rewarding 360 degree view. The visit continues through various exhibitions and down to the two lower levels of vaulted cellars with a close-up of the remarkable great well of the house. Most of the basement rooms are used to house a small museum of local archaeology and culture. There are more rooms (some 32 in all), corridors and dungeons on upper levels.

The village
The main street, Rue Jauffret, leads from the Place du Marché, with a few arcades, past the former 17th-century Protestant Temple. This reverted to the Catholic Church in 1685 and has been known as the church of the Madeleine ever since. The interior was decoratively restored in 1932 by Giovanni Mazutti. At the end of the street is the only remaining ancient town gate. At Rue des Eyzins is the Musée du Parchemin et de l'Enluminure (*open April–June, Sept 3–7; July, Aug 11–1 & 3–7; T: 05 53 20 75 55*), with reconstructions of medieval workshops demonstrating the making of parchment and illuminations.

Along the Dropt
A few kilometres northwest of Duras at **Esclottes** is one of the oldest Romanesque churches (11th century, rebuilt in the 13th) in the region, with sculpted capitals representing *Christ in Glory*, the four Evangelists, the *Adoration of the Magi* and *Tobias and the Fish*. On a high bluff at **Monteton** is the movingly simple Romanesque church of Notre-Dame with a gable belfry, and a view from the terrace of 13 other belfries. The interior is equally uncomplicated, the buttresses linked by arches and the *Hand of God blessing the World* on the altar.

At neighbouring **Allemans-du-Dropt** the church of Ste-Eutrope is basically 12th-century and was decorated in the 15th century with an extraordinary group of murals, discovered in the 20th century. Over the chancel is a horseshoe arch in Mozarab style. The paintings include the *Last Supper* on the north wall, and in the chancel the *Carrying of the Cross*, *Crucifixion*, *Entombment* and the *Resurrection*. In *Christ in Judgement*, a spirited St Michael overcomes demons and the condemned are carried off to Hell like eggs in a basket. Behind the altar are the coat of arms of the lords of

Allemans and St-Martin. The church of St-Gervaise at **La Sauvetat-du-Dropt** boasts a fine 12th-century choir, but was damaged by a cyclone in 1242 (see the inscription). Rebuilt in the 16th century, the choir and portal are flamboyantly decorated. An old bridge over the Dropt here has a series of round arches followed by a series of 13th-century arches.

Eymet

One of the best-preserved *bastides* in the Dropt Valley is Eymet, founded in 1270 by Alphonse de Poitiers as part of a line of French defences on the southern boundary of the Périgord. The site has been occupied since the dawn of time: standing stones point to Bronze Age activity nearby, traces of Roman villas have been discovered, and a priory was established here by Moissac c. 1000 (*see p. 330*). This was near the junction of two Roman roads and the castle remains are built on the 11th-century *castrum*. In 1279 it came under the control of the Plantagenets who added fortifications c. 1320 (destroyed in 1830). Eymet's history was turbulent but it remained mainly English despite a particularly bloody battle in 1377 against du Guesclin's men (*see p. 109*). When the siege was over, the southern gate had to be partly demolished because a huge war machine had become stuck there, and has been called the Porte de l'Engin ever since. The town supported the Protestant Jeanne of Navarre, and Henri of Navarre frequently passed through Eymet.

It has retained its attractive central Place de la Bastide, surrounded typically by a variety of medieval arcades and façades. North of the square is the 12th- and 13th-century keep of the old château, and in a slightly later building is a small Museum of Archaeology (*open July, Aug Mon–Sat 3–6.30; Thur, 10–12*).

Lauzun

South of the Dropt, Lauzun is a quaint place with some surprises. It was the birthplace in 1632 of Antoine Nompar de Caumont, favourite of Louis XIV, who became Maréchal de France and, scandalously, the lover of the Grande Demoiselle, niece of the king. The home of the Dukes of Lauzun was the château begun in the 13th century although the main building, which has an octagonal tower, is 15th–16th-century. The two parts are linked by a domed pavilion built by the Maréchal in the 17th and 19th centuries. The small church is mainly Gothic although a tiny part of the west front is Romanesque and it contains some good furnishings including the 17th-century altar, retable and carved panels. In the neighbourhood, although they take some searching out, are some tiny examples of Romanesque churches at Queyssel, Maurillac and St-Colombe.

Villeréal

The small community of **Villeréal** further east, overlooking the right bank of the Dropt, is an Alphonsine *bastide* founded in 1269 with a wonderful covered market on 14th-century wooden piers with a 16th–17th-century second floor, and also a fortified church.

BASTIDES

These were the planned towns of the Middle Ages, of which some 300 still exist in southwest France between Bordeaux and the Pyrenees. Medieval new towns were not exclusive to southwest France but their density and the word *bastide* (from Occitan or old French *bastir*, to build) certainly are. They offered a means to administer the domains of the ruling factions, the Counts of Toulouse (crucial following the Albigensian Crusades, *see p. 251*) and of Aquitaine. From 1154, the Dukes of Aquitaine were also the Plantagenet kings of England, and as tension increased with the French Capetians, *bastides* were a means of establishing administrative supremacy and, later, military domination. During some 300 years of struggle between the English and the French, the Haut-Agenais (Lot-et-Garonne and Dordogne) was the frontier zone between territories, accounting for the high number of *bastides* here. They date mainly from the beginning of the 13th century to c. 1370. There are five main groups according to founder: the Counts of Toulouse; Alphonse de Poitiers (1249–71), who inherited land in the southwest through his wife, Jeanne de Toulouse; the Kings of England; and the Kings of France from 1281 onwards; the last category, foundation by *paréage*, was a joint arrangement between a founding authority (the overlord) and the ecclesiastical or secular owner of the land, when the deeds of foundation were drawn up defining the rights and benefits of each of the signatories. A *chartre des coutumes*, crucial to the inhabitants, set out civil and political liberties or constraints, legal obligations and economic objectives, the most important privilege being the status of freeman. Some *bastides* were built on virgin territory, others on or near a pre-existing community. Sites were chosen for their natural advantages, on top of a hill or in proximity to a main route or junction, a ford, or good agricultural land. The overall shape was regular (square or rectangular) as far as topography allowed: one of the major characteristics is the rectilinear grid plan with a large open central square for trading. The land was divided into equally sized *ilots* or building plots, usually long and narrow, which were allocated to prospective inhabitants. The church was nearly always set back diagonally from the centre. The community would be granted the right to hold markets and to build market halls (*halles*) which often incorporated weights and measures and communal bread ovens. Administration was controlled by consuls whose *maison commune*, or meeting place, was in certain instances built in or over the *halle*. The main streets are called *charretières*, the minor ones *carrerots*, and *androand* are the narrow spaces separating the houses for drainage or firebreaks. The arcades around the central square were not part of the original construction but were added when permission was granted to extend façades over the public walkway. *Bastides* were not necessarily fortified from the outset, and many acquired ramparts and gates later on.

Monpazier

The ultimate *bastide* in the southwest is Monpazier, which has conserved much of its original character. It is a rectangle 400m by 220m, with sections of the walls still standing and the four gateways virtually intact. A contract to found this town was entered into between Edward I and Pierre de Gontaut-Biron in 1284. Strategically placed between the Agenais and Périgord, it completed a chain of English defence and colonisation which had begun in 1267. It fell to the French, returned to the English in 1316, and during Anglo-French hostilities changed hands several times between 1360 and 1453. In 1574 it was taken by the Protestants. Serious peasant revolts broke out in the region in 1594 and 1637 and the leader of the latter, Buffarot, was horribly executed on a wheel in the square.

The main streets arrive at the corners of the large place which is empty except for the covered *halle*, a forest of chestnut timbers. In it are the old grain measures. Jostling for room around the square and abutting awkwardly at the corners, the old houses adhere strictly to the original uniform dimensions with each façade and roofline expressing a complete independence of style developed over the centuries, as do the variety of cool arcades spanning the walkways, flooded with pools of light and shade on a bright day. The church, off the main square, was begun at the same time as the town but modified in the 15th and 16th centuries. The sculpted portal was remade in the 16th century, and on it is a Jacobin proclamation: *Le peuple français reconnaît l'existence de l'être suprême et de l'immortalité de l'âme* ('The French people believe in the existence of a supreme being and the immortality of the soul'). Inside are some rustic Romanesque capitals and some very fine 14th-century choir stalls with carvings. Opposite the church is the 14th-century Maison du Chapitre on three floors with Gothic bays, where tithes were collected.

This is a strawberry-growing area, with delicious late local fruit, and it also produces tobacco and the ubiquitous maize. The source of the Dropt is at Capdrot, to the east of Monpazier.

Château de Biron

Guided visits July–Aug 10–7; April–June, Sept–mid-Nov 10–12.30 & 2–6, closed Mon; mid-Nov–mid-Dec, Feb–March 10–12.30 & 2–5.30, closed Mon, Fri, Sat; mid- to end-Dec, 10–12.30 & 2–5, closed Mon; closed Jan; T: 05 53 63 13 39.

The awe-inspiring silhouette of the Château de Biron greets you from its lofty position, and small houses cluster at the foot of the knoll. The château is the product of several stages of construction determined by the vagaries of history and the fortunes of the Gontaut-Biron family, who owned it for some 800 years (*see box overleaf*).

Visiting the château

The château is on several levels, irregular in shape, and arranged around a large outer or lower courtyard and a more compact upper *cour d'honneur*. The visit begins in the lower court, dominated by the main part of the château to the west and a church opposite. There is some Renaissance detail in the 16th-century loggia. The surprisingly large chapel, one of the masterpieces of Biron, was built in the early 16th century and displays late-Gothic and early Renaissance characteristics. It consists of two superimposed naves, the upper one opening into the courtyard for the use of the nobility, and the lower serving as the parish church accessed from the village. The upper chapel originally contained a superb group of sculptures, of which two tombs are still in place; although damaged, their quality is quite apparent. The tomb nearest the altar is that of Pons de Gontaut (d. 1524) and has scenes from the *Life of Christ* and of *Lazarus*. The other tomb commemorates the Bishop of Sarlat, Armand de Gontaut (d. 1531), who built the chapel, and is decorated with the *Three Virtues*. The chapel has stellar vaults and pendant bosses. The missing works, a very fine *Pietà*, and an *Entombment* comprising eight figures in a wooden frame, were sold in 1907 and are now in the Metropolitan Museum of Art, New York.

Around the *cour d'honneur* are the remains of the 12th-century fort, including the keep and the main living quarters redesigned in the 15th century with mullioned windows. The large Neoclassical building (17th century), built by the Maréchal de Biron before his disgrace, contains the council chamber of the Etats Généraux, which dates from pre-revolutionary France and was convened by the king to treat important matters of state. Inside is a huge kitchen, some fine fireplaces and precious parquets. The water supply, as in most castles, was from a cistern under the courtyard. At the end of the courtyard, an arcade and peristyle with 18th-century columns form a loggia with views over Périgord Noir.

HISTORY OF CHÂTEAU DE BIRON

Biron was the seat of one of the four great baronies of Périgord (the others were Beynac, Bourdeilles and Mareuil). The first baron, Gaston de Gontaut, a very distant ancestor of Lord Byron, built a fort in the 12th century to protect his territory from the neighbouring Agenais. A later baron with Cathar sympathies felt the wrath of Simon de Montfort (*see p. 251*) and the consequent destruction of much of Biron in 1212. It was besieged during the Hundred Years War (*see p. 14*). In the late 15th century Pons de Biron, one of many soldiers who returned from campaigns in Italy with Charles VIII, had money to spend and new ideas of comfort and elegance, and was given permission to remodel his castle in a style akin to those of the Loire valley. More changes were effected by Baron Armand de Gontaut (1524–92), Maréchal de France, who fought with Henri IV against the Catholics. His son Charles was elevated to duke in the 1598 by the king, but soon fell from grace and was beheaded at the Bastille in 1602. After the Religious Wars the moats were filled in. The family fortunes revived in the 18th century with the inheritance of Lauzun and more alterations were made. Viollet-le-Duc (*see p. 95*) brought his talents to the restoration of the castle in the 19th century.

THE MARMANDAIS

The Marmandais, surrounded by the Dropt, the Garonne and the Lot, was traditionally given over to market gardening, although now cereals and vineyards are cultivated. The Marmande tomato, plump and tasty, was perfected at the end of the 19th century, and tobacco was introduced in the 18th century; there are a few surviving wooden tobacco drying sheds. The vineyards of the little-known Côtes-du-Marmandais extend over both banks of the Garonne, around Seches, Cocument and Beaupuy.

MARMANDE & ENVIRONS

Described as *'Marmande la jolie'*, an accolade awarded by 1940s mayor, M. Grossot, Marmande depended for centuries on the Garonne for its living. The bronze statue, *La Pomme d'Amour*, which has become the emblem of the town, is of a young girl with a tomato, a reference to the legendary properties (erotic, exotic, aphrodisiac) of the fruity vegetable. It sits in the rather heartless Place Clemenceau, with the Hôtel de Ville on the south. Close by is the Musée Municipal Albert-Marzelles (*open Tues–Fri 3–6; Sat 10–12 & 3–6; T: 05 53 64 42 04*). It is essentially a museum of local history. The town's ancient source of fresh water is remembered by the Nine Fountains (19th century) on Place des Fontaines. Rue L. Faye leads to the Church of Notre-Dame (13th–17th century), whose redeeming feature is its Renaissance cloister. Of the original building begun in 1275, partly rebuilt in 14th and 15th centuries, only the main façade and porch, and the last bays of the aisles have survived following a fire and explosion in 1648 when choir and tower had to be rebuilt. The central vault boss has six *fleurs de lys*, which suggests a date prior to the reign of Charles VII (1354-80) who replaced multiple fleur-de-lis on the royal coat of arms with three as symbol of the Trinity, the object of royal devotion. Below the rose window with trefoil tracery is a tribune and one of the best Cavaillé-Col organs in Aquitaine. There is a 17th-century *Entombment* in wood. The cloister (1545) on the south was desecrated during the Religious Wars and contains the late 16th-century doorway of the Caillade chapel. In 1950 the cloister and adjoining land were transformed into classical French gardens, with box topiary and lindens. West of Notre-Dame is the Place du Marché and further west, in Rue Labat are some of the best old facades (15th–16th centuries) in Marmande. On the banks of the Garonne, is the Lavoir des Cinq Cannelles and the *Chemin de Ronde*.

Just north-west of Marmande, giving views over the town, is Beaupuy, a hilltop village with a wine co-operative. Castelnau-sur-Gupie was a 13th-century English *bastide* dominating the valley, as St-Pierre-de-Londres should have been, but only the church was built and most of that was demolished in the 18th century; there are a few storiated capitals in the porch. Seyches further up the same road, has a tower-gateway and was an English possession. The Dukes of Biron hailed from the village of **Gontaud-de-Nogaret** which has an exceptionally pretty church with 13th-century façade and 12th-century transept and apse.

Rembrandt: *Christ on the Cross* (1631), in the church of St-Vincent, Mas d'Agenais.

MAS D'AGENAIS

The now modest village of Mas d'Agenais on the Garonne started out as Roman *Velenum Pompejacum* and here, in 1877, the fine marble statue of *Venus* (now in the Musée des Beaux-Arts, Agen, *see p. 343*) was uncovered by a farmer in his field. There is a solid market hall with 17th-century timbers and attractive restored houses. The Fontaine Galiane (along Rue Galiane) is also under a timber structure. South of the main square, via the Roman Gate, is a view over the Garonne and the Canal.

Church of St-Vincent

The main attraction of Mas is the painting *Christ on the Cross* (1631; *pictured opposite*) by Rembrandt in the Church of St-Vincent (buy *jetons* from the Tourist Office or shops to illuminate the work), but the church itself comes a very close second. The church is one of the best in the region, such was the importance of Mas during the Middle Ages. It was begun in 1085 after the destruction of a 6th century church, and completed about 40 years later. Viollet-le-Duc (*see p. 95*) and Abadie rebuilt the west front in 1862, and the wooden spire was taken down in 1873, resulting in a somewhat severe exterior. There is much to delight inside, however. Entering through the south transept, the layout can be seen to be Benedictine, similar to Moirax (*see p. 345*) with a barrel-vaulted nave and aisles, barely projecting transepts, and tripartite east end. The crossing was rebuilt in the 16th century as was the five-sided chapel. The richly carved capitals are worth close investigation. To the left of the entrance is a Merovingian (7th century) capital, to the right the *Sacrifice of Abraham*, and opposite on south-east pier, *Daniel in the Lions Den*. Between the southeast chapel and the apse is an arcade with three decorative capitals. The east window capitals are carved with an *Annunciation* and *Visitation*, *Supper at Emmaus*, *St Michael Slaying the Dragon* and *Martyrdom of St Vincent*. In the south aisle, near the Gothic Sacré-Coeur Chapel is *David and Goliath* and opposite, *Samson and the Lion*. Furnishings include an early Christian (4th–5th centuries) marble sarcophagus in the southwest aisle, 17th-century stalls by Jean Tournier from Gourdon (*see p. 173*) in the apse and, most importantly, Rembrandt's painting in the north chapel. A stark but powerful rendition of *Christ on the Cross* (1631), it is part of a group of seven Stations of the Cross commissioned by a Dutchman. The Dufour family, who originated from Mas d'Agenais, purchased the work and donated it to the town in 1804. Its authenticity was confirmed in 1960; the rest of the cycle is in Munich.

AIGUILLON & ENVIRONS

Aiguillon has a prime site, where the Baïse and the Lot join the Garonne, and is central to the *département*, but its past is more impressive than its present. A Roman encampment, then a French *bastide* founded in 1300 by Philippe the Fair, it became the residence of the notorious and decadent Duc d'Aiguillon who received Madame du Barry, the mistress of Louis XV, here in the 18th century. The Neoclassical château of the Dukes, begun in 1765 (*no admission*), surveys the river from its clifftop. There are old houses in the medieval quarter, where Rue Sabathier arrives at the 12th-century Château de Lunac. The locks and weirs on the Garonne were neglected in the 20th century, and only 4.5 km between St-Léger and Nicole, close to Aiguillon, linking the Baïse and the Lot, are now navigable.

Small river or canal-side towns around Aiguillon include **Tonneins**, on a rocky promontory from which there is an excellent vista of the Garonne. It used to be an important cigarette producing town. The story of the Garonne and shipping, and tobacco is told at the Espace Exhibition Garonna (*open July, Aug 3–5; March–June, Sept–Oct, by appointment only; T: 05 53 79 22 79*). The classic *bastide* of **Damazan** (13th century) on the Canal latéral, has a central square with arcades and *halle* with *Mairie* atop. Likewise, **Buzet-sur-Baïse**, is a watery flatland where the Canal, the Baïse and the Garonne meet, with multiple locks, a river marina, canal walk and boat rides.

THE PAYS D'ALBRET

NB: This section and the following two chapters are covered by the map on p. 320.

The area between the Garonne and the forests of the Landes de Gascogne, known as the Pays d'Albret or Néracais, was associated with the powerful Albret dynasty from the 11th century. Its capital is Nérac, where the greatest of all the Albrets, Henri III of Navarre (1553–1610) who became King Henri IV, and his queen, resided, gathering around them a court to rival that at the Louvre. The gently undulating fields and woodland are crossed by numerous small rivers, notably the Baïse and the Avance.

PROTESTANTISM AND THE ALBRETS

In 1527 Marguerite d'Angoulême, sister of François I and author of *The Heptameron*, married Henri d'Albret, King of Navarre. A cultured woman, Marguerite introduced the humanist ideas of the Renaissance to Nérac and the great thinkers of the day were drawn to her court. Marguerite's daughter, Jeanne d'Albret, converted to the Protestant faith under the influence of Théodore de Bèze (1519–1605), a disciple of Jean Calvin (1509–64), both of whom visited Nérac. She took with her much of the Agenais and ordered the complete substitution of the Protestant faith in the Béarn (*see p. 483*), with far-reaching consequences. The first active centres of Protestantism were Nérac and Oloron, followed by Ste-Foy, Bergerac and Agen. Jeanne created the Protestant Academy of Orthez. She made her son, Henri III of Navarre (*see p. 485*), who alternated between Catholicism and Protestantism six times for various reasons, head of the Protestants when the Religious Wars broke out.

NÉRAC

The old buildings clustered around the remains of Henri IV's château on the left bank of the Baïse at Nérac create a picturesque ensemble. This town draws the crowds for its historic associations with France's favourite monarch, although the remains of the Château de Nérac are relatively modest. The river carves a wide course here on its way north and is spanned by two bridges, new and old.

HISTORY OF NÉRAC

The Albret family inherited the property from the abbey of Condom in the 11th century. Their astute politics, judicious marriages and successful wars resulted in great power and wealth until the Gascon princes dominated a kingdom extending as far as Pau (*see p. 484*). In 1572, when he was 19 years old, Henri of Navarre married Marguerite de Valois (la Reine Margot; *see p. 92*). In 1576 Henri based himself in Nérac where he spent some of his best years enjoying the good life and firmly establishing his reputation as the Vert Galant, for his numerous amorous adventures. In 1578 with the arrival of his wife and his mother-in-law, Catherine de Médicis, the provincial court of Nérac became as showy as that of the Louvre. Nérac was abandoned for ever in favour of Paris when Henri acceded to the French throne in 1589. After the Wars of Religion, Louis XIII had the citadel destroyed. In the 18th century a thriving agricultural economy developed, exporting wheat, wine, flax and linen. Terrible flooding in December 1952 meant that the Baïse was declared non-navigable until the 1990s, when repairs began.

Château de Nérac

Open June–Sept 10–12 & 2–7; Oct–May 10–12 & 2–6; closed Mon; T: 05 53 62 21 11.
The Château contains an exhibition dedicated to the Albret family and a museum of local archaeology. The year after Henri IV's death in 1610, the château burned down with the loss of the archives. Originally it consisted of a four-square building around a courtyard with towers at each angle, dry ditches and a fortified entrance. All that remains is one wing and what you see was originally an internal façade onto the courtyard, a pretty example of 15th–16th-century transitional architecture, between the late Gothic and early Renaissance. It is possible that this wing contained Henri's apartments and, at the river end, doorways and a fireplace hang suspended where once there was a corner pavilion. The building is just one storey high and dominated by a steeply raked roof with red tiles. Along the length of the façade is a loggia with basket-handle arches supported by carved capitals; the twisted columns appear to continue through the cornice below to culminate in sculpted bosses. There is little of architectural interest inside; the ground floor displays local archaeological finds; the exhibition on the first floor gives a detailed account of the court of Nérac and its political and cultural importance.

Exploring the town

The Church of St-Nicolas was rebuilt 1759–87 in sober Neoclassical style on the site of an earlier church consecrated in 1096. It received two steeples in 1855. Most of the furnishings are 19th-century, including the organ and the stained glass with Old and New Testament scenes. In streets behind the church are some 16th-century houses and the 17th-century Hôtel de Ville (with a fine Gallo-Roman mosaic floor), while near the Pont Vieux in Petit Nérac is the 16th-century Maison de Sully. At the end of the Pont Neuf is La Garenne, a park created by Jeanne d'Albret's husband, Antoine de Bourbon, on the river bank. There is a fragment of Gallo-Roman mosaic near the entrance as well as a fragment of the Roman villa, and several fountains in the park. Notable is a positively flesh-creeping 19th-century statue, *Fleurette noyée* by Daniel Champagne, in memory of Fleurette, the first of Henri of Navarre's many conquests who drowned herself in despair when abandoned by her royal lover. The king of Navarre's park is the setting for Shakespeare's *Love's Labour's Lost*.

ENVIRONS OF NÉRAC

Lavardac was a French *bastide*, founded in 1256 on the banks of the Baïse, and a major river port for shipping Armagnac. Nearby, on the Gélise River at **Barbaste**, is an extraordinary and unique fortified mill, the Moulin-des-Tours (*open mid-June to–Aug Mon, Thurs–Sat, 3–6.30; Sun 10.30–12.30 & 3–6.30; T: 05 53 65 09 37*). The mill and the old bridge are 13th-century. The mill became the property of the Albrets in 1308 and Henri of Navarre took pleasure in the title Meunier de Barbaste. Milling was limited to the core of the building, while the four towers, the tallest of which is 29m high, were reserved for defence. It was used as a mill until the mid-19th century, but the mill wheels were removed when it was taken over by a cork manufacturer, and it was badly damaged by fire in 1937. The 19th-century Maison Aunac on the river adjacent to the Moulin-des-Tours, has been brought back to life as Le Château Imaginaire (*open July–Aug 10–12 & 2–7, and Tues, Thu 9–1; April–June, Sept–Oct and holidays 2–6; Christmas and Feb hols, 2–6; T: 05 53 97 25 15*). This magical fairyland enlists the help of interactive installations, holographs, mirrors and sculptures, and was concocted by 25 artists.

Xaintrailles, to the northwest, is a hilltop village on the old Roman way, La Ténarèze. The château, rebuilt in the 15th century, was the birthplace of Joan of Arc's companion in arms, Jean Poton de Xaintrailles. The *bastide* of **Vianne** preserves almost perfectly intact its set of ramparts, towers and fortified gateways. Within is less interesting, although the chequerboard layout has been respected. It was founded as Villelongue in 1284 by Edward I's seneschal, Jourdain de l'Isle, lord of Mongaillard, and was later named after de l'Isle's aunt. In the medieval cemetery near the north gate is a tiny Romanesque church with a fortified bell-tower and large west door. The barrel-vaulted interior has some lively carved capitals. The village has had a tradition of glassmaking since the 1920s. On Friday evenings in summer there is an open-air market of regional products.

PRACTICAL INFORMATION

GETTING AROUND

• **By air:** Agen airport, T: 05 53 77 00 88
• **By train:** Paris to Agen. Bordeaux to Agen, Moissac, Montauban, Toulouse. Périgueux to Villefranche-du-Périgord, Monsempron-Libos (for Fumel), Trentels-Ladignac, Penne-d'Agenais, Pont-du-Casse, Agen. Paris, Bordeaux, Marmande, Tonneins , Aiguillon, Agen.
• **By bus:** Agen to Mont-de-Marsan via Nérac. SNCF bus : Agen (train station) - Aire-sur-Adour - Pau; Agen - Nérac - Mont-de-Marsan; Agen - Villeneuve-sur-Lot.

TOURIST INFORMATION

Agen 107 Blvd Carnot, BP 237, T: 05 53 47 36 09, www.ot-agen.org
Aiguillon Pl. 14 Juillet T: 05 53 79 62 58, email ot.confluent@wanadoo.fr
Auvillar Pl. de la Halle, T: 05 63 39 89 92, www.auvillar.com
Barbaste Pl. de la Mairie, T: 05 53 65 84 85, mairie.barbaste@wanadoo.fr
Beaumont-de-Lomagne 3 Rue Fermat, T: 05 63 02 42 32, www.info82.com/beaumont
Clairac 16 Pl. Viçose, T: 05 53 88 71 59, www.clairac.com
Duras Blvd Jean-Brisseau, T: 05 53 83 63 06, otsi.duras@wanadoo.fr
Pays de Duras, T: 05 53 93 71 18, www.paysdeduras.com
Eymet Pl. de la Bastide, BP4, T: 05 53 23 74 95, www.eymet-en-perigord.com
Fumel Pl. Georges-Escandes, BP 56, T: 05 53 71 13 70, www.fumel.fr
Granges-sur-Lot Mairie, T: 05 53 79 11 66, email tourisme-granges@worldonline.fr
Lavardac Ave du Général-de-Gaulle, T: 05 53 65 94 69, mairie.lavardac@ville-lavardac.fr
Layrac Rue du Dr Ollier, T: 05 53 66 51 53, email ot.layrac@tele2.fr
Marmande Blvd Gambetta, T: 05 53 64 44 44, www.mairie-marmande.fr
Miramont-de-Guyenne 1 Rue Pasteur, T: 05 53 93 38 94, www.ville-miramontdeguyenne.fr
Moirax Mairie Le Bourg, T: 05 53 87 13 73
Monflanquin Pl. des Arcades, T: 05 53 36 40 19, www.cc-monflanquinois.fr
Monpazier Pl. des Cornières, T: 05 53 22 68 59, email ot.monpazier@perigord.tm.fr
Nérac 7 Ave. Mondenard, T: 05 53 65 27 75, www.ville-nerac.fr
Puymirol 7 Pl. Maréchal Leclerc, T: 05 53 95 32 30, www.mairie-puymirol.fr
Tonneins 3 Blvd Charles-de-Gaulle, T: 05 53 79 22 79, office-tourisme-tonneins@wanadoo.fr
Vianne Pl. des Marrionniers, T: 05 53 65 29 54,
Villeneuve-sur-Lot 47 Rue de Paris, T: 05 53 36 17 30, www.ville-villeneuve-sur-lot.fr

ACCOMMODATION & RESTAURANTS

Agen

Rue Voltaire at the centre of the town is called *la rue des restaurants* and has a friendly atmosphere. Closed to traffic Thursday– Saturday evenings in summer.
€€ **Le Mariottat**. The garden and shady terrace around a handsome 18th-century *hôtel particulier* make a beautiful setting

in summer to appreciate Eric Mariottat's gourmet cooking and a warm welcome from Christiane. In winter the restaurant is sleek and elegant, a fit setting for cuisine described as *terroir- contemporaine*, the best of the Southwest presented in a modern idiom. The menus are €23 (weekday lunch); Aquitaine €35, Poisson €49 and Surprise €58. 25 Rue Louis-Vivent, T: 05 53 77 99 77, www.restaurant-mariottat.com

Agnac
€ Chambres d'hôtes Château de Péchalbet. On the borders of the Lot-et-Garonne and the Dordogne, Henri and Françoise Peyre's lovely 17th-century mansion has five very attractive guest rooms with traditional furniture. The building sits in 40 hectares of woodland and meadows and has a large pool. *Table d'hôtes* can be booked in advance. (west of Eymet), T: 05 53 83 04 70, http://pechalbet.free.fr

Aiguillon
€ Chambres d'hôtes Le Clos Muneau. A spacious *maison de maître* on the edge of the town with a garden, and pool, which gives the impression of being in the countryside. There are two guest rooms and suite. 28 Rue Victor Hugo, T: 05 53 79 58 84, www.clos-muneau.com

Beaumont-de-Lomagne
€ Chambres d'hôtes La Beaumontoise. ■ A home in the centre of the town offers two attractively understated bedrooms. Breakfast is served in the pretty lounge, there is a little garden, and *table d'hôtes* of good simple produce and cooking is available. 52 Rue de Maréchal Foch, T: 05 63 26 00 42, www.beaumontoise.net

Barbaste

€ La Table du Meunier, Moulin des Tours. In an old underground mill near the magnificent Moulin des Tours, a choice of regional cooking or Gascon crêpes. T: 05 53 97 06 60.

Boé
€€ Château St-Marcel. Close to Agen, an impressive 17th-century château reached by an avenue of ancient cedars through woodland. There is a large pool and tennis courts. There are 17 bedrooms decorated in a modern and unfussy style, and 6 which are traditional—all different. The cooking is regional and traditional, and served in the attractive brick-arched restaurant. T: 05 53 96 61 30, www.chateau-saint-marcel.com

Duras
€ L'Hostellerie des Ducs. An oasis of calm in an old monastery run by the Blanchet family which has maintained its excellent reputation for a long time. The restaurant and terrace, where good home cooking is the rule, overlook the grounds and the pool. The 16 pleasant rooms are all different. Blvd Jean-Brisseau, T: 05 53 83 74 58, www.hostellerieducs-duras.com

Francescas
€ Relais de la Hire. An 18th-century mansion in a hamlet near Nérac and Agen, the large house is behind a high wall which encloses a garden. Jean-Noel Prabonne produces top-quality cuisine based on seasonal availability. The menus range from €20, €30 to €56. 11 Rue Porte-Neuve, T: 05 53 65 41 59, www.la-hire.com

Monpazier
€ Hôtel/Restaurant Edward 1er. This adorable little 19th-century property with castle-like pretensions has ten elegant, quiet rooms rooms and two suites.

There is a lovely pool, garden, terrace and cooking is based on fresh Périgordian produce with menus from €29. 5 Rue St-Pierre, T: 05 53 22 44 00, edward1er@chateauxhotels.com

Penne d'Agenais

€ **La Maison sur la Place**. Traditional cooking of a rare quality and with a touch of originality, in a charming setting in the village centre. Ring Tuesday-Sat. T: 05 53 01 29 18.

Pont-du-Casse

€€ **Chambres d'hôtes Château de Cambes**. In a totally calm environment 5 minutes from Agen, this beautiful château stands at the foot of a cliff in 7 hectares of grounds, with streams, a lake and heated pool. Originally a summer retreat for medieval Agen notables, a shelter to aristocrats during the Revolution, and a base for local *maquisards* during the last war, Karen and Neil Dixon now provide five luxurious and restful suites. *Table d'hôtes* available by prior reservation, around €35. T: 05 53 87 46 37, www.chateaudecambes.com

Pujols

€€ **Restaurant La Toque Blanche**. A long-established reputation combined with a perfect hilltop village setting, it has a winter garden, large and small dining rooms, and terrace. Dishes are based on local produce and wines and the cuisine French traditional. Set-price menus are €25 (weekday lunch), €38, €54 and there is a *menu dégustation*. T: 05 53 49 00 30, www.la-toque-blanche.fr

€€ **Restaurant l'Epicurien di Villa Smeralda**. Fairly recently opened, the chef was formerly at Tonneins which received a Michelin star. The setting, in the centre of the village, is very attrac-tive, with a beautiful terrace. The food is excellent. Le bourg, T: 05 53 36 72 12.

Puymirol

€€€ **Hôtel/Restaurant Les Loges de l'Aubergade**. ■ A very elegant hotel cre-ated in a personal manner by Michel and Maryse Trama in a building which once belonged to the Counts of Toulouse. The courtyard has been used to advantage, and the rooms are embellished with lush fabrics and atmospheric lighting. The cloister is beautifully adapted as a setting to appreciate Trama's superb culinary skills—the restaurant has recently been awarded a third Michelin rosette. Cookery courses are held at the Atelier des Sens. 52 Rue Royale, T: 05 53 95 31 46, www.aubergade.com

St-Sylvestre-sur-Lot

€€€ **Hôtel/Restaurant Château Lalande**. A dreamy hotel-restaurant with pools arranged like Roman *thermae* and exceptional gastronomy. The restaurant and 22 rooms and suites are sophisticat-ed, with antiques, fine rugs and fabrics. Anthony Ayçaguer is the driving force in the kitchens creating dishes such as *Dos de Sandre rôti au gros sel, embeurré de pommes de terre de Noirmoutier, écrevisses et pancetta sautés*; menus €37 to €99. T: 05 53 36 15 15, www.chateau-lalande.com

La Sauvetat-sur-Lède

€ **Chambres d'hôtes Chateau de Saint-Sulpice**. A handsome 16th–19th-century château in open countryside above the Lède with spacious accommodation: 3 family suites and 2 bedrooms, with chandeliers, fireplaces and *toile de Jouy* on the walls. The décor in the guests rooms is original, including the old music room of 1810, now the guest din-ing room; and the circular sitting room.

Outside are a terrace and pool; June's passion is horses. The owners organise theme weekends; *table d'hotes* and lunch picnic baskets can be ordered. Prices are good value. June and Frédéric Filliette, T: 05 53 01 46 44, www.chateausaintsulpice.com

Sérignac-sur-Garonne

€€ Hotel/Restaurant Le Prince Noir. A former 17th-century convent near the Garonne, 12k from Agen, is a quiet hideaway. Around a large interior courtyard, there are 22 bedrooms with comfortable armchairs and antique bedsteads; in the grounds a pool and tennis court. The cuisine is regional based on local produce - duck and goose; prunes and strawberries; menus €18€–32. Rte de Mont-de-Marsan (D119 west of Agen), T: 05 53 68 74 30, www.le-prince-noir.com

Tonneins

€€ Côté Garonne. A gourmet bistrot with accommodation where the cooking combines the best of the Southwest. Meals are served in a beautiful setting overlooking the Garonne. The cuisine is highly imaginative: roast foie gras with gingerbread, pears and chutney for example. Menus €15–39. All the décors are modern, including the 5 charming bedrooms. 36-38 Cours de l'Yser, T: 05 53 84 34 34, www.cotegaronne.com

Tournon d'Agenais

€ Restaurant le Beffroi. A delightful address in the centre of the village, and a young chef who cooks imaginative versions of local cuisine, original in both their preparation and presentation. This attractively decorated restaurant is very popular with locals. Place de la Mairie, T: 05 53 01 20 59.

MARKET DAYS

Agen Wednesday and Sunday; Saturday on the Esplanade du Gravier
Auvillar Sunday farmers' market
Biron Wednesday in summer farmers' market
Duras Monday; Saturday, Tuesday June–September
Eymet Thursday; July-August Tuesday evening
Layrac Friday
Marmande Tuesday, Thursday, Saturday
Monpazier Thursday
Nérac Saturday Tuesday evenings, June–September
Penne d'Agenais Sunday
Tonneins Wednesday, Friday, Saturday
Villeneuve-sur-Lot Tuesday and Saturday; farmers' market Wednesday;

FESTIVALS & EVENTS

February: *Festival de Guitare*, biennial festival of jazz, country, blues from around the world, Nérac
May: *Festival International d'Orgues de Babarie*, biennial (04, 06 etc.) festival of barrel organ and mechanised music, Bon-Encontre, near Agen
Printemps du Théâtre et arts associés, spring theatre and associated arts, Agen
July: *Festival de Jazz*, Aiguillon
Evocation Historique, re-enactment of the town's history, Duras
Musiques en Pays de Serre, Madaillan, Penne d'Agenais, Tournon
Foire aux Fruits, festival of produce from France's largest orchard, Prayssas
August: *Festival International des Menteurs*, celebration of the art of lying Moncrabeau

THE GERS

The heart of old Gascony, the land of swashbuckling swordsmen and musketeers, virtually coincides with the modern *département* of Gers (the 's' is pronounced). The Gers, the most westerly of the eight *départements* of the Midi-Pyrénées, turns historically and culturally to Aquitaine rather than to the Languedoc but the Gascon language, still sometimes heard in a market place, is a local version of Occitan. The landscape is characterised by shallow valleys and softly undulating ridges determined by the Gers and other small rivers which rise in the foothills of the Pyrenees and fan out on their way north. Some 37 per cent of the sparse population of the *département* is concerned with agriculture. Vines are cultivated on the slopes in the north and west, while sweeping fields of wheat and maize cover the plains. The Gers may not have the sharp contrasts of landscape of the other departments of the Midi-Pyrénées but it does offer such varied experiences as *corridas* (bullfights), motor racing and jazz. It is also synonymous with Armagnac brandy and a hearty rustic gastronomy, with dishes based on goose fat.

HISTORY OF GASCONY

The Duchy of Gascony was formed in 852, defined by the wide arc of the Garonne to north and east and the Pyrenees to the south. Gascony was joined to Aquitaine in 1036, and was subjected to English domination in the 12th century, resolved only in the 15th century at the end of the Hundred Years War. The proliferation of *castelnaux* (communities protected by castle walls), *sauvetés* (protected by the Church) and *bastides* (planned towns with economic and political advantages) between the 11th and 14th centuries are an integral part of the Gers. As time went on, Gascony was controlled by three main feudal dynasties: Foix-Béarn, Armagnac, and Albret. In 1527 the House of Armagnac passed to Henri II d'Albret through his marriage to Marguerite d'Angoulème and their daughter, Jeanne d'Albret, inherited all three great Gascon domains. At her death in 1572 these territories came under the control of her son, Henri of Navarre, who became Henri IV of France (*see p. 485*) and were reunited with France on his accession as King in 1589.

THE LOMAGNE

Between the Rivers Gers and Garonne is the Lomagne, a former duchy of Gascony, astride the meeting point of the Gers, Tarn-et-Garonne and Lot-et-Garonne. An important agricultural area famed for the production of white garlic, its main town is Lectoure.

LECTOURE

Lectoure is at ease behind its refined and genteel Neoclassical façades, and solid as the narrow ridge of rock that it is built upon. The three main monuments in Lectoure, the cathedral, the museum and the Fountain of Diana, are at the east end of the town which has one main street running one-way, east–west.

HISTORY OF LECTOURE

Lectoure, capital of the Lomagne, was the site of an *oppidum* occupied by a Gallic tribe, the Lactorates, who judiciously surrendered to the Roman invaders c. 120 BC. Subsequently the Gallo-Roman city, capital of *Novempopulania*, flourished on the plain at a crossroads. The high ground was reserved for the temples dedicated to Jupiter and, more importantly, to Cybele, ancient Phrygian earth goddess, in whose cult the ritual sacrifice of the bull and ram, symbols of strength and fertility, was important. A remarkable find of altars decorated with bull's heads (now on display in the museum) was made in 1540 when the city wall was demolished east of the cathedral. In the Middle Ages, Lectoure was the main residence of the Viscounts of Lomagne and then became the headquarters of the powerful Counts of Armagnac, until the Siege of Lectoure, between November 1472 and March 1473, when Louis XI's troops invaded and ransacked the town and murdered Count Jean V. Soon afterwards the town was reborn as a royal seneschalcy, only to suffer again during the Wars of Religion.

Cathedral of St-Gervais-et-St-Protais

In the 13th century Bishop Giraud de Monlezun took a pledge of allegiance to Edward I of England; he also built an episcopal residence and repaired the cathedral. The plain west façade was erected in the 15th century and since then subjected to many modifications and obvious restoration. Supported by two angle buttresses, the low arch of the entrance is a 19th-century replacement and the series of ten niches above the door has almost melted away, such is the fragility of the limestone. The fenestration is modest, with only a three-light window and a small oculus. The belfry on the north is still impressive, though the original version was demolished by Louis XI's army during the siege of Lectoure when the cathedral was part of the city defences. A tall spire was erected in the 15th century, but had to be demolished, along with the upper level of the belfry, in the 18th century. The five stepped levels, more ornate towards the top, are supported by angle buttresses which lost their statues in the Revolution. A tall isolated gabled buttress on the north flank of the cathedral indicates the incomplete rebuild of the choir in the 16th century. The east and south sides of the cathedral can be seen from the adjacent Jardins des Marronniers and the courtyard of the Hôtel de Ville respectively.

The interior

Inside, a choir with apse and ambulatory in the style of the north of France was grafted to the single nave and the transition from nave to chancel is effected by an awk-
ward triumphal arch partly obstructing the view of the high choir vaults. The two
square bays of the nave are defined by six massive piers, the cores of which are
Romanesque and were designed to carry domes in the manner of Cahors or Souillac;
perhaps this plan was never completed, because at the end of the 12th century the
nave was vaulted. Repairs to the nave were carried out in 1480, and at the beginning
of the 16th century vaulted chapels were inserted and more alterations followed in the
17th and 18th centuries. The reconstruction of the chancel and apse began in the
16th century, at which time the five square chapels in the east were completed with
massive triangular sections of masonry between them. Only in 1600 were the ten
cylindrical piers introduced to create the ambulatory. The choir vaults have three
polychromed pendant bosses and the carved early 17th-century choir stalls were
placed here in the 19th century. The chapel to the left of the choir has an 18th-cen-
tury altar and elegant wrought iron, as well as a white marble statue of the *Assumption
of the Virgin*, probably Italian. The Sacré-Coeur chapel has a series of 17th-century
easel paintings of the *Passion*.The former baptistery contains a Museum of Sacred Art.

Musée Archéologique de Lectoure

Guided visits on the hour, 10–11 & 2–5; closed and holidays; T: 05 62 68 70 22.
The Hôtel de Ville (1676–82), contiguous with the cathedral, was originally the episcopal palace. A majestic, regular but unadorned building with numerous windows, its
brick vaulted kitchen and cellars have been transformed into a fascinating museum of
archaeology, opened in 1972. The entrance to the museum is below the magnificent
cantilevered staircase set off by the scrolling outlines of the wrought-iron balustrade.
The seven rooms of the museum are arranged chronologically, the first part dedicated to local palaeontology. The Gallic era is represented by burial pits of the second
half of the 1st century BC, sculptures, pottery—including huge *amphorae* for wine—
and coins. The showpiece, 20 pagan altars from the 2nd and 3rd centuries, are mainly in Pyrenean marble and decorated with the head of a bull (taurobole) or a ram
(criobole). The engraved inscription on each stone records the date of the initiation
ceremony involving the sacrifice of a bull or ram, and the name of the receiver of the
rites. This unique collection of altars was always recognised as exceptional, yet in
1591 they were re-used at the base of the pillars of the *halle aux grains* where they
stayed until 1842; by 1874 they were in the *Mairie*. There are other pagan and
Christian funerary monuments, sarcophagi, and mosaics exhibited in an attractive
vaulted chamber dated 1680, one with an awesome portrayal of the god Oceanus.

Exploring Lectoure

On leaving the Hôtel de Ville turn left and left again down to the bottom of Rue
Fontelié to the **Fontaine de Diane**, a spring and pool covered by a 13th-century
vaulted construction with a double-arched opening and 15th-century iron *grille*.

Water from this spring was used at the royal tannery, further down the street, now the Maison d'Ydrone retirement home. This important workshop (built 1752–54) was one of the most advanced in its day and employed over 100 people. A double flight of steps leads down into the yard, and above the industrial building is a pretty iron-work gable which once contained the works' clock.

Turn left up the Chemin de Ste-Clair which follows the old city walls enclosing public gardens, cross the main road and continue on to the northwest side of town and the former home of the executioner, the 14th-century Tour du Bourreau, part of the old town walls. Wind your way back through the old streets past the Hôtel de Castaing-Bastard in Rue Lagrange, now converted to a hotel-restaurant (*see p. 393*), an elegant building with fine stucco and fireplaces inside.

Back on Rue Nationale, just after the corner with Rue des Frères Danzas is the 13th-century Tour d'Albinhac. To the west of the town is Cours d'Armagnac and, on the site of the castle of the Counts of Armagnac, is the hospital, begun in 1760 and completed in 1809–12. Behind the hospital on Allées Montmorency are the remains of the castle where the Duc de Montmorency was imprisoned after the battle of Castelnaudary (Aude) before being executed in Toulouse in 1632 for opposing Richelieu (*see p. 16*). Complete the amble along Boulevard Jean Jaurès, built on the southern ramparts.

ENVIRONS OF LECTOURE

West of Lectoure, **Terraube** is a typical Gersois village with a dramatic château, prop-erty of the Galard family since the 10th century. In the other direction, to the north-east between Lectoure and Miradoux are three sights: at **St-Avit-Frandat** is the 17th-century Château de La Cassagne (*guided visits mid-July–Sept, closed Mon; T: 05 62 68 83 24*), whose main curiosity is a replica of the Great Council Chamber of the Knights of St-John of Jerusalem at Malta, known as the Salle des Chevaliers de Malte; the medieval (14th–16th centuries) Château de Plieux (*open summer 3-7, closed Tues; win-ter Sat, Sun 3–7; T: 05 62 28 60 86*) shelters a permanent collection of contemporary art; and the 14th-century Church of Ste-Blandine (*open mid-April–mid-Oct 8-7; T: 05 62 28 67 95*) at Castet-Arrouy, has a remarkable 19th-century interior.

The oldest *bastide* in the Gers, **Miradoux**, was founded in 1253. It has an impos-ing but battered church, with a bare west end except for one rose and a pedimented Renaissance doorway. Across from the church is the Hôtel de Ville and built up against it a 16th-century market hall. **Flamarens**, further northeast, is a tiny place with a château (13th–15th centuries) with one wing and a round machicolated tower look-ing out over the countryside. It was badly damaged by fire in 1943 and is under restoration (*occasionally open*). The Grossolles family owned the château from 1466 to 1882 and the arms of Hérard de Grossoles, Bishop of Condom (1521–43), with the date 1541, are above the door of the spectacularly ruined church.

At the heart of the village of **Lachapelle** sits the miniature rustic Baroque church of St-Pierre (13th century). Attached to the château and originally its private chapel, it became the parish church (*open July–Aug 10–12 & 2–7; May–June, Sept–Oct 2-6;*

March–April, Nov–Dec, Sun and holidays, 2–5; T: 05 63 94 12 28). Tiny though it is, the interior was entirely decked out in 1776 by the craftsman Muraignon Champagne with an all-encompassing scheme of gilded and painted woodwork, panels, pilasters and mouldings. Around the nave a superimposed series of arcades and loggias imitates the interior of a theatre. There are also furnishings of a similar quality to the woodwork, including a pulpit and altars of the same date, a 16th-century statue of Ste-Quitterie, some late 16th–early 17th-century choir stalls with carved misericords, a 17th-century *Virgin and Child*, a relic of St Prosper (born in Aquitaine c. 390) that came from Rome in 1777, and a two-eagle lectern presented by Napoleon III.

Château de Gramont
Guided visits May–Sept 10–12.30 & 2–6; Feb-April, Oct–Nov 2–6; closed Mon Feb–June, Sept–Nov; closed holidays; T: 05 63 94 05 26.
Due east of Lectoure is this part-Gothic, part-Renaissance restored castle beside the river Arratz, the ancient frontier between Gascony and Languedoc (now the boundary between Tarn-et-Garonne and Gers). The entrance for visitors is through the Simon de Montfort tower opposite the church, where there is a small exhibition. The château is composed essentially of two unequal wings. The smaller, known as the Châtelet, abutting the Simon de Montfort tower, is the older, dating from the time of the Montaut family, and incorporates elements from the 13th, 14th and 15th centuries. The monumental main entrance, with the arms of the Montaut family above, was erected in the 17th century. The arrow slits and cross windows are 19th-century fantasies.

Inside is a large courtyard with the later and much larger wing (c. 1535–40), in bluish-grey limestone, on the north; here the Corinthian and Ionic orders are used casually. Steps lead up to the two doorways on the elevated ground-floor level. The garden façade, flanked by pavilions, is slightly more ordered, with pedimented smaller windows and larger ones with entablatures. Inside the main entrance on the north, also reached by an exterior platform, is a staircase with late-Gothic vaults with heavily moulded ribs. The interior proportions and décor have been restored as far as possible, and the Grande Salle has a particularly fine monumental Renaissance fireplace.

FLEURANCE

Fleurance, situated on the Gers River, south of Lectoure, and conveniently located between Agen and Auch, is one of the best-known *bastides* and one of the main commercial centres of the Gers today. The co-founder, Eustache de Beaumarchais, was instrumental in the creation of many *bastides* in Gascony and the Toulousain, often naming his foundations after foreign towns (e.g. Pampelonne, Grenade, Cologne).

Exploring Fleurance
The buildings that surround the 60 square metre arcaded central square are 18th-century but were undoubtedly laid out to the plan of the original *bastide*, founded c. 1272. The houses on the west and east are the best conserved and many have good wrought-

iron. The wonderful Neoclassical market hall (1834–37) is a serious work on two floors designed by an architect from Auch called Ardenne. At its exterior angles are fountains with graceful statues in bronze, by A. Durenne, representing the four seasons.

The amply proportioned church of **Notre-Dame et St-Jean-Baptiste** was begun during the last third of the 13th century. Three successive campaigns of building, between the 14th and 16th centuries, and a difference in the level of the site from west to east of about 4m, contributed to the mixture of materials and the unevenness of the exterior elevations as well as to the varying heights and arrangement of the roofs. To absorb the thrust of the high nave, small flying buttresses in brick were used for the first time in the region. The west elevation, entirely in stone, was deprived of much of its decoration during attacks on the town by the Huguenots. Twelve corbels above the portal signify the existence at one time of a covered gallery. The lower part of the belfry is said

to be an ancient Gallo-Roman tower and the octagonal Toulousain-style belfry, in stone, was completed at the beginning of the 15th century.

The interior is dark, lit only by small clerestory windows, and typically of the Midi, there is little integral decoration. The three earlier east bays of the nave have quadripartite vaults and the west bays tierceron ribs. The showpiece of the church is undoubtedly the three windows of the east end with Rayonnant tracery and stained glass by Arnaud de Moles and his workshop. They are thought to have been executed between 1506 and 1520. On the left in the main panels are St Laurence, Mary Magdalene and St Augustine; above is a *Pietà* and below the *Martyrdom of St Laurence*, *Noli me Tangere*, and *St Augustine's Conversion*. The central window (*pictured left*) has a *Trinity* flanked by *Christ Resurrected* and the Virgin, with a choir of angels, and the *Crucifixion*. The third is a Jesse window crowned by the Virgin enthroned in a large flower.

Among the furnishings is a 15th-century statue of the *Virgin and Child*—Notre-Dame-de-Fleurance—in the St-Jean chapel, the source of numerous miracles during the Wars of Religion, and three paintings by J.-B. Smets, of a family of Flemish painters from Auch in the 18th century.

Central window (1506–20) by Arnaud de Moles and his workshop, at the east end of Notre-Dame et St-Jean Baptiste, Fleurance.

EAST OF FLEURANCE

St-Clar, south of Gramont (*see p. 375*), is a *bastide* on a hill, founded jointly in 1289 by Edward I of England and the Bishop of Lectoure, Géraud de Monlezun, on the site of an earlier *sauveté*; this resulted in two arcaded squares corresponding to the different periods of development. The older area, the Castelviel, is now partly restored but its old church (12th and 14th century) is in a poor state and cannot be visited. The later *bastide* has retained its original orthogonal layout around the main square with a covered market hall, which consists of a simple roof supported by timber posts, contiguous with the rebuilt *maison commune* (19th century). There is a small Musée Départemental de l'Ecole Publique (*open June–Sept 2–7; Oct–May 2–6; closed Mon, Tues.*) based on the old school of 1877, a rustic affair which had two classes for boys and two for girls and is a rare example of a pre-1882 school, the year that the Jules Ferry Law laid down the basis for general public education. In fact the classroom here dates from the 1930s, and a number of supporting items are on display.

Beaumont-de-Lomagne

Beaumont-de-Lomagne is a pleasant *bourgade* with a mighty 14th-century covered market supported by a veritable forest of timbers. In the square is a statue to the mathematician Pierre Fermat (1601–65), who was born here and lived in the building now used by the Tourist Office. Fermat's Last Theorem (that the equation $x^n + y^n = z^n$ has no whole number solutions where n is greater than 2) flummoxed mathematicians until a proof was announced in 1994 by the British mathematician Andrew Wiles. The castle-like church has a beautiful Toulousain-style belfry built 1390–1480. Beaumont, like St-Clar, has important markets for the high-quality white garlic grown in the Lomagne. The markets are not, unfortunately, held under the beautiful 14th-century market hall but at the *marché au forail* on Tuesdays and Saturdays in the summer.

THE TÉNARÈZE

Named after a line of hills between the Adour and the Garonne, this area has long been the north–south corridor linking the Garonne and the Pyrenees. On the edge of the Landes forest, it is best known for the Armagnac vineyards, offering many opportunities to visit Armagnac distilleries. The main town, Condom, plays an important role in the brandy business.

CONDOM

Condom is the major town of the Gers and capital of the Ténarèze, the central section of the *département*. Refreshed by the Baïse River, used in the 19th century for transporting valuable cargoes of Armagnac to Bordeaux, the town is still one of the three main brandy centres, along with Auch and Eauze, and has handsome 17th- and 18th-century white stone *hôtels particuliers* reminiscent of Bordeaux. It is variously described as the town of seven churches or of a hundred towers (supposedly 100 fortified residences were built by 100 noble families). The most important church now is the former cathedral of St-Pierre. The etymology of the town's unforgettable name is either a synthesis of *condate* and *dum*, meaning a hill at a confluence, or is derived from *condominium*, a jointly controlled stronghold, as it was when the Vascon people from the Iberian peninsula, ancestors of the Gascons and the Basques, settled here c. 721.

HISTORY OF CONDOM

Condom is little mentioned until the 11th century when a Benedictine abbey was established and it became a stage on the *Via Podiensis*. It was elevated to episcopal see in the 14th century but the Hundred Years War caused havoc until 1453. Just over a century later, having adhered to the Reformation, it was the theatre of more unrest during the Wars of Religion and the cathedral was ransacked in 1569. Peace was restored with the Edict of Nantes in 1598 and the rebirth of the town dates from the 17th century. Its most celebrated bishop was the great orator Jacques Bénigne Bossuet (1627–1704), named Bishop in 1670, but his contribution to the diocese was somewhat ephemeral as he was always busy elsewhere—he was tutor to the son of Louis XIV and spent most of his time at Court.

Cathedral of St-Pierre

The town centre is Place St-Pierre, dominated to the north by the Cathedral of St-Pierre. The Benedictine abbey dedicated to St Peter, an important centre of learning, reached its apogee in the early 14th century, and in 1317 Pope John XXII elevated Condom to bishopric with 130 parishes, a status it kept until the Revolution. The present cathedral was designed at the end of the 15th century by Jean Marre (d. 1521), who rose through the ranks from prior at Eauze and Nérac to confessor to the king, before becoming Bishop of Condom. By 1511 work on the cathedral was already at an advanced stage and by 1521 the only parts still to be finished were the choir stalls and the roof. Bishop Hérard de Grossoles completed the work in 1524 and the cathedral was consecrated in October 1531. The south flank of the cathedral facing the square shows the transition between Flamboyant and Renaissance. The building is solidly buttressed all round and there is a 40m square tower over the west end.

The interior

Inside it is clear that the large aisleless 16th-century building, which does not have an extended transept, is an addition to the 14th-century Ste-Marie chapel at the east and the two parts are not exactly aligned. The wide nave with tiercerons has no triforium gallery but is lit by the clerestory windows with *grisaille* glass. The nave piers have clustered shafts and carved capitals but the lierne-vaulted choir is surrounded by undecorated cylindrical columns. The stone *jubé* is the third version, made in 1844 by the Virebent workshop in Toulouse, and forms a pseudo-ambulatory. The stained glass of the choir was made in a local workshop in 1861. A little light relief is added by an interesting group of vault bosses repainted in 1841, among them, above the choir, St Sauveur, dedicatee of the first church, and St Peter, the present patron in pontifical dress with the keys; Jean Marre is represented by a sheep (*marrou* is Gascon for ram). Angel musicians evoke the celestial choir as well as the sumptuous liturgy of the 16th-century cathedral famed for its organ and counter-tenor chants and above the nave is the royal coat of arms of Anne of Brittany, a portrait of Louis XII, and the *fleur de lis*.

The original late Gothic or early Renaissance pulpit, with an openwork baldaquin, is still in place. Of the large chapels on the north, the first contains the tombs of Bishops Marre and Milon and the third a carved walnut altar of 1704 salvaged at the Revolution from the pilgrim chapel, Notre-Dame-de-Piétat. A monument to Bishop de Grossoles stands in the sixth chapel. In the west tribune is the 17th-century organ built locally by Daumassens.

The town centre
The west door opens into Place Bossuet with a worked metal cross of 1824. North of the cathedral is the cloister, built by Bishop Grossoles in the 16th century in a similar style to the cathedral. There are double arcades on the east and west, somewhat excessive for the space, and in the northeast corner a doorway with Italianate decoration. The upper level has been occupied since 1861 by the Hôtel de Ville, and the cloister serves as a public thoroughfare. On the north, between the old episcopal palace and the cloister, is the episcopal chapel, now part of the entrance to the Palais de Justice, also built in the first half of the 16th century. An imposing Renaissance door links the chapel with the Hôtel de la Sous-Préfecture, the old episcopal palace begun in 1764 by the last bishop.

The magnificent U-shaped stables (2 Rue Jules-Ferry) with timbered ceilings have been converted to house the Musée de l'Armagnac (*open April–Oct 10–12 & 3–6, Nov–Dec, Feb–March 2–5; closed Tues and holidays; T: 05 62 28 47 17*). Created in 1954, it retraces the history of the *eau-de-vie* and explains its production.

Round the corner at 21 Rue Jules-Ferry is the grandiose Hôtel de Polignac (1780–85), now a school, with colonnades and wrought iron, built by the Abbot Marie Dorlan de Polignac, Prior of Layrac, on the ruins of the old citadel. The west façade overlooking the river is equally impressive. Further down the street is the former 18th-century seminary of Bishop de Milon, now the Lycée Bossuet. Rue des Eclosettes leads back via Rue des Jacobins to the covered market and from the southeast corner of the square the narrow Rue Voutée leads into Rue Gambetta, a lively, pedestrian street with the post office in the old Neoclassical Hôtel de Ville and the pretty 17th-century Hôtel de Lagarde, now the Trois Lys hotel (see p. 392). In Allée Général de Gaulle (Rue Jean-Jaurès) are stately 18th-century residences built on the line of the old fortifications, such as the Hôtel du Bouzet de Roquepine (1763) with *oeil de boeuf* windows. The adjacent Château Cugnac-Armagnac is laid out around three sides of a courtyard and closed to the street with formidable railings. It incorporates the ancient Armagnac distillery, Maison Ryst-Dupeyron, and can be visited (*enquire at T: 05 62 28 08 08, www.rystdupeyron.com*). Opposite, at the angle with Rue des Cordeliers, is Hôtel de Cadignan (1775).

From Place de la Liberté turn right into Rue Cauzabon where on the left is the Louis XV-style Hôtel de Galardon with a pilastered portico and mascaron. Place du Lion d'Or and Rue Charron, which lead back to Place St-Pierre, also have some pretty houses. Rues Ichon and des Armuriers run down to the banks of the Baïse and Pont des Carmes, south of which are gardens.

ENVIRONS OF CONDOM

Close to Condom, at Béraut, is the **Musée d'Art Naif (M.A.N.)** in the Château d'Ensoulès (*open July–Aug 10–7; May–June, Oct, 10–7, closed Tues, Wed; Nov–April, 10–5, closed Tues, Wed; T: 05 62 68 49 87, www.museeartnaif.com*). This recently opened museum has paintings from all over the world and is based on the private collection of Albert Laporte, who over the last 48 years has accumulated some 2,500 works. The works are shown in rotation, with about 800 on display at a time, including thematic exhibitions. Naive art is the work of artists who are self-taught but who may nevertheless be professional. A variety of techniques are used: embroidery, works on glass, collage, ceramics. The profusion of densely hung paintings over two floors is almost overwhelming. The subjects are mainly undemanding, optimistic, colourful and mundane; they are frequently amusing and liberally peopled; detail and narrative is strongly characteristic. The darker side of Naïve Art is Art Marginal, including movements such as Art Brut. The work which launched the collection is *La Jungle* an exotic landscape by the French artist Raymond Riec; there is a series of 40 works by the Polish immigrant painter Wiacek illustrating scenes from his life; and the Brazilian Emani Pavaneli paints in the way that Botrero sculpts. Coelho Isablino's *Labyrinth of Paedophiles* is decidedly disturbing, although the collection as a whole is light-hearted and optimistic.

Larressingle

From a distance, the bluff mass of the walls and battlemented towers of Larressingle (*T: 05 62 28 26 25*), a short distance west of Condom, is an extraordinary sight (*pictured opposite*) described locally as a pocket-sized Carcassonne. The church was fortified in the 12th century and later a 270m rampart was thrown around the church and castle, surrounded by a ditch. Recognised by the popes in the 13th century as the property of the abbeys of Agen and Condom, it became the official residence of the bishops of Condom until the end of the 16th century when they moved to Cassaigne (*see p. 382*), taking most of the transportable timber elements with them.

The barrel-vaulted fortified entrance on the west, where there was once a drawbridge, is very narrow and the protection afforded by the walls and towers to the houses huddled up against them gives the enclosure attractive intimacy. Opposite the entrance is the semi-ruined, massive castle keep on four floors, with signs of later

The fortified church (12th century) and castle of Larressingle.

alterations and additions to make it more habitable. Nestling behind is the little 12th-century church of St-Sigismond; its west façade has a porch with Romanesque capitals and the *Lamb of God* in the tympanum. The half-dome of the 12th-century church was pierced when a two-bay extension was added to the east end in the 13th century. The route to Santiago passed this way, and the other road from Larressingle (between the cemetery and the *Mairie*) will take you down to the old pilgrim bridge, the Pont d'Artigues. The Camp de Siège Médiéval (*open July–Aug 11–7; May–June, Sept 11–5.30 closed Wed; Oct–April 2–5 closed Wed; guided visits with demonstrations July–Aug at certain times; T: 05 62 68 33 88, www.larressingle.asso.fr*), has replicas of medieval siege machines such as a trebuchet and a *couillard*.

Fourcès and Montréal

One of the most enchanting *bastides* in the Gers is the little circular village of Fourcès north of Montréal. A bridge over the Auzoue leads into the centre under the watchful eye of the 16th-century château, now an elegant hotel (*see p. 392*). This tiny community has only about 350 inhabitants but is decked out in blooms during the flower festival on the last weekend of April. The village probably developed around a primitive fortification, long disappeared, and was later enclosed in an all-embracing wall, fragments of which remain, as does the pretty bell-tower astride the lane on the west. The old houses, some with arcades and others half-timbered, which go back to the 13th and 14th centuries, link arms to enclose the plane-shaded central square.

Montréal, built on an escarpment, was one of the first *bastides* founded in Gascony, in 1256. By the time it was finished in 1289 it was already under English domination. It has the typical regular layout with a central square, arcades and a large church off-centre, with aisles and primitive capitals and corbels in the east, bearing the scars of Protestant iconoclasm, particularly around the south door. At the tourist office is the two-room Musée des Fouilles de Séviac (*open July–Aug 10–1 & 2-7; March–June, Sept–Nov 10–12 & 3–6, Sun and holidays 3–6; T: 05 62 29 42 83*) which displays many items found since 1868 at the Gallo-Roman villa at nearby Séviac (*see below*), southwest of Montréal.

Fouilles de Séviac

Open July–Aug 10–1 & 2–7; March–June, Sept–Nov 10–12 & 3–6; Sun and holidays 3–6; T: 05 62 29 42 85.

The Gallo-Roman archaeological site, has a low-key setting that belies its importance as one of the largest in Gascony, covering 2 hectares. Excavations in 1959 uncovered a classic Gallo-Roman villa with peristyle which dates from the 2nd to the 5th centuries. A large interior courtyard 35 metres square is itself bordered by a gallery 4m wide; the living quarters consist of mainly rectangular rooms and, around them, another gallery. On the east is a large building with an apse heated by a hypocaust and to the south, separated from the villa by an interior courtyard in which marble columns have been found, are the vast *thermae* (bath complex) with white and green marble slabs and mosaics still in place in the piscina.

Séviac has some remarkable and well made 4th- and 5th-century mosaics. Of around 30 surviving pieces of varying size, some are surprisingly complete. The background colour is a creamy white and the designs are picked out in terracotta red, pink, olive green, dark blue and yellow ochre. Nearly all are geometric repeat patterns but a few have stylised fruit and vegetal designs. During the Merovingian era (6th and 7th centuries) the villa was divided into smaller dwellings with transverse walls. On the southeast are traces of Merovingian Christian sanctuaries with a baptistery and necropolis.

Mouchan

Mouchan, southwest of Condom, has a small but satisfying 12th-century church (*open mid-June–mid-Sept, Wed-Sun 10-12 & 3-7*) in the typical yellowish-orange stone of the region with an 11th-century square tower, all that remains of the former Cluniac priory of St-Austrigile. There are simple carvings on the exterior and inside are 31 decorated capitals, mainly with a stiff leaf design similar to that seen at Flaran (*see page opposite*), but also interlacings, and five with figures or animals. One of particular note, in the east end of the church, is carved on three faces with little scenes inscribed in arches.

Château de Cassaigne

Open mid-June–mid-Sept 9–12 & 2–7; mid-Sept–mid-June 9–12 & 2–6, closed Mon; T: 05 62 28 04 02, www.chateaudecassaigne.com

Not far from Condom is the Château de La Cassaigne, set in 27 hectares of vines. It attracts 40,000 visitors a year, both to visit the building and to sample the Armagnac. The 13th-century castle became the summer palace of the bishops of Condom at the end of the 16th century. It was remodelled in the stylish comfort of the Renaissance by Bishops Jehan de Monluc and Jean Duchemin, who were both very attached to it and died here. Their work forms the core of the building, but it was again altered during the time of Bishop Louis de Milon (1693–1734), who was responsible for the restrained elegance of the present west entrance façade. Work continued on the gardens in the 18th century. The Faget family, descendants of the *Intendant* of the last bishop, have owned the property since 1827. A visit to the château includes the kitchen with a beautiful brick vault, likened to an outsize bread oven and a tasting.

At Mansencôme, just south of Cassaigne, the Château of Busca Maniban (1649; *open April–Oct 2–6, closed Sun and holidays; T: 05 62 28 40 38*), is a classic 17th-century building in a marvellous setting above the vineyards. On offer is a visit to the house and the distillery. There is a typical Gascon *pigeonnier* nearby.

ABBAYE DE FLARAN & VALENCE-SUR-BAÏSE

Open July–Aug 9.30–7; Feb–June, Sept–early Jan 9.30–12.30 & 2–6; closed 3 weeks in Jan; T: 05 62 28 50 19.
On the banks of the river at Valence-sur-Baïse, 8km south of Condom, is the Abbaye de Flaran. The best-preserved Cistercian edifice in the Gers, it is a handsome group of 12th- and 17th–18th-century buildings which were carefully restored after a fire in 1970. Apart from their architectural merit, they are used as a centre for cultural events and for information on the pilgrimage routes. Of special interest, although independent of the Abbey, is the **Simonow Collection** of 16th–20th-century art, more than 300 works on loan for an extended period of time.

History of the abbey
Flaran was founded in 1151 and donations of land and property during the second half of the 12th century enabled the construction of an important and very beautiful monastery. The upheavals of the 14th and 15th centuries took their toll. Placed in the hands of secular abbots at the end of the 15th century, it continued to decline and in 1569 the abbey suffered devastating attacks by the Protestants. In 1573, however, Abbot Jean de Boyer started restoration work on the church and repairs to other buildings were carried out until 1603. In the 18th century a general remodelling of the abbey was effected, particularly the guest quarters.

Visiting the abbey
The entrance to the abbey is across the great courtyard with the church to the east and stables and outhouses to the west, and through the former *quartier d'hôte*, the prior's residence, conceived on the lines of a small Gascon château in 1759 with a grand staircase and stucco decoration. The passage on the ground floor leads to the cloister which has been rebuilt twice since the 12th century. All that remains of the 14th-century reconstruction is the west gallery, with rectangular piers subdivided by paired columns and capitals with vegetal motifs or hybrid animals and figures. The remaining galleries are very simple constructions with timber and tile roofs, and an upper

floor on the north. The refectory on the north of the cloister was reduced in size at some point and adorned with elegant stucco work (c. 1730–80). The kitchen and the warming house, either side of the refectory, were altered in the 18th century. The old cellars have been renovated to contain an exhibition dedicated to St-James Major, with sculptures and other references and information on the pilgrimage to Santiago de Compostella in Spain (*see p. 11*). On the east of the cloister are the 12th-century monastic buildings, the *armarium* (library), sacristy and the very gracious **Chapter House**. The latter has nine ribbed bays in brick supported by four coloured marble columns and simple capitals and opens onto the cloister with three richly moulded recessed bays supported by capitals on short marble shafts.

Above the Chapter House was the dormitory, communicating directly with the church. The variety in the fenestration on the garden elevation indicates alterations in the 15th and 17th centuries, and in the 18th century it was extended when individual and more comfortable rooms replaced the dormitory, an ironic decadence of the original Cistercian ethos. On the walls of the upper gallery (north), originally closed, are 18th-century mural paintings.

At the heart of the abbey is the beautiful church of **Notre-Dame** (begun c. 1170), a rare example in the southwest of quintessential Cistercian architecture with minimal decoration and maximum light. It has a wide transept, square chancel and semicircular main apse with two apsidal chapels on either side decorated on the exterior with a band of small arcades. These disappeared from the central apse when a brick-and-timber rising was added, possibly in the 17th century. The crossing is vaulted with rectangular ribs and the three-bay nave (raised c. 1220) received a pointed barrel arch. A small rose window was inserted in the west. The south aisle is barrel-vaulted but the north is ribbed. The numerous capitals all have stylised foliate, geometric or interlace motifs, and over the door from the cloister is a simple chrism. The west door has geometric friezes and reused marble columns.

The garden, also classed as a historical monument, is surrounded by water—a canal and the river. The garden façade was embellished by a monumental gateway in the 18th century.

The Simonow Collection

The Simonow Collection is housed in two rooms on the upper floor of the prior's lodging (access via the main staircase). The paintings on display are a high-quality, eclectic group of mainly 19th-century works, ranging from *Arab Bazaar* by Sir Frank Brangwyn (1867–1956) to a still life by Matisse, along with works by Rodin, Monet, Braque and Courbet. The earlier works include drawings by Rubens, Tiepolo and Piazetta. Among English artists represented are Constable with a charming drawing *Landscape with Sea*, and Jacob Epstein with a bronze *Portrait of Meum* (1916). Suzanne Valadon (1865–1938) is represented twice, including a portrait of her son Maurice Utrillo entitled *Mon Fils* (1910). There is also a *Portrait of M. Simonow and his Dog Sue* (*pictured opposite*) by Zdzisław Ruszkowski (1907–90) who introduced Simonow to the art scene in Paris in 1972.

Zdzislaw Ruszkowski: *Portrait of M. Simonow and his Dog Sue* (1981).

Valence-sur-Baïse and St-Puy

Valence-sur-Baïse is a 13th-century *bastide* founded by the Comte d'Armagnac, with a 14th-century church. This was the land of Blaise de Monluc (1500–77), Maréchal de France, whose *Commentaires* were written partly in response to the reputation he acquired for his harsh treatment of the Protestants during the Wars of Religion when he was attempting to quell disturbances in Guyenne. At the many-times rebuilt Château de Monluc (*open 10–12 & 3–7; Sun and holidays 3–7; Oct–April closed Sun and holidays; T: 05 62 62 28 55 70*) at St-Puy, you can discover more about wine, Armagnac and the Armagnac-based liqueur, *pousse-rapière*, a potent aperitif, in its beautiful vaulted cellars.

ARMAGNAC

Armagnac brandy is probably France's oldest distillate of wine, certainly older than cognac or calvados. When it was first produced in the 15th century it was taken for medicinal purposes only but during the 16th century it started to acquire a different status. Production peaked in the 19th century, then stemmed by the phylloxera epidemic in 1878. The area which comes within the Armagnac appellation was defined in 1909 and covers nearly 13,000 hectares, mainly in the Gers but also in neighbouring Landes. The *appellation* is divided into three areas according to soil type: Bas-Armagnac or Armagnac-Noir to the west on the edge of the Landes, is the largest area (7,548 hectares), with acidic, predominantly sandy soil which produces perfect grapes for distillation; the limestone of Haut-Armagnac to the east and south (157 hectares) has grapes better suited to wines; the central region, Armagnac-Ténarèze (5,127 hectares) has a mixture of clay and chalk with sand. White wine, low in alcohol and high in acidity, is produced for distillation from three main grape varieties, Folle blanche, Ugni blanc and Colombard. Distillation has to take place by 31st March following the harvest and the alembic, or distilling vessel, is particular to the region. The wine is heated twice but distilled only once (whereas cognac is distilled twice), and maturation is in oak casks and not in the bottle, which gives it a particular bouquet of prune and violet. Depending on the number of years left to age in wood, Armagnac is sold under the *appellations* XXX (less than two years), VSOP (four years) and Napoleon (five years or more). Aperitifs based on Armagnac are the sweet Floc de Gascogne, red or rosé; and La Belle-Sandrine, made with passion fruit.

LA ROMIEU

The two towers of the church high above the countryside signal La Romieu, a walled village of just over 540 inhabitants on the site of a Benedictine abbey founded, so it is said, by two monks returning from Rome c. 1062. The village's name, from the Latin *romaeus* meaning pilgrims, was first mentioned in 1082. It was granted *bastide* status in the 14th century at the wish of its great benefactor, Arnaud d'Aux—cousin of Bernard de Got, first pope at Avignon (*see p. 92*)—who was born at La Romieu c. 1260. The village was English from 1279 to 1453. After an illustrious career, Arnaud was made cardinal in 1312 and that year envisaged the construction of his funerary monument, composed of collegiate church, cloister and residence, inaugurated on 30th July 1318.

The **Collégiale de St-Pierre** (*open May 10–6.30; June–Sept 10–7; Oct–April 10–12 & 2-6; T: 05 62 28 86 33, www.la-romieu.com*) is an unexpected and interesting example of Gothic architecture, approached through the 14th-century cloister which originally had two, possibly three levels. The Rayonnant bays, with two trefoil and one polyfoil opening in each, are divided by slender columns.

The aisleless church, supported by massive buttresses, has a five-bay nave with the four tombs of the Cardinal and his nephews, also damaged. Below the octagonal tower on the east is the sacristy, entirely decorated with some remarkable 14th-century murals. The eight walls are covered with octagonal medallions containing portraits of founders, biblical figures or geometric patterns and the vaults with a variety of angel musicians and censer angels. The other, square, tower is all that is left of the Cardinal's palace.

BAS ARMAGNAC & THE MADIRAN

NB: This section (to p. 390) is covered by the map on p. 414.

The Bas Armagnac, also known as Armagnac Noir, is the western side of the Gers and the heartland of Armagnac brandy (*see box on opposite page*), where vast stretches of vines overlap with forests. The Madiran is a small wine-producing region between the towns of Riscle and Maubourguet and Lembeye further south, along the valleys of small rivers which flow north into the Adour.

EAUZE

Eauze was the ancient city of the Elusates people. *Elusa* became one of the three main political, administrative and commercial centres, with Auch and Lectoure, during Roman occupation of *Novempopulanie*. The busy commercial town was created by Charles IX in the 16th century when he granted the right to hold a market. Now the Armagnac capital, Eauze holds an Armagnac fair in Ascension week and is one of several towns in Bas Armagnac which hold *corridas*.

Musée du Trésor d'Eauze
Open June–Sept 10–12.30 & 2–6; Feb–March, Oct–Dec 2–5, and in the morning by appointment; T: 05 62 09 71 38.
A museum has existed in Eauze since 1976, but the discovery of the 'Treasure of Eauze' in 1985 marked a turning point and a new home was found in the heart of the town. When the Musée du Trésor d'Eauze, in Place de la Liberté, was completed in 1994 the

Treasure was returned to Eauze by the National Antiquities Museum at St-Germain-en-Laye. The museum is small and modern, spanning three floors. On the lower floor (a walk-in safe) is the great 'Treasure', presented vertically. It comprises an amazing 28,003 silver Roman coins dating from the 3rd and 4th centuries, as well as 45 coins in bronze and 3 in gold. Juxtaposed, in a horizontal display, is an outstanding collection of jewellery including exquisite necklaces, bracelets and earrings studded with precious stones and intaglios. The next level (ground floor) explains different periods of prehistory and displays prehistoric tools and a model showing the evolution of the town. The top level has objects reflecting daily life and religion in the Roman era.

Maison Jeanne d'Albert and Eglise St-Luperc

The town's most famous house, on the central arcaded square, Place d'Armagnac, is the timber-framed Maison Jeanne d'Albret. Jeanne's son, Henri of Navarre (*see p. 485*), was taken ill here on 15th June 1579 and was cared for by his queen Marguerite de Valois (La Reine Margot; *see p. 92*) for 17 days. There are small streets with timber-framed houses in varying degrees of dilapidation. The octagonal belfry tower, in stone and yellowish brick with a distinctive roof, indicates the 15th–16th-century church of St-Luperc. Long, narrow and aisleless with a three-sided apse, the interior is enlivened by the fact that the walls are not rendered, adding colour and texture to an otherwise plain church (except for the 1977 murals in the apse) with little fenestration. The painted bosses contain the coats of arms of France and Eauze and of Jean Marre, prior of Luperc and Bishop of Condom (*see p. 379*) in the 16th century.

NOGARO & ENVIRONS

Nogaro is the small rural capital of Bas Armagnac. It has two particular attractions: motor racing in April and September, at the Circuit Paul-Armagnac; and an interesting church. It is a village with plenty of half-timbered houses and the oldest Armagnac distillery; it is also well-known for *courses landaises* (*see p. 421*) held every three years. This was a *sauveté* (place of refuge) on the pilgrimage route to Spain created by the Archbishop of Auch in 1060 and has one of the largest Romanesque churches in the Gers, although it was much modified in the 17th century, and again in the 19th. There are Romanesque elements around the north door, including Christ and the symbols of the Evangelists. The vault of the three-bay nave was rebuilt in brick in the 17th century but the arches with ovolo moulding between the nave and aisles date from the end of the 11th century. The capitals in the east end are sculpted with, from left to right: acanthus leaves; a centaur between two horsemen; *Daniel in the Lions' Den*; musicians; *Christ with Zacchaeus*, who climbed a sycamore tree the better to see Jesus; and *Jesus in a Boat with the Two Sinners*. The sacristy was a 16th-century addition. There are also Romanesque murals and the church has been restored. The collegiate buildings which, with the church, once contributed to the protection of the town now shelter what is left of the cloister, transformed into a garden. Just one bay of the outer wall of the old cloister gives a clue to the beauty of the original carvings.

WINES OF THE MADIRAN

Although its history is long, the region's viticulture went into crisis at the beginning of the 20th century and was reduced to only 6 hectares in 1953. Vines now once again cover over 1,000 hectares and the wines are gaining recognition. Introduced and perfected by the Benedictines of the abbey at Madiran in the 11th and 12th centuries, the wine was used for communion and was appreciated by pilgrims on the Santiago road. It was awarded appellation contrôlée status in 1948 but its first official recognition were the *lettres de noblesse* (letters patent) issued by François I and the court of England in the 16th century. The wines used in the production of the exclusively red wines of Madiran, rich in tanin, are the Tannat, a local variety of black grape, Cabernet Franc and a small amount of Cabernet Sauvignon. The most recently conferred appellation in the region was the Côtes-de-St-Mont in 1981. Pacherenc, the delicious white wine of the Vic-Bilh, the old name of the region around St-Mont, is produced from local grape varieties with curious names—Arrufiac, Gros Manseng, Courbu and Petit Manseng—plus a little Sémillon and Sauvignon.

St-Mont

St-Mont is the most interesting village of the Madiran, with a cooperative winery, the Union des Producteurs Plaimont (*see p. 391*). As its name suggests the village is perched on a hill and overlooks the Adour Valley. There are pretty pebble and brick houses lining the street up to the tall stone church at the summit, which has conserved a small number of remarkable Romanesque capitals. The area in front of the church is landscaped and next to it are the abandoned buildings of the 18th-century priory. The **Abbaye de St-Mont** (*the key to the church is at the Mairie, open Mon–Wed 9–11.30, also Tues 2–4.30; or at the Mayor's house, T: 05 62 69 61 28.*) dedicated to St John the Baptist, was founded in 1045 by Bernard II of Armagnac, called Tumapaler, and was attached to Cluny in 1055. The abbey's history is obscure but it was ransacked by the Protestant troops of Gabriel Montgomery in 1569 and then rebuilt. After the Revolution all the buildings except the church were sold. The interior is wonderfully light and spacious; the aisleless nave is not quite lined up with the apse. All that remains of the 11th-century building are the south transept and apse and part of the south wall of the nave. The vaults were added and the north side of the church altered at a later date, around the late 12th or early 13th century. The oldest and finest capitals from the first building campaign, at the entrance to the south apsidiole, are vegetal on the left and show lions in tendrils on the right, displaying an affinity to the work at St-Gaudens in the Collegiate church (*see p. 545*). There are stylistic similarities to Jaca (Spain) in the next two, slightly later capitals on the southwest, one with a double Corinthian motif, and the other with the theme of David and his Musicians, as well as a reused capital in the southeast of the main apse with the story of Balaam's Ass.

EAST OF ST-MONT

Termes d'Armagnac has a splendidly massive 13th-century keep towering over the Adour Valley. The Tour de Termes d'Armagnac and Musée du Panache Gascon (*open June–Sept 10–7.30, closed Tues morning; Oct–May 2–6, closed Tues; T: 05 62 69 25 12*), is the only part remaining of the castle built on the border (*terminis*) between the ancient territories of Armagnac and Béarn. This was the château of Tibault d'Armagnac who, alongside several hundred other Gascons, fought with Joan of Arc. The spectacular vantage point of this lofty edifice (36m) is reached through six levels of thematic tableaux dedicated to Gascon gallantry. The church next door has a magnificent 18th-century gilded retable.

Nearby **Aignan**, the first residence of the counts and therefore first capital of Armagnac, has traditional houses and an arcaded square. Now it is an important commercial centre for brandy with a cooperative which can be visited. The church has conserved several 12th-century carved elements around the portal and, inside, some good capitals decorating the two apses. It was modified in the late 13th century when the massive square belfry was topped by a distinctive roof and lantern.

Lupiac is a modest village with a large square and timber arcades, described as the *berceau d'Artagnan* at the heart of the Pays d'Artagnan. The villages around here have capitalised on Alexandre Dumas' hero because the man behind the myth, Charles de Batz-Castelmore, was born some time between 1610 and 1620 at the Château of Castelmore (*privately owned*) about 4km north of Lupiac. Although Dumas embellished the facts, Charles de Batz, who adopted his mother's name, did have an illustrious career in the service of Louis XIV. He died during the siege of Maastricht in 1673 and legend has it that he is buried at Lupiac, but of this there is no proof. The St-James chapel (or Notre-Dame-de-la-Pitié) was founded by Charles de Batz, uncle of the musketeer, in 1605 (*see p. 501*). In the chapel, the Centre d'Artagnan (*open July–Aug 10.30–7; Sept–June 2–6, closed Mon; T: 05 62 09 24 09*), explores the musketeer's life.

On the Osse River in the centre of Gascony is the small town of **Vic-Fézensac**, a popular centre for tourism and best known for the Whitsun *corrida*. The medieval town was divided between the Counts of Armagnac and the archbishops of Auch, causing constant tension. In the 18th century the town was physically cut in two when Baron d'Etigny drove the main road through the middle of the old market square. The most interesting part of the church, founded in 1190 by the bishops, is the Romanesque chevet with some of its original decoration and some 15th-century paintings in the south. The 15th-century nave was repaired and covered with a timber roof in the 17th century, while the altar and font are 18th-century.

Lavardens, a picturesque Gascon village clinging to a rocky bluff, was a stronghold of the Counts of Armagnac in the 13th century and was inherited in 1496 by Marguerite d'Angoulême. The streets are narrow and steep and five of the old towers of the *enceinte* still survive. The huge château (*open July–Aug 10–7; April–May, June–Oct 10.30–12.30 & 2-6; Nov–Dec, Feb–March 10.30–12 & 2–5; closed Jan; T: 05 62 58 10 62, www.chateaulavardens.com*) which dominates the village was dismantled by

Henri of Navarre's troops in 1577 and can be visited. It holds important temporary exhibitions. Rebuilding began in 1620 under the direction of the architect Pierre de Levesville but was interrupted by a plague epidemic in 1653. It changed hands twice in the 18th century and after 1820 it was more or less abandoned until 1970, when restoration work was undertaken. The west part of the château is the most elegant, standing proud above the valley; although it has few rooms there are some quite outstanding tiled floors.

PRACTICAL INFORMATION

GETTING AROUND

• **By Bus:** Agen to Auch via Lectoure, Fleurance. Agen to Pau via Condom; Bordeaux to Auch via Condom. Condom to Auch via Valence-sur-Baïse; Condom to Mont-de-Marsan via Nogaro, Barcelonne-du Gers; Condom to Barbotan-les-Thermes via Eauze; Condom to Lectoure and Fleurance.

TOURIST INFORMATION

Aignan Pl. Colonel Parisot, T: 05 62 09 22 57, si.aignan@wanadoo.fr
Beaumont-de-Lomagne 3 Rue Fermat, T: 05 63 02 42 32, www.info82.com/beaumont
Condom Pl. Bossuet, T: 05 62 28 00 80, www.tourisme-tenareze.com
Eauze Pl. d'Armagnac, T: 05 62 09 85 62, http//eauze.net
Fleurance 1121 bis Rue de la République, T: 05 62 64 00 00, www.tourismefleurance.free.fr
Fourcès Mairie, T: 05 62 29 50 96, www.fources.fr
La Romieu Rue du Docteur Lucante, T: 05 62 28 86 33, www.la-romieu.com
Lectoure Pl. du Général-de-Gaulle, T: 05 62 68 76 98, www.lectoure.fr

Montréal-du-Gers Pl. de la Mairie, T: 05 62 29 42 85, otsi.montrealdugers@wanadoo.fr
Nogaro 81 Rue Nationale, T: 05 62 09 13 30, www.nogaro.fr
St-Clar Pl. de la Mairie, T: 05 62 66 34 45, www.saint-clar-de-lomagne.com
Valance-sur-Baïse Mairie, T: 05 62 28 59 19, si.valencesurbaïse@club-internet.fr
Vic-Fézensac 22 Pl. Julie-St-Avit, BP 28, T: 05 62 06 34 90, www.vic-fezensac.com

WINERIES

Aignan Cave d'Aignan, Route de Nogaro, T: 05 62 09 24 06
Madiran Cooperative winery: Maison du Vin du Madiran et Pacherenc, Le Prieuré, T: 05 62 31 90 67
St-Mont Union des Producteurs Plaimont, Caves des Producteurs Plaimont, T: 05 62 69 62 87
Nogaro Cave des Producteurs Réunis, Route d'Aire, T: 05 62 09 01 79

ACCOMMODATION & RESTAURANTS

Beaumont-de-Lomagne
€ **Le Commerce**. Great value food and

good traditional French fare in the restaurant where menus range from €16.50–29.50. The simple rooms are comfortable and light. 58 Ave du Maréchal-Foch, T: 05 63 02 31 02, http://hotellecommerce.com.

Bouzon-Gellenave

€ **Chambres d'hôtes Château de Bascou.** A wine-producing *domaine* of the Côtes de St-Mont region with 3 rooms decorated around different themes in the typical 19th-century Gascon house surrounded by a shady park with pool. The living room picks up the theme of jazz, a tribute to the annual festival at Marciac, and *table d'hôte* is also available by reservation. 5km west of Aignan (via D48), T: 05 62 69 04 12, chateau.du.bascou@free.fr

Condom

€ **Hôtel Continental.** This 24-room hotel with one suite on the banks of the Baïse has been totally renovated. It is arranged around an interior garden and the rooms are pleasant and comfortable using warm shades. The restaurant, Les Jardins de la Baïse, which also has a terrace, serves original and tasty dishes based on local produce. 20 Av. Maréchal Foch, T: 05 62 68 37 00, www.lecontinental.net

€ **Hôtel/Restaurant Les Trois Lys.** ■ In the centre of the town, this all-time favourite hotel in an elegant 18th-mansion has 10 large, elegant rooms, some with original features. Karin Faggion concocts delicious variations on typical Gascon cuisine such as *Bisque de crabe et ses ravioles, Tajine de confit de canard aux figues*, and *Macaron moelleux au chocolat noir* and menus €13–30. 38 rue Gambetta, T: 05 62 28 33 33, www.les-trois-lys.com

€ **Restaurant Table des Cordeliers.** ■ This is a highly successful and carefully thought-through transformation from 15th-century monastery to 21st-century gourmet restaurant. The wonderful dimensions and light of the old chapel lend themselves to elegant dining. Run by the Sampiétro family, the welcome and service is impeccable and the food is a unique experience. Choices include *Escalope de foie chaud au grué de cacao, Médaillon de veau, méli-mélo de légumes de saison*, and *Pyramide crémeuse au safran, pommes fruits rôties, crème glacée aux noix*. Menus range from €20 during the week to €60. 1 Rue des Cordeliers, T: 05 62 58 43 82, www.latabledescordeliers.fr

Fleurance

€ **Chambres d'hôtes En Marsan.** An avenue of trees leads to this fine 19th-century house with annexes which have been entirely renovated to provide 3 rooms accommodating 11 people in comfort. The spacious family property has memorabilia of the owner's father, artist and caricaturist. Outside are a pool and terrace and other activities are available. Plenty of restaurants in the area. Route de Terraube, Mme Martine Cottin, T: 05 62 06 08 20, www.cottin.org

Fourcès

€€ **Château/Restaurant de Fourcès.** The château, which dates back to the 12th century and once protected the picturesque circular *bastide*, has been beautifully restored to create interesting spaces. The garden is next to the stream, and the pool is under the castle walls. Also a high-class restaurant. T: 05 62 29 49 53, www.chateau-fources.com.

€ **Chambres d'hôtes Château du Garros.** ■ This vast house built in 1822 is decorated with a great deal of talent in an elegant combination of traditional French/English and Indian combining beautiful colours. There are three spacious and luxurious double rooms with a heady, romantic aura. A large living room and charming breakfast room are available for guests. Anne Carter, T: 05 62 29 47 89,www.chateaudugarros.com

Lavardens

€ **Chambres d'hôtes Mascara**. A peaceful spot owned by a passionate gardener. The house has blue shutters, an azure pool, and four restful, understated rooms. The living areas have been created from the old *chai* where wine was kept. It is in an excellent position not far from Auch. Monique and Roger Hugon, T: 05 62 64 52 17, monique.hugon@free.fr

Lectoure

€ **Hotel/Restaurant Le Bastard**. ■ The well-appointed hotel with 29 bedrooms occupies an elegant late 18th-century town house with views over the surrounding countryside and pool/terrace. Under the direction of Jean-Luc Arnaud, the restaurant is especially sought after, the gourmet meals served in an attractive dining room with large windows. Menus €15–56. Rue Lagrange, T: 05 62 68 82 44, www.hotel-de-bastard.com

Manciet

€ **Hotel/Restaurant La Bonne Auberge**. A well established restaurant in an ancient building on the main square of the village. Simone et Pépito Sampiétro (parents of the owners of La Tables des Cordeliers) and their daughter guarantee a warm welcome and excellent cooking based on seasonal produce. It has 14 comfortable rooms at

reasonable rates, and menus 14€-43€. T: 05 62 08 50 04.

Miradoux

€ **Chambres d'hôtes Lou Casâu**. A warm welcome and attractive surroundings on offer at this 18th-century house at the heart of the *bastide*. There are 3 rooms named after racehorses, a family passion, where 19th-century elements have been conserved. It has a garden, pool and terrace. 5 Pl. de la Halle, André and Béatrice Lanusse-Cazale T: 05 62 28 73 58, email www.chemindecompostelle.com

Montaut-les-Creneaux

€ **Restaurant Le Papillon**. The green setting and light wood décor is very elegant and inviting. Local produce based on the land as well as seafood are used. The cooking is imaginative and at times combines both fish and foul in dishes such as *Sole fourrée au foie gras*, or keeps them separate in a traditional *Cassoulet* or *Filet de bar aux endives confites*. Menus €13–39. RN21, Route d'Agen, T: 05 62 65 51 29, lepapillon@wanadoo.fr

Projan

€ **Hôtel Château de Projan**. In the west of the Gers, not far from Aire sur l'Adour (Landes), set in tranquil, wooded surroundings with a lake and views towards the Pyrenees, the château combines the old settings with a collection of contemporary art. The welcome is personal, and delicious dinners accompanied by local wines are served in intimate surroundings enhanced by an open kitchen (menus €25–52). The eight bedrooms have 18th-century furniture and modern art. (D946), T: 05 62 09 46 21, www.projan.com

St-Clar

€ **Chambres d'hôtes La Garland Jean-François and Nicole Cournot**. Rooms in a large, arcaded stone house which is part of the 13th-century market place, with an enclosed garden. The three neatly pretty ensuite rooms look out over the square and there is a sitting room for guests with library and TV. Pl. de la Mairie, T: 05 62 66 47 31, nicole.cournot@wanadoo.fr

St-Puy

€ **Chambres d'hôtes La Lumiane**. The house on the edge of a picturesque village dates from 1688, and has five charming, light rooms with antique furniture, three in the converted wing with separate entrance. There is also a sitting room for guests, a large enclosed garden, terrace and pool which is overlooked by the old church. Madame Eman also provides an excellent *table d'hôte* every evening. Monsieur and Madame Eman, T: 05 62 2895 95, http://lalumiane.net

Sarragachies

€ **Chambres d'hôtes Domaine de la Buscasse**. The handsome 17th–19th-century house 15km west of Aignan is in the middle of Côtes-de-St-Mont winemaking region. An avenue of limes, calm surroundings with wonderful views towards the Pyrenean chain, and 15 hectares of vines are the setting for three very light and bright double rooms. Fabienne and Jean-Michel Abadie, T: 05 62 69 76 07, www.buscasse.free.fr

MARKET DAYS

Aignan Monday
Beaumont-de-Lomagne Saturday and small-scale wholesale garlic market Tuesday and Saturday

Condom Thursday
Eauze Thursday
Fleurance Tuesday, Saturday
Jegun Wednesday
Lectoure Friday
Miradoux Saturday
Montréal-du-Gers Friday
Nogaro Wednesday and Saturday
St-Clar Thursday
Valance-sur-Baïse Wednesday
Vic-Fézensac Friday

FESTIVALS & EVENTS

March: *Le Vignoble en Fête*, wine festival, St-Mont
April: *Marché aux fleurs*, flower market, Fourcès
Easter: *Coupes de Pâques*, motor racing, Nogaro
May: *Fête des Fleurs*, flower festival, Riscle. *Foire aux Grands Eaux-de-Vie d'Armagnac*, Armagnac fair, Eauze. *Festival International des Bandas et y Peñas*, colourful spectacle with a Spanish flavour and over 2,000 musicians, Condom
May/June: *Pentecôte à Vic - Féria de Toro*, Whitsun bullfights, Vic-Fézensac *Foire aux Grandes Eaux-de-Vie d'Armagnac*, festival of brandy, Eauze
July: *Fête de l'Ail*, celebration of white garlic, Beaumont-de-Lomagne *Coup de Théâtre dans les Vallons, Festival du Théâtre dans les rues*, street theatre, Roquelaure. *Nuits Musicales en Armagnac*, Condom, Flaran, Lectoure *Fête Médiévale*, sound and light, Termes d'Armagnac. *Féria*, all types of bullfighting and teasing, Eauze. *Festival Tempo Latino*, Latin American music and dance, especially salsa, in the arena and streets, Vic-Fézensac

SOUTHERN GERS

AUCH

Auch is centrally placed in the *département*, and midway between Aquitaine and Languedoc, on an escarpment above the River Gers. The greatest monument of Auch, the late Gothic cathedral, stands silhouetted against the sky with the *ville haute* or old town clutching at its skirts. Narrow medieval lanes contrast with the elegant 18th-century Allées d'Etigny and monumental steps descend to the river. The modern city of Auch is a major, market town and *Préfecture* of the Gers, and has spread out onto the plain in the Gers valley.

HISTORY OF AUCH

The first settlers of the *oppidum Elimberris* were a Celtic tribe, the Auscii. Defeated by the Romans in 56 BC, *Augusta Auscorum*, one of the main cities of Roman Aquitaine, developed on the right bank of the river. From the 9th century the population returned to the hill and built a simple oratory, the core of the medieval *cité*. As the town of Auch expanded it came under the shared authority of the consuls of Auch, the Count of Armagnac, the Archbishop of Auch and the Prior of Saint-Orens. Between 1715 and 1768 Auch became a separate *généralité* or administrative centre, covering a huge territory between the Garonne and the crest of the Pyrenees. The 18th century was the high point for Auch, largely due to its *Intendant* from 1731 to 1767, Baron Antoine Megret d'Etigny, who invigorated the economy of the town and the region with a huge road-building programme linking Auch with the mountains and the Canal du Midi. The Province of Gascony disappeared in 1789 and the larger part of it became the Gers.

Cathedral of Sainte-Marie

The cathedral was one of the last Gothic cathedrals in the southwest, begun at the end of the 15th century, just after Albi cathedral was completed. It replaced a Romanesque church consecrated in 1121. At about the same time a canons' residence had appeared on the south and an episcopal residence on the north while to the east was a steep escarpment. Despite these constraints, the cathedral, designed by Jean Marre, bishop and architect of Condom cathedral, extended to the south as well as to the east where it was supported by a crypt built into the rock. The first stone was laid in 1489, the unfinished building consecrated in 1548, and finally completed in 1680.

The exterior

The exterior shows the evolution of styles over the 200 years of construction. Viewed from the north or south, it appears to be a Flamboyant building with flying buttresses and a shallow transept. In total contrast is the west end. The three entrances, begun in 1560, were the work of the architect Jean de Beaujeu. The north and south portals and the four buttress-towers flanking them had risen to the height of the aisles by 1567 and were completed c. 1635. Above each portal is a Flamboyant rose window beneath a triangular pediment. The decoration of each doorway is transitional, juxtaposing Flamboyant aedicules with pinnacles, crockets and delicately carved Italianate friezes. The massive but elegant west elevation, completed by 1680, uses an exclusively Classical idiom. The three round-arched entrances correspond to the nave and aisles and lead to an open portico, closed by railings in the 18th century.

The interior

The interior is regular and harmonious, unencumbered by integral ornament, an intrinsic feature of southern Gothic architecture. The simple quadripartite vaults and transverse arches are emphatically outlined but spring from shafts which are pared down to the minimum, while sharply profiled aisle arches spring directly from the smooth round piers without the hint of a capital. The blind triforium under low basket arches is more like a Renaissance balcony. Five pentagonal radiating chapels surround the apse while the rest of the 21 chapels are square. This very plain interior is the foil to two great treasures: the stained-glass windows and the magnificent carved choir enclosure. Both were installed by the time the cathedral was consecrated in 1548, when the chapels and ambulatory were vaulted, although the choir had a temporary timber roof and the nave was still a skeleton, because the parish cemetery stood here.

The series of 18 Renaissance stained-glass windows (1507–13) were made by Arnaud de Moles for the ambulatory chapels. To produce the intense reds, blues, greens and golds, he took advantage of new advances in glass-making and in the techniques of abrasion and annealing (slow cooling). The iconographic programme brings together monumental figures from the Old and the New Testament, a line-up of prophets, patriarchs, sibyls, saints and apostles, with small scenes relevant to their prophesies or lives. The themes were probably furnished by the incumbent archbishop and donor of the stained glass, Clermont de Lodève (1507–38), a member of the great Amboise family. There are three key storiated windows. The *Creation* cycle in the first chapel north has figures of Adam and Eve and small scenes above and below of the *Creation* and the *Fall*. The three windows in the main apse dealing with the theme of the Crucifixion have magnificent *fleur de lis* in the upper register. In the central bay is *Christ on the Cross* with the Virgin, St John and Mary Magdalene. The window in the left bay contains Isaiah, the Apostle Philip and prophet Micah, and on the right King David, James the Great as a pilgrim, and a prophet. The *Resurrection* window, on the southwest, combines Christ's apparition to Mary Magdalene, *Noli me Tangere*, in the

Stained glass window (16th century) by Arnaud de Moles in Sainte-Marie at Auch.

central bay, and the *Incredulity of St Thomas* with a small scene of the *Supper at Emmaus*. At the top Auch is represented by its coat of arms, and above the main figures are Claude de France, daughter of Louis XII, and her betrothed, the future François I, representing the two branches of the Crown, the Valois and the Orléans. At the base are more prophets and apostles and the arms of Clermont de Lodève.

The choir

The visit to the choir enclosure (entrance fee), intended as it was to separate worshipping clerics from the lay public, is a world apart from the main body of the church. It is a completely enclosed area, one of three in the Midi-Pyrénées—with Albi (*see p. 249*) and St-Bertrand-de-Comminges (*see p. 542*)—to survive church reforms in the 17th century. The 113 choir stalls that line three sides are an extraordinary *tour de force*. Carved from heart of oak, richly patinated, the sanctuary contrasts in texture and abundance with the plain stone and the radiant stained glass. The enclosure was probably completed c. 1552–54 but there is no recorded date for the start of the work, calculated at c. 1510–20. Gothic in essence, with late Flamboyant-style baldaquins, the iconography of the age of humanism brings together biblical and mythological figures.

The choir stalls are on two levels. The carved reliefs of the high backs of the upper 69 develop the theme of the *Creation*, starting with Adam and Eve in the northwest. Proceeding anti-clockwise, the male-female alternation is maintained with figures representing the Old Law, including Moses; sibyls and prophets juxtaposed with the Evangelists, Apostles and allegories of virtue; David in several scenes leading up to his accession as King; sibyls and prophets representing Fidelity and Infidelity, and Fortune and Misfortune; Babylon and the tests of exile in the shape of more sibyls and prophets. The programme culminates with Saints Peter and Paul, the joint founders of the Christian Church, and above the entrance to the choir are St Jerome, St Augustine and the Virgin. The lower stalls carry scenes from the life of Christ from the *Annunciation* to the *Crucifixion* in high-relief panels on the end stalls. The misericords are decorated with lively and sometimes provocative anecdotes and the armrests with chimerical beasts and demons. Barely a surface is left undecorated.

The crypt and chapels

The crypt, built to support the east end, has five undecorated radiating chapels corresponding to the main chapels. The 7th-century sarcophagus of the Bishop-Saint Léothade, from the former Benedictine abbey of St-Orens d'Auch, is the most interesting piece. The cathedral treasure is in the former sacristy. The St-Sépulchre chapel, in the southeast where the first stone was laid, is the only chapel of the apse without glass because it is against the canonical buildings. Its contains an important sculpted group enacting the *Entombment* (c. 1500): Joseph of Arimathaea and Nicodemus at the head and feet of the body of Jesus as he is lowered into the tomb; the Virgin carrying the crown of thorns; St John; Mary Magdalene; and Maries Salome and Cleophas. This particular group is flanked by four soldiers and covered by a gilded baldaquin with a *Trinity* and numerous angels. All ten chapels of the nave were dedicated to Our Lady when the sculptor Jean Douillé was commissioned in 1662 to make 13 retables. Just two retables have survived complete, and part of another. The most noteworthy, in the chapel of the Assumption on the right of the west door, was restored in 1964. Among other furnishings are the early 16th-century ciborium above the 19th-century altar in the St-Sacrament chapel; a reconstruction (1803) of the mausoleum of Baron d'Etigny, originally at St-Orens d'Auch but demolished at the Revolution; and the 18th-century pulpit. The 17th-century *jubé*, at the west of the choir, elements of which are now scattered around the cathedral, was replaced in 1860 by a new ensemble with painted décor, stalls and altar of white marble. This arrangement was itself altered in 1970 when the altar was moved forward. The choir organ above the west end of the enclosure was given by Emperor Napoléon III and Empress Eugénie; an instrument designed for French Romantic music, it is signed Aristide Cavaillé-Col. The main organ in the west end below the rose window is one of the finest in the region and is used for concerts during the summer music festival. Built by Jean de Joyeuse, its installation was completed in 1694. The case is carved in chestnut and is decorated with caryatids, eagles and angel musicians, with Our Lady in the centre and reliefs of King David and St Cecilia on the lower part.

EXPLORING AUCH

South of the cathedral

Place de la République is the market place in front of the cathedral and the tourist office is in the pretty timber-framed Maison Fedel on the north side. South of the cathedral Place Salinis, created c. 1863, is shaded by *micocouliers* (nettle) trees, typical of the Midi. Towering 40m above it is the 14th-century Tour d'Armagnac against the former canons' residence, originally built as a prison with a cell on each level.

East of Place Salinis the famous **Escalier monumental**, built c. 1863 to the detriment of the old fortifications, descends to the banks of the Gers and the lower town via six flights of steps and three terraces. Covering the central section of the top terrace (from where, in favourable conditions, you might see the Pyrenees) is a vast horizontal relief of words wrought in iron, called *L'Observatoire*. Conceived in 1991 by a Catalan artist, Jaume Plensa, it is engraved with the biblical text of the Flood and recalls the disaster of 1977 when the Gers burst its banks. Its opposite half, the *Faux Refuge*, is on the opposite bank across the footbridge. Firmin Michelet's bronze statue of D'Artagnan (*see p. 390*), erected in 1931 on the level below, is less avant garde. The top terrace of the monumental steps leads to the Pousterles, ancient steep lanes with names such as Coulomates (*colombes*) and las Houmettos (*ormeaux*), linking the lower and upper towns, and to the old town gate, the Porte d'Arton.

At the end of Rue de la Convention on Place Garibaldi is the former pilgrim Hôpital de St-Jacques, rebuilt in 1765. In a tiny courtyard on Rue d'Espagne is a splendid staircase. Place Salustre-du-Bartas, is named after a Gascon poet (1544–90) born near Cologne (Gers), whose statue is in the square. The municipal library is installed in the former 17th-century Carmelite chapel and can be visited.

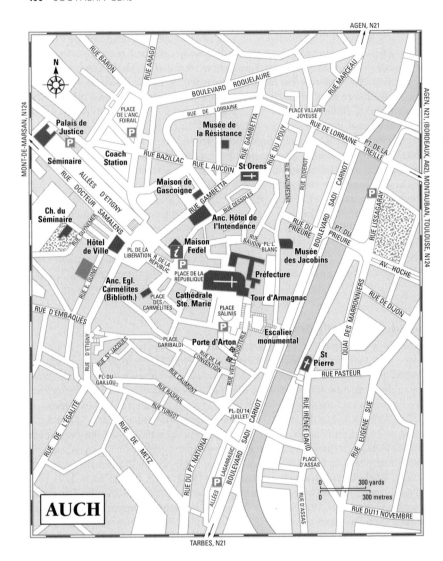

Northwest of the cathedral

The large Place de la Libération with a circular fountain was one of Intendant d'Etigny's creations, and overlooking it is the Hôtel de Ville (1777) which has a room with portraits of illustrious Gersois and a small theatre. At the end of the shady Allées d'Etigny, a statue of the great man, erected in 1817, surveys his work. North of Place de la Libération on Rue Gambetta the Maison de Gascogne, the restored 19th-century grain market, is now used for shows and exhibitions, and the post office opposite has taken over the former Hôtel de l'Intendance (1759). Rue Dessoles is a lively, pedestrianised street (the old Camin Dret) with the 19th-century Neoclassical church of St-Orens at the north end and some notable restorations of *hôtels particuliers* at nos 40 and 45. During Whitsuntide, R. Boiziot, butcher, on the corner of Rue Bazeilles, might well be selling the much sought-after quality beef from the bulls executed during the *corrida* at Vic-Fézensac (*see p. 390*). The street leads back uphill to the tourist office. The former 18th-century episcopal palace is now occupied by the *Préfecture*.

The **Musée des Jacobins** (*open May–Sept 10–12 & 2–6; Oct–April 10–12 & 2–5, closed Mon and holidays; T: 05 62 05 74 79.*), at 4 Pl. Louis Blanc, also known as the Musée d'Auch, occupies the old Jacobins convent north of the cathedral, a 15th-century building radically modified in the 17th century, acquired and restored by the town in 1976. The museum has some fine Gallo-Roman exhibits displayed, with the medieval items, in an attractive gallery looking out on the garden. The collections include some brightly coloured Gallo-Roman frescoes (from 20 BC to the 1st century AD) found in 1962 at Villa la Sioutat, 9km from Auch. Among the funerary objects is a touching epitaph to a dog called Myia, and a beautiful perfume flask (after 2nd century AD) found intact in a sepulchre at la Hourre, Auch. There are also medieval carvings, examples of 18th-century decorative arts, ceramics, 18th- and 19th-century paintings, and a regional ethnological collection (19th–20th centuries). The museum also has a very rich Latin American collection donated by Guillaume Pujos in 1921, focussing on Pre-Colombian Mexican and colonial art.

THE ASTARAC

The area south and west of Auch, known as the Astarac, was a small medieval fiefdom between Armagnac, Fézensac and Bigorre, from the 10th to the 15th centuries, and has a good array of picturesque Gascon *bastides* around Mirande, as well as several small, rustic churches.

MIRANDE & ENVIRONS

Mirande on the banks of the Baïse is one of the largest and best-preserved of the *bastides* of southern Gers. It was conceived in 1281 as a *paréage* between the Counts and the Abbots of Berdoues, and was the old capital of the Astarac, and later a garrison town. Alain-Fournier (1886–1914), author of *Le Grand Meaulnes* (1912), did his officer training here. The town's outstanding feature is the massive porch-tower of the church, straddling the street. The large square is surrounded by arcades in warm yellowish stone and has a pretty bandstand in the middle. At 13 Rue de l'Eveché is the small but well-presented **Musée des Beaux-Arts et Arts Décoratifs** (*open Mon–Fri 9–12 & 2–6; Sat 10–12 & 3–6; closed Sun and holidays; T: 05 62 66 68 10, www.gers-gascogne.com*), in a purpose-built gallery of 1983. It contains 15th–19th-century Italian, Flemish and French paintings, including a number of charming portraits and works attributed to Nicolas Largillière and J.B. van Loo; among the landscapes are one or two from the School of Barbizon. There is an important group of *faïence* from the main French producers and from the southwest and a few pieces of medieval sculpture.

The aspiration that Mirande would be raised to the status of episcopal see accounts for the grandiose proportions of the **Church of Ste-Marie**, begun in 1409. The most original part of the building, which had to be fitted into an area surrounded by already existing streets and houses, is the west tower and porch. The road runs under the porch, above which flying buttresses support the four-level belfry with turrets and a complex roof. Flying buttresses are used on the north and south elevations, unusual in this part of the world, and although the church gives an impression of homogeneity, only the openings on the southern façade are original. In each façade is an identical portal with a statue of St Anthony on the north and St John the Baptist on the south. The Flamboyant west portal, now closed, was heavily restored in 1877–80. The St-Sacrament chapel contains some 15th-century glass, the *Virgin and Child* and *St Michael slaying the Dragon*, with the arms of the town. The remainder of the glass was made by Thibault of Clermont-Ferrand in 1860–61.

St-Clamens and St-Élix-Theux

South of Mirande, isolated in a field between Berdoues and Belloc, is the tiny rustic Chapel of St-Clamens. The key is held at the farm opposite. This remarkably unaltered 11th-century chapel was built on the foundations of a Gallo-Roman temple and, to prove it, under the makeshift porch on the south, is a white marble pagan funerary monument, discovered in 1886, decorated with reliefs and an inscription to Arulianus, possibly the owner of a Gallo-Roman villa. The minuscule windows of the apse are flanked inside and out by 8th- or 9th-century capitals and columns and inside are 12th- and 16th-century wall paintings in a perilous state. In front of the altar is an outstandingly beautiful white antique marble sarcophagus (probably 4th century), found on the site c. 1820. The carving on the lid is a possible allegory of the passing of life represented by a wheel pushed by four winged figures, with a winged head at each corner. The base is more deeply engraved with a portrait of the defunct in a medallion supported by four figures, and either side of it are scenes representing the seasons. The weather-beaten Gothic font was formerly kept outside, and there are two 18th-century statues.

Between St-Michel and Moncassin is the remote 16th-century chapel of **St-Elix-Theux**, worth visiting for its marvellous site on a ridge between the Baïsole and the Petite Baïse and for the superb farm buildings around here, using adobe bricks (sun-baked bricks) and pebbles in a chequerboard pattern.

Barran to Bassoues

North of Mirande, Barran is a well-kept *bastide*, close to Auch, with golden stone houses and a good market square. It also has a strangely contorted church spire covered in grey slate which, although very celebrated, is less than satisfactory: it twists irregularly and looks suspiciously like a case of warped timbers. **Montesquiou**, a picturesque village with an aristocratic name and home of the maternal family of d'Artagnan, is a small *castelnau* on a hill with a medieval fortified gate. There are prehistoric sites in the neighbourhood, a 12th-century belfry on the church, and every July there is an important cattle fair here called La Madeleine.

The massive keep (43 m) of the village of **Bassoues** signals an important *bastide* founded by the Archbishops of Auch in 1279, not far from a monastery acquired in the 13th century. The other major curiosity is the beautiful 16th century timber-framed *halle* which straddles the road, similar to the one at Gimont (*see p. 409*), with some pretty houses either side. The Donjon de Bassoues (*open July–Aug 10-7; April–June, Sept–Oct 10–12 & 2–6, closed Tues; Nov–March check times; closed Jan; T: 05 62 70 97 34, www.bassoues.net*), a huge square tower with angle buttresses and machicolations (1368) is a magnificent piece of military architecture. It contains a permanent exhibition on *sauvetés*, *castelnaux* and *bastides* in Gascony. Next to the keep is the former archbishops' residence, which was altered in the 16th and 17th centuries.

The 15th-century parish church, aisleless Gothic and rather empty, is near the market, built into the slope of the hill. In the cemetery on the western edge of the village, past the keep, is the 15th–19th-century basilica containing the tomb of the local hero St Fris, nephew of Charles Martel (*see p. 167*), who died in mortal combat against the infidels near Bassoues in the 8th century. The legend of his death is remembered over the south and west doors.

MARCIAC & ENVIRONS

One of the best-known villages in the region is Marciac, a quiet 13th-century *bastide* where the population of around 1,200 increases massively each August for the annual jazz festival founded in 1979. The main concerts are held under a zebra-striped marquee on the rugby pitch, and the effervescence bubbles over into the arcaded central square and surrounding streets during the day. The exhibition **Territoires du Jazz** (*open 1st to 15th August 10–7.30; April–July, 16th Aug–Sept 9.30–12 & 2.30–6; Oct–March, Mon–Fri, 9.30–12 & 2.30–6.30, Sun 11–1; closed Sat and holidays; T: 05 62 08 26 60, www.bastidesetvallonsdugers.com*) is a musical journey through jazz from its origins to the present.

The crocketed spire of **Notre-Dame-de-Marciac** marks one of the loveliest churches in the Gers, built in yellow stone in the 14th century to the east of the main square. The spire, which stands on a square tower, was completed in 1865 to a height of approximately 90m, making it the highest in the *département*. There are matching early Flamboyant portals on the north and south and a narthex was added in the 15th century and closed by a wrought-iron *grille* in the 18th century. The entrance is through the south door. The church has a four-bay nave with aisles with large screened chapels flanking the choir. There is a shallow pentagonal apse and two smaller chapels in the east. The western part of the nave was partly rebuilt after suffering at the hands of Protestant iconoclasts in the 16th century when the original octagonal piers and pointed arches were replaced by cylindrical pillars and round arches. The church was vaulted in 1869 when some restoration was accomplished. The nave is lit by a series of rose windows in the clerestory.

There is some rich and interesting sculpture in the east of the church which shows a curious nostalgia for the archaic forms and iconography of Romanesque art. The capitals at the entrance to the main apse present *Daniel in the Lions' Den* and *Samson and the Lion*, and in the south apsidal chapel are various episodes from the *Life of St Eligius*, patron saint of blacksmiths. The carvings at the bases of the clustered shafts in the choir are also noteworthy. The Flamboyant west porch, enclosed in the 15th century when the two chapels either side were added, has some decorative sculpture of varying quality; there are also large sculpted bosses in the narthex.

East of Marciac, at **St-Christaud**, there is a great Gothic building in brick with diamond openings, built c. 1250 on a knoll to watch over the pilgrim route (*see p. 11*). **Tillac**, to the southeast, is a perfect 13th-century *castelnau* with a narrow arcaded street bordered with timber-framed houses, two ancient town gateways with towers, and a 14th-century church with, if you are unwise enough to press the button, a recorded message and guided visit. The church (c. 1334) was badly damaged by fire in the 19th century, destroying the 17th-century timber roof. The choir stalls on the left are 18th-century but the rest are neo-Gothic. There is a gilded retable (1741) from the famous Ferrère workshop (*see p. 525*) in the Asté (Pyrenees) and behind it a ciborium with Renaissance decoration.

VALLEYS OF THE SAVE & THE GIMONE

The villages of the two almost parallel valleys of the Save and Gimone Rivers, southeast of Auch, show the influence of the Toulousain in the predominantly brick buildings, which include the impressive fortified church of Simorre. This region is renowned for its production of foie gras. The main towns are L'Isle-Jourdain and Gimont.

L'ISLE-JOURDAIN & THE SAVE VALLEY

This is a relatively important town of around 5,000 people which was once the capital of the lands belonging to the de l'Isle family. Count Raymond de l'Isle and his countess accompanied Raymond IV, Count of Toulouse and de l'Isle's cousin, on the First Crusade (1096–99) and while in Palestine the countess gave birth to a son. His baptism in the waters of the Jordan is remembered in the name of the town. Raymond's brother, Bertrand de l'Isle (1044–1124), became Bishop of Comminges (*see p. 539*) and was canonised in the 13th century. The dynasty died out in the 15th century and the county was sold in 1421 to Jean IV, Count of Armagnac.

The town has two squares. The older, Place Gambetta—called the *marcadieu*—with arcades on two sides, is on the edge of the route built by the *Intendant* of Auch, d'Etigny. The other square contains the late 18th-century *Hôtel de Ville*, a sophisticated Italianate building in brick with a rusticated ground floor and wrought-iron balconies above. Adjacent is the Neoclassical brick market hall (1819), with a mass of elegant octagonal pillars, converted to house the **Musée Européen d'art Campanaire** (*open June–Sept 10–12 & 2.30–6.30; Oct–May 10–12 & 2.30–5.30; closed Tues, 1–15 Jan; T: 05 62 07 30 01*.), which has a collection of bells from all over the world and presents the six stages involved in making bells and chimes. L'Isle-Jourdain was the birthplace of Claude Augé (1854–1924), creator of the *Dictionnaire Complet Illustré* (1889), which became the *Petit Larousse Illustré* in 1906, and the building opposite is named after him.

L'Isle adhered to Calvinism and, in common with most Protestant towns, the majority of its pre-17th-century monuments (castle, fortifications, and church) were destroyed. The only fragment of medieval architecture remaining, against the northeast of the church, is the brick keep of the château dismantled by Richelieu in 1621. The church was raised to collegiate status in 1318 by Pope John XXII (*see p. 179*). In the late 18th century it was replaced by the severely Neoclassical church of St-Martin, designed in 1785 by Jean-Arnaud Raymond, which takes the form of two superimposed Greek crosses using the monumental Doric order. The interior was entirely decorated in the 19th century, the vaults by Engalières (c. 1879) and the walls by Terral (c. 1889). The reliquary chapel on the south contains the relics of St Bertrand-de-L'Isle, Bishop of Comminges (1040–1123) and of St Odo, second Abbot of Cluny (879–942), and a relic of the True Cross.

Château de Caumont

Guided visits, July–Aug daily 3–6; May–June, Sept–Oct, Sat, Sun and holidays 3–6; T: 05 62 07 94 20, www.caumont.org

At Cazaux-Savès, above the Save Valley, the château is situated on high ground with a spectacular view of the Pyrenean range. The present residence was begun c. 1535 on the site of a medieval fortress by Pierre de Nogaret la Valette, who had accompanied François I on his campaigns in Italy. He endowed his property with elements of Renaissance elegance and comfort without altering the basic medieval structure. The defences were dismantled after the Wars of Religion and the château was damaged by fire in the 17th century. When James MacMahon, an Irish mercenary, married Pauline de Montgaillard la Valette in the late 18th century, he chose to adapt the château to the then highly fashionable *style troubadour* (early Gothic revival), ruining much of the property and himself. He also made an unsuccessful bid to breed merino sheep.

The main building, screened by neo-Gothic outbuildings, is in alternating brick and poor-quality stone from Auch. It is arranged around three sides of a courtyard whose level was raised by MacMahon and lowered by the present owners, who have restored most of the windows. At the exterior angles are square towers with steeply pitched roofs, and between these flanking the north entrance (16th century) are two stair-towers with pepper-pot roofs. The east façade has a gallery supported by huge stone corbels, the west (17th century) has a rusticated loggia on the ground floor, and the south is also 17th-century. Throughout the interior there are examples of the rom-

FOIE GRAS

This is a major product of the southwest of France, especially Gascony and the Périgord and is produced from both geese and ducks. The Egyptians reputedly noticed that migrating geese naturally overfeed thus extending their livers before long flights. The production of foie gras in Gaul was promoted by the Romans who fed the geese on figs. From *jecur ficatum* (*la foie due au figue*, liver thanks to figs) came, *figuido* (8th century), *fedie*, *feie* and finally 'foie'. Although geese and ducks virtually disappeared from the southwest with the Romans, they were known to be present in the Béarn in the 14th and 15th centuries. The turning point came in the mid-16th century with the introduction of maize from the Americas, which proved to be an ideal foodstuff for poultry. About the same time the Jews of eastern Europe inherited Egyptian know-how for producing foie gras and it was eventually turned into a highly fashionable delicacy by Louis XVI and his court.

There are more ducks (over 4,000,000) than geese (130,000) reared in the Gers, and this imbalance is general throughout the foie gras producing areas. The ducks (Mulard ducks are used, a cross between the Barbary and common Pekin duck) and geese are reared free-range, once they have their adult plumage, until they are brought into the feeding sheds for the last two or three weeks of their lives. Here *gavage* or feeding takes place two or three times a day, depending on the species. In the Gers, good quality white maize is used. The fattened liver is not diseased and will return to normal if the bird is released. As farmers will explain, in order to make good quality foie gras, it is important to keep the livestock healthy and happy.

The products associated with duck and geese are high in polyunsaturates and therefore contribute to the low incidence of heart disease in the southwest (along with the red wine of course). The fashionable drink to serve with foie gras is a high-quality sweet white wine—Sauternes, Monbazillac or Jurançon for example—but this is not to everyone's taste. Goose foie gras is considered slightly more delicate and sweeter than the duck and there is a confusing range of ways to serve it. Fresh, the liver can be cooked (fried) in slices at a high temperature as a main course or starter. Foie gras *mi-cuit*, is 100 per cent foie gras, cooked and pasteurised and available in jars or cans. Most traditional is the *foie entier* (whole), in its sterilised form, conserved in jars or cans and served cold as a starter. There are also mixes: *mass* is 100 per cent foie gras but reconstituted; *parfait* is minimum 75 per cent; *mousse*, *galantines* or pâtés, are minimum 50 per cent foie gras mixed with pork or another meat. Sometimes the foie gras is flavoured with truffles. These products can be bought at the specialist markets (*marchés aux gras; see Samartan p. 413*), in general markets, in stores, and directly from the producers.

antic intentions of McMahon. The vast hall or Salon Troubadour painted in neo-medieval *trompe l'oeil*. The second salon (1840), is in *style Pompéien* or Malmaison style. Also open to view are the library behind the door in the tower, the kitchen and the cellars, the first-floor corridor transformed by MacMahon and the bedroom known as La Chambre du Roi where, legend has it, Henri IV slept. Most moving is the little chapel created by MacMahon and his son-in-law the Marquis de Castelbajac, one of Napoleon's generals and Ambassador to Napoleon III, for Caroline MacMahon, Marquise de Castelbajac, who died aged 18 in childbirth.

Samatan

The small town of Samatan is the location for the most famous of all the *marchés au gras* (foie gras markets) in the region. Although not for the squeamish, these are reassuring indications of the ritualistic importance that the French still put on the production, selection and purchase of food. At Samatan the markets are held on Mondays on the edge of the town in three huge sheds beside the car park. The *foies* (livers), weighing anything from 400g to 900g, are set out on long trestles in one of the three sheds and the trading is done rapidly by barter. There are three markets: the first for foie gras itself (*see box opposite*), at about 9.45; at 10.45 the poultry carcasses are sold; and at 11.30 is the *marché de volailles*, live poultry and other animals. Not surprisingly, Samatan has a **Musée du fois gras et des Traditions Populaires** (*open July–Aug 10–12 & 4–6; Sept–June 10–12 & 3–5, closed Sun, Tues; T: 05 62 62 55 40.*)

Free-range geese, farmed in the Gers to produce foie gras (*see box opposite*).

Lombez

The community of Lombez is gathered around the **Cathedral of Ste-Marie** which shares the square with a fine covered market with brick pillars, and its walls with the houses to the south. The diocese, founded in 1317, was one of several in the region created by Pope John XXII (*see p. 179*) and lists 32 bishops until its suppression by Pius V in 1801. A plaque to the right of the west entrance records the visit of the Italian poet Petrarch in 1330, arranged by Bishop Jacques Colonna (1328–41), himself of Italian extraction, who made Petrarch an honorary canon in 1335. The old Tribunal (now the *Mairie*) has a permanent exhibition dedicated to the poet.

The rather severe exterior of the brick church is characteristic of the Midi Toulousain with tall buttresses around the chevet, mirandes below the roof, and a five-tiered octagonal belfry with mitred bays. The foundations, belfry and first bay were constructed c. 1346 and the west end has the typical blank face of meridional Gothic relieved only by a small roundel and the Flamboyant entrance in stone.

The interior

The interior is divided into two by an enfilade of pillars, similar to the Jacobins church in Toulouse (*see p. 593*), but the north section is smaller than the south. Beside the first pillar on the left is a trap door which opens to reveal the floor level before it was raised as protection against flooding. The restored 12th-century baptistery in the northwest, below the tower, was part of an earlier church. It has an eight-rib vault and contains a remarkable collection of treasures. Outstanding is the lead baptismal font referred to by Eugène Viollet-le-Duc in his *Dictionnaire Raisonné* (*see p. 95*): it is made of two separate pieces, the lower decorated with religious figures in medallions in the style of the 13th century and the upper part with a frieze of profane scenes of antique design. It was possibly made up of two disparate pieces stored in the workshop. The stopper in the base suggests it was used for total immersion which was practised until the 9th century. Other items worth noting are a late 15th-century sculpture the *Dead Christ*; 17th-century choir stalls in walnut, less grandly carved than those of Auch but with some splendid atlantes on the episcopal throne; the altar in Carrara marble was consecrated in 1753, and has a bas-relief by François Lucas; the wooden balustrade from the chancel (1671–1710); some quality 18th-century ironwork by G. Bertin; and the 18th-century organ. The brilliantly coloured 15th–16th-century glass by the followers of Arnaud de Moles (*see p. 376*), restored in the 19th century, illustrates scenes from the *Life of Christ* and from the *Passion*.

L'Isle-en-Dodon

L'Isle-en-Dodon, also on the Save, is a classic *bastide* with a central square surrounded by arcades; a Neoclassical brick *Hôtel de Ville* and *halle*, and several timber-framed houses. The 14th-century church has a fortified east end with battlemented towers and an octagonal belfry over the west porch. A Gallo-Roman stone altar is embedded in the east wall and the vivid 16th-century stained glass expresses a debt to the work of Arnaud de Moles (*see p. 376*).

GIMONT & THE GIMONE VALLEY

Gimont is the only town in France where a main road runs straight through the middle of the covered market. Founded by the Cistercian abbey of Planselve (*see below*) in 1266, as a *paréage* with Alphonse de Poitiers, Gimont clings to a narrow promontory above the Gimone River, hence the constricted layout. Originally surrounded by arcades, the massive market hall has 28 octagonal piers supporting a timber roof, and was heightened and rebuilt in the 19th century—there are two dates, 1331 and 1825, on pillars east and west. The foie gras markets are not in the old hall but in the *marché aux grains* down the hill to the north. In the market hall during May there are *courses landaises*—possibly not the moment to choose to drive through (*see p. 421*).

The church of Notre-Dame, northeast of the market hall, was planned in 1292 but the date above the porch is 1331. It is mainly in brick: the later belfry is built over the vaulted stone sacristy with a Flamboyant window on the north, whereas the upper brick part is 16th- or early 17th-century. The church contains some interesting items, including a 15th-century pulpit, an 18th-century altar in Caunes marble, and a small 15th-century *Virgin*. The most famous work is a 16th-century triptych of the *Crucifixion* from nearby Planselve which, according to Flemish tradition, has a painted central panel and carved wings. There are relief sculptures of the Virgin, St Lazarus and an Angel of the Last Judgement, and Mary Magdalene and St Martha on the outside.

Just outside Gimont, the **Abbey of Planselve** (*contact Tourist Information for visits*) was an important Cistercian abbey whose origins in 1142 are well documented. It maintained a hospice and chapel for pilgrims on the edge of the property and prospered until 1557 but deteriorated at the hands of absentee abbots, during the Wars of Religion and the Revolution, until in 1802 demolition began. The buildings are almost entirely in brick. The little that is left is unusual and interesting. The property was enclosed in a long brick wall, and the entrance is through the 14th-century gatehouse which contains a model of the monastery in 1737. There are two beautiful *pigeonniers* near the Gimone.

South of Gimont

Near Saramon, which has Renaissance houses, south of Gimont, is **Boulaur**, a serene and appropriately *bon locus* for the only active Cistercian community of nuns in the Gers who some years ago took over a long-abandoned Fontrevist house founded in 1142 (*visits possible outside the hours of mass; check on T: 05 62 65 40 07.*) Note the barns to the left with wooden latticework typical of southern Gascony. The 13th- and 14th-century abbey church with *mirandes* and a watchtower was restored in the late 20th century. The spacious interior has painted décor in the manner of the Jacobins in Toulouse. Most of the buildings and the fine wrought iron of the church are 18th-century.

The formidable brick church of **Simorre**, further south, now stands in a large empty square but was once part of a Benedictine community, its abbey documented since the 9th century. After it was destroyed by fire c. 1140, the present site was chosen. Some 600m of walls and a ditch protected the religious as well as the secular community, both under the control of the abbots. A cloister was built in 1240 and the new brick church, begun in 1292, was blessed in 1309 when a long drawn-out feud between the abbots and the Counts of Astarac was coming to an end. The octagonal belfry and sacristy were added in 1350, and from 1442 the church was lengthened towards the west, using stone, while in the 15th century the abbey buildings were embellished. With many changes during the 16th century, fire damage in the 17th century and repairs and demolition from 1756 until the Revolution, the monastic buildings were lost. In 1843 Simorre's historic and architectural importance was recognised and Viollet-le-Duc stepped in to restore and modify the church between 1844 and 1858. Restoration was also carried out in 1960.

A sturdy version of Toulousain Gothic with shallow articulation of the elevations, it has a military appearance emphasised by the continuous crenellations added (or extended) in the 19th century. The 14th-century stone façade was originally preceded by a porch with a Flamboyant doorway and you can see the gable embedded in the southwest wall. On each of the short transept arms is a small bell-tower. The striking exposed brick nave was entirely rib-vaulted in the 14th century. Over the crossing is an octagonal lantern on pendentives and ribs, with mitred openings. Although the west end is blank, the fenestration is surprisingly rich in the east part, with fine 14th-century tracery and a variety of stained glass, the oldest (1357) in the upper part of the square east end. Five windows of the choir and south transept have stained glass dated 1482, and one 1519. The stained glass opposite the south door is 1525, and there is a 19th-century imitation of the original style in the north transept window. The very fine carved choir stalls, sadly mutilated in parts, were a gift in 1517 from Jean Marre, a monk of Simorre who became Bishop of Condom (*see p. 378*). In the north transept there is an interesting 15th-century *Pietà* with several figures. The sacristy has murals of 1380 (*for opening times and guided visits, T: 05 62 65 36 34*).

Near Simorre, between Gaujan, on the Gimone valley, and Meilhan, the courage of the Resistance during the Second World War is commemorated by a tall carved columnar monument marking the site where 84 members of the Maquis (the underground French resistance movement) died on 7th July 1944.

North of Gimont

North of the Auch-Toulouse road is **Mauvezin**, a village on a hill between the Arratz and the Gimone rivers. It was once an important stronghold but in the 17th century the castle was divided up and the fortifications dismantled. It is laid out around a vast empty square surrounded by mainly 18th-century whitish limestone houses, with the 14th-century market hall on stone piers to one side. The post office is in a 16th-century building, and the *hôtel de ville* is 17th-century.

Solomiac is a late *bastide* (13th century) on the Gimone with a 14th-century market hall and 15th–16th-century *couverts* around it.

Curious and picturesque, **Sarrant** is a polygonal shaped village arranged around its church, with a 14th-century tower over the old town gateway.

East of Mauvezin, at **Cologne**, is arguably one of the prettiest *bastide* squares and covered markets. Wide-open and spacious, it is surrounded by houses harmoniously combining brick, stone and timber, all well restored, the oldest on the north and south. The *halle* itself is 14th-century. This is a simple structure, with a small square building in the centre (now used for exhibitions) from which the roof radiates out, supported by stone piers at the angles and wooden pillars elsewhere, the whole thing topped by a small belfry. There are still 15th-century grain measures under the market hall.

PRACTICAL INFORMATION

GETTING THERE & AROUND

• **By train:** Between Auch and Toulouse via Gimont, L'Isle-Jourdain.
• **By bus:** Run from Auch to: Bordeaux via Condom; Agen via Fleurance; Montauban via Mauvezin; Mont-de-Marsan via Vic-Fézensac, Nogaro, Aire-sur-l'Adour; Mont-de-Marsan via Marciac, Plaisance-du-Gers, Riscle; Tarbes via Mirande, Miélan; Lannemezan via Masseube; Toulouse via Gimont, l'Isle-Jourdain; Toulouse to St-Plancard via Samatan, Lombez.

TOURIST INFORMATION

Auch 1 Rue Dessoles, BP 174, T: 05 62 05 22 89, www.mairie-auch.fr
Bassoues Au Donjon, T: 05 62 70 97 34
Cologne 12 Pl. de la Halle, T: 05 62 06 99 30, domisyndicat@wanadoo.fr
Gimont 83 Rue Nationale, T: 05 62 67 77 87, www.ot-gimont.com
L'Isle-en-Dodon T: 05 61 94 53 56, mairie.social@wanadoo.fr
L'Isle-Jourdain Maison du Tourisme, Rte de Mauvezin, T: 05 62 07 25 57, ot-isle-jourdain@wanadoo.fr
Marciac Bastides et Vallons du Gers, Pl. du Chevaliers d'Antras, T: 05 62 08 26 60, www.bastidesetvallonsdugers.com
Masseube Val de Gers et Hautes Vallées, 14 Ave E. Duffréchou, T: 05 62 66 12 22, www.masseube.net
Mauvezin Pl. de la Libération, T: 05 62 06 79 47, officedetourismedemauvezin @wanadoo.fr
Miélan Pl. du 8 Mai, T: 05 62 67 52 26 32300 Mirande 13 Rue de l'Evêché, T: 05 62 66 68 10, email bienvenue@ot-mirande.com
Montesquiou, T: 05 62 70 96 59, si.montesquiou@wanadoo.fr
Samatan 3 Rue du Chamoine Dieuzaide, T: 05 62 62 55 40, www.samatan-porte-du-gers.com
Saramon Mairie, Grande Rue, T: 05 62 65 49 71, www.saramon.net
Simorre Rue de la Mairie, T: 05 62 65 36 34, si.simorre@wanadoo.fr

ACCOMMODATION & RESTAURANTS

Auch
€ **France**. Opposite the cathedral, in a former post house, is a hotel with 27 comfortable rooms individually decorated in a variety of styles, some simple, some more elaborate; a buffet breakfast

is available. In good Gascon tradition, the *Belle epoque* style restaurant, Le Jardin des Saveurs, under chef Roland Garreau, serves an inventive variation on traditional ingredients. Menus €25–49 Excellent wines and ancient Armagnacs. 5 Pl. de la Libération, BP 124, T: 05 62 61 71 71, roland.garreau@wanadoo.fr.

Beaumarchés

€ **Chambres d'hôtes Labeyrie**. The house has passed through several generations of the family before becoming a welcoming and peaceful spot, close to Marciac and the world famous Jazz Festival and within sight of the Pyrenees. There are three rooms painted in warm colours with ancient furniture and wood floors as well as a living room for guests. Outside is a kitchen garden and plenty of green space as well as a private lake for fishing. Marie-Edith Samson-Larrieu, T: 05 62 69 49 11, www.multimania.com/alabeyrie

L'Isle Jourdain

€ **Hostellerie du Lac**. The hotel is beside the lake near the centre of L'Isle Jourdain. There is a terrace for outside dining which is next to the water. Although the rooms are basic, but quite large, and the large restaurant is somewhat old-fashioned, the prices are good and the food is copious and well-cooked with plenty of local goodies such as foie gras and *magret de canard* presented in a variety of ways. T: 05 62 07 03 91.

Gimont

€ **Château de Larroque**. The romantically elegant château-hôtel is set in vast wooded grounds, and has a swimming pool and tennis court. Convenient for Toulouse and Auch, this is foie gras country. Of the 16 rooms, all with views, there is a choice of romantic with heavy drapes, or modern. Owned by the Fagedet family, André is *chef de cuisine*, and creates dishes full of taste and flavour. Rte de Toulouse, T: 05 62 67 77 44, www.chateau-larroque.com

€ **Le Coin du Feu**. 25 reasonably-priced rooms have balconies overlooking the pool and courtyard. There is a large dining-room which features a central fireplace where good local produce is at the basis of the food served here. Bd. Du Nord, T: 05 62 57 96 70, www.le-coin-du-feu.fr

Juilles

€ **Chambres d'hôtes Au Soulan de Laurange**. Gérard Crochet and Alain Petit offer accommodation for up to 10 guests in this charming 18th-century Tuscan style home, with a flowery terrace, wonderful views over the côteaux de Gers; *table d'hôte* by reservation on certain days; pool. Chemin de la Devèze, T: 05 62 67 76 62.

Marciac

€ **Les Comtes de Pardiac**. A modest but comfortable and bright hotel on the main square of the 'Jazz' village. The 25 rooms are mainly small but pleasant, and include a suite and two family rooms. There is buffet breakfast inside or on the terrace. T: 05 62 08 20 00, www.hotel-comtespardiac.fr

Mirande

€ **Les Pyrénées**. In the heart of Gascony, this hotel, has 22 spacious and pleasant rooms and 2 suites and a modern restaurant serving traditional Gascon food based on local ingredients such as foie gras, duck and beef. 5 Ave d'Etigny, T: 05 62 66 51 16, perso.wanadoo.fr/hotel-pyrenees.

Monferran-Saves
€ **Chambres d'hôtes Le Meillon.** A farmhouse with a huge garden, pool and panoramic views of the Pyrenees. There are five rooms on the first floor, and *table d'hôte* most days. Anne-Marie and Jean-Raymond Lannes, T: 05 62 07 83 34.

Pujaudran
€ **Le Puits St-Jacques.** In a former pilgrimage staging post, this is a gastronomic restaurant serving imaginative dishes based on regional produce. Pl. de la Mairie, T: 05 62 07 47 11.

St-Maur
€ **Chambres d'hôtes Domain de Loran.** Warm welcome offered at this handsome Gascon house with two towers in beautiful grounds with a lake and a games room for guests. The accommodation can take up to 12 people, in 4 rooms, 2 of them family rooms. Jean and Marie Nedellec, T: 05 62 66 51 55.

MARKET DAYS

Auch Thursday, Saturday
Bassoues Sunday
Beaumarachés Saturday
Cologne Thursday
Gimont Wednesday; *marché au gras* during the winter
L'Isle-en-Dodon Saturday
L'Isle-Jourdain Saturday
Lombez Saturday
Masseube Tuesday
Marciac Wednesday

Mauvezin Monday
Miélan Thursday
Mirande Monday
Samatan Monday; July–August occasional Fridays; foire au foie gras, August; *marché au gras* Monday in winter
Saramon Saturday
Seissan Friday, also *marché au gras* Oct–April.

FESTIVALS & EVENTS

April: *Festival National du Film d'Animation*, animated film festival, Auch. *Marché aux fleurs*, flower market, Fourcès
May: *Fête des fleurs*, flower festival, Riscle
Courses landaises, cattle running, Gimont
June: *Festival Eclats de Voix*, festival of voices, Auch
Festival 'Flamenco, Toros y Cocina', Spanish festivities: Flamenco, Bulls and Spanish cuisine, Gimont
Festidrôle, festival of comedy, Simorre
July: *Festival de Country Music*, Mirande
August: *Jazz in Marciac*, the most important jazz festival in southwest France, Marciac
Festival Médiéval, music and dance, Sarrant
Festival du Musique Classique, 'Coeur d'Astarac', Heart of Astarac classic music festival, Mirande
September: *Festival Africain*, Samatan

LES LANDES

The *département* of Les Landes, the second largest in France, takes its name from a landscape of uncultivated moorland and marshes known as *landes* or *lannes*, which has been transformed into one of regimented pine forests and drifting sand dunes. A large part is crossed by dead-straight roads and the population is scattered. This landscape ends at the celebrated silver beaches of the Atlantic on the Landais coast, part of the Côte d'Argent, and gives way to oaks, maize and vines in the Sud Adour (the Chalosse and Tursan), between the River Adour and the Gave de Pau. To the east of the *département* is Armagnac Landais, the smallest geographic region of the Landes, historically and geographically part of Gascony.

THE LANDAIS COAST & FOREST

The long straight shoreline of the Landes, is known as the Côte d'Argent. It extends over 106km of sandy beaches and attracts many French visitors in the summer. The only hiatus is the military zone between Biscarrosse-Plage and Mimizan-Plage, with no public access. The typical forest and dune landscape—which extends north into the Gironde and south to the Basque coast—is punctuated by lakes and criss-crossed by small rivers, but permanent communities are small and infrequent. The Coastal Way follows part of a secondary pilgrimage route to Spain (*see p. 11*).

BISCARROSSE & ENVIRONS

Biscarrosse enjoys a magnificent position between two large lakes, Cazaux-Sanguinet and the Etang de Biscarrosse-Parentis. Its long association with pioneering aviation from 1930–55 is celebrated in the Musée de l'Hydraviation (*open July–Aug 10–7; rest of year 2–6, closed Tues and holidays; T: 05 58 78 00 65*). The museum is dedicated to two pioneers: Henri Fabre (1882–1984), who built and flew the first sea-plane on 28th March, 1910, and Pierre-George Latécoère (1883-1943; *see p. 583*) whose workshops can be seen. There is also a Musée des Traditions et de l'Histoire (*open July–Aug 9.30–7; mid-Feb–May 2–6, June, Sept, 10–12 & 2–6, closed Sun, Mon; other times by appointment, T: 05 58 798 77 37*). The history of the town is illustrated through a variety of memorabilia, and rural life evoked by a mini-farm and working beehive.

Mimizan to the Etang de Léon
Mimizan, where Gallo-Roman and medieval settlements were engulfed by sand, offers floral walks around the Etang d'Aureilhan. The richly sculpted Gothic doorway and belfry (13th and 15th centuries), the only remaining evidence of the Abbey Church of Mimizan, has been restored (*open mid-June–mid-Sept 10–12.30 & 2–7, closed Sun and*

holidays; other times by appointment; T: 05 58 09 00 61). It includes an unusual group of polychrome sculptures with *Christ in Majesty* surrounded by the symbols of the Four Evangelists flanked by St Peter and St Paul, as well as murals. On the Coastal Route to Spain, the bell-tower was a symbol of encouragement to pilgrims.

St-Julien-en-Born has the only lighthouse (*open July–Aug Tues and Thurs 10–12.30 & 2.30–4.30 T: 05 58 42 89 80*) in the Landes, 38m high with 183 steps, with views over the forest and the Atlantic. The village of **Lit-et-Mixe** developed on the old Roman coastal road and has a small local history museum. To the east, the typical Landais village of **Lévignacq** has an outstanding church, fortified in the 13th–14th centuries, with a curious curved spire. The church contains 15th- and 18th-century painted decoration. The 13th-century church at Vielle-Saint-Girons to the south is one of the oldest on the coast. A popular excursion from the **Etang de Léon** nearby is the trip on a *galupe* or *barque* (flat-bottomed boat) on the Courant d'Huchet (*departures April–Oct, at 10 for 2 hours, and 2.30 for 3–4 hours, by reservation only, T: 05 58 48 75 39*). This is the only way to see the Huchet, the most significant of the small rivers or *courants* typical of the Landes which run directly to the sea, and an opportunity to enjoy the lush vegetation along its banks, including wild orchids.

LANDES CÔTE SUD

The Landes Côte Sud, from Moliets to the Adour Estuary, is more densely populated and equipped to receive larger numbers of visitors. Inland at Soustons, is a memorial to François Mitterand (1916-96) who had a home here for 31 years.

Hossegor-Capbreton

The most popular seaside resort on this part of the coast is Hossegor-Capbreton, two small ports either side of an estuary which have merged into one community. Hossegor is typical of the Landes coast with sand dunes, pines and seafront, numerous hotels and sports and leisure activities, including golf. Its development as a resort began early in the 20th century and, while not on the scale of Arcachon or Biarritz, it has enormous appeal and character. A major asset is the saltwater lake, which began as a freshwater pond created when the Adour was redirected in the 16th century. The construction of a canal linking it to the ocean in the 19th century—an attempt to prevent the build-up of silt in the channel—transformed it into a tidal saltwater lake. The fight goes on and the channel is constantly dredged mechanically.

The main building in Hossegor centre is the Sporting-Casino (1930), adjacent to the *fronton*, a wall against which to play the Basque game *pelota*; there is an indoor *jai alaï* hall, a *fronton* with three walls (1956; *see p. 448*). Very special to the town are the colourful façades (c. 1925) on the seafront around the semicircular Place des Landais, and houses of similar style (c. 1920–40) are repeated along the wide promenade. There is a pleasant 6km walk all around the lake. One of the first hotels on the east bank, the Hôtel du Parc, is now the post office, and among the pine trees on the west bank are villas of the 1920s and '30s, the most beautiful of which is the Villa Julia.

The port at the confluence of the Bourret and Boudigau rivers divides Hossegor from the older **Capbreton**, the only fishing village between Arcachon and Anglet. In the Middle Ages this was the largest community on the Landais coast and the 17th-century engineer Vauban (*see p. 67*) considered expanding the port into a naval base. At the western extremity is l'Estacade, a rebuilt mid-19th-century wooden jetty, with views of the coastline and Pyrenees. The fishing port, marina and the fish market are across the Boudigau and around the Port de Pêche are some lively restaurants. The Municipal Casino, overlooking the entrance to the port, contains the Ecomusée de la Pêche (*open July–Aug 10–12 & 2–6.30; April–June, Sept 2–6; Oct–March, Sun and holidays, school vacations, 2–6; T: 05 58 72 40 50*), with aquariums, models of boats and fishing equipment as well as an explanation of the Gouf de Capbreton, the geological phenomenon of an underwater canyon which reaches extraordinary depths: at 5km from the coast it is around 400m deep, at 20km 1000m, and at 50km 1400m. In the old centre, the Church of St-Nicolas offers a panoramic view from the tower. Inside the church is an interesting series of engraved plaques in memory of ships' captains and crews, a 14th-century *Christ* and a fine 15th-century *Pietà*, both carved in wood.

Soorts a little way inland still has some 19th-century farmhouses, as well as one of the oldest golf courses in France, created in 1930. The environment is carefully protected and at Seignosse-Bourg around the Etang Noir there is a 50 hectare nature reserve (*guided tours, T: 05 58 72 85 76*). The inland village of **Tosse** has a pretty 12th-century restored church and Landais farmhouses in timber and brick. The Etang Blanc is a favourite place for fishing and walking, and at **St-Vincent-de-Tyrosse** is a Romanesque church (11th–12th centuries), restored in 1926 in a curious Romano-Byzantine style. **Réserve Naturelle du Marais d'Orx** (*open all year; guided visit by appointment, T: 05 59 45 42 46*), is marshy terrain of some 800 hectares close to Labenne (N10) which was dried out in the 19th century but has been allowed to return to its natural state since becoming a protected nature reserve in 1989. On one of the most important migration corridors of Europe, more than 200 species of migrant birds collect here annually.

FORÊT DE LANDES

The Landes forest is a vast triangular swathe of territory extending over nearly 11,000 square kilometres across much of the *département* of Les Landes and part of Gironde. Before the 19th century, the centre of the Landes was mainly open moorland (*lande*), essentially flat and sandy, with numerous small rivers and shallow wells, with patches of marsh as well as small woods with both broad-leaf and evergreen trees. Dominating the landscape were endless stretches of poor grass grazed by sheep, watched over by shepherds who walked on stilts 1.5m tall in order to cover long distances rapidly and to watch over distant flocks. In the late 19th century, maritime pines were planted to improve and stabilise the land and in 50 years the countryside was transformed. This relatively young forest is the largest in Western Europe and is covered with a network of hiking tracks and cycle routes through the enfilades of trees where green ferns and violet heather flourish.

Ecomusée de la Grande Lande, Marquèze

Access is by train (April–Nov) from Sabres station approximately every 40min and the trip takes 10min; it is important to check departure times. Trains run June–mid-Sept 10–12 & 2–5.20, last return 7; April–May, mid-Sept–Oct, Mon–Sat, 2 until 4.40, Sun and holidays from 10–12 & 2–4.40; T: 05 58 08 31 31, www.parc-landes-de-gascogne.fr

The Parc Naturel Régional des Landes de Gascogne was created in 1970 in order to maintain the balance between tourism and the natural environment. The open-air museum at the heart of the Parc Naturel Régional reconstructs traditional life in the *landes* before the wholesale planting of pines. The museum is laid out as a pre-1850s *airial*, an isolated, self-sufficient rural community of peasants who grouped together on grassy areas of common land. Here are preserved a number of typical rural buildings; the dwellings are painted white and the others are farm buildings, including a *poulailler perché* (raised chicken coop). There is also livestock. Exhibits relate to the main occupations of the Landais peasant: shepherding, farming, milling and tapping for resin. The finest house is the *maison de maître* (c. 1900), a low, timber building that was inhabited by the ploughman, anchorman of the community, and his family. The precious oxen were part of the family and a place was reserved for them inside the house. Sheep were considered more lowly but were far more numerous, and had many uses. By the river is a working mill, and in the pine woods resin is tapped for turpentine, an industry which developed with the growth of the forest. Another aspect of the Ecomusée is the Graine de Foret, at Garein (*open mid-April–Oct 8–12 & 2–7; Nov to mid-April, 2–6; T: 05 58 08 31 31*), which is a discovery trail through the forest.

ARMAGNAC LANDAIS

The most easterly part of Les Landes is an area of contrasting landscapes, where the forest of the Landes and the farmland and vineyards of Armagnac overlap. Its vulnerable position between the territories of France and England in the Middle Ages made it a battle ground, and *bastides* were founded at strategic points by both sides.

MONT-DE-MARSAN

Situated where the Douze and Midou unite to become the Midouze, Mont-de-Marsan is known as the town of three rivers, with some 30,000 inhabitants. Crowds gather for the Fêtes de la Madeleine in July, and for *férias* and *courses landaises* at the arena.

The town which developed around the *castelnau* established by the Viscount of Marsan between the Douze and Midou c. 1133 became an important stage on the pilgrimage route thanks to the Benedictine priory of La Madeleine. The town was strongly defended with ramparts on both banks and the Porte de Roquefort and Château de Nolibos, possibly built by Gaston Fébus (*see p. 571*) in 1344, to the east. The château was demolished in the 17th century. A suburb soon developed on the opposite bank of the Midouze at the river port from where grain and wine were transported to Bayonne, and during the Hundred Years War the walls were extended around it. In the 18th century trade picked up, rich families built grand mansions and the town was cleaned up and opened out. Mont-de-Marsan became capital of the *département* of Les Landes created in 1790, and was endowed with administrative buildings.

Exploring Mont-de-Marsan

Just east of Place du Général-Leclerc, where the Tourist Office is located, two footbridges cross the Midou to the old part of town. The further one, Passerelle des Douves, leads past gardens to a terrace below the old castle. The other, Passerelle des Musées, brings you down to Rue Lacataye and the **Musée Despiau-Wlérick** in the 14th-century Lacataye keep (*open 10–12 & 2–6, closed Tues and holidays; T: 05 58 75 00 45*). The museum has a unique and rich collection of early 20th-century sculpture, including works by Bourdelle and Rodin, and of two local sculptors, Charles Despiau (1874–1946) and Robert Wlérick (1882–1944). From the top of the building is a good view over the town. Some 20 sculptures are also placed in the gardens and streets of the town.

Beyond the museum are sections of the old ramparts, and along Rue Victor-Hugo are the 19th-century Neoclassical buildings of local administration, including the *Préfecture*, the *Hôtel du Département*, the *Palais de Justice* and the old *Gendarmerie* and prison. The church of La Madeleine, rebuilt 1825–30 by D.-F. Panay to harmonise with the other public buildings, contains a main altar (18th century) by the Mazetti brothers from Avignon whose work is in several Landais churches.

Behind the *Préfecture* in Rue Maubec are two stone houses described as Romanesque, but probably 13th-century. Rue G. de Gourgues south of the church brings you to Place de Général-de-Gaulle, once the site of the 12th-century castle but now replaced by the theatre and market. Cross the Pont de l'Hôtel-de-Ville at the confluence of the Douze and Midou, and turn west to the Pont de Commerce, the area of the old port and of the Cales, or quays, of the Midouze. The houses around Place Joseph-Pancaut were built by wealthy merchants in the 18th century. The arena at Plumaçon (1899, enlarged 1933), the venue for *corridas* and fairs which has 7,000 seats, can be visited by appointment (*T: 05 58 75 06 09*).

LABASTIDE-D'ARMAGNAC

The most attractive *bastide* in the Armagnac Landais is Labastide-d'Armagnac, east of Mont-de-Marsan. It was founded in 1291 by Bernard IV d'Armagnac to defend his territory against troublesome neighbours in the Marsan, and its charter was ratified by Edward I in 1294. Labastide lost its walls and gates in the 17th century but has retained much of its medieval character.

Place Royale is large and empty, enclosed by attractive façades and continuous arcades combining stone with brick and timber. Unusually for a *bastide,* the church opens onto the square with a towering belfry porch (15th century), thought originally to be part of the fortifications; the interior is painted with 19th-century *trompe l'oeil* and contains a 15th- and 16th-century polychrome wood *Pietà*. Adjacent to the church is the *Mairie*, above the old market hall which still has a grain measure. Reputedly the view over the square from the Maison Malartic opposite the church, which was visited several times by Henri IV, was the inspiration for Place des Vosges in Paris. Labastide was an important Protestant centre for the region and suffered the consequences. Maison Clave on Rue Castay contains murals which appear to date from the Protestant period, and near the west exit to the village is a simple building dated 1607, described as *Le Temple extra-muros*, or Protestant church, which has been turned into an exhibition centre for *bastides* in Gascony; enquire at the tourist office for opening times. At Château Garreau is the Ecomusée de l'Armagnac (*open April–Oct 9–12 & 2–6, Sat 2–6, Sun 3–6; Nov–March, Mon–Fri 9–12 & 2–6; T: 05 58 44 88 38*) all about distilling, with no less than 11 stills.

Environs of Labastide-d'Armagnac

Two kilometres east of Labastide, at Geoü, the chapel Notre-Dame-des-Cyclistes (*open July–Aug 10–12 & 3–6, closed Sun morning; May–June, Sept–mid-Oct 3–6, closed Mon, Sun morning; T: 05 58 98 11 46*) is a tiny, restored 11th-century Romanesque building on the site of a 4th century Roman villa. The French national sport of cycling is honoured here, and the church has been completely given over to cycling memorabilia.

A few kilometres west is the slightly busier **Saint-Justin**, which was granted *bastide* status in 1280 as a result of a *paréage* (*see p. 358*) between the Hospitallers of St John of Jerusalem and the Vicomtesse de Marsan. A section of the ramparts with three octagonal towers and an attractive arcaded square shaded with lindens have survived along with some good buildings, including a fine Renaissance timber-framed house.

The privately owned **Château de Fondat** (*for guided visits, enquire at the tourist office in St-Justin*), outside St-Justin, is a deliciously Romantic concoction which began as a large farm estate built in 1607 by a Scotsman, Lord Argelouse. Heavily remodelled in the 19th century, it is set in interesting gardens with old trees and a dovecote on stilts.

SOUTHEAST OF MARSAN

In the village of **Bascons**, southeast of Mont-de-Marsan, is the Musée de la Course Landaise (*open Wed–Fri 2–7; T: 05 58 5 91 76*), which has been entirely renovated. It contains memorabilia, the history and spread of the sport (*see box opposite*) in the Landes and also a documentation centre. Close by is a simple 13th-century rural chapel, Notre-Dame-de-la-Course-Landaise, which is the scene of an annual pilgrimage at *Ascension*. The village also has a typical arena. Pomarez, in Chalosse in the south of the region, is considered the Mecca of *courses landaises*.

The **Château de Ravignan** (*guided visits, July–Sept, Sat–Sun 3–7; May–June, Sept–Oct, by appointment only; T: 05 58 45 26 44*) to the east, at Perquie near Villeneuve-de-Marsan, is one of the best in the Landes. It was begun in the 17th century and completed in the 19th century. The elegant Classical building is set in a *parc à la française* and contains good furniture and objets d'art and a collection of costumes from the court of Louis XVI.

BASCO-LANDAIS SPORTS & FESTIVALS

Courses landaises have been practised at least since the 15th century and possibly earlier. This bloodless teasing of bovines is the main event of village *fêtes* in the Landes and took its present form c. 1830/40 when certain rules were established and oxen were gradually replaced by cows. The performance takes place in an arena, the objective being to provoke the animal and the art to avoid its charges gracefully. To the mainly Spanish terms employed are added the French *l'écart, la feinte* and *le saut* (swerve, false swerve and leap). The *saut* is perhaps the most spectacular and has different versions, such as *le saut les pieds dans le béret. Courses landaises* are followed most enthusiastically in the Chalosse, the Tursan, Armagnac, in northern Béarn and the Bigorre where they take place more than 450 times in some 80 arenas from May to September. The *corrida*, introduced into the south-west during the Second Empire by Empress Eugénie, is a bull-fight in the Spanish tradition, with matadors and *novilleros* who exhaust the animal before killing it. A *ganaderia* is where the bulls or cows for fighting are bred. *La fête*, or *heste*, in the Landes and Gascony combines *courses landaises* with a colourful summer street celebration when *bandas* (brass bands) animate the streets at night and in certain towns lasts for five days. The *féria* is an annual festival with bull-fighting.

THE SUD ADOUR

South of the River Adour the pine forests of the Landes de Gascogne are replaced by the gentle hills and fields of maize of Gascony, most of which lies in the neighbouring *département* of Gers. The region around Montfort is still described by its old name, La Chalosse, and in the southeast, centred on Geaune, is the Tursan, which differs from the Chalosse by virtue of its vineyards. The old name of the land south of Dax, of which Peyrehorade was the capital, is the Pays d'Orthe.

AIRE-SUR-L'ADOUR

The bustling market town of Aire-sur-L'Adour is on two levels, the lower part on the banks of the Adour, and the *quartier du Mas* on rising ground to the southwest. Aire is at the heart of an agricultural region where the economy depends largely on the production of geese and ducks, and the *marché au gras* is one of the busiest in France.

The lower town
The Tourist Office is on the south bank of the Adour east of the bridge. The old bridge was washed away by serious flooding in 1743 and 1795, and rebuilt only in 1834 thanks to Madame de Berry, for whose visit six years earlier a wooden bridge had been

hastily erected. Further along the river is the arena where the *courses landaises* (*see box on p. 421*) are held during the traditional festivities in June.

From the tourist office, Rue Maubec leads south past a working Carmelite convent with a 19th-century chapel, on the site of the 12th-century episcopal mills. Beyond is the former **Cathedral St-Jean** (the bishopric transferred to Dax in 1933). It was begun in 1092, but a bay was demolished during the Hundred Years War and in 1569 Protestants attacked the church and massacred the prelates. The severe west façade combines stone and brick, relieved only by the undecorated door and a plain oculus, and the slate-roofed belfry is set slightly back. Inside, the nave is vast and dark with extensive painted décor of 1860. Of the Romanesque building, relatively intact until the 18th century, only the brick choir, transepts and some capitals have survived. The north transept is barrel-vaulted, but the south is ribbed. In 1766 the apse was replaced by a huge rotunda and the stalls, woodwork and main altar in coloured marble are also 18th century. The nave was radically altered in the 19th century when the arches were punched through and aisles added. The 1750s' organ was restored in the 1990s. There are occasional visits to the tower and to the sacristy. In the latter, which has Romanesque openings and 14th-century ribbed vaults supported by a central column, chasubles and church treasures are on display.

South of the cathedral is the former episcopal palace, rebuilt in 1647, which now houses the Hôtel de Ville. It has a fine stone staircase, panelled Salle du Conseil, and a small museum of Gallo-Roman mosaics. Across from here on Rue Labeyrie is the large early 20th-century covered market with the *marché au gras* next door. The commercial centre is along the two parallel main streets, Gambetta and Carnot, and the present Crédit Agricole in Rue Gambetta was the *halle aux ceréales*. At the corner of Rues Labeyrie and Libération is the restored 14th-century Maison de l'Officialité, with Gothic and Renaissance windows, where local magistrates used to meet. The canal belonging to the cathedral chapter was dug in the 16th century to provide water for the mills and the bishops' palace and linked Aire with Barcelonne-du-Gers to the east.

From Rue Labeyrie head south and uphill along Rue Felix-Despagnet towards the quartier du Mas and the Romanesque church of Ste-Quitterie. It is a fair walk; by car, head in the direction of Pau.

Quartier du Mas and Basilica Sainte-Quitterie

Church open. For guided visits Tues–Sat, mid-May–Sept, ticket office next to the church, T: 06 77 02 43 44; other times by appointment, T: 05 58 71 47 00.

The Mas was inhabited from Gallo-Roman times onwards. An early Christian sanctuary was established here, and in 1092 the existing abbey was taken over by Benedictine monks. The church, dedicated to St Peter, was begun in the 11th century, incorporating a 4th-century mausoleum sheltering the venerated relics of a young Christian girl identified as Quitterie, a Christian Visigoth princess. She refused to abandon her faith to marry a high-ranking pagan Visigoth, Euric, was pursued, took refuge in Aire, and was beheaded here in 476, at the foot of the hill of Mas where a spring gushed forth water. Quitterie gathered her head in her hands and carried it up the hill to the site where the church now stands. The area around the abbey developed into a veritable cultural centre protected by walls, ditches and a château.

The exterior

The oldest part of the church visible from the exterior is the east end (11th–12th centuries). A walk gives an understanding of the site and there are sarcophagi from an ancient Christian burial ground to the north. The north wall has a stone base of around the same date, but the upper part was rebuilt in the 14th century in brick following a fire during a local revolt in 1288. The massive west front, also part stone (13th century), is enhanced by two levels of continuous arcades. The brick section, including the square belfry, with recycled Gallo-Roman columns on the two lower levels, was also part of the 14th-century alterations, although the last stage of the belfry is 18th century. The Gothic porch was attacked by the Protestants in 1569 when fire scorched the stone, and angels, apostles and prophets on the arches were destroyed; the figure of St Peter on the central *trumeau* survived until the 18th century. The carvings on the tympanum represent the *Last Judgement* with *Christ in Majesty*, the Virgin and St John, framed by the instruments of the Passion. Below are the *Expulsion of Adam and Eve from Paradise*, and *Hell*, with the damned in cauldrons, or led by chains attached at the neck through the jaws of Leviathan. Traces of colour are faintly discernible in places.

The interior

Immediately inside the door are holy water stoups, the one on the right supported on an old nave boss carrying the arms of Foix, and the other a Roman capital in marble on a Visigoth stone sculpture. In the nave, the Classical pillars were erected after the Wars of Religion in the 17th century. When the Romanesque nave was rebuilt in the 14th century, the floor was raised to the level of the choir, which had to be high enough to accommodate the roof of the crypt. At the same time a large window was opened in the north transept. More light was let into the nave in the 16th century by four new openings. The transept floor was raised to the height of the choir in the 17th century.

The choir gives an idea of the grandeur and beauty of the original church. In 1886, stalls and panelling were removed to expose 12 damaged Romanesque capitals supporting arcading lavishly decorated with delicate friezes and interlacing. Two capitals near the altar represent scenes from the Old Testament including *Balaam on his Ass* and the *Song of Songs*. Four capitals carry scenes of the Vices and the appropriate punishments, and the six others carry foliate designs and animals. Some of the arcading was removed when the choir was subjected to an elaborate Baroque décor of coloured marble and stucco, the work of the Mazetti brothers in 1771. The centrepiece of the altar is *Ste Quitterie in Glory*. The end of the apse is still concealed beneath 18th-century decoration but the northeast chapel was dedicated to St Philibert in the 19th century, when it was entirely restored. Here are eight 12th-century capitals, one carrying a *Visitation* and scenes of vice, animals or monsters. The waiting area between the apse and apsidal chapel was created in the 14th century: here the insane were retained (or restrained, there is still evidence of the manacles) while their families descended into the crypt to pray for sanity to be restored. Stairs lead down to the original 4th–6th-century mausoleum or crypt, built around a spring which was no doubt the site of an ancient cult; the floor is scattered with Gallo-Roman fragments. Here lies the splendid early Christian (4th century) sarcophagus of Ste Quitterie in white Pyrenean marble. The relics have disappeared but the iconography of the reliefs on the sarcophagus is important proof of the early existence of Christianity in this region. The carvings on the lid show the *Sacrifice of Abraham*, the *Healing of the Paralytic*, *Jonah and the Whale* (always a monster in early Christianity), and *Tobias and the Giant Fish*. On the main face from left to right are the *Raising of Lazarus*, *Daniel in the Lions' Den*, the *Good Shepherd* carrying the Lamb between the Church, with Ste Quitterie in her arms, and a veiled female representing the Synagogue, *Adam and Eve with the Serpent*, and what might be the *Creation of Man* or the *Baptism of Christ*. Jonah features again on the end faces. In the 11th-century chapel of St-Desiré opposite are 14th-century paintings with the coats of arms of the great Gascon families, and the *Annunciation*, *Nativity* and *Adoration of the Magi*. The miraculous fountain whose water was considered to have healing properties, site of Quitterie's martyrdom, is on Rue du Château below the church.

THE TURSAN

Among picturesque villages and sights in the vicinity of Aire-sur-l'Adour are the small 15th- and 19th-century Château du Lau at Duhort-Bachen (*guided visits by appointment only June–Sept 2-6, closed Thurs, Sat, T: 05 58 71 51 89*). The capital of the old region of Tursan, **Geaune**, southwest of Aire, was a *bastide* established by the English in 1318. **Pimbo**, south of Geaune, was a pilgrimage halt on the journey from Le Puy to Compostela (*see p. 11*): the 12th-century collegiate Church of St-Barthélémy (*open Mon-Fri 10–12 & 2–6; T: 05 58 44 46 57*) provided shelter. It is mainly 14th-century, with a few fragments of Romanesque sculpture. This was the oldest *bastide* in the Landes, jointly founded in 1268 by the Canons of Pimbo and the representative of Henry III. It also has a botanic garden.

Samadet, stretched out along a ridge west of Geaune, is a little town of pretty coloured façades which produced *faïence* in the 18th century. The Musée de la Faïence et des Arts de la Table (*open April–mid–Oct 10–12 & 2–7; Nov–March 2–6; closed Mon; T: 05 58 79 13 00*) was created to safeguard the memory of the production of faience. Earthenware, which had appeared in France in the mid-16th century, gained in popularity because of restrictions on silverware at the time of Louis XIV. The Manufacture Royale was established in Samadet in 1732–1838 thanks to the Marquis de Roquepine, Abbot and Baron of Samadet, who took advantage of local deposits of clay as well as quantities of wood and sand to start manufacturing locally. From 1732 the Manufacture Royale de Fayance de Samadet enjoyed huge success and was sold all over the southwest, eventually closing in 1840. The museum has a wide range of objects decorated in a variety of colours. It also traces the evolution of tableware in France from the Middle Ages to the present day with 10 displays of tables with their settings.

Eugénie-les-Bains, a commune established in 1861 north of Geaune, has become a green oasis on the edge of the desert of the Landes. Empress Eugénie, the last Empress of France, beneficently offered her patronage to the town after reputedly sheltering there during a storm in 1859. It has an arena and water and rose gardens, but above all this spa town is heralded as both premier *village minceur de France* and gastronomic centre. Since 1975 the chef Michel Guérard has pioneered *cuisine minceur* here, proving that good food can be part of a calorie-controlled diet. The hotels and restaurants are dominated by the Guérard dynasty. The spa waters cure obesity.

West of Eugénie-les-Bains, the 14th-century Tour Maubourguet at **St-Loubouer** is where Gaston IV of Foix (1436–72) brought together the Estates of Lannes (Tursan, Chalosse and Dax) and made them swear allegiance to Charles VII. The Romanesque church has a fortified belfry and 12th-century sculptures. At Larrivière, is another church dedicated to sport, Notre-Dame-de-Rugby (*open daily 9–7; Mairie T: 05 58 45 92 79*), with *ex-voto* tributes to the oval ball, including the motifs in the stained glass.

SAINT-SEVER

Saint-Sever, on the edge of the Chalosse, was once a major halt for pilgrims on the road between Bordeaux and the Pyrenees. The abbey church is the theatre of a magnificent group of 11th–12th-century sculpted capitals. The town is sheltered by the Belvédère de Morlanne, a natural balcony of rock commanding the river valley.

HISTORY OF SAINT-SEVER

The Romans occupied the *oppidum* on the hill of Morlanne, but the town is named after Severus, a Christian from Eastern Europe, sent by the pope to evangelise the area. He was successful in his mission, but early in the 5th century was beheaded by Vandals. He took up his head and walked, a spring gushed forth, and the area became a site of pilgrimage. Guillaume Sanche, Duke of Gascony, fulfilled his vow that if successful in battle he would rebuild the sanctuary dedicated to Severus, founding the abbey in the late 10th century. Around 1025 the first church was built, with a vast apse, two apsidal chapels and probably a timber roof. In the 11th century a precious illuminated manuscript, the *Béatus* (or *Apocalypse of Saint-Sever*), was compiled at the abbey (*see picture overleaf*). Grégoire de Montaner (Abbot 1028–72), of noble birth and trained at Cluny in Burgundy, assured a privileged position for St-Sever. When in 1060 the monastery was ravaged by fire, Grégoire initiated an ambitious project of rebuilding inspired by the architecture established by the Cluniac Benedictines. Shortly before his death, the main altar was consecrated and by the 12th century much of the structure of the church was in place. An earthquake in 1372, the Hundred Years War and the Wars of Religion did terrible damage. Under the auspices of the Congregation of Saint-Maur in the 17th century, there were major repairs and alterations. It is now the parish church.

A page from the 11th-century manuscript, the *Apocalypse of Saint-Sever* or the *Béatus*, illuminated by Brother Stéphanus Garcia, depicting The Lamb surrounded by stars; the beheading of the false prophet and the Beast; and the vanquishing of the Devil and the Dragon.

Abbey Church of St-Sever

Open May–Oct 8–12 & 2–7; Nov–April 9–12 & 2–6, Sun 8–12.

The exterior of the church is in a mixture of styles, in poor condition in places, rebuilt in others, but still essentially Romanesque. The nave is short in relation to the unusually long chevet, and the tall apse with a domed roof was remodelled in the 17th century. The 19th-century restorers created the neo-Romanesque west end to replace a 17th-century Classical doorway and reopened the small door in the north transept; the belfry on the northern transept dates from 1930. The tympanum in the north door is Romanesque, albeit badly damaged, and reuses two Roman capitals from Morlanne.

The interior

The interior is a forest of columns and pillars, with carvings that warrant close inspection. The chevet is orchestrated by six apsidal chapels in echelon, three each side, which increase in size and height to culminate at the east in a deep apse, the same layout used at the second abbey church of Cluny (Burgundy) in the 10th century. The walls between the chapels are pierced to form arcades linking one to the next. This is a rare arrangement for southwest France and the result is an exceptionally large two-bay choir which, along with the choir and transepts, has 12th-century barrel vaults. Each transept has an elegant gallery above the chapel which gives access to the upper part of the choir chapels, a system usually associated with northern France. The southern gallery is closed by a screen. The main altar and baldaquin are Baroque but under the wooden floor of the apse are fragments of mosaics, part of the extraordinarily rich decorative programme in the Romanesque period. A variety of materials indicate different building campaigns or alterations. The three round pillars in the southwest, the rib vaults of the aisles (except for the southeast bay) and the Rayonnant tracery are the result of building campaigns in the 14th–15th centuries, while the barrel-vaulting of the short nave is 17th–18th-century.

The carved capitals, some 150, are a magnificent testament to the importance of Saint-Sever in the 11th–12th centuries. Those of the chevet, completed by the end of the 11th century, place the abbey church among the major creative centres of the first wave of Romanesque sculpture, and show certain similarities with those at St-Sernin in Toulouse (*see p. 588*) and Conques (*see p. 218*). The second wave of construction and decoration began in the early 12th century. Some of the capitals appear disproportionately large, and many were repainted in the 19th century, in an attempt to re-create the medieval colours. Recycled Roman elements include a number of marble columns and one capital in the middle chapel north of the choir. The earliest capitals on the north of the chevet demonstrate a free interpretation of antique models with vigorous variations on the acanthus or smooth leaf designs. The form of the capital and abacus adapts according to its role or position, and there are different techniques used in the carving. Balls and lions start to appear in the north and are expanded on and added to on the south of the chevet, suggesting the same workshop. Complicated designs incorporating interlacing appear, and more lions, including two particularly elegant ones on the south of the middle chapel; another, with a figure between two lions, may be a reference to Daniel in the Lions' Den. Birds of increasing complexity include a deeply cut image where the feet of two birds meet above a man's head. The storiated capitals are from a later period, and include a *Christ in Majesty* with St Peter, on the angle of the north transept and aisle and, near the west door, are (north) an enigmatic painted scene in which four figures help four more to scramble up through foliage; and opposite, easily decipherable, *Herod's Feast* and the *Beheading of John the Baptist* on three faces of the capital. The organ was renovated by the Cavaillé-Col workshops in the 19th century; there is a gilded wooden altar (17th century) from the Jacobins (*see p. 593*) in the north aisle. From the sacristy there is access to the cloister, built in the 17th century and restored.

The Convent of the Jacobins

From the cloister, in Rue du Général-Durrieu, are some good 18th–19th century houses; no. 21 is 16th-century. This street meets Rue Lamarque, and to the left is the convent of the Jacobins or Dominicans (c. 1280), which contains a small and interesting museum (*see below*). The convent was established under the patronage of Eleanor of Castile, Edward I's queen, outside the town walls. In the 14th century the walls were extended to encompass the convent and at this time the first repairs were carried out. It was again extensively repaired and rebuilt c. 1660 following Protestant attacks. The cloister had only two wings in the 14th century, but was replaced by the present irregular four-sided one in the 17th century. To the east it is linked by three arcades with the chapter house, in which murals have survived. You enter the large brick church from the cloister. Recently restored, it is unadorned and impressively spacious, its main asset being the splendid timber roof.

Musée du Couvent
Open July–Sept 2.30–6; other times, check with the Tourist Office.
The Musée du Couvent is on the west of the cloister, through a small door and upstairs. Although dusty and forgotten, it contains a fascinating collection of Gallo-Roman finds from Morlanne (4th–8th century), the Gallo-Roman villa at Augreilh (4th century), fragments of the 11th–12th century abbey church, and pieces from the Jacobins. There is an exhibition dedicated to the remarkable 11th-century manuscript known as the *Apocalypse of Saint-Sever* or the *Béatus (pictured on p. 426)*. The town owns one of only three reproductions produced in the mid-19th century by Count Auguste de Bastard d'Etang, using a then-revolutionary process of chromolithography that came as close as possible to duplicating the artist's original work. The original, in the Bibliothèque Nationale in Paris, was produced in the abbey by Brother Stéphanus Garcia de Castile at the time of Abbot Grégoire. It consists of an illuminated transcript in French of the text of the Apocalypse of St John, and originally included the commentary of Béatus de Libiena (c. 786), who instigated the cult of St James at Compostela (*see p. 11*). The colours of the illuminations, the work of several artists, are particularly brilliant. The illuminations are presented here in slide form with a commentary

THE CHALOSSE

The Chalosse is a fertile region watered by the River Louts and renowned for beef cattle and foie gras. There are examples, or partial examples, of Romanesque churches in the Chalosse going back to the 6th century in Nerbis, Montaut, and St-Cricq Chalosse; to the 11th century at foundations in Bergouey, Doazit, Larbey, Caupenne; and to the 11th and 12th centuries at Laurede, Baigts and St-Aubin.

Hagetmau

In the east of the region, on the outskirts of the small town of Hagetmau, south of St-Sever, is the Romanesque **Crypte St-Girons** (*open July–Aug 3–6, closed Tues; at other times enquire at the Mairie, T: 05 58 05 77 77*), a tiny vestige of a once-important abbey dedicated to the 4th-century saint. The crypt was the traditional burial place of Girons and contains a remarkable group of sculptures. The abbey survived until 1904, when it was demolished leaving just the present low building. It was restored 1905–08, but little work has been done since. Steps descend into a marvellous space which is an extended polygon with a Gothic ribbed vault. The saint's tomb was placed at the centre of the crypt, framed by four free-standing antique marble columns. The 14 capitals of these columns plus the two engaged columns and eight stone wall piers are 12th-century. The capitals carry sculptures which are deeply cut and display a variety of figures, birds, lions and imaginary beasts. Of the free-standing capitals, one has confused scenes of damnation, another a vigorous image of a man and birds, and the third is clearly recognisable as the parable of Lazarus and Dives. The engaged capital on the south wall carries the *Deliverance of St Peter from Prison*.

Around Brassempouy

At **Maylis** is an Olivetian abbey (a branch of the Benedictine order) dedicated to Notre-Dame, which is famous for the Gregorian chant sung regularly at mass (Sun 11, weekdays 11.45; T: 05 58 97 72 81), and for the *tisane* produced here. The village is on a ridge with views over the Chalosse, and the church is restored neo-Gothic with a statue of Our Lady. A short distance to the south is a beautifully simple 14th-century chapel in dark stone restored by the monks.

This corner of France is rich in prehistory and near **St-Cricq-Chalosse**, a flowery village with a tiny arena, is Le Chemin de la Préhistoire (*Summer programme of activities, T: 05 58 79 86 37 or 06 24 60 00 57*). This ambitious journey through prehistory travels backwards from Neolithic to Middle-Paleolithic, with hands-on prehistoric activities such as making flints, producing fire and throwing pots.

A celebrated site in the annals of prehistory is the village of **Brassempouy**. Here, in the Grotte du Pape, 3km from the village, an ivory carving known as the *Venus of Brassempouy* or the *Lady with the Hood* came to light in 1894 (now in the Musée des Antiquités Nationales near Paris). This beautiful little head (36.5mm long) was carved from mammoth tusk some 23,000 years ago and is considered one of the oldest carvings ever found. The Musée de la Dame de Brassempouy (*guided visits only June–Sept 11*

& 2–7; Oct–15th Nov, 15th Feb–March 2–5.30, closed Mon; T: 05 58 89 21 73), specialises in female representations in prehistory and, as well as copy of the head, describes excavations during the 19th century, and has more from other parts of Europe. There are visits to the caves during digs. The Jardin de la Dame (open July–Aug 10–12 & 2.30-7; April–June, Sept–Oct, 2.30–5.30; closed Mon, T: 05 58 89 25 89) is an opportunity to find out about prehistoric man's environment, how he made tools and fire, hunted and cooked. Also in the village is the part-Romanesque church built on the castle mound.

Château de Gaujacq

House open mid-Feb to mid-Nov, guided visits at 3, 4 and 5; June also at 6; July–Aug also 11, 2. Garden open 2.30–6.30; both closed Wed and mid–Dec to mid–Jan; T: 05 58 89 01 01.
The charming Château de Gaujacq and its Plantarium lie between Brassempouy and Bastennes This beautiful site was occupied in the Gallo-Roman and medieval periods. The present château was built in 1693 by the Marquis de Sourdis, godson of Henri IV and brother of Cardinal François de Sourdis, Archbishop of Bordeaux (*see p. 20*). The house, Palladian and quite unusual in France, is single storey arranged around four sides of a rectangular garden court, with a continuous Ionic arcade of 44 arches. The gardens of the court are laid out fairly informally and some magnificent 150-year-old Magnolia grandiflora shade the house.

The visitor entrance is on the northwest, and the visit includes a large part of the privately owned and still inhabited château. The apartments for the numerous domestic staff in the 18th century—concierge, surgeon and gardener—are used for exhibitions. The main reception rooms on the southeast, with views towards the Pyrenees and the Luy Valley, have conserved their 17th- and 18th-century décor and furnishings, and some floors of Pyrenean marble. Louis XIV played billiards in what is now the large dining room and the small apartments of the Marquis de Sourdis have 17th-century panelling, some painted. One room is arranged as a memorial to Cardinal Sourdis, who died in Gaujacq in 1707. The delightful botanic gardens or Plantarium behind the house, created in 1986, contain, in eight main flower beds, a large collection of shrubs and perennials combining English informality with French structure.

Montfort-en-Chalosse

The main town at the heart of the Chalosse, a fertile region watered by the River Louts, renowned for beef cattle and foie gras, is Montfort-en-Chalosse, between St-Sever and Dax. The church goes back to the 11th century, with Gothic additions. On the outskirts of the town, the **Musée de la Chalosse** (*open April–Oct Tues–Fri 10–12 & 2–6.30, Sat, Sun and holidays 2–6.30; Nov–March, Tues–Fri 2–5.30, closed Mon and 15–31 Dec; T: 05 58 98 69 27*) reflects local rural traditions and the tranquillity of this part of the Landes in a beautifully restored *maison de maître* (1649), a substantial gabled farmhouse. Typically, it has one long and one short roof and deep overhanging eaves. The stone surrounds of openings are left exposed and the doors and shutters painted in *bleu de Chalosse*. Inside the farmhouse, the rooms—kitchen, dining room, bedrooms—are furnished in the style of a well-to-do 19th-century farming family.

DAX

The spa town of Dax on the south bank of the Adour is the second largest in the *département*. The long exploitation of the hot, muddy, mineral-laden water for which it is famous, used in the treatment of rheumatism and other complaints, has led to Dax's rank of *première station thermale de France*. Hotels and shops are therefore plentiful, and it is surrounded by parks and gardens.

HISTORY OF DAX

Roman *Aquae Tarbellicae* was established on an island and the city built on wooden piles. As the community spread onto the mainland the lake was filled in and by the 4th century an area of some 8 hectares was enclosed in walls 1465m long. Christianity was introduced in the 4th century by Vincent de Xaintes, bishop and martyr, whose relics were translated in the 11th century to the site of the present cathedral. A castle built in the Middle Ages, reputedly by Richard the Lionheart, was demolished in the 19th century, as were most of the Roman and medieval walls which had survived virtually intact until then, leaving some 300m standing. At this point Dax began to expand beyond its Roman confines and the spa facilities were modernised. Dax can now boast some 18 thermal treatment centres which attract around 55,000 *curistes* a year.

EXPLORING DAX

Across Place Thiers from the tourist office is Parc Borda, bounded to the south by the surviving fragments of Gallo-Roman walls. In the park is the arena built in 1913 for the summer *férias*. Many of the thermal baths and spa hotels are strung out along the river to the west, beyond which, in the Bois de Boulogne, is the Trou des Pauvres, an ancient public baths. The principal monument of the town is the Fontaine Chaude or **Source de la Nèhe**. The hot springs are contained in a rectangular pool enclosed in iron railings and a three-arched Doric portico, an early 19th-century successor to several Roman and medieval versions. The pool is fed by water at a temperature of between 60–64°C, which forces its way through more than 2000m of rock to arrive at the surface rich in minerals. It can be sampled from taps disguised as lion-heads decorating the fountain.

South of Rue Fontaine-Chaude are pedestrianised streets leading to the cathedral. Behind the elegant wrought-iron gate of the Hôtel St-Martin-d'Agès (1650), in Rue Cazade, is the local archaeology museum, the Musée de Borda (*open 2–6, closed Tues, Sun and holidays; T: 05 58 74 12 91*), named after the mathematician and sailor Jean-Charles de Borda, born in Dax in 1733. He explored new techniques in shipbuilding and created new navigational instruments. It houses Gallo-Roman and medieval finds, including 1st-century AD bronzes found in Dax in 1982, mosaics, ceramics and sculpture. There are also 18th–19th-century paintings and a room dedicated to Borda. In the Musée Georgette Dupouy at the same address (*open daily 2–6; T: 05 58 56 04 34*) is a collection of works by Georgette Dupouy (1902–92) and other 20th-century artists, Réné Sautin (1881–1968) and Nicholas Eeckman (1889–1973). The Crypte Archéologique at 27 Rue Cazade is all that remains of a 2nd-century Gallo-Roman temple, part of which can be seen from the street (*guided visits only, Feb–Nov, Tues–Sat 4pm, from Musée de Borda*).

A statue in Place de la Cathédrale refers to the legend that the properties of the muddy water of Dax were recognised when a Roman centurion's ailing dog was cured after falling into a warm spring. The Cathedral of Notre-Dame is Neoclassical (rebuilt 1683–1719) and has an interesting Gothic portal inside. A cathedral existed here from 1102. The Romanesque church apparently suffered badly at the hands of the English in 1295, as a Gothic version was begun in the second half of the 13th century. This building survived until desecrated by Huguenots in the 17th century. With the exception of the façade and sacristy, the ruins were demolished. The post-Reformation cathedral, designed by Pierre Battut, was inspired by the 17th-century domed church of St-Paul-St-Louis in Paris and consecrated in 1755. The Gothic sacristy was demolished in 1890, and in 1894 the Gothic doorway of the Apostles was moved to its present location.

PAYS D'ORTHE

Various routes converge on the north bank of the Gaves Réunis at **Peyrehorade**, the main town of the Pays d'Orthe. The town has a particularly good market and is one of the few places where *pibales* (elvers) are still fished in the winter. It has few monuments apart from a portion of the 16th-century Château Montréal built by the Viscounts of Orthez and the keep of the Château d'Apremont.

HASTINGUES

The tiny *bastide* of Hastingues, perched on a promontory commanding the valley of the Gaves Réunis, was named after John Hastings, the English Governor of Gascony, when founded in 1289 by Edward I. Of the fortifications added in 1303, just one gateway and a section of wall remain. It was attacked in the 16th and 17th centuries, but several 15th- and 16th-century houses have survived on the square and main street, the most notable among them being the *Mairie*.

The Aire d'Hastingues (motorway service area) on the A64 between Orthez and Bayonne has made a feature of the fact that it is a few kilometres from the crossroads of three of the four major pilgrimage routes to Santiago de Compostela (*see p. 11*). The Exhibition Centre (*open May–Sept, 8.30–8; Oct–April 9-6*) is in a building which was inspired by the scallop shell, symbol of the pilgrimage. The visitor is led along symbolic routes which develop the historic, spiritual and practical themes of the pilgrimage.

ABBAYE D'ARTHOUS

Open April–Oct 10.30–1 & 2–6.30; Nov–March 2–5; closed Mon; T: 05 58 73 03 89.
Between Hastingues and Peyrehorade, in what was originally a remote wooded valley, is the former Abbaye d'Arthous, founded c. 1167 by Premonstratensian friars from Case-Dieu in the Gers. Although badly desecrated over the centuries, substantial and lengthy restorations have been carried out in the recent past. The Premonstratensians were dedicated to preaching, poverty and work. Successful cattle breeders, their abbey grew rich from donations of land and animals and the reception of pilgrims. In 1289, during the English occupation of Aquitaine, the abbot and Edward I signed a *paréage* to found Hastingues (*see above*) on abbey lands. Unscathed during the Hundred Years War, it was badly damaged in 1523 during the war between François I and Charles I of Spain (Emperor Charles V), and again in 1571 by Protestant iconoclasts. There were phases of rebuilding in the 17th and 18th centuries, but by the time of the Revolution the monastery was much depleted and only three canons remained. Used as a farm after 1791, the abbey continued to deteriorate until it passed to the Conseil Général of the Landes in 1964. The Musée de l'Histoire du Pays d'Orthe here uses the latest modern technology to evoke the local history.

Visiting the abbey

The exterior of the chevet, the highlight of the church, has double engaged columns running the entire height of the apse, and the three small windows are framed by smaller columns and capitals. The decorations include billet mouldings, carved corbels with a variety of decorative motifs, and sculpted capitals. One capital on the southeastern side of the apse represents the *Flight into Egypt.*

Beyond, gates lead into a courtyard, enclosed by the church to the south, and to the north and west by 17th-century buildings in fairly good condition, although little remains on the east. The church, dedicated to Notre-Dame, was probably begun soon after the foundation of the abbey and spans the transition from Romanesque to Gothic.

The vast, aisleless nave was divided in two in 1727 and the damaged western part acquired a secular use. The east end is tripartite and the transept arms do not extend beyond the chapels. The vaults over the apse and north apsidal chapel are Romanesque, whereas the south chapel has early rib vaults and the transept slightly pointed barrel vaults. The ribs of the crossing are 14th-century, and the nave originally had a wooden ceiling supported by diaphragm arches springing from capitals; it was vaulted much later. The capitals in the apse have similar foliate designs to those on the exterior but are technically more confident. The capitals in the south transept are more evolved, although damaged, and include one with stylised vegetation from which a centaur shoots an arrow. In the south nave is a rare surviving example of interlacing and flowers. Carving on the old tympanum of the west door represents, on the right, the *Virgin and Child*, with Joseph and a star, and on the left two Magi, but the central part has disappeared.

SORDE L'ABBAYE

A powerful Benedictine abbey was situated here near a ford where a Roman villa had once existed. A toll bridge was built in 1289 and two years later the village acquired *bastide* status. Some remnants of the protective walls of the old town survive and the main street, Rue Laville, runs past what is left of the west gate and leads to the square on the north flank of the abbey. At right angles to the main street is a road running past the west front of the church to the river and the old abbey mill (c. 1100), transformed into a small hydro-electric generating station in 1923. A salmon ladder is a reminder of how important these fish were to the abbey in the Middle Ages but now the numbers have declined, and salmon have been replaced as a major source of income by kiwi fruit cultivated on the islands in the Gave. Four of the five medieval dykes still exist.

Church of St-Jean-de-Sorde

The Church of St-Jean-de-Sorde was begun at the end of the 11th century, and has retained its overall Romanesque outline, although only the large main apse at the east end dates from that period, flanked by heightened Gothic transept chapels. The north transept (12th century), in an attractive combination of stone and brick, with scorch marks, is unusually flanked by a square tower on the northwest. The surround of the transept door flows over onto the base of the tower and is an interesting example of Romanesque art. The seven consecutive arches, supported by columns and capitals, show versions of the *Wise and Foolish Virgins*, the *Months of the Year* and the *Signs of the Zodiac*. An image of *Christ in Majesty* on the tympanum is just recognisable. Gothic elements were added to the upper part of the transept, including a *chemin de ronde*, blind tracery, a pointed arch framing a simple rose window, and a pendant over the door.

Detail from the 11th-century mosaics in the Church of St-Jean-de-Sorde.

HISTORY OF SORDE L'ABBAYE

Since prehistoric times man has lived here where the river was fordable and the cliffs provided shelter. In the Gallo-Roman period it developed into a staging post on the Bordeaux–Pamplona road. The abbey, first mentioned in a document of 975, grew rich and powerful from donations and pilgrims who stopped here before crossing the Gave d'Oloron, the last major obstacle before the Col de Roncevaux (*see p. 476*). Sorde abbey was marked by the Franco-Spanish conflict in 1523, by the Wars of Religion in 1569 and in 1665, in common with many important abbeys, it came under the control of the Congregation of St-Maur, who restored and rebuilt it. At the Revolution, the abbey buildings were confiscated and sold, and the church passed to the parish. The owners of the abbey gave the property to the abbey of Belloc (near Bayonne) in 1980, and they returned it to the commune in 1995. The abbot's house is still privately owned.

The interior

The cavernous interior bears witness to many alterations and there is little evidence of the original church except in the east. The southwest pillar of the transept still carries its old capitals and, despite major restoration to the apse in the 19th century, the capitals at the entrance to each of the transept chapels are apparently original. They present episodes from the *Life of Christ*, and north, *Daniel in the Lions' Den* and *Christ's Arrest in the Garden of Gethsemane*, and south, the *Virgin and Child* and *Presentation at the Temple*. The greatest surprise, however, is the magnificent 11th-century mosaics behind the main altar, possibly inspired by the Roman mosaics in the abbot's lodgings (*see below*), and decorated with geometric patterns, intersecting spheres, animals and birds. The main altar is an elaborate affair in 10 different marbles produced by the Swiss-Italian brothers Mazetti from Avignon in 1784. The five-bay nave, on a bit of a slant, has always been aisled. It was remodelled in the late 13th or early 14th century and re-vaulted in the 17th century, leaving the 12th-century vault responds with no function. In the nave is a model of the church in the 18th century.

The monastic buildings

Entrance behind east end of church. Guided visits (some in English) April–Oct 10.30–12 & 2.30–6.30, closed Mon; Nov–March Mon–Fri 9–12 & 1.30–5; T: 05 58 73 09 62.

Beneath the terrace overlooking the Gave in front of the vast main wing of the abbey, is a unique underground gallery or cryptoporticus, built c. 1710. Steps lead down to a long passageway with arcades along its length on the river side and a series of 14 cells, some with their original doors, where supplies were kept. Below this level is a dock and fish tank, where salmon were landed and prepared for the kitchen. The only other underground gallery of this kind in France is at Haute-Combe in Savoie.

PRACTICAL INFORMATION

GETTING AROUND

• **By train:** Bordeaux, Sanguinet, Biscarrosse, Parentis-en-Born, Morcenx, Dax and Puyoô, Tarbes (some stations served by bus). Bordeaux, Morcenx, Dax, St-Vincent-de Tyrosse, Labenne, Boucau, Bayonne, Hendaye. Mont-de-Marsan via Dax or Morcenx, Bordeaux or Bayonne. Bordeaux, Dax, St-Vincent-de-Tyrosse, Bayonne/Hendaye. Bordeaux, Dax, Pau/Tarbes

• **By bus:** Marmande, Gabarret, Barbotan-le-Thermes, Cazaubon, Villeneuve-de-Marsan, Mont-de-Marsan. Agen, Gabarret, Barbotan-le-Thermes, Cazaubon, Villeneuve-de-Marsan, Mont-de-Marsan. Agen, Aire-sur-l'Adour, Pau, Dax, Grenade-sur-l'Adour, Mazères-sur-l'Adour, Aire-sur-l'Adour, Tarbes. Mont-de-Marsan to: Labastide-d'Armagnac; Agen; Hagetmau; Cazaubon; Marmande; Aire-sur-l'Adour; Pau.

TOURIST INFORMATION

Aire-sur-l'Adour Hotel de Ville, T: 05 58 71 64 70, otsi.aire@wanadoo.fr
Biscarrosse-Plage 55 Pl. du G. Dufau, BP 1, T: 05 58 78 20 96, www.biscarosse.com
Capbreton Ave G. Pompidou, T: 05 58 72 12 11, www.capbreton-tourisme.com
Dax 11 Cours Foch, BP 177, T: 05 58 56 86 86, www.dax.fr
Eugénie-les-Bains 147 Rue R. Vielle, T: 05 58 51 13 16, www.ville-eugenie-les-bains.fr
Geaune Rte. de Chalosse, T: 05 58 44 50 01, tourisme.tursan@wanadoo.fr
Hagetmau Bâtiment Administratif, Pl. de la République, T: 05 58 79 38 26, www.tourismehagetmau.com
Hossegor Place des Halles, BP 6, T: 05 58 41 79 00, www.hossegor.fr
Labastide d'Armagnac Pl. Royale, T: 05 58 44 67 56, www.labastide-d-armagnac.com
Lit-et-Mixe 23 Rue de l'Eglise, BP 3, T: 05 58 42 72 47, www.litetmixe.com
Montfort-en-Chalosse Pays de Montfort, 25 Pl. Foch, T: 05 58 98 58 50, ot.montfort.chalosse@wanadoo.fr
Mimizan-Plage 38 Av. Maurice Martin, BP 11, T: 05 58 09 11 20, www.mimizan-tourisme.com
Mont-de-Marsan 6 Pl. du Général-Leclerc, BP 305, T: 05 58 05 87 37, www.mont-de-marsan.org
Peyrehorade Pays d'Orthe, 147 Av. des Evadés, T: 05 58 73 00 52, ot-peyrehorade@wanadoo.fr
St-Justin Pl. des Tilleuls, T: 05 58 44 86 06, saintjustin@aol.com
St-Sever Pl. du Tour de Sol, T: 05 58 76 34 64, www.saint-sever.fr
Seignosse Av. des Lacs, BP 11, T: 05 58 43 32 15, www.tourisme-seignosse.com
Soustons Grange de Labouyrie, BP 53, T: 05 58 41 52 62, www.soustons.fr

ACCOMMODATION & RESTAURANTS

Biscarosse-Plage
€ **La Caravelle**. A charming and quiet spot on the edge of a large lake surrounded by pines and palms, the hotel has a deck by the water, and comfortable rooms reasonably priced. Close by are the ocean and a golf course. 5314 Rte

des Lacs, Lac Nond Ispe, T: 05 58 09 82 67, www.lacaravelle.fr

Capbreton

€€ **Cap Club Hôtel/Restaurant**. This is a new hotel with outstanding modern architecture which takes advantage of the exceptional setting. Designed for fitness fanatics, it has fabulous facilities for all levels : gym, relaxation, sauna, balneotherapy. Of the 75 bedrooms, 65 have ocean views and 15 have fitted kitchenettes. The restaurant, la Table de la Dune, has panoramic ocean views. 85 Av. du Marechal de Lattre de Tassigny, T: 05 58 41 80 00, www.capclubhotel.com

Dax

€ **Hôtel/Restaurant Le Richelieu**. This is an old *relais de poste* conveniently placed close to the town centre with 20 comfortable rooms. There is also a restaurant with patio; menus €14 (midday), €20 and €36. 13 Ave Victor-Hugo, T: 05 58 90 49 49, www.le-richelieu.fr

Eugénie-les-Bains

Michel and Christine Guérard own the following three establishments. For all reservations and information: T: 05 58 05 06 07, www.michelguerard.com

€€€ **Hôtel/Restaurant Les Prés d'Eugénie**. The largest of the Guérard properties occupies a Spanish-colonial-style building with balconies and arcades, fashionable in Eugénie's day. All white, it is in exotic gardens with lush vegetation. Nearby is the thermal spa in an authentic Landais house. As for the restaurants, Michel Guérard's masterful cooking allows two approaches: watch the calories with *cuisine minceur*, or gorge on the best of gastronomic cooking (three Michelin rosettes).

€€ **Le Couvent des Herbes**, is an enchanting 18th-century building around the the *jardin du curé*. The accommodation is of very high quality.

€€€ **Hôtel Les Logis de la Ferme aux Grives/Restaurant Auberge de la Ferme aux Grives** is an enchanted old farmhouse with a terrace, flower and vegetable gardens. The restaurant incorporates original décor including a huge fireplace and old bread oven, with hams suspended and the spit turning. Menus from €40. The rooms are utterly charming with exposed beams and wood floors, and canopied beds.

Gabarret

€€ **Hôtel/Restaurant Château de Buros**. A handsome 19th-century pile in Armagnac country with 20 romantically draped and swathed rooms. It is a calm and relaxing place with plenty of facilities (pool, tennis court, billiard room and 4-hole golf in the grounds). Northeast of Gabarret, T: 05 58 44 34 30, www.chateaudeburos.com

Grenade-sur-l'Adour

€€€ **Hôtel/Restaurant Pain Adour et Fantasie**. In a 17th-century château on the banks of the Adour. Philippe Garret cooks mouth-watering food from the best and the freshest of local produce and the set-price menus vary from €35 to €82. There is a pretty dining room and terrace is ideal for riverside meals. The rooms are spacious and luminous. Pl. des Tilleuls, T: 05 58 45 18 80, www.chateauxhotels.com/fantasie

Hossegor

€€ **Hôtel Les Hortensias du Lac.** ■ An authentic basco-landais lakeside house set among pine trees, it is low lying and quiet. The rooms are thoughtfully arranged, with calm modern décor in pale colours; some have balconies.

There is a lakeside terrace, comfortable lounges, and the hotel exudes a general feeling of well-being and no detail is overlooked. 1578 Ave du Tour-du-Lac, T: 05 58 43 99 00, www.hortensias-du-lac.com

€ **Hôtel/Restaurant Le Pavillon Bleu**. A modernised hotel with 21 very comfortable rooms in an excellent position by the lake over which most rooms have a view, and some balconies. The restaurant has recently become a popular and recommended place to eat. 1053 Ave du Touring-Club-de-France, T: 05 58 41 99 50, www.pavillonbleu.fr

Labastide-d'Armagnac

€ **Chambres d'hôtes La Citadelle**. This property is between the pretty Labastide-d'Armagnac and the thermal centre of Barbotan. It is set in a garden with terrace. It has one room for guests, and two *gîtes* which are sometimes used as *chambres d'hôtes*. Chemin de Broustet, Créon d'Armagnac, T: 05 58 44 85 39/06 86 11 89 65.

Magescq

€€ **Hôtel/Restaurant Relais de la Poste**. ■ A family-run establishment with balconies and flowers, in the pine forests of the Côtes-Sud not far from the coast. The rooms are modern and the high-class, creative combinations of Landes cuisine offered by Jean Coussau has earned two Michelin rosettes; for example, *Caviar d'Aquitaine et les blinis de maïs à la crème fleurette*. 24 Av. de Marenne, T: 05 58 47 70 25, poste@relaischateaux.fr

Mimizan

€ **Hôtel/Restaurant Au Bon Coin du Lac**. A rustic and refreshing setting with superb lake views, close to the *promenade fleurie*. Madame Antich maintains high standards in the hotel and extends a warm welcome. The light and roomy restaurant has lovely views and the cooking is under the direction of chef Jean-Pierre Caule who creates light and colourful dishes. 34 Ave du Lac, T: 05 58 09 01 55, www. auboncoindulac.com

Mont-de-Marsan

€€ **Hôtel/Restaurant Le Renaissance**. A couple of minutes from the town centre, this Neoclassical manor house with 24 large modern and restful rooms and a suite, is in a rural setting. Two rooms and the suite open onto the garden, where there is a pool. Traditional cuisine in the contemporary restaurant. Rte de Villeneuve, T: 05 58 51 51 51, http://le-renaissance.com

Moustey

€ **Restaurant le Domaine**. A small, very friendly family-run restaurant opposite the two churches of Moustey. The house dates from 1880 and there is an original *lavoir* and two covered terraces. It is on a typical Landais *airial*, a green space of 1.5 hectares on the edge of the forest, where horses graze. Set-price menus €11–26. 11 Rue du Docteur Fauché, T: 05 58 08 20 03.

Port de Lanne

€ **La Vieille Auberge**. This very pretty 18th-century Gascon inn with loads of character at the centre of the village is run by Mireille and Albert Lataillade. It has 10 rooms with all modern comforts, and one has a fireplace. There is also a pool set in the magnificent garden. The prices also are attractive. 66 Pl. de l'Eglise, (D117 west of Peyrehorade), T: 05 58 89 16 29, vieille.auberge@wanadoo.fr, or www.logis-de-france.fr

Renung

€ **Chambres d'hôtes Le Château Benauge**. This is a superb medieval fortified commandery in the Adour Valley close to Eugenie-les-Bains. It has been beautifully restored by its British owners, the Goodyears, to provide 6 guest rooms, each with private entrance opening onto the courtyard or gardens, and underfloor temperature control. The room in the round tower has jacuzzi and all have underfloor temperature control. 29 Chemin de Benauge, T: 05 58 71 77 30, www.benauge.com

Sabres

€€ **Auberge des Pins**. A Landais farmhouse with timbered façade and long sloping roof in large grounds with gardens in a village at the heart of the Landes forest. Michel Lesclauze and his mother Suzanne assure the the best of Landaise cuisine from carefully chosen produce; Wide-ranging menus are €18 (weekday lunch), regional €32, seasonal €45, gourmand €61, and Sunday lunch €28. T: 05 58 08 30 00, http://aubergedespins.fr

St-Paul-Lès-Dax

€€ **Restaurant Le Moulin de Poustagnacq**. A lively place where imaginative cooking combines with an old moulin in the forest, with gardens and terrace on the river. The menu is based on local produce, from the land and the sea. Menus €28, €35 and €65. T: 05 58 91 31 03, www.moulindepoustagnacqu.com

Soustons

€ **Chambres d'hôtes Le Domaine de Bellegarde**. This beautiful 1900 residence was entirely restored in 2002 by a group of friends who fell for the area. It is located in a quiet spot not far from the coast. There is a pool, billiard room, and tennis court on the property. 23 Av. Charles de Gaulle, T: 05 58 41 24 06, www.domainebellegarde.com

MARKET DAYS

Aire-sur-l'Adour Tuesday, Saturday
Dax Saturday, Sunday
Eugénie-les-Bains Wednesday
Hagetmau Wednesday, Saturday
Montfort-en-Chalosse Wednesday
St-Sever Saturday

FESTIVALS & EVENTS

February–March: *Carnaval*, weekend festivities with costumed cavalcade, Dax
April: *Festival Art et Courage*, celebration of courses landaises (*see p. 421*), Pomarez
June: *Festival des Abbayes*, promotion of religious buildings through classical concerts, Pays d'Orthe and Chalosse
Fête patronale, local festivities, Aire-sur-l'Adour
July: *Music d'Arts*, music festival in a small village, Brassempouy
Dax Festival, *Féria*, festival lasting about 5 days, with bullfights, *courses landaises*, cavalcades and concerts, Dax
Festival Paso Passion, three-day Spanish music festival with bandas (bands), Dax
August–September: *Festival des Nuits d'Eté*, Pays d'Orthe.
September: *Toros y Salsa*, bullfighting and dance, Spanish/Mexican food, Dax

PYRÉNÉES-ATLANTIQUES

The Basque region of France, Pays Basque, is part of the modern *département* of the Pyrénées-Atlantiques in the southwesternmost tip of France. A small world of its own, it encompasses the old provinces of Labourd, Basse-Navarre and Soule and its limits are the Adour River to the north, the Gave de Mauléon to the east, Spain to the south and, to the west, the Atlantic ocean. The Pays Basque is linked historically, geographically and linguistically to the Spanish Basque region, but as part of French Aquitaine it also has many differences. With the benefit of both the Atlantic coast and the Pyrenees, there is a stunning variety of scenery and the climate is mild, especially on the coast; the mountain weather is notoriously variable. The main towns, Bayonne and Biarritz, are close geographically but poles apart in character. Different again are the old coastal port of St-Jean de Luz and St-Jean Pied de Port in the foothills of the Pyrenees. Very specific to the region is the domestic architecture, as are the post-Reformation galleried churches. The Basque people proudly defend many of the region's characteristics and customs, including the language, Euskara, and sports, notably variations of *pelote*.

HISTORY OF THE PAYS BASQUE

The Basques have populated this part of Europe since time immemorial and have retained their identity despite being infiltrated and conquered. In the 9th century the semi-legendary Inigo Arista founded the dynasty of Navarre and made Pamplona his capital. Two centuries later, Sanche III le Grand (1000–35) annexed many Spanish territories, giving him control of the passes through the Pyrenees used by pilgrims. Navarre passed to the Kingdom of Aragon in 1076, then recovered its independence until the 13th century when, for one reason or another, it passed back and forth between French and Spanish dynastic houses. It became French in 1285 and returned to Aragon in 1425. In 1484 the title King of Navarre passed to the house of Albret through the marriage of Jean d'Albret to Catherine de Foix. This provoked Ferdinand of Aragon to annex and divide the Navarre peninsula in 1512. Jeanne III d'Albret inherited only Basse-Navarre, a tiny province north of the Pyrenees (the area around St-Jean-Pied-de-Port), and from her it passed to her son, the future Henri IV of France. It was absorbed into France finally in 1620.

The Labourd, on the coastal region, which had existed since 1023, and the Soule, on the border with the Béarn (*see p. 483*), were indistinct parts of the Duchy of Gascony and became loosely attached to English Aquitaine. Soule reverted to the House of Foix in 1449 and both ceded to France in 1451. The Treaty of the Pyrenees, which definitively laid down the frontier territories of Spain and France, was signed in 1659 and gave both sides the security to confirm local liberties or customs, such as the authority of human justice, *fours* in France, *fueros* in Spain. At the Revolution these local privileges were suppressed and the Pays Basque experienced a harsh period with a decline in the fishing industry and the burden of war with Spain. In 1813 the war spread into Labourd as the Imperial army retreated under general Soult. The city of Bayonne held out until the French defeat at Orthez (*see p. 493*).

The start of the fight for Basque liberty began in 1895 with the founding of the Basque Nationalist Party (*Partido nacionalista vasco*), whose objective was to unite the seven Basque provinces of France and Spain. Its founder, Sabino Arana Goiri (1865–1903) created the word *Euzkadi* (Basque Country), adopted by the Basque community and introduced the *ikurrina*, the red flag with a green and a white cross. Autonomy was granted to the Spanish Basque regions in 1936 but General Franco's regime rescinded this, resulting in the birth of ETA (*Euzkadi ta Azktasuna*, Freedom for the Basques) in 1959. The French nationalist movement Embata, created in 1960, was much less active.

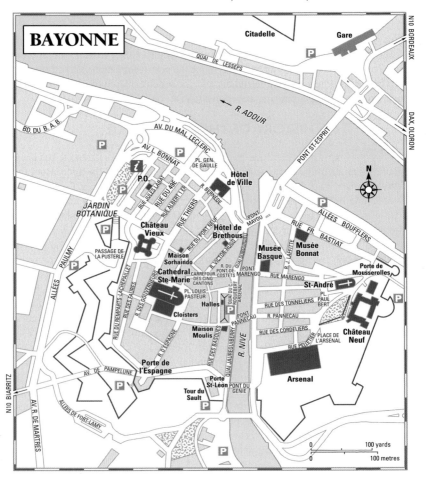

BAYONNE

Bayonne is a busy city at the confluence of the Nive and Adour with elegant and colourful river frontages and a uniquely confident charm. It is just 7km from the Atlantic coast, spans the Basque–Gascon frontier, and is the capital and main commercial centre of Pays Basque. As the second largest urban centre in the *département* of the Pyrénées-Atlantiques, with 42,000 inhabitants, it is a close rival to Pau. It has two excellent museums, the Musée Bonnat and the Musée Basque, is famous for its ham and the production of chocolate, and gave its name to the bayonet (*baïonette*). *Les Fêtes de Bayonne*, an important festival inspired by that of St Firmin in Pamplona, is held during the first week of August. Bayonne was the first French city to formalise the *corrida* (*see p. 421*).

HISTORY OF BAYONNE

The Romans had a fortified encampment above the estuary in the 4th century, called *Lapurdum* (the origin of the province of Labourd). The name Bayonne appeared only in the 11th century. Part of the Duchy of Aquitaine, in 1125 it received a charter of emancipation and came under English domination between 1151 and 1452. Richard the Lionheart separated the city from the Labourd in 1174 and as a result fortifications were built and a new cathedral begun in the mid-13th century. Bayonne became a shipbuilding and naval outpost for the English, whom it supported during the Hundred Years War, but in 1451 it returned to France. Around this time, sand blocked the mouth of the Adour estuary at Capbreton, causing disastrous flooding and altering the course of the river to run into the ocean some 30km further north. A revival occurred in the 16th century due to the city's strategic position vis-à-vis Spain, and because in 1578 Charles IX's engineer, Louis de Foix, redirected the Adour to create a new mouth, Boucau-Neuf, 6km to the west of the city. Bayonne was protected by its girdle of defences during the Wars of Religion and the Fronde (*see p. 16*), but Louis XIV instructed his engineer Vauban to construct more fortifications and a citadel as protection against Spain. The maritime trade with Europe and the West Indies, cod and whale fishing in the New World, and shipbuilding, supported the town in the 18th century. It was declared a free port in 1784, by which time maritime activity had moved further downstream. In 1814, Bayonne held out, proving its motto *Nunquam Polluta* ('Never Defiled'). The railway came in 1854 and the town expanded beyond its cordon of fortifications to spread westwards along the Adour, leaving the old centre largely unaltered. Continuing restoration is re-enhancing the magnificent houses, with woodwork painted crisply in *sang de boeuf* red, greens and blues against white walls. The docks at Boucau and Anglet handle 4,500,000 tonnes of shipping annually.

VIEUX (GRAND) BAYONNE

Central Bayonne has three ancient *quartiers* based on commercial and military traditions: Vieux (Grand) Bayonne lies around the cathedral on the west bank of the Nive;
Petit Bayonne on the east bank; while St-Esprit is on the north bank of the Adour.
Vieux Bayonne has always been the busy commercial centre and several of the street
names still refer to local trades or guilds. The building of 1842 which encompasses
the Hôtel de Ville and Municipal Theatre, on Place de la Liberté at the mouth of the
Nive, has a mosaic in the forecourt of the arms and motto of the town. Just beyond
the Hôtel de Ville, at the end of Rue Victor-Hugo, Hôtel de Brethous (1732), was
occupied by the young Hugo when he accompanied his father, a General of the
Empire, to the acceptance by Napoleon of the surrender of Spain in 1808. Rue Victor-
Hugo is aligned with the bridges, Pont Mayou and Pont-St-Esprit, that span the Nive
and Adour in an area that was originally marshland, with houses propped on timber
supports. Until the end of the Middle Ages the streets perpendicular to the river were
canals where cargoes were off-loaded, lined with arcades with living quarters above.
Wooden bridges were eventually erected, Pont Mayou (Main Bridge) being the first.
By the 17th–18th centuries, quays for receiving merchandise had been built to replace
the canals.

Rue du Port-de-Castets, opposite Pont Marengo, leads to the Carrefour des Cinq
Cantons, the site of the Roman east gate and of the first stock exchanges in France.
This was the medieval gathering-place for tradespeople between the upper and lower
towns. At the heart of the pedestrian area is an impressive variety of old buildings,
notably the grand Maison Sorhaindo on Rue Orbe, where Louis XIV stayed before his
marriage to the Infanta Maria-Theresa (*see p. 460*). Rue du Port-Neuf (off Rue Orbe)
was a canal lined with arcades—now mainly rebuilt—and is famous for its *choco-
latiers*, descendants of the first chocolate houses in France (*see box on p. 447*). The
dark ambrosia can be sampled at Cazenave, whose reputation rests on drinking
chocolate, or Daranats, best known for chocolate bars.

Three of the typical tall and narrow Bayonnais buildings in Rue de Salie have been
rehabilitated, the façades conserved and the original colour schemes strictly adhered
to. On the walk up Rue Argenterie and Rue du Pilori towards the highest part of
Bayonne, the tall apse of the cathedral comes into sight on Place Pasteur. In the
Middle Ages this was the site of the gallows and of the old *maison de vesiau* or *hôtel de
ville*, which became the *Palais de Justice* in the 19th century.

Cathedral of Ste-Marie

*Open Mon–Sat 7.30–12 & 3–7, Sun 3.30–6.30; no visits during services or morning of hol-
idays; T: 05 59 59 17 82.*
The Cathedral of Sainte-Marie, in Pl. Mgr. Vansteenberghe, at the apex of Vieux
Bayonne, is the exception to the rule of most Gothic churches in this region because
it was almost entirely modelled on the cathedrals of northern France. It was begun in
1258 to replace a Romanesque structure destroyed by fire, and was therefore built

during English occupation of Aquitaine. It was completed in the 15th century. There were additions in the 16th century but during the 18th century, unsympathetic to Gothic architecture, and the Revolutionary period, the building was allowed to fall into disrepair. Restoration work began in the 19th century under the supervision of Emile Boeswillwald.

The exterior

From Place Pasteur there is an uninterrupted view of the very fine 13th-century east end, with radiating chapels between pinnacled buttresses and double lancet windows with oculi reminiscent of Reims. The balustrade was restored in the 19th century. By the time the transepts, nave and aisles were constructed in the 14th century the Rayonnant style of Gothic architecture had taken over and flying buttresses introduced. The north porch, with two polygonal turrets, lost its sculptures during the Revolution and was clumsily restored, but a magnificent bronze door-knocker (15th–16th centuries) has survived. At the beginning of the 16th century, a Flamboyant sacristy and chapter house were added. At the west there was already a south tower (end 15th/16th centuries), and in the 19th century a north tower was begun to balance it. This was completed only in the 20th century—the white stone is 19th-century and the yellow 20th-century—and both towers were topped off with matching spires. The gable between them carries a copy of the original *Pietà*, and the balustrade above the rose window is a restoration. The restored porch is a mixture of Rayonnant and Flamboyant, its statuary destroyed in 1793–94.

The interior

Inside the relatively narrow 13th-century choir is surrounded by an ambulatory and chapels; the seven-bay nave was built in the 14th century. Typical of Rayonnant architecture are the fine responds and mullion shafts, thin vault ribs, triforium and clerestory, giving an impression of height (26m) and lightness. Rib bosses in the east bring together the leopards of England and the *fleurs de lis* of France; brightly painted in the south transept vaults are the arms of Bayonne complete with sailboat, castle and five sailors surrounded by the four Evangelists. The glass in the upper part of the nave dates from the 16th and 17th centuries, restored in the 19th and 20th centuries, and represents the *Creation* (south) and the *Nativity* and scenes from the New Testament (north), whereas the rose window in the west is modern. In the south aisle is a rose window with mouchette tracery and 15th-century glass; the most celebrated window (1531) in the second chapel on the north shows the story of the *Canaanite Woman* with donor figures. It is also well worth asking to see the 16th-century Flamboyant-style sacristy which protects an almost intact 13th-century double portal. Influenced by Reims, it carries the *Adoration of the Virgin* and *Virgin and Child* on the left, and a *Last Judgement* on the other side. The main altar is 19th-century, with a ciborium in gilded wood designed by Boeswillwald; the Baroque pulpit sculpted in mahogany from the Canaries and the organ case are both 18th-century.

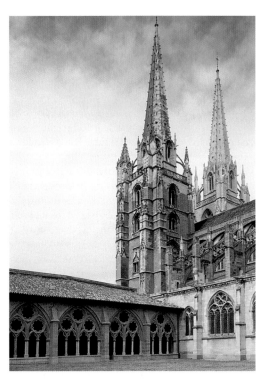

The cloister (12th–16th centuries) and towers of Ste-Marie.

The cloister

The splendid cloister (*open June–Sept 9–12.30 & 2–6; Oct–May 9–12.30 & 2–5; T: 05 59 46 11 43*), entered from Place Pasteur, on the south side of the cathedral, was built in the 12th–13th centuries and reworked in the 15th–16th centuries. It has three surviving wings: the north was demolished in the 19th century. It is particularly spacious and unusual in that it starts at the level of the third bay of the nave and encompasses the transept. The west aisle, which has delicate tracery of four lancets and three oculi, is the oldest and may in parts survive from the earlier construction. The south tracery has slight variations, and the east gallery has similar tracery and vault bosses to the south, although the ribs spring from corbels sculpted from large pieces of limestone. The cloister was originally used as a cemetery and there are the remains of tombs and tombstones; it was also used for guild meetings.

Chateau Vieux

The former Bishops' Palace, opposite the west door of the cathedral, is now the municipal library and behind it is the Château Vieux, a low, heavy building with four towers and curtain walls, begun at the time of the Viscounts of Labourd in the 11th–12th centuries but much altered. The keep was demolished in the 17th century when Vauban was extending the fortifications. It was used by the English seneschal 1154–1451 and occupied by the Black Prince who imprisoned Bernard du Guesclin (*see p. 109*), here in 1367. And it was from here that, after François I's defeat at Pavia in 1525, the Duc de Montmorency sent a ransom of 2000 écus to free the royal children held hostage. This district, the highest part of Bayonne, is riddled with about 200 vaulted cellars, constructed from the 13th to 18th century to protect merchandise from fire and used as shops and stores. Visits are organised by the tourist office.

BAYONNE'S CHOCOLATE HOUSES

Bayonne was the first city in France to manufacture chocolate. Cacao beans and cocoa were discovered by Cortez in Mexico in 1518 and were carried from the New World to Spain in 1585, but did not reach France until the early 17th century. The introduction of the chocolate trade to Bayonne was attributed to Sephardic Jews, expelled from Spain and Portugal at the time of Ferdinand and Isabella and the Inquisition. Around 1619 they settled in the St-Esprit *quartier* outside the main part of Bayonne. The cocoa merchants among them traded directly with the Americas and the word 'chocolate' was documented in Bayonne for the first time in 1670. The trade thrived so that by the mid-19th century there were some 33 chocolate producers. After a downturn in the 20th century, the Académie du Chocolat was established in 1993 and there are once more several chocolate houses in Vieux Bayonne (*see above, p. 444*), as well as a chocolate museum in Biarritz (*see p. 458*), and south of Pl. Louis Pasteur, the Fabrique du Chocolatier Puyodebat (*66 Rue d'Espagne, open Sept–May 3.30–6, closed Sun, Mon; T: 05 59 59 20 86*).

To Porte de l'Espagne

West of the Château Vieux, alongside Rue du Rempart-Lachepaillet, is the Passage de la Pusterle, through ramparts built by Vauban in the 17th century, with a gateway decorated in antique style to the glory of Hercules. On the other side of the ramparts is a small **Jardin Botanique** (*open mid-April–mid-Oct 9.30–12 & 2–6, closed Sun, Mon*), with Japanese overtones, and some 1,000 species.

Rue des Faures was the blacksmiths' street where the first *baïonnette* was forged in the 16th century, and is now a neighbourhood of antique shops. Here, too, there is one of the last craftsmen making *makilas*, the traditional Basque walking-stick ideal for pilgrimages and hiking. The wood used is from the medlar: it is initially carved while still attached to the tree, cut six months later and dried over several years. Secreted in the handle is a fine steel blade. (There is also a maker of *makilas* at 37 Rue Vieille Boucherie.)

At the end of Rue d'Espagne is Porte de l'Espagne where the three successive building campaigns of the fortifications can be distinguished: the Gallo-Roman section and the bases of semi-circular medieval towers; a section of the 16th-century wall; and Vauban's construction. On the left of Rue Tour-du-Sault is a little square, La Plachotte, with a fragment of the Gallo-Roman walls and a fine Renaissance tower. The Tour du Sault is a section of the old barrier protecting the port. The gardens south of the old tower shelter a fountain dedicated to St Léon, patron saint of Bayonne who, after spreading the gospel in the north of Spain, returned to Bayonne but was beheaded for his troubles by Norman pirates. Where his head fell a spring gushed forth; the martyr picked up his head (not uncommon) and ran 300 steps to this place where first a tomb, and then a chapel, were erected.

Along the river

Rue des Basques, parallel with the river, has conserved its 13th-century layout and is lined with jettied houses sporting wrought-iron balconies. From Quai Jaureguiberry is a classic view of the elevations and quays of Petit Bayonne, and at the Pont Pannecau end stands the very splendid 17th-century timbered Maison Moulis, altered in the 19th century, which appears to be three houses, but is in fact one, with three *corps-de-logis*. It was originally painted in ox-blood to protect the timbers from damp. It overlooks the market hall, rebuilt in the 1990s in 19th-century style, with small restaurants inside. The buildings around the square are mainly 18th–19th-century.

PETIT BAYONNE

Pont Marengo and Pont Pannecau link Quai du Commandant-Roquebert and Vieux Bayonne to Petit Bayonne, the 'new borough' or Borc Nau, established on the marshes in the 12th century and then populated by important religious communities. Now the picturesque narrow streets and regular façades shelter the town's two major museums. In times gone by, female miscreants were punished by being dipped in the river from Pont Pannecau; the Musée Basque owns a replica of the type of cage used. The large complex of buildings to the south of Pont Pannecau is the refurbished Arsenal. Rue des Tonneliers, to the north, home to the coopers' guild and base for corsairs, was originally an arcaded canal. This street leads to Trinquet St-André, one of the oldest enclosed *pelote* courts in the Pays Basque where Louis XIV reputedly played *jeu de paume*. Check the sporting calendar at the tourist office for games. Next door is the neo-Gothic Church of St-André which contains a painting of *The Assumption* by Léon Bonnat (*see p. 450*).

PELOTE BASQUE

Traditional to the Pays Basque, *pelote* (meaning 'ball') is a game played out-of-doors against a *fronton* (wall) by two teams of three players or *pelotaris*. The name comes from the Roman handball game *pila*, which evolved into *jeu de paume* (real tennis) in France and fives at Eton College in England. Pelote Basque falls into three basic categories—*main nue*, played with the bare hand; *chistera*, using a wicker basket; and *pala*, played with a wooden racquet—but there are something like 21 variations on these themes. The *chistera* is a long curved wicker basket attached to a leather glove, worn like an extension to the player's arm to throw and catch the ball. It developed first in Spain out of a need to protect the players' hands, and spread to the Labourd. Today there is only one *chistera*-maker in France, based in Anglet (Fabrique Gonzales, 6 Allée des Liserons, visits Mon, Wed, Fri, at 5 pm, T: 05 59 03 85 04). *Cesta punta* is a more modern and spectacular version of *pelota main nue*, played in a covered court with three walls (*jaï alaï*); introduced some 30 years ago, it is reputed to be the fastest ball game in the world.

Château-Neuf

Place Paul-Bert is the centrepiece for the annual *Fêtes de Bayonne* and *the courses de vaches* (*see p. 469*). The Château-Neuf Petit Bayonne, with two enormous round towers, was built on the orders of Louis XI after Bayonne was attached to France. Completed in 1498, it faces towards the town to keep an eye on the troublesome Bayonnais, and has 17th- and 19th-century additions. It is now used for temporary exhibitions in conjunction with the Musée Basque (*see below*). In the fortifications behind the Château-Neuf, reinforced by Vauban in the 17th century, is the Porte de Mousserolles, which still has its drawbridge. Further west, just off Place de l'Arsenal at 41 Rue des Cordeliers, is Ibaïalde, a traditional producer of *jambon de Bayonne*. Here you can watch the curing process and taste the famous regional ham which was originally shipped through Europe via the port of Bayonne. The top-quality ham carries the Ibaïona label and has an *appellation contrôlée*.

Musée Basque

Open July–Aug, 10–6.30, Wed until 9.30; May–Oct 10–6.30, closed Mon; Nov–April 10–12.30 & 2–6; closed Mon and holidays; T: 05 59 46 61 90.

The Musée Basque et de l'histoire de Bayonne is housed in the Maison Dagourette, 37 Quai des Corsaires and exhibitions are held at the nearby Château-Neuf (*see above*). The 17th-century Maison Dagourette was heavily disfigured, especially in the 20th century, but some of the original façade survived hidden, and restoration began in 1991. The entirely renovated and revitalised museum re-opened in 2001. Its objective is to develop an understanding of Basque culture in the seven provinces of the Pays Basque, both French and Spanish. The presentation has been attractively adapted to the revamped interior by using traditional materials and simple vitrines. It is designed to encourage a fresh look at ethnography and makes use of sound, moving images, works of art, documents, models, photographs, and costumes to give an overall image of the Basque culture. The annotations are in French, Basque and Spanish.

The collections are arranged thematically under standard ethnological headings: 'Agro-Pasturalism', 'Architecture of the House', 'Vessels and Furniture' (note the *zuzulu*, a handy bench-table for fireside meals), and 'Clothing' (with clogs and berets). Canalisation and the port of Bayonne are examined in 'Maritime and River Activity'; 'Economic and Financial Activities' covers the money exchange and mint in Bayonne in the 17th to 19th centuries. 'Games, Sports and the Arts' includes *pelote* Basque and *quilles* (skittles) as well as rugby and bull-fighting; 'Popular Religion', 'The Cathedral' and 'Bereavement in Pays Basque' include architecture along the pilgrimage route, 18th-century woodwork from the choir of Bayonne cathedral, and the superstitions associated with death. More specifically Basque are the sections on 'Religious and Literary History', showing that the birth of a Basque conscience started to evolve with the first translation of the Bible into Basque in the 16th–17th centuries; it also covers the integration of Jews in the 16th–17th centuries and the 'Rediscovery of Pays Basque', which looks at the Basque indentity as it developed in the Romantic era (19th–early 20th centuries) under the influence of philosophers, linguists, writers and

Albrecht Dürer: Head of a Stag (c. 1503) in the Musée Bonnat.

artists, culminating in the creation of the Basque museum in 1922. The section on 'Neo-Basque' is the continuation of this history through to the creation of a new mythology of the Basques in the 20th century.

Musée Bonnat

Open July–Aug 10–6.30; May–June, Sept–Oct, 10–6.30, closed Tues; Nov–April 10–12.30 & 2–6; closed Tues and holidays; T: 05 59 59 08 52.

Musée Bonnat, 5 Rue Jacques Lafitte, is an art gallery housing works of great variety and quality in a specially designed building of 1901, and is an enduring tribute to Léon Bonnat (1833–1922). Bonnat was born in Bayonne in 1833, brought up in Spain and trained as an artist in Madrid, and travelled to Rome. Back in France he became a successful portraitist and was sufficiently wealthy to fund his avid acquisition of paintings, objets d'art and above all drawings, from all periods. He donated his collection and many of his own works to Bayonne in 1891, making this one of the best provincial museums in France. Frequent temporary exhibitions are themed around the numerous works in reserve.

The entrance is arranged around an arcaded atrium with wrought-iron arches painted a fresh viridian. The large triptych by Bonnat's most notable pupil, Henri-Achille Zo, shows Bonnat and his Basque and Bearnais Pupils, with Bayonne in the background. Space is devoted to the drawings and engravings of Paul Helleu (1859–1927), a sensitive draftsman and portraitist who served as the model for Elstir in Proust's *A la Recherche du Temps Perdu*. Bonnat's extensive collection of Egyptian, Greek and Roman antiquities is in the Salle des Antiques on the lower-ground floor.

First Floor: The majority of the paintings, subject to reorganisation from time to time, are on the first floor. Numerous works by Bonnat himself include the powerful and unrelenting portrait of Mme Léopold Stern (c. 1863; *pictured opposite*) and *Job* (1880), a tribute to Spanish painting. The museum owns portraits by Degas of Léon Bonnat and of his brother-in-law Enrique Melida. French 19th-century painters are well represented, and the collection includes finished and unfinished studies by Girodet, Géricault, Delacroix and Corot

Léon Bonnat: portrait of Mme Léopold Stern (c. 1863).

and works by the great animal sculptor, Antoine-Louis Bayre. There are also paintings by Courbet. The preponderance of works by Ingres includes one of his most enticing small paintings, *The Bather* (*pictured opposite*), an odalisque where smooth flesh, twisted scarf and plaited hair are combined to stunning effect. A large decorative panel of *Le Doux Pays* (1882) by Puvis de Chavannes emulates Florentine fresco painting and proposes an idealism that was admired by the Symbolists. Other European works include sketches by Rembrandt, Rubens and van Dyck and there are drawings and preparatory works by Giovanni Bellini, Leonardo da Vinci, Michelangelo, Raphael and Titian. There is a sensitively observed *Head of a Stag* (c. 1503; *pictured on p. 450*) and other drawings by Dürer. English painters are represented by Reynolds'

Study of Colonel Tarleton, c. 1782, and by a fine portrait of Henry Fuseli by Sir Thomas Lawrence.

Spanish collection: Bonnat greatly admired Spanish painting and consequently the collection of Spanish works (15th–19th century) is particularly rich, with a beautiful *Adoration of the Magi* (15th century) from the School of Valencia, and works by El Greco, Murillo and Ribera among others. There are three major works by Goya, *Self Portrait* (1800), a preparatory study for the Castres version (*see p. 343*), *Last Communion of St José de Calasanz* (1819), and the large portrait of the Duc d'Osuna (1816), reading a letter. There is a 14th-century statue of Christ, once part of a group now in the Musée des Augustins in Toulouse (*see p. 600*) and among the objets d'art is a 15th-century Florentine painted chest.

EUSKARA: THE BASQUE LANGUAGE

A mystery surrounds the language spoken in this corner of Europe, yet it is the most important unifying element of the region. It does not have the Indo-European roots of many other European languages and it preceded the Roman conquest. Its closest similarities are with the languages of the southern Caucasus. It is sophisticated and complicated grammatically, but it never had its own written language and in the Middle Ages took on Latin characters. It is pronounced phonetically. The vowels are as in other European languages, but the consonants vary: for example, 'z' is pronounced as the 'ss' in French, 'x' as 'ch', and 'tx' as 'tch'. Some form of Euskara was once spoken throughout Aquitaine in pre-Roman times. There are now four recognisable dialects across the whole Basque region. It is spoken by 21 per cent of Basques and used by more than half of those living in Basse-Navarre and the Soule. In 1919, the Academy of the Basque Language, Euskalzaindia, was formed; since 1960, some primary and secondary schools have taught in Euskara; and in 1984 a university syllabus in Basque was introduced.

Jean-Auguste-Dominique Ingres: *The Bather*, in the Musée Bonnat.

QUARTIER ST-ESPRIT

Across the Adour is the *quartier* of St-Esprit and Vauban's citadel, with four bastions. Of the Gothic collegiate church of St-Esprit, dedicated by Louis XI, all that remains is the wide central nave and narrow aisles, but it contains a beautiful polychromed wooden group of the *Flight into Egypt*. It was in this *quartier* that Sephardic Jews from Spain, who introduced chocolate to Bayonne, settled in the 17th century (*see box on p. 447*).

BIARRITZ

Biarritz, the Atlantic coast's answer to Nice, is a town of some 30,000 inhabitants (increasing to around 110,000 in summer), which benefits from a dramatic craggy coastline indented with coves and softened by *hortensias* (hydrangeas) and tamarisks. A fashionable resort from the mid-19th century to the Second World War, it saw elegant or eccentric mansions, more Deauville than Pays Basque, bestowed upon it by residents and visitors, and acquired a particularly racy reputation in the 1920s. It is now the playground of surfers. Since the 1990s the town has had a new lease of life as a seaside holiday resort. Although very crowded during the summer, it remains the gateway to the Pays Basque and its countless hotels and other facilities, as well as the mild climate, make it an excellent off-season centre. The town also offers a wealth of festivals and entertainment, as well as its own ballet company.

HISTORY OF BIARRITZ

Under English sovereignty in the 12th century, whaling was the main industry of the small, protected port of *Beiarrids*, and since 1351 a whale has featured on the town's coat of arms. The creatures were beached at high tide and every part was used—the tongue being a particular delicacy. By the end of the 17th century the whales had moved on and men were forced to hunt them as far away as Newfoundland and, as in St-Jean de Luz, *corsairs* or privateers took over. The pleasures of sea-bathing were already appreciated locally and by the mid-18th century had received official approbation in the interests of health. Eugénie de Montijo launched Biarritz on the international scene in 1854 when she returned to the site of her childhood holidays, bringing her husband, Napoleon III. Charmed by the place, he built Villa Eugénie for their summer visits and they came regularly until 1868. In the wake of the Imperial couple followed crowned heads and aristocrats from other European countries, including Queen Victoria in 1889. Throughout the Belle Epoque, Biarritz glittered with thousands of visitors annually, all anxious to be seen. In 1918 Picasso arrived with his wife, the dancer Olga Kokhlova, and the roaring '20s saw the likes of Cocteau and Hemingway as well as the Windsors, Frank Sinatra and Rita Heyworth in the 1950s who all joined in the fun after the Second World War. Over the period flamboyant and stylish villas appeared alongside hotels and casinos. The English were responsible for the first golf course at Biarritz. The town suffered from German occupation and Allied bombing in 1944. Despite the introduction of surfing by the film director, Peter Viertel, in 1957, it was not until 1991 that the town began to host an international surfing competition every July. Part of the rejuvenation of Biarritz has involved the conservation of its architectural heritage, and now some 800 buildings from the 1860s to 1950s are protected.

Pointe St-Martin

The Pointe St-Martin, on the coast to the north of the town, is a good starting-place for a view of the whole bay across to the Atalaye plateau and the Virgin rock. For an even better view, climb up the 248 steps of the lighthouse (built 1831–32; *open July–Aug 10–12.30 & 2.30–7; May–June, Sept 2.30–6.30*) on Av. de l'Impératrice. At 73m above sea-level, the layout of this part of Biarritz comes into focus, with the golf course established in 1888. Initially Biarritz developed in two distinct areas, around the church of St-Martin towards the interior and around the old port behind the Atalaye plateau. As this coastline became fashionable, the land around the old *quartiers* was divided into numerous *lotissements* (building plots) linked by a complex system of avenues and streets.

BIARRITZ ECLECTICISM

The style, or non-style, of a type of domestic architecture found in coastal resorts from around 1830 up until the Second World War is described as *eclectisme*, an expression coined by the philosopher, Victor Cousin. Nowhere is this better demonstrated than in Biarritz's gloriously idiosyncratic private villas. Eclecticism borrows from all styles and periods in a totally pragmatic way, to produce neo-Gothic, neo-Louis XIII and Neoclassical hybrids; Hispano-Mauresque rubs shoulders with neo-Basque or Norman-urban-seaside, which slot in between Belle Epoque, Art Nouveau and Art Deco. In Biarritz materials are varied: brick is often used, as is stone from the nearby quarries of Bidache, or wood and plaster, and later reinforced concrete; there are multiple roofs, gables, turrets, verandas, balconies, bay windows and columns; and decorations include glazed brick and tiles, wrought-iron, ceramics, terracotta mouldings, stained glass, and polychromy of all kinds.

The Lotissement Impérial

The most important estate, the Lotissement Impérial, owned 15 hectares between Pointe St-Martin and the Hôtel du Palais until 1880, when it was sold and divided up into 270 plots. Typical of the fashionable residences that appeared are Villa Etchepherdia (Green House) at 7 Rue d'Haitzart (1900) as well as 1 Av. Mac Croskey; and Le Manoir at 2 Av. Mac Croskey, which belonged to Bolo Pacha, a colourful character who was shot for spying in 1918. Avenue de l'Impératrice offers many lively examples of eclectic architecture, particularly nos 54, 36, 18, 17 and 15. The domed Russian Orthodox Church (1890–92) dedicated to St Alexander Nevsky is the work of Oscar Tisnes. The unmistakable **Hôtel du Palais** (1904–05), with glorious ocean views, replaced the Villa Eugénie which was sold in 1881 to became the Palais Biarritz, hotel and casino; that opened in 1894 but burned down in 1903. The present Belle-Epoque building by Niermans, architect of the Negresco in Nice, combined

Municipal Casino (1929; renovated 1994), by Laulhé, overlooking the Grande Plage, Biarritz.

the existing ground floor and added a wing using reinforced concrete camouflaged as brick. La Rotonde restaurant was designed by Alfred Laulhé, and very good teas are served in the gracious lounge.

Behind the Hôtel du Palais on Rue Pellot is the **Imperial Chapel** (*open mid-July to mid-Sept, 10–12.30 & 2.30–7, closed Sun; mid-April–mid-July, mid-Sept–mid-Oct, Tues, Thur, Sat 3–6; mid-Oct–Dec Thur 3–6*). Built in 1864–65 for Eugénie, a devout Catholic, the chapel is the epitome of Eclecticism and the only remaining imperial relic. Designed by Boeswillwald, with the advice of Mérimée, it is a simple shape with a porch and semi-circular apsidiole, using stone and glazed brick. The interior is colourfully decorated in a busy combination of Romano-Byzantine and Hispano-Mauresque motifs, floral and geometric, and *azulejos*. The chapel, which was consecrated at the time of the war in Mexico, is dedicated to Notre-Dame-de-Guadalupe whose image, painted by Louis Steinheil, is on the ceiling above the altar.

Some of the old hotels, most now converted into apartment blocks, in Avenue de la Reine-Victoria are worth studying, such as the Continental (1881–89) at no. 2, by Pierre Louis, similar to the Louis XIII style of Eugénie's original villa and one of the first buildings erected after the sale of the imperial estate; the Hotel Carlton (1910) by Cazalis; and the Majestic (1913, adapted in 1925) by Godbarge. The attractive Hostellerie Victoria (no. 12) is a Deauville-type villa, and no. 11, Etche Handia (Great House, c 1908), was built by Alfred Laulhé for himself in brick and stone with pretty details.

The town centre and Grande Plage

In comparison with the *lotissement*, the town centre has a greater mix of commercial buildings, casinos, palaces, modest houses, squares and public gardens. The years 1924–29 were a period of expansion when most of the buildings along the sea front were rebuilt. Gracing the Esplanade du Général-de-Gaulle overlooking the Grande Plage is the splendid Art Deco municipal casino (1929; *pictured opposite*) by Laulhé, on the site of the Moorish-style baths of 1858. The casino was about to be replaced by a hotel complex but was saved and renovated in 1994; along with the gaming tables and slot machines there is a large restaurant here with sea views. Around the corner at 4 Rue Gardères is one of the earliest Art Deco buildings (1926) in this area. Villa Larralde at nos 3–9 was the property of an English banker during the mid-19th century and was praised by Viollet-le-Duc as an example of modern stone architecture; Coco Chanel lived and worked here for a while. Avenue Edouard VII is a busy commercial street with the most outstanding Art Deco building in Biarritz, the Hôtel Plaza (1926–28), notable for its mosaics, glass and wrought-iron, designed by L.-H. Boileau and Paul Perrotte, as was the old Au Bon Marché (1928–29), transformed into the *Mairie*. East of here on Square d'Ixelles is the tourist office.

At the western end of the Grande Plage is the touristy Place Bellevue, dominated by the large Espace Bellevue (1858), the first hotel-casino on the Basque coast but altered many times and turned into a convention centre in 1999. Place Bellevue opens into Place Georges-Clémenceau with the Grand Hôtel (1860).

Not far away is the Musée Historique (*open 10–12.30 & 2–6.30, closed Sun, Mon; T: 05 59 24 86 28*), in the former Anglican church on Rue Broquedis. It retraces Biarritz's history, from its beginnings around small fishing and agricultural communities to its blossoming as a fashionable resort, with reference to paintings, costumes, artefacts and documents.

Where Rue Gambetta meets Rue Mazagran is the former workshop of the *couturier*, Jean Patou, designed by Louis Süe (1925), while at no. 4 is the old Hotel d'Angleterre by Tisnes, architect of the Russian church, begun pre-1870, with additions in 1878 by Pierre Louis and by Laulhé in 1929. Beyond Place Bellevue is Place Eugénie, a church, gardens and a cliff walk to the Plateau d'Atalaye, with more views and the little port. The Port des Pêcheurs, protected by the Basta rock, was created in 1870 and is a fun place for a drink or seafood meal. The unmistakable **Villa Le Goéland** is a prime example of eclecticism. An endearing mixture of Anglo-Norman-style brick and timber with neo-Gothic angle turrets and roofs of every shape, the original house was transformed and embellished c. 1903–04 by the Parisian architect Gaston Ernest to benefit from its position on the plateau. It now has *chambres d'hôtes* (*see p. 466*). It looks out towards the Rocher de la Vièrge, named after the statue of the Virgin erected in 1865 on the headland lashed by breakers: it can be reached via a metal footbridge made in Eiffel's workshops.

Opposite the Virgin rock is the **Musée de la Mer** (*open July–Aug 9.30–midnight; Easter, June, Sept 9.30–7; Christmas and Feb school holidays, and May Sat, Sun and holidays 9.30–6; other periods 9.30–12.30 & 2–6; T: 05 59 22 75 40*). The museum, built in

1932, shows its age. Nevertheless, it has over 150 species of fish and invertebrates native to the Bay of Biscay, a shark grotto and seal tank (feeding at 10.30 and 5), and exhibits of local interest in connection with fishing and whale hunting, the history of sea-bathing, geology and ornithology. There is a café on the terrace with ocean views.

Port Vieux

Until the 17th century, the main activity of the sheltered Port Vieux was whaling. In the 19th century it was recognised as ideal for sea-bathing and a bathing station was built c. 1858; the present one dates to 1951–52. South of the cove, on a rocky headland, is one of the most symbolic buildings in Biarritz, Villa Belza, an extraordinary edifice with terraces and outcrops, towers and turrets, named after the West Indian governness who saved the Dubreuil children during the Revolution.

Above Boulevard du Prince de Galles is a tamarisk-covered walk with views of the Côte des Basques, the beach at the foot of the Falaise d'Hurlade where surfers gather. Take the upper route, along the Perspective de la Côte des Basques, to admire a number of grand houses. To visit the chocolate museum, continue south from Carrefour d'Hélianthe. Musée du Chocolat, 14–16 Avenue Beau Rivage (*open July–Aug 10–6; rest of year 10–12 & 2.30–6; closed Sun outside school holidays; T: 05 59 41 54 64*), offers a video history of chocolate, which was introduced to France during the reign of Louis XIV (*see p. 447*), as well as sculpture in chocolate.

Turning inland along Rue Gambetta, across Avenue Carnot, and then left into Rue de la Fontaine you come to the house, nos 6–8, which belonged to Queen Natalie of Serbia in 1905. A right into Rue Peyreloubilh and and downhill along the Passage du Chapeau-Rouge takes you past a pretty Andalucian-style house. Left and right brings you back onto the Plateau d'Atalaye.

Further inland, down Avenue Foch, is the Gare du Midi, transformed into a modern theatre, and behind it, at 1 Rue Guy-Petit, is Asiatica, the museum of Oriental art (*open Mon–Fri 10.30–6.30, Sat–Sun 2–7; holidays 2–6; guided visit Wed 3 pm; T: 05 59 22 78 78*). The museum has a rich collection of some 1,000 high-quality works from India, Nepal, Tibet and China. In Rue St-Martin is the Church of St-Martin, the oldest church in Biarritz, first mentioned in the 12th century. It has been subject to several transformations, including in the 16th century; the porch was rebuilt in 1844. The nearby Château Gramont was built by Mayor Jules Labat in 1866 to replace his existing villa with something grander and more fashionable.

TOWARDS ST-JEAN-DE-LUZ

Bidart and Guéthary occupy the gap on the coast between Biarritz and St-Jean-de-Luz. Follow the Corniche into Bidart from the N10 to arrive at the chapel of Ste-Madeleine (rebuilt 1820) and views from the clifftop. **Guéthary** is the smallest community on the Basque coast, with a *fronton-mairie*, museum and tiny port and the prettiest clifftop railway station. The **Ecomusée de la Tradition Basque**, just north of St-Jean-de-Luz (*open July–Aug 10–6.30; May–June, Sept, Mon–Sat 9.30–11.30, 2.30–5.30; Sun,* *and holidays 2.30–5.30; T: 05 59 51 06 06*), is an excellent introduction to Basque life, history and culture and complements the Basque museum in Bayonne (*see p. 449*). The exhibits are carefully presented in an old Basque farmhouse and include traditional crafts, smuggling, Basque sports, festivals and dances, and the symbolism of the white, red and green Basque flag and Basque cross. Outside are rustic buildings.

ST-JEAN-DE-LUZ

The seaside resort and small seductive town of St-Jean-de-Luz, in the lee of the western Pyrenees, is undoubtedly the most attractive on this coast. A remarkable church, narrow streets lined with 17th–19th-century houses, fishing boats and a pretty beach in an oval bay, as well as a wide choice of hotels and restaurants, all contribute to its charms but also cause congestion in the summer. The Pyrenees and the valley of the Nivelle, Bayonne and the Atlantic coast are on the doorstep.

HISTORY OF ST-JEAN-DE-LUZ

The name of the town is misleading, being unconnected with *lux* or 'light', but instead a contraction from the Basque, *Donibane Lohitzun*, in French St-Jean-de-Marais, a town on the marshes where houses were supported on chestnut props. St-Jean-de-Luz has the only fishing port of any importance on this part of the coast and depended on whaling from the 11th century, first locally but later off the American coast. With the loss of the New World fishing territories in 1713, Luzien fishermen turned to cod and sardine, although tuna became king fish around the 1950s, and today anchovy, hake and conger eel are also landed. The town's seafaring history includes piracy and the more legal form, privateering, for which the Corsaires Basques required a *lettre de marque* granting royal approval to arm their ships as protection against the Spanish and English. Many an astute Luzien shipowner made his fortune from these privileges by using his vessel in 'commercial' ventures. St-Jean prospered in the 16th–17th centuries and enjoyed its greatest moment of glory on 9th June 1660, when it hosted the marriage of Louis XIV and the Infanta Maria-Theresa, according to the Treaty of the Pyrenees (*see p. 463*). Terrible storms and high tides wiped out part of the old town in the 17th and 18th centuries, leading to the construction of protective breakwaters in the 19th century, and by the end of that century, tourism had already taken a strong hold.

The old town

Close to the Nivelle and west of the Tourist Office is the busy, tree-lined **Place Louis XIV**, with a bandstand. This is the heart of the old town and focal point for many activities especially in the summer. The Maison Louis XIV (*guided visits July–Aug*

The seafront at St-Jean de Luz.

10.30–12.30 & 2.30–6.30; June–July, Sept 10.30–12 & 2.30–5.30; T: 05 59 26 01 56), on the corner of the Place and Rue de la République, was used by the young King on the occasion of his marriage to the Spanish Infanta Maria-Theresa, and from here he reputedly threw celebratory gold coins to the crowd below. The house was built in 1643 by a shipowner, Johanis de Lohobiague, and has passed down through his family. Many of the rooms were altered by later generations but there is some good furniture, many mirrors, and rediscovered painted beams. In the royal bedroom is a portrait of the king aged 22, in the year he married his bride (also 22), and a bed specially installed here at the time. The Infanta stayed for five days after the union which, by court convention, should have been consummated publicly; but Anne of Austria tactfully closed the drapes. From the south-facing gallery is a view of the port and the convent (1650) on the Ile des Récollets where Louis XIV attended mass every day. The alleyway alongside the house contained the guillotine in the 18th century. The adjacent building is the Herriko Etxea or *Mairie*, built in 1654, with an equestrian statue of Louis XIV by Bouchardon.

The port

Visitors gravitate towards the port where huge tunas were once landed in vast quantities. The colourful fishing boats still sail from here, but most of the fish is whisked away to the processing plants on the other side of the river at Ciboure, and the *vente à la criée* (fish auction) on the quay has been reduced to a whisper. On a clear day the peak of La Rhune (*see p. 471*) can be seen, presiding over the town. On the quay is the unmistakable Maison de l'Infante or Joanoenia (*open mid-June–mid–Oct 11–12.30 & 2–6.30, closed mornings Sun/Mon; T: 05 59 26 36 82*). A pretty Italianate building of 1640 in brick and stone, with superimposed loggias flanked by square towers on the main façade, it is mainly used for temporary exhibitions. The house belonged to the ennobled whaling family of de Haraneder, who provided Louis XIII with two ships to take supplies to French troops during the siege of the Ile de Ré at the time of the Wars of Religion. There are one or two interesting elements inside, such as the Renaissance fireplace with a coat of arms and some fine painted ceilings.

The Musée Grevin (*open April-Oct 10–12 & 2–6; July, Aug until 6.30; school holidays 2–6; T: 05 59 51 24 88*), is a waxworks museum presenting major historic events. In Rue Mazarin is the pretty red-and-white Maison Grangia Baïta, Wellington's head-quarters in 1813. This street leads to the entrance to the port and the lighthouse, at the southern end of the beach. Across the harbour entrance is the Fort de Socoa.

The seafront

The houses along the seafront of St-Jean-de-Luz date mainly from the 1920s and are connected to the beach by footbridges spanning the 19th century seawall, built to prevent the town from becoming one big sandcastle (the sand, however, was washed away naturally some 50 years ago). Apart from one 1970s' high-rise block, the bay is lined with attractive small houses and hotels, and closed at the far end by the Sainte-Barbe headland.

In Rue de la République, at no. 17, the Maison Eskerrénéa (16th century) is one of the few houses that resisted the maurauding Spanish in 1558 and consequent conflagrations. This narrow pedestrian street is jam-packed with jostling holidaymakers in the summer, as is Rue Gambetta, where numerous restaurants offer local dishes. Along both are shops and boutiques selling Basque linens, espadrilles and berets, Basque *macarons* (made with butter), *mouchous* (macaroons with cream), *turons* (almond confectionery) and fudge, not to mention *gateaux Basques* and a whole range of sauces and spices based on the famous Basque *piments d'Espelette* (*see p. 472*). At 20 Rue Gambetta is the Maison Goritienea, a typical house of the Labourd, built by the Corsaire Labrouche. It was used by Maréchal Soult prior to Wellington's arrival. Rue Garat leads back to the seafront.

Church of St-Jean-Baptiste

The Church of St-Jean-Baptiste, a sombre affair from the outside, off Rue Gambetta on Rue Garat, was completed in the 17th century having been reconstructed piecemeal from the 15th century onwards to replace a church which burned down in 1419; the belfry was truncated in the 18th century by lightning. The building was incomplete when Louis XIV and Maria-Theresa were married here in 1660, and it is possible that the king donated money for the church, the only one at that time in fact, although the town had a population of about 22,000. The entrance used by the royal couple was later walled up and replaced by another further west in 1664. This in its turn was embellished in 1868 with Flamboyant-style décor and a statue of St John the Baptist.

The interior

The plain stone exterior of the church gives way to wood, gilding and colour inside with a timber roof, likened to a ship's hull, over a simple but vast single space (49m by 21m). Wooden galleries on three levels were added at the end of the 17th century. Uniquely, St-Jean-Baptiste remained independent from the Bishopric of Bayonne, enabling it to keep for itself all funds raised, and only baptisms (not deaths) were recorded here. Much of the interior decoration has a strong Spanish character, especially the dressed statues and the sumptuously gilded Baroque retable, which fills the whole of the apse. It was made in Bidache and installed after the royal wedding (the light switch is behind the last column on the right). Arranged on three levels, it presents a multitude of gilded saints below God the Father and a pelican, symbol of Christ's sacrifice. In the centre of the upper level is the *Assumption of the Virgin* above St John the Baptist. To the right of the altar is a painting of the *Adoration of the Magi* (1727) by Jean Restout, a reference to the traditional celebration of the Epiphany in St-Jean. The large *ex-voto* boat was presented by Empress Eugénie in 1856 in thanks for a lucky escape when her ship was wrecked off the coast, when all but one rescuer were saved. The great organ of 1656, made by Gérard de Rodez, counterbalances the altarpiece; the decorative pulpit dates from 1878.

Ciboure

Across the Nivelle stands Ciboure, in Basque Ziburu, from *zubiburu* (head of the bridge). On the island in the Nivelle is the former Récollets convent; it is now offices but the fine 17th-century cloister has survived. The Dutch-style building on the bank of the Nivelle (opposite the Maison de l'Infante) was the birthplace of the composer Maurice Ravel on 7th March 1875. Ravel (d. 1937) lived most of his life in Paris but returned to the area where he found inspiration for the famous Boléro suite. Henri IV planned the Fort de Socoa to protect the town from the Spanish, but it was not built until the 17th century; it is now a centre for young people.

Several Art Deco villas were built here in the 1920s: one of the most classic and complete examples is Villa Leïhorra at 1 Impasse Muskoa (*closed; details of occasional openings available from the Tourist Office*). Built 1926–29 by the architect Joseph Hiriart, the house is arranged around a patio decorated with mosaics, and has stained glass by Gruber and decorations by Daum and Schwartz.

On higher ground at Urrugne an octagonal tower, the Tour Bordagain, is the only remains of a 12th century fortified church. On the N10 the Château d'Urtubie (*guided visit including snack, mid-March–Oct, 11 & 2–7; T: 05 59 54 31 15*), is now a hotel (*see p. 467*) and thoroughly renovated. The château was originally a keep authorised in 1341 by Edward III, which was added to until the 18th century and has remained in the same family since its construction. In 1463 Louis XI stayed here, Louis XIV made it a viscomty in 1654, and both Wellington and Soult were received here during the Napoleonic Wars. Further west is the Parc Florénia (*open August 10–8; April–July, Sept 10–7; Oct–March Mon–Sat 9.30–12 & 2–6, Sun 12–6; T: 05 59 48 02 51*) a pleasant and varied botanic and flower garden covering 16 hectares.

ROUTE DE LA CORNICHE

The Route de la Corniche or Corniche Basque follows a relatively unspoilt coastline with views of Spain and Mont Jaizkibel (500m) at the end of the Pyrenean chain. The route brings you to the last town in the southwest corner of France, **Hendaye**, a holiday resort with a good sandy beach on the Atlantic coast and a marina on the Bidassoa River. Opposite is the Spanish town of Fontarabie. The river marks the frontier between France and Spain and the Île des Faisans (or Île de la Conférence), now reduced by the flood tides to a narrow wooded bar, which was regularly used for exchanges between the two countries. In 1469 Louis XI of France and Henri IV of Castile met here; François I was released nearby after his capture in Pavia in 1525, in exchange for his two sons; in 1615 two more royal marriages were agreed; and in 1659 the Treaty of the Pyrenees was signed here (*see box below*).

East of the bay, on the Pointe Sainte-Anne, the Domaine Abbadia is a nature reserve of 64 hectares, mainly for the protection of some 30 species of birds as well as other fauna and flora.

There are magnificent views over Urrugne and La Rhune from the churchyard of Notre-Dame-de-Soccori, a former pilgrimage site, although the 14th-century church was rebuilt in the 19th century.

TREATY OF THE PYRENEES

This treaty settled endless frontier disputes between Spain and France. After three months of negotiation, Cardinal Mazarin for France and Don Luis de Haro for Spain signed the treaty on 7th November 1659, on the Île de la Conférence (or des Faisans) near Hendaye. Spain ceded certain territories to France, notably Roussillon, the Artois and several strongholds to the north. It was agreed that Louis XIV would marry the Infanta Maria-Theresa, daughter of Philip IV of Spain, who would renounce her rights to the Crown of Spain, in return for a payment of 500,000 gold *écus*. In 1861 Queen Isabella of Spain and Napoleon III inaugurated a monument to this important agreement.

Château d'Antoine d'Abbadie

Open June–Sept, Mon-Fri independent visits 12.30–2, Sat–Sun 2–6, guided visits Mon–Fri 10–11.30 & 2–6; Feb–May, Oct–mid-Dec, Tues–Sat guided visits 2–5; closed mid-Dec–Jan; T: 05 59 20 04 51.

Higher on the headland is the idiosyncratic Château d'Antoine d'Abbadie. This remarkable neo-Gothic confection was built between 1857 and 1879 by Antoine Thomson d'Abbadie (1810–97), explorer, scientist, astronomer and polyglot who was born in Ireland of a devout Catholic family from the Basque region. Educated in France, he travelled widely in Europe, the Middle East and North Africa, but Ethiopia, whose languages he studied, held a particular fascination for him. The château was recently renovated, inside and out, and is now positively sparkling.

In the course of building his castle, Abbadie fell out with two architects before calling for advice on the master of Gothic revivalism, Eugène Viollet-le-Duc (*see p. 95*), in 1864. Viollet drew up the overall plans for the building from afar, being occupied with Roquetaillade in the 1860s and 1870s, and put his collaborator Edmond Duthoit to the task. Externally the château epitomises the neo-medieval enthusiasm of the period, with asymmetric plan and elevations, giving the effect of a random agglomeration of parts over the centuries of the kind sought-after in 19th-century England. The château has three distinct wings, for working, for living, and for religious devotions.

The interior is very much Duthoit's domain but adapted to the particular tastes of his patron. The *horror vacui* décor is a confusion of neo-Gothic and Art Nouveau, with a particular colour scheme for each room, including black for the entrance hall and red for the Salon Arabe. Scattered around are references to Abbadie's eclecticism, such as Irish shamrocks, a neo-medieval fireplace, a quotation from the poet Robert Buchanan, Kufic inscriptions and family mottos. The furnishings range from late-Gothic style chairs to fashionable divans, Oriental drapes and a *porte-torchère* (lampstand) modelled on a young Ethiopian, Abdullah.

As well as the observatory, built to catalogue the stars, one of the more curious installations in a house of curiosities is a small tunnel bored through its walls. Antoine intended to study the refraction of light by focusing his telescope onto the highest point of the horizon, the summit of the Rhune. Unfortunately the rest of the house got in the way, hence the hole through it. The experiment turned out to be a failure: the exit of the tunnel, next to the main entrance, is marked with a stone surround inscribed *ez i kusi, es i kasi* ('I have seen nothing, I have learned nothing').

PRACTICAL INFORMATION

GETTING AROUND

• **By air:** Biarritz/Bayonne International Airport, T: 05 59 43 83 83, www.biarritz.aeroport.fr
• **By train:** Paris/Lille, Bayonne. Bordeaux, Bayonne, Biarritz, Guéthary, St-Jean-de-Luz , Ciboure, Hendaye.
• **By bus:** Airport shuttle bus (*navette*) to: Biarritz centre, Anglet-Plage, Bayonne; St-Jean-de-Luz; Hendaye. Bayonne, Biarritz/Anglet-Plage; Bayonne, Biarritz, Bidart, Guéthary, St-Jean-de-Luz, Ciboure, Urrugne, Béhobie, Hendaye, Irun Bayonne, Capbreton, Hossegor, Seignosse, St-Jean-de-Luz, Ascain, Col de St-Ignace, Petit Train de la Rhune, Sare

TOURIST INFORMATION

Anglet 1 Av. de la Chambre d'Amour, T: 05 59 03 77 01,

www.anglet-tourisme.com
Bayonne Pl. des Basques, BP 819, T: 05 59 46 01 46,
www.bayonne-tourisme.com
Biarritz Square d'Ixelles, T: 05 59 22 37 00, www.biarritz.fr
Ciboure 27 Quai Maurice Ravel, T: 05 59 47 64 56, www.ciboure.com
Hendaye 12 Rue des Aubépines, T: 05 59 20 00 34, www.hendaye.com
St-Jean-de-Luz Pl. du Maréchal-Foch, T: 05 59 26 03 16,
www.saint-jean-de-luz.com
Urrugne Maison Posta, Pl. René Soubelet, T: 05 59 54 60 80,
www.urrugne.com

GUIDED WALKS, BOAT TRIPS & FERRY

Bayonne
Themed walks from the Tourist Office: July–Sept, Mon–Sat, 10am (English on Thursday); Oct–June, Sat at 3pm.
Boat: Le Bayonne from Allées Bouffleurs, Adour and tributaries, T: 06 80 74 21 51

Biarritz
Walks from the Tourist Office, July–Aug, Mon 10am, Friday 6pm.

Hendaye
Port de Sokoburu: Goelette Haut Couthelain, as far as Spain, T: 06 16 70 89 33; Hendayais II, T: 05 59 47 87 68 or 06 14 85 72 65

St-Jean-de-Luz
Port: Nivelle III, mid-April–Sept, T: 06 09 73 61 81; Marie Rose, April to mid-Oct, T: 05 59 26 25 87

Ferries
Henday- Fontarrabie (Spain), Bateau Marie Louise, all year, T: 06 07 02 55 09
St-Jean-de-Luz-Ciboure-Socoa, mid-June to mid-Sept, T: 05 11 69 56 93

ACCOMMODATION

Anglet
€€€ **Le Château de Brindos**. A magical site with a private lake which was bought by Serge Blanco and was totally overhauled to reopen in 2002. Really something special, it manages to maintain a slightly Spanish atmosphere evoking the days when it was favoured by Madrileños. The gastronomic restaurant is under the sure hand of maestro Antoine Antunes. 24 luxury rooms and 5 suites. Closed in winter except for the Christmas period. 1 Allée du Château (quartier de Brindos, near the airport), T: 05 59 23 17 68,
www.chateaudebrindos.com

Bayonne
€ **L' Hôtel des Arceaux**. This small hotel in the ancient centre of Bayonne was recently taken over by Frédéric and Sébastien who extend a personal welcome to guests. Totally renovated, the interior is contemporary and colourful and though the 17 rooms are not huge, they are cheerful. The huge lounge with reddish/orange walls and old furnishings is often inhabited by the cat. 26 Rue Port Neuf, T: 05 59 59 15 53, www.hotel-arceaux.com

€ **Chambres d'hôtes Le Mamelon Vert**. Philippe and Jacqueline Lespagnon are genuinely pleased to welome you to their large elegant house overlooking Bayonne and the Chiberta forest. Two bedrooms are spacious while the other 2 are more suited to children. Philippe plays the flute and there is a piano and pool at the disposal of guests. 1, Chemin de Laborde (take the red bridge, Pont Grenet), T: 05 59 74 59 70, www.mamelonvert.com

Biarritz

€€€ **Hôtel Palais**. Napoleon III's gift to Eugénie overlooking the ocean became their summer residence in 1850s. Rebuilt and extended in 1903 as a palatial hotel. Of the 154 vast rooms, 20 are suites and 2 are royal suites. Some of the rooms have the charm of another era. There are three restaurants, one of which has a Michelin star. 1 Ave de l'Impératrice, T: 05 59 41 64 00, www.hotel-du-palais.com

€€ **Château du Clair de Lune**. This romantic lodge set in mimosas on the edge of Biarritz towards Arbonne is surrounded by 8 hectares of grounds. Of the 17 rooms, ask for one in the château rather than the new annexe for the full effect. No hotel restaurant, but Campagne et Gourmandise (*see Restaurants, opposite*) is next door. 48 Av. Alan-Seeger, Rte d'Arbonne, T: 05 59 41 53 20, www.chateauduclairdelune.com

€€ **Hôtel Edouard VII**. ■ In 2002 Pascal and Sylvie Boulineau lovingly restored this venerable hotel in the centre of Biarritz, creating utterly delightful accommodation. There is a little interior garden, a splendid staircase, and huge rooms decorated in an understated, English style. Garden-room, with bunk-beds is particularly suited to families. 21 Av. Carnot, T: 05 59 22 39 80, www.hotel-edouardvII.com

€ **Hôtel/Restaurant Le Val Flores**. An adorable Logis de France hotel and restaurant 700m from La Grande Plage, open February–December. Very feminine in presentation, with pale colours heightened with rose and blue, the 21 rooms are impeccable. Also a pretty garden and terrace for *al fresco* dining.

Traditional and gastronomic choices in the restaurant. They also hire bikes. 48 Av. de la Marne, T: 05 59 24 07 94, www.hotel-valflores.com

€€€ **Chambres d'hôtes Villa le Goéland**. One of the most emblematic domestic buildings of the resort opened to guests in 2003. It benefits from panoramic all-round views. Everything is on a huge scale, including the three bedrooms, Motebello, and complemented by the furnishings collected by owner Paul Darraignez. Of the three bedrooms, Goéland has a superb private terrace. 12 Plateau de L'Atalaye, T: 05 59 24 25 76; www.villagoeland-biarritz.com.

Ciboure

€ **Hôtel Lehen Tokia**. ■ A listed Art Deco building situated in the high part of Ciboure with an amazing view of the bay of St-Jean-de-Luz. The décor is a happy combination of Art Deco and Basque. Of the 7 pleasant bedrooms named after precious jewels, the Diamond Suite is pure Art Deco. There is also a pretty little garden and pool. Chemin de Achotaretta, Colline de Bordagain, T: 05 59 47 18 16, www.lehen-tokia.com

Hendaye

€ **Hotel Le Valencia**. The hotel has the amazing advantage of being right next to the shore, and 5 of the 20 rooms (3,4,5,6 and 23) open directly onto the ocean. Modern and freshly redecorated in light colours, it is closed in December. 29 Blvd de la Mer, T: 05 59 20 01 62, www.hotelvalencia.net

St-Jean-de-Luz

€€€ **Hôtel du Parc Victoria/Restaurant Les Lierres** ■. A magnificent hotel in a late 19th-century *hôtel particulier* surrounded by wonderful woodland and flowers, in which is a magnificent pool with terraces and 'beach', and garden rooms. The hotel's 9 rooms and 9 suites are elegantly furnished, mainly in the spirit of the 30s, with careful attention to detail. Les Lierres restaurant has three rooms, one pure Art Deco, the Winter Garden, and one for private dining; in summer meals are served by the pool. The talented young chef, Eric Jorge, specialises in beautifully presented inventive dishes. 5 Rue Cépé, T: 05 59 26 78 78, www.parcvictoria.com

€€€ **Le Grand Hôtel/Restaurant, 43 Blvd Thiers**. The truly grand and luxurious palace-hotel, in a marvellous position overlooking the beach, re-opened in 2001; the pink and white Art Nouveau façade is listed. Closed in winter. T: 05 59 26 35 36, www.luzgrandhotel.fr

€€ **Hôtel La Devinière**. A little oasis of delight and refinement with 11 rooms which is open all year. The rooms are all individually decorated, thanks to the talents of the owner's wife who is an antiquarian. Close to the Casino and beach, on a pedestrian street, there is also a *salon de thé*. 5 Rue Loquin, T: 05 59 26 05 51, www.hotel-la-deviniere.com

€€ **Hôtel les Goëlands**. The 30 rooms, in two solid Basque houses, were renovated in spring 2005. Catherine and Pampi Bernard are the third generation to run this hotel, which is well adapted to families with small children. It was the first in Aquitaine to receive the *Clé verte* label for its 'green' approach. There is a restaurant for residents. 4-6 avenue d'Etcheverry, T: 05 59 26 10 05, www.hotel-lesgoelands.com

€ **Hôtel Ohartzia**. ■ The Ohartzia is popular. It couldn't be more central, behind St-Jean-Baptiste church, and is close to the beach, nevertheless quiet with a charming interior garden. The 17 rooms are basic yet comfortable, and good value. 28 Rue Garat, T: 05 59 26 00 06, www.hotel-ohartzia.com

Urrugne

€€ **Château d'Urtubie**. This historic stately home owned by the Count and Countess de Corral, stands in lovely gardens. The 5 *chambres prestiges* and 5 *chambres charmes*, have recently been refurbished and the furnishings are all 18th- and 19th-century. Some have views of the grounds, and one room is in the tower. No dining in the château, but there is a restaurant opposite. On the N10, T: 05 59 54 31 15, www.chateaudurtubie.fr

RESTAURANTS

Bayonne

€€ **Le Bayonnais**. A serious restaurant on the banks of the Nive. The inventive chef creates tasty and delicious dishes which depend on seasonal availability 38 Quai des Corsaires, T: 05 59 25 61 19.

€€€ **Restaurant Le Cheval Blanc**. ■ A top-class restaurant which Jean-Claude Tellechea inherited from his father, and maintains an excellent reputation for his Basque cooking. He incorporates local ingredients, such as the Ibaïona ham, or sheep's milk cheese, and wonderful chocolate desserts. 68 Rue Bourgneuf, T: 05 59 59 01 33.

€€€ **Restaurant François Miura**. This is one of the great addresses in the

Basque region. Miura makes full use of the flavours of the excellent products he puts into his dishes which include delicate sea food combinations such as *Chipirons farcis aux pieds de porc*, and *feuillantine au chocolat*. 24 Rue Marengo, T: 05 59 59 49 89.

€€ **Restaurant La Grange**. ■ Carefully balanced cooking, full of flavours are the trademark of Jacques Diharce who has trained in a variety of great restaurants. He brings his expertise to traditional dishes such as classic *rognons de veau grillé*. 26 Quai Galuperie, T: 05 59 46 17 84.

Biarritz

€€€ **Campagne et Gourmandise**. A discreet and unaffected establishment reflecting the character of the owners, André and Annick Gaüzère, whose welcome is warm and professional. André's cooking is inventive and thoughtful, including *Gâteau léger de langoustines laqué d'épices* and *Baba aux pommes rôties*. 52 Av. Alan Seeger, T: 05 59 41 10 11.

€€€ **La Maison Blanche**. ■ A beautiful modern and simple setting for the excellent restaurant where the cuisine is under the sure guidance of Tomas Anciart. The menus (gourmand or *du marché*) and the à la carte, and all elegantly presented dishes are based on the best of the pays Basque. Such delights include *Autour de l'asperge verte, le quatuor de saveurs en chaud-froid; Carré d'agneau en croûte de sésame, gratin de petits artichauts, tempuras à l'ail confit et tortellini frit au parmesan*, and a dessert based on a variety of ways to serve strawberries. Tonic Hotel, 58 av. Edouard VII, T: 05 59 24 58 58, www.maisonblanchebiarritz.com

€€ **Le Clos Basque**. ■ An attractive place with a shaded terrace where you can sample the cuisine of Béatrice Viateau, an excellent example of traditional Basque but with a modern touch. Menus are adapted to the seasons and change frequently, and specialities include *Foie gras et pain perdu*. 12 Rue Louis Barthou, T: 05 59 24 24 96.

€-€€ **Au Plaisir des Mets**. Jean-Noel Aguerre's cooking is based on the best sea food and products of the land. The setting is also unexpected and intimate. 5 Rue du Centre, T: 05 59 24 34 66.

€-€€ **La Tasca**. a glamorous, modern and chilled bar which opened in 2003. Great tapas, and a small choice of *plats du jour* to accompany the wide variety of drinks on offer. , 51bis Av. Gambetta, T: 05 59 22 54 24. Open until 2 a.m.

€ **Café Cosi**. A café open from 9 to 9 serving light meals, brunches and lunches, in the centre of town. It puts on new displays of paintings about every three weeks. 9 Rue Larralde, T: 05 59 24 41 00.

Bidart

€€€ **La Table des Frères Ibarboure**. In a wonderful setting in the wooded countryside, brothers Martin and Philippe combine classic Basque cooking with imaginative artistry inspired by fresh produce. Dishes include *Ravioles de morue, Foie chaud de canard aux agrumes*, and *Desserts au chocolat de Bayonne*. Chemin de Thaliena, T: 05 59 54 81 64.

€-€€ **La Tantina de la Playa**. The sea reigns here: it is before your eyes as you eat the fresh sea food *à la plancha*, a simple way of cooking which retains all the natural flavours of the ingredients. Typical Basque dishes of the day are chalked up on the slate. Plage de Bidart, T: 05 59 26 53 56.

Ciboure
€€ Chez Dominique. ■ Very close to the port where the fish is brought in, Georges Piron's inspired but simple cooking benefits from the fresh seafood. His generous dishes include *Carpaccio de langoustines et tartare de cèpes, Medaillon de lotte*, and *Foie gras poëlé, truffe glacée au thym*. Quai Maurice Ravel, T: 05 59 47 29 16.

Hendaye
€ Ez Kecha. For anyone who is enthusiastic about wine, the bar has about 20 on offer by the glass, and several hundreds of *crus* to choose from. These can be accompanied by light snacks. Lieu-dit-Vin, 3 Route de Béhobie, T: 05 59 20 67 09.

Guéthary
€–€€ Villa Janénéa. Gaelle Thibon was second chef at Watergate, Washington. She works with the best local products which are carefully chosen and cooked so that their fresh, natural flavours and goodness are retained. 352 Av. du Général de Gaulle, T: 05 59 26 50 69.

St-Jean-de-Luz
€€ Olatua. The chef, Olivier Lataste, has brought new life into classic dishes from the Basque and Landes regions. He innovates from available fresh produce to create the *plats du jour*. 30 Blvd Thiers, T: 05 59 51 05 22.

€–€€ Chez Maya. This is one of the best places to eat along the coast with a light and innovative approach to local cuisine from Frédéric, grandson of the original owner. 4 Rue St-Jacques, T: 05 59 26 80 76.

€–€€ Chez Pablo. ■ Chez Pablo guarantees regional cuisine, generous servings, resolutely Basque decor and bistrot ambiance. In the same family for four generations, it serves local favourites such as *pibales* (in season), cod, and their famous *chiprions farcis en su tinta* as well as a good-value *plat du jour*. Rue Mademoiselle Etcheto, T: 05 59 26 37 81.

€ Bodega Chez Kako. A fashionable meeting place recommended for its good, down-to-earth cooking including *tapas, piquillos*, grilled fish of the day or *côte de boeuf*. 18 Rue Marechal Harispe, T: 05 59 85 10 70.

FESTIVALS & EVENTS

February: *Carnaval* St-Jean-de-Luz
March: *Bi Harriz Lau Xori*, Basque festival of song, cinema, theatre and poetry, Biarritz. *Foire aux Jambons*, celebrating Bayonne ham, Bayonne
Carnaval de Printemps, Biarritz
May: *Biennale des Arts plastiques de Navarre*, St-Jean-de-Luz. *Journées du Chocolat*, celebration of the product and visits to producers, Bayonne
June: *Fête des Casetas*, the bars and 'bodegas' set up shop on the Côte des Basques beach, Biarritz
June–August: *Fêtes patronales de la St Jean*, St-Jean-de-Luz. *Internationaux de Cesta Punta*, pelota/jaï alaï/cesta punta championships, St-Jean-de-Luz
July: *Cesta Punta Basque et Pelota*, Biarritz. *Nokia Biarritz Surf Festival*, big names in surfing come to Biarritz. *Courses de trot à l'Hippodrome des Fleurs*, trotting races, Biarritz
August: *Les Fêtes de Bayonne*, five-day festival with dancing day and night, traditional sports and corridas (the latter until September), Bayonne
Gant d'Or, the Golden Glove professional Pelota Tournament, Biarritz

PAYS BASQUE

THE LABOURD

Some of the prettiest villages, often with the *fronton*, *Mairie* and church assembled around the centre and set in idyllic scenery, are scattered through the foothills of the Pyrenees and the countryside of the Labourd. An ancient province of Pays Basque (*see p. 441*), the Labourd includes the coastal towns of the previous chapter, and stretches inland to Espellette and Cambo-les-Bains. The Pays Basquais provinces of Basse-Navarre and then Pays de Soule lie further east along the foot of the mountains.

THE NIVELLE VALLEY

The valley of the Nivelle links St-Jean-de-Luz and **Ascain**, where a 'Roman' bridge—in fact 16th-century—crosses the river. Here Notre-Dame-de-l'Assomption is typical of medieval Basque churches, enlarged in the 16th–17th centuries, with a massive porch-tower. The interior is brighter than the church of St-Jean-de-Luz (*see p. 461*), with painted corbels, ceiling and chancel arch. Galleries on three sides are supported by stone columns and the pulpit is suspended from the first level. There is some good quality carving, and an 18th-century altarpiece above the raised altar.

BASQUE CHURCHES

Basque churches, as found in the Labourd or Navarre but not in the Soule, are generally sober from the exterior, heavy and strong like a fortress, with sturdy stone walls. Many were damaged during the Wars of Religion in the 16th century and rebuilt mainly in the 17th century. A large porch, often incorporated into a west tower, provides shelter from the vagaries of the climate. Inside is a large, single space, covered by a wooden roof, flat or arched and usually painted. Wooden galleries on the side walls, possibly added later, are polished and sometimes carved. The men sat in the galleries, the women in the nave. A small pulpit, often highly decorated, is usually attached to the north gallery. The main altar, by contrast, is often an exuberance of Baroque motifs, colour and gilding, expressing the strength of local enthusiasm for scenes, statues, twisted columns, swags and vines. In the churchyards are many discoidal stelae, reminiscent of Celtic crosses.

St-Pée-sur-Nivelle

St-Pée-sur-Nivelle (St-Pierre) has some good 17th- and 18th-century houses along the main street, notably the Maison Altzola (1676), where the timbers of the two upper floors are painted in traditional ox-blood red and rest on a stone base. The plain entrance of the church, restored in 1606, opens to reveal a magnificent altarpiece under a shell-like vault, filling the whole of the apse, with numerous gilded statues arranged around St Peter. Only a romantic ivy-clad ruin remains of the Château d'Ibarron (15th and 17th century) to the west, which burned down in 1793.

Sare and La Rhune

The most emblematic of French Basque mountains, La Rhune, rises to 905m above the village of Sare, and on its slopes are the remains of cromlechs and fortifications. Excursions may be made up La Rhune on a little wooden milk train dating from 1924 called **Le Petit Train de la Rhune** (*leaves from the station of Col de St-Ignace: mid-April–mid-Sept, departures at 10am and 3pm; July–Aug, every 35 minutes from 9am; mid-March–mid-April and Oct, at 10am and 3pm, except Mon and Thurs; T: 05 59 54 20 26. There is also a bus connection from St-Jean de Luz.*). The journey to the summit, the frontier with Spain, takes about 40 minutes. Small wild horses, or *pottoks*, a recognised breed related to pit ponies, graze on the mountain.

One kilometre from the station is **Ortillopitz** (*open April–Oct; T: 05 59 85 91 92*) a beautiful old house which is a monument to the traditional life of the Basque region. The white-painted timber-framed farmhouse with original furnishings was built in 1660 on the remains of a house of 1540. It conserves the old staircase, cider cellar, stone sink and outside, in the 3 hectares of land which surround it, are reminders of the former self-sufficiency of the property.

Sare is a lovely village deep in the countryside, with remarkably beautiful old houses, a Museum of the Gâteau Basque and a cider press. The belfry-gable of the parish church of St-Martin carries a 17th-century inscription, and under the west porch is a modern *Pietà*. Inside are galleries and a raised altar with five retables and painted chancel arch. The village was appreciated by Napoleon III and Eugénie, to the extent that in 1867 Sare dedicated the chapel of Ste-Catherine to the Empress. The small oratories around the village were built from the 17th century onwards at the behest of local fishermen. The vast series of caves, Les Grottes Prehistoriques de Sare *en son et lumière* (*open July–Aug 10–7, Easter–June, Sept 10–6; Oct 10–5; Nov–Dec, Feb-March 2–5; T: 05 59 54 21 88*) have a new presentation, with geological information, displays on the origins of the Basque people, and a megalithic park. Unfortunately all prehistoric traces were damaged in the 20th century.

Aïnhoa

The jewel of the Labourd is Aïnhoa, founded in the 13th century by Premonstratensian friars as a staging post on the pilgrimage route to Santiago. It flaunts perfect Basque houses with wide central doorways, ranged along its one main street. Most were rebuilt in the 17th–18th centuries after the village was ransacked by the Spanish in 1629. The houses traditionally face east and some carry decorative friezes, dates or inscriptions. At the end of the lane beside the *Mairie* is a 19th-century chapel dedicated to Notre-Dame-de-l'Aubépine (hawthorn). The church has an unusual octagonal lantern and slate-covered spire on a square base. The rounded east end is 14th-century, while the remainder is a plain building of the 17th and 18th centuries. Inside is the usual arrangement of galleries, but here the walls are painted white to show off the woodwork and the gilded altarpiece. Immediately behind the church is the *fronton*.

THE BASQUE HOUSE

The Basque house (*etche* or *extxea*) is particularly attractive yet functional, well adapted to the needs of an extended family and to local climate and materials. Generally wide, low and large, the timber-framed structure stands on a stone base, with the beams painted red or green to create striking geometric patterns. The red-tiled gable roofs are typically long and shallow with deep eaves like Swiss chalets; sometimes the pitch is uneven because the house has been extended in one direction to accommodate a growing family. The buildings are carefully orientated against bad weather, their backs turned to the west or northwest, windows and balconies facing the rising sun. The wide doorways were designed to allow loaded carts through, and the ground-floor space was divided between the animals on the north, to provide warmth, and the family. In some cases the family rooms were on the floor above. The attic, sometimes with triangular openings, where crops were dried also acted as insulation. Some of the most striking examples of this type of Basque house are in the Labourd, in villages such as Sare, Aïnhoa and St-Pée-sur-Nivelle but there are slight regional variations and differences in materials. The less colourful style of the Basse-Navarre is typified at Baïgorry, and further east, in the Soule, the houses are still more sombre, and roofed in flat tiles or slate. Such was the importance of a house that many a description—*etcheverry* ('new house'), *etchegaray* ('house on the hill'), *etchegorri* ('red house')—was adopted as the family name.

Espelette

The red-and-white façades of Espelette, are adorned in the summer and autumn with strings of red pimentos (small hot peppers). Successfully grown here for generations, the moderately piquant *capsicum annuum* was introduced from the Americas in the 17th century to flavour chocolate and is now sold fresh, dried, as powder or paste, and flavours many Basque recipes. (More can be learned about the pimento at Accoceberry Piment d'Espellette, Route Zubizabaletako bidea, T: 05 59 93 86 49). Espelette has typical 16th–18th-century Basque houses, and an old château. The modest 17th-century church in the lower part of the village has carved wooden galleries and turned balusters, a painted wooden ceiling and a 17th-century gilded altarpiece.

CAMBO-LES-BAINS & THE NIVE VALLEY

The upper town of Cambo-les-Bains stands on a plateau overlooking the Nive Valley, where the spa developed in the 19th century around two hotwater springs. It is clustered around the typical Labourdine single-nave church, with galleries and ubiquitous Baroque retable which is beautifully cared for. On the edge of the town, surrounded by woodland, is the former house of Edmond Rostand (1868–1918), author of *Cyrano de Bergerac* (1897).

Rostand's house, which he called **Arnaga** (*guided visits July–Aug 10–7; April–June, Sept 10–12.30 & 2.30–7; Oct 2.30–6; March, Sat, Sun 2.30–6; T: 05 59 29 70 57*), is now a shrine to the poet. Rostand first came to Cambo in 1900 to recuperate from pleurisy and made such a good recovery that he decided to establish a base here; the building of a neo-Basque house set in large formal gardens began in 1903. The project was closely supervised by Rostand and most of the rooms have their original décor, incorporating wood panelling, painted decoration, *trompe-l'oeil* and coloured glass, while some are themed (Chinese, Empire). A small bedroom was reserved for Rostand's creative activity and its walls are now papered with documents referring to his origins. The exterior timbers have recently been repainted in red, also the original colour. The gardens frame views of the mountains around Itxassou and contain a pergola inspired by the Gloriette at Schönbrun in Vienna.

Itxassou and environs

In the deeply green and lush Nive Valley is the village of Itxassou, divided on the one hand around a square with *fronton* and *Mairie*, and on the other around the simple but impressive 17th-century church. The church is painted white and has a red roof and square tower, and it stands in a graveyard where there are a number of discoidal stelae. The interior was endowed with a Spanish-style retable and galleries in the 18th century, and there are wooden statues including a 17th-century *Virgin* carved in wood.

Further south along the valley is **Bidarray**, perched on a high plateau with a minute but solid 12th-century church with a 17th-century façade and belfry gable, built in the distinctive sandstone of the Basse-Navarre.

Ossès boasts a church with a tall white-and-pink octagonal belfry unlike anything else in Pays Basque, built with help from Antoine de Bourbon and Jeanne d'Albret (*see p. 364*). Inside is a sumptuous red-and-gold retable liberally scattered with cherubs and foliage set in a pink sandstone sunburst. On the Irissarry road is the remarkable Maison Sastriarena, with a massive carved lintel bearing the date of its restoration, 1628.

St-Etienne-de-Baïgorry

Stretched out along the Nive in the Vallée des Aldudes, the village of St-Etienne-de-Baïgorry has Basque-style houses with carved lintels. The road crosses a pretty bridge spanning the Nive des Aldudes, which at times runs red with mountain mud (*ibaï gorri* means 'red river'). Nearby is the church of St-Etienne, and under the 18th-century tower is an entrance reputedly reserved for the *cagots*. The most unusual feature is the Baroque organ in the manner of southern Germany.

The charming little Château d'Etchauz (11th and 16th century; *guided visits April–Oct at 2.30 and 4.30; mid-Nov–March, by appointment only; closed Sat, Sun and Mon all year; T: 05 59 37 48 58; also chambres d'hôtes, see p. 481*), former seat of the Viscounts of Baïgorry , is a superb example of medieval architecture with two round towers and two Renaissance watchtowers.

Beyond St-Etienne a narrow wooded valley leads through wild landscape to the Col d'Urquiaga, and to the west is a spectacular drive to the Col d'Ispeguy through land where France and Spain traditionally share grazing rights. The wine from the vineyards around Baïgorry and Irouléguy claims the evocative *appellation* Irouléguy.

BASSE-NAVARRE

ST-JEAN-PIED-DE-PORT

In a hollow surrounded by mountains is the picturesque *bastide* of St-Jean-Pied-de-Port ('at the foot of the pass'). The old capital of Basse-Navarre, it controlled the ancient and busy route to Spain over the Col d'Ibañeta via Roncevaux; the border is 8km away. The attractive houses overhanging the Nive, the old city wall and gateways (17th century), markets and festivities, all draw the crowds.

HISTORY OF ST-JEAN-PIED-DE-PORT

St-Jean-Pied-de-Port has always served as a resting-place for travellers, merchants and armies on the road to Spain through Roncevaux, protected by the fortress of St-Jean-le-Vieux, which was destroyed by Richard the Lionheart in 1178. From the 10th century it became a major route for pilgrims to Santiago de Compostela, and with the revival of interest in their route, modern pilgrims now gather here, sometimes in large groups. The fortress was replaced at the end of the 12th century by the present *bastide*, founded by the Aragonais kings of Navarre, and it became the capital of Basse-Navarre. The commercial success of St-Jean-Pied-de-Port was assured and a flourishing leather industry developed. The marriage in 1484 of Jean d'Albret with Catherine de Foix added King of Navarre to the family's already illustrious titles but the War of Navarre (1512–30) between the Aragonais and the Bourbons-Albrets resulted in the division of the territory. Only the small segment, Basse-Navarre, was retained by the Albret. With the accession of Henri IV to the throne in 1589, St-Jean reverted to France and was used as a frontier garrison town during the Franco-Spanish War in the 17th century. Its military role was revived in the 19th century as a base for expeditions against Spain.

Exploring St-Jean-Pied-de-Port

From Place Charles-de-Gaulle, opposite the elegant 17th-century Hôtel de Ville, the road heads south to the bridge over the Nive from which is a classic picturesque view, looking upstream, of balconied Navarrais houses standing in the river, the old bridge and the church, against a backdrop of wooded slopes. From Place Floquet turn left on Rue Urhart to the Rue d'Espagne leading south to the Porte d'Espagne and the road to Spain. This is now a tourist-trodden street, but has always been the commercial area, lined with handsome 17th–18th-century stone houses with overhanging roofs and carved joists. Turn back to cross the old bridge and pass under the fortified belfry tower, Porte Notre-Dame, complete with studded doors and portcullis where stone seats were provided for the poor waiting for the hospice to open. In the 14th century there was a wooden bridge which could be raised, but until the 11th century the only crossing was a ford. The riverbank alongside the church takes you to the Eyheraberry or 'Roman' bridge, the first built here in stone: it is probably no earlier than the 13th century, and was rebuilt in 1634. The church was once an integral part of the fortifications, and steep steps behind it climb up to the *chemin de ronde* and the Citadel.

The Church of **Notre-Dame du Bout du Pont** is a severe affair although the violet tints of the stone add warmth. The lower parts of the walls are Gothic (14th century), while the remainder is 17th–19th-century. The bare interior with nave and aisles is unlike the Basque churches of the Labourd, with just two galleries in the west and two windows in the east presenting the arms of the town and of the province.

Rue de l'Eglise, opposite the church, is spanned by the 13th-century Porte de Navarre in the old fortifications, and steps again climb to the *chemin de ronde*. There are some fine jettied houses with characteristic stone lintels carved with dates, names and professions. Rue de la Citadelle rises steeply between 17th- and 18th-century houses, and one 16th-century timber-and-brick house. The Prison des Evêques (*open end-March–Oct*), built in 1584, was a prison only in the 18th century. Adjoining is the Maison des Evêques, a reminder that there was an episcopal see here during the Great Schism (14th–15th centuries). Rue de France leads to another gate with steps in the walls, and no. 39 is the pilgrim hostel. The street is straddled by the Porte St-Jacques. Pilgrims from different parts of Europe converged on Ostabat about 20km northeast and arrived in St-Jean-Pied-de-Port this way. The present hiking routes, the GR10 and GR65, follow the old pilgrimage roads (*see p. 11*). A right bend takes you up to the plateau of the Citadel, attributed to Vauban (*see p. 55*) although his involvement was minimal. It is now occupied by a school; to visit, enquire at the tourist office. The views from here towards the town, the Pays de Cize and the Cols of Ibañeta and Bentarte are glorious. The Citadel replaced a castle damaged by the Spanish in the 16th century, and c. 1644 the present fort, after plans by Deville, began to take shape. Additions suggested by Vauban, including covered paths, and further alterations in the 18th century made this a modern defensive system and St-Jean-Pied-de-Port the main stronghold between Pamplona and Bayonne during a period of almost permanent conflict between France and Spain.

EXPLORING BASSE-NAVARRE

A short and beautiful excursion into the countryside from St-Jean leads along the mountain-valley road (D301), to St-Michel and the village of Esterunçuby. The N135 over the Col d'Ibañeta drops down to the vast plateau of Roncevaux, familiar from the Chanson de Roland and pilgrimage history, a monastery going back to the 12th century, and the Gothic collegiate church with the tomb of Sanche VII (*open 10–2 & 4–8*).

BATTLE OF RONCEVAUX

The route via Roncevaux (Roncevalles) has been known since time immemorial as a relatively less difficult way through the Pyrenees, but became legendary after the attack on Charlemagne's army on 15th August 778. While returning from the siege of Saragossa to put down a revolt in France, the rearguard under the command of Roland was ambushed by the Vascons in the narrow Col de Bentarte. The exhausted Frankish battalion, impeded by the military hardware and supplies they were moving, were slaughtered to a man. The event, Roland's heroic death, even his sword Durandel, were immortalised in the medieval epic poem *La Chanson de Roland*. Following this battle, Charlemagne created the Kingdom of Aquitaine.

St-Palais

St-Palais northeast of St-Jean was a new town founded in the 13th century at the confluence of the Bidouze and the Joyeuse, and became the capital of Basse-Navarre in the 16th century. A fertile region, it is an important agricultural centre where maize has been cultivated since the 16th century. There is a small museum of history and pilgrimage, Basse-Navarre et des Chemins de St Jacques in the interior courtyard of the *Mairie* (*open July–Aug 9.30–12.30 & 2–7, Sun and holidays 10–12.30; Sept–June 9.30–12.30 & 2–6.30, closed Sat, Sun; T: 05 59 65 71 78*). The most famous house is the Maison des Têtes, opposite the church of St-Paul, with images of the Albret dynasty. Just 3km south on Mont St-Sauveur, the convergence of the pilgrimage routes from Le Puy, Paris and Tours, and Vézelay (although another tradition cites Ostabat) is marked by the Stèle of Gibraltar.

The Grottes d'Isturitz et d'Oxocelhaya

Guided visits July, Aug 10–6; June–Sept at 11, 12, and 2–5; mid-March, April–May, Oct–mid-Nov 12–5; T: 05 59 29 64 72.

These two caves at Saint-Martin-d'Arberoue, between Hasparren and St-Palais, are superimposed. They have impressive natural formations and were frequented and decorated by prehistoric man from the Mousterian to Magdalenian periods. A number of objects were found, and copies exist in in a small local museum.

La Bastide-Clairence

La Bastide-Clairence is a proud little village where Gascon and Basque influences blend harmoniously. It was founded on the banks of the Joyeuse, a tributary of the Adour, in 1312 by Louis le Hutin, King of Navarre with the objective of reconnecting Navarre, which had just lost its coastal territories, with the outside world via the Adour. The town was populated by immigrants from the Bigorre in Gascony, and the layout—along straight, parallel arcaded streets around a central square—is more typically Gascon than Basque, although the colourfully decorated half-timbered houses are not. The impeccable main street, with a number of artisans' workshops, runs uphill to the church, built in the 14th century, the only stone building until the 17th century. Surrounding the church is an unusual arcade paved with tombstones which was, and remains, the burial place for local people. Until the end of the 18th century, the Etats Généraux of Navarre held their meetings here, and the graveyard of a Jewish community has been preserved nearby. There are rustic carvings on the church porch and the interior is arranged in a typically Basque manner.

Bidache

Bidache is on the old boundary between France, Navarre and the Béarn, and has the striking ruins of the Château de Gramont silhouetted on a cliff above the little Bidouze River. In 1320 this territory came under the control of the Dukes of Gramont who still own the property, mainly 16th–17th century, which was set on fire during the Revolution. What remains is skeletal in places. The main Classical pedimented entrance is wedged between two round 14th-century towers, and a substantial amount remains of the north wing with Renaissance elements. There are similarities inside with Cadillac (*see p. 84*). A wing of c. 1600 and a medieval tower have also survived.

PAYS DE SOULE

This is the meeting point of Pays Basque and the Béarn in the south of the Pyrénées-Atlantiques and also the most rugged part of Pays Basque. The foothills are green and lush, but the scenery becomes more dramatic towards the Spanish border. The area is crossed by spectacular mountain routes over the high pass of Col Bargargui (1327m) or the Col d'Aphanize (1055m) and there are two passes into Spain at the Port de Larrau and La Pierre-St-Martin (*see p. 501*). The smallest of the three French Basque provinces, Pays de Soule was ceded at the end of the 15th century by Louis XI to his nephew, François-Phébus de Foix, King of Navarre. A year after the death of the king, Soule was detached from the Béarn and returned to the Crown of France. Nevertheless, it continued to be part of the diocese of Oloron, which came under the King of Navarre. The Soule remained staunchly Catholic at the Reformation but the churches were ruined by the Protestants.

Three routes across the Soule link St-Jean-Pied-de-Port and the Gave de Mauléon. The highest and most spectacular, the D18 across the Haute Soule, goes through the

Forêt d'Iraty to Col Bargargui. Tucked under the highest peak hereabouts, the Pic d'Orhy (2017m), is the sombre mountain village of **Larrau**, which grew around a pilgrim hospice and church, the latter restored in 1656 with its Romanesque apse still intact. In a landscape of ravines, the most accessible is the Crevasses d'Holzarte (Holçarté), a relatively easy walk (best in spring or autumn, *T: 05 59 28 51 28*) on the GR10 to a footbridge spanning the crevasse. Very isolated (D113) is a tiny Romanesque church, Ste-Engrâce (*T: 05 59 28 60 83*), which shelters some carved and polychromed capitals of Solomon and the Queen of Sheba, *Salome's Dance*, the *Virgin and Child* and the *Epiphany*, and a superb Baroque altarpiece. South of Ste-Engrâce are the truly spectacular Gorges de Kakouetta (*mid-March–mid-Nov T: 05 59 28 60 83 or 05 59 28 73 44*) and Gorges d'Ehujarre; access mid-March–mid-Nov 8am to nightfall.

The lower route (D417), branches off at Mendive, with panoramic views from the Col d'Aphanize (off the D117). Certain rugged mountain churches in this area contain elaborate Baroque altarpieces, and at Aussurucq (D147) is a typical *clocher pignon trinitaire*, belfry with three gables. The **Château de Trois-Villes** (*guided visits 10–12.30, Sat–Mon, April, May, Sept; T: 05 59 28 54 01*) at Elicabia, is a small 17th-century château built by the Comte de Tréville, Captain of the King's Musketeers.

The third route into the Soule (D918) is via the Col d'Osquich where, in October during the migration season, the hunting of *palombes* is still permitted by the traditional and distressing method of trapping them in nets.

MAULÉON-LICHARRE

Mauléon-Licharre on the Gave is the main town of the Soule. Mauléon was the *bastide* around the medieval castle on the hill and Licharre, below, was formerly an independent commune and is a major centre for the manufacture of *espadrilles* (linen and twisted cord sandals). The castle was built in the 12th century and was held by the English in 1307; in 1449 it was handed over to the Counts of Foix. It is possible to walk around the ramparts. Inside is an exhibition of its history; to visit, contact the tourist office.

Château d'Andurain de Maytie
Guided visits July–mid-Sept 11–12 & 3–6; closed Thur, Sun mornings and holidays; T: 05 59 28 04 18.
A very handsome example of late-Renaissance architecture on the main square, the château was built at the end of the 16th century by Pierre de Maytie in open countryside. His son, Arnaud de Maytie, Bishop of Oloron, restored the Catholic faith to the diocese and two other members of the family were bishops of Oloron in the 17th century. The most impressive feature of the exterior is the enormously high roof, partly covered in *bardeaux*. The façade is asymmetrical and flanked by angle pavilions which were heightened in the 18th century; the mullioned windows have broken pediments on the ground floor; and in the roof are three elaborate dormers decorated with masks. There is a corbelled balcony over the main entrance. The entrance for

visitors is through the left-hand pavilion. The house is privately owned and the alterations made by successive occupants are part of its charm. The visit includes the main reception rooms, including the dining room altered to 19th-century tastes and the salon with a 17th-century monumental Italian-style fireplace; a precious 16th-century patchwork and *appliqué* bedspread given to the household by Jeanne d'Albret; and Louis XV style chairs with their original yellow tapestry fabric. Straight flights of stairs of a sophisticated construction lead to the apartments of the three bishops and another magnificent fireplace. There is a prayer book presented by Louis XIII and a remarkable collection of 16th–17th century rare books.

PRACTICAL INFORMATION

GETTING AROUND

• **By train:** See also Bayonne/ St-Jean de Luz (*p. 464*) . Bayonne, St-Jean-Pied-de-Port . Pau, Oloron-Ste-Marie
• **By bus:** St-Jean-de-Luz, Ascain, Col de St-Ignace, Petit Train de la Rhune, Sare, Grottes de Sare
St-Jean-Pied-de-Port , St-Etienne-de-Baïgorry. Dax, Mauléon. Cambo-les-Bains , Bayonne. Bayonne, St-Palais, St-Jean. St-Jean-Pied-de-Port , St-Etienne-de-Baïgorry

TOURIST INFORMATION

Ascain Le Bourg, T: 05 59 54 00 84, www.ascain-tourisme.fr
Bidache Pl. du Fronton,
T: 05 59 56 05 11,
com.de.communes.bidache@wanadoo.fr
Cambo-les-Bains Av. de la Mairie,
BP15, T: 05 59 29 70 25,
cambo.les.bains.tourisme@wanadoo.fr
Espelette Chateau des Barons
d'Ezpeleta, T: 05 59 93 95 02,
www.espelette.com
La Bastide Clairence Maison Darrieux,
T: 05 59 29 65 05,
www.labastideclairence.com
Mauléon-Licharre 10 Rue J-B. Heugas,
T: 05 59 28 02 37,
www.pyrenees-baseques.com
St-Etienne-de-Baïgorry Elizondea,
T: 05 59 37 47 28,
www.pyrenees-basque.com
St-Palais Pl. Charles-de-Gaulle, T: 05
59 65 71 78,
www.tourisme-saintpalais.com
St-Pée-sur-Nivelle Pl. de la Poste, T: 05
59 54 11 69,
www.saint-pee-sur-nivelle.com
St-Jean-Pied-de-Port 4 Pl. Charles-de-Gaulle, T: 05 59 37 03 57,
www.pyrenees-basque.com
Sare Herriko Etxea, T: 05 59 54 20 14,
www.sare.fr

ACCOMMODATION & RESTAURANTS

Aïnhoa
€€ **Hôtel/Restaurant Ithurria** ■ .
This typical 17th-century Labourdin house was a staging post on the Route to Santiago. Run by the Isabal family, it has 28 very refreshingly understated rooms, gardens and a pool. Some of the best food in the region is cooked here

by Maurice and Xavier while Maritchu and oenologist Stéphanie supervise the dining room. The cuisine is based on quality local produce, and among irresistible choices are *Petits piments doux farcis à la morue, Saumon frais de l'Adour, Pigeon rôtie a l'ail doux, Cassoulet Basque aux haricots rouges*, and *Délice à l'Izarra*. Menus €32–48. Rue Principale, T: 05 59 29 92 11, www.ithurria.com

Ascain

€ **Chambres d'hôtes Ferme Haranederrea**. On the outskirts of Ascain, on the way to the Col de St Ignace, is an authentic Basque farm belonging to the same family since 1800 and still home to three generations. Nothing too modern, nothing too bright, this is a rustic setting, well polished and simple, where the owners extend a warm, unpretentious welcome. T: 05 59 54 00 23.

Barcus

€€ **Hôtel/Restaurant Chilo**. A 'gourmet' auberge whose owner, Pierre Chilo, is one of the best cooks in Pays Basque. The dishes are varied and inviting. Menus from €18 (weekday lunch) to €62. The little hotel with pale blue shutters, looked after by Martine, is a delight, with cosy rooms, a fireplace in the lounge, and a lovely pool. D24 southeast of Mauléon, T: 05 59 28 90 79, www.hotel-chilo.com

La Bastide-Clairence

€ **Chambres d'hôtes Le Clos Gaxen**. On the edge of the village, the typical white Basque house stands on a hill in a beautiful rural setting. It has three simple but charming bedrooms and good bathrooms where careful attention is given to detail and each is named according to its view. Outside is a pool, and in the fields the owners' horses peacefully graze. *Table d'hôtes* by prior reservation. Route d'Hasparren, T: 05 59 29 16 44, www.leclosgaxen.com

Cambo-les-Bains

€ **Chambres d'hôtes Domaine de Xixtaberri**. Unusual, spacious, strong colours, old beams and stone and, at 678m, truly panoramic views. The rooms are in a separate building from the domain where myrtles, cherries, and pimentos are grown, and guests can help gather them. *Table d'hôtes* in the main building. Route d'Hasparren, T: 05 59 29 22 66, www.xixtaberri.com

€ **Maison d'hôtes Rosa Enia**. An amazing house, huge and eccentric. Built by Edmond Rostand's doctor, Professor Grancher, 1896, where the likes of Sarah Bernhardt were received. The owner's sister kept elephants and parts of the house were built to accommodate them. There are five guest rooms and *table d'hôtes* is available. T: 05 59 93 67 20, www.rosa-enia.com

Espelette

€ **Chambres d'hôtes Maison Irazabala**. Overlooking the 'pimento' village, three generations of the family live in the traditional Basque house with inherited furniture and polished wood floors. Under the influence of its owner, Sylvie Toffolo-Fagoaga, the setting is unpretentious, serene and welcoming and the two large restful rooms named after nearby mountains, Artzamendi and Baïgura. T: 05 59 93 93 02, www.olhaldea.com/irazabala

€€ **Euzkadi**. This is as regional cooking used to be, with family recipes gathered and cherished by chef André Darraïdou. Rue Karrika Naguise, T: 05 59 93 91 88.

Ispoure

€ **Chambres d'hôtes Ferme**

Etxeberria. Etxeberria is a family farm in the Basque region at the foot of the Irouléguy vineyards with 4 guest rooms. There is a very warm welcome from Mme Mourguy, and the family will be delighted to show you the vineyard and organise donkey rides. T: 05 59 37 06 23.

Itxassou

€ **Hôtel/Restaurant Du Chêne**. An attractive place run by Geneviève Sallaberry in the middle of the village, with blue beams in the dining room and wonderful traditional country cooking. Meals also served on the wisteria draped terrace. It has 16 rooms, some with large bathrooms and old-fashioned baths. T: 05 59 29 75 01.

Larrau

€ **Hôtel/Restaurant Etchémaïte**. Not far from the Pic d'Orhy, in a rural setting, a small family-run mountain auberge renovated with simplicity and charm. There is a fireplace for winter days, and some rooms have mountain views. T: 05 59 28 61 45, www.hotel-etchemaite.fr

Mauléon

€ **Hôtel/Restaurant Bidegain**. An institution which has been taken over by Pierre and Martin Chilo. The setting is of another era, but it is starting to return it its former glory with inspired and attractive versions of regional dishes, such as *Noix de boeuf au vin d'Irouléguy*, *Piquillos farcis à l'axoa de veau*, and *Gaufres à l'ananas caramélisés*. 13 Rue de la Navarre, T: 05 59 28 16 05.

St-Etienne-de-Baïgorry

€ **Hôtel/Restaurant Arcé**. ■ A hotel of great charm on the banks of a small river has passed through five generations of the Arcé family. Christine is in charge of the hotel which has pretty rooms overlooking the river, and larger ones towards the mountains. Pascal waves his magic wand in the kitchen, maintaining the high standard of the meals served in the riverside restaurant or on the terrace. In season he uses fresh wild herbs, local cherries, Landes asparagus and trout from the Nive served smoked. There is also a pool. Follow the signs through the village past the church, T: 05 59 37 40 14, www.hotel-arce.com

€ **Chambres d'hôtes la Maison Jauregia**. This charming 16th-century house belonging to Daniel Hargain, built at the foot of the Iparla peaks, is full of austere character. Inside a magnificent oak staircase leads to three large rooms with simple decoration blending old and new. This is a great base for hikers and those who love the outdoors, as Daniel is also guide. No *table d'hôtes* but a restaurant nearby. T: 05 59 37 41 02, daniel.hargain@wanadoo.fr

€ **Chambres d'hôtes Château d'Etchauz**. The château (11th and 16th centuries), the oldest in Pays Basque, was built by the Viscounts of Baigorry and overlooks the village. It was sold in 1848 to Harry d'Abbadie d'Arrast, script writer to Charlie Chaplin who visited several times. Restored in the 1990s, it has 7 large and individually styled rooms. T: 05 59 37 45 58, www.chateauinfrance.net

St-Jean-Pied-de-Port

€€ **Hôtel/Restaurant Les Pyrénées**. In the town centure, the former post house has a pretty interior garden and pool, and the 20 rooms have been updated while the restaurant (one Michelin star) is one of the best. Chef Firmin Arrambide has earned a reputation for his subtle and delicate touch as well as constant and unique reinventions of Basque recipes. Among them at *Saumon frais de l'Adour à la Béarnaise* (seasonal) or *Lièvre à la royale*. T: 05 59 37 01 01, hotel.pyrenees@wanadoo.fr

€ **Hôtel/Restaurant Ramuntcho**. Cathy and André Bigot ensure that you enjoy your stay in their small, friendly hotel. The 17 rooms are simple, and some benefit from wonderful views of the Pyrenees. In the restaurant with red tablecloths you can eat good, local dishes such as *Poulet Basquaise*, local trout and cured ham, at reasonable prices (menus €12–28). 1 Rue de France, T: 05 59 37 03 91, http://perso.wanadoo.fr/hotel.ramuntcho /index.htm

€ **Chez Pecoïtz**. A Basque country house in the mountains near the Irouléguy vineyards, where hearty, family cooking is on the menu. There are also rooms available. At Aincille, southwest of St-Jean-Pied-de-Port, T: 05 59 37 11 88.

St-Pée-sur-Nivelle
€ **Le Fronton**. Jean-Baptiste Daguerre is full of new ideas and interesting combinations while maintaining the flavours of the original products.

Sare
€€ **Hôtel/Restaurant Arraya**. ■ A truly delightful hotel in a 16th-century pilgrimage hospice at the heart of the beautiful village. The building and its décor are beyond reproach. A stunning wooden staircase leads to 23 pretty rooms imbued with the fragrance of old polished wood and fresh flowers. There is a pretty restaurant and terrace with food which matches the high quality of the establishment. On the menu are such delights as *Les ravioles de Xangurro* (crab)

sur fumet d'étrilles, and *Gâteau Basque à la confiture de cerises noires servi tiède avec sa crème vanillée*. Closed in winter. T: 05 59 54 20 46, www.arraya.com

€ **Chambres d'hôtes Maison Aretxola**. On a little hill with the mountains behind and two streams, all is silent and calm here. The interior is most attractive, combining old stone and furniture with cotton fabrics and stencilled decoration and 3 rooms are available to guests. Route des Grottes, T: 05 59 54 28 33, www.aretxola.com

MARKET DAYS

Cambo-les-Bains Friday
Espelette Wednesday
Hasparren Tuesday (alternate in winter); Saturday
Mauléon Tuesday, Haute Ville; Saturday, Pl. des Allées
St-Palais Friday
St-Pée sur Nivelle Saturday
St-Jean-Pied-de-Port Monday
Urrugne Thursday May–November

FESTIVALS & EVENTS

January: *Foire aux Pottoks*, traditional Basque event around the local horse fair, Espelette
April: *Arnaga Côté Jardins*, top-quality crafts and garden fair, Cambo-les-Bains
July: *Errobiko Festibala/Festival de la Nive*, Itxassou. *Foire artisanale aux produits fermiers*, evening market, Mauléon
August: *Concours d'Irrintzina (cri Basque)*, long rallying call used in Basque mountains, *Fête de l'Espadrille*, celebration of the espadril (canvas shoe), Mauléon

THE BÉARN

The Béarn covers the eastern part of the *département* of the Pyrénées-Atlantiques, stretching from the plains of Gascony, across the fertile foothills of the Pyrenees, to culminate at the Spanish border at the Cols de Somport and Portalet. It presents a distinctive character and its traditions, language and local industries are fiercely protected. The arms of Béarn feature two gold cows, symbolic of the active pastoral life of the region where sheep and cattle are moved to the mountains in the summer during transhumance. Local products include cotton and linen textiles, espadrilles, golden Jurançon wine and the famous Basque beret, which has Béarnais origins. The main town is Pau; other centres are the towns of Oloron-Ste-Marie and Orthez and the magnificent valleys of the Aspe and Ossau. The Béarnais language is a form of Occitan, derived from Latin, the same root as Provençal or Toulousain. It remained the official language of the Béarn from the 13th century to the Revolution, and can still sometimes be heard.

HISTORY OF THE BÉARN

The Béarn was an independent province until 1589 and was wholly united with France only in 1620. Its name originates from a people called the Venarni who crossed the Pyrenees and settled near Lescar. Between the 11th and 13th centuries, local viscounts became vassals of the Aragonais kings. In 1188, Count Gaston VI of Moncade (1173–1214) established the *Droit Béarnais*, with a unique set of laws and liberties including the right to transfer a title or inheritance through female descendants. Gaston VII of Moncade (1229–90) reorganised the legal system and divided the Béarn into *vics* (districts). Forced to stand firm against the opportunist English, Gaston built fortifications and moved his capital to Orthez. Around this time the Béarnais language took over from Latin. Gaston III Fébus, Count of Foix and Viscount of the Béarn (1343–91), inherited the territory through his mother and established his capital at Pau. Gaston IV (1436–72), another warrior, took the French side, regained the territory lost to the English, and married Eléonore of Navarre. The viscounts acceded to the crown of Navarre in 1481 but in 1512 the Spanish, angered by the Béarnais' support of the French, split the territory. They kept Haute Navarre, and Basse-Navarre became part of the Béarn, bringing to Henri d'Albret (1517–55) and his descendants the title King of Navarre. Under his daughter, Jeanne d'Albret, the province wholeheartedly embraced the Protestant faith, which resulted in terrible destruction of lives and buildings, especially in 1569: Jeanne and her son, Henri III of Navarre, in La Rochelle at the head of the Protestant armies, were taken prisoner by Charles IX who ordered Terride to take the Béarn. When Henri acceded to the French throne as Henri IV in 1589 he famously declared, *'Je donne la France au Béarn'* ('I give France to the Béarn'). After Henri's death, reunification was brought about by Louis XIII.

PAU

The capital of the Béarn, Pau is a large town between the plain and the mountains, on a ridge high above the Gave de Pau, and with a pleasantly mild climate. On a clear day, there is a heady view of the Pyrenean range to the south from the famous Boulevard des Pyrénées. The town's reputation and its most prestigious monument, the Château de Pau, owe much to Gaston Fébus, who built the medieval castle in the 14th century, and Henri IV, who was born there two centuries later. Pau became very fashionable with English and American expatriates in the 19th century: they left their mark on the town in the shape of elegant villas and luxuriant gardens, rugby, and the oldest golf course in France. The Musée des Beaux-Arts was built in the 1930s to conserve one of the best collections in Aquitaine, and Pau is also proud of its gardens and rare old trees.

HISTORY OF PAU

The town derived its name from the wooden palisades or *paü* in Béarnais, erected to protect the cattle and trade routes and developed in importance around the château of Gaston Fébus when it became the administrative capital of Foix-Béarn. Pau's old churches were razed during the religious turmoil of the 16th century but following the reunification of the Béarn with France in 1620 Roman Catholicism was re-imposed on the region and a *parlement* established, with the dual role of justice and administration, while honouring Béarnais law. A period of prosperity ensued, which is reflected in the elegant buildings in the town centre. In the 18th century foreigners, particularly British, were drawn to the Pyrenees; Napoleon passed through the town in 1808, and Wellington in 1815. The latter's cavalry officers filled their time fox hunting, and in 1840 Lord Oxenden created the Pau Hunt. Gradually the fashion for Pyrénéisme combined with the promotion—by a Scotsman, Dr Alexander Taylor—of the curative properties of the gentle air made Pau a smart resort for foreign visitors. Over time the British visitors became residents, built villas set in English-style gardens, and gave a singularly Anglo-Saxon character to the urban centre, which can still be detected in the legacy of fine gardens. The foreigners also introduced mains drainage, street lighting and the first golf course, and St Andrew's is one of the few English parish churches still active in France. The Boulevard des Pyrénées was laid down and lined with elegant hotels and residences. Since 1908–14, when the Wright brothers patronised the local school of aviation, Pau has been also associated with the aeronautical industry and, after natural gas was discovered in the 1950s, Elf Petroleum based its headquarters here. The University of Pau, founded in the 1960s, now has some 15,000 students.

HENRI III OF NAVARRE, HENRI IV OF FRANCE

Statue of Henry IV in the Château de Pau.

Henri III, King of Navarre, was born in the Château de Pau on 13th December 1553 to Antoine de Bourbon and Jeanne d'Albret. Through his mother he inherited his title and his Protestant persuasion; through his father he inherited the crown of France. In 1572 Henri married Marguerite de Valois, daughter of Henri II, and narrowly escaped the St Bartholomew's Day massacre of Protestants in Paris by temporarily rejecting the doctrines of the Reformation and escaping to Nérac (*see p. 365*). Recognised by Henri III as the legitimate successor to the throne of France, he took the name Henri IV in 1589, then had to conquer his kingdom, winning battles at Arques (1589) and at Ivry (1590).

He was forced to renounce his Protestant beliefs again in 1593—he is famously quoted as saying *'Paris vaut bien une messe'* ('Paris is well worth a Mass')—and made his entry into the capital in 1594. Although Henri spent very little time in Pau he is referred to locally as *'Noste Gran Henric'*, and generally as the *Vert Galant* (Old Charmer). Despite the religious problems of his reign and his reputation with the ladies, he is remembered as a good and popular king. He was a man of his time, and was also courageous, diplomatic and tolerant. By the Edict of Nantes (1598) he ended the Wars of Religion that had raged since 1562, and established interior religious stability. By the Peace of Vervins (1598) he made peace outside the kingdom. He undertook the work of restoring royal authority, reorganising France and improving communications helped by the Protestants, Sully and de Serres, and the Catholics, d'Ossat and Jeannin. Finances were rapidly put in order, agriculture was encouraged, and the cloth and silk industries were revived. The King extended the eastern boundary of France by forcing the Duke of Savoy to make over some of his territories (1601) and Quebec was founded (1608). Henri IV united his fiefdoms with the Crown of France (1607), with the exception of Basse-Navarre and the Béarn (incorporated in 1620). He was assassinated by Ravaillac in 1610. His son, from his second marriage to Marie de Médicis in 1600, was Louis XIII.

EXPLORING PAU

A visit to Pau is determined by the Boulevard des Pyrénées, which stretches 1800m from the château at the west (the older section, constructed in the 1850s) to Parc Beaumont at the east (completed by 1900). Almost in the middle is Place Royal, tree-lined and graced with a statue of Henri IV (1843) by Raggi, erected on the instructions of Louis-Philippe to replace an effigy of Louis XIV destroyed at the Revolution. North of Place Royal is the tourist office. Rue Henri IV and its extension, Rue Louis-Barthou, are lined with smart boutiques. At the western extremity of Boulevard des Pyrénées is the Château de Pau, set in an ancient park with beautiful trees.

Château de Pau
Guided tours (in French), mid-June–mid-Sept 9.30–12.15 & 1.30–5.45; April–mid-June, mid-Sept–Dec, 9.30–11.45 & 2–5; Nov–March 9.30–11.45 & 2–4; T: 05 59 82 38 19.
The château, a combination of medieval citadel and Renaissance palace, with 19th-century alterations during the Restoration and Second Empire, stands defiantly above the Gave de Pau. It contains a fine collection of furniture, paintings and tapestries and three rooms are designed as a journey through French history of the 16th and 17th centuries.

History of the château
A 12th-century fort with three towers standing guard over the valley was transformed by Gaston III Fébus into one of the most important citadels protecting his territories. Between 1372 and 1379 he added the great brick *donjon carré* (33m high), a watch-tower (the Tour de la Monnaie), and raised the existing main wing by a storey. Further changes had been made by the mid-15th century but, more importantly, after the marriage of Henri d'Albret to Marguerite d'Angoulême in 1527, the latest influences from the Loire Valley were introduced, and between 1529 and 1535 the medieval castle was transformed into a Renaissance palace with large mullioned windows and a grand staircase with straight flights, a step ahead of the Louvre.

The birth in Pau in 1553 of the future Henri IV (*see box on p. 485*), first of the Bourbon dynasty, secured the reputation of the château although Henri returned rarely to Pau and made no alterations to the building. His last visit was in 1587. His sister, Catherine de Bourbon, lived here until 1592. When the Béarn returned to the French crown, the château was used as a prison or barracks and fell into neglect. With the return of the Bourbons after the Revolution an attempt at consolidation was made and the great restorer, Louis-Philippe (King of the French, 1830–48), who saw some political advantage in resurrecting Henri's IV's birthplace, employed Lefranc, a pupil of Fontaine who created the Empire style. The Tour Louis-Philippe was erected to match and balance the existing Tour Mazères, creating the classic view of the Château de Pau from the west. The décor of the royal apartments is a unique example of the period 1838–48. From c. 1853, Second Empire craftsmen completed Louis-Philippe's work for Napoleon III and Eugénie, for whom Pau was a convenient halt on the way south, in predominantly Renaissance and neo-Gothic styles. The 14th-century tower to the east was renovated, the north wing made habitable, and the old buildings to the east were demolished and replaced in 1862 by a neo-Renaissance portico, along with a high tower imitating the 15th-century buildings of the north wing. Between 1864 and 1872, under the direction of Auguste Lafollye considerable work was carried out on the exterior of the south wing and the interior decoration of the chapel. He also extended the grand staircase and made a detailed study of the existing castle, published in 1882. The statue in Pyrenean marble of Gaston Fébus in the costume of a bear hunter, by Henri de Triqueti, was placed in the park facing the Pyrenees. To the west of the chateau, towards the Pyrenees, are garden terraces and the park.

Visiting the chateau

The château stands on a *motte* which was consolidated with a stone *glacis* in the 14th century, restored in the 19th. The entrance is on the right of the courtyard through the neo-Renaissance portico. Gaston Fébus's massive brick tower is to the left, and next to it is access to the south terrace. The visit includes rooms in the west and south of the château on three floors. In the 16th-century rib-vaulted kitchen is a model of the pre-16th-century château. The **Salle aux Cent Couverts** contains an immense oak table large enough to seat 100, dating from the time of Louis-Philippe (1841), and the statue of Henri IV (1605) wearing the orders of Saint-Michel and Saint-Esprit, in Carrara marble by Pierre de Franqueville. Louis XIII signed the Act of Union (Edict de l'Union) of Béarn and Navarre and supremacy of the Catholic Faith in this room on 20th October 1620. The Salle aux Cent Couverts leads to the grand staircase (1528–35), with a coffered ceiling, decorated with Henri and Marguerite's intertwined initials, but extended and altered in the 19th century.

On the first floor of the south wing is a sequence of reception rooms from the 14th century, which were panelled and decorated at the time of Louis-Philippe. The **Salon de Famille**, originally Jeanne d'Albret's bedroom and possibly the true birthplace of Henri IV, was later decorated entirely in the style of Napoleon III. In the west wing are the more intimate rooms of the private Appartements de l'Empereur et de l'Impératrice, including the Appartement de l'Impératrice Eugénie with 15th-century fireplace and doorway.

The **Chambre du Roi**, Henri IV's birthplace, is on the second floor, its décor dating from 1845–47. The focus of attention here is the tortoiseshell cradle. Such a shell was inventoried in the *cabinet de curiosités* of Pau and Nérac belonging to the Albrets in 1561–62. In 1582 a new shell had been acquired and by the 17th century, ambiguous references were made to the cradle of Henri IV, although nothing points to it being more than a simple wooden one. Gradually, the two objects merged into one myth. By the 18th century the shell had acquired the status of relic and attracted 'pilgrims'; its veneration developed into the custom of carrying the tortoiseshell in procession through the town. This led to its association with the Béarnaise identity and it became the centrepiece for elaborate festivities in the 18th century, when Henri IV was definitely in vogue. By 1793 attitudes had changed and the precious shell was burned or, so the story goes, replaced by another in the nick of time. From 1822 the tortoiseshell cradle was presented in a setting of lances, banners and a white-plumed helmet. Also on this floor are the apartment where Abd al-Qadir was imprisoned in 1848 after France's victory over Algeria, and the Salle des Peintures.

The magnificent tapestries, displayed throughout the apartments, were chosen by Louis-Philippe from the royal reserves. They include some 100 hangings from 10 series woven at the Gobelins manufactory in Paris and in Brussels between the 16th and 18th centuries. The styles and iconography vary widely, although they represent predominantly mythological scenes (*Story of Psyche*, *Marriage of Flora and Zephyr*, *Arabesque Months*), as well as aristocratic activities such as *Maximilian's Hunts* (Gobelins, 1685, the remainder in the Louvre), after designs by Bernard van Orley, or outdoor scenes (*Child Gardeners*).

Among the wide range of furniture and rare objects from the 16th–19th centuries throughout the apartments are a superb Renaissance bed (1562), and 18th-century copies of Japanese vases. Memorabilia includes Henri IV's jewel case (1607), in black walnut and mother of pearl, and a beautiful inlaid backgammon board (c. 1600).

Paintings, engravings, sculptures and decorated porcelain celebrate good King Henri, such as Bosio's well-known statue of *Henri as a Child* (1822) and Sèvres vases with scenes of his reign; paintings include the *Adoration of Henri IV's Cradle by the Inhabitants of the Ossau Valley* by H.P. Poublan and *The Birth of Henri IV* (1827) by E. Devéria. Ingres' *Don Pedro of Toledo kissing the Sword of Henri IV* is one of four versions painted 1814–21. Also in the collection is a magnificent portrait of Henri's father, Antoine de Bourbon (1557) from the studio of François Clouet.

To the Musée des Beaux Arts via the old town

The house opposite the château belonged to Duc de Sully, Maximilien de Béthune (1560–1641), Henri IV's Protestant Superintendent of Finances. Rue du Château leads into Rue du Maréchal-Joffre, formerly the Grande Rue, lined with 17th- and 18th-century mansions. The medieval town was surrounded by walls, extending from the level of the arcaded Place Reine-Marguerite, an ancient square, arcaded on one side and site of markets and the scaffold in the Middle Ages, to the present Rue du Maréchal Foch. From the square, the narrow Rue René Fournets brings you into the Quartier du Hédas, built over a stream which became a covered drain in the 19th century. This is the oldest area of the town and in the Middle Ages was the centre of a variety of activities which depended on water from the stream, such as washing and tanning.

To the east of Rue Fournets, on Rue Tran, is the *Musée Bernadotte* (*open 10–12 & 2–6, closed Mon; T: 05 59 27 48 42*), birthplace in 1763 of the cooper's son, Jean Baptiste Jules, who joined the revolutionary army, became Maréchal de France under Napoleon, and was elected heir to the Swedish throne in 1810. As Charles XIV, he was the first of the present Swedish dynasty. Follow the street to Place des Sept-Cantons, and turn left onto Rue Montpensier, where there are reminders of the Englishness of Pau in the 19th century, including the church of St Andrew in Rue Planté. Return to Rue Joffre, cross Place G.-Clemenceau, and follow Rue Foch to Rue Mathieu-Lalanne on the right, and the fine arts museum.

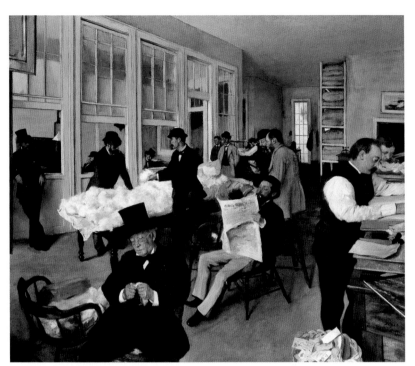

Edgar Degas: *A Cotton Exchange in New Orleans* (1873)

Musée des Beaux-Arts

Open 10–12 & 2–6, closed Tues; Rue Mathieu Lalanne, T: 05 59 27 33 02, www.musee.ville-pau.fr

This important collection consists mainly of paintings, a varied but rich selection of predominantly 17th–18th-century Spanish, Italian and Northern European works, and French works with a local emphasis from the 19th–early 20th centuries. Inaugurated in 1864, with 25 paintings, the museum was expanded by the La Caze donation and helped by a financial bequest from textile magnate Emile Noulibos (d. 1875). It moved into the present building in 1931, although forced to close between 1942 and 1953.

A Cotton Exchange in New Orleans (1873; *pictured above*) was painted by Edgar Degas during a visit with his brother to the family business in New Orleans. In the painting, Degas' brother is shown engrossed in the *Daily Picayune*, which announced the liquidation of the family company that year. The palette is subtle and limited to the contrast of white cotton, newspaper and sleeves with black business suits. The space is defined by diagonals and uses the abrupt cut-off point which is a characteristic of Degas' style. The painter planned to sell the work to a Lancashire cotton magnate, but instead it ended up in Pau in 1876, and was purchased by the museum with money from the Noulibos bequest. This was the first work by Degas to enter a museum during his lifetime.

Spanish, Italian and North European collections: Among the Spanish works are 15th-century religious paintings from Aragon, one of several versions of *St Francis receiving the Stigmata* (c. 1595) by El Greco, and a moving painting of *St Jerome* (1633) by José de Ribera. Italian paintings include works by Ghislandi (Fra Galgario), Piazzetta and Giuseppe Ricci, whose *At the Station* (c. 1890) is a beautifully observed yet puzzling scene in the waiting room of a maritime station. There are works from Northern Europe by Jan Brueghel the Elder, Jacob Jordaens, and two by Rubens. Among the paintings from Holland is Nicolas Berchem's *Return of Tobias* (1670–80); and English works include portraits by George Romney and Sir David Wilkie. There is the mandatory landscape by Corot, *Fontainebleau, the Gorges d'Apremont* (1834).

French collection: The majority of the French works are from the 19th and 20th centuries including several examples of

Orientalism, by Benouville, Guillaumet, Cormon and others. The Belle Epoque is represented by Léon Bonnat (*see p. 450*) with a portrait of *Madame Maurice Pascale and her Dog, Tiny* (1905), Ernest Bordes, Henri Zo among others. There are a number of landscapes by local artists and a Turneresque watercolour, *Le Cirque de Gavarnie* (1882), Gustave Doré. There is a also a good group of works by painters on the peripheries of Impressionism and Fauvism, such as Carolus-Duran; a Symbolist work by Fantin-Latour, *Dances* (1891); Guillaumin's *Creuse Landscape* (c. 1900), a Fauve-influenced landscape; and two by the Bordelais painter, André Lhote, including *14th July, Avignon* (1923); Albert Marquet; Berthe Morisot's *Pasie Sewing* (1881), a delicate painting of soft greens and violets; and Jean-François Raffaelli. There are also works by Kees van Dongen and Edouard Vuillard, a pastel, *Demolition, Rue de Calais* (1927); and a small collection of later 20th-century works.

Around the museum

Close to the museum, the Triangle is a popular café area. Southeast of the museum, at the eastern end of Boulevard des Pyrénées, is Parc Beaumont, 10 hectares of garden sold to the city by the celebrated writer Countess Anna de Noailles (1876–1933) and designed by Henri Martinet in 1898 in the English horticultural tradition with bandstand and lake. Some of the original trees have survived more than a century, and a new feature is the Anna de Noailles trail leading to the rose garden. The park surrounds the Palais Beaumont (1900), which began life as the Belle-Epoque Winter Palace and was recreated as casino in 1930 with a Neoclassical façade and grand hall. Early in the 21st century it was transformed again by François Lombard, adding winter gardens, conference centre and pool in front of the south façade. The light, glazed building with tremendous views has a pleasant restaurant. Opposite the casino is the former Jesuit College, established during the Counter-Reformation in 1620.

THE JURANÇON

The Jurançon is the area west of Pau, between the Gaves de Pau, d'Ossau and d'Oloron. It is famous for its white wines, favourite of Henri IV. The landscape consists of small narrow valleys and hills with panoramas of the Pyrenees, and large 17th–18th-century Béarnais farmhouses, sober but dignified, with marble lintels, roofs covered in flat tiles and decorated with a double *génoise* moulding under the eaves.

WINES OF THE JURANÇON

The vineyards cover some 1,000 hectares over about 40km along the steep slopes of the Gave de Pau, facing the Pyrenees. The vines thrive in pebbly ground and a mild climate that combines rain carried from the west and the sunshine of the south. The vineyards are mainly small and sometimes perilously steep, planted at an average of 300m above sea-level to avoid spring frosts. The delicious white wines, dry and *moelleux*, are produced from regional grape varieties, Gros Manseng, Petit Manseng, and small amounts of Courbu, Camaralet and Lauzet. The Maison des Vins in the Commanderie du Jurançon, Lacommande (*open mid-June–mid-Sept 10–12 & 3–7, Sun 3–7; remainder of the year, Wed–Sun, 2–6; closed Sun Jan–March; T: 05 59 82 70 30, www.vins-jurancon.fr*), promotes wine from a selection of independent producers in the region and offers tastings. Tastings also at Cave des Producteurs de Jurancon, 53 Av. Henry IV, Gan (*open by appointment, 8-12 & 1.30–7 and Sun in July and Aug; T: 05 59 21 67 03*).

Monein

The thriving town of Monein, set in a fertile plain, flourished from the mid-15th to the 17th centuries and was resolutely Calvinist during the Reformation. The **Church of St-Girons** (1464–1530) is the largest of the period in the Béarn and is famous for its roof timbers. The tall tower (40m), like a land-locked lighthouse, is supported by massive angle buttresses and a stair-tower. The 60m-long church is constructed in stone, pebble and brick and the steep roof is covered in slate which replaced the original wooden shingles in 1964. Although powerful, it was never a fortified church and owes its scale to the wealth of the town.

Inside the porch is the surprisingly ornate Renaissance entrance to the nave. The double arch is decorated with foliage and angels carrying the instruments of the Passion, and the jambs are also carved. To the right is the Flamboyant door leading to the belfry and roof space. Inside, the nave has simple vaulting, and one aisle half its width and the same height on the north. The window tracery is Flamboyant, the latest glass installed in the 16th century, and the apse six-sided. A restoration begun in 1999 uncovered painted décor of *fleur de lis*, which has been reproduced. Behind the main altar is an early 18th-century Counter-Reformation retable made in the town, with the symbol of the four Evangelists. The church was Protestant for 60 years but was not damaged, simply cleared of its ornament.

A climb to the roof is presented as a *son-et-lumière* show (*guided visits July–Aug at 11, 3, 4 and 5; Sun and holidays at 4 and 5; Sept–June, Sun–Fri at 4 and 5; T: 05 59 21 29 28*). This magnificent structure (50m long, 18m high, 20m wide) used 1,000 hearts of oak and took three years to assemble. The purpose of the huge tower is to protect and support the *charpente* with its two parts, one covering the nave and the other the north aisle.

THE BÉARN DES GAVES

Closely linked with the history of the Béarn are the old capitals of Lescar and Orthez, the cathedral of Lescar and the castles built along the Gaves de Pau and Oloron to defend the Béarn.

LESCAR

Lescar, just west of Pau, is a pleasant residential town with a magnificent 12th-century cathedral. At the foot of the escarpment dominating the Gave de Pau was the site of ancient *Beneharnum*, a Gallo-Roman *oppidum* and, from 506, the seat of a diocese. Virtually wiped out by the Normans in 840, it re-emerged on the hill in the 10th century as Lescar and in 1125 the cathedral was begun on the site of a monastery. Lescar became one of the main religious centres of the Béarn, containing the relics of St Galactoire, the first bishop, and the mausoleum of the Kings of Navarre.

Cathedral of Ste-Marie
Open to visitors; guided visits Friday at 3pm, Saturday at 2pm; T: 05 59 81 15 98
Despite a turbulent history and unfortunate restoration in the 19th century, the cathedral remains a magnificent building. It was begun by Bishop Guido (Guy de Lons) in 1125, damaged by fire in the 14th century, and the furnishings were wrecked in 1563 on the orders of Jeanne d'Albret, after which it became a Protestant church. Further destruction ensued in 1569 when Huguenot troops under Montgomery ransacked the town and cathedral. When the Catholics returned in 1620, essential rebuilding of the vaults was carried out. At the Revolution the cathedral became a Temple of Reason. With the Concordat in 1802, Lescar lost its status as cathedral and from 1843 parts of it were demolished or disappeared under cement and plaster.

The south wall reveals the diverse stages of construction: evidence includes walled-up Romanesque doorways and Gothic windows. Set in a stone frame near the south door is the tombstone of the founder, Bishop Guido, above an inscription recording that it was placed here by Bishop Jean de Salettes in 1620. The east end—best viewed from the cemetery—is Romanesque and highly decorated with carved corbels and billet moulding, some restored. The neo-Romanesque west end dates from the 17th century.

The interior

The interior is light and spacious, with a four-bay barrel-vaulted nave supported by mighty pillars, and in the aisles are transverse barrel vaults abutting the nave. The crossing was rebuilt in the 17th century and the 12th-century apse and side chapels have semi-domes. There are some good 12th-century storiated capitals (some may be copies). In the south aisle and around the transept they include *Adam and Eve*, *Cain and Abel*, and scenes from the *Life of Daniel*, the *Sacrifice of Abraham* and *Herod's Feast*. There is also the *Birth of Christ*, the *Flight into Egypt*, and a *Christ in Majesty* in the apse. On the floor of the apse is an unusual mosaic (12th century, discovered and restored in the 19th century) depicting a hunt, with lions and wild boar as well as birds and a donkey, which pursue or are being pursued by two huntsmen, each with an oliphant (ivory horn). One is dressed in a 12th-century tunic and the other, described as Moorish, seems to have one good leg while the other is a wooden peg. The Latin inscription records that Bishop Guido commissioned the work. The site of the former sepulchre of the Kings of Navarre, whose remains were discovered in 1929, is indicated by a bronze plaque before the altar. In the crossing are some 17th-century wooden stalls with low-relief carvings of Christ, Apostles, the Virgin and local saints. The large gilded altarpiece in the north aisle and the organ case are both 18th-century.

ORTHEZ

The Gave de Pau flows northwest, through the historic market town of Orthez. The capital of the Béarn for 200 years, its more recent claim to fame is the Orthez-Pau basketball team, and its best monuments are the 13th-century fortified bridge and the Tour Moncade.

HISTORY OF ORTHEZ

The town developed on a major crossroads where a bridge already existed and became an important halt for pilgrims on the Vézelay–Santiago road in the 12th century. Gaston VII of Moncade built a fortified stone bridge, the church and the château and made Orthez his capital. Gaston Fébus altered the bridge and gave the town its motto *'tourqey si gaouses'*, loosely translated as 'take us if you dare'. In the 16th century Orthez was the main Protestant town in the region and suffered the consequences in 1569 during the Wars of Religion when the Protestants threw the Catholic priests into the *gave* from the bridge. Orthez then settled down to a period of prosperity when the Protestant Academy, established in the former Jacobin Convent, was raised to the status of university in 1583, but with the re-establishment of the Catholic Church and the final absorption of the Béarn into France in 1620, its moment of glory was over. In 1814 Wellington won a victory over the Napoleonic army of General Soult here.

Exploring Orthez

The Tourist Office is in the Maison de Jeanne d'Albret, a pretty building (15th–17th centuries) with mullioned windows and stair-tower. Behind it are a 17th-century *colombier* (dovecote) on tall, stilt-like columns typical of the region, and a small formal garden. On the second floor of the house, the Musée du Protestantisme (*open 10–12 & 2–6, closed Sun and holidays; T: 05 59 69 14 03*), gives a fascinating account of Protestant life in the Béarn and Pays d'Adour in the 18th and 19th centuries with the aid of documents, ecclesiastical furnishings and engravings.

The Maison is situated between the *bourg vieux*, which developed in the 12th century near the bridge, and the *bourg neuf*, which dates from the Renaissance. From Rue Bourg-Vieux (its extension is Rue de l'Horloge), lined mainly by 18th-century houses with large entrances and sombre façades masking courtyards, turn right into Rue des Aiguilletiers, which runs parallel with the *gave* and the railway line. In front is the tower of the **Pont-Vieux**, one of the few surviving bridges with medieval defences. Built in the 13th century, probably with two towers and removable wooden sections at each end, it was altered in the 14th century. The 2m-high parapets were damaged in 1814 when the French were retreating before Wellington, and the tower was restored in the 19th century by Boeswillwald. Pilgrims used to make a halt on the route to Santiago on the other side of the bridge at the Hospice St-Loup.

Near the Pont-Vieux are old houses characteristic of the region with steep, tiled roofs; *génoise* mouldings are found on the richer houses. Facing the *gave* at 22 Rue des Aiguilletiers is the workshop of M. Guy Pendanx, one of the champion metalworkers of France; and on the corner is a little tower where the ladies sat to watch the world go by. Turning right, takes you past the Salle de la Moutète, 'temple' to the famous basketball team, and the covered market. Opposite, in Rue Lasserre, is the Maison Badcave, a heavily restored 15th–17th-century house, part timber-framed, with wattle and daub infill, steep roof, dormers and a balcony.

Rue de la Moutète brings you to the **Church of St-Pierre**, which was part of the defence system of the town outside the walls. It was begun towards the end of the 13th century, completed about a century later, and turned over to the Protestants after the Wars of Religion. There were several campaigns of rebuilding and the neo-Gothic belfry and porch, which protects the original entrance, are 19th century. The 14th-century nave is narrower and higher than the apse and transepts, the chancel is 13th-century Gothic, and the brick vaults have carved bosses. The rose window and décor are also 19th century. Above the door is a work by Bonnat, the *Beheading of St Denis*.

From Place Marcadieu follow Chemin Gaston-Fébus, along the line of the town wall which was also the outer defence of the château, towards Château Moncade (*open May–Sept; check times at Tourist Office, T: 05 59 69 37 50*). To the left, where the road bends to meet Rue Moncade, are vines planted in 1991 to commemorate the death of Gaston Fébus 600 years earlier. All that remains of his headquarters is the truncated tower, fixed at 33m, with false crenellations, and the outline of the *corps de logis*. There is an exhibition in the tower and after the climb up a narrow spiral staircase, the views from the top are rewarding.

SALIES-DE-BÉARN

Salies-de-Béarn is a picturesque village and spa on the Saleys River whose existence depends on salt deposits. The salt spring here was already exploited during the Bronze Age and the town grew around the spring, in the present Place du Bayaà. It is commemorated by a fountain with a wild boar (1927), referring to the supposed discovery of the spring by wounded quarry, but the pool was covered in 1867. By 1587 a corporation had been established and tight regulations laid down for the collection of salt water, allowing each family who lived in the town the right to collect a certain volume in a certain length of time. Salt is essential for the production of *jambon de Bayonne* and during the second weekend in September this is re-enacted at the Fête du Sel. The locals had the right to sell salt in the Béarn and Bigorre along the old salt routes, but when the 16th-century exemption from salt tax ended, the town exploited the curative properties of the mineral instead. By the 19th century, salt-water baths were considered to cure a variety of problems. The modern spa offers general fitness programmes lasting for just an hour to a week. The Musée des Arts et Traditions Béarnais (*open mid-May–mid-Oct 3–6, closed Sun, Mon; T: 05 59 38 00 33*) is in a 16th-century house on Place du Bayaà. The Musée du Sel in Rue des Puits Salants (*hours as above*) is a small museum of the history of salt extraction. In the wall outside is a reconstruction of a *coulédé*, where the salt water was poured and stored; there is a genuine example at 8 Rue Pont Mayou. The houses on stilts in the river near Pont de la Lune are a particular feature of Salies.

SAUVETERRE-DE-BÉARN & ENVIRONS

This *sauveté* was founded by the Bishops of Dax and Oloron in 1071. In the 12th century, when Orthez, Salies-de-Béarn and Sauveterre were taken from the control of the Viscounts of Dax and became part of the Béarn, and Gascony passed to the English, the strategic importance of this site was obvious. Gaston VII of Moncade fortified Sauveterre, and Gaston Fébus completed the defences in the 14th century to make it one of the most important towns in the region during the Middle Ages, at the centre of the Kingdom of Béarn-Navarre. This came to an end with the loss of the Haute Navarre, and the increased importance of Navarrenx (*see below, p. 496*).

Exploring Sauveterre-de-Béarn

Place Royale (18th century) and the elegant Hôtel de Ville (16th century) that now houses the Tourist Office were outside the town walls. The old east gate, Porte de Miqueu, was at the start of Rue St-André, on the pilgrimage road; adjacent is the Esplanade, high above the valley. The Romanesque **Church of St-André** has a massive fortified belfry over the crossing which was part of the town defences. Built at a period of transition (late-12th /early-13th century), the layout is indeed Romanesque with aisles, transept and apses covered in half-domes, whereas the west door and the vaults of the nave and aisles are Gothic. Major work was carried out c. 1869. The small north door is simply adorned with a chrism but the later west doorway, heavily restored, has an arrangement similar to Oloron (*see p. 500*), with twin sub-tympana spanned by an arch, the difference being the central pendant boss instead of a trumeau. It is decorated with Christ in a mandorla and the symbols of the Evangelists, the sun and the moon, two angels squeezed in at the extremities and more angels in the voussoirs. The soaring interior is surprising, and in the east are some 12th-century capitals of note including a *Nativity* on the eastern respond of the north aisle, and on the northeast crossing, Gluttony and Slander.

West of the church is the shell of Gaston of Moncade's 33m-high Tour Montréal, sheer with the cliff face. Descend the steps from here to the foot of the tower and follow the banks of the *gave*, past some of the six fountains of Sauveterre, the arcades of the Maison du Sénéchal de l'Hôpital and the chapel of St-Joan. The picturesque half-bridge, the Pont Fortifié, also known as Pont de la Légende, dates from the time of the two Gastons and was the entry to and exit from the Kingdom of Navarre. It originally had a wooden drawbridge, allowing access to the Île de la Glère, and the isolated pier dates from 1732 when an attempt was made to lengthen it. Attached to the bridge is a famous local legend: in 1170, Sancie, the wife of Gaston V, was suspected of causing the death of her deformed baby and was thrown into the river, but survived,proving she was innocent. A footbridge further west crosses to the island.

Domaine de Laàs

Open July-Aug 10–7; May–June, Sept–Oct, 10–12 & 2–7, closed Tues; T: 05 59 38 91 53. East of Sauveterre (D936/D27) is this 17th-century château set in a 12 hectare park. It contains a superb collection of furniture, tapestries and paintings brought together by Louis Serbat, former President of the French National Society of Antiquaries, who purchased the property in 1946. There is a Flemish slant to the paintings, but also works by Fragonard and Vigée-Lebrun (*see p. 603*). The park and gardens, which can be visited, overlook the Gave d'Oloron.

Navarrenx

Navarrenx played a major role in the history of the Béarn. This small *bastide* overlooking the Gave d'Oloron was founded in 1316 but was not fortified until the 16th century as part of Henri II d'Albret's ambition to reconquer the Spanish part of Navarre, including Pamplona, following the reduction of his territory to a small corner north of the Pyrenees. The fort, virtually the first of its kind in France, was designed by an Italian engineer, Fabrici Siciliano, and built 1538–47 with forward angle bastions, a century before Vauban's career was launched (*see p. 67*). The efficacy of the structure was tested, not against the Spanish but the French, in 1569 during the Wars of Religion. It held out as a safe place for Protestants for two months against a Catholic siege led by Terride, followed by a harrowing massacre of the defendants. The town fell gradually into decline but has been carefully restored.

From the bridge on the south (13th century, enlarged 18th/19th century), enter through the well-preserved Porte St-Antoine, protected by a fine *echauguette* and a bastion called La Cloche. This leads to an open square surrounded by the severe garrison accommodation, where a plaque publicises the amorous adventure of Franz Liszt and Caroline de Saint-Cricq at Navarrenx. A flight of steps leads up to the ramparts and ends at a complex of defensive structures with underground galleries. The walls to the east were demolished for the Oloron road, but on the north side much survives. The Gothic Church of St-Germain dates from 1551–62 and the 19th century, and la Fontaine du Siège was restored in 1989. In the old Arsenal is an exposition of the history of the bastide, *Navarrenx à travers les siècles*. Recently the first fully French cigar arrived on the market at the Comptoir du Tabac des Gaves et de l'Adour in Navarrenx. Robusto cigar production is in the barracks of 1537 at the heart of the village.

Gurs

Between Navarrenx and l'Hôpital St-Blaise, at Gurs, is the grim reminder of the largest internment camp (*T: 05 59 39 98 00*) in the south of France, through which 18,500 people—mainly Spanish Republicans, then German and foreign Jews—passed between 1939 and 1944. It was built in 42 days in 1939 and it is marked with a monument by an Israeli artist, Dani Karavan.

L'Hôpital St-Blaise

Audio guide and light show April–Nov 10–7; T: 05 59 66 11 12.

All that remains of L'Hôpital St-Blaise, the commandery established on the pilgrimage route by the Knights of Malta, is the remarkable little church which has undergone a 10-year restoration. Squat and rustic, in the form of a Greek cross, a central octagonal belfry was added later; the roof is of wooden shingle. Despite its simplicity, the architecture combines severe 12th-century Romanesque with exuberant Hispano-Mauresque. The west door has been recarved, and on the tympanum is Christ in a mandorla surrounded by the symbols of the four Evangelists. Inside is very simple, the four naves covered by slightly pointed vaults and enhanced by the restoration and lighting and a few Baroque additions. The most exciting feature is the eight-pointed star vault of the cupola, created by intersecting ribs springing from corbels and supported by squinches, reminiscent of the cupola at Ste-Croix in Oloron. Other Moorish touches are the narrow plate-tracery windows decorated with simple shapes.

OLORON-STE-MARIE

Standing in the foothills of the Pyrenees, where the Gave d'Aspe and the Gave d'Ossau meet, Oloron-Ste-Marie was formerly a rather sombre town but is now looking much more cheerful, with fresh paint and flowers. The rearing of sheep and cattle (*les Blonds des Pyrénées*) forms an important part of the local economy, as do the linen and cotton industries, which originated in the production of cloth to protect working oxen from heat and insects.

HISTORY OF OLORON-STE-MARIE

The present town was built on the site of an Iberian, then a Roman settlement, *Iluro*. It was destroyed in the 9th century but revived at the end of the 11th century by Centulle V, Viscount of Béarn and Count of Bigorre, who granted a charter of privileges establishing a staging-post on the pilgrimage route to Spain. Two distinct areas evolved: a fortified town on the cliff between the two *gaves*; and the episcopal city around the cathedral to the west. Only in 1858 were the two reunited as Oloron-Ste-Marie. Today the three historic quarters of the town are equipped with markers which give information to visitors on the important sites, in four languages, and there is also a children's version. The information markers are activated by a bracelet available at the Tourist Office. The weaving of traditional fabrics can be seen at Tissages Lartigue, Avenue Georges Messier (*Tues 10.30–12, Thurs 2–4; T: 05 59 39 50 11*).

EXPLORING OLORON

The Tourist Office of the Piémont Oloronais is on the first floor of the Villa Bourdeu, a fine 19th-century building at the heart of the town and an attraction in itself. Conceived as if it were a station concourse of c.1900, it leads visitors through a virtual voyage of discovery of the Piedmont Oloronais. On the ground a giant map indicates the different areas: Oloron Sainte-Marie and the neighbouring villages, the Barétous Valley, the Aspe Valley and the Tunnel du Somport into Spain, and the Ossau Valley with the peaks and lakes and the Le Petit Train d'Artouste (*see p. 505*).

From Place de la Résistance, the market place with the Fontaine Henri (19th century), cross Place A.-Gabe, leaving the 19th-century church of Notre-Dame behind you. After Pont Ste-Claire spanning the Gave d'Ossau, turn left into Rue de la Filature—its name a reference to spinning—through an archway and climb up the winding Rue des Chevaux to the Biscondau and a view of the ramparts. Place St-Pierre is surrounded by 17th–18th-century houses and the 18th-century church of St-Pierre, now deconsecrated. Rue Centulle leads on up to the top of the Ville Haut, or Old Town, built on the ancient *oppidum* and gathered around the Romanesque church of Ste-Croix, the oldest monument in Oloron.

Eglise de Sainte-Croix
Open 8–8.
The church stands on the site of a 6th-century sanctuary dedicated to the first bishop, Gratus, which was destroyed by the Normans in the 9th century. Reputedly the first stone of the present building was laid in 1070 by Bishop Amat as a centre of worship for the new town. The belfry was added later, and is in Gothic style. Under the orders of Jeanne d'Albret, Ste-Croix became a Protestant church between 1569 and

1621. In 1640 the east end was damaged when the château to the east, containing explosives, blew up. Although listed as a historic monument in 1841, Boeswillwald considered it hardly worth saving and the responsibility fell to Abbot Menjoulet. He saved the church in the 1850s, but also added an extension to the west with a statue of the Virgin. In 1960, the 19th-century porch was demolished, the statue placed in front of the cemetery, and the west front returned to its primitive state. The exterior is impressive and austere with a massive off-centre belfry in Gothic style, a tall cupola, heavily restored apse, and rustic west front. The Romanesque south door has marble columns and pillars supporting a suite of six round arches and two badly damaged capitals representing *Damnation*, a woman attacked by griffins, on the left, and opposite, *Life Eternal*, a dove and chalice.

The interior
The nave vaults are supported by cruciform pillars on decorated plinths, and capitals with flat palm-leaf or ball-flower carvings although on the south are atlantes. The most unexpected structure in the building is the cupola, an 18m-wide octagon supported on a round drum with four false pendentives, painted in *trompe-l'oeil* to look like scallop shells. The arches intersect to create a Moorish eight-pointed star similar to, although older than, the cupola of the Hôpital St-Blaise (*see p. 497*) and following the pattern of those in the mosque in Cordoba, Spain. Significantly the Béarn came under the control of Aragon in the late 11th century. The Romanesque capitals are more ornate towards the east end. On the high arches of the chancel, though difficult to see, are the *Adoration of the Magi*; the *Baptism of Christ*, *St John the Baptist in Prison*, *Herod's Feast* with Salome performing acrobatic feats, and the *Temptation in the Desert*, with Christ richly dressed and the demon depicted twice. A console in the south chapel carries a curious representation of the Trinity as a head in triplicate. The smaller capitals of the blind arcades in the apse are easier to see; they show *Adam and Eve*, *Cain and Abel* and the *Sacrifice of Isaac*.

Towards the cathedral
In Rue Dalmais are two monuments: the 13th-century **Tour de Grède**, one of the major structures in the Quartier Ste-Croix.once played an important defensive role but was turned it into a habitable property in the 14th century, including opening windows and doors. Still inhabited in the first half of the 20th century, it has been entirely restored and offers marvellous views of the Pyrenean mountain chain. The **Maison du Patrimoine** (*open July–Sept 10–12.30 & 3–7, closed Mon*) is a small museum of local history housed in the gracious 17th-century Maison Marque which has conserved the fine original staircase, chestnut panelling and mullioned windows. As well as local archaeology and ethnography, there is documentation regarding the internment camp at Gurs (*see p. 497*). There is also a medieval garden of medicinal plants, some claiming undreamed of cures.

From Place Manjoulet to the west of the church, next to the cemetery, you reach the Promenade Bellevue with a view over the town and the *gave*. Steps lead down to Rue

L.-Barthou, an attractive shopping street, and a left turn over the bridge spanning the Gave d'Aspe leads to Place de Jaca from which is a view towards the Pyrenees. A short detour left down Rue Adoue, the road to Spain built in 1751, brings you to a small bridge, Pont de Forbeig. From Place de Jaca, Rue de Révol leads to the cathedral.

Cathedral of Ste-Marie

Open 8–8.

The Cathedral of Ste-Marie was built at the time of Gaston IV and Bishop Roger de Sentis between 1102 and c. 1150 but was damaged over the centuries, c. 1212 by *routiers* and in 1302 by a storm, after which the apse and part of the nave were rebuilt in Gothic style with flying buttresses. It was converted to the Protestant faith, subjected to wholesale iconoclasm in 1569, and a major renovation was begun in 1602. When it was returned to Christian worship, after the Revolution, in 1801, the cathedral had lost its status and become a parish church. Around 1860 Viollet-le-Duc visited and restoration was begun.

The exterior

The exterior, visible from all sides, is forbidding. The apse is 14th-century, with radiating chapels. There is a crenellated tower on the south, and another at the west above the porch protecting the most celebrated part of the cathedral, the Romanesque west door (restored in the 19th century, and again in 2001), the only obvious survival of the 12th-century church. The carvings are endearing and lively, enhanced by the use of contrasting materials, yellowish limestone and white marble. The tympanum is composed of marble slabs—which may prove to be recycled Gallo-Roman stelae—carved with the *Descent from the Cross*, unusual in this position, showing the Virgin, St John and others present at the entombment of Christ, as well as the Sun and the Moon represented as small figures. Beneath Christ is a chrism and bull's head and above the doorway, divided by a central marble trumeau (19th century) representing two captives in chains, are sub-tympana. On these are heavily restored images of *Christ in Glory* between two lions, and a figure holding two monsters by the throat. To either side are high reliefs: on the left, a scene of a demonic beast devouring his victim; and on the right, a horseman, suggesting the punishment of evil and the Church triumphant. In the outer arch of the entrance are the Four and Twenty Elders of the Apocalypse, each holding a viol, lute or rebec, or a long-necked phial. On the inside arch is a busy scene of the preparations for the Marriage at Cana, exactly as if this were the prelude to a 12th-century wedding in the Béarn. The wooden doors were given to the cathedral by Henri IV after his marriage to Marie de Médicis, when the Catholic religion was reinstated.

The interior

The interior was rebuilt almost entirely in the 14th century, the apse with five chapels and the only ambulatory in the Béarn. One Romanesque pillar on the south of the choir has survived as well as four 13th-century piers of the nave, but the vaulting is

14th-century, the transept chapels 15th-century, and the side chapels, endowed with Counter-Reformation altarpieces, were added in 1749. The wooden pulpit of 1523 from Mauléon (*see p. 478*), with painted and gilded decoration, restored in the 17th century, has a depiction of St Charles Borromeo, an outstanding Catholic reformer.

The cathedral treasury includes a curious piece of 19th-century furniture called a *chapier* which contains a splendid collection of priestly vestments worn by the Bishops of Oloron from the 16th to 19th centuries, in silk, damask and brocade with silver thread. Tradition claims that they were given by such as François I, Marie de Médicis and Empress Eugénie to the bishops. The early 18th-century crèche is considered one of the most impressive of its kind in France: as well as the set-piece *Nativity*, painted and enhanced by gold leaf, it has has an unusual group of seven freestanding figures carved in oak which were gilded in silver and then painted. Dressed in regional costume, they represent different social classes and one sports a beret.

Crypt de l'Eglise Notre Dame

Crypt open June–Sept 10–12 & 3–6; rest of the year by appointment at Tourist Office.
In Pl. Gambetta, the church was built 1869-87, this is the youngest church in Oloron, designed by the architect of imperial palaces, Joseph-Auguste Lafollye in Romano-Byzantine style with a belfry of 52m. It has paintings in the apse by Paul Delance, who won the *prix de Rome* and was a student of Gérôme, and the organ of 1851 was made by Vincent Cavaillé-Coll. The crypt, which has several parts, has been splendidly restored and can be visited.

THE BARÉTOUS

Between Pays Basque, Spain and the Gave d'Aspe, south of Oloron, is the Barétous, an agricultural region forever associated with the characters who inspired Dumas' *Three Musketeers*. Although the musketeer châteaux cannot be visited, this is beautiful walking country at altitude or in the foothills, rich in flowers and forest. With the accession of Henri IV to the throne, many *cadets* or younger sons took advantage of the opportunities that opened to the Béarnais to seek their fortune and adventure in Paris. Immortalised by Alexandre Dumas, the Three Musketeers, *cadets* of Gascogne et du Béarn, were based on real characters. D'Artagnan came from the Lupiac (*see p. 390*) in Gascony, whereas the others were Béarnais. The character of Aramis was based on a lay abbot from Aramits in the Barétous; Porthos was born in 1617 in Pau and legend claims he owned a château at Lanne in the Barétous; Athos, in reality Armand de Sillègue, came from a village near Sauveterre which inspired his fictional name. Monsieur de Tréville, captain of the Musketeers, was in fact Arnaud Jean du Peyrer, born in Oloron in 1598, and builder of the Château de Troisvilles (*see p. 364*), near Tardets.

High in the mountainous frontier, **La Pierre St-Martin** (1640m) is a centre for excursions and winter sports and famous for an ancient frontier treaty, La Junte de Roncal (1375), which is celebrated every year on 13th July at the Col de la Pierre St-Martin on the Spanish border, giving the Barétous grazing rights on Spanish soil.

VALLEYS OF THE ASPE & THE OSSAU

Directly south of Oloron-Ste-Marie is the Valley of the Aspe and southeast is the Valley of the Ossau. Both are ancient pilgrimage routes, crossing the border into the Spanish state of Aragon at Col du Portalet and Col du Somport respectively, and the two valleys are linked across the Plateau du Bénou and the Col Marie-Blanque. The scenery is spectacular but distinct in each valley; the houses and barns are mainly simple, solid stone buildings with steep, slate-covered roofs and the occasional grand entrance with a grey marble surround or sculpted dormer window. There are some small Romanesque churches but more usually the churches are 16th-century and, typical of the mountain region, contain a proliferation of 17th- and 18th-century fittings. The Route de Fromage Ossau-Iraty (the cheese route) indicates places where you can sample *pur-brebis*, the delicious local sheep's milk cheese (*see box on p. 505*).

VALLEY OF THE ASPE

For about 45km from Escot the *gave* runs through a steep and wooded valley, sometimes narrowing into a gorge, sometimes slightly wider to create a fertile plain. The villages are small and isolated, turned in on themselves, yet they line the most direct route from Bordeaux to Saragossa, followed by Roman armies, thousands of 12th-century pilgrims, and medieval tradesmen who all had to trail over the Col de Somport (1650m); the modern route into Spain takes you through tunnels and under the Col. Pilgrimages slowed with the Reformation which took a strong hold in the valley and there is still Protestant worship in the area. The four distinct centres of the **Ecomusée de la Vallée d'Aspe** are an indispensable introduction to local history and rural life: they are situated in locations relevant to their subject, at Sarrance, Accous, Lourdios-Ichère and Borce.

Sarrance

At the centre is the small Place de l'Eglise enclosed by the church, the *lavoir*, a monumental fountain, and 17th–18th-century façades. The history of Notre-Dame began in 1345 when Premonstratensian friars founded a monastery, which drew pilgrims in ever increasing numbers to the statue of the Virgin, including Louis XI in 1461. Although the cult of relics was incompatible with her reforming ideals, Marguerite of Navarre mentioned Sarrance, where she withdrew to write, in *The Heptameron*. The monastery was destroyed in 1569 by the Protestant forces of Jeanne d'Albret and later sold, but the monks returned in 1605 and rebuilt the chapel and hostel although the pilgrimage never regained the momentum of the 15th century, being eclipsed by Bétharram (*see p. 508*).

The present church of 1609 has a curvilinear façade and an imposing octagonal belfry with concave faces and statues, topped with an arcaded cupola covered in slate. The inside is far more rustic and gaudily decorated, with pendant bosses over the nave, and has chapels on the north. The gilding is thorough, and on the walls are coloured reliefs. The sanctuary was entirely restored in 1865 and on the gilded half-dome is a Tree of Jesse. The chapel dedicated to St Norbert, founder of the

Premonstratensian order, contains a retable with a gilded post-Reformation *Virgin and Child*, and reliefs which probably come from the 18th-century Calvary, and depict the *Agony in the Garden* and the *Sleeping Apostles*, with an embossed leather antependium. The St-Martin chapel contains a replica head of the Black Virgin attached to a dressed statue in an ornate niche, and naive coloured reliefs (18th century) recount the legend of the Virgin of Sarrance, a statue that repeatedly re-appeared beside the spring where it had first been found by an ox. Against the south wall is an unusual two-tier cloister, much rebuilt, and in the gardens off the cloister is a walk uphill along the route of the Calvary that existed in the 18th century.

Below the church is the **Ecomusée Notre-Dame-de-la-Pierre** (*open July–Sept 10–12 & 2–7; Oct–June, Sat, Sun and holidays 2–6; T: 05 59 34 55 51*), where the legend of the Virgin of Sarrance, the church, the village and the reintroduction of the pilgrimage in the 1930s are delightfully recreated using audio-visual displays, commentary, music, sculptures and reliefs, and a model of the valley. The original head of the statue of the Virgin, simply and roughly carved in dark stone, is part of the collection of local religious artefacts. The chapel on the main road marks the location of the miracle.

Lourdios-Ichère, Bedous and the border

At Lourdios-Ichère, between Sarrance and Bedous, is another part of the **Ecomusée: Un Village se Raconte** (*same opening times as Notre-Dame-de-la-Pierre; T: 05 59 34 44 84*), is a museum which tells the story of a once isolated village based on a 19th-century document written by the school teacher. Interiors of the period are reconstructed and the exhibition traces the dependence of village life on livestock and the rhythm of the seasons. It constitutes an excellent introduction to the valley and rural customs, such as the *meule de fougère* (stacks of bracken used in place of straw). Outside, about 100m to the left of the museum, the exhibit continues along a discovery trail.

Further south is the Plaine d'Accous, with **Bedous** the most active of the villages, with streets lined with 16th–18th-century houses. A pretty route from here towards Aydius arrives in the picturesque hamlet of **Orcun**, huddled close to the hillside around a tiny chapel, quite plain on the outside (*open daily 3–4, although someone might unlock it at other times on request*), transformed in the 17th century into a miniature stage set, with every surface painted and every statue gilded.

The road to Accous, on the old pilgrimage route, passes the oldest church in the valley at **Jouers**, which has some striking corbels around the exterior of the apse. In the narrow streets of **Accous** are some notable houses and a monumental Mairie on the square. The Fermiers Basco-Béarnais, part of the Ecomusée (*open July–mid-Sept daily 9.30–1 & 2–7; mid-Sept–June 9.30–12 & 2–6, closed Sat, Sun; T: 05 59 34 76 06*), is a cheese-producing co-operative with three *saloirs*.

South of Accous, the road to the right at l'Estanguet takes you up to the **Cirque de Lescun**, one of the most beautiful landscapes of the Pyrenees, looking towards the Billare range, habitat of the rare native bear, whom you are unlikely to meet. The road continues on to Etsaut and **Borce** and the last of the quartet of museums, Hospital St-Jacques de Compostelle, Borce (*opening times, T: 06 81 32 58 32*). The exhibition, in an old pilgrim hospice with a 12th-century chapel, explores the origin of the pilgrimage to Compostella and the conditions of the journey.

The Espace Animalier is a museum-park concerned with the fauna of the Pyrenees and has two indigenous bears, Myrtille and Ségolène, in a new space. There are also domestic animals. It is close to the new Maison du Parc National at the village of Etsaut (*open May–Oct 9.30–12.30 & 2–6.30; remainder of year by appointment; T: 05 59 34 88 30*) with an exhibition on the Brown Pyrenean Bear and information on the National Park. The last community before the border is Urdos, on the edge of the Parc National des Pyrénées (*see p. 515*).

GAVE D'OSSAU

The Gave d'Ossau tumbles down from the high Pyrenees through the mountain scenery of the Vallée d'Ossau, which starts at Sévignac-Meyracq. The lower valley as far as Laruns is wide, open and fertile, supporting small communities, but the valley narrows further south and is more enclosed as it climbs towards Gabas and beyond, with the Pic du Midi d'Ossau (2884m) looming in the background.

Arudy is a small town with old houses, a *lavoir*, and a church rebuilt in the 16th century. Behind the church the Maison d'Ossau, a 17th-century building with a slate roof and sculpted pediment, contains the local history and ethnography museum and a permanent exhibition on the Parc National des Pyrénées (*open July-Aug 10–12 & 3–6; Sept–June 2–5, Sun 3–6, closed Mon, Sat; T: 05 59 05 61 71*).

Bielle is the ancient capital of the valley and mountain pastures owned collectively are still administered from here. There are some good 16th-century houses, an 18th century château, and the church is 16th-century with a late Gothic doorway typical of the Béarn.

South of Bielle, **Laruns** is a busy town at the start of the high valley, with traditional summer celebrations in mid-August and a cheese fair in October. The Fromagerie Pardou (*T: 05 59 82 60 77*) offers a guided visit to cheese cellars and a tasting. Across the *gave*, strung out on the ridge opposite Laruns, is a series of small villages overlooking the valley. At **Aste-Béon** is the Falaise aux Vautours (*open June–Aug 10.30–12.30 & 2–6.30; May, Sept 2–6; school holidays 2–5; T: 05 59 82 65 49*), where vultures and other birds of prey can be observed live on film via a camera installed in a cliff.

At the centre of the little community of **Béost** is a pretty ensemble of a church with a fortified house to the east and the medieval *abbaye laïque* to the west (altered in the 16th and 18th century), described as the Château d'Aramits (*T: 05 59 05 30 99*), of musketeering fame (*see p. 390*). The church has conserved its Romanesque apse and around the south door (14th century) are some re-sited Romanesque elements including marble reliefs of Christ teaching and resurrected, with Apostles and angels. The rest, including the tall belfry, is 15th century. Inside are some carved capitals and a marble Pietà (15th century). On the corner opposite the church is a primary school where only the Béarnais language is used, and there are some attractive houses with inscriptions and dates as well as a superb *lavoir* in need of restoration.

Eaux-Bonnes and the border

The old communities of Béost, Assouste and, higher still, Aas, barely more than a hamlet, are older than the now more important spa town of Eaux-Bonnes. The curative properties of its waters were first tested in the 16th century when François I came to recover from injuries sustained in battle in Northern Italy. In 1800 Napoleon had a road constructed so that he could send his wounded soldiers for treatment, and in 1809 what is now the *Mairie* was built to house them. During the heyday of the spa it was visited by well-known artists such as Devéria and Delacroix. The road from Laruns winds up through sequoia trees planted more than 100 years ago by the Empress Eugénie, who first came here as a young woman in 1840. She was also responsible for the *promenade horizontal*, for improving the English garden and, more ambitiously, for the Route Thermale, the D918—running through two high passes, the Col d'Aubisque (1709m) and the Col du Soulor (1474m)—linking Eaux-Bonnes with Argelès-Gazost (*see p. 518*). People come here now for the treatment of bronchitis and asthma.

To the south, the road runs through Eaux-Chaudes before reaching **Gabas** (1000m), the last village before the Spanish border and the night stop during the *transhumance* of cattle in the summer. The two *gaves*, d'Ossau and de Brousset, meet here, on the edge of the national park, making it an excellent starting-point for excursions to the Lac de Bious-Artigues and the petit train. This small village handles about 80 per cent of the local production of ewes' milk cheese, some 10,000 cheeses, which are refined here in salting cellars. The tiny chapel (*key at the Bar Turon opposite*) with a porch (1121) was one of the last stops on the pilgrimage route before crossing the Pyrenees into Spain.

Southeast of Gabas the cable car from Artouste-Fabrèges, which has restaurants and shops, will take you up to the **Train Touristique du Lac d'Artouste** (*operates end May–Sept; T: 05 59 05 34 00*), the highest train in Europe. Allow at least three hours for the 10km return train journey and one hour at the top at an altitude of about 2000m.

FROMAGE DE BREBIS

The shepherd milks the ewes by hand in the mountains twice a day during the summer and begins the process of transforming the milk into cheese. This involves heating the milk, churning, moulding, separating and salting it. The cheeses are sent to a *saloir* in the valley to complete the maturing process. Each cheese is individually processed (wiped, salted and turned) each day and stored on wooden slats. The cheeses may remain in the *saloir* for up to 18 months, but most are sold after six. Twenty-five litres of milk is needed for each 5kg cheese. The shepherd has the right to one out of every 12 cheeses he makes. Side products are the *grueil* or *petit-lait* (whey), sold at the markets and flavoured with sugar and coffee, and *caillé* (curd), sold only by specialists. The Route du Fromage Ossau-Iraty-Brebis-Pyrénées across the Béarn and Basque regions has 46 locations where you can sample and buy local cheeses (map from Tourist Information offices).

BÉARN-ADOUR

The region on the border with Gascony, north of Pau and Tarbes, is described variously as the Béarn-Adour or the Vic-Bilh Montanérès (*vic-bilh* meaning 'old country') and embraces part of the vineyards of Madiran and Pacherenc (*see p. 507*). In this rolling countryside with fields of maize the villages are often grouped around Romanesque chapels and 16th-century manor houses.

From c. 1070 until the 13th century, **Morlaàs** was the capital of the Béarn, and the viscounts granted to its inhabitants important privileges called the *for de Morlaàs*, the impetus behind the town's development in the 12th century. On the edge of a plateau dominating the plain, the site is not unlike that of Lescar, and is now a rural suburb of Pau with a few picturesque old houses and a market. The church of Ste-Foy (12th century) had one of the finest sculpted portals in the Béarn and parts of it are on display at the Tourist Office (*open July–Aug, Tues–Sat, 10-12, 2-4; rest of the year Mon, Tues, Thurs, Fri; T: 05 59 33 62 25*). The church benefited from large donations from Count Centulle V, in expiation for his marriage to a blood relative, and came under the protection of the abbey of Cluny from 1079. The west front remains of interest despite a total rebuild (1857–1903) and there are many references in iconography and layout to Ste-Marie at Oloron (*see p. 500*). The recarved central trumeau has atlantes in chains and above the door the *Massacre of the Innocents*, the *Flight into Egypt*, *Christ in Majesty*, St Matthew and St John are depicted. The successive arches framing the tympanum are decorated with ducks, and the Twenty-four Elders of the Apocalypse; among the souls of the saved is Boeswillwald, Inspector of Historic Monuments. The statues of the 12 Apostles in the door jambs are also 19th-century. The interior of the church has a mainly 14th- and 17th-century nave with 19th-century aisles; the east apse has Romanesque capitals painted in the 19th century, including the *Martyrdom of St Faith*, who appears again on a south window capital.

CHÂTEAUX OF THE BÉARN-ADOUR

In the direction of Tarbes, the **Château de Montaner** (*open July–Aug 10–7; April–June, Sept–Oct 2–7, closed Tues; T: 05 59 81 98 29.*) is a fort built by Gaston Fébus to protect his territory from the English and converted in the 14th century into a palace. The great brick *donjon*, one of the most remarkable in the southwest, stands on a mound guarding the entrance and the circular enclosure. The church of St-Michel at the foot of the hill was rebuilt in the 14th–15th century in brick and pebbles, and inside are interesting murals (c. 1490–1530), restored in the 1980s.

Château de Mascaraàs-Haron (*guided visits mid-May–mid-Sept 10–12 & 3–6, closed Tues; T: 05 59 04 92 60*) is near Garlin, north of Pau. A pretty building overlooking the Vic-Bilh, it was used as a hunting lodge by Jeanne d'Albret, and altered in the 17th–18th centuries. It boasts one of the most important decorative ensembles in this part of the Pyrénées-Atlantiques, with 16th–18th-century works of art and an old library

Close to the border with Gascony, the **Château de Crouseilles** (*open May–Sept, 9–1 & 2–7, Sun 10–7; Oct–April 9.30–12.30 & 2–6, Sun 1–6; T: 05 59 68 10 93*), is a vineyard with a recently renovated 18th-century building where the best of Madiran and Pacherenc *crus* can be tasted. There are also numerous activities, visits to the vineyards, and displays of crafts during the summer.

The **Château de Momas** (*open for guided visits April–Oct, Sat, Sun afternoons, or by appointment; T: 05 59 77 14 71*) is privately owned and in its restored gardens are thousands of rare species of plants and ancient vegetables cultivated by Madame Teillard, the great grand-daughter of a botanist and chemist who brought medicinal plants from Porto Rico.

Château de Morlanne

Guided visits to the exterior only; work on the interior ongoing at time of writing; July–Aug daily 10–7; April–June, Sept–Oct, Wed–Mon 2–7, closed Tues; T: 05 59 81 60 27.

A magnificent sight with immaculate brickwork, perfect crenellations and pleasantly landscaped, the château was extensively restored in the 1970s in the spirit of the 14th century by its last owners, Raymond and Hélène Ritter. Gaston Fébus purchased the land in 1373 to defend his western territories. From the 15th century the castle changed hands several times, eventually falling into disrepair, and was subjected to alterations in the 19th century. By the time of its rescue in 1969 by the historian and writer, Raymond Ritter, the *donjon* was only half its present height. Using other Fébusian fortresses as models, notably Montaner, thorough restoration was carried out. The castle is built on a *motte* with a towering *donjon*. It has five sides around a courtyard, is built in brick and the main buildings are on the west. The interior is the showcase for the Ritters' collection of antiques and paintings: among the wealth of objects displayed is a 12th-century *Christ in Majesty* from the Toulousain, Louis XV commodes, furniture by Georges Jacob, a Dutch roll-top writing desk, an elaborate Italian jewel cabinet, an Empire period Egyptian-style bed, and furniture from Alsace, M. Ritter's birthplace. The fine collection of paintings includes works by Canaletto, Fragonard and Pannini.

NAY & THE GAVE DE PAU

Strategically placed on the river southeast of Pau is the *bastide* of Nay, centred on the vast arcaded Place de la République, which has a very busy market. The most prestigious building on the square is the Maison Carrée, and Nay prides itself on perpetuating certain traditional craft industries such as the manufacture of berets and cattle bells. It was founded in 1302 by Marguerite de Moncade, in conjunction with the Augustine monastery in Gabas, where a community already existed close to the bridge built in the 12th century on the vital route linking France and Spain. The local cotton, linen and woollen industries prospered, and the force of the river torrents was harnessed to power the mills. Many buildings were lost during a fire in 1543. The church of **St-Vincent** was rebuilt afterwards. The massive stepped belfry tower, originally integral with the 14th-century walls, ends in a curious octagonal structure added in the 19th century. The door next to the tower is a survival of the 13th century, but the window tracery is Flamboyant, as is the very fine south door with a decoration of *choux frisés*.

The **Maison Carrée** (*open July–Aug 10–12 & 3–7, closed Mon; May–June, Sept–Oct and school holidays 10–12 & 2–6, closed Mon/Sun; Nov–April, Tues–Fri, 3–6; T: 05 59 61 34 61/05 59 13 99 65*), is a superb example of Renaissance (c. 1550) domestic architecture, influenced by Italy and adapted to France, as in Toulouse and Lyon. The builder was a Spaniard, Pedro Sacaze, who had made his fortune in the cloth trade and in pastel (*see p. 315*). After many years of neglect, the Maison Carrée was painstakingly renovated in the 1990s and a museum installed. The street façade has mullioned windows above arcades, and dormers in the steep roof. The house is composed of two main wings, north and south, linked by galleries which enclose a courtyard. There is a garden behind the south wing. The west gallery consists of a sophisticated two-tier loggia above the arcades, using the Classical orders in their established sequence, and an attic storey. Only one column is fluted: the project was interrupted by the Wars of Religion. There are relief portraits of the proprietor and his wife on the north façade. Pedro Sacaze's son-in-law, François de Béarn, Captain Bonasse, a staunch Catholic, continued the work but was killed by Protestant troops during the siege of Tarbes and Jeanne d'Albret confiscated the house. Consequently the matching east gallery was never completed and a simpler wooden version links the two wings, which is perhaps less elegant but nevertheless fascinating, as some of the wooden panels which enclose it are original 16th century examples. The museum contains a collection of Béarnais furniture (17th–19th century) and local ethnology as well as a model of Nay in the 16th century.

The famous *béret Basque* in fact originated in the Béarn. A film and exhibits explain the story at the Musée du Béret, Place St-Roch (*open July–Aug 10–12 & 2–7; April–June, Sept–Christmas, Tues–Sat 10–12 & 2–6; Jan–March, Nov Wed and Sat 2–6; Tues 10–12 & 2–6; T: 05 59 61 91 70*). Mystery still surrounds the evolution of this quintessentially French rural head-covering. The Fabrique de Sonnailles at 24 Rue des Pyrénées (*open by appointment only Mon and Sat 2–5; T: 05 59 61 00 41, www.daban.fr*), is one of only two workshops where sheep bells, each with its own particular sound, are made.

Lestelle-Bétharram

The nearby village of Lestelle-Bétharram, a site of pilgrimage for some 800 years and dedicated, like Lourdes, to the Virgin, was frequently visited by Bernadette Soubirous (*see p. 516*). The chapel was badly damaged by Protestant troops in 1569 and rebuilt between 1614 and 1710 at a period when an increasing number of miracles revitalised the site. The exterior is of grey marble decorated with white marble statues of the Virgin and Child and the four Evangelists. In contrast the interior is heavily ornate, every surface decorated with gilt and paintings (1690–1710). On the front panels of the tribune above the west entrance are scenes of the early miracles performed in the chapel, and below are depictions of the ancestors of Christ. The 19th-century statue of *Our Lady of Beau-Rameau* by Alexandre Renoir on the main altar evokes the miracle of a drowning girl saved by the Virgin, who holds a branch out to her. Another apparition of the Virgin to local shepherds is the subject of the retable (1620–30) in the south aisle chapel. The severe mausoleum of St Michel Garicoïts, Bernadette Soubirous' mentor, was designed by the architect Gabriel Andral and consecrated in 1928. The local history museum is the Musée du Patrimoine des Pères de Bétharram (*open Easter–mid-Oct 9–12 & 2–6, mid-Oct–Easter Sat, Sun 9–12 & 2–5; T: 05 59 71 92 30*). South of the town, the Grottes de Bétharram (*open daily April–Oct 9–12 & 1.30–5.30; Feb–March, Mon–Thurs 2.30 and 4; Fri 2.30 only; T: 05 62 41 80 04*) are a spectacular five-level network of caverns, visited partly by boat and partly by *petit train*.

PRACTICAL INFORMATION

GETTING AROUND

• **By air:** Pau-Pyrénées international airport, T: 05 59 33 33 00, www.pau.aeroport. fr.
• **By train:** At Pau, a funicular (free) links the train station below Blvd des Pyrénées to the town centre. Paris, Pau. Pau, Toulouse; Pau, Bordeaux; Pau, Gan, Buzy, Bayonne, Oloron-Ste-Marie. Pau, Orthez. Oloron, Lanfranc; Oloron, Arudy.
• **By bus:** Agen, Sarrou, Carlin, Auriac, Sauvagnon, Pau. Mont-de-Marsan, Aire sur l'Adour, Sarron, Garlin, Pau. Buzy, Bielle, Béost, Laruns, Artouste. Oloron-Ste-Marie, Sarrance, Bedous, Accous, Canfranc (frontier).

TOURIST INFORMATION

Pau Comité départemental du Tourisme Béarn-Pays Basque, 22ter Rue Jean-Jacques de Monaix, T: 05 59 30 01 30, www.tourisme64.com
Pau Tourist Office, Pl. Royale, T: 05 59 27 27 08, www.pau.fr
Arudy Pl. de l'Hôtel de Ville, T: 05 59 05 77 11, www.ot-arudy.fr
Bedous Vallée d'Aspe, Pl. Sarraillé, BP 11, T: 05 59 34 57 57, www.aspecanfranc.com

Les Eaux Bonnes, 64440 Gourette, T: 05 59 05 33 08, ot-eauxbonnes@wanadoo.fr
Maisons du Parc, Pyrénées Atlantiques **Etsaut Vallée d'Aspe**, T: 05 59 34 88 30, pnp.aspe@espace-naturel.fr
Lembeye Pl. du Marché, T: 05 59 68 28 78, Office du Vic-Bilh Montaneres, 7 Pl. du Corps Franc Pommiès, T: 05 59 68 28 78, ot.vic.bilh@wanadoo.fr
Laruns Vallée d'Ossau, T: 05 59 05 31 41, email ossau.tourisme@wanadoo.fr
Morlaas Place Sainte Foy, T: 05 59 33 62 25, morlaas.tourisme@wanadoo.fr
Nay Pl. de la République, T: 05 59 61 34 61, www.ot-nay.fr
Oloron-Ste-Marie Allées de Comte de Tréville, T: 05 59 39 98 00, www.ot-oloron-ste-marie.fr
Lescar La Cité, T: 05 59 81 15 98, ot.lescar@wanadoo.fr
Navarrenx 17 rue St-Germain, T: 05 59 66 14 93, www.béarn-gaves.com
Orthez Maison Jeanne d'Albret, Rue Bourg-Vieux, T: 05 59 69 02 75, www.mairie-orthez.fr
Salies-de-Béarn Rue des Bains, T: 05 59 38 00 33, www.béarn-gaves.com
Sauveterre-de-Béarn Mason Rospide, Pl. Royale, T: 05 59 38 58 65, www.béarn-gaves.com

ACCOMMODATION & RESTAURANTS

Arroses

€ **Chambres d'hôtes**. Comfortable rooms in an old farm around a beautiful *maison de maître* in the Madiran vineyards. The rooms and bathrooms are very spacious, calm and comfortable, and there is a swimming pool and horse riding at the farm. The *table d'hôtes* (€14) is excellent. Between Pau and Tarbes. M. J. Labat, 64350 Arroses, T: 05 59 68 16 01.

Bielle

€ **Hôtel/Restaurant L'Ayguelade.** South of Arudy, in the Ossau Valley close to the D934, the Ayguelade has been in the Lartigau family for three generations. The welcome and service reflects this experience, and this is one of the best restaurants in the Ossau Valley with creative cooking (menus €13–35). The bedrooms are each different. T: 05 59 82 60 06.

Jurançon

€€ **Hôtel Castel du Pont d'Oly.** A well-known and popular address run by Monique and Christian Marcoux. The very best products are combined by the talented chef to create a seasonal choice. Menus from around €28.The house is prettily restored and has rooms over-looking the garden and pool. 2 Ave Rauski, RN134, T: 05 59 06 13 40, www.hotel-restaurant-pau.com

€€€ **Restaurant Chez Ruffet.** ■ This top-quality restaurant serving the best regional products with panache is the domain of a great and talented chef, Stéphane Carrade, artist of regional cuisine. The menu changes weekly, and among the creations are *Bar de ligne cuit sur une pierre du gave or La fleur de cour-* *gette farcie au pied de cochon.* Carrade has new projects for his establishment which will delight foodies. The menus €23–110, *à la carte* €59–72. 3 Ave Charles-Touzet, T: 05 59 06 25 13.

Laruns

€ **Chambres d'hôtes Casa Paulou.** Jean-Bernard Mourasse has created roomy and very attractive accommodation in the restored barn. The owners are mountain enthusiasts and are happy to advise you on visits in the region. 6 Rue Bourgneuf, T: 05 59 05 35 98.

Lestelle-Betharram

€€ **Hôtel/Restaurant Le Vieux Logis.** Hotel-restaurant which has passed from father to son since 1951. Originally a family house, it has been transformed into hotel situated between Béarn et Bigorre near the Grottes de Bétharram. The rooms are modern and there is a swimming pool. In the restaurant the dishes are classic but refined, and good value, with menus from €24 to €40. Route des Grottes, T: 05 59 71 94 87.

Monein

€€ **Hôtel Château Lamothe.** This small château in the heart of the Jurançon vineyards has become a 10-room hotel surrounded by a park and 100-year old trees and more recent lavender, oleander and palms. Lovely views, pool and pool house, tennis courts and pelota *fronton*. The rooms are all different, one with original floors and four-poster, and an attic room in yellow. 53 Av. des Vallées, T: 05 59 21 20 80, chateau-lamothe@wanadoo.fr

Morlanne

€ **Ferme Auberge Lauzet Grand-Guillotte.** This is a friendly place where the owners rear sheep and ducks and the food they serve is based on their own produce. Delicious are *Le canard à l'orange and Foie gras frais aux pommes* At lunchtime there is an €11 menu, and others €15–25. Rue du Château, T: 05 59 81 61 28.

Orthez

€ Hôtel/Restaurant Au Temps de la Reine Jeanne. ■ This attractive hotel in the historic centre of the town was beautifully renovated in 2004. Comprising a series of old houses, the bedrooms are spacious and refined, and the public rooms decorated with good taste. There is jacuzzi and sauna and a pretty patio. The restaurant is one of the best in the Béarn des Gaves, serving dishes full of flavour inspired by the availability of produce from the local market; menus from €15 to €34. 44 Rue Bourg-Vieux, T: 05 59 67 00 76, www.reine-jeanne.fr

€ Auberge Saint Loup. The old pilgrimage hospice with a fireplace is prettily presented using warm colours. The reception is friendly and the innovative cuisine is very much of the region, an adaptation of grandmother's recipes, such as *Filet de veau cuit au foin, L'émincé de porc aux oignons confits* and *Pain d'épices terrace*. The menu changes every 15 days. Set menus from €14 to €42, and a la carte €34. 20 Rue Pont-Vieux, T: 05 59 69 15 40.

Pau

€€€ Hôtel/Restaurant Parc Beaumont. This audacious modern building opened in 2004 in a superb position on the edge of Parc Beaumont close to the Boulevard des Pyrénées, taking full advantage of terrific views. The interior is ultra chic. The restaurant Le Jeu de Paume is under the direction of innovative and contemporary chef Christophe Canati, recognised with a Michelin rosette in 2001 in a previous establishment. 1 Av. Edouard VII, T: 05 59 11 84 00, www.hotel-parc-beaumont.com

€ Hôtel Le Roncevaux. An attractive establishment in an old building in the town centre close to the château and the Blvd des Pyrénées. It combines old-world charm and modernity with lots of wood panelling in the public areas and 39 bedrooms (3 with four-posters). 25 Rue Louis-Barthou, T: 05 59 27 08 44, www.hotel-roncevaux.com

€ Hotel Central. Excellently situated in the centre of the town, this bright little hotel has smallish, cheerful bedrooms, American billiards and bar. Rooms are reasonably priced. 25 Rue Leon Daran, T: 05 59 27 72 75, www.hotelcentralpau.com

€€€ Restaurant Chez Pierre. A restaurant whose reputation has been established over two generations. The wood-panelled décor has echos of Pau's English influences, but the cooking is resolutely Béarnais. Menus from €34. Upstairs, Le Bistrot de Pierre offers more modest repasts at more reasonable prices. 16 Rue Louis-Barthou, T: 05 59 27 76 86.

€€€ Le Majestic. With a very varied choice on offer from chef J.M. Larrère, Le Majestic is considered one of the best addresses in Pau. Calm and elegant throughout, the décor has been recently updated and there is a garden in 19th-century style. Menus start at €17 (midday), and in the evening from around €26; average price €35-€45. 9 Pl. Royale, T: 05 59 27 56 83.

€ Chez Olive. The restaurant occupies a 12th-century building opposite the castle, and specialises in a modernised version of traditional southwestern cooking. In good hands, the same family has run it for 57 years. The menus range from €19, and the à la carte between €19 and €40. 9/11 Rue du Chateau, T: 05 59 27 81 19.

Sauveterre de Béarn

€€ **Chambres d'hôtes Le Domaine de Bétouzet**. The steep-roofed, part-17th/part-18th century home of Florence Verspieren stands in beautifully tended grounds facing the Pyrenees, surrounded by a pool, a pigeonnier and artists studios. The lounges and dining room combine modern art and antique furniture harmoniously. The five stunning bedrooms have masses of space. In fine weather meals are served on the shady terrace (prebooked *table d' hôtes*, €30–35). Andrein, near Sauveterre de Béarn, T: 05 59 38 91 40, www.betouzet.com

Sévignacq-Meyracq

€ **Restaurant Les Bains de Secours**. This lovely restaurant with rooms, rural but refined, is tucked away in an isolated part of the Ossau Valley south of Pau. The old Béarnais farm is the setting for Jean-Pierre Paroix's personal and wonderfully subtle cooking with dishes of notes such as *La confit de canard en pot au feu or La salade de sole aux cèpes*. Menus range from €15–30. There are 7 bedrooms where peace and quiet is assured. T: 05 59 05 62 11.

MARKET DAYS

Arundy Tuesday, Saturday
Bedous Thursday
Laruns Saturday
Monein Monday
Lembeye Thursday
Morlàas Friday (fortnightly); local produce Saturday
Nay Main market Tuesday, local produce Saturday
Navarrenx Wednesday, Saturday
Orthez Tuesday; marché au gras Nov–March
Salies-de-Béarn Thursday; organic Saturday

FESTIVALS & EVENTS

February: *Grand prix d'equitation de la ville de Pau*, Major horse-riding events, Pau
April: *Fête des fleurs*, spring flower show, Château de Momas
June–July: *Transhumance*, movement of sheep and cattle to the mountains, Aspe and Ossau Valleys
July: *Junte de Roncal*, ceremony held on the 13th in connection with an ancient treaty with Spain, Col de la Pierre St-Martin (D132) *Fête d'Orthez*, five days of féria—bullfighting, berets and bandas, Orthez. *Fête du fromage*, Etsaut
August: *Monein fête ses fruits et ses Vins du Jurançon*, everything stops for the *hesta* - tasting of fruit and wine, Monein. *Hesta de Noste Dama*, traditional festival of local music—flute and tambourine—and costumes, Laruns, Ossau Valley. *Fêtes des Vins de Madiran*, wine festival, Crouseilles
September: *Fête du Sel* (La Heste de la Saü), with salt carrying and ham rolling, craft market, concerts, parade; Salies-de-Béarn.
La Garburade, celebration of the traditional soup, Oloron-Ste-Marie
October: *Fête de l'Arbre au Château de Momas*, an opportunity to see the horticultural collection of about 30 nurserymen, Momas

HAUTES-PYRÉNÉES

The Département des Hautes-Pyrénées, often referred to as the Bigorre, the old province to which it roughly corresponds, benefits from a wondrous variety of landscapes. The mountain peaks of the central Pyrenean range in the south rise to over 3000m and include one of the best known, the Pic du Midi-de-Bigorre (2877m), while the natural amphitheatre, the Cirque de Gavarnie, is among the most spectacular of many natural sites of great beauty. The natural assets of the mountains are protected by the Parc National des Pyrénées (*see below, p. 515*) in the southwest along the Spanish border. The *département* stretches north through the foothills of the Pyrenees with picturesque mountain villages, to the gentle slopes of the Madiran between Gascony (Gers, *see p. 371*) and the Béarn. Mountain torrents are known here as *gaves* or *nestes*, the main ones being the Gave de Pau, which flows north and west, through Lourdes, an important site of pilgrimage; the Grande Neste, which marks the eastern border of the Bigorre; and the Adour which waters the main town, Tarbes, and the plain beyond. The Adour valley has been the main route to the mountains since ancient times.

THE PYRENEES

The Pyrenees, which form a huge natural barrier between France and the Iberian Peninsula, are in fact two ranges running more or less east–west with a tiny break in the middle, the Vallée d'Aran, south of Luchon in the Central Pyrenees. The highest peak in the French Pyrenees is Vignemale (3298m) south of Cauterets, and many other peaks are over 3000m; the highest of all, the Pic d'Aneto (3404m), is in Spain. Although the peaks in the Pyrenees are not as high as in the Alps, there are Pyrenean valleys at a higher altitude than Alpine ones. The highest section overall is in the central-west Pyrenees, covered by the *départements* of the Hautes-Pyrénées, Haute-Garonne and Ariège-Pyrénées. A multitude of rivers, including the Garonne, rise in the mountains and flow towards the north, carving out valleys and gorges. It is an area of breathtaking natural beauty offering a great choice of outdoor activities. As in all mountain regions, the weather is very changeable, even in the summer when mist or rain can suddenly descend; snow can close the high passes from November to May. There are cultural and scenic differences across the length (about 150km) of the range. The west is greener and more lush, influenced climatically by the Atlantic and culturally by Gascony and Aquitaine, while the eastern part is more Mediterranean and arid, and is historically part of the Languedoc. There are also distinct cultural, climatic and geographic differences on either side of the divide. The southern slopes, turned towards the Iberian peninsula and Africa, can guarantee more hours of sunshine, while the French Pyrenees, which rise more suddenly and steeply from the plain, have more dramatic panoramas and a greater variety of landscape. Conversely there are cultural similarities binding all the mountain people together. The Basque country is a case in point; the people here are often closer to their Spanish than their French neighbours.

HISTORY OF THE PYRENEES

By the 5th century Iberian tribes had settled as far north as the Garonne, and after the Romans crossed the mountains and colonised the region at the beginning of the last millennium, the local people were described as Bigerri or Bigerriones by Julius Caesar. During the Gallo-Roman era the mineral water spas, as well as the marble quarries, were an important natural resource. The Visigoth and Carolingian empires extended either side of the Pyrenean range, as did the Kingdom of Aragon, and the word Bigorre appeared in the 6th century as the name of a diocese. The frontier between France and Spain, which runs more or less along the crests, was determined by the Treaty of the Pyrenees in 1659 (*see p. 463*). Both licit and illicit trade across the border continued for centuries. The Pyrenees thrived during the 18th century but suffered hugely in the 19th century when local industries such as mineral extraction, marble quarrying, farming, forestry and weaving went into severe decline, precipitating huge depopulation which left many of the more remote villages with only tiny permanent communities. Closer to the present, during the Spanish Wars and the Occupation of France in the Second World War, the mountains provided refuge to many.

A main industry today, along with tourism, is *la houille blanche*, hydro-electric power generated by seven power stations. The energy potential of mountain torrents was recognised by Aristide Bergès (1833–1904), born near St-Lizier, and first harnessed in 1869. Iron ore is still extracted in the Ariège, where there is also a talc quarry, a cigarette paper works and the only tungsten mine in France. There are many cattle and sheep, and cheese is made in the mountains, but the major industry by far has become summer and winter tourism. The spas are the oldest resorts and of the 17 spa towns in the Midi-Pyrénées region, 13 are in the Pyrenees. The water acquires its curative properties by picking up minerals, and sometimes heat, underground for anything from a few to several hundreds or millions of years. Different spas offer different cures—the range is astounding. Some spas also double as ski resorts, of which there are 21 in total; many cablecars and lifts also operate in summer enabling walkers and non-walkers to reach the higher slopes. Tourist centres provide a vast range of information on walking, categorising different levels from very easy walks taking up to three hours (*promenades*) to hikes taking several days (*randonnées*), with details of guides and lists of mountain refuges.

PARC NATIONAL DES PYRÉNÉES

The Parc National des Pyrénées was created in 1967 in order to conserve the beautiful landscape as nearly as possible in its natural state. It aims to be a haven for wildlife and a heaven for hikers. The park stretches along the length of the Pyrenees from the upper valley of the Aure in the east (Haute-Pyrénées) to the upper valley of the Aspe in the west (Pyrénées-Atlantiques), covering 45,700 hectares along the Spanish border, from an altitude of 1067m to its highest point, the Pic du Vignemale (3298m). On the other side of the national border is its Spanish equivalent, the Parque Nacional de Ordesa (15,000 hectares), reached on foot through the Brèche de Roland at Gavarnie. There are 118 lakes, many rivers and torrents, and no habitation, although 50 per cent of its area is used for grazing. Around the central zone is an outer area of 206,352 hectares where life goes on, but complements the objectives of the park. Within this is a special area, the Réserve Naturelle de Néouvielle (2,300 hectares), which also comes under the protection of the national park, and south of Gavarnie is its Spanish continuation, the Parque Nacional de Ordesa y Monte Perdido.

The flora and fauna of the whole park are protected. The abundant flora includes valerian, orchid, fritillary, asphodel, gentian, saxifrage, edelweiss, *rhododendron ramondia des Pyrénées*, *jacinthe sauvage* (wild hyacinth) and *lys des Pyrénées* (lily of the valley): 160 species are endemic to the Pyrenees. Fauna includes two indigenous species of butterfly and a curious little animal that has survived in small numbers, the desman, a sort of aquatic mole with an extended snout; also the izard (a Pyrenean antelope), marmot, and many varieties of raptors, tetrax and game. Tragically, the Pyrenean brown bear is an endangered species, having been hunted to near extinction; approximately 14 to 16 have been identified at time of writing. Solitary and nocturnal, it can reach 200kg in weight and measure 2m in height. The Maison du Parc at Etsaut (*see p. 504*) has an exhibition on the Pyrenean bear. A few bears from Slovenia, close genetically to the local breed, have been introduced here (and in the Massif Central).

Access to the park in Hautes-Pyrénées is via the Valleys of Azun, Cauterets, Luz-Gavarnie and Aure; in Pyrénées-Atlantiques via the Valleys of Apse and Ossau. Much of the park can be driven through, and there are 350km of paths, refuges for long-distance walkers and picnic areas. Campsites and *gîtes* are confined to the periphery, as is skiing. The limits of the park are marked by posts which have an image of the head of an izard. The park is safeguarded by *garde-moniteurs* who welcome the public and have expertise in all aspects of the mountains. The main tourist information office is at Parc National des Pyrénées, 59 Route du Pau, 65000 Tarbes (*T: 05 62 44 36 60, www.parc-pyrenees.com*). Maisons du Parc (five in Hautes-Pyrénées and two in Pyrénées-Atlantiques) are open during the holiday season (*see p. 533*).

LOURDES

Lourdes is one of the prime places of pilgrimage in Europe, set in the beautiful valley of the Gave de Pau. It is the product both of the traditional veneration of the Virgin in the Pyrenees and of successful promotion, much the same as that which elevated Santiago de Compostela in Spain to such an important European shrine in the Middle Ages.

HISTORY OF LOURDES

The history of Lourdes began on the limestone promontory dominating the Gave de Pau, where in the 11th century the Counts of Bigorre built a stronghold. It was subsequently occupied by the English and then by Gaston Fébus, Count of Foix (*see p. 571*), before the region reverted to the French by the Treaty of the Pyrenees in 1659. Lourdes would probably have remained a fairly insignificant town but in 1858 its fortunes were completely reversed when Bernadette Soubirous (1844–79), a poor and devout child of 14, received 18 visions of the Virgin of the Immaculate Conception in the Massabielle grotto beside the *gave*.

VISITING LOURDES

Each year more than five million people, many sick or disabled pilgrims, from some 130 countries, pour into the valley from the Sunday before Easter to mid-October, by plane (to Tarbes), by specially adapted trains, or by road. There are 22 consecrated sites where mass is celebrated daily in different languages. There is also a video on the history of the Visions and the Message of Lourdes and several museums and shows with religious themes. The extent of the facilities makes Lourdes an excellent base, although it can be an emotionally difficult place to visit. The material exploitation, from the souvenir shops to the risk of pickpocketing, is probably a characteristic of pilgrimage towns down the ages, although there are also modern attractions such as the waxworks and the recently opened Aquarium des Pyrénées. Even a non-participating observer can find the experience of the youth Mass on a Saturday evening, or the torchlight procession every evening at 20.45, and the overwhelming atmosphere of solidarity, contagiously moving.

The old town

The town is divided by the Gave de Pau. The Marian City, built around the Massabielle grotto, is to the west. A visit to the old town, to the east, is centred around the castle and the sites connected with the Soubirous family. The latter include the 19th-century parish church of Sacré-Coeur in Rue Lafitte, which shelters the Romanesque font used for Bernadette's baptism on 9th January 1844; the Cachot de Bernadette, Rue des Petits-Fossés, where she was living when she had her first vision in 1858; in Rue Bernadette-Soubirous the Moulin de Boly (*open April–Oct 9–12 &*

2–6.30; Nov–March 3–5 and mornings in vacations; T: 05 62 42 16 36), birthplace of the saint on 7th January 1844. No. 2 Rue Bernadette-Soubirous (*open daily mid-April–Oct 9-12.15 & 2.15-7, Sun open at 10, T: 05 62 94 22 51*) was the saint's home from 1858 until she entered the Convent of St-Gildard at Nevers in 1866. The Moulin Lacadé, which her father ran, and which Bernadette used to visit, is in the same street. She died in Nevers in 1879 and was canonised in 1933.

The Château-Fort de Lourdes, on the opposite side of the *gave*, dates from after 1407 and was modified in 1590. It subsequently became a prison and was damaged at the beginning of the 19th century but restoration work began in 1828 and the museum was installed here in 1922. The **Musée Pyrénéen** (*open April–Sept 9–12 & 1.30–6.30; Oct–March 9–12 & 2–6; Fri 2–5; T: 05 62 42 37 37*) provides an interesting resumé of the prehistory and palaeontology of the Pyrenees, its natural history and local traditions, and a good introduction to mountain culture. Among the 18 rooms are the Ramon de Carbonnières room, dedicated to Pyreneeists who conquered the high peaks from 1796 to 1956, including Count Henry Russell who made 33 ascents of Vignemale between 1861 and 1904. The rural life section has curious *cires de deuil*, spaghetti-like coiled candles still used in some villages at funerals to represent the dead and protect the living; and there are elements of medieval architecture.

An unusual collection is on display at the **Musée Christhi**, at 24 Rue de la Grotte (*guided visits from 3p.m.; closed Sun, Nov, and holidays; T: 05 62 42 62 53*), which has a unique collection of coloured advertising cut-outs and other paper imagery for popular brand names between 1870 and 1920.

The Marian City

The Boulevard de la Grotte is the main route to the sanctuaries. To accommodate the vast numbers who gather here, the Esplanade des Processions was built in 1875 and divides into sweeping walkways leading to the two superimposed basilicas at the apex. The neo-Gothic Basilica of the Immaculate Conception, designed by Hippolyte Durand, consecrated in 1871, is built immediately above the Grotte de Massabielle where the Virgin of the Immaculate Conception appeared to Bernadette. On the lower level is the neo-Byzantine

The dome of the Basilica of the Rosary and the spire of the Basilica Superior, Lourdes.

Basilica of the Rosary, designed by Léopold Hardy (1883–89), which can accommodate 1,500 people. In the grotto a sentimental 19th-century marble statue of the Virgin by Carrate watches over the continuous file of the faithful. Two further basilicas, cavernous, concrete, and functional were designed in the 20th century to accommodate thousands of worshippers, wheelchairs and stretchers. The oval underground Basilica of St Pius X, consecrated in 1958 by Cardinal Roncalli, later Pope John XXIII, resembles a vast fallout shelter and can hold nearly 30,000 pilgrims. The impasto stained-glass decorations by Jean-Paul and Germaine Sala-Malherbe make a desultory attempt to cheer it up. More recent is the church of St-Bernadette opposite the grotto, inaugurated in 1988, made up of two adjacent amphitheatres.

An escape from the crowds (or, perhaps worse, from the desolate town when empty of pilgrims) can be made on the funicular (*open mid-July–mid-Oct 10-7; end-March–July, mid-Oct–mid-Nov 10–6; T: 05 62 94 00 41*) from Av. F. Lagardère that runs up to the Pic du Jer (948m), south of Lourdes. At the summit is a large cross, illuminated at night.

THE LAVEDAN

The wide valley of the Gave de Pau flows through one of the most beautiful and thriving areas of the Pyrenees, the Lavedan, in the western part of the Bigorre between Lourdes and the Spanish border. The lower Lavedan is pleasantly green, with pastures and broad-leafed trees, but further into the higher terrain the scenery becomes more rugged, the vegetation changes and there are spectacular waterfalls, culminating in the best known natural site in the whole range, the Cirque de Gavarnie.

ARGELÈS-GAZOST TO ARRENS

The *sous-préfecture* of the Hautes-Pyrénées, Argelès-Gazost, south of Lourdes at the junction of three valleys, attracts crowds on market day. It capitalised on its potential as a spa in the late 19th century and the waters are used in the treatment of oedema and phlebitis. The old town, built on the flank of the hill, has some interesting streets and 16th- and 17th-century houses, and near the 17th-century Tour Mendaigne (next to the tourist office) is a sunny terrace overlooking the Gave de Pau. Nearby is the Donjon des Aigles in the ancient **Château de Beaucens** (*open Easter–Sept, demonstrations in the afternoon, T: 05 62 97 19 59*) built c. 1000 on a rock from which eagles (and other raptors) and their handlers demonstrate their skills. At the new Parc animalier des Pyrénées (*open Jun–Aug 9–7, April–May, Sept 9–12 & 2–6, Oct 1–6; T: 05 62 97 91 07, www.parc-animalier-pyrenees.com*), many of the region's wild animals, including brown bears and wolves, can be observed at close quarters

On the road to the Col d'Aubisque, there is an extraordinary concentration of tiny, rustic mills, some restored and fitted out, at **Arcizans-Dessus**. In the first is the Moulin Musée (*open July–Aug 3–6; rest of year by appointment; T: 05 62 97 52 54*). At **Aucun** is a museum of local history, customs and trades, the Musée Montagnard du

Lavedan (*open during school holidays at 5, other times by appointment; T: 05 62 97 12 03*). Next to the museum is the little church of St-Félix, part 11th-century and part Gothic. Above the south door is an 11th-century monogram of Christ with a bird and a lamb, possibly relocated when the church was altered in the 15th century. The apse, with a billeted cornice and simple carvings, is also 11th-century. On the west is the entrance to the old cemetery and a porch used by the municipal authorities known as *coussous* for meetings, and the doorway and font was once reserved for the *cagots*—medieval marginals who participated at Mass only from a distance. On the north are two baptismal vats used for the immersion of ailing newborn babies. The most interesting pieces are the 16th-century baptismal font and holy water stoup, both in granite. The former is decorated with curious mundane scenes, such as a goat chewing a tree, and an acrobat on his hands; the latter has even stranger primitive carvings of animals and figures.

The much-modified 12th–13th-century church of **Marsous** contains a large 16th-century polychrome *Christ on the Cross*, and some 17th- and 18th-century woodwork, retables and paintings. 800m south of the village, hidden by buildings on a hillock at the junction with the D105, is the spectacular 18th-century chapel of Notre-Dame-de-Pouey-Laün. It was erected on the site of a pilgrim hospice built into the solid granite of the hill. The exterior of the domed chapel is soberly Classical, but the interior is known as the *chapelle dorée* (gilded chapel) because of the abundance of gold leaf used on the ornate Baroque interior, the work of the Ferrère brothers from Asté (*see p. 525*). The retable of the main altar is resplendent with vine-entwined cabled columns and an *Assumption* on the pediment above a statue of Our Lady of Pouey-Laün.

The Arrens valley enters the Parc National des Pyrénées at Porte d'Arrens, a region of romantic mountain lakes where in springtime the valley blooms with wild flowers. In the village of **Arrens** the church of St-Pierre probably dates from the 13th century, the end of the Romanesque period in this region. The porch has a Romanesque tympanum with Christ surrounded by the symbols of the four Evangelists and some Gothic decoration. In the graveyard wall to the right of the entrance are the remains of a Gothic window protecting the *bénitier des cagots*, a font or stoup used by medieval outcasts. The church furnishings include a large polychromed wooden statue of Christ (possibly 13th century) above the Romanesque altar in the north chapel, and a Renaissance consuls' bench. Above Arrens is the Col du Soulor (1474m), a favourite stopping-place with wide mountain panoramas, a rustic chalet-café and local cheese for sale. The road climbs even higher with restricted access to the Col d'Aubisque (1709m).

SAINT-SAVIN

On the alternative route south of Argelès is St-Savin, where well-kept houses, *embans* or *couverts* and three hotels around the irregular square look down to the valley some 580m below. The abbey was a victim of the Revolution but the solid Romanesque Abbey Church (1140–60; *open May–Oct 9–7; Nov–April, 9–6; T: 05 62 97 02 23*), dedicated to St Savin, a 6th-century hermit who lived at Pouey-Aspé, still stands. Altered in the 14th century, when the walls and belfry were raised, it is enlivened by the play of light and shade on the *mirandes*, the buttresses and the octagonal drum of the belfry, with the distinctive candle-snuffer spire of the region. In the shape of a regular Latin cross, with a main apse and two apsidal chapels, sturdy pillars and buttresses, it is covered with a timber and slate roof (14th century). On the tympanum of the main west doorway is a rare image of *Christ in Majesty* dressed in priestly garments, surrounded by the symbols of the four Evangelists. The south door (19th century) is decorated with a Romanesque chrism, and on the cornice of the south apsidal is a tetramorph.

The church has a remarkable number of interesting furnishings. Inside the west door is a ten-sided Aragonese stoup (1140) and font (10th and 18th centuries). Further into the nave, opposite the pulpit (17th century), is an impressive Spanish-style *Crucifixion* (14th century), carved in wood and polychromed. The nave is dominated by the Renaissance organ (1557) with 16th- and 18th-century decoration including three mechanised wooden masks below, activated by the organ pedals. In the south transept is a Romanesque font called the *bénitier des cagots*, carved in granite and supported by two little figures back to back. The St-Catherine chapel has a 12th-century table and Renaissance retable of the *Descent from the Cross*, and in the chapel of St-Pierre there are an 8th-century table and 19th-century tabernacle. The main altar is the 11th-century black marble tomb of St Savin and behind it stands part of a 14th-century gilded *Tower of the Eucharist*. Either side of the choir are two large 15th-century panels with paintings on wood of scenes from the Life of St Savin and his miracles. The 5th-century martyr was crucified on a wheel. The 28 choir stalls are walnut, and the arms of Mgr de Foix (Abbot 1540–1606) are on the officiate's stall. There are also 15th- and 17th-century paintings.

A door from the north transept leads to the sacristy and the 12th-century chapter house, the only part of the monastic buildings still intact, with simply carved capitals and bases. The window capitals have shallow reliefs of bearded heads facing inwards and masks towards the cloister, and a variety of symbolic images.

A small museum of treasures (*open Easter–Oct*) includes a 15th-century reliquary in the form of a château with turrets at the angles, three outstanding 12th-century statues of the *Virgin and Child* and masonry from the former cloister.

CAUTERETS

The best-known spa town in the Pyrenees for many centuries, Cauterets has a formidable array of thermal springs with curative properties for respiratory complaints as well as rheumatics. It can also claim the longest list of illustrious visitors. Jeanne de Navarre and Gaston Fébus came here in the 14th century; Rabelais in the 16th century; and Marguerite de Navarre, sister of François I, reputedly wrote part of her *Heptameron* (1559) here. A new influx of the great, including J.-J. Rousseau, benefited from a new road in 1763; but the town's finest era was the 19th century when Romantic fervour for nature and the picturesque, combined with the patronage of King Louis of Holland and Queen Hortense, drew about 25,000 *curistes* a year, helped by improved transport, monumental hotels and the exploitation of further thermal springs. Victor Hugo wrote about Cauterets in 1843. By 1882 the population had reached nearly 2,000. The first tarmac road in France was built between the Raillère Baths and the Griffons Baths in 1903. Baudelaire, Tennyson, Chateaubriand, George Sand, Edward VII, Gabriel Fauré and Claude Debussy all came for the cure. After a period of decline the town is once again thriving. A ski resort was established in 1964 in the Cirque du Lys (1850–1250m), reached from Cauterets by cable car.

At 1000m above sea-level and on the river, this is a lively centre. The old train station, a delightful wooden building (1897) in a combination of alpine and American western styles, can be visited but no longer functions. The Musée 1900 in the Residence d'Angleterre (*open 10–12 & 3–6.30, closed 15th Nov–15th Dec and holidays; T: 05 62 92 02 02*), is a local ethnological museum with displays of elegant costumes (1850–1925), articles associated with mountaineering, and a *cuisine de l'epoque*.

The most famous of the town's numerous public gardens is the Esplanade des Oeufs. There are many thermal baths; a memorial to Marguerite de Navarre near the Neoclassical gold-and-grey Thermes de César in the older part of town; Belle Epoque grandeur on Boulevard Latapie-Flurin; and the Russian Princess Galitzine's villa in Avenue du Mamelon-Vert. Eight kilometres south is Pont d'Espagne, the start of more walks in the national park and the country of the Lac de Gaube (1728m) and also of Henry Russell (*see p. 517*), the 19th-century Irish mountaineer, known in France as '*pionnier du pyrénéisme*'.

LUZ-ST-SAUVEUR

The main town in the Barèges Valley is Luz-St-Sauveur (711m), made up of Luz and the spa of St-Sauveur to the south, which benefited from the patronage of Napoleon III. He and the Empress Eugénie both suffered bad health, and spent some months at St-Sauveur. They endowed the town with a spectacular bridge completed in 1861, its single arch suspended 65m above the Gave de Pau. Luz is a charming medieval town, with houses embellished with pearl-grey marble and slate roofs around the remarkable fortified **Church of St-André**. A primitive sanctuary, built here at the end of the 11th century by the St-André family, was handed over to the Hospitallers of St John of Jerusalem in the 14th century. The Hospitallers fortified the church and dug a ditch around it to protect the inhabitants of the town from the Miquelets, Aragonese bandits. This little church has retained many of its medieval characteristics including the battlemented wall completely surrounding the church and its graveyard, each merlon protected by a piece of schist held down with a large stone. The arsenal tower to the north was built to defend the original entrance and in the vault of the passageway is a 14th century fresco restored in 1867. The stepped gable-belfry is typical of the Luz Valley, with two open arcades containing the bells, and at the angle of the nave and right transept is the high clock-tower. Over the south porch is a high relief of Christ surrounded by the four Evangelists, badly damaged in 1793, with a monogram of Christ surmounted by a painted *Hand of God*; the capitals and bases of the columns supporting the tympanum are also decorated. Inside are the 12th-century font with a

The road towards the Cirque de Gavarnie.

cover, the splendid 18th-century pulpit, and confessionals. To the left of the entrance to the St-Joseph chapel a 13th-century child's tomb was for a long time used as a holy water stoup.

Just outside Luz, at **Viella**, the part-Romanesque church of St-Michel (*if locked, key held at the auberge*) has a recently restored retable, dated 1730, executed by father and son Soustre, sculptor-carpenters from Asté. Incorporating a profusion of putti and gilded grapevines, one of the richest in the Hautes-Pyrénées. Further up the valley, **Barèges** (1250m) is a small, essentially modern, resort with plenty of modest hotels. It is the highest spa town in France and the oldest winter sports centre in the Pyrenees, established as such in 1921. It was difficult to reach because of poor roads, but by the 18th century Colbert was able to exploit the potential of the spa waters for treating the military. The route over the Col du Tourmalet (*see p. 526*) was improved in 1730 and some years later the route through the gorges was built. The thermal baths, in an elegant building in shades of grey, were built in 1861. The Jardins botanique du Tourmalet (*open mid-May to mid-Sept 10–7; T: 05 62 92 18 06*) cover two hectares with a collection of 2,500 species of mountain plants in their natural surroundings.

GAVARNIE & THE CIRQUE

South of Luz, the road bifurcates at the village of Gèdre (1000m) and after passing the rocky disorder of the Chaos de Coumély, the right fork continues climbing to Gavarnie, at 1365m the highest village in the Pyrenees. The deservedly famous **Cirque de Gavarnie** is a sheer wall of snow-capped rock, a vast natural amphitheatre averaging

1676m in depth, 890m wide at the base and fanning out in three stages to stretch 11km between Pic de Pinède and Pics Gabiét. It was created some 20,000 years ago when an immense glacier slid down the valley towards Lourdes, scooping out the fragile limestone rocks. Its crest is the border between Spain and France. Around it are a group of peaks over 3000m and across the border in Spain is Mont Perdu (3355m).

The village developed at the time of the pilgrimages to Santiago when a commandery was established for the protection of travellers. The mainly 14th-century church, originally the hospice chapel, stands on the old pilgrim route. The village, also a ski resort, was an important centre for *Pyrénéisme* in the 18th and 19th centuries. It is an easy walk from the village to the Hostellerie du Cirque (1570m)—there is alternative transport on donkey or horseback—to view at closer quarters the amphitheatre and the Grande Cascade, the highest waterfall in Europe, crashing out from the back of the Cirque to drop some 423m. There is a vast choice of walks, some much more demanding than others, and a ten-hour trek into Spain and back through the gap known as the Brèche de Roland, according to legend carved out of the rock by Roland's faithful sword Durandal.

THE ADOUR VALLEY

NB: This section and those following are covered by the map on p. 538.

BAGNÈRES-DE-BIGORRE

Bagnères-de-Bigorre is a pleasant spa town in the wide Campan Valley on the banks of the Adour. Its mineral waters are used in the treatment of rheumatoid arthritis, psychosomatic and respiratory problems. Typical of the domestic architecture of Bagnères are the open-work wooden balconies, known as *style thermal*. The old town is bordered to the east by Allées des Coustous, site of the bustling market, and Place des Thermes to the southwest. Conserved in a small garden at the angle of Rue des Thermes and Rue St-Jean are the Gothic portal of the church of St-Jean, and the remains of the cloister of the Jacobins convent destroyed at the Revolution. Also in the area are the 15th-century tower of the Jacobins, Tour de l'Horloge, and the Maison de Jeanne-d'Albret (1539). The church of St-Vincent (c. 1366), northeast of the old quarter, has a 14th-century belfry gable and the remains of a fine Renaissance porch (1557), but the belfry and lateral chapels to the choir were not added until the 19th century. There is a Baroque pulpit, and 20th-century scenes of the Passion decorate the east end. The organ, rebuilt in 1708, has been entirely restored.

The extensive gardens on the slope on the west side of Place des Thermes colourfully frame the spa buildings, which consist of the Neoclassical marble façade of the thermal baths of 1823 with additions of 1860, and the Musée Salies (*open July–Aug, Wed–Sun 3–7; rest of the year Wed–Sun 3–6*), built in 1930. The museum mounts temporary exhibitions, and contains a modest collection of paintings organised thematically with works by Daubigny, Chassériau, Isabey Jongkind, and the Orientalists against a bright-red background. There are also floral works by a local painter, Blanche Odin (1865–1957), and ceramics and sculptures.

Aquensis, La Cité des Eaux (*www.aquensis-bagneres.com*) is a new thermal centre open to the general public with pool, sauna, hammam, beauty and massage treatments, in a modern building. The Musée du Vieux Moulin, Rue Hount Barade (*open Jan–Oct 10–12 & 2–6; closed holidays; T: 05 62 91 07 33*), has a collection of old objects and machinery associated with domestic life, agriculture and cottage industries, especially weaving.

The Musée d'Histoire Naturelle, Vallon du Salut (*T: 05 62 95 85 30*) which opened in 2003 in the old baths at Vallon du Salut, is the public face of the Conservatoire Botanique Pyrénéen. Two major themes are addressed, a land in motion and evolving biodiversity through regular temporary exhibitions on nature and the environment. There is also a giant maquette of the Haute Bigorre, and the 18th-century gallery of the baths with marble fittings on the history of Bagnères as a thermal centre.

THE BARONNIES

East of Bagnères are the Baronnies, an unspoilt section of the foothills of the Pyrenees spanning the area between the Adour and Nestes valleys. A labyrinth of narrow roads links small communities built on the wooded slopes along the valleys of the Arros and the Luz. The point where these two rivers meet, Bonnemazon 10km northeast of Bagnères, was the site chosen c. 1140 by Cistercian monks, originally from Morimond in Burgundy, for the **Abbey of Escaladieu** (*open May–Sept 9.30–12.30 & 1.30–6.30; Oct–April 9.30–12.30 & 1.30–5, closed Tues; T: 05 62 39 16 97*). Although wilfully damaged and laid waste from the 14th to 16th centuries and again in the late 18th century, it still evokes the majestic tranquillity of all Cistercian abbeys. The restored buildings are used for concerts, conferences and exhibitions. The entrance is through the 17th-century gatehouse to the west of the church. All that remains of the cloister, partly enclosed by buildings but completely devoid of galleries, is the ghost of its physical presence and an aura of claustral peace enhanced by swallows, a catalpa tree, some fragments of masonry and an 18th-century fountain.

To the south, bordering the road, the impressively simple abbey church (1143–63) has also retained its grace and harmony despite mutilation. A Latin cross 44m long, the nave was reduced to six bays in the 14th century when the apse was also destroyed. The nave has pointed barrel-vaults and is flanked by interconnecting chapels which form rhythmically satisfying aisles when viewed along their length. The truncated east end was closed by a flat wall in the 16th century and two flat-ended chapels were built into each transept. In the 17th century the south transept received the distinctive octagonal belfry which dominates the street elevation of the church. The pillars of the nave show traces of the original 12th-century stone stalls which were replaced by wooden ones at the end of the 16th century. Immediately next to the north door are the three round-arched bays of the *armarium claustri*, and the sacristy, its original doorway and window almost intact. The layout of the chapter house is unusual, comprising six full and three half bays. The ribbed vaults are supported by four marble columns while a stone bench runs round the edge. It opens onto the cloister through a triple-arched round-headed doorway flanked by double windows. On the floor above, the narrow lancets with brick surrounds indicate the monks' dormitory, and under the blocked-off staircase leading to it is the 14th-century prison.

Beyond the auditorium is a corridor to the garden bounded by the river. A doorway in the north wing opens into an entrance with a 17th- and 18th-century staircase leading to the 17th-century rooms now used for exhibitions. The *scriptorium* (common room) below is very attractive. West of the entrance is the warming room, with a marvellous flagstone floor, the only room with a fireplace.

The ruins of the **Château de Mauvezin** (*open mid-April–mid-Oct 10-7; mid-Oct–mid-April 1.30–5.30; T: 05 62 39 10 27, www.chateaudemauvezin.com*, 2.5km east, occupy a grassy hillock, the site of an ancient *oppidum* and a Roman *castrum* above the village of Mauvezin, dominating the Arros Valley, the Baronnies and an ancient route between Dax and St-Bertrand. The strategic position of the castle was not lost on the Counts of Bigorre in the 11th century, nor on the English when Aquitaine, including the Bigorre, came under the control of the Black Prince in 1360. After a long siege in 1373, the fortress capitulated. Gaston Fébus (*see p. 571*) bought the estate in 1377 and rebuilt the château as a link in the chain of forts controlling traffic across the Midi. A classic medieval stronghold with a square keep (34m high) in the south side and a square courtyard (30m square) with powerfully buttressed walls enclosing a 12th-century cistern. It is now the headquarters of the Escole Gastou Fébus, a Gascon language society.

SOUTH ALONG THE ADOUR

The Adour Valley runs south of Bagnères, growing increasingly winding with ever more spectacular scenery as it leads deep into the mountains, on the way to Gavarnie (*see p. 522*) and Arreau (*see p. 526*).

At **Asté** are the Grottes de Médous (*open April–Sept 9–7; April–June, Sept, Oct 8.30–11.30 & 2–5.30; T: 05 62 91 78 46*). These grottoes are rich in exotic stalactites and stalagmites. The visit covers 1km and includes 200m by boat on an underground section of the Adour. In the same village during the 17th and 18th centuries were two families famous for the production of Baroque church sculptures, the Soustre and the Ferrère. This tradition is remembered in the Maison des Ferrères et du Baroque Pyrénéen (*open Sat, Sun, 10–12 & 2–5.30; T: 05 62 91 76 49*). Three generations of the Ferrère dynasty carved and gilded elaborate structures featuring cupids, vines and twisted or cabled columns between 1647 and 1808. The altarpieces were often combined with paintings by local artists, and can be found in many churches in the *département*.

Beaudéan was the birthplace of Baron Dominique Larrey (1766–1842), surgeon to Napoleon and the *Grande Armée*, who invented the mobile hospital otherwise known as an ambulance. His birthplace, Maison Larrey (*open May–Sept 2–6, closed Mon; Oct-April 2-6, close Mon, Tues; T: 05 62 91 68 96*) can be visited.

The right fork takes you over the Col de Tourmalet (2115m) linking the valley of Haut Adour with the Gaves Valley. The distant views are spectacular and the pastures filled with a profusion of flowers including, in July, vast patches of dark-blue Pyrenean iris. La Mongie is a graceless modern ski resort. After 17km you reach the Col and the route to the **Pic du Midi-de-Bigorre** (2865m), which dominates the landscape for miles around and is easily recognisable by the Observatory at its summit. A cable car was installed in 2001, and a visit goes up to Level 6 of the Observatory, at 2877m. (*reached from La Mongie: open June–Sept 9–4.30, last return 7; Oct–May, closed Tues, from La Mongie 10-3.30, last return 5.30; T: 08 25 00 28 77, closed March; T: 05 62 56 70 65, www.picdumidi.com*). The history of the Pic first as meteorological centre, and later also as observatory, goes back to the 18th century. As well as a glazed viewing gallery with the most spectacular panoramas and a maquette of the site, visitors can discover the world of space and wonder at the ever more sophisticated scientific knowledge pioneered by Charles de Nansouty and Xavier Célestin Vaussenat. There are images of the sun's surface thanks to equipment such as Sidérostat and a large animated model of the 2m telescope of astronomer Bernard Lyot.

THE NESTES

The area takes its name from the ancient name for mountain streams or *nestes*, and strictly speaking marks the old boundary of the province of Bigorre. Rural communities, built in schist and slate, have ancient but modest churches, decorated with murals or frescoes from the 12th century through to the 16th. They are not always easy to locate, and are frequently closed for protection, but visits can be arranged through the local tourist offices.

ARREAU

Arreau (730m) has the typical steep slate roofs with attic windows and subdued silver-grey colours of all the mountain towns. It used to be the capital of the Four Valleys—Aure, Magnoac, Barousse and Neste—and is well placed between the mountains, the plain, and Spain (via the Tunnel de Bielsa). A visit to the town, built between the Neste d'Aure (Robinson Crusoe's route through the Pyrenees) and the Neste de Louron, is accompanied by the sound of water rushing into the valley.

On the right bank by the water is the **Château des Nestes** (*open summer school holidays 9.30–12.30 & 1.30-7, Sun 9.30–12.30; winter school holidays 9.30–12 & 2–6; other times 9.30–12 & 2–5.30, closed Sun and Mon; T: 05 62 98 63 15*), a commandery protecting the sanctuary of St-Exupère in the 11th century, a judiciary building in the 17th century, a mill and grand residence in the 18th century, and which now contains a collection of antique tools and holds temporary exhibitions. The **Chapel of St-Exupère** opposite is dedicated to the 5th-century Bishop of Toulouse who was born in Arreau. His story is told on one of the six archaically decorated Romanesque capitals of the portal which is flanked by pink marble columns and outlined by three carved voussoirs. On the tympanum is a chrism typical of the high valleys of the Nestes and Bigorre; the octagonal tower has triple windows. Inside the porch is a wooden coffer for offerings. Most of the chapel is in Flamboyant Gothic style and a 16th-century wrought-iron screen protects a Romanesque stoup. Next door is the fine building known as the Maison St-Exupère (1554), and overhanging the river is the balcony of the Maison de la Molie (18th century) with marble columns.

On the other side of the bridge, on Grande Rue, is the famous Maison aux Lys (16th century), its façade timbers carved in a *fleur-de-lis* pattern as a reminder of the moment when, at the end of the 14th century, the inhabitants opted for allegiance to Louis XI and the Crown of France rather than to the successor of the Count of Armagnac, Jean V. The rounded, flower-like swastika of the Pyrenees can also be seen, used liberally to decorate doors and façades.

SOUTH TO ST-LARY-SOULAN

South of Arreau is **Cadéac**, which has a 16th-century church and the chapel of Pène-Tailhade straddling the road, their slate roofs glinting in the sun, past Guchen to **Ancizan**, where the is a local museum, the Musée de la Vallée d'Aure, *La vie d'autre-fois (open school holidays, 10–12 & 2–7; other times, 10–12 & 2–6 closed Mon, Tues, and Nov-Dec; T: 05 62 39 97 75)*.

The neat silver-grey village of **Vielle-Aure** is in a beautiful setting, its pleasant 16th-18th-century buildings in striking contrast to the modern ski resort of Soulan above it. Just off-centre, the small church of St-Barthélemy has a Lombardy-style east end, massive piers and a Romanesque altar, but has been modified since the 12th century. Murals were added in the 15th century and a Flamboyant door in the 17th century. Scallop shells and a statue of St James testify to this alternative pilgrimage route into Spain via the Rioumajou Valley.

Vielle-Aure's more dynamic neighbour, **St-Lary-Soulan** (836m), whose much-restored 12th-century Church of Ste-Marie to the north of the town near the baths was, like Vielle-Aure, on the same pilgrimage route. Two Romanesque carvings, a Christ and a chrism, are reused on the exterior and the church preserves an eye-catching Baroque retable from the now-demolished church of St-Hilaire. St-Lary-Soulan is popular with walkers and skiers, one of the six gateways to the national park, the Maison du Parc is in a 16th-century building (*see p. 533*). The Maison de l'Ours (*open summer 9.30–12.30 & 1.30–6.30; winter 9.30–12.30 & 1.30–5.30; rest of year, Wed–Sun 9–12.15 & 1.45–5.30, closed Mon, Tues; T: 05 62 39 50 83*), is dedicated to safeguarding bears and unravels the fact from the myths attached to these unfortunate creatures in the Pyrenees. It has two bears, Apollon and Bingo, born in a circus cage.

St-Lary is on the doorstep of the **Réserve Naturelle du Néouvielle**, containing the Lac d'Orédon. Here carmine wild roses and lilac asters, thistles, dianthus, saxifrages in all varieties, dark-blue gentians, and ancient pines thrive. Some 1,250 flowering plants have been identified, above all in June and July: not much blooms before May but many flower through August and September. The 15 lakes of the Reserve are also home to an exceptional variety of flora and fauna, including 570 types of algae. The road, quite winding in places, is closed in the winter.

NESTE DE LOURON

Southeast of Arreau is a series of Romanesque chapels (at Autist, Bourisp, Cadéac, Gouaux, Guchen, Loubajac, Ourde, Samuran and those described below) with 16th-century murals, on the old pilgrim route (*To protect these fragile works, visits are arranged from the Maison du Tourisme de la Vallée du Louron, at Bordères-Louron, T: 05 62 99 92 00 or 05 62 99 95 35*). The Renaissance decorations, either tempera on wood or fresco on plaster, were added to these simple structures after the Council of Trent in 1563, coinciding with increased prosperity in the valley resulting from a growth in trade with Spain, particularly in wool, following the discovery of the New World in 1492, and from the integration of the region into France. At **Vielle-Louron**, for example, the plain exterior of St-Mercurial gives no clue to the stunning interior decoration painted in intense colours. Several themes cover the walls: an *Annunciation*; a vivid *Last Supper*; scenes from the *Passion*, from the *Flagellation* to the *Entombment*; and *St-Mercurial fighting the Infidels*. On the vaults are the Tree of Jesse, a tetramorph, and Christ surrounded by the Apostles. In the lateral chapel, now the sacristy, is a *Last Judgement* with a very explicit image of the jaws of Leviathan.

The Vallée de Louron is very beautiful: the once tiny and remote community of **Génos** (about 150 residents), with a ruined château, lake, swimming pool, hotels, two ski resorts, and in recent years a thermal baths, Balnea, attracts 30,000 visitors in the summer. St-Blaise, at **Estarvielle**, is a Romanesque church remodelled in the 16th century, with a Baroque retable which partly obscures the paintings. On the north side is *Christ carrying the Cross*, and on the south a *Descent from the Cross*. Framed by the central part of the retable is a *Crucifixion* representing the moment when Christ's side was pierced by Longinus's lance and the soldiers playing cards on Christ's tunic. Close by at **Mont**, the Church of St-Barthélemy is exceptional for having exterior painted decoration. In an oratory in the cemetery are frescoes relating to the Life of St Catherine of Alexandria, signed 'Bona'. Under the church porch is a *Crucifixion* and there is a large *Last Judgement* on the wall between the buttresses. The nave paintings, dated 1574 and attributed to Melchior Rodigis, have scenes from the Passion, Christ before Pilate and Christ with the four Evangelists as well as Isaiah announcing the Birth of Christ. The north chapel contains scenes from the Life of John the Baptist and a *Visitation*, *Annunciation* and *Nativity*. The two painters' styles are quite distinctive, but both use contemporary dress for their figures.

Arixo, Rue des Pic du Gourg Banc, **Loudenvielle** is a modern exhibition of the habitat, the churches and the religious art in the Louron (*open during school holidays: habitat and religious art, 10–12 & 2–6; churches 6–7; film at 9; T: 05 62 99 97 70*). The Col de Peyresourde (1569m) marks the departmental boundary with the Hautes-Garonne, after which the road drops down towards the Luchon Valley (*see p. 549*).

NESTE D'AURE

North of Arreau, on the Neste at **Sarrancolin**, is an interesting and original church in the shape of a Greek cross. It is crowned by an admirable belfry with triple round arches on small columns on the upper level and a candle-snuffer spire with spirelets. The first abbey church was built here by Benedictines from Simorre in 952 and was replaced in the 12th and 13th centuries. It is dedicated to a local martyr, St Ebons, and by some quirk of fate the superb 13th-century reliquary made to contain the saintly remains is still in the church despite being thrown in the Neste at the time of the Revolution and being carried off by thieves in 1911. It is a wooden casket covered with gilded and enamelled copper and is one of the finest in France. On one face are Christ, a king (possibly St Louis), St Ebons, Apostles and saints; on the other scenes from the Birth of Christ; and on the gables at each end are St Peter and St Paul. Following a fire c. 1570, the choir was enclosed by a wrought-iron screen and contains the late 16th century choir stalls and misericords and the altar and retable of 1651. In the north transept is a 17th-century gilded polychrome relief with the *Annunciation, Visitation, Martyrdom of St Lawrence* and *Jesus preaching at the Synagogue*.

In the village, all that is left of the protective walls is the old door called the Tour de la Prison and there are some fine 15th- and 16th-century jettied houses. High quality marble in shades of coral, grey, yellow, green and red, was extracted here from antiquity until the first half of the 20th century despite an earthquake in 1749. The marble is being quarried again, and visits are organised by the Arreau Tourist Office.

East of La Barth-de-Nest, at **Nestier**, is La Calvaire du Mont-Arès, a curious enfilade of 11 rounded bare stone oratories and a chapel, the first one more-or-less underground, which mount the grassy slope of Mont Ares. Constructed in stages during the mid-19th century they had almost disappeared before being restored in the late 1980s. At the summit is a simple altar in the ruins of a chapel. During the summer open-air plays are performed in the small modern amphitheatre outside the restored monastery.

The **Grottes de Gargas** at Aventignan (*guided visits July–Aug 10–12 & 2–6; rest of year, enquire at the site; T: 05 62 39 72 39*) contain a baffling series of more than 200 hands represented in silhouette, other prehistoric decorations and geological concretions. Prehistoric man used the caves over a long period during the last Ice Age, but the decoration is the work of late-Palaeolithic man, between 25,000 and 30,000 years ago. The hands, mainly in red or black, are in ten clusters of up to 43 silhouettes in the first gallery of the lower cave, and there are more further on, including in the Sanctuaire des Mains. The silhouettes were created by projecting pigment from the mouth, but their intention and interpretation have no definitive explanation. A frequent feature of the hands is that one, sometimes two, fingers are incomplete although the thumb always features. In different parts of the caves are the 148 animal images, probably executed over a long period, but due to difficulty of access and their fragility only a few can be seen and the visitor has to make do with a number of reproductions. Some of the drawings, the majority of which represent oxen, bison and horses, are easy to decipher, whereas others are unfinished or piled up on each other like a tangled skein of thread.

TARBES

Tarbes, capital of the Bigorre, is the second largest urban agglomeration in the Midi-Pyrénées and main town of the *département* of the Hautes-Pyrénées. It began as a Roman settlement in the Adour Valley on the important Bayonne–Toulouse route. It is now the most dynamic industrial centre in the region, although a somewhat characterless garrison town relieved by fountains and green areas.

EXPLORING TARBES

Start out from Place de Verdun (north of the tourist office), and turn left on Rue Abbé Torné. The characteristic building material of the Tarbes plain is smooth round pebbles, with stone or brick courses, often arranged in a herring-bone pattern. The **Cathédrale de la Sède**, begun at the end of the 12th or early 13th century, and extensively restored, is an interesting combination of brick, stone and pebble in a mixture of styles, from Romanesque at the east, with a massive octagonal belfry, to Neoclassical at the west. On the south flank are the remains of a Romanesque cloister. The interior décor is predominantly 18th-century, its main features the wooden stalls and panelling, the wrought iron, chequered floor, and the altar and baldaquin by Marc Arcis, using coloured Pyrenean marble. Above the crossing is an octagonal lantern on pendentives. The restoration of the 17th-century organ was completed in 1993.

One block north of Rue Abbé Torné at 2 Rue de la Victoire is the **Maison Natale du Maréchal Foch** (*open May–Sept 9–12 & 2–6.30, Oct–April 10–12 & 2–5, closed Tues, Wed; T: 05 62 93 19 02*). Birthplace of Field-Marshall Foch (1851–1929) Commander of the Allied Forces in 1918, gathered here in the 18th-century house is a collection of memorabilia which either belonged to the great man or are reminders of his popularity.

North of Place de Verdun up Rue Massey is the **Jardin Massey**, a 14-hectare green oasis bequeathed to the town by Placide Massey (1777–1853), naturalist and director of the Orangerie at Versailles. The park, created 1829–52, has a collection of rare and exotic trees and several sculptures, including busts of the writer Théophile Gautier (1811–72), born in Tarbes, by his daughter Judith, and of the poet Jules Laforgue (1860–87) by Michelet. It also contains four galleries of a 14th-century cloister salvaged from the former Benedictine abbey of St-Sever-de-Rustan (*see p. 531 opposite*). The iconography of the capitals includes scenes from the Old Testament, the *Creation of Adam and Eve* and original sin, the *Birth of Christ*, the *Passion* and martyrdoms, as well as allegorical themes and foliate capitals.

The Musée Massey et des Beaux-Arts (*under restoration. Information from Tarbes Tourist Office*), is installed in Massey's former house, designed by Jean-Jacques Latour. It was begun in 1852 at a time when Hispanic styles were in vogue through the influence of Empress Eugénie, Spanish wife of Napoleon III. The museum has an archaeological collection with a remarkable Bronze Age mask of the local god Ergénd, and European paintings from the 16th century to the present giving pride of place to a painting by Utrillo; also of note are an *Adoration of the Magi* by the School of Jan Scorel, and landscapes by William Didier-Pouget.

The main commercial quarter of Tarbes is east of Place de Verdun. Rue Brauhauban is a presentable pedestrian street lined with some good 18th and 19th century houses, among them Gautier's birthplace at no. 2. Turn right to Place du Marcadieu, dominated by the grand Duvignau fountain (1896) evoking the four valleys of Bigorre—Aure, Bagnères, Argelès and Tarbes—at the heart of the market quarter with its splendid *halle*, a typical construction of the 1880s in iron.

The **Haras National** (*guided visits Mon–Fri at 10, 11, 2, 3, 4; last Sun of month at 2.30 and 4; T: 05 62 56 30 80*) is southwest of Place de Verdun, on 70 Av. du Régiment de Bigorre. The cavalry stud was established in Tarbes at the order of Napoleon. It is graced with a beautiful group of Empire buildings designed by the architects Devèze, Larrieu and Ratouin in 1881. The light and airy stables, for pampered horses, have been restored using original materials: pebbles and cobblestones for the floor, marble for the troughs, loose-boxes (some of the first examples) in solid oak, and a curved ceiling in chestnut, with false marbling reproduced inside and out. Equestrian events are held here regularly.

THE LANNEMEZAN

The area to the east of Tarbes is known as the Lannemezan, the flat land north of the town of the same name. At the hamlet of **Moulédous** resides a Baroque retable of traditional style, returned to its original gilded splendour in 1982–86. It may have come from either or both the workshops of two families of artists from Asté (*see p. 525*), the Ferrère and the Soustre. The central panel represents the *Assumption of the Virgin* with a saint-bishop and St John the Baptist, with God the Father above flanked by St John and St Matthew. The church is kept locked. To visit, ring M. Marcel Duffau (*T: 05 62 35 71 45*) in advance, and collect the key at the house opposite

Abbaye de St-Sever-de-Rustan

Guided visits, in summer 2–6; out of season, by appointment; T: 05 62 96 69 85 or Mairie 05 62 96 63 93)

The former Abbaye de St-Sever-de-Rustan on the banks of the Arros. A Benedictine community existed here early in the 11th century and seems to have flourished until the 14th century, when it was overtaken by the Hundred Years War, then abused by secular abbots, and finally overrun by Protestant troops in 1573. The restoration was begun in 1646 by the Congregation of St-Maur, and in the 18th century the abbey received secular decoration typical of the period and of the St-Maur abbots; but the Revolution brought everything to a halt and parts of the abbey were sold off.

The cloister of St-Sever de Rustan ended up in the Jardin Massey in Tarbes and the organ in the church of Castelnau-Magnoac, but the church, the sacristy and monastic buildings can still be visited. The Romanesque portal in the south wall of the abbey church has been in this position since the 18th century. Part of the nave is also Romanesque, with a round-arched window curiously inserted in the south buttress. The carved capitals, like the storiated capitals of the nave, have stylistic links with the late 11th-century carvings at St-Sernin, Toulouse (*see p. 588*). A Gothic-style east end seems to have been hastily and clumsily added during rebuilding in the 16th century, and the church bears the traces of several stages of modification or adaptation. The major legacies of the 18th century are the monastic buildings, some beautiful wood panelling in the sacristy, the monumental staircase in the southwest of the former cloister and some fine stucco-work.

Trie-sur-Baïse

To the southeast is Trie-sur-Baïse, notorious for the largest pork markets in France and for the annual competition to find the person who can produce a sound most like a pig. This *bastide* was founded in 1323 by Jean de Trie and has kept its original layout despite pillage by the English in 1356 and destruction in 1569 during the Wars of Religion. The cloister of the oldest church in Trie belonging to a Carmelite monastery has been reconstructed in the Cloisters Museum, New York. The very large central square has a graceful 19th-century iron *halle* encompassing the stone Mairie. On the south side, the parish church of Notre-Dame-des-Neiges was begun in 1444, the date of the peace treaty between the English and the Counts of Foix and Bigorre.

Notre-Dame de Garaison

Against the wall of the church at Monléon-Magnoac stands one of the old town gates; inside the church are wood carvings from the sanctuary of Notre-Dame de Garaison (*usually open; T: 05 62 99 49 41*) to the south. The sanctuary represents the long tradition of Marian devotion practised throughout the Pyrenees, notably along the pilgrim route from Notre-Dame-de-Rocamadour in the Lot to Montserrat in Catalonia, passing St-Savin, Aragnouet, Luz, Bourisp and Gavarnie. Garaison was the site of a medieval cult dedicated to Our Lady of September. In 1515 a young shepherdess, Anglèze de Sagasan, received visions of the Virgin near the fountain of Garaison telling her to create a new chapel, and anticipating by some 200 years the apparitions of the Virgin to Bernadette de Soubirous at Lourdes; construction was undertaken by 1540 and the chapel was restored in the following century. It remained an important centre of veneration until the 19th century.

The Gothic-style sanctuary, built in brick with rib vaults, is entirely decorated with 16th- and 17th-century murals and has furnishings from the 15th/18th century. It is part of a stunning group of buildings—now used as a Catholic boys' school—built around a semi-formal garden. The 17th-century main door, graciously painted in shades of blue, is a foretaste of the unusual but colourful decoration of the church. The narthex has paintings dated 1699 inspired by a popular book about Garaison published in 1646, and naive paintings recounting the appearance of the Virgin, dressed in white, to Anglèze. The tempera *ex-voto* paintings on the walls of the nave are reminders of some of the many miracles and cures associated with the site.

PRACTICAL INFORMATION

GETTING AROUND

• **By train:** Paris–Tarbes/Lourdes
Toulouse–Lannemezan–Tarbes
Shuttle service from Lourdes and
Tarbes to ski resorts
• **By bus:** Shuttle buses
Tarbes–Lourdes. From Tarbes buses
run to Bagnères-de-Bigorre/La-Mongie,
Vic-Bigorre, Maubouguet, Mont-de-
Marsan, Rabastens de Bigorre, Auch,
Lannemezan, St-Lary Soulan,
Montréjeau, Montgaillard, Bagneres-
de-Bigorre, Lourdes, Argeles-Gazost,
Luz-St-Sauveur, Soumoulou, Pau,
Tournay, St Lary, Trie-sur-Baïse,
Aéroport-Pau-Pyrénées.
From Lourdes buses runs to Barèges,
Cauterets, Bagnères-de-Bigorre,
Montgaillard, St-Pé-de-Bigorre and
Pau.
Buses run from Luz-St-Sauveur to
Gavarnie

TOURIST INFORMATION

Argelès-Gazost 15 Pl. de la
République, T: 05 62 97 00 25,
www.argeles-gazost.com
Arreau Château des Nestes, T: 05 62
98 63 15, www.vallee-aure.com
Arrens-Marsous Maison du Val
d'Azun, T: 05 62 97 49 49,
www.valdazun.com
Bagnères-de-Bigorre 3 Allées
Tournefort, BP 226, T: 05 62 95 50 71;
Barèges Pl. Urbain-Cazaux, T: 05 62 92
16 00, www.bareges.com
Cauterets Pl. Foch, BP 79, T: 05 62 92
50 50, www.cauterets.com
Gavarnie T: 05 62 92 49 10,

www.gavarnie.com
La Barthe-de-Neste Neste Barronnies,
T: 05 62 98 87 02,
www.ot-neste-baronnies.com
Lannemezan 73 Rue Jean-Jacques
Rousseau, T: 05 62 98 08 31,
www.lannemezan. com
Lourdes Pl. Peyramale, BP17, T: 05 62
42 77 40, www.lourdes-France.com
Luz-St-Sauveur Pl. du 8 Mai, T: 05 62
92 30 30, www.luz.org
St-Lary Soulan 37 Rue Vincent Mir,
T: 05 62 39 50 81, www.saint-lary.com
St-Laurent-de-Nestes Pl. de la Mairie, T:
05 62 39 74 34, www.neste-nistos.com
Tarbes 3 Cours Gambetta, T: 05 62 51
30 31, www.tarbes.com
Trie-sur-Baïse Maison du Pays de Trie,
31 Pl. de la Mairie, T: 05 62 35 50 88,
www.triesurbaise.com

ACCOMMODATION & RESTAURANTS

Argeles-Gazost
€€€ **Hôtel Miramont/Restaurant Le
Casaou.** Extremely charming and stylish hotel in pretty surroundings with a
lovely separate garden annex with 8
rooms, Les Jardins du Miramont. The
Restaurant Le Casaou is light and spacious and designed for unhurried
enjoyment of local specialities by chef
Pierre Pucheu who ranks among the
best chefs in the Département. He uses
seasonal produce including local lamb,
haricots Tarbais and Madiran wine. 44
Av. des Pyrénées; T: 05 62 97 01 26,
www.hotelmiramont.com
€€ **Hôtel/Restaurant Beau Site.** This
hotel really is in a beautiful site, with
views all around. The hotel has 16 com-

fortable rooms, panoramic terrace and a small garden. Carefully prepared home cooking is served in the restaurant. 10 Rue du Capitaine Digoy, T: 05 62 97 08 63, www.hotel-beausite-argeles.com

Arreau

€ Hôtel/Restaurant d'Angleterre. This ancient *relais de poste*, now run by Madame Aubiban, boasts a long tradition of hospitality and a mention by the Irish mountaineer, Henry Russell, in *Souvenirs d'un montagnard* (1889). On the way to the Pyrenees it is a simple and welcoming base, with 20 rooms, garden and heated pool. On the Luchon road, T: 05 62 98 63 30, www.hotel-angleterre-arreau.com.

Asté

€ Hôtel/Restaurant d'Asté. Situated in the Haute Adour region with plenty of opportunities for sport or relaxation, summer or winter, the hotel is in a leafy setting and a sunny terrace. The rooms are restful and uncluttered. In the bright restaurant where Guy Perseré is chef, the excellent dishes include *Pavé de Merlu de ligne en nage de Palourdes*, or *Filet de canard rôti et sa compote d'oignons de Trébons*, with menus from €13 upwards. Rte. des Cols, T: 05 62 91 74 27, www.hotel-aste.com

Bagnères-de-Bigorre

€€ Hôtel /Restaurant Pyrénées Sport. Just outside the spa of Bagnères, in a beautiful setting, the hotel is well placed to take advantage of all that is on offer in the Pyrenees. There are 54 bright, modern rooms with minimalist decor by Philippe Starck and in the Restaurant La Fabrique the chef conjures up wide-ranging dishes from good local produce such as *porc noir Gascon*, and *agneaux de pays*. Rte des Cols, Gerde, T: 05 62 95 53 11, www.citecycle.com

Barèges

€ Auberge du Lienz - Chez Louisette. ■ A delightful mountain *auberge* which at 1600m, opposite the majestic Pic du Midi de Bigorre, is in summer bathed in green and in winter is the snowy slopes of Tourmalet. The good old-fashioned home cooking is especially renowned for its sweet and tasty mutton Barèges-Gavarnie, served as *cotelettes*, *gigot* or *civet*, on a platter of local slate. Or there is tender *Pied de cochon farci aux morilles, Truite fario fourrée aux cèpes*, and for pudding, bilberries, raspberries and liquorice as found in the mountains. Rte. du Lienz, T: 05 62 92 67 17.

Cadéac

€ Hostellerie du Val d'Aure. Cathy and Guy Bonnet run this attractive hotel/restaurant close to Arreau/St-Lary in a 3ha park. There is a garden with terrace, magnificent mountain views, a large swimming pool and tennis court, and the rooms are pleasant and unfussy, some with balconies. A sample of dishes served in the rustic restaurant includes *Oeufs de caille au foie gras et cèpes, magret de canard gras à l'orange*, and *Filet de sandre rôti aux noisettes*. Rte de St-Lary, T: 05 62 98 60 63, www.hotel-valdaure.com

Castelnau Magnoac

€€ Restaurant Dupont. Pierre Dupont's restaurant has the charm of a large family house which for many generations has introduced its guests to the way of life and gastronomy of the Southwest of France. T: 05 62 39 80 02.

Castelnau-Rivière-Basse

€ Hostellerie du Château Montus. Deep in the Madiran vineyards, the owner of this property helped revive the reputation of the local wine. The old manor house, with a large terrace and great views, is arranged around an interior courtyard. The décor, inspired by the mythology of wine, is boldly individual bordering on the bizarre. The 15 rooms are grandiose and the bathrooms enormous; the colours are strong and the details exotic, even erotic: scenes from the karma sutra on a bedroom ceiling. Meals are served exclusively to residents. T: 05 62 31 70 20.

Cauterets

€ **Hôtel/Restaurant Lion d'Or**. The Lasserre sisters run this hotel in a sweetly old-fashioned 19th-century building, close to the spa, to the cable car and the town centre. There are 25 delightful rooms, all different, with pretty details—a little lace here, lavender sachet there—some with balcony. Denise, mother of Bernadette and Rose Marie, concocts simple but tasty meals which are served in a friendly, intimate dining room where hotel silverware from the 1830s is still used. 12 Rue Richelieu, T: 05 62 92 52 87, www.hotel-lion-dor.net

Gavarnie

€€ **Grand Hotel Vignemale**. ■ A tall, chalet-style building of 1907, in the village but separated from it by the Gave de Pau, facing south with sublime views of the Cirque, its waterfalls and snow-clad peaks. The slightly outmoded elegance of the marble clad lobby is offset by a friendly welcome and information on the region. A great place for rest, fresh air and exercise, with comfortable, slightly cottage-like but spacious rooms with that famous view. The restaurant with *table d'hôte* around €30 is reserved

for hotel guests, and serves simple, healthy mountain meals. Open in season (May–Oct). T: 05 62 92 40 00, www.hotel-vignemale.com

Loubajac

€ **Chambres d'hôtes**. The typical Bigourdan house and 12ha farm with sheep and poultry - 5 ha are in front of the house, is open all year. The rooms are attractive and uncluttered, and outside is a large garden and spectacular mountain scenery. The food served at the *table d'hôtes* is based on the produce of the farm. Jean-Marc and Nadine Vives, 28 route de Bartres (D940 northwest of Lourdes), T: 05 62 94 44 17, www.anousta.com

Lourdes

€€€ **Grand Hotel de la Grotte**. In a commanding position on the rocks below the castle overlooking the sanctuaries and the Gave, this top class luxury hotel was built in 1872 and in the same family for 4 generations. With bags of traditional elegance and modern comfort, the 80 rooms are luxurious and vary in character, some under the eaves, some with views. There is a choice of eateries, including bistrot with terrace, brasserie for all-day food, and a top-of-the range gourmet restaurant. 66 rue de la Grotte, T: 05 62 94 58 87, www.hotel-grotte.com

€€ **Hôtel/Restaurant Beau Séjour**. Turn of the 20th century charm on the wide avenue opposite the station, there are wonderful views from the terraces and rooms. Throughout the hotel warm reds and ochres are used to discreetly elegant effect, including the bedrooms, which are large and to a high standard of comfort. The brasserie has a large patio and the restaurant is very attractive with painted mural. There is a shuttle bus between the hotel and the religious city. 16 Av. de la Gare, T: 05 62 94 38 18, www.hotel-beausejour.com

€€ **Restaurant Le Chalet de Biscaye.**
Ginette and Jean-Michel Verducou run an outstanding restaurant with a large choice of modern cuisine as well as a return to the traditional. Delicious suggestions include *Les tripes cuites au chaudron, Les goujonnettes de Bar à la fondue de pomodore, Le pavé de sandre rôti au tamarin sabayon de livèche*, and for lovers of desserts, *Un praline à l'ancienne or Un success au chocolat blanc et gianduja*. 26 Rte. du Lac, T: 05 62 94 12 26.

Pinas

€ **Chambres d'hôtes Domaine de Jean Pierre**. A former agricultural property in the Lannemezan, close to St-Laurent-de-Neste, well positioned for exploring mountain or plain, the large house is covered with Virginia Creeper and surrounded by extensive grounds with views of the Pyrenees. The rooms are very light, spacious and elegantly simple. Breakfast is served on the terrace or in the lovely beamed dining room. Marie Sabine Colombier, 20 Rte. De Villeneuve, T: 05 62 98 15 08, www.domainedejeanpierre.com

Pouzac

€ **Chambres d'hôtes les Chambres de Zoé**. A very pretty old house which once belonged to Lafaille, one of Napoleon's Generals, in a village near to Bagnères-de-Bigorre. It has been carefully restored in an eclectic style and good decorative sense by the much-travelled owners. A large entrance arch leads from the street to a galleried interior once used for drying crops, and each room is personalised by theme and colour. 5 Rue Général Lafaille, T: 05 62 95 41 93.

St-Lary-Soulan

€ **Hôtel/Restaurant La Pergola**.
Delightful hotel at the foot of the Pyrenees with wooden balconies overlooking a garden and trees and aromatic plants. The 20 comfortable rooms are described as either 'cosy', 'montagne' or 'élégance'. The cooking under the direction of Jean-Pierre Mir, is outstanding with both traditional and gastronomic dishes on offer, and there is a hearty buffet breakfast for those with an energetic day in mind. Rue Vincent Mir, T: 05 62 39 40 46, www.hotellapergola.fr

St-Savin

€€ **Hôtel/Restaurant du Viscos**. Close to Argelès-Gazost, Vallée des Gaves, Monsieur and Madame Saint Martin have a charming hotel close to the church of St-Savin with pretty rooms embellished with delicate drapes. Jean-Pierre Saint Martin is a master of invention, rediscovering lost flavours and creating unusual combinations for the pleasure of diners in the dining room or on the terrace. Menus from €21–50, and for something a bit different the 'Randonnée Gourmande en Bigorre' menu. T: 05 62 97 02 28, www.hotel-leviscos.com

Tarbes

€€€ **Restaurant L'Ambroisie**. In an old presbytery of the diocese of Tarbes, Daniel Labarrère puts heart and soul into his cooking which is based on seasonal availability, with dishes such as *Noix de St Jacques au pamplemousse vert sur endives fondues*. 48 Rue Abbé Torné, T: 05 62 93 09 34.

€€ **Restaurant Le Fil à la Patte**. The food here is excellent value for money. André Sanchez only works with fresh produce, which he shops for at the market every day. The menus follow the seasons and are always colourful and full of flavour. 30 Rue Georges Lassalle, T: 05 62 93 39 23.

Viscos

€€ **Hotel/Restaurant La Grange aux Marmottes**. In a magical mountain village, at 850m, in the Pays Toy close to Luz, Mme Sénac runs this friendly hotel and restaurant, with beautiful views, garden and pool. There are 10 rooms and 2 suites in two renovated barns where rustic and modern meld successfully. Some of the culinary delights of the establishment are *La selle d'agneau du Pays Toy farcie*. T: 05 62 92 88 88, www.lagrangeauxmarmottes.com

MARKET DAYS

Arreau Thursday
Argelès-Gazost Tuesday, Saturday
Arrens-Marsous July–August Sunday
Bagnères-de-Bigorre Saturday
Barèges Summer, Wednesday
Cauterets Friday
La Barthe-de-Neste Sunday
Lannemezan Wednesday, *Marché aux ovins* (sheep), to see
Lourdes Thursday (every two weeks), Saturday
Luz-St-Sauveur Monday
Maubourguet Tuesday
Pierrfitte-Nestalas Saturday
St-Lary-Soulan Saturday
St-Laurent-de-Nestes Summer Friday
Sarrancolin Tuesday, Saturday
Tarbes Thursday, Halle Brauhauban Saturday and Sunday
Trie-sur-Baïse Tuesday *Marché au porc* (to see)
Vic-en-Bigorre Saturday

FESTIVALS & EVENTS

February: *Anniversaire de la Première Apparition*, first apparition to Bernardette Soubirous on 11th February, Lourdes. *Semaine de l'Astronomie*, week of astronomy, Cap Astro, Barèges and La Mongie, T: 06 82 80 83 41

April: *La Hestayade*, gathering of Occitan choirs, Ibos (near Tarbes), T: 05 62 90 03 98

June: *Festival Eldorando*, international festival of hiking, with walkers from all over the world in the Pyrenees for 4 days, with music and celebrations, Val d'Azun, T: 05 62 97 49 49

July: *Le Tour de France Cyclist*, the great cycle race passes through the Pyrenees every year. *Equestria*, festival of the horse, Tarbes, T: 05 62 52 30 31 *Défi Pyrénéen*, bicycle race between Argelès-Gazost and Bagnères-de-Bigorre T: 05 62 95 50 71

August: *Sur les Chemins de St-Jacques-de-Compostelle*, festivities along the pilgrimage route, Sarrancolin, Arreau, Antignan, Guchen, Vielle-Aure, St-Lary, Aragnouet, all in the Aure Valley, T: 06 10 75 41 16. *La Pourcailhade*, pig festival and pig-noise championship, Trie-sur-Baïse, T: 05 62 35 50 88

September: *Moutouades, Fêtes des Cotelettes*, return of sheep from the mountains, Luz-St-Sauveur. *Championnat International de Chiens des Pyrénées*, Pyrenean mountain dog championships, Argelès-Gazost, T: 05 62 97 00 25

December: *Fête de l'Immaculée Conception*, Festival of the Immaculate Conception (8th), Lourdes

HAUTE-GARONNE

The Département d'Haute-Garonne is determined by the Garonne River which rises in the Pic d'Aneto in Spain to flow north into France, turns northwest towards Toulouse then north again. The different areas or *pays* encompassed in Haute-Garonne include the Comminges and Central Pyrenees, the Volvestre and Lauragais, and the Toulousain, which guarantee a rich diversity of scenery and architecture. Among a variety of historic sites some of the best are the hilltop village of St-Bertrand-de-Comminges dominated by a magnificent Gothic cathedral, and on the plain below the Basilica of St-Just-de-Valcabrère; the Gallo-Roman Villa of Montmaurin; the village of Rieux in the Volvestre south of Toulouse; and the Canal du Midi east of Toulouse.

THE COMMINGES

Modern Comminges is an administrative subdivision of the *département*, which loosely follows the boundaries of a medieval province of the same name spanning the Garonne Valley, between the plains of Gascony and the central Pyrenean chain. St-Gaudens is the major administrative centre in the Comminges, with St-Bertrand-de-Comminges the most important historic site.

HISTORY OF THE COMMINGES

Evidence of prehistoric, Iron Age and Celtic man has been found in this *pays* and according to a 4th-century text by St Jerome, Comminges was annexed by Pompey in 72 BC on his return from the Iberian Peninsula, although this has not been confirmed. The people who gathered here were known as the Convenes and by 15 BC their city, *Lugdunum Convenarum*, had become the capital of part of the province of *Aquitania*. Christianity was probably introduced by 250 AD and *Lugdunum*, an episcopal city in the 4th century, flourished until the arrival of the Visigoths c. 408–409. By the 6th century the town was known as *Convenae*. In 585, during the Frankish invasions, it was reputedly devastated, and then faded into obscurity until the 11th century and the arrival of Bertrand de l'Isle, the future St Bertrand. The Comminges was a semi-independent province in the Middle Ages, reaching the extent of its power towards the end of the 12th or early 13th centuries under the first four counts (of Comminges), all called Bernard. Comminges was absorbed into the kingdom of France in 1456, and pilgrimages to St Bertrand's relics were in full swing by the 17th century. After the Revolution, they were revived some time around 1805.

ST-BERTRAND-DE-COMMINGES

St-Bertrand-de-Comminges is a major showpiece: a wooded cliff provides the backdrop to the Gothic cathedral which rises in overwhelming proportions above a medieval walled village set on a small mound. At its feet are more medieval buildings, Gallo-Roman sites and the Romanesque church of St-Just-de-Valcabrère, and in the distance are the mountains. Wherever you look, Gallo-Roman elements are reused, or medieval stone is recycled. Despite its tiny population (about 250), St-Bertrand welcomes some 200,000 visitors a year but, like most small towns, it is unlikely to be busy at either end of the day. There is an annual festival in July and August with concerts in the cathedral, at St-Just and at St-Gaudens.

Site Antique de St-Bertrand-de-Comminges

To the northeast, below the hill, are the remains of successive archaeological sites from the Gallo-Roman to early Christian periods. The vestiges revealed by the excavations date from c. 20 BC up to the 6th century. When the settlement was elevated to the status of colony in the 2nd century it expanded to cover some 30 hectares stretching from the foot of the hill to the banks of the Garonne and as far as the Romanesque church of St-Just (*see p. 544*).

The temple of the forum and its enclosure, west of the road, were built during the reign of Augustus (27 BC–14 AD) and abandoned by the 4th or 5th centuries. The adjacent *thermae*, of the same period, were rebuilt on a larger scale with hot and cold baths, *piscina* and hypocaust. Part of the *cardo* (the north–south axis) divided this from the vast *macellum* (market), east of the road on the site of an earlier basilica. The market had three monumental entrances and a large open space in the middle bordered by a double row of stalls to the south and one row to the north. A large porticoed square was a later addition to the market complex. Between it and the forum, a small round monument has been reconstructed: its precise function has not been identified but it may have marked the intersection of the Roman roads to Dax and to Toulouse. The late 2nd-century northern *thermae*, northwest of the forum are the most complete, with easily identifiable *piscina*, *natatio*, *frigidarium*, *tepidarium*, and *praefurium*. Parts of just three terraces of the early 1st-century theatre are visible on the hill behind the car park; the rest disappeared when the road was built in the 18th century.

In the attractive lower town, near the little parish church of St-Julien, is the overgrown site of an early Christian basilica (5th century); marble sarcophagi scattered around indicate its use as a burial ground. There is also a magnificent example of a Comminges barn nearby, with hooped or semi-circular timbers in the upper part.

Exploring the *cité*

There are three approaches to the hill village which is still confined within the medieval ramparts: on foot through Porte Cabirole (east) or Porte Majou (north), or by car via Porte Hyrisson and car park (west; a *petit train* runs to Porte Hyrisson). Porte Majou, originally the main entrance to the medieval town, was rebuilt in the

St-Bertrand-de-Comminges (left) and the basilica of St-Just-de-Valcabrère (right).

18th century and used as a prison. On the inside is a Roman funerary stele and, out-side, the arms of Cardinal de Foix (15th century). On foot you are more likely to enter through Porte Cabirole which has Roman inscriptions on the outer wall. The little building opposite, which incorporates some medieval masonry, stands on the remains of the barbican. Passing under the archway, a short distance up on the left is the half-timbered Maison Bridaut (rebuilt 1577) with a Renaissance tower. A left turn at the Hôtel Oppidum—the 15th-century house on the right has medallions under the eaves on the right—then a right turn past an 18th-century fountain, brings you out in the centre of the *cité* and face-to-face with the great looming west front of the cathedral.

On the left is the neo-Gothic church of **Les Olivetains**, part of a former monastery attached to the Sienese branch of the Benedictine order established here in the 19th century. The buildings are occupied by the Tourist Office, an extensive bookshop, museum and art gallery (*open July–Aug 10–7; April–June, Sept–Oct 10–6; rest of year 10–5*). The 19th-century chapel is used to exhibit an ensemble of statues and sculptures known as the Trophy (c. 24 BC), an allegory of Augustus' conquest of Gaul and Spain. A trophy originally consisted of a tree-trunk erected by a victorious army and decorated with the spoils of battle. It became the motif of a triumphal monument in ancient Greece and then in Rome, where it expanded into a large ensemble of sculptures. Some 115 fragments were discovered in 1926 and 1931 in ditches near the remains of the Roman temple at St-Bertrand and have been pieced together. The grouping is not necessarily accurate, but is based on the best information available given the wide disparity of the pieces.

Cathedral of Ste-Marie

Open daily. No visits Sunday morning; T: 05 61 89 04 91. Fee payable to visit the choir.
Bertrand de l'Isle, great Church reformer and builder, Bishop of Comminges 1083–1123, was responsible for the first cathedral, consecrated in 1200. In 1218 Bertrand was canonised and *Lugdunum Convenarum* became St-Bertrand-de-Comminges. Bertrand de Got, Bishop (1294–99) and later Pope Clement V (*see p. 92*), initiated, supervised and financed, through the intermediary Canon Adhémar de St-Pastou, the transformation of the cathedral to accommodate the influx of pilgrims. The building was completed at the time of Bishop Hugues de Châtillon (1336–52).

The exterior
Work started c. 1307 at the east, with the chevet. The Romanesque nave was incorporated into an aisleless Gothic structure and 14 gabled and pinnacled buttresses support the walls which were extended upwards. At the west, under the Gothic carapace, elements of the old church are visible in the narthex and the first three bays with simple lancets. The austere façade was enlarged and the belfry raised in the 14th century. The west portal, approached by marble steps and submerged in a deep recess, has richly sculpted décor. On the marble Romanesque tympanum is the *Epiphany* watched by St Bertrand, and the lintel carries a relief of the twelve Apostles. The five capitals of the porch carry figures and animal motifs similar to the west porch of St-Sernin in Toulouse.

The interior
The massive narthex conserves capitals and half-barrel vaults from the 11th–12th-century church. Built in silvery-grey local stone, the fairly small cathedral (55m by 16m and 28m high), with five radiating chapels and no transept, has simple quadripartite vaults and little integral decoration except painted bosses bearing the coats of arms of the bishop-builders. The calm of the Gothic church is disrupted by the ornate 16th-century choir enclosure of burnished oak, the *jubé* of which is at the level of the second bay of the nave. This consists of a gallery with pendant bosses and 20 figures above including God the Father, an Ecce Homo, Apostles and virgins, and on the two lower panels are polychromed statues including St Bertrand, St Roch and St Sebastian.

Placed on the diagonal on the north of the first bay, to serve both the choir and the nave, is the equally ornate three-tiered Renaissance organ, supported on a coffered platform by five fluted columns, which was donated by Bishop Jean de Mauléon (1523–55). Incorporated is the 16th-century pulpit which faces the parish altar in the St-Sacrement chapel, added in 1621. The chapel contains the famous crocodile *ex-voto*.

The chancel, windows and treasury
The closed partitions of the wooden church-within-a-church separate the chancel or choir enclosure from the body of the cathedral. The bequest of Jean de Mauléon, inaugurated at Christmas 1535, this is one of the rare complete choir enclosures left in France, and one of three in the Midi-Pyrénées, with Albi and Auch. It provided an area where the clergy could perform Mass unobserved and undisturbed by the pub-

lic who would, nevertheless, hear it from the ambulatory. The exterior is relatively sober, the full glory of the carved oak being reserved for the inner sanctum. Arranged in two tiers around three sides of the choir are the 66 stalls assigned, according to status, to canons and church dignitaries—the 38 in the upper row, with sculpted backs and canopies, were reserved for higher ranks. The tribune, on the reverse of the *jubé*, has at its centre the ambo from where the deacon read aloud the Epistle and Gospel. The iconographic programme leads the faithful, via saints, prophets, sibyls, virtues and various biblical characters, towards salvation. The carving is profuse and harmonious, using a variety of woodcarving and marquetry techniques: the large figures on the back of the upper stalls are in relief; on the stall ends the images are carved in the round and take the form of little scenes such as the *Tree of Jesse*, the *Temptation of Adam and Eve*, the *Virgin and Child*, the *Four Evangelists*, and the *Temptation of Christ in the Desert*; and marquetry is used on the episcopal throne as well as the seats of the celebrant and his acolytes for the images of St Bertrand, St John the Baptist and St John the Evangelist. In addition to the religious, mythological and allegorical mix typical of the 16th century, executed with exuberance and humour, are animal motifs on the carved armrests. Throughout the carvings of the choir stalls are versions of foliate heads or 'green men'.

The decorative wooden retable, which received a garish coating of paint and gilt in the 18th century, has an extraordinary frieze of 27 lively paintings of the Life of Christ and the Virgin. The main altar, in Sarrancolin marble, dates from 1737 and the lectern is 18th-century. At the east end of the choir enclosure is the 15th-century stone mausoleum of St Bertrand in the form of a large casket. The side facing east is covered with scenes of the life of the saint painted in the 17th century, with a silver reliquary bust containing St Bertrand's head on the altar. The other side forms a small passageway and in the central cavity is the large silver and ebony casket containing the body of the saint.

Of the 15 windows of the cathedral, three in the east contain 16th-century stained glass, similar in technique to Auch (*see p. 396*). In the central panel is the kneeling figure of the donor, Jean de Mauléon, with scenes of the *Nativity* and the *Baptism of Christ*; in the north the *Annunciation*, and in the south the *Presentation at the Temple*. The Flamboyant Notre-Dame chapel (late 14th–15th century) contains the 15th-century marble tomb of Hugues de Châtillon who was responsible for its construction.

The Ste-Marguerite chapel (14th century) is the entrance to the chapter house and treasury which contains, among other things, two medieval embroidered copes, with scenes of the Passion and the Virgin and Child, given by Clement V to celebrate the translation of St Bertrand's relics on 16th January 1309, and brilliant *opus anglicanum* embroideries produced by workshops in London.

The cloister

On the south flank of the cathedral is a rare surviving Romanesque cloister, albeit much remodelled. Since the 19th century the south gallery arcades, built above the ramparts, have been open towards the countryside, bringing a garden-like gaiety to what is normally an enclosed contemplative space. The layout is unavoidably lopsided with three 12th-century aisles, west, south and east, with eight, twelve and five bays respectively. Pairs of slender columns and double capitals support round arches and a light timber-and-tile roof. The central western pier is made from the drum of a Roman column carved with the four Evangelists, heavily inspired by antiquity; on the capital above are the *Labours of the Months* and the *Signs of the Zodiac*. The best capitals are on the west and include an elegant foliate design, *Adam and Eve*, *Cain and Abel* and four with decorative motifs. The only indication of the former monastic buildings is the trefoil entrance and walled-up Gothic window of the chapter house. The cloister served for a time as a burial place: in recesses in the vaulted late-Gothic north gallery, known as the Galerie des Tombeaux, are sarcophagi with epitaphs of seven canons and benefactors.

St-Just-de-Valcabrère

Open daily July–Sept 9–7; May–June 9–12, 2–7; April, Oct 10–12, 2–6; in winter, Sat, Sun, and school holidays 2–5; T: 05 61 95 49 06.

The basilica of St-Just-de-Valcabrère (1.5km from St-Bertrand) is an outstanding Romanesque building in a pastoral setting. To enjoy the famous view (*pictured on p. 541*) of St-Just surrounded by cypresses, with the casket-like cathedral in the distance, take the narrow road before the church, and then the unmade track on the right.

The exact dates of the basilica are not known, but it seems likely that a church was begun in the 11th century, slightly before the first church at St-Bertrand, on the site of an early Christian necropolis near the ruins of the Gallo-Roman town plundered for its stone. Numerous antique carvings and early Christian funerary monuments were used in its construction.

The church has a simple, well-proportioned belfry. Incorporated in the gateway are 1st-century AD inscriptions and a medieval chrism. On the tympanum of the 12th-century north entrance is a relief of *Christ Enthroned*, framed in a mandorla, with two censer angels and the four Evangelists. Either side of the entrance are marble statue-columns with traces of colour, similar to the Evangelists' pillar in the cathedral cloister (*see above*). A little scene on each capital identifies the main figure, from left to right: the *Decapitation of St Just*; the *Stoning of St Stephen*; a man inviting a woman—probably St Helen—to mount a horse watched by an angel, a possible allusion to the pilgrimage of the mother of Constantine; and the *Arrest and Flagellation of St Pasteur*. On the south side of the church are fragments of pre-Romanesque walls and of a Romanesque cloister, and embedded in the wall of the church is an engaging antique carving of a theatrical mask. The splendid east end is a complex structure progressing from rectangle to polygon via a round arch and squinches.

The interior

The variety of textures and colours in the interior is very beautiful. The church consists of four uneven barrel-vaulted bays, half-barrel vaults in the aisles, and a trilobed east end less complicated inside than out. Massive pillars separate nave and aisles. Behind the basin-shaped table covering the altar is a facsimile of a document found in 1886 recording the dedication of the altar to St Stephen (Etienne), St Just and St

Pasteur in October 1200. A sarcophagus supported on a vaulted passage behind the altar contained the relics of St Just and St Pasteur, and pilgrims could either pray below it or climb the steps to touch it. The richest decoration in the east bay includes paired marble columns standing against the piers on antique bases, and two inverted antique friezes as well as a frieze of acanthus leaves. On the south wall a tombstone dated 347, and another in the pier to the right of the entrance, testify to the introduction of Christianity by the 4th century. Two hollowed-out Roman capitals standing on columns against the two northwest pillars are used as holy water stoups.

Barbazan and Valentine
Across the Garonne from St-Bertrand is the charming spa of Barbazan where the waters were taken as a cure for malaria during the colonial era but are now used to combat stress, with gardens and a small thermal establishment.

Between Barbazan and St-Gaudens is the *bastide* of Valentine, built near the site of a large 4th-century Gallo-Roman villa. (*open all year by request, Mairie, T: 05 61 89 05 91*). Several Christian churches were built here on the ruins of a 4th-century temple, the last becoming part of a Benedictine priory in the 13th century, destroyed in the 18th century by Protestants. In the 19th century the town was famous for its blue faïence, examples of which can be seen in the Musée Municipal in St Gaudens on Blvd Bepmale (*open 9-12 & 2-6, closed Sun, Mon and holidays; T: 05 61 89 05 42*).

ST-GAUDENS

St-Gaudens is *sous-préfecture* of Haute-Garonne, the main industrial centre in the Comminges and an important market town. The farmers' market on Thursdays has been held on the same site for 700 years and there are numerous fairs and a large cattle market serving a region famous for its veal. St-Gaudens stands on a high ridge above the Garonne with what would be a marvellous panorama of the Pyrenees if it were not marred by the unfortunate situation of the steaming factories of Cellulose du Rhône et d'Aquitaine in the valley below. Medieval pilgrimage routes to Santiago (*see p. 11*) from St-Giles, St-Girons and St-Bertrand once converged here.

Eglise Collégiale de St-Pierre et St-Gaudens
Open 9-12 & 2.15-6, Sun 9-12, T: 05 61 94 77 61.
The story of this church goes back to the persecution of a Christian community in this region c. 5th–6th centuries. It is traditionally associated with La Caoue, on the Luchon road, where a tiny oratory was erected and rebuilt in the 20th century. According to legend, the decapitated Gaudens set off with his head under his arm to the site of the present church. The cult was officially recognised and drew numerous pilgrims in the Middle Ages and a chapter of canons was established here by the Bishop of St-Bertrand until the Revolution. A church was begun during the period of ecclesiastical reform between 1056 and 1063 by Bishop Bernard II, of the family of the Counts of Toulouse. At the end of the 11th and beginning of the 12th centuries—

the time of the great pilgrimages and of the chapter's increasing fortune—a grander church was begun, inspired by St-Sernin in Toulouse. Bernard II's unfinished church was incorporated into the new one, and for a short period stone-carvers of remarkable skill worked in the collegiate church.

The exterior

Part of the 11th-century building is conserved in the walls of the three east bays and a large portion forms the lower part of the apse, but much of the decoration was lost in the 19th century when the building was profoundly altered. The cloister on the south, begun towards the end of the 12th century, was destroyed c. 1810 but has been re-created in golden stone. Here the new capitals, modelled on seven originals, prove the influence of the Toulousain cloister workshop. The 13th-century chapter house contains a small museum of religious art from the Comminges. The west door of the church is 19th-century as are the belfry (1874) and the two-level roof (1887). The north entrance is 17th-century although the marble relief in the tympanum was probably salvaged from the 12th-century portal destroyed in the 16th. This is an elaborate and elegant version of a chrism in a circle decorated with lozenges and supported by four angels emerging from clouds.

The interior

The interior is rather dark: there is a lighting box at the west end. The barrel-vaulted nave has five unequal bays with galleries in the two east bays. When the decision was taken in the late 11th century to build a church with a gallery, the east bay was already complete. To minimise disruption to worship, work began in the second bay with the construction of a tribune or gallery, after which an adjacent tribune was built and the existing vault was raised. Lack of funds then put paid to the ambitious scheme for a galleried nave and the remainder of the church is closer to the one envisaged by Bernard II. From this brief period date the eight finest capitals (once attributed to the 19th century) influenced by the Spanish workshops on the pilgrimage road. The iconography of the capitals principally addresses morality and original sin. Their execution is vigorous and the carving crisp. On the capitals of the north pier are lions in foliage (west) and monkeys in obscene positions, attached with ropes around their necks to men who seem to be leading them (east); on the south pier, a man is devoured by a lion while his companions try to save him (south) while Adam and Eve flank the serpent (east), and the west capital has a man leading an animal by a rope. The oldest capital in the south chapel has a horseman among foliage and interlacings. The tribune carvings, including the scene of a baptism, were carried out slightly later and do not show the same virtuosity as the Spanish-influenced ones. Virtually all the Romanesque décor of the chevet has been replaced by 19th-century paintings by Lamothe (1858) of the religious history of Comminges. The stalls are 17th-century but were damaged during the Revolution. In the aisles are late 18th-century Aubusson tapestries of the *Triumph of Faith* and the *Transfiguration*. In the background of the tapestry of the *Martyrdom of St Gaudens*, made for the church, is a panorama of the town c. 1760. The organ is 17th-century.

NORTH OF ST-GAUDENS & THE GARONNE

The pleasant alluvial plain between the Garonne and the Save Rivers was crossed by the ancient routes between Agen and *Lugdunum Convenarum* (Comminges) and Toulouse and the Spanish peninsular.

Musée et Villa Gallo-Romain, Montmaurin

Open April–Sept 9.30–6; Oct–March 9.30–12, 2–5; T: 05 61 88 74 73.
At the southern end of the Gorges de la Save is the important archaeological site of Montmaurin, the largest excavated Roman villa in France. In the mid-1st century AD a major villa was constructed at the centre of cultivated land. The site was abandoned towards the end of the 2nd or early 3rd centuries, when the Save burst its banks, until the mid-3rd century. Around 330 AD the main building of the earlier construction was transformed into a luxurious residence, and c. 350 more buildings were added, arranged around successive inner spaces to create a unified architectural ensemble of great beauty. Although it was consumed by fires later in the 4th century, the parts excavated evoke the harmonious layout of the villa. The setting is enhanced by well-maintained hedges and a scattering of dark cypress trees.

Furthest from the public entrance is the hemispherical main courtyard that was the ancient entrance and reception area. Contained within the hemisphere is a temple. Following on is a large courtyard with peristyle flanked by living accommodation on the northwest—the southeast has not been excavated—and beyond is a second courtyard with fishponds surrounded by the summer quarters, with some fragments of mosaic still in place. To the northwest of the large courtyard is the *thermae*, the most complete section, comprising *nymphaeum*, *piscina*, hypocaust, hot and cold baths, a garden surrounded by slender columns, and a pergola facing out towards the landscape.

In the village, the very modest museum of Montmaurin next to the *Mairie* is devoted to the prehistory and Gallo-Roman history of the area which includes the 30,000-year-old Mandibule de Montmaurin, the jawbone of a Palaeolithic man of the Aurignacian period found near Aurignac in 1949.

St-Plancard

Hidden among cypresses in the cemetery just outside the village of St-Plancard, on the Save River, is the delightful 11th-century chapel of St-Jean-des-Vignes. The key is held at the *café tabac*. It has a perfectly simple shape, with an apse each end and one chapel on the south; the roof timbers rest directly on the walls, which are pierced by three small windows in the east, and the walls carry some precious 11th-century murals discovered in 1943. The features are stylised, the colours delicate and images faint, but it is possible to decipher a *Christ in Majesty* surrounded by the Evangelists, and a *Crucifixion* on the east wall; and in the south chapel, Christ enclosed in a double mandorla surrounded by numerous figures, with the *Hand of God* above and the *Temptation of Adam and Eve* to the right. On the arch of the chapel is a decorative frieze.

St-Martory

St-Martory spans the Garonne at the crossroads between St-Lizier and St-Bertrand. It once used its natural resources to manufacture paper. St-Martory was the birthplace of Norbert Casteret (1897–1987), speleologist and co-pioneer of pot-holing in France. In 1931 he confirmed the source of the Garonne as the Pic d'Aneto in Spain. Among his important discoveries in the vicinity, an area riddled with grottoes, were drawings and the oldest statues in the world (of a bear and two lions) at Montespan (*closed to the public*), southwest of St-Martory, in 1923. The church on the north of the river is difficult to visit because of traffic on the main road, making it advisable to park on the south and walk across the three-arched bridge, built in 1724, which has preserved its monumental toll gate decorated with the French cockerel and Louis XIV's sun emblem. A menhir and Gallo-Roman funerary stele are erected near the remodelled church of 1387, which has a 12th-century marble font, a Romanesque door and a 16th-century terracotta *Pietà*. The château on Place de la Poste (16th century, restored) can be visited by appointment with the Tourist Office.

Aurignac

Aurignac is a pretty village on the ridge of a hill. Over the town gate is a Flamboyant belfry and the 15th-century church porch has rare cabled columns from the Crucifix chapel demolished in 1791. The capitals are cubic inside and hexagonal outside. Discoveries of bones and other objects in nearby caves, 1.2km away on the D635, were made in 1860–61 by Edouard Lartet and marked an important advance in research on Cro-Magnon man, explained at the Musée de la Préhistoire (*closed for an indefinite period during reconstruction; T: 05 61 98 70 06*). The period 30–27,000 BC (known as Aurignacian), saw the appearance of figurative art. One of the most important finds in the area was the small (14.7cm) but curvaceous *Venus of Lespugue*. The original is in the Museum of National Antiquities at St-Germain-en-Laye near Paris. A sign on the road between Aurignac and Alan indicates the site of a very well-conserved Gallo-Roman piscina with marble facings, in a bucolic farmyard.

Alan

Alan, on the D10 midway between St-Bertrand-de-Comminges and Toulouse, was the happy choice in 1270 of the Bishops of Comminges as the site of a residence. Successive bishops left their mark on the buildings over five centuries, and time has taken its toll, but there are some reminders of past glories at the **Palais des Eveque de Comminges** (*open June–Sept Sat, Sun 10–12 & 3–7; T: 05 61 98 90 72*). Jean-Baptiste de Foix-Grailly, elected in 1470, undertook major revisions including a monumental Flamboyant porch adorned with the Béarn cow from his coat of arms. The palace was saved in 1969 by the opera singer Richard Gaillan, and is used for concerts and exhibitions. A kilometre south of Alan, the **Hôpital Notre-Dame de Lorette** (*open Sun afternoon; T: 05 61 98 98 84*), was built by Bishop du Bouchet in 1734 to care for the sick. Privately owned and lovingly restored, the pharmacy, cloister with monumental well, and chapel can be visited.

CENTRAL PYRENEES

Enclosed in a deep wooded valley at the southern extremity of France, Luchon is sometimes described as *La Reine des Pyrénées*. The town's official name is Bagnères-de-Luchon and in a minor way it is the inland region's answer to a coastal resort, a typical spa town with many hotels, gardens, the third largest thermal station in France in summer, and in the winter, skiing.

LUCHON

The properties of the sulphurous waters of the former Gallo-Roman city of *Ilixon* were already recognised by 25 BC and appreciated for six centuries until the location returned to obscurity between the 5th and 10th centuries. The town's rebirth in the 18th century was due mainly to Baron d'Etigny, the King's *Intendant* at Auch (*see p. 395*), who visited the town for the first time in 1759. He was responsible for a new access route and for instigating a programme of works to link the old town with the baths, a radical exercise in Haussmanism before its time. By 1827 the town owned 78 springs and this heralded the beginning of a fashionable period for the spa, which was patronised by the rich and famous from all over Europe—Flaubert, Mata Hari, Lamartine, Alexander Dumas fils, Bismarck and Leopold II of Belgium—until the beginning of the 20th century. Both Luchon and St-Béat claim the balcony that inspired the duplicitous scenes in Cyrano de Bergerac. In 1993, a cable-car was opened from the centre of town to the ski-resort of Superbagnères (1797m).

The Musée du Pays de Luchon, 18 Allées d'Etigny (*open 9–12 & 2–6; closed holidays; T: 05 61 79 29 87*) covers in ten rooms the local archaeology, the mountains, winter sports, local history and architecture. The grander buildings along the dead-straight Allées d'Etigny date from the mid-19th century and near the end of this linden-lined avenue there is the faint but distinct aroma of sulphur. The Parc des Quinconces, with its catalpas and tulip trees, bandstand, pond, pony rides, and a statue of d'Etigny by G. Crauk (1889) surveying it all, was created in 1849 after the Etablissement Chambert was built in 1848 to replace baths destroyed by fire in 1841. Its elegant colonnade is of St-Béat marble (*see p. 551*). The Pavillon du Prince Impérial was built in 1960 and in 1970 the glass, steel and grey-marble Vaporarium, with natural saunas, was the first in Europe. To the east of Allées d'Etigny is the casino, surrounded by another park of 4 hectares with pond, grotto and exotic plants. There is also a botanic garden, the Arboretum de Joueou on the Route de l'Hospice de France.

MOUNTAIN CHURCHES WEST OF LUCHON

In the vicinity of Luchon are 31 Romanesque churches (*for their protection viewable inside only through visits organised in the summer by the Bibliothèque Pour Tous, 9 Avenue Jean-Boularan, Luchon T: 05 61 79 04 12*). With their bell-towers and slate spires, these little mountain churches are beautifully integrated with the landscape. Several can be found near the D618, west of Luchon. The Vallée d'Oueil, a pastoral valley running north–south, leads to two rural 12th-century churches built in schist, **Benque-Dessus** and **Benque-Dessous**—the latter has slightly better-conserved Romanesque characteristics while the former has Gothic murals. The little church at **St-Paul d'Oueil** has a sculpted tympanum, and the minuscule St-Barthélemy at **Saccourvielle** is endowed with one of the loveliest bell-towers in the area.

St-Aventin

St-Aventin at the foot of the Vallée de Larboust, has the most outstanding of the area's small churches, the presence of venerated relics of the local saint accounting for its importance. The structure is typical of the first Romanesque style in the Midi (early 11th century): bare walls, small windows and a blind arcade around the east end. The easternmost of the two towers is the older, and a simple gable was replaced by a taller tower with double, triple and quadruple openings in ascending order above the stepped west façade. Apart from some Gallo-Roman stones embedded in the south wall (*pictured below*), most of the sculptures date from the second half of the 12th century. Above the porch, Christ, in a mandorla supported by angels, is surrounded by the four Evangelists holding their symbols. On the capital to the right is the *Martyrdom of St Aventin*, and on the left the *Massacre of the Innocents* and *Mary Magdalene anointing Christ's Feet*. A pillar faced in marble east of the portal is carved with a *Virgin and Child*, the Virgin's hair centrally parted, with animals around her and under her feet, and on the east face is Isaiah, stylistically similar to the sculptures at St-Just at Valcabrère (*see p. 544*). On the buttress to the right is a relief showing the legend of St Aventin's relics being discovered by a bull.

The pilasters in the nave and aisles are proof that the original building was designed to be vaulted, but not with the vaults we see now. The surprisingly high nave is flanked by narrow aisles and the interior is decorated with a series of paintings from the end of the 12th century through to the end of the 13th or 14th century. Some are faded and difficult to decipher as they were hidden under plaster until the end of the 19th century. On the apse walls St Sernin and St Aventin are in the place of honour, their names written in the banderoles. In the dome are visions of glory, with a cycle of the Life of Christ in the upper register. In the nave

Carvings on the church at St-Aventin.

Christ's image is represented in a medallion supported by six angels, and the *Hand of God* between Cain and Abel framed in another, while on the intrados of the large arcades are Adam and Eve, probably painted in the 14th century. There are several Romanesque pieces such as a holy water stoup carved out of a capital, another stoup with strange reliefs, a wrought-iron screen and a crudely executed marble crucifix.

Neste d'Oô and the Col de Peyresourde

A further kilometre west another valley runs south along the Neste d'Oô leading to a series of natural lakes at 1504m or more, reached only on foot. Almost opposite this turning is the little church at **Billière** with an apse at each end. The 11th-century church of **Cazaux-de-Larboust** has 15th century frescoes, which include *Christ in Majesty* and the *Four Evangelists*, *Mary and the Apostles*, *Adam and Eve*, the *Birth of Eve*, the *Temptation* and the *Expulsion from Eden*, and the *Last Judgement*.

Going west another 2km on the main road you come to a little 9th–10th-century church isolated in the middle of a field at the foot of the **Col de Peyresourde**, with a multitude of names, St-Pé-de-la-Moraine, Moraine de Garin, Sants-Tristous, or other variations on these themes. It has a simple belfry-wall with antique bells, a staircase to the roof, and tiny windows, and a number of Gallo-Roman marbles with pagan imagery incorporated into the construction both inside and out. It also has a mosaic stone floor with a rare early representation of the Christian sign, the fish.

ST-BÉAT

Between Luchon and St-Béat, northeast of Luchon, are the marble quarries at Marignac and the Lac de Géry. St-Béat, built on both banks of the still narrow defile of the Garonne in the southern part of the old province of Comminges (*see p. 539*), is grandly called the Key to France, a title it acquired in the Middle Ages because of its position close to the Spanish border.

St-Béat is famous for the marble quarried here during Roman times and used extensively in the southwest, although there was a break in production during the Middle Ages. The quarries were reactivated when fashions changed in the late 17th and 18th centuries and the marble was used in such prestigious palaces as Versailles as well as in many more modest locations, including the houses of St-Béat itself, and for many Baroque altarpieces in the region. The quarries can be visited (*Tues–Sat 2–6, by appointment T: 05 61 79 77 07*).

North of the town are the ruins of an 11th-century château with 12th- and 15th-century walls (*open Tues–Sat, 2–8 by appointment, T: 05 61 79 77 07*); its keep, rebuilt in the 19th century, stands sentinel over the valley. The church (*guided visits of the church and its treasure, same arrangements as château*) was built in 1132 and has been tastefully restored. On the tympanum is a *Christ in Majesty* and the symbols of the four Evangelists; the four decorated capitals include an *Annunciation* and *Visitation*. It has a collection of mainly 16th–18th-century furnishings, and a 12th-century *Virgin in Majesty*. Another building worthy of note in the town is the Consuls House (1553).

THE VOLVESTRE

The Volvestre derives its name from a Celtic tribe, the Volques, who settled around Toulouse about 2,000 years ago, and refers to the valley region southwest of the city, lying midway between the plain and the mountains. It is bounded to the west by the Garonne, which at various times between 1259 and 1453 marked the border between Languedoc and English Guyenne. Almost parallel with the Garonne, slightly to the east, is the the Lèze Valley, and the Volvestre is crossed by the Arize. Many of the towns in this area are built in brick.

St-Sulpice-sur-Lèze was one of many *bastides* founded by Alphonse de Poitiers. Built entirely in brick, the Place de l'Hôtel-de-Ville is one of the most impressive of its kind, surrounded by arcades and timber-framed houses. Where the Arize meets the Garonne, is the *bastide* of **Carbonne**, founded c. 1256 by Alphonse de Toulouse. The finest of three superb dovecotes is the 16th-century Pigeonnier de Grilhon in the gardens of the retirement home on Av. Prosjean. Built in brick, it is topped off with a dome and lantern. The principal monument of the town is the 14th-century Church of St-Laurent in the east near the Garonne. Near the church is the former home of sculptor André Abbal (*open June–Aug, Sept, 10–12, 3–7, closed Tues; Oct–May, Sat, Sun 3–6, T: 05 61 87 58 14/05 61 87 82 67*) whose works in stone are exhibited in the gardens as well as indoors. Temporary exhibitions of contemporary art are also mounted here.

RIEUX-VOLVESTRE

The most seductive of the brick towns of the Volvestre, bordering the meandering Arize, is Rieux-Volvestre, with its old streets, timber-framed houses, covered market and the fine 'fortified' **cathedral of Ste-Marie**. Rieux was given a diocese in 1317 by the beneficent Cadurcien Pope John XXII (*see p. 179*), and the Franciscan bishop Jean Tissendier rebuilt the cathedral in brick in the second quarter of the 14th century, incorporating the nave and chancel of earlier edifices. The sophisticated octagonal belfry, the pride and joy of Rieux, is a variation on the theme of the Jacobins Church in Toulouse (*see p. 593*), its tall lower level composed of blind arches surmounted with stone quatrefoils. Each angle of the octagon is outlined by an engaged column in pink marble, the three upper stages each set back from the level below, the whole crowned with a balustrade.

The interior has an unusual arrangement with three large chapels on the north and none on the south. The nave and choir of the older church were incorporated and more modifications were carried out in the 17th century during the time of the three bishops Bertier, when two chapels and the choir were rebuilt.

The **Treasury of the Cathedral** (*accompanied visits from the Tourist Office: July–Aug 2.30 & 4.15; April–June, Sept, Mon–Sat 2.30 & 4.15; Oct–March, Mon–Sat 2.30 & 3.45; T: 05 61 87 63 33*) contains a number of important ecclesiastical items. The most important treasure of Ste-Marie is the unique 17th-century reliquary bust of St Cizi. This effigy of the Roman fighter of Sarrasins and patron of the town was made in 1671/2 by Pierre Desnos of Toulouse, in wood plated with 5kg of silver.

MONTESQUIEU-VOLVESTRE & ENVIRONS

Montesquieu-Volvestre, to the south, is a *bastide* of 1246, founded by the counts of Toulouse near an existing château on the banks of the Arize. Protected by the verdant slopes of the Plantaurel range, it has been the most important town of the Volvestre since 1317. A brick town with a regular layout, its best features are the covered market on 20 octagonal pillars and the Gothic (14th–16th century) church opposite, dedicated to St Victor, whose relics it once claimed to own. This has a massive, gabled west elevation and a tall belfry that is a 15th-century interpretation of the usual 13th- and 14th-century Toulousain model, on the south side. The tempo is doubled, so that it has 16 rather than the usual eight sides, each face with a narrow lancet window. Inside are a number of interesting pieces, including an *Entombment* group (16th century) in painted stone, a wooden *Crucifixion* (15th century) and, in the northeast, an *Adoration of the Shepherds and the Magi* (16th century) painted on wood. There is a Baroque pulpit and a painting by Despax, the *Martyrdom of St Victor* (18th century). The crypt was rediscovered in 1983 and restored; it dates from c. 1390, was blocked up in 1747, and contains four reliquary busts.

Typical of the *clocher-murs* of medieval churches in around Montesquiou (at St-Christaud, Latour, Castagnac, Canens and Gouzens) arguably the finest example is at **Montbrun-Bocage**. Inside the Romanesque building is a remarkable series of 15th-century murals (*to visit, enquire at the Mairie, Mon-Thurs 9-12, T: 05 62 98 10 82*). The village provided refuge to Protestants expelled from Mas d'Azil (*see p. 567*).

CAZÈRES-SUR-GARONNE

Back on the Garonne, Cazères-sur-Garonne is a cheerful town on a wide expanse of the river in the foothills of the Pyrenees. The Gallo-Roman town of *St-Cizy* developed on the road linking Toulouse and Dax. It belonged to the Comminges in the 12th century before coming under the control of the Counts of Toulouse and benefited from the rights of passage to traders and pilgrims across the river between Languedoc and Foix, and from a long tradition of shipping. The old town is on a promontory above the left bank of the river, enclosed in modern boulevards. The Tourist Office is to the northwest of the old centre, installed in La Case de Montserrat, a timber-framed house built in 1547. Purchased by the Benedictine abbey of Montserrat in Spain, it was used by the Procurer General of Montserrat who travelled in France and beyond, collecting donations to cover the costs, for three months, of pilgrims on the road to Montserrat and Santiago. The church of **Notre-Dame-de-Cazères** was built in the 14th century and, until 1795, had a very different west end from the present one; the upper part was demolished by order of the Convention and the present unusual façade dates from 1885–96. The church has a long history as the centre of a Marian cult associated with a spring on the Garonne. Opposite the church is the metal *halle* of 1904 with statues (1905) at either end by Frédéric Tourte, an assistant to Bourdelle (*see p. 324*), symbolising the principal agricultural activities of the region at the time.

The road alongside the church, Rue Ste-Quitterie, marks the primitive *cité* and crosses the Hourride, where there is a fountain of 1562, to arrive via Rue Massenet at the Promenade du Campet overlooking the Garonne. At the foot of the church is the Grotte de Notre-Dame-de-Cazères, an oratory erected in 1630 following a plague epidemic. To the south, next to the bridge, is the old wooden boathouse. Cazères had an important boat-building industry, especially at the end of the 19th century, and the last boat, a trawler, left this workshop in 1948 to go to Sète on the Mediterranean. The very attractive 19th-century bridge, rebuilt after the floods in 1875, has recently been restored. Follow Boulevard P.-Gouzy away from the bridge. In Rue des Capucins is the Capuchin monastery (1612–19) with a cloister of 1717, which can be visited.

THE LAURAGAIS

The Lauragais, southeast of Toulouse, follows the corridor between the Pyrenees and the Montagne Noire (Black Mountains) and the route to the Mediterranean, and is crossed by the Canal du Midi. It is an undulating and fertile land with a particular windswept charm as the wide, exposed valley is frequently buffeted by the *vent d'autan*, the southwesterly once harnessed here with windmills. Historically the Lauragais is interesting for its many Cathar communities in the 12th and 13th centuries, and in the next centuries, pastel (*see p. 315*) was intensively cultivated in the valley.

The *bastide* of **Montgeard** was founded in 1319 on a slope dominating the plains of the Lauragais. A pastel baron, Durand de Montgeard, was the principal benefactor of the brick church which was modelled on St-Cécile in Albi. The west tower with rounded buttresses was built in 1561, although the upper part is modern and the narthex has sculpted stone inserts. The interior is rendered and painted in splendid *trompe l'oeil* on a blue background, the ribs, tiercerons and bosses in gold, red and green. The elegant alabaster font is dated 1516, and there are four Renaissance alabaster reliefs—on the southwest wall, in the two chapels near the altar and above the pulpit—of the *Assumption*, *St Catherine*, the *Coronation of the Virgin* and the *Mystical Throne*. In the village a small 16th-century château (*visits by appointment April–Oct Sat, Sun 10.30–6.30; T: 05 61 81 52 75*), was built by the same Durand, who bought his seigneurial rights from Catherine de Médicis, Countess of Lauragais. A watchtower of the same period, on the angle of a wall at the end of a path alongside the grounds of a 17th-century house, was built to survey the precious fields of pastel.

The fame of **Avignonet-Lauragais**, standing sentinel over the valley, rests on an incident in May 1242, when a group of about 60 armed men commanded by Pierre-Roger de Mirepoix descended from the Cathar stronghold of Montségur (*see p. 562*). Aided and abetted by the locals, they avenged the persecution of heretics by slaughtering all the members of the recently installed Inquisition, including Inquisitors Guillaume Arnaud and Etienne de Saint Thibery. As a consequence the fate of Montségur, the last Cathar sanctuary, was sealed and early in 1243 the Council of Béziers decided to destroy it.

THE CANAL DU MIDI

Although an overland trade route had crossed the valley for more than 1,000 years, carrying goods from the Mediterranean to Toulouse and on to the Atlantic via the Garonne, the problem of transporting increasing quantities of grain, especially maize, from the Toulousain to the Languedoc arose in the 17th century. It was solved by Pierre-Paul Riquet's great engineering feat, the Canal Royal du Languedoc, now called the Canal du Midi. Louis XIV's minister Colbert obtained royal approval for Riquet's scheme in 1666 and work began in 1667. In less than 14 years, 240km of canal was dug by a workforce of 12,000 head (three women equalled two heads). Over 60 locks, single, double and multiple, coped with the considerable slopes, and water was channeled from a reservoir at St-Ferréol in the Montagne Noire to Naurouze, the highest point, from where the canal flowed downhill in each direction. Riquet died, exhausted and penniless, in 1680, a year before the canal's completion. In 1856 the Canal Latéral à la Garonne was realised and canal barges could make the entire journey to Bordeaux, instead of off-loading at Toulouse on to river craft. The canal is now a UNESCO world heritage site.

St-Félix-Lauragais

On a high vantage-point on the D622, the 13th-century *bastide* of St-Félix-Lauragais offers a splendid view east to the Montagne Noire and south to the Pyrenees. Around the square are timbered houses and opposite the market, the 17th–19th-century house where the composer Déodate de Séverac (1873–1921) was born. On the north of the village, overlooking the plain, is the château dating from the 12th/18th centuries which hosted the first Cathar synod in 1167 in the presence of the Cathar Bishop Nicétas.

Revel

The largest town in the Lauragais is **Revel**, a *bastide* founded in 1342 by Philippe VI who laid down in the charter the dimensions of the houses and the length of time allowed to erect them. The huge 14th-century *halle* (now housing the Tourist Office) in Place Philippe VI-de-Valois has ancient roof timbers around a central stone building with Serlian windows and a lantern belfry. Revel has been the capital of quality reproduction furniture, marquetry and all associated crafts since 1888 when a specialist cabinetmaker from Versailles, Alexandre Monoury, settled here and opened a school. The **Conservatoire des Métiers du Bois in Rue Moulin** (*open Tues–Thur, Sat 10–12; March–Sept 2–6, closed Mon; Oct-Feb 2–5.30, closed Mon; T: 05 61 27 65 50*) is an exhibition which follows the process from tree to objet d'art; check opening times at the tourist office. Samples of modern cabinetmaking can be seen at Espace Art et Meuble on the Castres road (*open Tues–Sat, 10–12 & 2–6.30; Mon 2.30–6.30; T: 05 61 83 56 58*).

PRACTICAL INFORMATION

GETTING AROUND

• **By train:** Toulouse and Montréjeau via Muret, Carbonne, Cazères-sur-Garonne, Martres-Tolosane, Boussens, St-Martory, St-Gaudens, and between Toulouse to Carcassonne, via Bram, Castelnaudary, Avignonet.

• **By train:** There are buses between Montréjeau and Luchon; St-Gaudens and Luchon; St-Béat and Fos; Muret and St-Sulpice-sur-Lèze; Boussens and St-Girons; Castelnaudary and Sorèze via Revel.

TOURIST INFORMATION

Bagnères-de-Luchon 18 Allées d'Etigny, T: 05 61 79 21 21, www.luchon.com
Barbazan T: 05 61 88 35 64, office-tourisme-barbazan@ wanadoo.fr
Cazères-sur-Garonne 13 Rue de la Case, T: 05 61 90 06 81, syndicat-dinitiative2@wanadoo.fr
Montesquieu-Volvestre 20 Pl. de la Halle, T: 05 61 90 19 55, ot.montesquieu@wanadoo.fr
Montréjeau 22 Pl. Valentin Abeille, BP 6, T: 05 61 95 80 22, office.tourisme.montrejeau@wanadoo.fr
Rieux-Volvestre 9 Rue de l'Evêche, T: 05 61 87 63 33, www.tourisme-volvestre.com
St-Béat Mairie, Ave de la Gerle, T: 05 61 79 45 98, office-Tourisme-Saint-Beat@wanadoo.fr
St-Bertrand-de-Comminges Les Olivetains, Parvis de la Cathédrale, T: 05 61 95 44 44, olivetains@wanadoo.fr
St-Gaudens 2 Rue Thiers, T: 05 61 94 77 61, www.stgaudens.com

Villefranche-de-Lauragais Square G. de Gaulle, T: 05 61 27 20 94

ACCOMMODATION & RESTAURANTS

Ausseing
€ **Chambres d'hôtes La Cazalère**
Isabelle Perusat has transformed a former Templar pilgrim hostel into a showcase for artists of all kinds. The three suites have pure, clean contemplative décor and each is different: Yaïch, in the tower, has a view towards the Pyrenees; the Suite des Artists is a large space in the old barn; and Purcell looks out onto a wheatfield. Guests can use the kitchen, dining room and other living areas. There is also an enclosed garden and terrace. *Table d'hôtes* also provided. T 05 61 97 04 50 or 06 12 17 97 84.

Auterive
€ **Chambres d'hôtes La Manufacture.**
A classic old brick building that was originally used for making sheets which was purchased as a home by Doctor Basset in 1880 and has been passed down through five generations. Many original features have been safeguarded and there are five large and light guest rooms on the first floor. In the grounds, the pool that was used to rinse the linen is now a swimming pool and lawns shaded by a superb 100-year-old cedar. 2 Rue des Docteurs Basset, T: 05 61 50 08 50, www.manufacture-royale.net

La Pomarède
€€ **Hostellerie du Château de la Pomarède.** On the edge of the Haute-Garonne, in the Aude, since 1998 the old 'Cathar' castle of 1052 has been an elegant hotel/restaurant. Gérard and

Nathalie Garcia have created a beautiful setting with spacious rooms and beautiful terrace. Talented chef Gérard produces unexpected culinary pleasures which skillfully blend tastes and textures from fresh produce bought at Revel market. Menus €25, €45, €75. T: 04 68 60 49 69, www.hostellerie-lapomarede.fr

Montgaillard-Lauragais
€€ Hostellerie du Chef Jean/Restaurant du Vieux Puits. This is a lovely spot in a hilltop village near the Canal du Midi in its own grounds. It has a winter and a summer pool, and sauna. The 14 rooms are quiet and not too pricey. The food is beautifully presented in the rustic dining room. Menus €26–60. T: 05 34 66 71 34, www.hostellerie-chef-jean.com

Montesquieu-Volvestre
€ Chambres d'hôtes La Halte du Temps. An oasis with palms and pool in this charming town with a view of the remarkable church tower. Marie Andrée Garcin's sober brick house dates from the 17th century and is enlivened by plants and has a shaded terrace for a leisurely breakfast. The 3 rooms and a suite are extremely pleasant. An excellent *table d'hôtes* is served. 72 Rue Mage, T: 05 61 97 56 10, lahaltedutemps@free.fr

Revel
€ Hôtel/Restaurant la Commanderie. This little hotel with 7 bedrooms is close to Revel's covered marketplace. The restaurant overlooks the terrace garden and cuisine gastronomic is served in two dining rooms with pink tablecloths and brick and stone walls. The menus are from €17 to €34. 7 Rue du Taur, T: 05 34 66 11 24.

St-Bertrand de Comminges
€ Hôtel/Restaurant Comminges. The hotel is in an old family house draped in wisteria and has been renovated. In the upper town, it is in a prime position opposite the cathedral where, once the day's visitors have departed, all is peace and quiet. Pl. Basilique, T: 05 62 88 31 43.

€ L'Oppidum. This hotel is in an old building near the top of the picturesque village from where you can hear the cow-bells in early morning. The bedrooms are light and unfussy rooms and the simple restaurant serves gastronomic and regional specialities; menus €15–32. Rue de la Poste, T: 05 62 88 33 50, www.hotel-oppidum.com

Saint-Gaudens
€ Hôtel/Restaurant Le Beaurivage. An ancient house dating from 1782 on the banks of the Garonne outside the town with 12 reasonably priced rooms. The cuisine is gastronomic and inventive, based on regional ingredients and fish; menus €16–77. Pont de Valentine, T: 05 61 94 76 70.

St-Félix Lauragais
€€ Hôtel/Restaurant du Poids Public. Between the Pyrenees and the Montagne Noire, this excellent address has a wonderful views of the Lauragais from the dining room and from the terrace. It is named after public scales here at one time where anything and everything was officially weighed. It has 10 rooms with good bathrooms. Claude Taffarello's cooking is wonderful. Menus range from €26 to the *menu dégustation* at €65. T: 05 62 18 85 00, www.auberge-du-poidspublic.com

Sauveterre-de-Comminges
€ Hostellerie des Sept-Molles. ■ This hotel-restaurant is in a beautiful rural setting not far from St-Bertrand de

Comminges. The rooms are spacious and comfortable with lovely views, and the welcome is warm. There is a pool and tennis court. The restaurant is equally attractive with terracotta colours and old dresser. Gilles Ferrau, who originated in the region, assures a very high quality cuisine incorporating excellent regional fare such local lamb, veal and fish, and wild mushrooms. Menus €29.50, €39 and gastronomic at €42. Just off the D9/D26. T: 05 61 88 30 87, www.hotel7molles.com

Valcabrère

€€ **Restaurant Le Lugdunum**. This restaurant run by Renzo Pedrazzini and his wife has an unusual vocation, to recreate historic cuisines. It conjures up the gastronomy of ancient Rome using combinations of sweet and sour, where spices and aromatic plants complement the dishes and the drinks. Les Espouges, T: 05 61 94 52 05 (N125).

Varennes

€ **Chambres d'hôtes Château des Varennes**. This imposing 16th-century château owned by Béatrice and Jacques Mericq is attributed to the architect Dominique Bachelier, and has a wonderful view over the Lauragais. In the Toulousain manner it is built entirely in brick and has a splendid 18th-century courtyard with double flight of steps facing the village. There are four immense rooms with high ceilings embellished with pretty fabrics and other individual touches. There is also a lounge, library and dining room for guests where exposed brick adds warmth, and *table d'hôtes* can be reserved. Outside is a pool, a large terrace and vegetable garden. T: 05 61 81 69 24, http://www.chateaudesvarennes.com

Villefranche-de-Lauragais

€ **Hôtel/Restaurant de France**. A simple and very reasonable hostelry with 23 rooms. The main reason for coming here is to sample a really good *Cassoulet royal* maison in the restaurant; menus €11–25. 106 Rue de la Republique, T: 05 61 81 62 17, www.hotelrestaurantdulauragais.fr

MARKET DAYS

Bagnères-de-Luchon Wednesday
Carbonne Thursday, Saturday
Cazères Saturday
Montesquieu-Volvestre Tuesday, Saturday
Revel Saturday
Rieux-Volvestre Tuesday
St-Béat Tuesday Friday
St-Gaudens Thursday, Saturday
Villefranche-de-Lauragais Friday

FESTIVALS & EVENTS

April: *Foîre à la Cocagne*, tribute to the pastel industry, St-Félix-Lauragais
May: *Fêtes du Papogay*, traditional archery competition to shoot down a wooden bird, Rieux-Volvestre
June: *Foîre de Messidor*, includes the eating of a giant cassoulet, Nailloux
July: *Regates*, regatta, Cazères-sur-Garonne
July–August: *Festival du Comminges*, outstanding musical event, St-Bertrand-de-Comminges and St-Just-Valcabrère
August: *Fête des Fleurs*, flower festival created by Edmond Rostand, Bagnères de Luchon

ARIÈGE-PYRÉNÉES

The Ariège-Pyrénées is a rugged and sparsely populated land, which catches the winds and the sun of the Mediterranean and the imagination with its decorated caves, tales of large and tenacious Cathar communities, and ancient châteaux. It benefits from the natural advantages of mineral water springs and an abundance of wildlife, shelters rustic Romanesque churches, and there are endless opportunities for exploration on foot, by bike or on horseback.

BASSE ARIÈGE

The valley of the Hers in the Basse Ariège crosses the Pré-Pyrénées, a lower (1000m), parallel range to the Pyrenees proper, consisting of the Plantaurel hills and the Monts d'Olmes. Without the obvious attractions of the high ranges, it still provides many vistas of great beauty enhanced by fields of golden sunflowers in July. There were numerous Cathar hideouts in this area, the most famous of which is Montségur.

THE VALLEY OF THE HERS

Mazères
South of Toulouse and north of Pamiers is Mazères, founded in 1253 by the neighbouring abbey of Boulbonne. It was one of the main *bastides* in the Basse Ariège, in the territory of the medieval Counts of Foix, powerful vassals of and rivals to the Counts of Toulouse. The Château of Mazères was the favourite residence of Gaston Fébus, the legendary Count of Foix (*see box on p. 571*), where he grandiosely entertained the French King Charles VI in 1390. Palace and abbey were destroyed by the Protestants during the Wars of Religion in the 16th century. Consequently Mazères presents a post-Reformation face, its 17th- and 18th-century houses and market influenced by the brick buildings of Toulouse. The one notable exception is the Renaissance Hôtel d'Ardouin and Musée de Vieux Mazères (*open Mon, Fri 9-12, Thurs 2-5, Weds morning by appointment; T: 05 61 69 42 04*). The mansion was built c. 1580 for a pastel merchant and has been transformed into the of the history of pastel (*see p. 351*) and of Gaston Fébus, among other things.

Vals
The tiny rural hamlet of Vals, east of Pamiers, has a small but sensational *église rupestre* (church hewn out of the rock; *open 9–7; T: 05 61 68 88 26*). One of the most ancient churches in the Midi, Sainte-Marie was erected at the site of a Celtic *oppidum* and pagan temple and is built into a small mound of puddingstone. At the west end, the tower-keep stands proud above ground. Adding to the drama, the entrance to the

sanctuary is through a natural cleft in the rock into which 23 steps are carved, leading up to the crypt-like nave of a 10th-century sanctuary, part-natural, part-manmade. To the east, on a slightly higher level, is the flat-ended barrel-vaulted 11th-century apse. This is decorated with 12th-century paintings discovered in 1956; there is a light switch left of the steps. Influenced stylistically by Catalonia, the paintings are executed primarily in red and black pigment, complemented by grey, yellow and white. The theme of Christ's birth is represented in the east bay by the *Annunciation*, the *Nativity* (where the Virgin is covered by a cloth decorated with circular medallions), the *Bathing of Jesus* and, in a fragment on the east wall, the *Adoration of the Magi*. In the vaults is the *Christ of the Last Judgement*, accompanied by the tetramorph and the Apostles two-by-two. On the north is the figure of Christ, his hand raised in blessing. The next level of the church has been much modified and has 19th-century plastered vaults. On the third level is a 12th-century chapel dedicated to St Michael which was transformed into a tower in the 14th century. The large arch was opened later. Outside on the north wall is a discoidal cross, probably from the cemetery.

Mirepoix

The main town in the Pays d'Olmes, Mirepoix is a *bastide* with some unusual characteristics. Like most others, it is laid out on a grid system around a central square, although here planted with grass and rose bushes, just the spot for a glass of Blanquette de Limoux, the local sparkling wine. The first *bastide* was founded in 1207 by Raymond-Roger of Foix, but it harboured a great many Cathars and two years later was taken by Simon de Montfort, who dispossessed Pierre-Roger de Mirepoix and installed Guy de Lévis. In 1229 De Lévis became the King's representative for the region, a sensitive area between Toulouse and pockets of Cathar resistance in the mountains. The original *bastide* was on the right bank of the Hers, too close to the river because in 1279, when the dam broke at Puivert 28km upstream, the village was washed away. Ten years later, a project to rebuild in a safer place on the left bank, near the castle and Benedictine chapel was carried out by Jean de Lévis, son of Guy. The layout of the town centre has not altered since the 13th century, although a fire in 1380 destroyed many buildings and the houses date from the 14th century onwards.

The first floors of the houses extend over the public right of way around the square, supported by timber posts and lintels creating a *couvert* (arcade); several are decorated. Outstanding is the 15th- and 16th-century Maison des Consuls on the north, its 25 joists sculpted at the extremities with a variety of strange animals and human heads.

Cathedral of St-Maurice

In a large, shady square created in the 15th century, the cathedral of St-Maurice is the third church on the site. It has an enormously wide nave, the second widest Gothic nave in Europe after Gerona in Spain. The problem of vaulting the 22m span was not resolved until the 19th century when the church was finally completed. The post-flood town encompassed a small Benedictine chapel which was rebuilt as a parish church in 1298, itself considered too modest when the Cadurcien Pope, John XXII (*see p. 179*), raised the status of Mirepoix to diocese in 1317. The first two bishops raised funds to build the chevet (1343–49), determining the ambitious dimensions of the nave, but work was interrupted from the mid-14th century by the Hundred Years War. Building started again with the eighth bishop, Guillaume de Puy (1394–1433), and surged ahead from 1493 during the episcopate of Philippe de Lévis, who was responsible for four main constructions: the octagonal belfry with its crocketed spire; the episcopal palace contiguous with the church; the new west wall; and the Renaissance door on the south. He also built the episcopal chapel above the north entrance dedicated to St Agatha, and opened the three Flamboyant windows. When Philippe de Lévis died in 1537, activity ground to a halt until a long time after the suppression of the diocese. Only in 1858 were the walls of the chevet raised and the choir vaulted. Viollet-le-Duc advised on the second campaign of work (1861–67), when the chapels were pushed back to enlarge the nave by about 3.3m in order to line it up with the choir, and the later walls were raised.

The strange arrangement of gables above each face of the apse, as well as the flying buttresses and slate roof—both atypical of the region—are all 19th-century. The Flamboyant north entrance has sculpted capitals but has lost its statues. The wide aisleless nave is disproportionate to the height (24m) and length (48m), making the vaults appear to bear down on the space. The interior décor is mainly neo-Gothic and little is left of the earlier furnishings with the exception of a funerary statue of Constance de Foix, wife of Jean de Lévis; the 14th-century bosses of the choir chapels sculpted by the Master of Rieux; and a 14th-century polychrome wooden crucifix of Catalan origin. The pulpit is all that remains of the 15th-century wooden fittings made locally. Next to it is a gilded retable presenting the fifteen mysteries of the Rosary. *The Crucifixion*, by the Flemish painter Larivière Viscontius, in the St-Maurice chapel is the only surviving example from a series of seven works by this painter, heavily influenced by Velázquez. The episcopal chapel above the porch has a fine painted tile floor of 1530, the most precious part being the labyrinth, which the faithful followed on their knees, the last to be placed on the floor of a Western church.

Camon

Camon, is a golden and peaceful village higher up the green valley of the Hers on the Mediterranean side of the Ariège south of Mirepoix. Legend attributes the foundation of the village to Charlemagne, although more certain is that a Benedictine abbey existed here in 923, coming under the protection of the abbey of Lagrasse in the Aude in 943, and designated priory in 1068. The village developed as a *sauveté* or refuge around the abbey but, like Mirepoix, it was devastated by the flood of 1279. It was rebuilt as a fortress at the end of the 13th century, and was enclosed in fortifications (1360–85) during the Hundred Years War. In 1494 the abbey and church were again destroyed. The village took its present form between 1503 and 1535 when the Bishop of Mirepoix, Philippe de Lévis, began another campaign of reconstruction of the abbey, improving the living quarters in the great rectangular tower, which then became known as the château, and enclosing the village in an *enceinte*. The defences were amended (1560–70) during the Wars of Religion by Cardinal Georges d'Armagnac, Prior of Camon, but with the dissolution of the priory at the end of the 18th century the château became private property.

The entrance to the village is through an elegant archway of 1684 with a clock, and an ancient bronze bell (1342) placed above it. The abbey and château (*guided visits only, enquire at the Tourist Office; out of season telephone T: 05 61 68 88 26*), rebuilt in 1526, has a cloister and frescoed chapel. The interior has 16th-century tiles, 16th-century murals of mythological scenes in the former prelate's study, and a bedroom with 20th-century painted décor by a local artist, Mady de la Giraudière. The church was rebuilt by Philippe de Lévis and its embellishment was continued by successive priors in the 17th and 18th centuries.

MONTSÉGUR

The most celebrated of all the Cathar strongholds, although nothing remains of their actual citadel, is Montségur, vertiginously perched at 1207m on a granite outcrop in the St-Barthélemy range. Visible from all around, unless enveloped in cloud, it is at its most impressively forbidding in winter. The site is one of the most stunning and the story the most moving of the whole saga of Cathar persecution (*see p. 13*).

Château de Montségur

Open Feb 10.30–4; March 10–5; April 9.30–6; May–Aug 9–7.30; Sept–Oct 9.30–6; Nov 10–5.30; Dec 10.30–4.30; closed Jan; guided visits at peak periods; T: 05 61 01 06 94 or 05 61 01 10 27.

For about 40 years the rock had an exclusively Cathar population. The Cathars, who were never builders, had persuaded Raymond de Péreille, a local member of the lesser nobility sympathetic to their cause, to rebuild his ruined château c. 1204. During the Albigensian Crusade (1209–29; *see p. 251*) Péreille's family occupied the keep and the Cathar population lived there in safety. With the annexation of Languedoc by France at the end of the Crusades, the region was put under the protection of a French governor, Guy de Lévis. In 1232 Guilhabert de Castres, the Cathar bishop, chose Montségur as a place of safety, bringing with him the elders of the Cathar Church and consequently elevating the site to the spiritual centre of the Cathar faith. The community grew to about 400 or 500 people, grouped around the château in a terraced village clinging to the rocky outcrop, probably with a complicated and extensive defensive system.

The site was not challenged until after 1240, when Raymond VII of Toulouse, reminded by the king of his undertaking to fight the Cathars, made a derisory attempt to take Montségur. The task was then assigned to the more resolute Seneschal of Carcassonne, Hugues des Arcis. The mounting crisis was compounded when, in 1242, Cathar knights slaughtered the Inquisitors at Avignonet in the Lauragais (*see p. 554*). In 1243 an army of some 1,500 men was raised and, with the blessing of the Archbishop of Narbonne, Pierre Amiel, laid siege to Montségur in May. The defence

The walls and keep of Montségur (late 13th century) looking northwest.

of the refuge was commanded by Pierre-Roger de Mirepoix, one of Raymond de Péreille's henchmen. The defenders, supported by their faith, by a continuous stream of supplies made possible by weaknesses in the blockade, and above all by the difficulties posed by the steep mountain, held out for ten months. Gradually, however, conditions deteriorated for the Cathars and by Wednesday, 2nd March 1244, a surrender was agreed and a 15-day truce negotiated, giving the faithful time to prepare for death by taking the *consolamentum* or last rites. On 16th March the château was evacuated and over 200 who refused to convert to Catholicism were burned at the stake for their heretical beliefs.

Guy II de Lévis became *seigneur* of the fiefdom of Montségur sometime after July 1245 and rebuilt most of the fortress (the ruins of which can now be seen), where a small garrison was installed until the end of the 15th century. The village on the hill was demolished or left to decay. Mentioned once in 1510, the château and its story lay forgotten until in 1862 the ruins were classified a historic monument and Napoléon Peyrat published his *Histoire des Albigeois* (1872), a romanticised version of the drama embellishing the legends of the site. A monument to those who were massacred was erected in 1960 at the foot of the mountain, and today the site attracts a large number of visitors.

Visiting the castle

The climb to the top by a well-trodden track takes about half an hour and is not too demanding, though fairly steep in places. The château is an irregular shape, the longest of the five sides on the north, with the main entrance on the southwest and a smaller one opposite. The interior space, about 700 square metres, is enclosed by high walls built into the natural rock with no openings, only regularly spaced hollows to receive wooden building supports. There are three flights of stone steps up to the *chemin de ronde* and at the northwest extremity the keep, originally accessed from the upper floor by a wooden ladder, has a spiral stair in the southeast angle to the lower level. There are a few signs of rudimentary comfort, such as a fireplace, vaulted ceilings and windows, and in the western part of the ground floor was the cistern. The east wall is very thick, about 4.2m, with grooves made to contain beams to support the platform for a catapult.

The village and environs

The village is southeast of the citadel, with the small Musée Historique et Archéologique (*open June–Aug 10–12.30 & 2–7.30; May 10.30–12.30 & 2–7; Sept 10.30–12 & 2–6; April, Oct 2–6; March, Nov 2–5; Feb, Dec 2–4.30; closed Jan; T: 05 61 01 06 94*). This contains explanations and information about the site, a model of Montségur at the time of the Cathars, and some of the best archaeological finds from local sites.

Between Montségur and Bélesta, is the waterfall of **Fontestorbes**, an eccentric torrent with the singularly fascinating habit of gushing for 35mins (if there is enough water) then, once the reserve is empty, slowing down to a trickle for 25mins.

The universally famous but almost abandoned village of **Montaillou**, with just 12 residents, is to the south of Montségur. The Cathar community established here in the Middle Ages was the subject of Emmanuel Le Roy Ladurie's book *Montaillou*, based on information contained in the Inquisition register of Jacques Fournier, Bishop of Pamiers, kept in the Vatican archives. A few houses, a rebuilt church and the ruined medieval château are all that remains.

THE ARIÈGE VALLEY

The Ariège flows northwards from its source in Andorra to join the Garonne south of Toulouse. The N20 follows this wide valley connecting the Toulousain with the Pyrenees, Andorra and Catalonia, with a tunnel under Puymorens. Here the climate is influenced by the Mediterranean and the landscape is one of extremes.

PAMIERS & ENVIRONS

Built mainly in brick like the towns of the Toulousain, Pamiers is the largest town of the Département of the Ariège but not the *préfecture*; that honour went to Foix in 1790. Although not an immediately appealing town, the water, important for the tanning and dying industries of the past, which runs through the canals and fountains is a singular feature much enhanced by judicious planting.

An abbey, first mentioned in 961, was built here at the site of the martyrdom in 507 of Antonin, Christian grandson of the Visigoth King Theodoric I. In 1111 the Counts of Foix came to a partnership agreement with the powerful abbots when Roger II, Count of Foix, returning from the First Crusade, built a château here named Apamie after a town in Asia Minor. During the Cathar crisis in the 12th–13th centuries the town remained orthodox and was rewarded for its constancy by elevation to episcopal see in 1295. Jacques Fournier, Bishop of Pamiers and of Mirepoix (1318–25), became third pope at Avignon, as Benedict XII (1334–42). Most of Pamiers' medieval buildings were destroyed during the Wars of Religion in the 16th century.

Exploring Pamiers

The Ariège was navigable from Pamiers to the Garonne during the Middle Ages, when canals were created for the dual purpose of defence and to run the mills, and a canal still delineates the old town. On its banks is a small public garden around a former mansion, now the municipal library, and the tourist office on Boulevard Delcassé. West of the gardens, in Rue du Collège, is a Carmelite chapel, founded in 1648 and rebuilt in the 18th century, arranged internally to correspond to a mystical ascension by successive levels to a high altar. The square tower outside was built as a keep by Count Roger-Bernard III in 1285.

The cathedral stands in Place Mercadal, the old town centre at the foot of the hill where the Counts' castle stood. **Cathedral of St-Antonin** was formerly the parish church of Notre-Dame du Mercadal and was rededicated when it became the cathedral in the 16th century. Apart from the octagonal belfry, modelled on the Jacobins church in Toulouse in the 14th century, which served as a watchtower, the building was demolished by the Protestants in 1577 and was reconstructed 1657–89. Only the badly mutilated Romanesque portal has survived from the earlier church. The already crude carvings of the capitals have suffered with time but it is just possible to make out a *Martyrdom of St John the Baptist*, *Adam and Eve*, *Cain and Abel*, *Daniel in the Lions' Den*, *Samson slaying the Lion* and, opposite the door, a *Martyrdom of St John the Evangelist*, the two St Johns being the patron saints of the very first church. The furnishings include a 16th-century wooden statue of Mary Magadalene and five 19th-century paintings of the legend of St Antonin.

On the perimeter of the square are the 18th-century *Palais de Justice*, the 17th-century seminary, now the *lycée*, and the *Mairie* has taken over the 17th-century episcopal palace; the present Bishops' Palace being on the south. Near the *Mairie*, on the west, the Porte de Nerviau is a fragment of the fortified enclosure separating two quarters, altered in the 15th century. In the gardens at the foot of the castella plateau there is a bust of the composer Gabriel Fauré (1845–1924), who was born in Pamiers.

The Tour de la Monnaie on Rue Charles-de-Gaulle was originally adjacent to a building of 1419 in which Count Jean I of Foix established a mint to make copper coins called Guilhems, to pay the troops who fought against William of Orange. This street leads to the present lively commercial centre and the church of Notre-Dame-du-Camp, rebuilt in the 17th century except for the massive 14th century rectangular façade flanked by two small towers. The portal was rebuilt in 1870 and the gloomy interior has nothing to detain the visitor. Further north is the belfry of the old Cordeliers church (1512).

On the left bank of the Ariège, the old church of Mas Vieux St-Antonin, or the **Abbey de Calloup** (*interior open on certain days in July, August and September; T: 05 61 67 52 52*), stands on the ancient pilgrim way to Santiago de Compostela in Spain. First mentioned in 961, parts of the building go back to the 12th century but it was damaged during the Wars of Religion, and between 1672 and 1738 it underwent successive campaigns of restoration. After the Revolution, along with many religious buildings, it was sold in 1791 by the State and used for agricultural purposes until it was acquired in 1989 by the Commune of Pamiers. At the time of writing the church is under restoration.

Le Vernet

In the *Mairie* at Le Vernet, north of Pamiers, is a room dedicated as the Memorial du Camp d'Internement du Vernet d'Ariège 1939–44 (*open 8.30–12 & 1.30–5, closed Wed, Sat, Sun; T: 05 61 68 36 43*) with grim reminders of the detainment camp established here for Spanish refugees in 1939 which went on to become an internment camp for foreigners during World War II until 1944, when the last inmates were transported to Dachau. Arthur Koestler described his experiences at Le Vernet in *The Scum of the Earth* (1941). Outside the village is a cemetery with the tombs of the 217 who perished in the camp.

WEST OF PAMIERS

Carla-Bayle

On a ridge between the Lèze and Arize valleys west of Pamiers is Carla-Bayle, a tidy little town with a wide view. The medieval stronghold became a Huguenot bastion and suffered heavily during the Wars of Religion. In the 18th century the community of Carla-le-Comte actively supported the Revolution and became Carla-le-Peuple, acquiring its present suffix in 1879 in tribute to its most famous son, Pierre Bayle. Bayle's birthplace houses the Musée Pierre Bayle (*open July–Aug 10–12 & 3–7; Jan–June, Sept–Dec, Wed, Sat, Sun, 2–6; T: 05 61 68 51 32*), an excellent museum retracing his life and work, and one of the best Protestant museums in the region. The house is arranged around an interior courtyard and the collection includes documents, engravings and acerbic cartoons. It also reconstructs Pierre Bayle's study and a kitchen of the period. Round the corner from the museum is the Protestant Temple which can be visited. Indistinguishable from other houses from the outside, it is a simple galleried hall with two spiral staircases, benches, an ancient stove, a piano and a wooden table. The date over the porch of the Catholic church is 1687; the date of the Revocation of the Edict of Nantes was 1685.

PIERRE BAYLE (1647–1706)

Bayle was a Protestant philosopher and the author of *Pensées sur la comète* and *Dictionnaire historique et critique* (1696–97). He was the victim of anti-Protestant persecution and settled with a French community in Rotterdam, where he published his works, in October 1681. His self-imposed exile saved him but not his brother, who was imprisoned and executed because of Bayle's publications. His famous plea for freedom of conscience—*C'est donc la tolérance qui est la source de la paix et l'intolérance qui est la source de la confusion et du grabuge* 'It is tolerance that is the source of peace and intolerance that is the source of confusion and mayhem'—prefigured the writings of John Locke and announced the spirit of the 18th century, although his liberalism also led to conflict with fellow Protestants.

Le Mas d'Azil

In the Montagnes de Plantaurel is Le Mas d'Azil, a *bastide* with a small museum of prehistory (*open July–Aug 10–6; June, Sept 10–12 & 2–6 closed Mon; April–May 2–6, Sun and holidays 10–12 & 2–6, closed Mon; March, Oct–Nov Sun and holidays 2–6; T: 05 61 69 97 71*) next to the 18th-century church. In the vicinity are dolmens and megaliths. The site is most famous, however, for the vast natural tunnel carved through the limestone range of the Plantaurel by the Arize, the Grotte du Mas d'Azil (*open as for the museum*), where primeval man, Cathars and Calvinists all apparently took refuge. Tools of the Magdalenian period can be seen.

FOIX

Foix, mid-way between Toulouse and Spain, is the ancient headquarters of the Counts of Foix on the west bank of the Ariège almost in the centre of the *département*. With a population of 10,000, Foix is one of the smallest *préfectures* in France.

THE COUNTS OF FOIX

The first Count of Foix, in the 11th century, was Bernard, the second son of the Count of Carcassonne; the dynasty, which established a *paréage* with the abbots of St-Volusien in 1168, ended in 1391 with Gaston Fébus (*see box on p. 571*). The Counts were neighbours of the Counts of Toulouse, whose dominance they challenged, and showed Cathar sympathies during the Albigensian crisis. After the annexation of Languedoc to France in 1229, they extended their domain southwards to Andorra and in 1290, when Roger Bernard III inherited the Viscounty of Béarn, the most splendid period in their history began.

Château des Comtes de Foix

Guided visits July–Aug 9.45–6.30; May–June, Sept 9.45–12 & 2–6; Oct, April 10.30–12 & 2–5.30; Nov–March 10.30–12 & 2–5.30; closed Mon and Tues except school holidays; closed Jan; T: 05 61 05 10 10.

The old streets Rues Lazema, des Grand-Ducs and Rocher de Foix lead up to the Counts' château high above the town, with three towers linked by battlemented walls

The Château des Comtes de Foix towering over the town.

silhouetted against the mountains. In the rock beneath the castle are caves which were inhabited in prehistoric times. Nothing is known about the first fort on the site, mentioned in the 11th century. The castle was besieged by Simon de Montfort during the Albigensian Crusade—but was finally occupied by cunning rather than force in 1214—and it was taken by the King of France, Philippe III the Bold, in 1272. Gaston Fébus frequently stayed here at the beginning of his reign but after 1364 more rarely, preferring Mazères. The square towers linked by a two-storey building seem to have been built by the end of the 13th century, the Arget tower to the north probably the oldest; and the round Fébus tower was added in the 15th century. The castle was saved in the 17th century when many others were destroyed at Richelieu's orders, and was used as a prison until 1862. It was given its 19th-century appearance during restoration and modification between 1885 and 1897 by Paul Boeswillwald, pupil of Viollet-le-Duc, including the bell-tower of the Arget tower.

Six rooms in the castle are devoted to the **Musée de l'Ariège**, which has exhibits ranging from local archaeological finds to displays of rural life and 19th-century building materials. It also has seven Romanesque capitals from the abbey cloisters, one recalling the persecution of St Volusien in 507, a collection of armoury and a Henri IV bed (16th century).

Exploring the town

In the 10th–11th centuries the town grew at the foot of the castle in the quarter around Rue du Palais de Justice (*see plan overleaf*) and the ancient church of St-Nazaire. The house at 30 Rue des Chapeliers was that of Monsieur de Tréville, a descendant of the Captain of the Musketeers at the time of Louis XIII. The *Préfecture*, opposite the church, has a grandiose but crumbling 19th century stone-and-brick façade with caryatids. The Church of St-Volusien once sheltered the saint's relics. Volusien, the 7th Bishop of Tours, found sanctuary in the Ariège Valley following victimisation by the Visigoths at the end of the 5th century and died a natural death here. The only relic of the 12th-century sanctuary which was rebuilt two centuries later, then damaged during the Wars of Religion, is the Romanesque portal with four sculpted capitals. The belfry dates from the 16th century and the choir was raised and vaulted the following century. Inside there is a band of Gothic-style painted carvings around the choir and a 16th-century coloured terracotta *Entombment*; the stalls (c. 1670) are from St-Sernin in Toulouse. In the Romanesque crypt is a 14th-century polygonal chapel. The church was restored in the 1960s.

Place St-Volusien was the ancient commercial centre of Foix. Rue des Marchands, leading out of it, was one of the grandest of the old city, containing the buildings of government and administration of the former province of Foix. East of the church, 37 Rue du Rival has a fine door dated 1617, and at the end of this street is the old bridge over the Ariège. There are several small squares with fountains in the old town, Place Dutilh, Place St-Vincent, and Place de Labistour, where one of the old city bastions stood; in Place du 8 Mai 1845 is an 18th-century portal.

Allées de Villotte, a wide tree-lined avenue at right angles to the river and built on the old ramparts outside the medieval *enceinte*, is now the main road of the town and

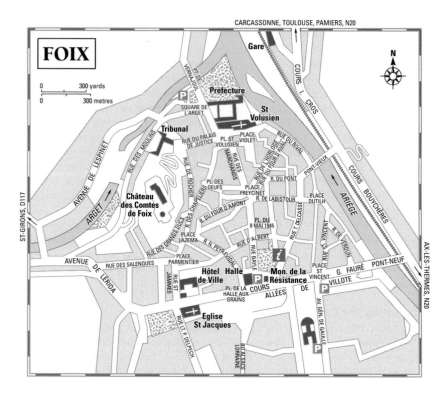

has a large grain market built in 1870. The Hôtel de Ville was built where the old pilgrimage hostel of St-James had stood and the hospital opposite the was the former Capuchin church of St-Jacques. Place Parmentier, the potato market in the 19th century, has some 16th-century half-timbered houses, and to the west of the roundabout there is a fine view of the castle from Pont de St-Girons. On the outskirts of town in the direction of Toulouse, at Couloumié, is the Musée de la Chasse et de la Nature (*guided visits 9–10.30 & 10.30–12 & 2–3.30 & 4.30–5; T: 05 61 65 04 02*). The visit introduces the history of hunting throughout the ages and the treatise on hunting written by the Count of Foix, Gaston Fébus (*see box opposite*).

Environs of Foix

At Montgaillard, south of Foix, are the **Forges de Pyrène**, which brings together 120 ancient trades on a 5 hectare site (*open June–Aug 10–7; June, Sept 10–6; Oct–mid-Nov 1.30–6, closed Mon; March–May, Tues–Fri 1.30–6, closed Mon; closed Jan, Feb; T: 05 34 09 30 60*), demonstrating the skills of the blacksmith, distillers, bakers, basket maker, and many others. Further upstream, the Pont du Diable at Marcu-Ginabat is a fortified bridge with two arcades, built in the 13th century. Nearby the Church of St-Louis has a rustic porch (12th century) with carvings.

GASTON FÉBUS

The legendary blond warrior Gaston III (1331–91) chose for himself the name *Fébus* (Occitan for Phoebus, the sun god). He inherited the Béarn in 1343 through his mother and dominated the Bigorre (*see p. 513*), although he did not govern it. His aim was to link his territories across the south with a chain of castles from Mazères to Pau, thus controlling an important east–west route between the Mediterranean and Bayonne. He made Pau his capital when he became Prince of Navarre and it continued to be a regular port of call. Unsurprisingly, his vast inheritance was fraught with political and military problems but he defended it on all sides: against the English in Aquitaine, the French in the east and against the armies of Armagnac to the northwest. In his castle at Orthez he wrote a book on hunting, the *Livre de la Chasse*. In 1380 he took solitary refuge in the great *donjon* of Pau after murdering his only son, who had tried to poison him, and there he wrote his *Livre des Oraisons* (Book of Prayers). He maintained independence until 1390 when, inexplicably, he surrendered to Charles VI by the Treaty of Toulouse, which named the King of France as his successor, although this could not be applied as no conquest had taken place. The line of the Counts of Foix ended with his death in 1391. The Bigorre was added to the huge county of Foix-Béarn in 1425 under Jean I, and passed eventually to Henri III of Foix-Béarn, King of Navarre, who acceded to the throne of France as Henri IV in 1589 (*see p. 485*).

ROUTE DES CORNICHES

The D20 from Bompas is a small winding route above the valley that avoids the main road. Just outside **Arnave** is the pre-Romanesque pilgrimage church of St-Paul, undoubtedly built on a pagan site, reached by a half-hour walk up a narrow footpath into the hills. Further on there is a turning to **Verdun** and the little church of St-Blaise, with belfry-porch and gable, the only building to survive a flood that destroyed the village in 1875. Overlooking the valley at **Axiat** is the small 12th-century church of St-Blaise, with a sturdy square belfry of superimposed triple and quadruple bays. The date of the portal is contested but could be as early as 1075, and the structure is built in superb ashlar, but unfortunately the interior decoration has been badly tampered with. Structural changes were made at the end of the 17th century when the nave was lengthened.

Lordat (900m) is a small village dominated by the proud ruins of what was one of the largest medieval castles in the County of Foix, possibly built in the 10th century. The 10min walk up provides splendid views, explained by three orientation tables, which include the military architecture. Three successive elliptical *enceintes* defended the castle keep from the east and south. One wall of the keep dates possibly from the first construction, but is difficult to confirm as the castle was rebuilt in 1295 and because of subsequent deterioration. It served as refuge to Cathars after the fall of Montségur (*see p. 562*) in 1244 and was dismantled in 1582.

There is a small, discreet Romanesque chapel at **Vernaux** (11th century? and 16th century), but one of the best churches on this route is **St-Martin d'Unac**. Built at the end of the 11th century at the time of Roger II of Foix, part of the nave and the 24m high belfry, with double openings on three levels, are survivors of the first church, which was enlarged in the 12th century when the three apses were added. Its main features are the decorations inside and out: the three east windows—outlined with billets, zig-zags, rosettes and stars—have columns and capitals in marble. Inside, around the choir, are some fine capitals whose quality suggests a link to the workshop of St-Sernin in Toulouse. On the south wall is a 15th-century mural depicting St Michael in the role of a knight, a pilgrim kneeling before him, an open book in his hands.

THE SOUTHERN ARIÈGE

Deep into the Pyrenees, close to the Spanish border, mountain torrents such as the Vicdessos, the Saurat, the Aston and the Oriège carve through some of the highest and wildest places of the *département* and have created a series of remarkable caves.

Painted *bouquetin* or mountain ibex (Magdalenian 17–10,000 BP) in the Grotte de Niaux.

Grotte de Bédeilhac

Open July, Aug 10–6; April–June, Sept–Oct and school holidays 2.30–4.15; T: 05 61 05 95 06, www.grotte-de-bedeilhac.org

These vast caves at the head of the valley of Saurat are of both geological and prehistoric interest. The caves were discovered in 1906, and it has been calculated that they were used by prehistoric man for over 10,000 years. Requisitioned during the Second World War by the French army, and then the Germans, who considered using them as an aircraft factory and even as an airstrip, the caves contain Magdalenian paintings, engravings of bison and horses and reindeer, and unique examples of animals modelled in clay, that are remarkably still in place. The main village, Saurat, is stretched out along the old road and the valley offers a variety of scenic walks and has a rare sandstone quarry worked entirely by hand by Sylvain Cuminetti (*T: 05 61 05 92 54*).

GROTTE DE NIAUX

Open all year but visits must be booked in advance; closed Mon from Nov–March except during school and public holidays; closed 25 Dec, 1 Jan; T: 05 61 05 10 10 or 05 61 05 88 37, www.niaux.net. Numbers are strictly limited for conservation reasons. The visit is a round trip of 1.5km over broken ground so good walking shoes and a warm sweater are recommended; lamps are supplied.

For the sheer beauty of their prehistoric paintings the caves of Niaux are among some of the most outstanding in southwest France. The first tourists came here in the 17th century, unsupervised, and carried off pieces of the calcite formations as souvenirs, leaving their graffiti in exchange. The majority of the paintings accessible to the public are concentrated in what is called the Salon Noir, a huge cavern about 700m into the cave. They date from the Magdalenian period, some 12,850–13,850 years ago, the last and most brilliant era, in creative terms, of the Upper Paleolithic. In 1925 a new gallery with a number of paintings was found beyond an underground lake, and discoveries continued to be made up to 1975. In total there are 104 animal paintings, three-quarters in the Salon Noir, most frequently of bison but also of horses, ibex, and a few aurochs, fish and deer, and many undeciphered signs and symbols. The animals are always represented in profile and the majority are painted, either in red pigment (iron ore) or black (manganese oxide or finely ground charcoal) over an outline sketch drawn first in charcoal or occasionally engraved. The motivation for these inspired creations can only be hypothesised. The effect of the paintings, especially in lamplight, is quite magical. They are profoundly moving, skillfully executed, sensitive to individual characteristics of texture and expression, yet drawn with an economy of line that has no temporal boundaries.

The Salon Noir and other galleries of Niaux are faithfully replicated at the Parc de la Préhistoire near Tarascon-sur-Ariège (*open July–Aug 10–8; April–June, Sept–Oct, Tues–Fri 10–6, closed Mon; Sat, Sun and holidays 10–7; T: 05 61 05 01 10*). The park covers 13 hectares and offers numerous exhibitions, demonstrations and hands-on experiences relating to prehistory. The Musée Pyrénéen at Niaux (*July–Aug 9–8; rest of year,*

10–12 & 2–6; T: 05 62 05 88 36) is a collection of over 3,000 objects which reflect life in the Ariège from prehistoric times to the end of the 19th century.

At Alliat, in the valley almost opposite Niaux, are the smallest of the caves in the region open to the public. **Grotte de La Vache** *(open July–Aug 10–6; April–June, Sept–Oct and school holidays 2.30–4.15; T: 05 61 05 95 95)*, which have paintings as well as carved objects of the Magdalenian era (12,000 to 15,000 BC) and archaeological debris from the Neolithic period.

VALLEY OF THE VICDESSOS

The Valley of the Vicdessos, southwest of Niaux, closes in on the river and leads to the village of Vicdessos and the multitude of lakes which are the beauty of this part of the high Pyrenees, most of them accessible only on foot. The Renaissance house at **Siguer**, a charming village on the D24, was the hunting lodge of the Counts of Foix. Slate was mined here at one time, but there are still red-tiled roofs as far south as Tarascon. The iron ore mines at **Rancié**, which had been worked since time immemorial, closed in 1929. Tourism and skiing have now taken over. There is a small exhibition of the history of the mine in the local Tourist Office, and at Sem is church dedicated to Ste-Barbe, patron saint of miners. Little more than a pile of stones marks the former Château de Montréal-de-Sos *(open all year, T: 05 61 64 87 53)* at the hamlet of **Olbier**, near Auzat, an important outpost of the Counts of Foix in the 13th century but long abandoned. It is a wonderful village abundant with flowers in the summer, along the stream and around the fountains, famous for the mountain races and for the traditional habitat of the shepherds, known as *orris*. **Saleix** is another delightful hamlet which has a 16th-century church with a one-handed clock. The road continues through the wild and rugged scenery of the Vicdessos region—dominated by the Montcalm (3078m), Canalbonne (2914m) and La Rouge (2902m) peaks, the landscape becoming ever more lunaresque over the Port de Lers (1517m)—to the popular lake, the Etang de Lers.

AX-LES-THERMES & THE FRONTIER

Ax-les-Thermes (720m), the last town of any significance before Andorra, was appreciated for the curative properties of the waters long before the Romans. Three valleys, the Ariège, the Lauze and the Oriège meet here, and the town has more facilities than most other centres in the Ariège. A novel feature of Ax is the Bassin des Ladres in the town centre, where all are welcome to strip off their boots or shoes and bathe their feet in the hot (77°C) sulphurous water. According to tradition, St Louis (Louis IX) founded the neighbouring hospital to treat leprous soldiers returning from the Crusades. The Mérens valley, which boasts the oldest Romanesque church of the Haute Ariège (10th–11th centuries), the remains consisting of the Catalan-style belfry with three levels of double openings, the walls of the apse and one apsidal chapel. This beautiful valley is also famous for its small black horses, descendants of those depicted in the Grotte de Niaux.

THE COUSERANS

The Couserans was an ancient viscounty, between the land of the Counts of Foix and the province of Bigorre, ruled by vassals of the Counts of Comminges. The designation is still used to describe the part of the Département of the Ariège west of Foix. Despite the barrier formed by the Pyrenees, there were close links between the Couserans and Catalonia and Aragon during the Middle Ages. The Spanish participated in pilgrimages to Notre-Dame-du-Marsan, near St-Lizier, and St-Lizier was a stage on the route to Santiago crossing the Pyrenees at the Col d'Aula. There is, however, no modern route from the Couserans into Spain. Many rivers rise in the mountains, forming a network of valleys which divide and sub-divide and divide again, making 18 in all. The main valleys are those of Bellongue, Biros and Bethmale, and three which join the Haut-Salat, the Ustou, Garbet and Arac. The smaller valleys can be entered by car but often just peter out in a track leading to the border. This is excellent hiking country, with well indicated and documented routes with an abundance of sub-alpine and alpine flowers above the forest line, as well as animals.

ST-LIZIER

On a hill beside the Salat, St-Lizier is a small town with the distinction of having two cathedrals, both founded in the 11th century, in the two separate quarters of the town. Notre-Dame-de-la-Sède, inside the *cité* walls, was the first. The sanctuary in the *bourg* is now known as the Cathédrale St-Lizier. One of the oldest and most prestigious music festivals in the region takes place at St-Lizier in July and August, when concerts are performed in the cathedral. Bishop Glycerius, of Spanish or Portuguese origin, who died c. 540, was reputed to have defended his city from Visigoths and Vandals. When canonised he became St Lizier.

St-Lizier Cathedral

Open 10–12 & 2–7; winter to 6. Treasury and Pharmacy, summer 10–12.30 & 2–7, closed Sunday morning; winter 10–12 & 2–6, closed Sun; T: 05 61 96 77 77.

The cathedral, built by Bishop Jourdain I in the late 11th century, probably on the site of a sepulchre, was consecrated in 1117 by St Raymond, Bishop of Barbastro in Spain. The many stages of reconstruction are evident from the exterior, the only remaining part of the 11th-century building being the south wall of the nave, visible from the cloister. The church was extended east with a transept and five-sided apse before the consecration. Gallo-Roman friezes and columns were haphazardly incorporated into the ashlar and a little later the walls were raised to take vaults.

The interior

The greatest glory of the cathedral is the Romanesque murals. The paintings in the choir, discovered in 1960, are on two levels and date from two different periods. The walls, erected and painted in the late 11th century, were tampered with when the choir vaults were reconstructed in the 12th century. Part of the original decorative scheme, in muted colours, has survived in the bays either side of the windows. This consists of friezes, heads and, framed by the painted architectural setting of blind arcades, pairs of standing figures, the Apostles in the apse and Kings and Prophets to the side. Below are images of the *Three Magi in the House of Herod*, the *Adoration of the Magi*, the *Annunciation*, *Visitation* and *Nativity*. The elongated figures are strikingly beautiful, the most moving being those in the *Visitation*, where Elizabeth and Mary are cheek-to-cheek, their haloes fused. The work is attributed to a 12th-century painter who worked in the Catalonian Pyrenees and in the Val d'Aran, identified as the Master of Pedret. The vault paintings, containing the arms of Bishop Auger de Montfaucon, which place them at the end of the 13th or early 14th centuries, are rather less eloquent, with a *Christ in Majesty*, surrounded by the symbols of the Evangelists.

The 12th-century murals in the north chapel, discovered in 1980 under a thick layer of plaster, are interesting for their rare iconography based on the *Revelation of St John at Patmos*. Two groups of three figures with haloes stand before the six gates of Heavenly Jerusalem, their arms outstretched towards the kings of the earth bearing treasures. Beneath are the symbols of the Evangelists and the figure of St John as he receives his vision from an angel. The words *Sanctus Andreas* can be deciphered on the north, and the east wall has a *Virgin Suckling the Infant Jesus* (c. 1300). The shadow of an inscription below the Virgin indicates that there was also an image of St John in the east end.

The cloister and treasury
The other major feature of St-Lizier is the fine Romanesque cloister, the only one in the Ariège, which is the result of two building campaigns, the first 1150–80 and the second in the 13th century, accounting for a variety of styles of capitals and different types of vaulting. In the 14th century the cloister was shortened by two bays when the transept was built, and the upper level was added in the 16th century. The 32 bays are supported by alternate single and double marble columns, with a cluster of four in the west gallery. The capitals are decorated with allegorical, geometric and vegetal designs, the most accomplished in the north gallery. The rare figurative images include *Adam and Eve*, in the north gallery, and *Daniel in the Lions' Den with Habbakuk* in the east. The treasury—in the sacristy off the cloister—contains a remarkable collection of treasures from the 11th to the 19th centuries of diverse origins, the finest being the elegant Renaissance reliquary bust of St Lizier, made by Antoine Favier of Toulouse, in embossed and gilded silver. The pharmacy of the hospice in the Hôtel Dieu, built in 1771 adjacent to the cathedral cloister, is complete with wooden cabinets and locally made jars, an operating table and a dictionary of pharmaceutical prescriptions.

The citadel
The **Cathédrale de Notre-Dame-de-la-Sède** (from *la Séda*, Occitan for episcopal see), of fairly modest proportions, was begun in the 11th century adjacent to the south ramparts and there is not a great deal left to visit. The apse, of the late 11th century, is the oldest part, and in the Romanesque chevet are reused Roman friezes; the three-

bay nave dates from the late 15th century. The choir stalls and altars are 17th-century and the wood-panelling is late 18th-century. There is nothing left of the cloister to the north, but the 13th-century chapter house with brick vaults has survived.

ST-GIRONS

St-Girons is the largest town in this part of the Ariège and is the *sous-préfecture*. A small dynamic commercial centre with a lively market, it is not of any particular architectural interest. Originally called Bourg-sous-Vic or Bourg-sous-Ville, in acknowledgement of its subordinate role to St-Lizier, it was called St-Girons when the remains of the Christian martyr Gerontius were brought here after the sack of St-Lizier by the Counts of Comminges in 1130. The advantages of its position in the wide valley where the three rivers Salat, Baup and Lez converge are obvious and the riverbanks are still St-Girons' strong point, with tree-lined walks and pleasant gardens surrounding the remodelled château of the Viscounts of the Couserans, now municipal offices. The parish church, rebuilt in the 19th century, has conserved its 15th-century belfry, and in the southeast of the town, the much-restored 12th-century church of St-Vallier still has its Romanesque portal.

VALLEYS OF THE COUSERANS

The road west from **Sentenac d'Oust** follows the Vallée de Bethmale, considered the most beautiful of all the Couserans valleys, scattered with the purples, pinks, mauves and blues of meadow flowers—wild orchids, wild thyme and bilberries—on the way up to the Col de la Core (1395m), such a popular place for walkers and motorists that it can almost become crowded in summer. Equally popular is the Lac de Bethmale, in a glade abundant with bees, berries and butterflies, raspberries and wild strawberries.

In **Samortein** there is a *sabotier*, Pierre Jusot (*T: 05 61 96 78 84 or 05 61 96 74 39*), one of the last in France, who makes legendary wooden clogs with long, curved and pointed toes, part of the traditional costume of Bethmale. His workshop can be visited. **Borde-sur-Lez** has a lovely old bridge leading to the hamlet of Ourjout and the 12th-century church of St-Pierre (*see below*). The wooded Vallée de Biros begins here. **Sentein** is the main town of the valley, important for mining and its thermal springs. It has a fortified church, the grandest of several little churches in this remote region with a reddish sandstone belfry, the third highest in the Couserans. The octagonal section of the belfry is 14th-century and the spire was added in 1749. Its Romanesque base is the baptistery, the entrance to which has an unusual arrangement of simple capitals on the outside supporting the arch and four columns inside. The body of the church was amended in the 14th century and has late 15th- to early 16th-century paintings in the east bay of the nave of Apostles, Prophets and Doctors of the Church, and in the west bay 12 figures in contemporary dress.

At **Castillon**, the Chapelle de St-Pierre (*exterior only, guided visits mid-July–mid-Aug Thurs at 10; book with the Tourist Office 05 61 96 72 64*) perched above the village with an impressive belfry and a statue of St Peter, originally belonged to the château demolished in 1632. The Vallée de la Bellongue rises to the Col de Portet d'Aspet (1069m) where the road drops down into the Comminges (*see p. 539*). **Audressein** is a pretty village at the start of the valley with a lovely 14th-century church, Notre-Dame-de-Tramesaygues, beside the river (*open daily in summer; guided visits mid-July to mid-Aug, Thurs at 10, reservation essential T: 05 61 96 72 64*). The deep porch has a series of *ex-voto* scenes in true fresco technique (restored 1987–88). The large figures of angels, St James and St John the Baptist are more sophisticated than the anecdoctal scenes presenting individuals in some sort of trouble or danger—sick, imprisoned, tumbling from a tree, departing on a crusade—who are all subsequently saved and are shown giving thanks to Our Lady.

PRACTICAL INFORMATION

GETTING AROUND

• **By train:** From Paris Austerlitz and Toulouse to Foix; from Toulouse to Latour-de-Carol via Pamiers, Foix. Tarascon-sur-Ariège, Ax-les-Thermes, Mérens-les-Vals, L'Hospitalet.
• **By bus:** From Toulouse to L'Hospitalet via Pamiers, Varilhes, Foix, Tarascon-sur-Ariège, Ax-les-Thermes, Mérens-les-Vals. Between Lavalenet and Foix, Chalabre, Saverdun; Mazères to Pamiers, Les Pujols. Between Foix and St-Girons; Serres-sur-Arget; Tarascon; Lavalenet; Pamiers and Auzat. Between Tarascon and Foix; Saurat and Tarascon; Ax-les-Thermes and Saverdun.
Boussens to St-Girons via Lorp, St-Lizier. Between St-Girons and La Bastide-de-Desplas; Aulus; Foix; Massat; St-Lary; Seintein, Ustou.

TOURIST INFORMATION

Aulus-les-Bains Centre Ville, T: 05 61 96 00 01, www.haut-couserans.com
Auzat Pays d'Auzat-Vicdessos, Rue des Pyrénées, T: 05 61 64 87 53, otauzat@club-internet.fr
Ax-les-Thermes, La Résidence, 6 Av. T:. Delcassé, T: 05 61 64 60 60, www.vallees-ax.com
Castillon T: 05 61 96 72 64, www.ot-castillon-en-couserans.fr
Foix 29 Rue Delcassé, T: 05 61 65 12 12, www.mairie-foix.fr
Le Carla Bayle T: 05 61 68 53 53, www.carla-bayle.com
Le Mas d'Azil T: 05 61 69 99 90, tourisme.arize.leze@wanadoo.fr
Mazères Vallée d l'Hers, Mairie, T: 05 61 69 31 02
Montferrier Pl. de la Montagne, T: 05 61 01 14 14
Montségur T: 05 61 03 03 03, www.montsegur.org
Pamiers Blvd Delcassé, BP 95, T: 05 61 67 52 52, www.pamierstourisme.com
Ste-Croix Volvestre T: 05 61 66 27 98, ot.volvestre.ariegeois@wanadoo.fr
St-Girons Pl. Alphonse Sentein, T: 05 61 96 26 60, www.ville-st-girons.fr
St-Lizier Pl. de la Cathédrale, T: 05 61 96 77 77, www.ariege.com/st-lizier

Sentein-Biros, T: 05 61 96 10 90, otbiros@free.fr

Seronais La Bastide-de-Serou, T05 61 64 53 53, www.seronais.com

GUIDED VISITS

Romanesque churches of the Couserans at Moulis, Arrout, Oujout and Sentein, visits mid-July to end-August, Fridays at 2–6.30 reservation essential at the Tourist Office, T: 05 61 96 26 60. Information for hikers: Foix CDT Ariègeois de la Randonnée Pédestre, 26 Faubourg de Planissolles, T: 05 34 09 02 09, www.wanadoo.fr/cdrp.09

ACCOMMODATION & RESTAURANTS

Aulus les-Bains

€€ **Hôtel La Terrasse**. A welcoming, family hotel-restaurant with a riverside location and a terrace overlooking the Garbet with pleasantly old-fashioned bedrooms and an attractive dining room. The cooking is based on traditional ingredients of the southwest, foie gras, *pigeonneau* (young pigeon), *filet de boeuf*; also fish and seafood. T: 05 61 96 00 98.

Ax-les-Thermes

€ **Le Grillon**. A quiet and pleasant hotel and restaurant with simple rooms in a chalet-style house. Deep in the mountains, the owner is also a mountain guide, and weekly outings are organised. The restaurant is reasonably priced and there are vegetarian dishes on the menu. Rue St-Udaut, T: 05 61 64 31 64 or 05 61 64 25 48, www.hotel-le-grillon.com.

Foix

€ **Lons**. In the centre of the small capital of the Ariège, a pleasant hotel which was formerly *relais de poste*. It has 38 decent bedrooms and the restaurant overlooks the river. 6 Pl. George-Dutilh, T: 05 34 09 28 00.

Mercenac

€ **Chambres d'hôtes Les Volets Bleus**. You will receive a warm welcome at this former *maison de metayers* which is charmingly furnished and set in the middle of an abundant garden. There are two pretty rooms available, one ground floor one first floor. *Table d'hôtes*, fitness room and jacuzzi. (6km from St-Lizier), Alain and Nicole Meunier, T: 05 61 96 68 55, www.ariege.com/lesvoletsbleus.

Mirepoix

€€ **Relais Royal**. ■ Occupying a beautifully restored 18th-century *hôtel particulier*, this is the first 4-star hotel in the Ariège. The original décor and fittings have been respected, such as the beautiful wrought-iron balustrade, wooden doors and terracotta floors. There are 8 very spacious bedrooms which combine the best of both worlds, traditional and modern, and the hotel has a pretty garden courtyard with pool. The elegant Ciel d'Or Restaurant offers French cooking at its best, *Asperges vertes tièdes, crème léger à l'orange, oeuf au plat à l'Espagnole*, or *Risotto aux primeurs du moment, poêlée de supion au basilic, jus à l'encre*; menus from €22 to €82. 8 rue Maréchal Clauzel, T: 05 61 60 19 19, www.relaisroyal.com.

Montferrier/Villeneuve d'Olmes

€ **Hôtel le Castrum**. Not far from Monségur, this is a top-quality hotel and restaurant surrounded by greenery and with a pool. The rooms are bright and modern and the restaurant prides itself in matching the appropriate wine to the dish. The chef produces creative dishes based on traditional regional cooking. The establishment also offers cookery and wine courses. Le Laouzet, T: 05 61 01 35 24, www.lecastrum.com

Montaut

€ Chambres d'hôtes Domaine de Pégulier. An elegant 18th-century mansion set in exceptional surroundings with park, gardens and heated pool all within sight of the Pyrenees. There are five tastefully arranged bedrooms of which two are south-facing suites accesses by a spiral staircase. The living rooms can be used by guests, and there is also *table d'hôtes* on offer. (3.5km from Saverdun), M. et Mme Maes-Lenoir. T: 05 61 68 30 65, www.chateaupegulier.com

St-Girons

€ La Clairière. The light and airy establishment is the near town centre. It has 19 spacious rooms, a terrace and swimming pool. The attractive restaurant is reputed for its modern cuisine, each dish a work of art. Av. de la Résistance, T: 05 61 66 66 66, www.ariege.com/la-clairiere.

€ Hôtel Eychenne This long-established family-run hotel occupies an old coaching inn. It has 42 large and uncluttered rooms with traditional furniture, and an inviting terrace/garden while the swimming pool adds a modern touch. The cooking is based on traditional ingredients of the south-west. 8 Ave Paul-Laffont, T: 05 61 04 04 50.

€ Chambres d'hôtes Relais d'Encausse. ■ In a peaceful setting not far from the town, with a warm welcome from the enthusiastic owners. Guests gather for a chat around the fireplace before a wholesome *table d'hôte*. T: 05 61 66 05 80. (From the D117 south of St-Girons take the tiny Rte de

Saudech and follow the signpost.)

€ Hôtel Horizon. Run by two generations of the Puech family, Francis and Maryse have renovated their father's hotel. There are 20 rooms competitively priced, a pool, tennis and other amenities. The restaurant has a terrace the cooking is an original slant on the traditional. Menus from €16.50 to €40; also with vegetarian alternatives. Lorp Sentaraille, on the D117 north of St-Girons, T: 05 61 66 26 80.

MARKET DAYS

Aulus-les-Bains in July-August Sunday
Bélesta Tuesday
Castillon 3rd Tuesday of the month; in July-August, Tuesday
Foix alternate Mondays, Fridays
Mirepoix Monday; Thursday farmers' market
Pamiers Tuesday, Thursday, Saturday
St-Girons Saturday
Vicdessos Thursday

FESTIVALS & EVENTS

June: *San Joan Beth e Gran*, festival of St John, valley of the Couserans and St-Girons
Festival of St-Jean, Ax-les-Thermes
July: *Fiesta et Festival International du théâtre*, international festival of theatre, Pamiers.
August
Médiévales de Mazères, the town rediscovers its medieval past in colourful and animated celebration, Mazères
Festival de St-Lizier, classical music in the cathedral, St-Lizier

TOULOUSE

Toulouse is distinguished by its mellow brick buildings and panoramas across the Garonne, which have inspired many comparisons with Tuscany or Spain. Toulouse's treasures are manifold: the largest Romanesque church and the best collection of 12th-century decorated capitals in Europe; the extraordinary brick church where the Dominican order began; and examples of elegant Renaissance town houses. It is also one of the rare places where crystallised violets are still confected and sold, after a revival of the industry in the late 20th century. The aeronautical and space industries contribute in large part to the modern prosperity of the metropolis and the surrounding area, while the university is the second largest after Paris. Fourth city in France, it is the capital of the vast Midi-Pyrénées region and provides the pulse that reverberates around a region whose furthest point north is some 200km away.

HISTORY OF TOULOUSE

The advantageous position of the fertile Garonne valley between the Atlantic, the Mediterranean and the Iberian Peninsula attracted Celtic settlers, the Tectosages, in 3rd century BC, followed about a century later by the Romans. Ancient *Tolosa* grew wealthy from the importation of wine, so that by the 2nd century AD it had acquired the status of colony, with 20,000 inhabitants. Only fragments of the 1st-century city walls remain in place, although the site of the ancient temple or *Capitolium* was discovered in 1992 during excavation work under Place Esquirol. The *Capitolium* was crucial to the history of the early Christian era and the martyrdom, in 250, of St Sernin (Saturninus), the first Bishop of Toulouse, who refused to worship pagan idols and died after being roped to a half-crazed sacrificial bull by crowds assembled on the steps of the *Capitolium*.

For a century from 418 the Visigoths made Toulouse their capital, after which came incursions by the Franks, Arabs and Normans. The history of the town and surrounding area as an almost autonomous principality began in the 8th century with the creation by Charlemagne of the county of Toulouse. In the feudal hierarchy this was part of the Kingdom of Aquitaine belonging to the French monarchy, but allegiance to the French diminished to a purely nominal status as the Counts' power increased, until they had dominion directly or indirectly over a vast territory where the language of Oc was spoken. By the 12th century, the boundary of the Languedoc covered an area loosely contained by the Dordogne, Gascony, the Montagne Noire, the Mediterranean and the Pyrenees, but was constantly in flux. The power of the princes and the Church developed side by side through the 11th and 12th centuries, economic prosperity and civil liberties stimulating urban growth and the Gregorian reforms (*see p. 623*) adding to the authority of the ecclesiastics. A new cathedral was begun in the 11th century, in 1096 the altar table of the unfinished church of St-Sernin was consecrated and in the same year Raymond IV of Toulouse led the First Crusade.

In spite of this activity in the orthodox Church, a breakaway fundamentalist Christian movement, described then as a heresy and now as Catharism, took root in the Languedoc. It resulted in the only crusade by the French against their own people, beginning in 1209, and was popularly known as the Albigensian Crusade (*see p. 251*). The foundation of the university in 1229 was a bid to counteract heretical beliefs through the teaching of theology and canon law.

The architectural style of the counter-heresy, generally referred to as southern or meridional Gothic, developed as religious orders created churches adapted to the liturgy and to preaching to large crowds, with one vast aisleless rib-vaulted space. The earliest extant model is the 13th-century nave of the cathedral of St-Etienne (*see p. 604*). The scarcity of stone in the alluvial basin of the Garonne contributed to the tradition of building in the elongated Roman-style brick which has become the hallmark of Toulousain architecture. Five serious conflagrations destroyed much of the town between 1463 and 1551 and in 1555 precise regulations were imposed forbidding reconstruction in wood and stipulating brick or stone.

The golden era of many towns in the region, not least Toulouse, began during a period of peace after the Hundred Years War (1337–1453) and ended with the start of the Wars of Religion in 1560. A variety of factors contributed to the prosperity of Toulouse and the Toulousain at this time: one was the definitive establishment in 1443 of the *Parlement*, a judicial and legislative institution, the second most important in France, elevating the town to the status of provincial capital; another was the commerce in indigo or *pastel* (*see p. 315*). The *pasteliers* were a merchant élite of about a dozen families whose members often rose to eminent positions in the municipal hierarchy and built Renaissance mansions. Renaissance Toulouse had close links with the humanists of Bologna University and also with the printing trade in Lyons, and from 1476 became the fourth town in France to have presses, although until the beginning of the 16th century documents were printed exclusively in Latin and Occitan. The introduction of maize to the region in the 17th century and the means of transporting it by canal (*see p. 555*) brought an era of renewed prosperity, and in the 18th century municipal schemes included the realisation of dykes, ports, bridges and a canal. Hand in hand with this came the demolition of medieval buildings, including the once-great church of Notre-Dame-de-la-Daurade. Toulouse, unlike other large towns in the Midi, adhered to the Revolution but after the suppression of the *Parlement* in 1790 became simply *chef-lieu* (county town) of the *département* of Haute-Garonne, created in 1790. Napoleon's popularity gradually waned—largely because of the decline in corn prices due to the blockading of ports and war in Spain—to the point where French troops under Marshall Soult, retreating before Wellington's army, were not welcomed by the inhabitants of the town. On 10th April 1814 Soult was defeated and the Duke was received as liberator of Toulouse, a pointless exercise, happening four days after Napoleon's abdication.

The end of the 18th and the 19th centuries brought the destruction of many religious buildings and parts of the old *cité*, to be replaced with new boulevards and public buildings. By the beginning of the Second Empire (1852) the population had increased to 100,000 but the industrial revolution had hardly touched this part of France. The building of the railway in 1856 linked Toulouse to the metropolitan north of France and helped to improve the economy but, until the eve of the First World War, Toulouse's largest factory was the state-owned tobacco factory on the banks of the Garonne. The leap into the 20th century was due, in the end, to its distance from the hub of activity and therefore of battle during the First World War, combined with plentiful supplies of manpower and energy (coal from Carmaux, hydro-electricity from the Pyrenees). The father of aviation, Clément Ader from Muret, made a primitive flying machine, *Eole*, which lifted off the ground in 1890, and is also credited with the invention of the word *avion* (aeroplane). Pierre Latécoère's boiler-making factory near Toulouse was converted to produce Salmson observation aircraft in 1917, and following the First World War Latécoère launched Aéropostale, with which the aviators St-Exupéry and Mermoz were both associated. Fighter planes were pioneered in the workshops of Emile Dewoitine; Concorde made its first flight in Toulouse in 1969; and Airbus Industrie is now an important employer in the region. The latest and most ambitious civil aircraft project is the double-decker Airbus A380 with 555 seats which made its maiden flight on 27th April, 2005. With France's space programme based here, Toulouse is also known as *Cité de l'Espace*. In June 1993 the first Metro line was inaugurated, and a second is underway at time of writing. There is ongoing restoration of the city's many monuments and the creation of new cultural centres. The population of the city numbers 426,700 and of greater Toulouse, 761,110.

PLACE DU CAPITOLE

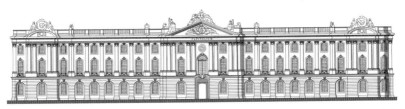

WEST ELEVATION OF THE CAPITOLE

The hub of Toulouse is the huge Place du Capitole. The square is a vast semi-pedestrianised area (created 1811–52) with pavement cafés and covering an underground car park. It springs to life on Wednesdays with a colourful market. The space is dominated by the brick-and-marble façade of the Capitole building (1750–60). The entrance to the historic rooms within the Capitole can be found in the northeast corner of the square.

THE CAPITOLE

Open Easter–Oct 9–7, Sun and holidays 10–7; Nov–Easter 9–5, holidays 10–7; T: 05 61 11 02 22.

Capitole is an unusual title for a place that everywhere else in France would be known as the Hôtel de Ville (town hall) and stems from a historical and etymological mutation. By the 11th century the elected council or chapter of the municipality—*capitulum* in Latin and *capitol* in Occitan—enjoyed considerable autonomy. *Capitulum*, *capitol* and *capitolium* (the name of the ancient temple) fused to become Capitole, denoting both the chapter and the *maison commune*, and its officers were known as *capitouls*. The *maison commune* was established here in the 12th century, deliberately distanced from the Counts' palace at the other end of town, now Place du Salin.

The exterior

The present façade—designed by Guillaume Cammas—was intended as a monumental screen for a disparate group of buildings which existed until 1873, when most were indiscriminately demolished. It now masks the town hall and the Théâtre du Capitole. The central pedimented portico is emphasised by eight columns in candy-pink marble from the Montagne Noire—to symbolise the eight *capitouls*—and there are large sculptures above the central portico by Marc Arcis, François Lucas and Louis Parant. The central archway leads to Cour Henri IV (1602–06) with a monumental gateway begun in 1546 by Nicolas Bachelier (d. 1556/57), the most original and talented Toulousain architect of the Renaissance. Above the arch is a statue in polychrome marble of Henri IV (1607). A marble plaque in the paving commemorates the execution of the Duke of Montmorency, Maréchal de France, Governor of Languedoc and godson of Henri IV, on 30th October 1632, for opposing Richelieu.

The back of the Capitole building is an 1883–84 replica of the west elevation set off by Place Charles de Gaulle, a public garden with fountains, where the Tourist Office is housed in a building called the Tour des Archives (1525–30), the only surviving part of the medieval Capitole. In 1873 it was restored by Eugène-Emmanuel Viollet-le-Duc (*see p. 95*), chief architect of the Monuments Historiques.

Galeries du Capitole

The Galeries du Capitole on the first floor include the Salle des Mariages with light-hearted décor dedicated to themes of love (c. 1916) by Paul Gervais. The next room has Impressionist-style murals by the local painter Henri Martin (*see p. 187*), including a frieze-like composition of a group strolling on the banks of the Garonne, among them Jean Jaurès, the socialist politician who came from the Tarn (*see p. 308*). The stuccoed and gilded gallery overlooking the Place du Capitole, the **Salle des Illustres** (1892–98), inspired by the Villa Farnese in Rome, was the creation of Paul Pujol. The statues represent illustrious citizens. The walls and ceiling carry historical and allegorical paintings of the great moments in the history of Toulouse including the siege by Simon de Montfort during the Albigensian crusades in the 13th century.

NORTH OF THE CAPITOLE

On the northwest of Place du Capitole, at the angle of Rue des Lois and Rue Romiguières, is the Hôtel du Grand Balcon (*closed*), a modest establishment haunted by the memory of aviation pioneers such as Antoine de Saint-Exupéry (author of The Little Prince) and Jean Mérmoz. Rue du Taur, the old north–south route that served the bourg of St-Sernin, leads through the old University area ending opposite the south flank of the celebrated Basilica of St-Sernin (*see p. 588*).

On Rue du Taur, between Place du Capitole and Place St-Sernin, is the brick church of **Notre-Dame-du-Taur** (begun c. 1300). It is identified by the impressive pedimented gable or *clocher mur*, typical of the Toulousain, with bells suspended in open arcades. According to legend, the church stands on the site of St Sernin's first resting-place (*see p. 588*). The south wall of the rather dingy interior carries a mural showing the genealogy of Jacob, with 38 figures.

The area west of Rue du Taur was the heart of the medieval university: Rue des Pénitents-Gris leads to Rue du Collège de Foix where, behind a wall, stands the former college founded in the 15th century by Cardinal Pierre de Foix (1386–1464). Archbishop of Toulouse at the age of 22, and from the powerful family of the Counts of Foix (*see p. 568*), Pierre de Foix also founded the University of Avignon. In the same street are the steeple and the gateway, all that remain of the great 13th- and 14th-century monastery of the Cordeliers, of the Franciscan order.

On the east side of Rue du Taur, at the intersection with Rue du Périgord, is Tour Maurand, a fragment of the oldest secular building in Toulouse. At 69 Rue du Taur is the monumental doorway designed by Nicolas Bachelier (c. 1555) for the Collège de l'Esquile, now the Cinémathèque, an important film library with particularly strong collections of American burlesque cinema, and Russian and Soviet cinema. It was founded in the 1950s, and now mounts regular exhibitions and maintains a comprehensive library of books on the cinema. (*T: 05 62 30 30 10; recorded programme information, T: 05 62 30 30 11, www.lacinemathequedetoulouse.com*).

Chapelle des Carmelites

Open May–Sept 9.30–12.30 & 2–6; Oct–April 9.45–12.30 & 2–5.30; closed Mon; T: 05 61 21 27 60.

Behind the pink façade and green door on Rue du Périgord, is the small counter-reformation Chapelle des Carmelites. The chapel is all that remains of the 17th-century Carmelite Convent, destroyed at the Revolution, whose foundation stone was laid in 1662 by Louis XIII during a break in his rampage through the southwest routing out Calvinists. The convent took 20 years to build and between 1741 and 1751 the walls and ceiling of this simple building were transformed by the painters Jean-Pierre Rivalz and Jean-Baptiste Despax with themes of theological and monastic virtues mixed with Old Testament prophets, scenes from the New Testament and the *Glorification of St Theresa of Avila*, reformer of the Carmelite Order. The chapel's exceptional acoustics, due to the wooden roof, make it a popular venue for musical performances.

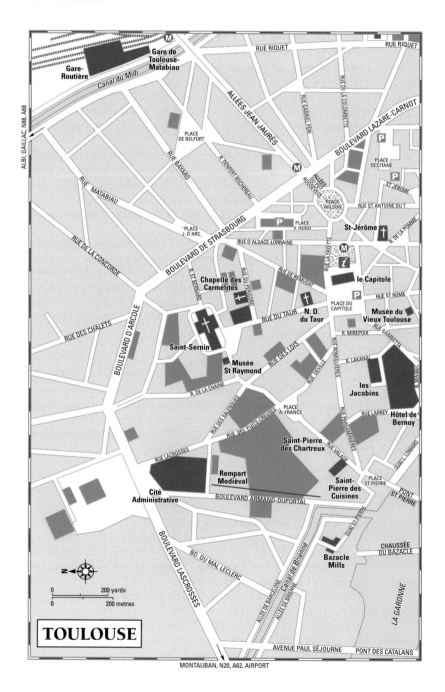

TOULOUSE

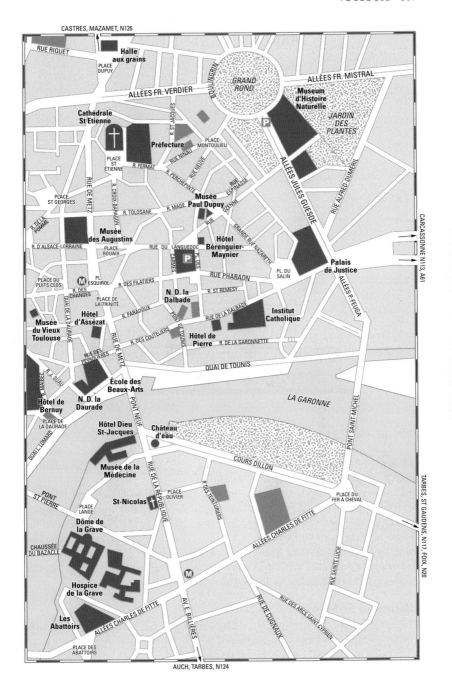

CASTRES, MAZAMET, N126

RUE RIQUET

PLACE
DUPUY

Halle
aux grains

ALLÉES FR. VERDIER

BOULINGRIN

GRAND
ROND

ALLÉES FR. MISTRAL

Museum
d'Histoire
Naturelle

JARDIN
DES
PLANTES

Cathédrale
St Etienne

Préfecture

R. ST. JACQUES

PLACE
MONTOULIEU

PLACE
ST
ÉTIENNE

R. FERMAT

RUE NINAU

RUE NEUVE

R. PERCHEPINTE

RUE ESPINASSE

RUE DE METZ

R. CROIX-BARAGON

PLACE
ST GEORGES

R. TOLOSANE

R. MAGE

RUE UZEINE

Musée
Paul Dupuy

ALLÉES JULES GUESDE

RUE ALFRED-DUMERIL

R. DE LA POMME

R. D'ALSACE-LORRAINE

Musée
des Augustins

PLACE
ROUAIX

RUE DU LANGUEDOC

PL. DES CARMES

Hôtel
Bérenguier-
Maynier

GRANDE RUE ST. NAZARETH

CARCASSONNE N113, A61

PLACE DU
PUITS CLOS

M

PL.
ESQUIROL

R. DES
CHANGES

R. DES FILATIERS

RUE PHARAON

PL. DU
SALIN

Palais
de Justice

ALLÉES P. FEUGA

QUAI DE LA DAURADE

PLACE DE
LA TRINITÉ

R. PARADOUX

N. D. la
Dalbade

R. ST REMESY

Institut
Catholique

PONT ST-MICHEL

Musée
du Vieux
Toulouse

Hôtel
d'Assézat

RUE DE METZ

R. DES COUTELIERS

PONT DE TOUNIS

RUE DE LA DALBADE

Hôtel de
Pierre

R. DE LA GARONNETTE

RUE DES
PEYROLIERES

QUAI DE TOUNIS

R. DE LA MAINE

R. J. SUAU

École des
Beaux-Arts

LA GARONNE

Hôtel de
Bernuy

N. D. la
Daurade

PONT NEUF

QUAI L'LOMBARD

PLACE DE
LA DAURADE

Hôtel Dieu
St-Jacques

Château
d'eau

COURS DILLON

PONT SAINT-MICHEL

TARBES, ST GAUDENS, N117, FOIX, N20

PONT
ST PIERRE

PLACE
LANGE

Musée de la
Médecine

St-Nicolas

RUE DE LA RÉPUBLIQUE

PLACE
OLIVIER

R. DES TEINTURIERS

PLACE DU
FER À CHEVAL

CHAUSSÉE
DU BAZACLE

Dôme de
la Grave

ALLÉES CHARLES DE FITTE

RUE SAINTE LUCIE

M

Hospice
de la Grave

AV. E. BILLIÈRES

RUE DES ARCS SAINT-CYPRIEN

Les
Abattoirs

ALLÉES CHARLES DE FITTE

RUE DE CUGNAUX

PLACE DES
ABATTOIRS

AUCH, TARBES, N124

BASILICA OF ST-SERNIN

BASILICA OF ST-SERNIN

Open July–Sept 8.30–6.15, Sun 8.30–7.30; Oct–June 8.30–11.45 & 2–5.45, Sun 8.30–12.30 & 2–7.30. Apse and crypt open July–Sept 10–6, Sun 11.30–6, closed Sat; Oct–June 10–11.30 & 2.30–6, Sun 2.30–5, closed Sat; T: 05 61 21 70 18. Binoculars are useful for viewing the carved capitals of the interior.

The basilica is the largest conserved Romanesque church in Europe and the most beautiful building in Toulouse. Small green gardens and mature trees soften its surroundings but most of the oval Place St-Sernin, created in the 19th century to the detriment of the monastic buildings, is a car park. Built in a combination of brick and stone, St-Sernin underwent a huge programme of repair, consolidation and 'de-restoration' at the end of the 20th century to secure, clean and return it to its putative profile of 1860/1872, before Viollet-le-Duc worked on it.

History of St-Sernin

The first shrine on this site was planned by Bishop Silve but built by Bishop Exupère c. 400 to shelter St Sernin's relics, translated in 402 or 403 from Bishop Hilaire's modest wooden oratory to the south. By the end of the 11th century a larger building was needed—and a more beautiful one desired—to accommodate the crowds of pious travellers en route for Santiago de Compostela in Spain (*see p. 11*), and also the needs of the resident clergy. The chapter was in funds as a result of the Gregorian disciplinary reforms, and the new church was begun in the third quarter of the 11th century in the form of a Latin cross, with double aisles flanking the nave and radiating chapels around the apse and on the east side of the transepts. The altar table is inscribed with the date of its consecration by Pope Urban II, 24th May 1096, and is signed by the stonecarver, Bernard Gilduin. Raymond Gayrard, saintly canon and former builder of bridges, took charge of the building works at the end of the 11th century when the chevet and the transept were already complete. By the time of his death in 1118 the three east bays of the nave had been vaulted and the body of the church was finished up to the level of the tribune windows, the part in stone and brick visible from the exterior. The collegiate church was elevated to abbey in 1117 and attention then turned to the construction of the cloisters and the monastic buildings, leaving the church unfinished, although there was a surge of activity in the 13th century under Abbot Bernard de Gensac (1243–64).

The exterior

The east end of the basilica is the most beautiful part of the building. The five semicircular radiating chapels clustered around the apse and the four chapels of the transepts create an undulating rhythm, with a secondary rhythm of colour contrasts set up by the use of brick for the mass and stone for the structural elements. All the elements are repeated in different tempos, resulting in a finely orchestrated yet powerful structure culminating in the 65m-high octagonal belfry. At the end of the 20th century restoration of the upper part, where there is an obvious lack of stone, reinstated the mirandes under the eaves. The belfry was built in four stages: the first stage with blind arcades covers the crossing dome, then come two levels with twin round-headed open bays surmounted by two stages with mitred bays built in the second half of the 13th century. The stone spire was added in 1478.

On each transept is a portal in the form of a triumphal arch, but both are now closed, and only the Porte des Comtes (c. 1082–83) on the south transept has kept some of its sculpted décor. Members of the leading family of nobles were buried in the small funerary recess on the left in sarcophagi from the early Christian burial ground close to the first church. Above the portal is an aedicule inscribed *Sanctus Saturninus*, suggesting it once contained the saint's effigy. The eight storiated capitals address the contrasting themes of salvation and damnation through the parable of Lazarus on the right-hand side, his soul depicted as a little naked body departing to heaven, as distinct from the figures on the left, who are guilty of the sins of avarice and lust and are being punished by monsters devouring their genitalia.

The delicately sculpted Renaissance archway, formerly part of the 16th-century enclosing walls, stands before the south door which is known as the Porte Miègeville (c. 1110–15), which used to run through the town centre, *mièja vila*. A projecting bay with a single arch and heavily sculpted cornice protects the all-important carved tympanum, one of the first examples of its kind. The iconography deals in a literal manner with the theme of the *Ascension*: Christ is assisted by angels who lift him physically by his waist. On the lintel below, the 12 Apostles contemplate the scene, flanked by the two men cited by the Acts who explain that Christ will return. The stylised twisted postures emphasise the awe of the scene, just as the deep carving of the folds stresses the solidity of the bodies and the upward fluid movement of the whole composition. There are stylistic similarities with the altar-table carvings by Gilduin in St-Sernin, and with the master of Jaca, Spain.

Three of the four capitals flanking the door are storiated. On the right is the *Expulsion from the Garden of Eden*; its counterpart on the left depicts the *Annunciation*, the antithesis to the *Fall*. The Angel Gabriel has his legs crossed, one of the earliest appearances in sculpture in the Languedoc of this convention for expressing movement (*see p. 601*). On the side face is a *Visitation* and the outer left capital graphically describes the *Massacre of the Innocents*. The fourth capital, with two lions imprisoned in tendrils, suggests the influence of the sculpture at Santiago. Carved consoles support the lintel: on the left is King David, the musician ancestor of Christ, between two lions; on the right, two round-faced figures wearing Phrygian bonnets sit astride lions, one foot bare and the other shod, an unexplained motif. In the right spandrel is St Peter holding the keys of heaven. The panel above, with two angels, was placed or replaced here in the 19th century, whereas the panel below, representing *Simon the Magician*, has never been moved. In the left spandrel St James is framed between bare tree-trunks, his name engraved in his halo, as it is at Santiago. Below him is a panel with two women astride lions flanking a male figure.

The west portal, begun after the Porte Miègeville (c. 1115–18), although unfinished, shows a progression from the others in quality and wealth of decoration. Eight capitals are deeply and vigorously carved with intricate vegetal forms twined around human figures and animals which cling on to the astragals with fingers or claws. Sculpted reliefs from this portal are in the Musée des Augustins (*see p. 600*). Above the double doorway is a gallery of five arches surmounted by a large rose window with no tracery. The narthex was not tampered with during the 19th century and still has its original mirandes. The two incomplete towers were brought to their present state in 1929.

The interior

The interior is harmonious and tranquil, unified by the regularity of the 11 bays of the nave and soft light from the aisles and the tribune. The barrel-vaulted nave is 21m high, divided by transverse arches springing from engaged columns supported by square pillars. The double aisles take the thrust of the high nave and also create beautiful diagonal views. The elegant tribune around the nave and transepts consists of a series of double openings, each pair divided by twin columns. The floor was lowered in the 19th century.

In the 1970s, when the 19th-century plaster and paint were removed to reveal the alternating brick and masonry, several medieval wall paintings were discovered in the north transept. Among these, on the last pillars of the north aisle, are an angel seated on clouds and a *Noli me Tangere*. The largest fresco is on the west wall of the north transept (c. 1180), using the arches to frame five scenes from the *Resurrection*, culminating with the *Lamb of God* in the vaults. There are other fragments in the north transept and 14th-century murals in the south transept chapel dedicated to the Virgin. The 12th-century *Christ on the Cross* in wood and gilt was heavily restored in the 19th century.

The finely carved choir stalls (1670–74) have similarities with those at the cathedral of St-Etienne (*see p. 603*). The famous altar table by Bernard Gilduin, carved on the chamfered edge, can be glimpsed through the 18th-century choir enclosure; there is a replica in the north transept. The crossing has been subjected to many structural alterations and decorative additions. It received painted decoration (recently restored) in the 16th century and a reredos carved by Marc Arcis in 1720. The final resting-place of St Sernin is beneath the Baroque baldaquin (1718–58), behind the altar. Etienne Rossat's sculpture of St Sernin was added in 1759.

The some 268 capitals are quite remarkable for their quality and quantity. Many are in the tribunes, and while the majority have vegetal designs of great skill, variety and beauty, some are storiated. They date from c. 1080 in the east to c. 1118 in the west. Many of them are difficult to see; and a full description here cannot be attempted. Upon entering the apse from the north transept, the oldest storiated capital is of Daniel between some rather benevolent lions, on the east capital of the southeast apsidal chapel. On the inner wall of the ambulatory are seven late 11th-century marble reliefs recalling carved ivories or metalwork on a monumental scale. The three smaller panels in the centre, attributed to Bernard Gilduin, may have been part of an altarpiece and are known to have been in this position since the 19th century. The central panel portrays a corpulent but dignified Christ framed in a mandorla and surrounded by the symbols of the four Evangelists. On his right is a cherub, on his left a seraph. Flanking these are two angels and two Apostles, in a larger format and possibly later. In 1258 the relics of St Sernin were raised from the crypt and placed under a heavy canopy in the church, and the crypt was then rib-vaulted. The lower crypt was vaulted in the 14th century and its central pier is reputed to be the only surviving fragment of the previous church. There are a number of reliquaries on display but the most valuable have been transferred to the Musée Paul Dupuy (*see p. 607*).

In the 17th century the ambulatory became the *Tour des Corps Saints* (Circuit of the Holy Relics), where carved and gilded shrines of the Counter-Reformation were placed in the chapels and aedicules, demanding some considerable aesthetic adjustment. These were removed and placed in the tribunes in the 19th century but restored and returned in 1980. There is also a 16th-century post-plague *ex-voto* offering suspended above the north ambulatory, and an altar table designed by Viollet-le-Duc in the main chapel. Sections of the organ case date from the 17th century and the instrumental part was replaced in 1888 by an organ from the workshop of Aristide Cavaillé-Col, adapted to the size of the building and to the sounds of the late 19th and early 20th centuries using many of the earlier pipes.

MUSÉE ST-RAYMOND

Open June–Aug 10–7; Sept–May 10–6; T: 05 61 22 31 44 or 05 61 22 21 85.

West of St-Sernin is the Archaeological Museum of Toulouse housed in the former Collège St-Raymond, an attractive brick building of 1523. Recently extended and renovated, it has a wide-ranging collection from the Bronze Age to the early Middle Ages. Finds made in the Midi include Iron Age (3rd–2nd centuries BC) jewellery such as splendid gold torques and bracelets from Lasgraïsses (Tarn) and from Fenouillet, near Toulouse; and from Toulouse come mosaics, trinkets, small bronzes and coins. The highlights of the collection are the antique sculptures discovered in the Villa Chiragan at Martres-Tolosane, notably the largest find of portrait busts in France. The museum also owns such treasures as a replica by a Roman sculptor of Praxiteles' *Venus of Cnidus*, copies of Myron's *Discobolus* and *Athena*, and a series of vigorously sculpted reliefs of the Labours of Hercules.

EAST OF ST-SERNIN

From Rue St-Bernard is a good view (best in winter when the trees are bare) of the chevet of the basilica. The Faubourg of St-Sernin was incorporated within the *cité* walls when they were rebuilt in 1346 at the time of the Hundred Years War. On Boulevard de Strasbourg, which follows the line of the medieval defences, a produce market is held most days. The building now occupied by Galeries Lafayette, at the junction with Rue de Remusat, a tentative Art Nouveau edifice in exposed metal and yellow brick, was built in 1908 as a department store. The main north–south thoroughfare, Rue d'Alsace-Lorraine, was carved through the medieval town in the late 19th century. Place Victor-Hugo manages to combine a car park (above) and the very colourful *halles* (below), which sells every type of sausage and cheese imaginable, and has a range of small restaurants in the mezzanine gallery on the west.

Place Wilson, a 19th-century oval space, encompasses a garden, fountain, specimen trees and statue (1898) of the bust of Pierre Godolin (1580–1649), the most celebrated Occitan poet of the 17th century, by Alexandre Falguière. Around the square are cinemas and pavement cafés. In Rue Pierre-Baudis, is the Théâtre National de Toulouse (formerly Théâtre de la Cité; *T: 05 34 45 05 00*), an effective combination of modern and ancient architecture, with a fragment of the Roman ramparts in the basement. It is an interesting exercise in the use of space, with a large foyer and café.

Place Wilson, with Allées du President Roosevelt and Allées Jean-Jaurès, was part of a grand scheme opening out towards the Canal du Midi. Traces of *céruse* (distemper) in pale *café-au-lait* or other pastel shades can still be seen on many 19th-century buildings. This was not simply frivolous camouflage but a serious attempt to brighten the streets at night and increase the safety of the public, following an order of 1783 by the city fathers. The building on the corner of Rue d'Alsace-Lorraine and Rue La Fayette was the first department store in Toulouse, Bazar Labit, which was replaced in 1877 by another store, the Maison Universelle, for which the present building was constructed.

SOUTHWEST OF THE CAPITOLE

LES JACOBINS

Open 9–7; T: 05 61 22 21 92. Fee payable to visit cloisters. The Refectory is open 10-7 during temporary exhibitions.

The second most celebrated religious building of Toulouse, the Ensemble Conventuel des Jacobins, is usually referred to simply as Les Jacobins. The first view of the church from from Rue Lakanal, is of the cliff-like apse. This stark yet impressive building, entirely in brick, was the first home of the Dominican Order founded in the 13th century; the name Jacobins was acquired from the Dominican community who settled in Rue St-Jacques, Paris. The monastery here was requisitioned by the artillery after the Revolution, altered and desecrated to the extent that in the 1840s the army deemed the building unworthy of repair. The church survived thanks to Prosper Mérimée and a lengthy programme of restoration but before this could begin some 5,000 cubic metres of soil, which had been used to raise the floor to street-level, had to be removed.

THE DOMINICAN ORDER

Dominic de Guzman (1170–1221), a pious Spanish cleric, discovered the extent of what is now described as the Cathar heresy in 1203 in the company of the Bishop of Osma as they crossed the Languedoc. On their visit to Pope Innocent III, in Rome the following year, they were encouraged to assist the Cistercians in their unsuccessful mission to bring back the 'heretics' to the Catholic Church. By 1206 Dominic had settled in the southwest with a group of preaching friars who lived a life avowed to poverty and discipline, setting an example closer to the Cathar Perfects than to the Cistercians. Recognised in 1217 by Pope Honorius III, the brotherhood developed and moved in 1229 to the present site, where the building of the first church began in 1230. Dominic left Toulouse after less than six months but his followers grew ever more powerful and resolute, to the extent that in 1233 Pope Gregory IX confided to the Dominicans the task of the General Inquisition. The prior, Pons de Saint-Gilles, and four brothers were named Inquisitors. On 4th August 1234 the church was consecrated and in the same year the Inquisition began its persecution. The Dominican Inquisitors lived and worked from Place du Salin, while the rest of the brotherhood lived a monastic life at the Jacobins.

The exterior

The church was built not to receive pilgrims but to preach to the masses. Its simple volumes, almost devoid of decoration, are a sober reminder of its predicative function and the avowed poverty of the Dominican order. Constructed entirely in warm russet-coloured brick and tiles, the exterior is articulated by tall angular buttress piers and narrow lancet windows in recesses, creating a rhythm of deep shadows. The only vestige of the church of 1234 are the late Romanesque-style arch and early Gothic capitals of the west façade, hidden until 1964 by 18th-century remodelling. A new campaign of building began in 1244 and continued for more than a century. The octagonal belfry of 1298, built to receive the great bell of the university, was undoubtedly inspired by the upper levels of the belfry of St-Sernin.

The interior

The entrance on the south is mainly a reconstruction of the 14th-century doorway with the coat of arms of Cardinal Godin, who bequeathed 4,000 florins to the church, in the vault. The interior arrangement of the church is unexpected. It is divided lengthwise by an enfilade of tall slender columns creating two equal sections, the south destined for the public, the north reserved for the clergy. On the ground in the first five bays, black marble slabs indicate the extent of the earlier building, which was extended eastwards with a five-sided apse (1244–53). This was later raised and vaulted (1275–92), and the first mass was celebrated on 2nd February 1292 in the main chapel dedicated to the Virgin. The rest of the church was raised to the same height 1324–1326 thanks to Cardinal Godin's contribution. The glory of the Jacobins church is the elegant column at the east from which spring 22 ribs, like the branches of a palm tree, to support the vaults 28m above ground. The effect is enhanced by the use of alternate red and green to outline the ribs.

From the beginning this simple and austere edifice was held in such high esteem that in 1368 Pope Urban V, penultimate pope at Avignon and former student of Toulouse, selected it as the resting-place for the relics of St Thomas Aquinas (d. 1274), who was canonised in 1323. Returned in 1974 to their original 13th-century position at the centre of the north nave, the relics of the saint lie in a gilded wooden casket (1827) beneath the main altar, a simple marble table.

Of the 11 chapels, the four eastern ones were enlarged in the 16th century, and in 1609 the axial chapel was converted into a rectangular shape with a four-sided brick dome and lantern. The painted wall and vault decoration, discovered under plaster, dates from the end of the 13th to the early 14th century, and is claimed to be 60 per cent original. Most of the medieval stained glass disappeared in the 19th century. The present windows in the chevet were installed between 1923 and 1930 while the modern glass in the nave was designed by Max Ingrand in 1951.

The cloister

In the northwest corner of the nave a small door leads to the cloisters, a dark green oasis of box hedges and cypresses in the red-brick frame of the monastic buildings. The cloister, with brick arcades supported by 80 pairs of slender marble colonnettes and grey St-Béat marble capitals with foliate designs, took shape between 1306 and 1310. It was mutilated after the Revolution to allow the horses which were stabled here to circulate, and original elements were scattered throughout the region. Some pieces were recovered and used in 1965–70 to return the cloister to its original form.

The central well has a new coping and in the northeast corner is the cover of the remains of the *lavabo*. The chapter house (1299–1301) has two slim hexagonal marble columns supporting the vaults on intersecting ribs, and traces of 17th-century mural paintings. The floor has been reconstituted from fragments of old tiles and tombstones. The St-Antonin Chapel, wedged between the chapter house and refectory in the northeast angle, was built 1337–41 by the Dominican Bishop of Pamiers as a chantry chapel and burial place, and is dedicated to the patron of his diocese. Irreparable damage was inflicted in the 19th century when it was transformed into the veterinary hospital for the artillery, although the rich 14th century painted décor of the Second Coming and the Legend of St Antonin has survived on the upper walls and vault. The great refectory, which replaced an earlier, smaller one in 1303, was damaged in the 15th century by an earthquake. It now houses exhibitions of modern and contemporary art. The entrance to the gallery is on Rue Pargaminières.

TO THE QUAYS & THE GARONNE

South of the Jacobins, the Lycée Fermat on Rue Lakanal was founded by three *capitouls* in 1566 as a Jesuit college and named after the mathematician Pierre Fermat (1601–65; *see p. 377*). The great entrance gate on the diagonal dates from 1606. It occupies a building begun c. 1502 by Jean de Bernuy, a Castillian who came to Toulouse to make his fortune in pastel. The **Hôtel de Bernuy** is a complete and delightful example of an early Renaissance *hôtel particulier*. The flat brick façade on Rue Gambetta has a late Gothic doorway sculpted by Aymeric Cayla (1504), concealing an early 16th-century courtyard which can be visited during the academic year. The return of the façade and the right side of the courtyard (1530) are the work of Louis Privat. In this small space is an abundance of Italianate motifs—busts in medallions, candelabra, deep cornices and a pierced balustrade. A perilously low coffered basket arch and vaulted passageway in the northwest lead to a second courtyard with a *tour capitulaire*, also by Cayla, with angle windows and busts. Jean de Bernuy, who guaranteed François I's ransom after his defeat at Pavia (Italy) in 1525, is said to have died in his own palace in 1556 during a small scale *corrida* to celebrate the arrival of his nephew.

Rue J. Suau, named after the painter born at no. 8, has one of the rare Art Nouveau houses in Toulouse at no. 4 (there is another in Rue Lakanal). The street opens out into the Place de la Daurade and garden beside the river. Downriver from here are the churches of St-Pierre-des-Chartreux, Rue Valade and **St-Pierre-des-Cuisines** (*open July–Aug 2–7, guided visit at 4; Sept–June Mon 9–1, guided visit at 11; T: 05 61 22 31 44*). The latter, which has been renovated, is used by the Conservatoire de Musique as an auditorium for concerts. The Gothic church in brick was built over the fragments of a 5th-century funerary basilica which can be seen in the archaeological crypt.

Beyond the bridge, either side of Quai St-Pierre, are the Canal de Brienne, built in 1768 and, the former Bazacle Mills or Espace EDF Bazacle, which contains an exhibition space (*open Tues–Fri 2–7; during exhibitions 2–7, closed Mon; Aug and holidays 2–7; T: 05 62 30 16 01*). The mills, established in the 12th century, brought their shareholders enormous profit, but a hydro-electric plant installed in 1889 put an end to milling. The site is now owned by Electricité de France.

Upriver from Place de la Daurade was once the site of the gardens of the Benedictine monastery of La Daurade. They were displaced in 1766–77 at the time of Lomenie de Brienne (Archbishop of Toulouse 1762–88), to create the Quai and the Port de la Daurade. Also lost was the gilded sanctuary called La Dorée, which stood on the site of the parish church of **Notre-Dame-de-la-Daurade** until 1759. The origins of this sacred precinct are a subject of debate but are usually cited as being of the 5th century. Negligible documentation exists to record the splendour of the polygonal domed structure covered with gold leaf and mosaics illustrating the *Life of the Virgin*. It became a Benedictine priory in the 11th century under the auspices of Cluny when a cloister was built. By 1759–61 the structure was so insecure that it had to be demolished. The cloister disappeared in 1811 but some of the magnificent 11th-century capitals were gathered up and are conserved in the Musée des Augustins (*see p. 600*). The present grandiose building was begun in 1772 and consecrated in 1838. The Marian tradition associated with this site is perpetuated in the *Black Virgin and Child*, a copy (1807) from memory of a 14th-century wood statue burned in 1799, venerated by pregnant women. The dim Neoclassical interior is decorated with a series of seven episodes from the *Life of the Virgin* by J. Roques, and a late 19th-century enamelled ceramic composition by Gaston Virebent provides the background to the *Black Virgin*.

Immediately adjacent to the church of La Daurade is the more lighthearted, *fin-de-siècle* École des Beaux-Arts by Pierre Esquié, inaugurated in 1895. The Quai de la Daurade provides a shady green walk on a hot dusty day. The **Pont Neuf** was begun in 1544, in use by 1603 and completed in 1632. The seven low arches are almost semi-circular and gill-like openings outlined in stone pierce the massive brick piers, a practical embellishment to allow floodwater to flow through. Now the oldest bridge across the Garonne, it once linked Languedoc, on the right bank, with Gascony on the left. From it there is a view of the dignified brick elevation of the Hôtel-Dieu St-Jacques (*see below*), and to the west the dome of the Hospice de la Grave, the successors to the plague hospitals and hospices for the poor founded in the suburb of St-Cyprien during the Middle Ages. Sheltering at the base of the Hôtel-Dieu is the last remnant of the old 15th-century Pont Couvert, at the narrowest part of the river.

Once across the Garonne there is a wonderful view back to the city. In the brick tower at the end of the bridge there is a photographic gallery, the **Château d'Eau** (*open 1–7, closed Mon and some holidays; T: 05 61 77 09 40*). Built in 1822, the year that Nicéphore Niepce pioneered photography, it may be the only gallery in the world installed in a circular water tower, interesting as such, as well as for its temporary exhibitions. Certain parts of the **Hôtel-Dieu St-Jacques** opposite can be visited and it contains a Museum of the History of Medicine (*open Wed–Sun 1–5; T: 05 61 77 84 25, www.musee-medecine.com*). Nearby is the 14th-century church of St-Nicolas with a reredos designed by J.-B. Despax (1768), one of the finest in Toulouse. South of the Château d'Eau is Cours Dillon and a grassy area beside the river.

Les Abattoirs: Espace d'Art Moderne et Contemporain

Open summer 12–8, closed Mon; winter 11-7; closed Mon; T: 05 34 51 10 60, www.lesabattoirs.org, M St-Cyprien-République, bus No 1.

Still on the left bank, but further north at the end of Pont des Catalans, is the Centre for Modern and Contemporary Art, Les Abattoirs. Brick abattoirs built in 1827 by Urbain Vitry, who became chief architect of the town, have been inventively transformed into an art gallery which consists of a large central hall, two levels of smaller galleries on either side (a Musée d'Orsay in miniature), and a basement. The centre also has a café, bookshop and multi-media library.

Selections are shown from the collection of some 2,000 works from the second half of the 20th century, by 667 artists from 44 countries, made up from donations and national collections. Particularly strong on artists of the 1950s–70s, there are representative samples of the major movements of the period from Europe, the United States and Japan, such as *Art Informel* (Lyrical Abstraction), COBRA (from Copenhagen, Brussels and Amsterdam), *Gutai* ('concrete' in Japanese), *Arte Povera* (an Italian movement identified by German Celant in 1967), and Transavantgarde (Italian neo-Expressionism). Artists represented include Robert Mapplethorpe, Robert Rauschenberg, Victor Vasarély, Marcel Duchamp, Jean Dubuffet, Hans Bellmer, Lucio Fontana, Sam Francis, Jean-Paul Riopelle, Antonio Tàpies, Armand-Pierre Arman, Brassaï, César, Combas and Hans Hartung. There are installations, interactions, videos and temporary exhibitions. Also here is a large stage backdrop designed by Picasso with Luis Fernandez for Romain Rolland's ballet *Le Quartoze Juillet* (1936), which is exhibited alternately with other works in the basement space.

This *quartier* has picked up with the new focus on Les Abattoirs. Nearby is the Centre Municipal de l'Affiche et de l'Art Graphique (*open Mon–Fri 9–12 & 2–6; T: 05 61 59 24 64*), which presents three exhibitions a year on a particular theme. The area along the river between the gallery and the Hospice de la Grave has been landscaped.

THE RIGHT BANK & HÔTEL D'ASSÉZAT

Rue de Metz, from Pont Neuf, was built in the 19th century to join the Garonne to the canal and bypass the ancient east–west route. During construction work the site of the Roman theatre was uncovered at the junction with Rue Peyrolières. **Quai de Tounis** follows the river from the Pont Neuf, originally important commercial wharves but now a recreation area. On the left is a street called Pont de Tounis because it was originally a bridge. It leads to Rue de la Dalbade and the eclectic west façade of the church of **Notre-Dame-de-la Dalbade** (*open 9–12 & 2–7, closed Sun afternoon; T: 05 61 52 68 90*). The brick mass of the 16th-century façade has a Flamboyant rose window above a stone portal with Renaissance motifs. In the tympanum is Virbent's eye-catching pastel-tinted ceramic copy of Fra Angelico's *Coronation of the Virgin* (1874). The church, the fourth on this spot, takes its name from the first, Notre-Dame de l'Eglise Blanche, and was built c. 1480–1550. Inside is a 17th-century polychromed processional statue *St Peter walking on the Water*, as the patron of the *Confrérie des bateliers et pêcheurs de Tounis*.

The long and narrow Rue de la Dalbade leading to Place du Parlement was traditionally inhabited by wealthy parliamentarians. A discreet exploration of courtyards is often rewarding. Next to the church at no. 32 is the Hôtel des Chevaliers de Saint-Jean de Jerusalem, built in the 17th century by Jean-Pierre Rivalz, inspired by the Chigi Palace in Rome. The **Hôtel de Pierre** at no. 25, built in 1538 for Jean de Bagis, is the most famous in the street. It bears the hallmarks of Bachelier's work (*see below*) in the arrangement of the window reveals around the courtyard as well as the powerful atlantes supporting the pediment of the west doorway. François de Clary added antique marbles recovered from the river bed in 1613 to the east and west wings of the courtyard and created the overpowering façade from stone originally intended for the Pont Neuf, to which were added huge sculpted motifs in 1857. Equally extravagant is the portal dated 1556 at no. 22, which marks the entrance to the fairly modest Hôtel Gaspard Moliner. Towards Place du Parlement, at 31 Rue de la Fonderie on the old Roman ramparts, is the Musée Archéologique de l'Institut Catholique (*for opening times, T: 05 61 36 81 00*), a small museum dedicated to archaeology, iron casting (cannons) and 19th-century agricultural tools.

The triangular Place de la Trinité, refreshed by a fountain inaugurated in 1826, was one of the first of many projects designed by Urbain Vitry. No. 57 is Neoclassical with a balcony, full-length statues and busts in niches. Rue des Marchands has a specially fine selection of the many caryatids which prop up parts of Toulouse, the best at no. 28, made by Auguste Virebent in 1840. The Virebent dynasty capitalised on the properties of clay and new manufacturing techniques to produce for this stone-poor city every kind of decorative element in terracotta.

Hôtel d'Assézat

Across Place d'Assézat is the Hôtel d'Assézat, the most famous of the pastel palaces and the finest Renaissance *hôtel particulier* in Toulouse. Pierre d'Assézat, seduced by the lure of the pastel industry (*see p. 315*), quit his native Rouergue, became a *capitoul* in 1552 and in 1555 engaged the eminent architect, Nicolas Bachelier, to build his mansion. Bachelier, who designed the north and west wings of the courtyard, came up with a very personal interpretation of the Classical idiom using brick and stone. Pairs of superimposed orders on the façades isolate the windows. At the junction of the two wings is a square stair-tower with a monumental entrance at the base. The tower extends upwards into a *tour capitulaire* topped with an elegant lantern. Pierre d'Assézat never saw the completion of his *hôtel*. In 1561 his election as *capitoul* for the second time coincided with the collapse of the pastel industry and exile because of his Protestant convictions. Bachelier's son, Antoine, completed the screen wall to the street c 1571. The extension to the east was never carried out and some of the original fenestration was altered in 1761. The building became the home of the Académie des Jeux Floraux, ancestor of the Académie Française, founded in 1323 to safeguard the language and poetry of Oc and organise an annual competition. In the 16th century the story arose that the funds originated from a rich beauty, Dame Clémence, as the flowers distributed to the laureates were made of silver. In the portico on the reverse of the south façade is a statue of this semi-mythical patroness, Clémence Isaure; it is, in fact, the remodelled tomb statue of Bertrande Ysalguier (d. 1348). On 3rd May each year, the winners of the competition are presented with flowers blessed on the altar of the *Black Virgin* of La Daurade; among those honoured by the society have been Ronsard, Chateaubriand and Victor Hugo.

Fondation Bemberg
Open 10–12.30 & 1.30–6, Thur until 9; closed Mon; T: 05 61 12 06 89.
The Hôtel d'Assézat now houses the very fine collection of the Fondation Bemberg, assembled by the writer and art lover Georges Bemberg over the course of a lifetime. This is a permanent display on two floors including over 40 European works, predominantly from the 16th and 17th centuries, among which are paintings by Lucas Cranach, Jean Clouet and Pieter de Hooch. There are also more than 80 French paintings from the late 19th and 20th centuries, of which 35 are by Pierre Bonnard, and others by Vuillard, Edouard Manet, Camille Pissaro, and the Fauves.

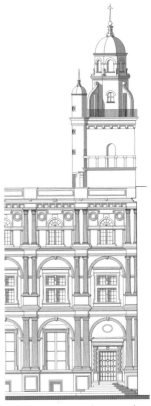

HÔTEL D'ASSÉZAT

Rue des Changes
Further along Rue du Metz, Place Esquirol is a large square where the recent discovery of the Roman Capitolium was made. Close by is the Musée des Augustins (*see overleaf*). Rue des Changes leads from here back to the Place du Capitole. This pedestrianised street, connecting with Rue des Filatiers and Rue St-Rome, was the main artery between the Capitole and the Parlement in medieval times. While the layout of the street and the plots have hardly changed, the fire of 1463 destroyed most of the buildings which were almost totally rebuilt by rich merchant families and pastel magnates. Parts of 15th–16th century houses remain at nos 16 and 19. Rue St-Rome—named after the Church of St-Romain, the very first Dominican monastery given by Bishop Foulque to Dominic de Guzman in 1216 (*see p. 593*)—continues towards the Capitole. No. 3 is one of the most beautiful Henri IV-style buildings in Toulouse, in alternating stone and brick with sculpted mullions, bossed door and arched boutiques partly uncovered; the courtyard, opening on to Rue Tripière, was remarkably restored in 1974. Tucked away in Rue Tripière are two interesting houses, built by *capitouls* in

1529 and 1617, acquired in 1898 by the journeymen carpenters and now the Musée des Compagnons (*open Wed 2.30–5.30, T: 05 62 71 58 91*). In Rue du May, the **Musée du Vieux Toulouse** (*open mid-May–mid-Oct 2–6, closed Sun and holidays; T: 05 62 27 11 50*) is installed in the 16th-century house of Antoine Dumay, doctor to Marguerite de Navarre, restored by Dr Simeon Durand in 1914. In the darkened rooms around an attractive courtyard are many objects relating to the history of Toulouse.

SOUTH OF THE CAPITOLE

From the southeastern corner of Place du Capitole, between the theatre and the Grand Hôtel de l'Opéra, south of Rue Poids de l'Huile, sandwiched between Rue St-Rome and Rue d'Alsace, a tangle of small streets radiates out from Place Salengro, created in 1849, with a pretty fountain and some well-restored façades. Place des Puits Clos has four pink marble columns saved from the retable of the church of La Dalbade (*see p. 597*).

East of Rue d'Alsace in Rue Lt.-Col. Pélissier, the secular order of the Pénitents-Bleus made their base in 1576 and, in 1622, commissioned Pierre Levesville to build their **Church of St-Jérôme**. This curious building exudes a secular atmosphere because the narthex is a passageway with display cabinets and is often used as a short-cut by shoppers. The church, with its curves, stucco and small loggias, decorated in the 18th century by the painter J.-P. Rivalz and sculptor Marc Arcis, resembles a Baroque theatre. The corridor comes out into Rue de la Pomme, a pleasant shopping street which brings you to the most congenial square in Toulouse, Place St-Georges, with a small garden, pretty façades and a host of inviting restaurants and pavement cafés. Its ambience undoubtedly derives from the fact that it is one of the oldest squares and was the main market for centuries. Rue des Arts runs alongside the church and chapter house of the former Couvent des Grands Augustins, begun in 1309, now the Musée des Augustins.

MUSÉE DES AUGUSTINS

Open 10–6, Wed 10–9; closed Tues; T: 05 61 22 21 82. Entrance on Rue de Metz.
The rich and wide-ranging municipal fine art collection is housed in an unexpectedly delightful setting. The religious community of the Augustinian monastery was disbanded at the Revolution and part of the premises was occupied by the École des Arts in 1804. It was partly demolished in the 19th century, then given its definitive role as museum and art gallery. Viollet-le-Duc's project for the museum in 1873 was carried out by his pupil, Denis Darcy, who built the western galleries between 1880 and 1896. From the reception hall a short flight of steps leads down to the large cloister completed in 1396, where a cloister garden has been created. On the left is a welcoming choir of upturned gargoyles from the old Cordeliers church. There are sarcophagi in the cloister aisles, and engraved medieval inscriptions (11th–16th centuries) in a small gallery on the west.

The museum has the most important collection of **Romanesque sculpture** anywhere in the world. The 350 pieces include capitals and other sculptures rescued from the cloisters of La Daurade, St-Sernin and St-Etienne. The eight oldest capitals (c. 1100) are from the first workshop of La Daurade and show a great affinity to the Moissac cloister capitals but include themes not found there. Two famous and enigmatic sculptures from the west façade of St-Sernin, the signs of Leo and Aries (first quarter of the 12th century; *pictured below*) are iconographically unique in Christian art. The St-Sernin cloister capitals (1118–25) show an advance in technical skill to create fluent carvings, mainly of animal and vegetal motifs. The cutting is deeper, more subtle, the detail more delicate and the plastic qualities of the carving enhanced. The group of capitals from the second Daurade workshop place greater emphasis on narrative dynamism than the first. One of the most celebrated capitals from St-Etienne, *Herod's Feast* (c. 1120–40; *pictured left*), portrays an overtly seductive Salome. Also from the cathedral are the very fine reliefs by Gilabertus of St Andrew and St Thomas and others from the same workshop.

Gothic sculpture is presented on the east of the cloister in the former sacristy, the chapel of Notre-Dame-de-Pitié (1341) and chapter house (14th–15th centuries). These include funerary objects such as the remarkable 14th-century *gisant* (recumbent statue) of Guillaume Durant, 16 statues from the Chapelle de Rieux, including Bishop Jean Tissendier presenting the chapel which was part of the Cordeliers church, and the exquisitely moving 15th-century *Notre-Dame-de-Grasse*. The youthful Virgin and her infant look outwards, away from each other, suggesting they were originally part of a larger group.

The 14th- and 15th-century church is used to display religious paintings by local artists such as Antoine Rivalz and Nicolas Tournier (*see p. 173*). Other European paintings include an early Murillo, one of three versions of the *Legend of St Anthony of Padua* (c. 1627–32) by van Dyck, Rubens' highly dramatic *Christ between the Two Thieves* (c. 1635), and a Perugino. The Bachelier reliefs (1544–45) made for La Dalbade can also be found here.

A wide range of 17th–19th-century secular paintings are exhibited in the upper galleries of the west wing, rebuilt in the 19th

The signs of Leo and Aries (early 12th century) from the west façade of St-Sernin.

Elisabeth-Louise Vigée-Lebrun: portrait of the Baronne de Crussol (1785).

century. Local painters such as Chalette and Roques are represented among others. Outstanding is the portrait (*pictured opposite*) of La Baronne de Crussol by Vigée-Lebrun. Elisabeth-Louise Vigée-Lebrun was one of the most successful portrait painters of her generation, skilfully committing many members of the aristocracy to canvas, including Queen Marie-Antoinette. The 19th century is splendidly evoked by the Salon Rouge where *pompier* works are hung in the manner of the Salons, one atop the other against a red brocaded wall. Delacroix, Ingres and Toulouse-Lautrec are also represented.

TOWARDS THE CATHEDRAL

An interesting route between the Musée des Augustins and the cathedral starts at Place Rouaix, which acquired its name before 1180, and along Rue Croix-Baragnon, a well-maintained street representative of the smart residential area on this side of town with some fine buildings and boutiques. At Place Rouix, the Chamber of Commerce has occupied the 18th-century Hôtel de Fumel, originally the residence of the presidents of the *Parlement*, since 1913. No. 15 Croix-Baragnon, the so-called Romanesque house (c.1300), is considered the oldest in Toulouse. Typical of the 18th century, the Hôtel de Castellane was constructed in brick and terracotta but given more prestige by being rendered to imitate stone. From the junction with Rue des Arts there is an impressive double view which helps to understand the geography of the town: towards the north is the belfry of the Augustins and, at the end of Rue Croix-Baragnon to the east, the strangely asymmetrical west front of the cathedral of St-Etienne. No. 1 Rue des Arts is a rare example of a timbered house from before the fire of 1463. Inside 22 Rue Croix-Baragnon are reused and replicated arcades from the 16th-century Hôtel Jean des Pins, demolished at the beginning of the 20th century. At no. 41 is one of the best early Louis XVI façades, with superb ironwork by Bernard Ortet, who worked at the Capitole and the cathedral in the 18th century.

The spacious triangular **Place St-Etienne**, the result of 19th- and 20th-century remodeling, has many 17th- and 18th-century houses. The Griffoul fountain in the centre of the square is the oldest in Toulouse. On the octagonal lower basin (1549) are spaces still awaiting the coats of arms of *capitouls*. Four columns support another basin, from the former provosts' dwelling, and the obelisk (1593) by Antoine Bachelier (*see p. 598*) incorporates four little figures spouting water, re-cast from four *mannikin pis* considered slightly improper in this location.

ST-ETIENNE CATHEDRAL

The cathedral is set off to advantage by the space surrounding it, although the building lacks the coherence of St-Sernin. The disturbing effect of the façade is due to a succession of modifications made since the 11th century. The cathedral in fact consists of two incomplete churches, one dating from the early 13th century and the other begun c 1272. The first documented reference to a cathedral dedicated to St

Etienne (St Stephen) is 844. At the time of Gregorian reform, Bishop Isarn, who was elected in 1071, stimulated moral and physical improvements including the rebuilding of the cathedral. The Romanesque church, transformed during the episcopates of a Cistercian, Foulque de Marseille (1205–31), and a Dominican, Raimond du Fauga (1232–70), is a prototype of the aisleless, rib-vaulted meridional Gothic church. When Bertrand de l'Isle-Jourdain (1270–86) was elected to the episcopate he planned to build a cathedral twice as large as the previous one to the east and north of the earlier nave. (When work began in 1272, the Rayonnant cathedral of Narbonne was under way; de l'Isle had been involved in settling a dispute in Narbonne over the site of the new cathedral, and was undoubtedly influenced by the work going on there.) After his death in 1286 the work was further slowed down when Pope John XXII reduced the size of the diocese, and it came to a halt at the end of the 14th century due to lack of funds. By this time the choir, up to the level of the triforium, and 15 chapels had been completed and were protected by a provisional wooden roof. Work did not take off again seriously for over a century, and it was not until a fire in 1609 devoured the timber roof and all the choir furnishings that the stone vault was begun in 1611 by Pierre Levesville, with money donated by Cardinal de Joyeuse. The work was not completed until the 20th century, when the north door was built.

The exterior

The earlier church seems to lean against the brick belfry but is in fact supported by two enormous brick buttresses at right angles to the façade. Between these, under a slightly pointed relieving arch, is a large rose window inserted when the façade was almost complete. The Flamboyant portal, inserted c. 1450, is decidedly off-centre because the architect, Martin Baudry, was at pains to save the baptismal chapel **(A)** north of the entrance. The belfry **(B)** is composed of a Gothic portion on Romanesque foundations, capped by the 16th-century gable belfry. From the gardens on the north you can see the large rectangular buttresses of the later Rayonnant building. Round the chevet, the south courtyard is where, until 1811, the Romanesque cloister and monastic buildings stood. The south buttresses are more elaborate than on the north. The south door entrance is midway between the two structures.

The interior

The effect of the interior is as disconcerting as the exterior because the two sections are not on the same axis and juxtapose two styles of Gothic architecture. They were separated by a wall until the beginning of the 16th century when Archbishop Jean d'Orléans attempted to begin the transept by building the massive round pillar **(C)** now standing incongruously between the two parts. On it is a memorial to Pierre-Paul Riquet, designer of the Canal du Midi (*see p. 555*).

Only three bays of the early 13th century church remain and anything that previously existed further to the east has been consumed by the great late 13th-century choir. To the west is the rather dark and cavernous section known as Raymond VI's nave **(D)** because of the east boss, carved with 12 pearls in the shape of the Cross of

ST-ETIENNE CATHEDRAL

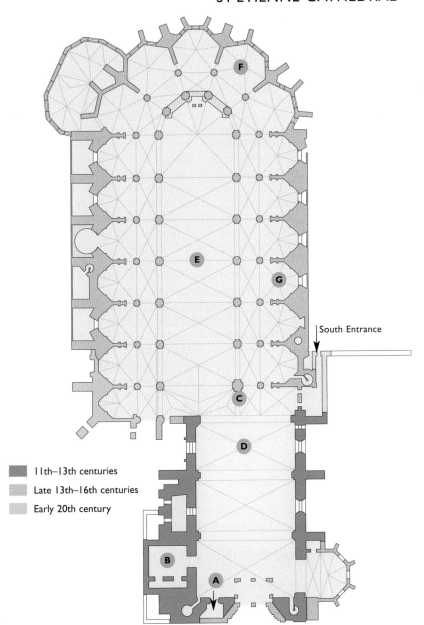

South Entrance

11th–13th centuries

Late 13th–16th centuries

Early 20th century

Toulouse. A vast single space with wide rounded vaults, it is supported by powerful rectangular ribs which spring from Romanesque capitals salvaged from the 11th-century church. The only light falls from the rose window, containing some original glass. This part of the building was nearing completion during one of Simon de Montfort's sieges of Toulouse, in either 1211 or 1217–18. On the walls are tapestries woven in Toulouse in the 17th century recounting the story of the Bishops of Toulouse.

The vast proportions of the five-bay choir **E** , with ambulatory and radiating chapels, dwarf the older nave. The shafts are little more than undulations on the surfaces of the cylindrical cores, and the capitals minimal, but the triforium is ornate. The height of the vaults at 28m is considerably lower than the planned 40m and the ribs spring from just above the triforium. Of the 15 chapels, the oldest date from 1279–86, but the majority were completed during the 14th century accounting for some interesting carved bosses, such as *St Louis Enthroned* (c. 1300) in the St-Joseph chapel **F**. The first chapel on the south, built in the 15th century by Archbishop Bernard du Rosier, is almost a church within a church. The majority of the stained glass is 19th-century, but there is some earlier, including panels from the end of the 13th century in the St-Vincent de Paul chapel **G**. This is the oldest stained glass in Toulouse, created from windows salvaged from the Jacobins, and depicts a Bishop and St Stephen, St Michael and the *Virgin and Child*. The glass in the St-Augustin chapel is also 14th-century, and that in the St-Louis chapel is 15th-century with portraits of Charles VII, King of France and the Dauphin, the future Louis XI. There is some 17th-century glass which shows a similarity with the work of Arnaud de Moles in Auch.

The furnishings are interesting, especially the double range of choir stalls carved in walnut 1610–13 by Pierre Monge of Narbonne. Their decoration includes pagan and mythological subjects which contrast with the little statue of the Virgin under the triumphal arch at the top of the episcopal throne. Also carved at the same time was the walnut case of the organ, perched some 17m above the floor. Restored in 1868 by Cavaillé-Col and again in 1976, it is often used for concerts. The tapestry hanging (c. 1609) by Jean du Mazet, from Castillon near Lombez, has scenes from the life of St Stephen. The Baroque retable of the main altar was designed by Pierre Mercier, and Gervais Drouet sculpted the central panel: the *Stoning of St Stephen* (1667). *The Four Evangelists* carved by Marc Arcis were added at the beginning of the 18th century. The polychrome marble is from the Carcassonne region, carried to Toulouse on the Canal du Midi. The more restrained ironwork of the choir enclosure (1766) is the work of Bernard Ortet, and the medallions were originally gilded. There are paintings by H. Pader and Nicolas Bollery (17th century) and by Despax (18th century), who delighted in the use of pastel colours. The 19th-century episcopal throne is by Auguste Virebent.

TO THE GRAND ROND & JARDIN DES PLANTES

Outside the west door of St-Etienne is the *Préfecture*, housed since 1800 in the former archepiscopal palace (17th century). The area southwest of the cathedral is the smart residential district of Toulouse. The old narrow streets lined with grand *hôtels partic-*

uliers with courtyards and gardens are attractive to explore. Rue Fermat is a street rich in Louis XVI façades and elegant ironwork; the tiny Place Stes-Scarbes has a modern fountain composed of six columns and a fine 18th-century balcony at no. 6. Rue St-Jacques leads to a fragment of the 1st-century Gallo-Roman enclosure, uncovered in 1962, and the vast Palais du Maréchal-Niel, built in the 19th century for Napoleon III's war minister in the style of a Parisian palace. Rue Ninau contains the charming **Hôtel Ulmo**, purchased in 1526 by Jean d'Ulmo, first president of the *parlement*, who had the house enlarged and embellished with a unique design for the main entrance consisting of a double flight of steps to a *perron* (platform) under a baldaquin. Rue Ninau leads to the green and pleasant spaces of the Grand Rond and the Jardins des Plantes. A former Carmelite property was used for the natural history collections forming the basis of the Jardin des Plantes and the science faculty, later to become the medical school. In 1865 the Musée d'Histoire Naturelle (*closed for renovation; T: 05 62 22 21 86, www.museum.toulouse.fr*) opened its doors to the public. It boasts the second largest collection of stuffed monkeys in France, as well as the first Prehistoric gallery, thanks to historians E. Cartailhac and Abbot Breuil (*see p. 131*). Simon de Montfort met his death near here, killed by a missile from a catapult on the city walls on 25th June 1218. In Avenue F. Mistral is the Monument à la Gloire de la Résistance (*1971; open 10–12 & 2–5; closed Sat, Sun and holidays. The Museum of the Resistance and Deportation is at 52 Allées des Demoiselles, Bus 10, 78, 79, open 9.30–12 & 2–6, Sat 2–5, closed Sun; T: 05 61 14 80 40.*)

Not far from the Jardin des Plantes,close to the Canal du Midi, at 17 Rue de Japon is the **Musée Georges Labit** (*open June–Sept 10–6; Oct–May until 5; closed Tues and holidays; T: 05 61 22 21 84*), a fascinating collection of Asiatic and Egyptian art and artefacts, housed in a purpose-built Moorish-style building set in gardens. George Labit (1862-99), the businessman who built the first department store in the city (*see p. 592*), ardent traveller and collector, gathered examples of works from distant and exotic places. The collection encompasses art of the last 3,000 years from India, Cambodia, Thailand, Indonesia, Tibet, Nepal, China and Japan, as well as Egyptian and Coptic antiquities.

MUSÉE PAUL DUPUY & VICINITY

Open June–Sept 10–6; Oct–May 10–5; closed Tues and holidays; T: 05 61 14 65 50.
Housed in the former Hôtel de Besson at 13 Rue de la Pleau, the building has been restored in a manner befitting this important decorative arts museum. Paul Dupuy, wealthy owner of the Toulousain department store Bon Marché, collected items that others rejected and installed them here after purchasing the building in 1905.

On the ground floor is the complete interior of the 17th-century pharmacy of the Jesuit college with its jars and bottles. The museum contains a variety of religious artefacts and the famous *cor de Roland*, an 11th-century carved ivory oliphant from southern Italy described in the 15th century as belonging to Roland, the legendary nephew of Charlemagne. Charmingly displayed on the first floor are porcelain and *faïence*,

17th-century Venetian glass and 19th- and 20th-century glass by Baccarat and Emile Gallé. The Salon de Musique has mainly 18th- and 19th-century instruments, and a marvellous pink room displays an exotic automaton called *La Leçon de Chant*, signed Robert Houdin, Paris 1844. The museum is probably most famous for its exceptional collection of clocks and watches of all kinds donated by Edouard Gelis, and it has recently added to this a series of magic lanterns and cinema apparatus. There are regular temporary exhibitions.

On Rue Ozenne is the Renaissance tower erected in 1533 by Guillaume de Tournoer or Tournier. When Rue de Languedoc was cut in the late 19th century, Hôtel Vieux-Raisin or **Bérenguier-Maynier** was spared, and after many years of neglect it has been thoroughly restored. The Gothic wall on Rue d'Aussargues was endowed with Renaissance windows after the *capitoul* Bérenguier-Maynier, a man of his time, acquired the house in 1515. He also added two wings to the principal dwelling. Jean Burnet became the owner in 1547 and, influenced by the work of architects such as Bachelier (*see p. 598*), built the front courtyard facing the Rue de Languedoc with a portico linking the two wings. All the façades are heavily adorned with caryatids, atlantes and fauns. Where Rue de Languedoc and Rue d'Ozenne meet is a top-notch confectioner and pastry shop, R. Pillon, selling a speciality cake called *Le Fénétra*, found only in Haute-Garonne and made with lemon and almonds. Further along Rue de Languedoc is one early 16th-century façade of the sober Hôtel de Pins, the house of Jean de Pins, Bishop of Pamiers and Rieux, scholar of Bologna and Italian ambassador to François I, who was condemned for his friendship with Erasmus.

THE TOULOUSAIN & FRONTONNAIS

The areas surrounding the city are more likely to be crossed than explored, but the predominance of brick, whether in châteaux such as Launac, Merville or Laréole, or small towns with their churches, such as Pibrac, Aussone or Muret, have a distinctive character. Here are the farms where the violets used in confectionary are cultivated, and to the north-east the ancient vineyards of Frontonnais.

On the outskirts of the city, the two main industries have a public face: to the north near the airport is the Airbus Industries Site, Parc Aeronautique, 10 av. Guynemer, 31770 Colomiers (*guided visit by bus and on foot, in English by request; advance booking required, T: 05 61 18 06 01; reservation@taxiway.fr; www.taxiway.fr; identification is essential; no photography.*) The visit of the largest aeronautical plant in Europe, home of the Airbus A380 (*see p. 583*), includes the huge assembly hall, the largest in the world, where you look down from a viewing platform onto the factory floor where the staff use bicycles to get about. Included are the inflight testing and delivery areas, and views of the Caravelle and Concorde, which can also be visited by arrangement.

The Cité de l'Espace (Space City), Av. Jean Gonord (*open July–Aug 9.30–7; March–June 9.30–5.30; Sept–Dec 9.30–5; Feb 9.30–5; closed Mon; T: 0820 377 223;*

www.cite-espace.com; Exit 17 or 18 from the périphérique east) is a sophisticated and informative theme park for all the family, which opened in 1999 on the edge of Toulouse. It is designed to give as much back up as possible to Toulouse's designation 'City of Space' and the scope of the exhibits ranges from a fragment of moon rock to the Ariane 5 Rocket.

Muret

On the west bank of the Garonne, south of the city, Muret was once the administrative capital of the Comminges (*see p. 539*). A decisive battle was fought here during the Albigensian Crusades between the combined forces of Raymond VI, Count of Toulouse and his brother-in-law Peter II of Aragon, against the crusading army of Simon de Montfort, representing the French king and the pope. On 12th September 1213 the defending army suffered a crushing defeat and Peter of Aragon was killed, giving de Montfort the opportunity to enter Toulouse. Muret was also an important stage on the pilgrim route to Santiago, but the 12th-century Church of St-Jacques was remodelled in brick in the 14th and 16th centuries. It is said that on the eve of the battle of Muret, and throughout the conflict, Dominic de Guzman (*see p. 593*) continued to pray in the church for the triumph of the Catholics over the heretics. Simon de Montfort attributed the miraculous victory to the pious devotions of the monk and in recognition a chapel was built, dedicated to Our Lady of the Rosary.

PRACTICAL INFORMATION

GETTING THERE & AROUND

• **By air:** Toulouse-Blagnac airport lies to the west of the city, T: 0825 380 000, www.toulouse.aeroport.fr. An airport bus runs every 20 mins, 5am to 11.30pm, to the town centre and bus station; T: 05 34 60 64 00, www.navettevia-toulouse.com For airport taxis, T: 05 61 30 02 54.
• **By train:** TGV service between Paris Montparnasse and Toulouse (5hrs); trains between Paris and Toulouse via Brive, Cahors and Montauban. From Toulouse to most main towns: Albi, Moissac, Foix, Auch, Bayonne, Tarbes and Carcassonne. The main station, Gare Matabiau, is

northeast of the centre on Blvd P.-Sémard, T: 08 91 67 68 69 (times), or T: 08 92 35 35 35 (information/sales).
• **By bus:** Buses leave from the Gare Routière, 68–70 Blvd P.-Sémard (next to the train station, at the end of Allées Jean-Jaurès), T: 0892 353 535; also Eurolines, T: 08 36 95 52 5/05 61 26 40 04, www.eurolines.fr; and Intercar, T: 05 61 58 14 53, www.intercars.fr
• **By metro:** The Metro runs north-east–southwest between Jolimont and Basso Cambo. The most central stations are St-Cyprien-République, Esquirol, Capitole, and Jean-Jaurès. Tickets are valid on city buses and metro. For all information concerning city buses and metro, Allo Semvat, T: 05 61 41 70 70.

TOURIST INFORMATION

Donjon du Capitole, 31000 Toulouse, T: 05 61 11 02 22, www.ot-toulouse.fr. Open June–Sept 9–7, Sun and holidays 10.30–5.15; Oct–May 9–6, Sat 9–12.30 & 2–6, Sun and holidays 10–12.30 & 2–5. Guided walking tours (2hrs; in English for groups by prior arrangement) leave from the tourist office every Saturday at 3, on Wednesdays in June and during school holidays.

ACCOMMODATION

€€€ **Grand Hôtel de l'Opéra**. Hotel of great charm in a 17th-century convent building, discreetly tucked away in a courtyard next to Place du Capitole just across the road from the Opera House, with well-appointed bar and lounges. Some rooms/suites have a magnificent views over the Place du Capitole and others look out onto the garden. 1 Pl. du Capitole, T 05 61 21 82 66, www.grand-hotel-opera.com

€€ **Hôtel des Beaux-Arts**. ■ The 18th-century building enjoys a prime location on the banks of the Garonne by the Pont Neuf and next to the Fine Arts Academy. The 19 individually presented bedrooms vary in decoration and size, and most have a river view. The Salon/bar is described as *chic anglais*. 1 Pl. du Pont-Neuf, T: 05 34 45 42 42, www.hoteldesbeauxarts.com

€€ **Hôtel de Brienne**. A modern hotel built in traditional brick on a leafy boulevard near the Canal de Brienne. The 71 comfortable and well-equipped rooms and 3 suites are not full of character but they are competitively priced. Blvd M.-Leclerc, T: 05 61 23 60 60, www.hoteldebrienne.com

€€ **Hôtel Mermoz**. ■ A practical and nicely appointed hotel between the station and city centre named after the famous aviator. There are 52 rooms which are light and unfussy. 50 Rue Matabiau, T: 05 61 63 04 04, www.hotel-mermoz.com

€ **Hôtel Albert Ier**. This hotel is very conveniently situated in the city centre, with Place du Capitole and St-Sernin on the doorstep. In a traditional Toulousain 19th-century building, it has pretty blue balconies outside and modern and fresh décor inside. There are 50 rooms, all different. 8 Rue Rivals/7 Rue J.F. Kennedy, T: 05 61 21 17 91, www.hotel-albert1.com

€ **Chambres d'hôtes Château Pontié**. On the outskirts of Toulouse, very close to Blagnac airport, this remarkable brick *maison de maître* with two towers, belonging to Chantal and Gilles de Faletans, has been an agricultural property since 1900. The three guest rooms are furnished with elegant original pieces, and for the use of guests are a dining room and two lounges. There is a pool and fishing in the private lake. At Cornbarrieu, 51 Rte. de Bouconne, T: 05 61 85 20 05, www.chateau-de-pontie.com

RESTAURANTS

€€€ **Restaurant Les Jardins de l'Opéra**. ■ The elegant courtyard restaurant of the Hôtel de l'Opéra (*see above*) is glass-walled to take advantage of the attractive surroundings and decorative pool in daylight, and enhanced by warm tones for the evening. Impeccable service and ultra-refined cooking is guaranteed by Maryse and Dominique Toulousy. Dishes are exquisite to look at and specialities include *Ravioli de foie gras frais de canard au jus de truffes, Escargots petits gris en vinaigrette, arlequin de cèpes et aubergines*, and *Souris d'agneau rôtie à l'os, gâteau de courgettes au basilic et croquette d'ail*.

€€€ **Michel Sarran**. One of the great Toulouse restaurants (two Michelin rosettes), it is an experience, both intimate and grand. In an *hôtel particulier*, the ground-floor dining room which opens onto a terrace-garden is a contemporary setting, and upstairs are small dining rooms. The *cuisine de création* is designed to please even the most discerning gourmets. Three menus: Capitol €45 (lunch only); Sarcens €75 and Surprise (for a group) €100. 31 Blvd A. Duportal, T: 05 61 12 32 32, www.michel-sarran.com

€€ **Café Bibent**. The most famous café on the place, with Belle Epoque décor where locals and tourists alike hang out. The cuisine is traditional and there is a large pavement terrace to sit back and watch the world go by. 5 Pl. du Capitole, T: 05 61 23 89 03.

€€ **Brasserie des Beaux-Arts**. ▪ The restaurant of the Hôtel des Beaux-Arts, the wood-panelled Belle-Epoque interior, pavement terrace, waiters in long white aprons, and white tablecloths lives up to the expectations of a traditional brasserie. The service is very professional and the food, based on seasonal availability including shell-fish in winter, is straightforward and well cooked. 1 Pl. du Pont-Neuf, T: 05 34 45 42 42.

€€ **La Brasserie Capoul**. A classic brasserie/bar (in the Hotel Grand Capoul) with busy and efficient waiters.

Good value *plats du jour* and seasonal food including cassoulet and seafood. Popular with locals and visitors alike, it is a great place to rendezvous. Eat in the mirrored interior, with bar, polished wood and leather benches, or on the lively pavement terrace. 13 Pl. Wilson, T: 05 61 21 08 27.

€€ **Restaurant Les Caves de la Maréchale**. Cross a small courtyard to the restaurant whose décor uses typical brick vaults to advantage to create an attractive and convivial atmosphere. The cooking is traditional, and includes cassoulet, with menus at €23 and €26. 3 Rue J. Chalande, t 05 61 23 89 88, www.lescavesdelamarechale.com

€€ **Chez Carmen**. Across the river, opposite the Museum of Modern Art, this extremely popular bistrot-brasserie (must reserve) is renowned for fresh, simple and fragrant food, especially succulent steaks and it specialises in old-fashioned recipes incorporating red meat, such as *daube* or *ragout*. The sister restaurant, **Le Chevillard**, 4 Boulevard du Maréchal-Leclerc, T: 05 61 21 32 02 has similar atmosphere and choices. 97 Allée Charles-de-Fitte, T: 05 61 42 04 95.

€€ **La Cantine du Curé**. ▪ In the old centre, this restaurant offers something out of the ordinary in its original approach to the produce of the southwest. Interesting creations and combinations include, for example, *Boudin au gambas*. The food is delicate and attractive and the owners' objective to be neither bistrot nor gastronomic but simply themselves and for the pleasure of their customers. Menus €28.50, €35, €40 and €55. 2 Rue des Couteliers, T: 05 61 25 83 42, www.lacantineducure.com

€€ **Restaurant Emile.** ■ In the oldest and one of the most attractive squares in Toulouse, Emile's has been around a long time. Eat inside the tall narrow house, or in summer on the pavement terrace. Traditional French cuisine: *Noisettes de biche*, *Pigeon au chou et au foie gras*, and *Soufflé au grand marnier*. Menus: lunch €17.50/€27.50; dinner €36/€45. 13 Place St-Georges, T: 05 61 21 05 56, www.restaurant-emile.com

€ **Restaurant Benjamin**. A bistrot-style setting with old beams and attractive atmosphere, the cuisine is traditional Southwest/Gascogne offering such staples as foie gras, duck and cassoulet. Close to Place to Capitole, there is always a plat du jour at midday, and menus €11/€12. Other menus at €17/€19.50/€23. 7 Rue des Gestes, T: 05 61 22 92 66.

Rouffiac-Tolosan

€€€ **Restaurant Ô Saveurs**. ■ At the pretty centre of the village north-east of Toulouse, this is a charming restaurant with simple décor. Daniel Gonzalez and David Biasibetti's *cuisine de passion* is based on top-quality products and they derive their inspiration from seasonal availability. Although rooted in traditional gastronomy, they take pleasure in unusual and subtle flavours and combinations: Menus: €20 weekday lunch; also €32, €45, and *dégustation* €70. 8 Pl. de Ormeaux, T: 05 34 27 10 11, http://o.saveurs.free.fr

MARKET DAYS

All markets function only in the morning, from around 6am to1pm.
Produce: Blvd de Strasbourg, Pl. Béteille, Pl. du Marché aux Cochons, Pl. Saint-Georges, Pl. Arnaud-Bernard, every morning except Monday; Pl. Salin, Tuesday and Saturday; St-Aubin, Sunday; Pl. du Ravelin (St-Cyprien), Friday

Organic market: (*marché bio*) Pl. du Capitole, Tuesday, Saturday
Books: (*bouquinistes*) Pl. Arnaud-Bernard, Thursday; Pl. St-Etienne, Saturday
Clothing and soft goods: Wednesday, Pl. du Capitole
Flea markets: (*brocante*) Allées Jules-Guesde, first Friday/Saturday/Sunday of each month; Pl. St-Sernin, Saturday and Sunday morning

FESTIVALS & EVENTS

March: *Cinémas d'Amérique Latine*, Latin American film of all kinds
June: *Fête du Grand Fénétra*, celebration of Fronton wine and folklore in Place du Capitole
July: *Festival Rio Loco*, music festival and songs by the river
Siestes Electroniques Open air concerts of modern music to relax to
July–August: *Toulouse d'Eté*, all types of music performed at different historic sites, Jacobins cloisters, La Daurade and the opera house and Toulouse Plage
September: *Piano aux Jacobins*, recitals in the cloisters. *Printemps de Septembre*, photography and video, dialogue between the arts
September–October: *Toulouse les Orgues*, organ festival taking advantage of the wealth of instruments in the town.

PLANNING YOUR TRIP

When to go

· July and August, are the most crowded months when school vacations and the French tradition of a general exodus from the cities between 14th July and the end of August makes early booking a necessity. However, even in high season it is still possible to find peace and quiet in the rural southwest. September is less frantic, with many of the same advantages. Less-frequented sites tend to close from 1st November and do not open again until March or April. The climate of southwest France is in general very pleasant. Temperatures range from a winter average of 10°C (50°F) to highs of 27°C (80°F) in July and August. Spring tends to be wetter than the autumn, but benefits from a wonderful range of wild flowers which last right through to July in the mountains. Autumn is generally glorious to the end of October or early November. Midsummer temperatures can rise to the low 30s (90–95° F) and occasionally to the high 30s (95–105°F), combined with high humidity inland, when the nights are stifling and cities such as Toulouse and Auch become unpleasantly steamy. At times the southern Atlantic coast enjoys higher temperatures than the Mediterranean, although the heat is tempered by ocean breezes. Towards the end of August heat builds up to spectacular thunder storms which do not necessarily clear the air. Meteorological information and forecasts can be found at www.meteofrance.com

French Government Tourist Offices abroad

Australia and New Zealand Level 13, 25 Bligh Street, Sydney NSW, T: 02 9231 5244, info.au@franceguide.com http://au.franceguide.com

Canada 1981 Ave MacGill College, Suite 490, Montreal, Quebec H3A 2W9, T: 514 288 20 26, canada@franceguide.com, http://ca-uk.franceguide.com

Ireland 30 Merrion Street Upper, Dublin 2, T: 1 560 235 235, info.ie@franceguide.com http://ie.franceguide.com

UK 178 Piccadilly, London W1J 9AL, T: 09068 244 123 (60p per minute), email info.uk@franceguide.com http://uk.franceguide.com

USA 444 Madison Ave, 16th floor, New York, NY 10022, T: 514 288 1904, info.us@franceguide.com http://us.franceguide.com

USA 205 North Michigan Avenue, Suite 3770, Chicago, Illinois 60601, T: 1 514 288 1904, info.chicago@franceguide.com http://us.franceguide.com

USA 454 Wiltshire Boulevard, Suite 715, Beverly Hills, Los Angeles, California 90212, T: 1 514 288 1904, info.losangeles@franceguide.com http://us.franceguide.com

Disabled Travellers

In the UK, Holiday Care Information Unit (*7th Floor Sunley House, 4 Bedford Park, Croydon, Surrey CR0 2AP, 0845 124 9974, admin@holidaycare.org, www.holidaycare.org.uk*) is a national charity which acts as a source of travel and holiday information for disabled and older people, their families and carers. RADAR (*Royal Association for Disability and Rehabilitation, 12 City Forum, 250 City Road, London EC1V 8AF, T: 020 7250 3222, radar@radar.org.uk, www.radar.org.uk*) is an organisation of and for disabled people. It provides information, campaigns for improvements and supports disability organisations.

In the USA, Mobility International USA (*PO Box 10767, Eugene, Oregon 97440, USA, T: 541 343 1284, www.miusa.org*) is a not-for-profit organisation whose mission is to empower people with disabilities through international exchange, information and technical assistance. Society for Accessible Travel and Hospitality (*347 Fifth Ave, Suite 610, NY 10016, T: (212) 447 7284, sathtravel@aol.com , www.sath.org*) is a not-for-profit educational organisation that campaigns on behalf of disabled and older travellers.

GETTING AROUND

By rail

The main train terminals are Bordeaux and Toulouse. These have links with the major centres in the region and with Paris, frequently by TGV (*Train de Grande Vitesse*), but travelling to smaller towns and cross-country needs detailed planning. TER (*Transports Express Régionaux*) indicates regional express services. TGV seats have to be reserved. It is very important to validate tickets (*composter*) with a date stamp at the orange machines at the entrance to the platform or risk paying a fine. SNCF discounts include passengers aged 12–25 years; up to four adults travelling with a child under 12 years old; and the over-60s. There are further discounts for two people on a return journey together; and for a return journey of at least 200km with a Saturday night away.

By bicycle

Cycling is a very popular pastime among the French. Bicycles and mountain bikes can be hired from certain train stations, campsites and *syndicats d'initiative*. Comité Régional de Tourisme d'Aquitaine publishes a brochure, *Aquitaine À Vélo*/Aquitaine by Bike, a bilingual brochure. There is no equivalent brochure in the Midi-Pyrénées. Some of the CDTs provide bicycle route maps (*circuits vélos*) free of charge. For other information and routes contact main tourist offices or: Fédération Française de Cyclotourisme, 12 Rue Louis-Bertrand, Ivry-sur-Seine Cedex, T: 01 56 20 88 88, www.ffct.org

On foot

Walking and hiking are very well catered for, with marked trails of every category from strenuous to gentle amble. There are several Grande Randonnée trails, official long-distance footpaths, which cross or begin or end in the region and include two main branches of the pilgrim route to Santiago de Compostela, the GR10 and GR36. These are described in various publications including *Topoguides*, published by the Fédération Française de Randonnée Pédestre (*14 Rue Riquet, 75019 Paris, T: 01 44 89 93 93, info@ffrp.asso.fr, www.ffrp.asso.fr*) and also by Randonnées Pyrénéennes (*Centre d'Information montagne et sentiers, 4 Rue Maye-Lane, BP 2, Ibos Cedex, T: 05 62 90 67 60, www.rando-pyrenees.net*).

OPENING TIMES

For museums and galleries these are subject to change and it is wise to check by telephone, in the press, or at local tourist offices. As a general rule, the national museums are closed on Tuesdays and the municipal museums are closed on Mondays. Many shut between 12 and 2 although the large museums tend to stay open all day, especially in the summer season. Last admissions are often 30–45 minutes before closing time. The same guidelines may also apply to other monuments. Some of the smaller churches may be manned during the peak months, but many close for lunch and some are permanently locked. When a key is needed it is advisable not to interrupt the key-holder at lunchtime. It is useful to have a torch to light high places in churches.

Small shops such as *tabacs* and *boulangeries* open around 7am, as do many cafés. Office hours are approximately 9–5.30/6. The two-hour lunch break is still sacred in most of southern France: shops and banks are also likely to close between 12 and 2. Most stores and shops stay open until 7 on weekdays and Saturdays but they will close on Sunday and may also close Monday. Only food stores are likely to be open on a Sunday morning. In holiday resorts opening times fluctuate seasonally.

Banks generally open 8.30–5 Monday to Friday, but are likely to be closed at lunchtime. In certain areas of the southwest they are open on Saturdays but not on Mondays. Opening times are posted outside the bank. Not every bank has a foreign exchange service, especially in small country towns.

ADDITIONAL INFORMATION

Emergency telephone numbers
Ambulance, medical/accident (SAMU: *Service Ambulance Medical d'Urgence*) T: 15
Fire department (*pompiers*)   T: 18
Police hotline   T: 17
General emergency for non-French speakers   T: 112

Markets
Smaller towns and villages hold a street market for produce once a week, but in larger towns more frequently. Toulouse and Tarbes have a produce market nearly every day. Trading usually starts at about 8 and ends towards 1pm. There are also dozens of

special markets, depending on the season or the region, and markets for things other than edibles, anything from plastic flowers to corsets. Details of market days in a selection of towns and villages are given in the relevant chapters.

Telephone and Postal services

Post offices are indicated by the sign PTT. Main post offices are open 8–7 on weekdays, and until 12 on Saturdays. Smaller village offices may close at lunchtime. Postage stamps (*timbres*) are on sale at all post offices and tobacconists (*tabacs*). Letter boxes are painted yellow. There are phone booths in some post offices. Public phone booths almost exclusively take phone cards (*télécartes*), which can be purchased in different denominations, or *unités*, at post offices, *tabacs* and some other stores.

T: 12 for directory assistance. To telephone outside France, dial 00 followed by the country code followed by the number (omitting the initial 0 if appropriate). To telephone France from abroad, dial 00 33 followed by the number with initial 0 omitted.

ACCOMMODATION

Prices in France are usually quoted per room, not per person, and do not normally include breakfast: note, however, that half- or full-board rates are quoted per person. Law requires that the tariff is posted in the room itself. The categories below are a very rough guide to prices which are subject to seasonal variations. Hotels which are specially recommended are marked (■). Details on Blue Guide recommended hotels and restaurants can be found at www.blueguides.com

€€€	€200+
€€	€100–200
€	below €100

Chambres d'hôtes (B&B) have an enormous range of accommodation and are gaining in popularity. They might be a simple room at a farm or a luxurious ensuite. As opposed to hotels, in the B&B tradition, breakfast is included. In many there is also the possibility of pre-booking *table d'hôtes*, a set menu/price home-cooked dinner eaten with other guests, which is often excellent.

French Government Tourist Offices (*see above, p. 613*) provide guides to **Logis de France**; **Châteaux & Hôtels de France**, privately owned chateaux; **Bienvenue au Château**, stately homes welcoming paying guests; and also Relais du Silence hotels. On www.franceguide.com, visitors can order or download brochures.

Relais du Silence provide accommodation in quiet surroundings. Central booking service: Paris, T: 01 44 49 90 00, F: 01 44 49 79 01, www.silencehotel.com

Gîtes de France et Tourisme Vert (*59 Rue St-Lazare, 75439 Paris Cedex 09, T: 05 49 70 75 75, F: 01 42 81 28 53, www.gites-de-france.fr*) provide details on rental accommodation in rural France.

FOOD & DRINK

Restaurants

There are restaurants of all categories throughout the region and rural *fermes auberges* also offer pre-booked meals. In this guide, restaurant prices denoted by Euro symbols (€) indicate a very approximate average price for lunch or dinner. Almost every restaurant has an *à la carte* choice as well as set-price menus. Where prices for menus have been included it does not mean there is no *à la carte* choice. Blue Guide specially recommended restaurants are marked (■).

Price per person
€€€ €80+
€€ €30–80
€ below €30

Lunch is normally eaten between 12 and 2, but may run on later in busier places; dinner is from 7.30 to around 10.30. In small towns and rural areas the closing times may be earlier. Restaurants are closed one day a week, often Sunday evening and/or Monday, so it is wise to check. Out of town lunch is still considered the main meal of the day (when the set menu comes into its own). If buying for a picnic, it is worth remembering that most markets and foodstores will close between 12 and 2.

CUISINE OF THE SOUTHWEST

In general the cooking of the interior of the region is based on the fat of the land, especially on duck, goose and pork, while the coast abounds in good fish and oysters. Excellent lamb is raised on the *causses* of the Quercy, in the Rouergue and around Pauillac in the Médoc as well as in the foothills of the Pyrenees; veal in the St-Gaudens area; beef in the Aubrac, the Chalosse and Bazas; and freshwater fish in the Rouergue. Seasonal produce plays an important part in the cuisine. Autumn is the time for dishes incorporating wild mushrooms, especially *cèpes* but also *girolles*, *morilles* and *pleurotes*, as well as chestnuts, walnuts and prunes; and in winter there are truffles and abundant foie gras, although the latter is becoming more of an all-year-round treat.

Soup: *Garbure* is a hearty Pyrenean or Gascon peasant soup made mainly from vegetables (butter beans (*haricots Tarbais*), potatoes and cabbage), with a bit of goose or duck thrown in. *Tourin* is made with onions and garlic. *Moutairol* is from the north of the region while *Le Ttoro* (pronounced Tioro) is a Basque fish soup with mussels and other fish, flavoured with onion and tomatoes. *La Rouquette*, the soup of the Bassin d'Arcachon, is made from crab and *loubine* (local name for bass or sea-perch).

Seafood and shellfish: Oysters are available in most restaurants on the coast, especially around Arcachon. They are usually served on the half shell and consumed alive. They may be sprinkled with a little lemon juice or vinegar but in the Arcachon Basin, rather curiously, they are frequently served with *crepinettes* (grilled sausages), foie gras or terrine and sometimes are deep fried or served *au gratin* (browned under a grill). Oysters are perfect with a good white Graves, Entre-deux-Mers or Premières Cotes-de-Bordeaux. Mussels may be served flambéed on a bed of pine needles. *Chipirons à l'encre*—squid cooked in their ink, with various other flavourings including Armagnac, or pimentoes from Espelette and tomato—is a very popular dish on the southern Atlantic coast. In the Gironde estuary, a curious serpent-like creature called a *lamproie* (lamprey, not strictly a fish but a primitive aquatic vertebrate) is still fished and cooked slowly in wine, leeks and shallots, as are the occasional sturgeon and *alose* (shad), eaten in the spring and served with a sauce; also seasonal are *pibales* (elvers). Freshwater fish include *brochet* (pike), *truite* (trout) and *sandre* (perch). *Le Marmitake* is a dish of the Basque coast, which was originally prepared by fishermen at sea from fresh tuna, potatoes, sweet peppers, onions, hot red peppers and white wine. *Estofinado*, a traditional dish eaten in the Lot Valley in the winter, is made from dried haddock (*stockfish*), potatoes, garlic and parsley.

Meat: Basic to the cooking of the southwest are poultry, duck, goose and pork. Think of the foie gras and pâtés of Gascony; the *charcuterie* (dried sausage) and *jambon cru* or *jambon de pays* (cured ham) from the Monts de Lacaune; and the best known, *Jambon de Bayonne* from the Valley des Aldudes. The duck and geese fattened up for foie gras also produce *magrets* (breast fillets) and *gésiers* (gizzards). *Confit* is poultry or pork preserved in its own fat and eaten hot or cold. *Saucisse de Toulouse* is fresh sausage sold by the kilo. Cassoulet is a regional dish from the Toulousain, particularly the Lauragais, and the Lot, based on white haricot beans, goose fat, goose or duck and Toulouse sausage, with local variations. *Pistache* is a variety of cassoulet cooked in the Pyrenees. *Sanglier* (wild boar) and *marcassin* (young boar), game and venison can be found in certain regions, and *salmis palombe* is a dish made from wood pigeon. *Peteram* is tripe as it is cooked around Luchon, in the Pyrenees; in the Quercy tripe is cooked with saffron, once an important crop here; and *tripoux de Naucelles*, in the Aveyron, is tripe cooked with ham and garlic in white wine.

Vegetables: White garlic produced in and around Beaumont-de-Lomagne (Tarn-et-Garonne) and pink garlic around Lautrec (Tarn) are both of a superb quality. There are also artichokes from Macau and asparagus from the Blayais, east of the Gironde, and the Landes. Pimentoes are cultivated in Pays Basque and many dishes incorporate them, including *la Piperade*, a type of ratatouille made of onions, garlic, pimentoes, tomatoes and ham bone for flavouring; but it may also be served in a type of scrambled eggs with ham and croutons. A typical Basque dish is *Hachoa*, incorporating hot red pepper powder (preferably from Espelette peppers), with diced veal and sweet peppers, which is cooked in a pan over the heat. Truffles are treated like gold dust: they are the ultimate complement to vegetable, egg and meat dishes and combine royally with foie gras. They are usually cooked, but they can be eaten raw.

Cheese: One of the great regional cheeses of the southwest is the blue of Roquefort, made from the milk of sheep raised on the causses of the Rouergue near Millau. A totally different but equally succulent *fromage de brebis* is Ossau-Iraty, made from the milk of Basque and Bearnais ewes, and served with *cerises noires d'Itxassou* (black-cherry jam). Cow's milk is used for Laguiole, a smooth, yellow, fairly hard cheese produced in the Aubrac and mixed with potatoes and cream to become *aligot*, and also for a number of Pyrenean varieties from Bethmale and the Couserans. The best of the goats' cheeses is *cabecou*, that made in Rocamadour in the Lot has an AOC, and *rieumes* from Haute-Garonne. Note that cheese is always served before the dessert in France.

Pastries and sweets: A *tartine* is buttered bread. *Croustade* is a flaky-pastry pie with a filling, usually apples; *pastis* is light-as-a-feather crisp pastry, with apples, sugar and butter and a dash of Armagnac or rum. *Gâteau à la broche*, found in the western part of the Pyrenees and in the Rouergue, is a conical cake that looks rather like a stalagmite. It has a high fat content and is cooked slowly on a revolving spit. *Fouace* is a semi-sweet cake with a little dried fruit to liven it up. *Gâteau Basque* is a light cake made with ground almonds and eggs, often cooked in a pastry base. *Macarons* are popular in the Basque country as well as St-Emilion; *mouchous* are two macaroons attached with *crème patissière*. Bayonne is the best place to sample chocolate.

WINE

Detailed information on wines is given in the appropriate chapters of the guide, along with information on visiting châteaux and vineyards, especially in major regions such as Médoc, Graves and St-Emilion. The majority of producers and distillers, private or cooperatives, will be happy to give a *dégustation* (tasting) and talk about their wines to those who have a genuine interest. It is advisable to make an appointment in advance.

Aquitaine

Some 3,000 châteaux and about 113,000ha fall into the world-renowned category Bordeaux and Bordeaux Supérieur. Near Libourne, on the banks of the Dordogne, are the vineyards of St-Emilion, Pomerol and Fronsac, which produce rich red wines. The Médoc, north of Bordeaux on the banks of the Gironde estuary, is the Mecca of fine red wines, which develop over time an exceptionally smooth and aromatic complexity. The Graves *appellation*, stretching south of the city on the west bank of the Garonne, bears a close resemblance to the Médoc: both vineyards benefit from pebbly or gravelly soil. Elegant dry white wines are produced in the Graves region, across the Garonne in Entre-Deux-Mers and on the right bank of the Gironde around Blaye. The golden sweet and semi-sweet wines such as St-Macaire, Loupiac, Barsac and Sauternes are grown on the banks of the Garonne about 40km south of Bordeaux.

A close neighbour to the Bordelais vineyards is the Bergerac *appellation* in Dordogne, which consists of 12 AOCs covering 12,000ha and includes Bergerac, Côtes de Bergerac (red and white), Rosette (white), Pécharmant (a quality red),

Montravel (dry and sweet whites), Saussignac (also sweet), and the great sweet white wine of Monbazillac. Among lesser-known wines are the Côtes de Duras and Buzet produced in Lot-et-Garonne, and in the Landes are the vineyards of the Tursan. On the borders of Aquitaine and Midi-Pyrénées, where the departments of Hautes-Pyrénées, Gers and Landes meet, are the reds of Madiran and the whites of Pacherenc-du-Vic Bihl. In Pyrénées-Atlantiques south of Pau, towards the mountains, are the delicious white wines of the Jurançon, both dry and sweet. Special to Pays Basque is the Irouleguy, local to St-Jean-de-Luz, vineyards originally planted in the 14th century by the monks of Roncevaux which have been extended over the last 20 years and produce whites and reds and obtained an AOC in 1970.

Midi-Pyrénées

The best-known wines of the Midi-Pyrénées come from the vineyards of Cahors and Gaillac. Cahors vineyards on the banks of the Lot to the west of the city of Cahors, produce only reds and the quality, like that of the wines of Gaillac, is constantly improving. The better wines can be laid down for at least 10 years. The Gaillac *appellation* takes its name from the town on the banks of the Tarn, and covers a wide range of wines, red, white, dry, sweet, rosé and sparkling. The Frontonnais is a small region between Toulouse and Montauban producing increasingly good wines.

Other lesser wine-producing areas exist in the Aveyron, on terraced vineyards around Marcillac, as well as at Estaing and Entraygues-et-Fel in the Lot Valley. In Tarn-et-Garonne are the wines of Côtes du Brulhois, Lavilledieu-du-Temple and Côteaux du Quercy. Production in these vineyards is on a small scale—many domaines are family businesses and produce *appellation contrôlée* as well as table wines.

OTHER DRINKS

Armagnac is a fiery brandy distilled in the northern part of the *département* of the Gers and the east of the Landes, around the towns of Condom and Eauze. *Pousse rapière*, a liqueur of orange and Armagnac with a sparkling wine, is also served as an aperitif.

The production of Basque cider (or *Sagardoa*) has a long history and some 70 cider brewers are in existence. It is claimed locally that the Basques taught the Normans all they know about apple wine. The small wooden stopper of the cider barrel is called a *txotx*, and this term is also used for the *cidre nouveau* celebrations beginning on the Friday following St Sebastian's day (20th January) and continuing until April.

Lillet, an aperitif created in Graves in 1887, consists of an assemblage of selected wines and fruit liqueurs aged in oak barrels for several months. Red or white, it is drunk chilled (6–8°C).

Floc (from the Gascon for flower) is an aperitif based on either red or white wine. Pineau (des Charentes) is made from grape juice added to Cognac, then aged in oak barrels. Patxaran, an alcoholic drink from the Navarre, is obtained by macerating plums in anis. The name comes from *baso aran*, the wild plum preferred in this recipe. Originally a domestic product, it is now produced industrially and is enjoyed throughout Spain.

GLOSSARY

Abacus Flat, horizontal element above a capital

Abri Prehistoric rock shelter

Ambo An early form of pulpit, where the Epistle and Gospel were read aloud

Antependium Frontal cloth on altar, pulpit or lectern

Apsidiole Small apsidal chapel

Ashlar Blocks of masonry evenly hewn to a high standard

Astragal A small semi-circular moulding of the type found at the top of a column, and below the drum of a capital

Atlante Supports in the form of sculpted male figures

Azulejo Glazed tile

Banderole An inscribed stone scroll

Bardeau/x Wooden shingle/s

Barri Suburb

Basket-handle arch Low, almost semi-circular arch (late medieval/Renaissance)

Bastide Medieval planned town (*see p. 358*)

Bat Valley (Pyrenees)

Bateau moulin Floating mill

Bâton écoté A moulding resembling a branch with pruned off-shoots

Billet Short cylindrical piece inserted at intervals into Norman moulding

Bolet an upper terrace or veranda reached by exterior steps leading to the entrance (Quercy)

Borie Rural dry stone hut

Boss Carving at the meeting point of vaulting ribs

Bourg Town or village

Burrin Flint tool with a chisel point

Cabane Hut or log cabin

Cagot Marginal or outcast person in the Middle Ages, of unknown origin, who lived and worshipped on the edge of the community or church

Calvinist Most French Protestants (Huguenots), followers of John Calvin

Capital A conical or pyramidal block, frequently with decorative carvings, between a column or pier and a horizontal block

Capitoul Municipal administrator of Toulouse until the Revolution

Cardo Latin for a main street running north–south

Castelnau A community coming under the jurisdiction of, and protected by, a new castle and walls

Causse A limestone plateau

Cazelle A rural dry stone refuge (Quercy)

Chai/s A wine and spirit storeroom

Charterhouse/chartreuse Carthusian monastery

Chartreuse Wine estate/country mansion in the Bordelais

Chauffoir Heated room in a monastery

Chemin de ronde walkway around the battlements of a castle

Chevet A French word to describe the east end of a church, including the apse and ambulatory

Chrism Chi-rho monogram of Christ, from the first two letters of the Greek word Christos

Chou frisé 'Curly kale' as applied to sculpture, predominantly 15th-century

Cirque Steep-sided hollow or natural amphitheatre

Cité The oldest part of a town

Clocher peigne Gable belfry divided vertically into two or three sections, something like a comb

Clocher pignon/clocher mur A church

belfry that is a flat extension of the gable or wall

Collégiale Collegiate church, i.e. with a chapter of canons

In commendam Where the tenure of a religious establishment was given to a cleric or layman, often absentee, who benefited from the income

Commune The smallest administrative division in France, each with a mayor

Concordat Agreement reached between the Holy See of Rome and Napoleon in 1802 regulating the connection between Church and State

Congregation of St-Maur Created in 1621 after the Reformation and Religious wars to assist religious communities that were *in commendam*

Cordeliers One of the first groups of Franciscans to settle in France (1226)

Corps-de-logis Main building or main wing of a building

Couvert Arcades or covered walk around the centre of a *bastide*

Croix pattée Arrow slit to accommodate a crossbow, introduced by the English

Decumanus Latin for a main street running east–west

Dégustation Tasting of food or wine

Département An administrative division in which the main executive is the *préfet*; most were created in 1790

Dolmen Megalithic tomb of large flat stones

Donjon Castle keep or tower above ground

Echaugette Suspended watchtower, often on the angle of a fortified wall

Ecuyer Equerry

Enceinte Enclosure

Enfeu Niche

Enfilade a line, series, suite of columns, windows, doors, etc

Ex-voto An offering given in fulfilment of a vow

Faïence Glazed earthenware

Faubourg Inner suburbs or outskirts

Flamboyant Late medieval style (15th–early 16th centuries) of French decoration and architecture (equivalent to Perpendicular in England)

Foire Fair; frequently an all-day market selling hardware, clothes etc.

Four banal Communal oven

Fronton Wall against which the Basque ball game pelote and its variations are played

Fronton-mairie Town hall with a wall that doubles as a fronton

Gabarre A traditional flat-bottomed river boat used on the Dordogne

Gariotte Rural dry stone refuge (Quercy)

Gave A mountain torrent (Pyrenees)

Génoise mouldings Cornice of superimposed Roman-style tiles

Gisement Mineral deposit in the ground

Glacis Defensive feature against cannon fire, consisting of a gentle slope at the foot of a wall

Gregorian reforms Gregory VII (St Hildebrand), Pope 1073–85, great spiritual leader of the medieval period, gave his name to ecclesiastical discipline and reform which had begun in the mid-11th century

Griotte Type of bitter cherry (morello)

Guyenne The part of Aquitaine owned by the English in the 12th–15th centuries

Gypseries Composition like stucco, made from lime (gypsum) with powdered marble or plaster which can be modelled

Halle couverte Covered marketplace

Hôtel particulier Privately owned town house or mansion

Huguenot French Calvinist or Protestant: by association with the name of a burgomaster from Geneva, Hugues Besançon, and a Swiss-German word meaning 'confederate'

Hypocaust Underfloor heating comprising hollow space

Imbrication Overlapping arrangement of tiles etc.

Impost Top corner of a pillar supporting an arch

Intendant Steward

Intrados Inner curve of an arch

Jacquemart Mechanical figure which strikes the hour with a hammer

Jacobin A member of the Dominican community, after the Rue St-Jacques in Paris; also a political group at the time of the Revolution

Jubé Rood screen or altar screen in a church

Jurade Medieval term used in connection with wine confraternities

Label-stop An ornamental boss at the end of a hood-mould (ie the moulding around an arch, doorway or window)

Lauze Traditional stone roof cladding in the Périgord and Rouergue. In Périgord the *lauze* is rectangular and held in place on steeply racked timbers by the sheer weight of the superimposed stones; in Rouergue the *lauze*, sometimes shaped like a fishscale, is attached to the timbers with a single nail or peg

Lavoir Public wash house, usually roofed but open at the sides

Lierne vaulting Tertiary rib in late Gothic vaulting which is decorative, not load bearing

Maison commune Medieval meeting place for town consuls (predecessor to the *Mairie*)

Mairie Town hall

Mandorla Oval shape, usually framing images of Christ (from Italian, almond)

Mascaron Decorative grotesque masque ornamenting a façade

Merlon Raised portion of a crenellated battlement, between the embrasures

Mirande Small opening immediately under the roof to ventilate the timbers, found in buildings in the Midi from the 13th century, sometimes incorporated into a *chemin-de-ronde*

Narthex The vestibule at the west end of a church between entrance and nave

Neste A pre-Celtic word for river (Pyrenees)

Occitan The modern name for the language of Oc, spoken in the Southwest

Oeil-de-Boeuf Bull's-eye style of window

Palombe Wood pigeon

Paréage The foundation of a *bastide* by agreement between local nobility, a representative of the King (seneschal) and the Church (abbeys or monasteries)

Parietal Denoting prehistoric rock art

Parlement Law courts equivalent to an assizes

Parvis Open space in front of or around a church

Pastel Dyers' woad, the leaves producing a high-quality blue dye, cultivated in parts of the Languedoc from the 14th–16th centuries

Pech, puech, puy Versions of an old (Occitan) word for hill or mound

Pendentive Concave spandrel leading from the angle of two walls to the base of a circular dome; means of effecting the transition from square or polygon to circle

Pénitents Members of secular confraternities who practised piety and charity and wore hooded costumes (blue, white or black) according to the order

Perron Exterior platform with steps

Pigeonnier Dovecote either integral with the farmhouse or freestanding, in a variety of forms (Gascony and the Quercy). Pigeons were an important source of food and fertiliser until the 19th century

Piscina Bathing pool; in a church, a container or basin that holds holy water

Pisé Floor made out of stones laid upright in a clay bed

Plate tracery decorative openings cut out of a solid piece of stone (12th–13th centuries)

Style pompier Refers to pompous and frigid academic paintings, reputedly derived from such works as David's *Sabine Women* (1799) where male nudes in firemen's helmets posed as classical Greek heroes

Pontet or **pountet** Construction joining two buildings, often spanning a public right-of-way

Préfecture Main town in a *département*

Présidial High-level tribunal or magistrates court (but lower than *parlement*) instituted by Henri III in 1552

Quilles Version of skittles

Rayonnant Gothic Style c. 1230–c. 1350, named after the pattern of radiating lights in rose windows

Région The largest administrative division in France, made up of several *départements*; created in 1972

Retable Freestanding decoration, painted or carved, behind the altar

Rinceau Low-relief frieze with a foliate or floral motif

Routier Hired mercenary (or a sort of highwayman)

Saintonge Old province where a distinctive style of Romanesque church architecture, with a highly decorated, many tiered west end, was developed

Sauveté/sauveterre Place of refuge or safety under the protection of the Church

Seneschal Agent of the king in charge of administrative or judiciary functions; suppressed in 1191, but the title remained to describe royal officers who had the power of bailiffs

Sigillated pottery Clay pots with impressed patterns applied with stamps or moulds, decorated with red slip and fired at a high temperature

Soleilho Open gallery on the top floor of a house, often used for drying crops

Spandrel Triangular surface between an arch, the horizontal drawn from the level of its apex and the vertical from its springing; also the area between two arches in an arcade; or the surface of a vault between adjacent ribs

Squinch Arch placed diagonally at the angle of a square tower—often in a system of concentrically wider and gradually projecting arches—to effect the transition to a polygonal or round superstructure

Star vault (also stella) vaulting where the *liernes* and *tiercerons* (types of rib) are arranged in the shape of a star

Stela Standing block, sometimes engraved or sculpted

Talus Slope at the foot of a fortified wall

Tetramorph The apocalyptic beasts each with the face of a man as seen in a vision by Ezekiel which became the symbol of the Four Evangelists

Tour capitulaire extended stair-tower built as a symbol of status and wealth

Transhumance Transfer of sheep and cattle from the valleys to summer pastures in the mountains

Trumeau Central pier supporting the lintel of a monumental doorway

Viguier Magistrate and representative of the king, who meted out justice in certain provinces until 1789

Voussoir Wedge-shaped stone of an arch

INDEX

Explanatory or more detailed references (where there are many) are given in bold. Numbers in italics are picture references. Dates are given for all artists, architects and sculptors.

cont/d from p. 4

Editor-in-Chief: Annabel Barber
Editor: Charles Godfrey-Faussett
Assistant editor: Judy Tither

Design: Anikó Kuzmich
Regional maps by Dimap Bt and Kartext
City maps, diagrams and floor plans © Blue Guides Limited
Architectural elevations: Michael Mansell RIBA & Gabriella Juhász
Floor plan: Imre Bába

The author would like to thank the Comités Regionaux de Tourisme for Midi-Pyrénées and Aquitaine, and the thirteen Comités Départementaux for all their practical help and advice, and also give special thanks to Solenne Odon and Marie-Yvonne Holley.

Photo Editor: Róbert Szabó Benke
Photographs by Phil Robinson: pp. 29, 59, 60, 89, 113, 180, 201, 254, 279, 332, 376, 397, 446, 456, 485, 517; Charles Godfrey-Faussett: pp. 219, 241, 264, 267, 268; Sanda Kaufman / Cleveland State University: pp. 105, 171, 191; Delia Gray-Durant: pp. 353, 355; Zoltán Serfőző pp. 460, 522; and Alexandre Peyrehorade p. 434.

Other images are reproduced by kind permission of: Bordeaux Tourist Office (p.24 photo: B. Lafosse); © Mairie de Bordeaux, photo: Lysiane Gauthier (p. 36; p.39 © Succession Picasso/DACS 2005); Centre des Monuments Nationaux / Abbaye de La Sauve-Majeure (p. 82); Les Eyzies Tourist Office (p. 132); MNP Les Eyzies (p. 134); Point Information Saint-Amand-de-Coly (p. 142); Villefranche-de-Rouergue Tourist Office (pp. 199, 234, 237); CRT Midi-Pyrénées (pp. 289, 381, 407, 541, 563, 568 photos: D. Viet); CDT Lot (p. 204); CDT Ariège-Pyrénées (p. 572 photo: B. Benoit); Luchon Tourist Office (p. 550); Foster and Partners (p. 283 © Ben Johnson); Musée Fenaille, Rodez, (p. 213 coll. Société des Lettres, photo: P. Soissons; p. 214 photo Méravilles); Musée Toulouse-Lautrec, Albi, Tarn (pp. 256, 258); © Musée Goya (pp. 304, 307 photos: P. Bru); Musée Arthur Batut (pp. 311, 312); Musée Ingres de Montauban (pp. 321, 322, 323, 325); Musée des Beaux-Arts d'Agen (pp. 342, 344); Musée des Beaux-Arts de Pau (p. 489); © BnF (p. 426); © RMN (pp. 451, 453 photos: R.G. Ojeda); © Musée Bonnat, Bayonne (p. 450 photo A. Vaquero); Musée des Augustins, Toulouse (p. 601, 602 photos: Daniel Martin); © Amis de Flaran (p. 385 photo: S. Bevan); Bridgeman Art Library (p. 362).

Printed in Hungary by Dürer Nyomda Kft, Gyula.

Your views on this book would be much appreciated. We welcome not only specific comments, suggestions or corrections, but any more general views you may have: how this book enhanced your holiday, how it could have been more helpful. Blue Guides authors, editorial and production teams work hard to bring you what we hope are the best-researched and best-presented cultural and historical guide books in the English language. Please write to us by email (editorial@blueguides.com), or via the comments page on our website (www.blueguides.com), or at the address given above (*see p. 4*). We will be happy to acknowledge useful contributions in the next edition, and to offer a free copy of one of our titles.